Wagner's Hitler

WAGNER'S HITLER

The Prophet and his Disciple

Joachim Köhler

Translated and Introduced by
Ronald Taylor

Polity

Copyright © this translation Polity Press 2000. First published in German
as *Wagners Hitler: Der Prophet und sein Vollstrecker* © Karl Blessing Verlag,
1997.

First published in 2000 by Polity Press
in association with Blackwell Publishers Ltd.

Reprinted 2000

Editorial office:
Polity Press
65 Bridge Street
Cambridge CB2 1UR, UK

Marketing and production:
Blackwell Publishers Ltd
108 Cowley Road
Oxford OX4 1JF, UK

Published in the USA by
Blackwell Publishers Inc.
350 Main Street
Malden, MA 02148, USA

A catalogue record for this book is available from the British Library

Library of Congress Cataloging-in-Publication Data

Köhler, Joachim, 1952-
    [Wagner's Hitler. English]
    Wagner's Hitler : the prophet and his disciple / Joachim Köhler ; translated and
    introduced by Ronald Taylor.
        p. cm.
    includes bibliographical references and index.
    ISBN 0-7456-2239-9
    1. Hitler, Adolf, 1889-1945--Political and social views. 2. Wagner, Richard,
    1813-1883--influence. 3. Antisemitism--Germany. 4. Holocaust, Jewish
    (1939-1945)--Causes. I. Title.

    DD247 .H5 K73 2000
    943.086'092--dc21   99-05847

Typeset in 10 on 12 pt Palatino
by Ace Filmsetting Ltd, Frome, Somerset
Printed in Great Britain by T. J. International, Padstow, Cornwall

This book is printed on acid-free paper.

CONTENTS

	Introduction by Ronald Taylor	1
1	*Ein Heldenleben*	6
2	The Last of the Tribunes	24
3	Dresden Burns	37
4	Studies in the *Ring*	51
5	Dragon-Slayer by Profession	67
6	The Future as Art	81
7	A Royal Failure	97
8	The Witch's Kitchen	115
9	A Lethal Subject	133
10	Pioneers	144
11	An Official Blessing	162
12	The Saviour Betrayed	178
13	Wagnerian Hero: A Self-Portrait	191
14	Blood Brotherhood	209
15	Life under the Mastersingers	242
16	Barbarossa Returns; Ahasverus Perishes	269
	Notes	296
	Bibliography	356
	Index	370

INTRODUCTION

The Germans have an awkward political history. Until the last quarter of the nineteenth century, strictly speaking, they had no national political history at all. Prussians, Saxons, Bavarians and the other tribal groupings cultivated their own particularist gardens and had their own centres of cultural and political appeal – the Prussians in Berlin, the Saxons in Dresden and Leipzig, the Bavarians in Munich, and so on. Not until 1871, when Bismarck created the Second Reich through blood and iron and the country gained a national capital and a national parliament – the same capital and a parliament building on the same spot as that to which the government of the German Federal Republic is now in process of returning – did Germany acquire the political status of a unified nation.

Since that time a confusion of Germanys – imperial, republican, totalitarian, republican again – has had to come to terms with a lengthening and ambiguous past dominated by two world wars and their consequences. Many chose to attribute the demise of imperial Germany not to the defeat by the allies of the German armies in the field, but to a cowardly 'stab in the back' by republicans and Jews back home. The economic and social collapse that followed the First World War, and the eventual failure of the Weimar Republic, were laid at the door of a crippling Treaty of Versailles, which also undermined Germany's ability to withstand with any degree of confidence the Great Depression of the early 1930s, and thus led directly to the rise of Hitler. So on to dictatorship, a shameless nationalist expansionism, the doctrine of the master race and ultimately the Holocaust, the Cold War in a divided Germany, then, since 1989, the collapse of the Wall and the restoration of a liberal democracy for the whole country.

On one plane this familiar chronicle may be taken as a sequence of events dictated by historical and political pressures. And undoubtedly there is a pattern of cause and effect, applied by historians with varying degrees of positivistic rigour, that can be laid over these hundred-and-fifty years as a pragmatic web of explanation. But maybe the roots of the problem lie deeper – embedded in the German national psyche.

In the shadow of the philosophy of Kant and under the liberating force of the French Revolution there emerged in Germany at the opening of the nineteenth century a demonstration, or series of demonstrations, of the autonomous power of the ego – the assertion, in philosophy and the arts, of the rights of self-expression of the individual creative self and the claims of the unfettered, free-ranging imagination. This romantic revolution, in company with the attractions of the philosophy of idealism, absorbed within itself the cults of the irrational, the unpredictable, the unknown, the mystical – everything opposed to the rationalistic, analytical values of the previous century.

The most perfect metaphor for this exalted spiritual condition is music – which, by virtue of its remoteness from the representational world of forms and concepts, is the most immediate and absolute of the arts, and in which resides the profoundest meaning of the universe and of the nature of liberated humanity within it. And no one expresses this liberation – spiritual, emotional, political, artistic – more triumphantly, more completely – and more threateningly – than Richard Wagner.

Few are the great artists around whom so much controversy has gathered and who have aroused such extremes of adulation and revulsion. Wagner makes total and unconditional demands on his audience. On the one hand these demands are the product of his theory of the *Gesamtkunstwerk* – a synthesis of the arts which will combine to expose the listener to a unified spiritual and dramatic experience. At the same time Wagner's operas present in its most powerful form the romantic doctrine of the absoluteness of music, its power to transcend temporal earthliness and embrace the infinite. In both the musical and ultra-musical dimensions of its significance, Wagner's art is the apotheosis of the romantic spirit. And because the romantic spirit is seen to appeal to an ultra-aesthetic consciousness, Wagner's music has come to exercise an irrational, ultimately non-musical power over men's minds – a power that has not avoided association with the destructive and the perverse. 'Music is demonic territory,' Thomas Mann reminded us.

One who found this particular devil irresistible was the young Adolf Hitler. In his native Austria, first in Linz, then in Vienna, he would scrape together the price of a standing-room ticket to see every performance he could of Wagner's operas, from *Rienzi* to *Parsifal*. Reminiscing during the Second World War in his 'Wolf's Lair' in East Prussia, he recalled that it had been at a performance of *Rienzi* in Linz in 1906 that he had first resolved to enter politics as 'a tribune of the people'. In 1933, shortly before his invasion of Poland, he paid a visit to Wagner's grave in Bayreuth. He had not forgotten that *Rienzi* in Linz. Standing by the Master's gravestone, he said to Winifred Wagner, the composer's daughter-in-law, 'That was when it all began.' It was also when it all ended. For it had been the music of *Rienzi*, he told his architect Albert Speer in 1938, that had inspired him with the conviction 'that he would succeed in uniting the German nation and making the Third Reich great'.

As it had begun, so it continued. In work after work, as Joachim Köhler shows in this book, Hitler found in Wagner characters with which to identify and concepts to apply to the circumstances of his political career. The uprising of the Roman citizens in *Rienzi* against the rulers who have betrayed them matched his pathological fear of being 'stabbed in the back' by members of his own party. The sight of the Reichstag fire in 1933 reminded him of the destruction of the Capitol at the end of Wagner's opera, while its overture became the symbolic accompaniment to his flag-waving party rallies. And as to Nuremberg, scene of these rallies, the great cry of 'Wach auf!' – 'Awake!' – that goes up in the final scene of *Die Meistersinger* found an echo in the Nazi challenge 'Germany Awake!' He was quick to cast himself in the role of a latter-day Siegfried, while his fanatical anti-Semitism feasted with delight on Wagner's vicious parody of Jewishness in the characters of the slimy dwarfs Alberich and Mime in the *Ring*. Later the mystical brotherhood of the Knights of the Holy Grail in *Parsifal* became the inspiration for the concept of an inner ring of party initiates to whom was vouchsafed intimate knowledge of the real meaning of the National Socialist movement. And so on. 'Theatre was the vein that ran through [Hitler's] entire life,' said Speer.

Nor was it only Wagner's theatre that overwhelmed the impressionable Hitler. In his thirties Wagner had been an impassioned political rebel, carried along by the inflammable idealistic rhetoric of the 1848 Revolution and a ringleader of the abortive uprising in Dresden which consigned him to exile for the next dozen years. Uncanny, to Hitler, was the parallel to his own career as leader of a failed coup that had landed him in jail and forced him to witness the proscription of his National Socialist Party. Moreover, Wagner, during his years in Swiss exile, had written a series of revolutionary essays in which he expounded his vision of the art and the society of the future, among them the infamous tract 'Music and the Jews'. For his part Hitler, during his year in Landsberg prison, wrote *Mein Kampf*, two turgid volumes of autobiography in which, for those with eyes to see and ears to hear, the political and cultural ambitions of the man who was soon to bring Europe to the brink of destruction were undisguisedly paraded.

Indeed destruction itself, both conceptually and in practice, forms a bond between the two men. As Wagner rejoiced in the sight of the Dresden opera house going up in flames during the revolt, and as the gods perish in the fires that consume Valhalla at the end of *Götterdämmerung*, so Hitler and his followers blasted and bludgeoned their way to power, making bonfires of 'degenerate' literature and ultimately incinerating the bodies of those they considered inferior and dispensable. Time and again Wagner called for the annihilation of the Jewish race, an alien body in an Aryan German state. Hitler took him at his word. And as in Wagner's operas the world is delivered from its distress and impotence by the emergence of a Saviour, a shining hero who might be called Lohengrin, or Siegfried, or Parsifal, so Hitler saw his own future as that of a national Messiah, a Man of Destiny preordained – witness his charmed survival of one assassination attempt after another – to lead Germany to its rightful position of world dominance.

Although the history of the world since the end of the Second World War shows that genocide is tragically still with us, the enormity of the German responsibility for the death of six million Jews during the years of the Nazi dictatorship still remains almost beyond the bounds of comprehension. Baffled and horrified outsiders ask how it was possible for one of the most cultured and civilized of peoples to have allowed itself to be made the instrument of such atrocities. At the same time the Germans themselves, still struggling to come to terms both with the legacy of the Third Reich and with half-a-century of a partitioned nationhood, cannot agree on where, even whether, to draw a line under the Nazi years and close the account. The question of collective guilt is tossed to and fro. How long, they ask, are we to continue professing public shame and contrition? When, wonder the generations born since the end of the Second World War, will these events, for which they can themselves have had no personal responsibility, be finally allowed to take their place in the objective passing of time? Countries can have their financial debts written off, so, under the banner of reconciliation, why not moral debts also? The old wound has been recently reopened by the arguments swirling round the plans for a Holocaust memorial to be erected in the rebuilt city centre of Berlin.

In *Wagner's Hitler: The Prophet and his Disciple*, Joachim Köhler argues that, as Hitler was the instrument of the Holocaust, so Wagner bears a responsibility, in the same historical continuum, for Hitler. What Wagner urged in words of rabid racial hatred and incitement to political violence, Hitler turned into chilling, murderous reality.

Scattered along the cultural trail that leads to Wagner lie the constituent elements of the German romantic tradition – the irrational, the egocentric, the intolerantly idealistic and the nationalistically utopian, collected under the spell of some of the most overwhelming music the world has ever known. Defiant heir to this world, socially and politically groomed for power by the custodians of Wagnerian values, Hitler took the stage to enact his megalomaniac Wagnerian visions of a Germany that would rule the world.

Wagner once described himself as 'the most German man' in the history of the nineteenth century; Hitler saw himself as Wagner's counterpart in the twentieth. Hitler called his ideal 'Germany'. What he really meant, writes Köhler, was 'Wagner'. It is a fateful correspondence that one ignores at one's peril.

RONALD TAYLOR

1

EIN HELDENLEBEN

Adolf Hitler was a failure as a politician and a failure as a military commander. He earned himself a permanent place in history as a mass murderer and as a megalomaniac who sought a confrontation with the whole civilized world. And on no one has mankind passed so crushing a verdict. Any search for a single word to epitomize what is barbaric and inhuman in the modern world inevitably leads to one name – Adolf Hitler.

He himself must have seen things differently. Failed politician as he may have been – a politician against his will, as he never tired of protesting[1] – he never ceased to claim that he had been chosen by fate to bring to an end the state of crisis in which he found his people. The fact that he plunged his people into even greater disaster was not to be laid at his door, he would have explained, but was to be blamed on those enemies of Germany who had brought chaos to the country after the First World War – a chaos of which he himself had been a victim. It was equally 'against his will', he went on, that he had become a military commander.[2]

Being the only one to realize that war was inevitable, he was left with no alternative, as German Chancellor, but to embark on this war in as proud a spirit as possible and justify it through a series of brilliant victories. No man who had never risen above the rank of private, and was totally ignorant of military strategy, had ever recorded such a series of successes in the field. That these triumphs quickly turned into defeats was due, in his eyes, to the overwhelming forces ranged against him and to the strategic realities. Risking all could mean losing all.

The man who took stock of his extraordinary life in his Berlin bunker in April 1945, and then, having drawn up his last will and testament, shot

Ein Heldenleben: 'A Hero's Life', an allusion to Richard Strauss's tone poem.

himself through the head, did not regard himself as a failure. In his view he had fulfilled the task, as far as conditions allowed, that destiny had laid upon him. If the ultimate victory had been denied him, then responsibility lay with the lack of a sense of true historical awareness on the part of the people in whose name he had acted. It was not he who had lost the war but the Germans, who had been unable to rise to the challenge. Let them now see how they could escape from the inferno.

In his own estimation he had done nothing but follow the voice that had summoned him to become the leader of the German people. Neither political power nor military success would in itself have sufficed. He pursued a goal that he had cherished from the beginning of his career, a goal that gave meaning to his life and compelled him to resolve on courses of action which no one else could have envisioned, let alone emulated. From the time this all-consuming vision appeared before his eyes, he waited only for the moment to fulfil it. It would then shine forth like a beacon, guiding first the German *Volk*, and ultimately the entire world, along the true way forward.

Hitler's private utopia, without a knowledge of which neither his achievements nor his atrocities can be properly understood, was entitled 'Richard Wagner'. It was a utopia that embraced both the magic of Wagner's music dramas and the philosophy behind his revolutionary writings. Hitler had been swept off his feet by performances of Wagner in the provincial town of Linz, and when he embarked on his political career, aided and abetted by others of like mind, he transformed these sublime experiences into a powerful political programme. The message enshrined at the heart of this programme – ethereal vision later converted into horrible reality – was guarded by Hitler and his band of disciples as though it were a holy relic. References to it were cast in riddles, its real meaning shrouded in silence.

The impious doctrine that bore the name of National Socialism was only a crude popularization of the esoteric message which instilled in the faithful first a sense of fear and apprehension, then a growing alarm and foreboding. They were denied access to the real meaning of the message. The Germans surrendered to a religion they did not know, adopting ritualistic practices they did not understand and blissfully dying for a corpus of religious rites into which they had never been initiated. No National Socialist had the slightest doubt that the Führer alone was in possession of true knowledge. And the Führer kept to himself what he had no desire to share with others.

A political and military failure Hitler may have been, a spectacular sinner before the Lord on the Day of Judgement, but in his own eyes, as the man called to put into practice the faith revealed to him and a handful of others, he was incontrovertibly the moral victor. As his idol, Wagner, had bidden him, he had united Germany and begun, albeit only tentatively, to transform it into an ideal 'Work of Art of the Future'. He had destroyed the 'degenerate' false gods of the early decades of the century and dangled before his people an intoxicating vision of perfect racial purity. As Wagner was the 'most German man'[3] of the nineteenth century, so Hitler set out to portray himself as his counterpart in the twentieth. He called his ideal 'Germany'. What he meant, however, was 'Wagner'.

Moreover, he had fulfilled one of his idol's most ardent wishes. The Bayreuth Festival, living heart of German cultural life, was now, for the first time, opened to the masses free of charge, and the soldiers returning from their heroic struggle on the eastern front against what Wagner had called the 'arch-enemy of pure mankind'[4] were personally invited by the Führer to Bayreuth to listen to that paean of praise to German art, Wagner's *Meistersinger*. And there was a second heartfelt desire of Wagner's, seldom openly expressed but raised to the status of doctrine by Wagner's son-in-law Houston Stewart Chamberlain, which Hitler later fulfilled as a chilling monument to his memory – the annihilation of the European Jews.

Hitler was fully aware of the extent of these atrocities, which he revealed to the Germans only in dark hints and half-truths. Indeed, he saw the Holocaust as his greatest achievement. In a memoir dictated shortly before he committed suicide he claimed that the world 'would be eternally grateful to me and to National Socialism for having exterminated the Jews in Germany and in Central Europe'.[5] For this reason alone he could never have seen his defeat, mirrored in the collapse of the Third Reich, as a personal failure.

At the end, to be sure, the familiar impression given by eye-witnesses is of a broken fifty-six-year-old man, at odds with himself and with those around him, awaiting his impending doom in a state of fear and trembling. But his final testament speaks a different language. There had been no change in his message, either in aim or in tone, since his days as a young revolutionary. All that had happened in the intervening years, everything for which he had been responsible down to the last unspeakable detail, had left not the faintest trace. It was as though the quarter of a century that separated his anti-Semitic debut in Munich from his anti-Semitic last testament in Berlin had been wiped out at a stroke. And when, shortly before his death, he married his secret mistress Eva Braun – out of gratitude for her loyalty, as he wrote – he was convinced that, in giving her his name, he was securing her place in history.

From *Der fliegende Holländer* to *Götterdämmerung* the union of two lovers in death is a fixed term in Wagner's mythological vocabulary. He offers them the ultimate redemption in death for what had been denied them in life. Faced with the question of his own death, Hitler invariably turned to the contemplation of a symbolic figure who sees death only as the gateway to a better life. Confident of 'the glorious re-emergence of National Socialism and with it the realization of a true national community', as he wrote on the day before he faced his own destiny, 'I shall die with a joyful heart'.[6]

The end of his own earthly journey was to be accompanied by a succession of deafening Wagnerian chords.

In geographical terms too his was a Wagnerian end. From the Reich Chancellery, where he had felt himself 'master of the whole world',[7] Hitler's path led to the underground bunker, described by one visitor as 'a God-forsaken mortuary'.[8] Such had been the descent from the Castle of the Gods to the 'sinister depths'[9] of the underworld portrayed in Wagner's *Ring des Nibelungen*, a descent from Valhalla to Nibelheim, 'source of darkness and death', as Wagner called it.

An SS man by the name of Rattenhuber had advised Hitler to move into the bunker because of the non-stop air raids.[10] Accustomed since the beginning of the war to taking refuge in underground lairs, and a loner by nature, Hitler took his courtiers and his 'Praetorian Guard' and cut himself off from the outside world. In a manner mockingly compared by his confidant Albert Speer to the quirks of Don Quixote,[11] he had always had a penchant for shutting himself up in rooms with artificial light. Now, for the final weeks of his life, he incarcerated himself in concrete once and for all.

As he lost his sense of time, so also he lost his sense of reality. Like Wotan with his Valkyries, he commanded armies of the dead, threw into battle divisions that no longer existed and played military games on the drawing board that only served to prolong the slaughter. 'The strategy that the Führer laid out before me,' wrote a despairing Goebbels in the bunker,[12] 'is grand and utterly persuasive – except that there is at the moment not the slightest chance of putting it into effect ... At times he seems to be living in the clouds.'[13] The same might have been said of Wotan, Wagner's God – and not only from the time when he faced defeat. That Hitler had previously been able to carry through his personal programme virtually without opposition, despite its unrealistic and impracticable nature, was due to the fact that he had always been granted the means to its achievement. Those days were now long gone, and his fantastic visions were now unashamedly revealing themselves as the chimeras they had always been.

Hermetically sealed in his bunker, Hitler knew he could see only the shadows of reality. But then, had not the external world itself, which had so miserably failed him and his hallowed ideals, become a mere shadow, a pale reflection of what might have been? Had not the theatre which he had made ready to receive the masterpieces of world drama turned out to be a rendezvous for a collection of barnstormers? It was a sense of black despair matched by the hopeless state of the war raging on the other side of the steel doors that sealed his bunker.

As the outside world disintegrated, it was to his inner world, described by Speer as 'hollow and empty',[14] that Hitler turned for a sense of stability. Like a film projected onto the screen of his consciousness, he was suddenly gripped by a vision that took him back to the days of his youth, a vision of the dying Siegfried, tragic hero of Wagner's *Götterdämmerung*. Here lay the way out of the threatening catastrophe. Siegfried embodied the miracle of spiritual metamorphosis, a transfiguration in death called by Hitler 'the divine transfiguration of the dying hero'.[15] The only sure path to immortality lay through death. Only the defeated warrior, in the world of Wagnerian mythology, was entitled to be reborn, and the same was true, in Hitler's variation of the theme, of the man who was a martyr to his people's 'religion of the future'. As this martyr, he would redeem his people through the panacea that Wagner had repeatedly proclaimed would deliver them from the horrors of reality. That deliverance might not come tomorrow but at some time in the future, perhaps even not until the next millennium. But come it would, 'one way or another'.[16] From the ashes left by the funeral pyre of National Socialism a glorious new dawn would then break.

But first, as with Jesus Christ and Siegfried, came the moment of betrayal – the kiss of Judas in Gethsemane, or Hagen's spear. Hitler too complained bitterly that he had been betrayed by those very people on whom he had showered the greatest favours. In a 'frenzied atmosphere of betrayal', as Goebbels described it,[17] there was talk of murdering the Führer. As early as 1942 Hitler told Hermann Giesler, his architect, that he 'lived and worked under the perpetual threat of being betrayed'.[18] After the attempt on his life in 1944 he left the impression of 'a man in a state of total despair',[19] according to his adjutant, even to the point of taking his own life – he, Hitler, instrument of destiny!

But as so often in the past, so now also he was spared. A few hours before committing suicide he remarked, with the sarcasm of a benefactor whose generosity has been ill rewarded: 'They ought to put on my gravestone "He was a victim of his generals." '[20] But at the same time he knew what no one else knew – that he was the victim of that power, converted into music by Wagner, which is bound to devour all would-be redeemers as long as there is still evil in the world. It was on this evil that Hitler had waged war since the beginning of his political career. How, barely heeded by the world, he had set about his task would be seen after his death. 'There is a great deal they do not know,' he muttered to one of his close acquaintances on the last day of his life. 'They will discover a lot of things that will surprise them.'[21]

The image of crucifixion came into his mind. Back in the 1920s, the time of *Mein Kampf*, he had visualized the German Reich being crucified by the Jews – a vision that Wagner had had of himself fifty years earlier. 'It is as though I were nailed to the cross of the German ideal,'[22] Wagner had said to Cosima, casting himself as the victim of those who have always murdered the saviours and redeemers of mankind. Convinced that world Jewry was set on destroying him and his work, Wagner had pondered on ways of forestalling their plans. Now Hitler had taken over from Wagner, doing whatever lay in his power to bring the Master's ideas to fruition and preparing to set out on his own Road to Calvary.

The Russian hordes moving in on Berlin were to Hitler, as to the preachers of the Wagnerian religion, mere pawns of the Jews. The closer they came to his bunker, the more he began to torture himself with the idea that they might pump poison gas down the ventilation shafts. He therefore had a new filter system installed; if he was to die, then it would be in the manner of his own choice, not at the hands of the enemy. He refused, he wrote, 'to put himself at the mercy of a foe who needed to stir up the masses with crude spectacles mounted by the Jews'.[23] What was in Hitler's mind? Did he envisage a second Golgotha, with himself as the new Saviour on the Cross, a vulgar peep-show in which, on another occasion, he imagined his tortured body, alive or dead, being put on public display? Such an end would be intolerable. As long as he held the reins of power, he would bid farewell to the strains of *Götterdämmerung*.

But the time might not yet have come. Maybe different music would be called for, the music, say, of the *Lohengrin* miracle. For inevitable as the end seemed, with betrayal surrounding him on all sides and the supremacy of subhuman forces established, the opposite might yet happen, a twist in the course of destiny, a Wagnerian salvation at the eleventh hour. Such a divine gesture would naturally be made only to the boldest and bravest, those who, like Hitler himself, were endowed with 'the titanic power',[24] as he called it, to set about the 'Herculean task'[25] of defending the Reich. What was now needed was tenacity, the tenacity to gain time not only for himself but for the achievement of the mission with which he had been charged. Shut up in his Berlin bunker, he was ready to give fate one last chance to perform a miracle. He could have escaped to his refuge at Berchtesgaden before the trap finally snapped shut, or found exile on some distant shore, like many conquered warriors before him. But he chose instead, a Wagnerian hero to the last, to persist in his impossible course, defying danger and holding out to the bitter end. All lay in the lap of the gods.

Hitler was utterly convinced that a man who did not believe in such miracles could not grasp the truth of myths. Back in his schooldays he had been confronted by this truth through Wagner's operas; now, as he approached his end, it would accompany him to the grave. Throughout his time in the bunker, proudly wearing the Iron Cross he had won in the First World War, he came more and more to ignore the reality of the moment in favour of a context of world history as a whole. Was history not rich in unexpected twists of fate? Had not the collapse of Germany in 1918, brought about by the treachery foreshadowed by Wagner in his *Ring*, been turned by his, Hitler's, sudden emergence into a glorious new beginning, a revolutionary new birth? The German *Volk*, once rent apart by a 'Jewish tyranny', had been vouchsafed a unity it had hitherto never known, a unity that would survive in triumph for thousands of years. But all this now seemed forgotten. And to think that this miraculous rebirth of the nation had taken place only twelve years earlier!

It was not the fluctuations of war that had to occupy one's attention, declared Hitler, but the course of history. When Goebbels' Ministry of Propaganda was bombed, he cheerfully consoled its chief with the promise to build him 'a new monumental ministry' on the very same spot after the war.[26] Even as a boy he had grandiose plans for such buildings in his head. For a man who thought in such millennial terms the present, especially a present as unedifying as that which now confronted him, faded into insignificance. What mattered was not time but eternity.

As the ceaseless thud of allied bombs penetrated the walls of his concrete prison, Hitler's mind went back to 'a distant artillery duel at the front'[27] – not the battle raging around him at that moment but the fighting in the trenches of Flanders from which he had narrowly escaped with his life. He was developing a chronic stoop,[28] his head began to roll from side to side, his left hand trembled so badly that he had to grasp it with his right, he was lame in one leg and the proud, strutting gait of the Nuremberg rallies had become a hobbling crawl. Yet, far from deflecting him from his mission, this made him all the more convinced that he was the reincarnation of the great Prussian monarch who, bloody but unbowed, had fought his way through one defeat after another until finally emerging victorious.

And now the figure of this Prussian hero, Frederick the Great, gazed down on him from the wall of his concrete cell. He had bought this portrait of 'Old Fritz' eleven years before and carried it with him as a talisman, packed in a wooden box, wherever he went. 'Take courage!' it said to him, whenever he looked at it. Through his victories for Prussia Frederick made himself a herald of the Führer, a shining example of how to win victory against seemingly overwhelming odds. When Hitler recalled how the sudden death of the Russian empress had brought about the miraculous deliverance of Prussia in the Seven Years War, tears are said to have come to his eyes.[29] Drawing a false analogy, he is reported to have been highly delighted when told of the death of President Roosevelt in April 1945.

Often he would sit in his bare room in the bunker, its dreariness reminding him of his days in Munich, and contemplate the portrait of Frederick the Great, the great survivor. He drew comfort from the picture, seeing in it his own mythical ego. As the lamps swung from side to side under the impact of the falling bombs, so the Prussian king's features also seemed to move. In the depths of the night, unable to sleep, Hitler could sometimes be seen gazing up imploringly at the great monarch. 'Sitting there motionless, as though in a trance', wrote an eye-witness, unobserved, 'with his chin cupped in his hand, he would stare at the picture for hours in the flickering candlelight. And the King even appeared to return his gaze.'[30]

There was also consolation to be derived from the future. That February Hitler had instructed Hermann Giesler to construct a model which should serve as a harbinger of better times to come – a scale model of his design for the river front of the town of Linz, on the Danube, a dream that had been in his mind since his schooldays. His plan, he was convinced, would one day make his home town the jewel of German cities. For it was here, let it be remembered, that he had first encountered the genius of Richard Wagner.

Now, forty years on, bending over his toy-town model, he took a child-like delight in having all the details pointed out to him as he strolled in his imagination down the magnificent streets which would make visitors aware of the intellect that had been at work there. What he could not do in reality he here acted out in play, imitating the different times of day by means of ingenious lighting effects or crossing his new Nibelungen Bridge, built to designs he had made in his youth. For hours he would gaze at his model, 'as though at a Promised Land which he would one day enter', as Giesler put it.[31]

Hitler had always had Wagner around him, as the contents of his safe proved. After hearing *Rienzi* in Linz, he had chosen the Master of Bayreuth to be his spiritual mentor. Then, barely twenty years later, Houston Stewart Chamberlain, intellectual leader of the Wagnerian cause, appointed him Wagner's successor, the man who, as the saviour of Germany, would fulfil all the Master's hopes.

Scarcely anyone knew of this commission. Both Hitler and the Bayreuth camp held their peace. Nor did they breathe a word about the precious treasure that was presented to him years later to set the seal on his secret appointment. A casual remark to Goebbels and Himmler that he was in possession of a number of original scores of Wagner's operas sounded as though he was referring to a collection of gramophone records.[32] In fact he was referring to a cache of priceless leather-bound volumes matched only by the vaults of Wahnfried; as well as complete manuscript scores of Wagner's early operas,[33] it included the orchestral sketch of *Der fliegende Holländer*, fair copies of *Das Rheingold* and *Die Walküre* and various other parts of the *Ring des Nibelungen*. It was a question, therefore, not merely of a series of irreplaceable documents such as no museum could boast, let alone a private individual, but of part of Wagner's bequest.

Hitler had come into possession of this Nibelungen treasure not by virtue of his position, nor through expropriation of the kind that was commonplace in the days of the Third Reich, but through the agency of Winifred Wagner, the composer's daughter-in-law, who is said to have negotiated its sale.[34] The volumes were presented to Hitler on his fiftieth birthday. In this way the most extensive collection of Wagner's works outside Wahnfried came into the hands of the man of whose kingdom Winifred herself, together with her Festival, had long been a courtier.

After the precious volumes had been handed to the Führer by the Confederation of German Industry in the course of the celebrations of what

had become virtually an annual national holiday, Hitler, to general astonishment, embarked on a scholarly résumé of the works as though they
were already his intellectual property.[35] The manuscripts had not been in
the hands of the industrialists for long. They originally belonged to King
Ludwig of Bavaria, to whom Wagner presented them in gratitude for his
generosity in financial matters. The manuscripts then passed into the care
of the administrators of the estate of the Wittelsbach dynasty, to which
Ludwig belonged, until Winifred Wagner became aware of their where-
abouts and laid her own claim to them. In the event the industrialists, with
whom Bayreuth had always had friendly relations, offered a substantial
sum to persuade the Wittelsbachs to part with the collection, and Hitler,
who regarded himself as the custodian of the Wagnerian heritage in succession to King Ludwig, accepted the generous gift without further ado.
He already knew that among the manuscripts was that of *Rienzi*, the work
with which everything had begun for him in Linz in 1906.

According to Winifred Wagner, Hitler was 'addicted' to Wagner's music;[36] others called it an 'obsession'.[37] But this was less important than the
reverse, namely that Bayreuth was 'addicted' to Hitler and built an 'obses-
sive' cult around him. Long before his political successes he had become
the anointed saviour of the Wagnerian religion. So when – under duress,
as the Wittelsbachs later complained – the precious bequest was disposed
of by being presented to Hitler on his birthday, it was not being disposed
of at all, because Hitler *was* Bayreuth, the blessed guardian of its holy relics.

His induction came shortly before the Putsch of 1923. With an unenvi-
able reputation as a rabble-rousing demagogue, and at the same time
cosseted by industrialists sympathetic to the interests of Bayreuth, he had
made himself *persona grata* to Houston Stewart Chamberlain, the ruthless
racialist thinker of the age of empire who had converted Wagner's
Weltanschauung into a philosophical system which he expounded in a
bestseller called *Foundations of the Nineteenth Century*. Chamberlain made
himself the high priest of a surging German nationalism, counting among
his admirers many of the country's intellectual elite and the aristocracy,
led by Kaiser Wilhelm II. A close friend of Cosima Wagner and the husband of her daughter Eva, he soon rose to become the custodian of the
Master's legacy.

Afflicted with what was probably multiple sclerosis, Chamberlain began to cast around for a successor. Like the wounded Amfortas, keeper of
the Holy Grail, who could only be relieved of his torment by the 'guileless
fool' Parsifal, he awaited the advent of the young hero who would put an
end to his suffering, rescue Bayreuth from its impotence and liberate Germany from the curse of the 'Jew-ridden Weimar Republic'.

Given the similarities between the room to which Chamberlain was confined in Bayreuth, where the curtains remained drawn the whole day, and

the underground cell in the Berlin bunker, Hitler might have been reminded of his suffering mentor huddled in his wheelchair, trembling and barely able to utter an intelligible word, a victim, as he saw himself, of the recent war and of the hostile forces that were spreading their tentacles over the Reich. Now, at the end of *his* war, it was Hitler's turn to tremble, to be gripped by the same paralysis that had earlier gripped Chamberlain. Nobody listened any more to the tyrant's raucous tones. He was no longer in touch with reality. Like Chamberlain, he saw the gulf open up inexorably before him.

Yet was not he too, again like Chamberlain, entitled to hope that there might be some way out? The clock said two minutes to twelve,[38] the perfect moment for a saviour to emerge from the shadows. Such had been the role he played in 1923 when he appeared as a living redeemer before the stricken Chamberlain. Receiving him as a man sent by God, Chamberlain rejoiced that 'at the moment of her greatest need, Germany should have given birth to a man such as Hitler'.[39] Nor was he mistaken. For years Hitler was to guide the fate of Germany and lead its people to what he saw as a glorious age. Now the one-time redeemer was himself confined to his dungeon, at the mercy of a superior enemy and left only to hope that fate would again work a miracle.

But the miracle of mercy had already been forfeited. He had made the whole of mankind his enemy. All too zealously he had embraced the prophecies of Wagner and his son-in-law; all too determinedly he had put into effect the policies expected of a man of action. For years, said Theodor Heuss, later President of the German Federal Republic, in 1932, eyes had been scanning the horizon for 'a new Siegfried who, in company with Wagner and Chamberlain, would emerge as the saviour of the German *Volk*'.[40] Or as Wolfgang Wagner, the present director of the Bayreuth Festival, put it, people were looking for 'an Aryan Messiah'.[41]

In 1923 the thirty-four-year-old Hitler was hailed as that Messiah. From his very first meeting with the barely articulate Chamberlain, at which Eva acted as interpreter, Hitler's political course was set. The influence of Bayreuth rested not on popular support but on individual conservative personalities and organizations. But in order to bring down the hated Weimar Republic it was not enough to be fanatically anti-Semitic – a hero was needed who would stand for the ideal of racial purity.

Three months after that meeting, Chamberlain, with the help of his scheming wife, published a pamphlet in which he laid out the radical new course for the future and introduced the Germans to their redeemer. Hitler, he wrote, with the authority of a man whose work had been compulsory reading in schools and military academies in imperial times, was a rare phenomenon whose courage was equal to Luther's and whose diplomatic skill matched that of Bismarck. In contrast to most politicians, Chamberlain went on, this man was not a mere 'peddler of empty phrases' but one who 'thought through the logic of his ideas and drew the relevant conclusions without flinching'. The central conclusion, stated back in 1850 by Wagner himself, was: 'One cannot declare allegiance both to Jesus and to those who nailed Him to the Cross.' Hitler, furthermore, not only shared the view, fundamental to the Bayreuth circle, 'that the influence of the Jews on German life had been utterly pernicious', but also had the 'abundant courage' necessary to act accordingly. Many had long recognized the danger and realized that 'measures had to be taken in order to counter it', but 'no one has dared to speak out openly or to put his conclusions into practice. No one, that is, except Adolf Hitler.'[42]

The pamphlet in which this self-fulfilling prophecy appeared received wide attention. Its effect on Hitler, who had gained prominence since the end of the war with a series of tirades against the Jews, was like that of a pronouncement by the Norns. He was the man of destiny, his path defined by fate. No longer was he a mere herald of the saviour to come – he *was* that saviour. He had sensed this since his visits to the opera house in Linz. It was all written in the stars.

To what extent the seventy-eight-year-old Chamberlain really knew the young Austrian firebrand we cannot tell. His knowledge came from the Wagner family, who had spoken enthusiastically about him for years; what was written about him may only have borne Chamberlain's name. At any rate he seems to have projected all his accumulated longings and visions onto Hitler and cast him as a mythical character in the fantasy world of Wagner's *Parsifal* – to Hitler's 'childlike delight'.[43]

In the course of a life now coming to an end in the depths of his musty bunker Hitler had acted out his vision, first by launching a *coup d'état* and subsequently spending a period in jail, then by seizing power in the Reich, and finally by making Bayreuth the centre of German cultural life. At the same time he had declared permanent war on 'Jewry' in all its forms, from Bolshevism to plutocracy and from degenerate art to the world of finance, pledging to annihilate those Europeans who could be included in a definition of the term. As he thought, so he behaved.

All this took place without his ever revealing the secret of his mission. As, on the one hand, he kept its origin in the Wagnerian world to himself, so, on the other, he laid a veil over its terrible consequences. What had begun with a lofty silence about his role as redeemer led to persistent lies about the 'final solution'. Only through absolute dictatorship could he realize his aims. Only as a mass murderer could he prove his credentials as a redeemer.

The homage that Chamberlain had paid him, followed by his initiation into the ranks of the Bayreuth disciples and his acceptance into the family, brought about a sudden flush of self-confidence. Hitherto he had registered his successes mainly in the atmosphere of taverns and beer-halls; now he knew that his fate was inextricably bound up with Wagner. *Rienzi* had been his awakening; the Master's writings, then almost totally forgotten, had converted him to the Wagnerian cause; and above all the *Ring* and *Parsifal* had provided a 'granite' foundation for his outlook on the world. Hitler saw the world through Wagner's spectacles and received Bayreuth's official blessing. They had waited a long time for this man to appear.

Mein Kampf became the most durable evidence of his vocation. Hitler's overweening self-estimation became contagious and led in Germany to a kind of religious mania, accompanied by displays of frenzied enthusiasm otherwise encountered only at mass demonstrations. Hitler's metaphysical vocation was made an item of national dogma. The crowds were swept off their feet not by what he was prepared to say but by the way he said it and the situation that he contrived in which to say it – in short, the unparalleled theatrical occasions that he created. And when the audiences for these performances, arrayed in uniform and drilled like soldiers, were themselves summoned to mount the stage, what had started as an obscene political display turned into an experience of collective revelation.

Nobody suspected that the Hitler state, a capricious assemblage of elements culled from Wagner's writings, accompanied by the heroic sounds of the music of the *Ring des Nibelungen*, could only be achieved after the 'Jewish question' had been solved. The gods in Valhalla had ordained that the destruction of their 'deadly enemy' must precede the age of the 'master race'. And though the air of intoxication had evaporated, the war been lost and Hitler's own life forfeited, he had to a large extent brought that destruction about.

Sitting in the midst of the thundering of the guns and composing his last testament,[44] Hitler could not conceal his satisfaction at his achievement. The words he dictated to his secretary sounded as though they had been whispered to him by Chamberlain, the arch-anti-Semite. The talk was of 'international Jewry slowly poisoning the whole world',[45] his final sentence, as the moment of death approached, calling for 'unremitting resistance' against the foe.

But the heart of his message remained veiled. Not even the 'love and loyalty' of and to the German *Volk*, of which he speaks again in his testament and from which he derived the strength to make his 'gravest decisions', could induce him to abandon the flowery language of the prophet of Bayreuth and say in plain terms what he meant. It was 29 April 1945, the day before he killed himself. There was no longer any cause for mystification – except for the fact that it was inseparably bound up with his secret role as Messiah. And this was a role that would not lapse even with his death.

As though trying to avoid at all costs the direct truth, Hitler couched his confessions and his attempted justification of his crimes in terms intelligible only to the inner circle. It was not he who had 'sought and provoked war', he claimed, but the Jews. Nor was it he who bore the responsibility for 'the ruin of our cities and the destruction of our artistic monuments':

the Jews alone bore the guilt for this 'murderous struggle'. If, his argument continued, he had felt compelled to take 'grave decisions, graver than any mortal had hitherto been called upon to make', then it had been not in his own interests but only 'out of love of and loyalty to my people' – as though the people had ever been consulted over such decisions. They were never asked, and the few who knew what was going on were bound to secrecy. The people would have been better off without the Führer's avowals of love and loyalty.

But it was not some obscure religion that had compelled him to make decisions such as 'no mortal' had made before and forced upon him one last cruel resolve. Nor did he make this final resolve as a politician or as a military commander, still less as the supreme representative of the German people. He made it as the man chosen to fulfil Wagner's prophecies and carry out the charge laid on him by Chamberlain.

The whole terrible sequence of his 'decisions', the mass murders by shooting and gassing, seemed to him, as he was dictating his testament, like acts of mercy. As Wagner had presented the downfall of the Jews as their 'salvation',[46] so now, his disciple explained, they were required, being those actually responsible for the war, to purge their guilt 'by more humane means'[47] – humane means such as shooting and gassing. Only the most brutal and callous of men, mocking his innocent victims as he himself waits for death, could have uttered such words. In homage to his God he plans secret orgies of killing in dark secret places in pits and ravines, in windowless chambers, in 'the bosom of night and death', as Wagner once put it.[48] 'Centuries will pass', he proclaimed, 'before, one way or another, the seed will germinate and the world can experience a shining new dawn.'[49]

But before transfiguration must come destruction. And if it did not come forthwith, he wrote, he would find himself unwillingly playing the principal role in another piece of theatre, 'this time enacted by the Jews'. For a whole week, reported Goebbels, the inhabitants of the bunker waited in 'a doom-laden atmosphere'[50] for the sound of a shot from the Führer's room – the shot of final deliverance.[51] He had given up his original idea of dying while fighting on the steps of his Chancellery. The only alternative was suicide in his concrete cell, followed by the Wagnerian immolation of the corpse. 'Let me perish in the flames of Valhalla,' Wagner cried.[52] In the event he died of a heart attack on a plush sofa in a Venetian palazzo.

His successor managed things better. The stage was set for *Götterdämmerung*, and on 12 April, in spite of the air raids, the Berlin Philharmonic Orchestra played Siegfried's Funeral March at their farewell concert,[53] a prelude to what was to follow. In *Götterdämmerung* Siegfried and Brünnhilde pass through the flames into redemption and eternity. Hitler's end was to symbolize the same progression, with the necessary reservations demanded by reality.

Hitler had obtained from Himmler cyanide capsules prepared in the concentration camp of Sachsenhausen.[54] For years cyanide, originally intended for use as a pesticide, had been used in the camps as a means of mass destruction. When a phial was broken in the mouth, a gas formed that stopped the flow of oxygen, causing the victim to suffocate and leaving a smell of bitter almonds.

Legend has it that Hitler, with his notoriously suspicious nature, tried out a capsule on his favourite dog, Blondi, observing the effect with an 'expressionless face'.[55] Since Hitler, like Wagner, was a fanatical opponent of experiments on animals, this is highly improbable. More likely is the explanation that he wanted the faithful Blondi to join him in death. And not only Blondi died before him but also her five puppies and any other dogs that could be found in the bunker. The massacre was carried out by an army sergeant with his revolver.[56]

This pointless killing formed part of the whole gruesome ritual of Hitler's death. As Brünnhilde had ridden into the flames on her steed, Grane, so he too, following Germanic tradition, planned to take his comrades with him on his final journey. In spite of his impending demise he had trained Wolf, his favourite puppy from Blondi's litter, entirely on his own and held him on his lap as he engaged in silent conversation with the portrait of Frederick the Great. No one else was allowed even to touch the dog.[57]

The name Wolf went back to Wagner, who had given Wotan, clad in his wolfskin, the pseudonym of Wolf. Hitler now adopted it as his own *nom de guerre*. He had spied for the German army in the 1920s under the name Wolf; the Wagner children in Bayreuth knew him as 'Uncle Wolf'; the place where the Volkswagen factory was built was named Wolfsburg; and the succession of places from where Hitler conducted the course of the war were disguised under various Wolf names. The little 'Wolf' now showed the big Wolf the way.

The sacrifice of the dogs in the bunker was actually Act Two of Hitler's drama. It had begun a week earlier, on 22 April, when, unnerved by the ever-increasing roar of the Russian artillery, he declared the war was lost and announced his intention to commit suicide. 'The Führer is a broken man', reported General Christian. 'When the Russians come, he will take the logical step and shoot himself.'[58] His resolve had a number of irrevocable consequences, among them the decision to sacrifice his most treasured possessions. These included an extensive collection of his architectural and artistic sketches which he once described as his 'most precious possession, the child of my own mind'.[59] But in the depths of his safe in the bunker there also lay the symbol of his devotion to the cause of Bayreuth – his collection of Wagner manuscripts. One can imagine him during those endless nights in the bunker, hunched over the scores in the flickering candlelight and gazing on an original letter of Frederick the Great's which had been included with the manuscripts. He was Wagner's heir, owner of his inheritance, as at the end of *Götterdämmerung* Brünnhilde seizes the ring, her inheritance, symbol of world domination, before riding off into the fire on her trusty Grane.[60]

Hitler may well have regarded his precious manuscripts as a comparable symbol of world domination, and as their rightful heir, he could do with them what he liked. In better days they had confirmed his metaphysical mission; now, in the moment of his defeat, they were to be his faithful companions on the journey to where all Wagnerian heroes, battered but not vanquished, found their rest. Not even those closest to him knew what was in his mind.

But they had their misgivings. Maybe they sometimes suspected that they had banked on the wrong Messiah. But Bayreuth thought in practical terms, and, heedless of the disaster facing the country, plans were put in hand, to Hitler's satisfaction, for the Bayreuth Festival in the summer of 1945.[61] In anticipation of better times to come, a new edition of Wagner's complete works was also set in train in the research centre that Hitler had founded. But since a task of this magnitude could not possibly be carried out without the Führer's express approval, Wieland Wagner, the composer's grandson, proposed to travel to Berlin himself in order to win over his godfather. However close the threat of the Russians and the Americans might be at the end of 1944, the new Wagner edition had to take precedence.[62]

Wieland sensed that he had to strike while the iron was hot. Not only did the imminent collapse of the Third Reich illustrate the urgency of embarking on the work, but also the project provided him with a pretext for gaining possession of the Wagner scores themselves. Winifred Wagner speculated that the Führer might in any case be considering giving them to Bayreuth.[63] Uncle Wolf, after all, could no longer have much use for them in the ruins of his capital. So why not part with them?

This is where Wieland's role came in. From the time of their first meeting in 1923 Hitler had loved the boy as though he were his own son and showered him with favours, according to his mother, including securing his exemption from military service. Wieland, for whom Hitler was a 'father substitute',[64] showed his gratitude by calling his son Wolf Siegfried. Charged with early responsibility for productions at Bayreuth, Wieland now made his precarious way through a war-torn Germany to Berlin on what Winifred called 'inheritance matters'.[65]

As Chamberlain had made Hitler Wagner's intellectual heir, and as Winifred, for her part, may have seen to it that he received the Wagner scores, the Wagnerian inheritance was intended to pass from Winifred to her oldest son Wieland. But Hitler had other ideas. He had set his own indelible seal on the interpretation of Wagner's philosophy and his was the name that would be linked for all time to the achievement of its objectives. 'Adolf Hitler has turned the Bayreuth ideal into the German ideal,' wrote a critic in 1936.[66] Eight years later he had the whole of Europe under his heel. When at the end of 1944 Wieland Wagner arrived in Berlin to ask to be allowed to take his grandfather's works back to Bayreuth, he found Uncle Wolf unsympathetic. 'The scores can be nowhere safer than here with me,' he said dismissively over supper.[67]

This remained the situation until 22 April. On that day Hitler ordered his safes to be emptied and the entire contents incinerated.[68] Over the following days the same was done in Munich and in the Berghof, his mountain retreat at Berchtesgaden, where he kept his sketches. No one was to lay hands on his most precious possessions. According to an eye-witness in Berlin, 'he ordered all his papers and documents to be brought out into the courtyard of the Chancellery and burned. That is being done this very minute.'[69]

After the abortive attempt to rescue their crown jewels, there was still a glimmer of hope for the Wagner family. On 23 April a transport aircraft took off from Berlin carrying what was described as 'top secret material of the utmost importance to the Führer'.[70] When the plane was reported shortly afterwards as having crashed, Hitler called it a 'disaster . . . in which important documents vital for an understanding of my actions and decisions' had been lost.[71] But although the machine had crashed, it had not burned out, which left a faint chance that the lost treasure might one day be recovered.

But it was not to be. It turned out that the missing boxes of papers had apparently contained not Wagner's works, but 'the original records of the Führer's so-called *Tischgespräche* [table-talk] since 1942'.[72] The scores themselves, however, were never found, in spite of investigations by Interpol instigated by Winifred Wagner after the war.[73] They were probably lost in the confusion of those final hours in the bunker.

A senseless act of destruction would in fact have fitted into the Wagnerian tradition, for while he was working on the poem of the *Ring* the Master himself, according to Chamberlain, 'had contemplated destroying all his scores'[74] – a custom continued in Bayreuth after his death, when vital personal documents and correspondence continued to be destroyed.

It was Chamberlain's biography of Wagner, published in 1895 by Bruckmann, a firm which was to become one of Hitler's most avid supporters in the 1920s, that turned the story of Wagner's life into a hagiography. His sublime thoughts had for Chamberlain the character of holy writ, a source of inspiration that must necessarily remain restricted to an inner circle of acolytes.[75] He spoke of his idol as of one risen from the dead, 'a man who had lived and suffered on earth and whose name should be cherished in our hearts as in a holy shrine[76] . . . a saviour in the mould of Jesus Christ'.[77] Hitler's ultimate goal, Chamberlain concluded, was to show mankind 'the road to salvation . . . from a world of wickedness and deceit, a world of murder and legalized plunder',[78] and to save it from the 'demoralizing influence of the Jews'.[79]

To achieve this, Chamberlain continued, Wagner – 'this pure, noble, totally selfless man devoted solely to the cause of art at its finest and most sublime'[80] – could not but become a martyr. Misunderstood by his own people, he was persecuted by those whose crimes he had exposed. 'No artist has ever evoked such merciless hatred' – words which made a special impression on Hitler. Tormented by the Jews, Wagner spent his 'sad and lonely last years in the isolation of Bayreuth', where, 'his health ruined by the deprivations and sufferings he had to endure', and his final victory to establish his Festival 'spurned and ridiculed', he breathed his last. 'It was a life brought to an end before its time.'[81]

Such was the legend disseminated by Chamberlain, evangelist of Bayreuth, the legend perpetuated by the young opera lover from Linz who had now found his life's vocation in the preservation of the Wagnerian bequest. Nor was it his vocation only in life. In death too, a death that recalled Wagner's vision of his agony on the cross, Hitler found himself beset by the same enemies that had 'brought the Master's life to an end before its time'.

Hitler's end was no less lonely, although at least he was to have the company of his dogs and his precious manuscripts – and of his mistress, another gesture to Wagner. The Dutchman with Senta, Tannhäuser with Elisabeth, Tristan with Isolde – all were united in death, in 'the kingdom of eternal darkness', as Wagner called it.[82] Cosima alone broke the divine ordinance, taking leave of her partner – in spite of their firm agreement – only forty-seven years later, by which time Hitler had long paid his respects in the Villa Wahnfried.

In the bunker, however, tradition was observed and Hitler died as bridegroom, with Eva Braun as his bride. The wedding took place after midnight on 19 April 'with all bureaucratic formalities',[83] followed by a champagne reception. The ceremony was conducted by a man called Wagner. The next day they mounted the funeral pyre together as Siegfried and Brünnhilde, intoxicated with thoughts of Valhalla. 'It was Eva's wish to join me in death,' dictated Hitler to his secretary. It will compensate us for that which my work in the service of my people denied us.'[84]

The rest of the ceremony followed step by step as he had planned it.[85] After bidding farewell to their faithful retinue, the couple went into Hitler's living room. As Frederick the Great looked down from the wall and the Russian guns rumbled all around, they swallowed the cyanide capsules Himmler had given them and Hitler shot himself through his right temple. The bunker breathed a sigh of relief.

When his servant Linge cautiously opened the door, the scent of bitter almonds was wafted towards him.[86] Five more members of the bunker staff followed, stood to attention in front of the sofa on which the two bodies lay and gave the Nazi salute. Then they solemnly carried the bodies up four flights of stairs to the open air. The dead Siegfried had been borne away in similar procession to the strains of Wagner's funeral march.

A few hours later radios throughout the country resounded to the sound of this solemn music. Maybe Hitler had listened to it before killing himself. Or maybe it had been the Liebestod from *Tristan und Isolde*, a piece which, according to his secretary, 'he had wished to hear in his final hour'.[87] The gramophone records lay to hand.

As the funeral procession emerged from the entrance to the bunker, it was met by the Russian artillery. Hastily the two bodies were wrapped in blankets, put in a pit and drenched in petrol. The shells were landing ever closer, and the pall-bearers retreated for a moment to the safety of the bunker, then came out again to set fire to the bodies. Coming again to attention, they raised their arms in a final salute as a pall of smoke rose high into the air, then sought a place to hide.

When darkness had fallen, the charred bodies were interred in a shell crater beneath a pile of rubble. A more piteous end can hardly be imagined. Yet even here a higher power seemed to be at work. For Rienzi, the Roman tribune at the centre of Wagner's opera, had also perished in the flames together with his sister, and been buried under the ruins of the Capitol. Hitler played out his role to the very end.

2

THE LAST OF THE TRIBUNES

B orn fourteen years before 'Brother Hitler', as he once called him,[1] Thomas Mann described in 'Wagner and Our Time' the 'spiritual intoxication' into which he was plunged by the works of a composer whom 'one must have experienced and understood if one is to have any comprehension of the modern world'.[2] Mann was referring to Richard Wagner, 'source of the most fertile, most profound experience of my youth'.[3] The opera he had heard in the Stadttheater in Lübeck had introduced him to a new, more stimulating, more sublime reality than 'the everyday drabness' of his family and his school life, which now shrank into the background.

Moreover this was a profoundly German art. The superiority of the Germans in intellectual matters throughout the nineteenth century, universally acknowledged, showed itself nowhere more strikingly than in Wagner's operas, where heroism and the search for God, ancestor worship and human progress all seemed to have found their ultimate expression. It was at an open-air concert in Rome that the twenty-year-old Mann first heard Siegfried's Funeral March from *Götterdämmerung*, an archetypal piece of 'German art'.[4] Part of the audience whistled and booed; others applauded wildly. The battle between the two sides raged to and fro until the leitmotif of Siegfried's sword rang out, 'its beat pounding out across the piazza', wrote Mann. 'Then, at its climax, with the crashing dissonance before the two great C-major chords, a mighty roar of triumph burst out, reducing the shattered opposition to silence.' At the moment twenty years later when Mann wrote these words, recalling 'the tears that ran down my cheeks at the sound of the Nothung motif', the First World War had just broken out. It was as though that earlier musical experience had been translated into political reality.

But it was not the blond warrior Siegfried, victor over the forces of darkness yet in the end himself to become a victim of their treachery, whom Thomas Mann, spurning 'milder words such as love and enthusiasm',[5] enshrined at the heart of what he called his 'passion' for Wagner: it was the shining knight Lohengrin, messenger of the Grail. Thirty years earlier, in the plush crimson splendour of the opera house in Munich, the Crown Prince Ludwig had sat in the royal box 'weeping in uncontrollable ecstasy at the spectacle'.[6]

Ten years after Thomas Mann it was the turn of Adolf Hitler, the twelve-year-old yokel from Linz, to be moved by the same music. 'I was swept off my feet', he later wrote of that evening, 'and my enthusiasm knew no bounds.'[7] For the country boy 'without friends and companions',[8] a failure at school and described by his teachers as 'obstinate, rebellious, opinionated and irascible',[9] Lohengrin, the outsider, was a gift from the gods. The other Wagnerian heroes soon followed, showing him with magic sword and holy spear the road that led to the Grail Castle. 'My burning desire from my thirteenth year onwards was to attend the Bayreuth Festival,' he later told Wagner's son Siegfried.[10] In *Mein Kampf* he remarked ironically that he would be eternally grateful for the mediocrity of the performances in Linz 'because they carried with them the assurance of better things to come'.[11] These 'better things' came when, at seventeen, he heard performances of world class in Vienna, among them one of *Tristan und Isolde* conducted by Mahler, with sets by Alfred Roller. So impressed was he by these sets that he frequently made drawings of them in his sketch books of the 1920s, and at his behest Roller's designs were incorporated in the nocturnal sets for Act Two of *Tristan* in the Bayreuth production of 1938.

Thomas Mann, from his superior vantage-point of cultural mentor, could establish an ironical distance between himself and the man he called 'the snuff-taking gnome from Saxony'.[12] Hitler could afford no such luxury. He imagined himself living the life of those he would have dearly loved to be. 'Only when the mighty waves of sound roll through space', he wrote, 'and the whistling of the wind yields to the frightful rushing billows of sound does one feel sublimity and forget the gold and velvet with which the interior is overloaded.'[13] The gulf between performers and listeners, between art and reality – indeed, between the Wagnerian in the audience and his heroic paragon on the stage – vanishes.

For Hitler, who as a schoolboy claimed 'no longer to believe in anything . . . and that everything had to be destroyed',[14] the opera house, with its funeral pyres and its burning castles, was the place where he could watch his dreams of destruction being turned into reality. Born a Catholic, he told an American reporter many years later that to attend a performance of Wagner was like going to mass.[15]

A friend and fellow-enthusiast called August Kubizek recalled one such occasion in November 1906. 'We were shattered by a performance of *Rienzi*,' he wrote. 'But although, when Hitler had been moved by a work, he usu-

ally began to talk about it the moment it was over, and subject the performance to severe criticism, this time he remained silent for a long time.'[16]
The hero, with whom the two friends were in the habit of identifying themselves, was in this case not a character from legend, like Lohengrin or
Parsifal, but an historical figure pledged to the overthrow of the existing
order. The revolutionary 'tribune of the people', his rise and fall portrayed
by Wagner to the accompaniment of fanfares, the roll of drums and triumphant processions, had really lived. When Hitler later wrote in *Mein Kampf*
that he had learned the lesson of history and become in his early days both
an artistic and a political revolutionary,[17] he could well have had the figure
of Rienzi in mind.

Kubizek goes on to describe a remarkable change that came over Hitler
after they had left the opera house. Hitler had suggested they walk up the
Freinberg, a hill above the Danube. Then his voice suddenly took a new
and quite extraordinary tone such as Kubizek had never heard before. 'It
was as though a quite different voice were coming from his mouth,' wrote
Kubizek, 'a voice which gripped him as powerfully as it did me.' It was the
voice of the tribune Rienzi, 'speaking as though to the assembled masses
before him'. In glowing images he declared it his mission 'to liberate the
people from bondage and reveal to them the joys of freedom'. As the 'real'
Hitler returned, ended Kubizek, 'the clocks on the church towers struck
three, as though heralding a new dawn'.[18]

Kubizek's account of these events, recorded decades later, was received
with considerable scepticism, seen as conforming too conveniently to Hitler's own interpretation of his career. Yet in its essence it may well be true.
Years later, in 1939, in a letter thanking his former friend for securing him
an invitation to Bayreuth, Kubizek referred to 'the youthful dreams which
you unfurled to me after we had seen those operas of Wagner's'.[19] When
the two men finally met again at Wahnfried, the Wagner family villa in
Bayreuth, Kubizek reminded the Führer of that night on the Freinberg.
'Hitler remembered the occasion down to the last detail,' he wrote.[20]
Winifred Wagner later confirmed the story. So did Albert Speer, Hitler's
architect, who wrote in 1938 that he had heard from Hitler himself that it
had been the 'divine music of *Rienzi*' that had inspired him with the conviction 'that he would succeed in uniting the German nation behind him
and making the Third Reich great'.[21] And later, in 1942, in his military headquarters of the so-called 'Wolf's Lair' in East Prussia,[22] he recalled that it
had been 'at a performance of *Rienzi* in Linz that he first had the idea of
becoming a politician – a tribune of the people'.[23]

On the occasion of Kubizek's visit to Bayreuth in 1939, shortly before
Hitler's invasion of Poland, the two men paid a visit to Wagner's grave in
the garden of Wahnfried – 'the spot that had always been the most sacred
of places for us', said the Führer.[24] This had been the moment when he
referred to that performance of *Rienzi* in Linz. 'I shall never forget', said

Kubizek, 'what he said in all gravity to Frau Wagner: "That was when it all began."'[25]

Hitler remained faithful to *Rienzi* throughout his life. Like the Roman tribune he sought to liberate the oppressed masses and offer them the prospect of a glorious future in the tradition of their forgotten ancestors – without repeating Rienzi's mistakes. And Wagner's 'grand tragic opera' of 1840 he saw as a paradigm for political action in the twentieth century.

One day in 1931 he was being driven in his supercharged Mercedes through villages decorated in his honour and lined with cheering spectators when he suddenly thought of spending the evening at the opera. Expressing a desire to see *Rienzi* in Weimar, he was asked by his travelling companion, a Party official called Otto Wagener, whether he did not find it an uncomfortable experience to sit in the theatre 'and watch a man of the people who had risen to the position of national leader being destroyed by a conspiracy on the part of those around him'.[26] Although in 1931 he was far from being 'the leader of his people', Hitler saw what Wagener was getting at and replied with a smile: 'On the contrary, I recognize, each time I see that opera, what mistakes I might be in danger of making, so as to avoid them when my time comes.'

There was a special relevance to Hitler's remark, for, according to Wagener, he was afraid that, as in Rienzi's time, there might be a counter-revolution from the right. 'A reactionary coup', he said on his way back from their evening at the opera, 'would amount to a betrayal both of us and of the German people.' In contrast to Rienzi, however, he reflected on the counter-measures he could take – 'another reason for being glad to see *Rienzi* again'.

This self-identification of Hitler's with Rienzi had its own private history. In his parents' house in the village of Leonding, outside Linz, he used to wrap a tablecloth round himself like a toga and pretend to be a 'Roman senator'.[27] As Party leader he took as his model Cesare Borgia, who, a century after Rienzi, had avoided those mistakes which had led to the tribune's downfall. Where Rienzi, despite the protests of the people, had shown mercy towards the nobles who had betrayed him, such generosity was not to be expected from Cesare Borgia, Macchiavelli's Prince. According to his Party comrade Otto Strasser, Hitler enjoyed telling the story of how Cesare, having invited the heads of the leading Roman families to a banquet in his house to celebrate their reconciliation, ordered a band of men in black to tie them up so that he could personally slay them one by one.[28] 'Hitler told this tale with relish,' said Strasser – whose brother Gregor, also present, met a similar fate years later at the hand of his Führer.

Hitler seems to have been particularly impressed by the fact that in Wagner's opera it is the people, as opposed to their benevolent tribune, who demand the death of the traitors.[29] Hitler suspected treachery everywhere, and set out to counter it by Borgia's methods. Watching the Reichstag fire in 1933, an event that reminded him of the destruction of the Capitol at the end of *Rienzi*, Hitler behaved like an avenging angel, according to Rudolf Diels, chief of the Gestapo. 'He was flushed with excitement and with the heat of the fire in the Reichstag dome,' reported Diels, 'raving totally out of control in a way I had never seen before and bellowing: "We shall show no mercy! Those who oppose us will be ground into the dust!"' Every communist official, Hitler thundered on, would be shot that very night and every communist deputy hanged: 'The people will not tolerate any act of clemency.'[30] They are words taken almost literally from *Rienzi*.[31]

There was another political mistake of Rienzi's from which Hitler learned his lesson. As he explained after his visit to the opera in 1931, Rienzi had no political party to back him up[32] but only the masses, with their fickle loyalty. As a lone fighter, he was vulnerable. In order not to be betrayed by the aristocracy, the landowners and the industrialists – those to whom Rienzi had offered the hand of friendship – there was only one way: 'We must strengthen and consolidate the Party and make it immune to the dangers of a reactionary nationalist Putsch from the right.' A pathological fear of betrayal, such as that to which Rienzi had fallen victim, pursued Hitler throughout his life and finally took complete possession of his mind. He adopted for himself the motto that Wagner had put into the mouth of his operatic hero: 'Death to the traitors!'[33]

On the other hand a tragic hero must not be allowed to escape his fate, for in his downfall lies his victory, and the inevitability of this process, which both frightens and inspires the audience, marks the dramatic climax of the action on the stage. In the finale of Wagner's opera Rienzi himself takes on heroic form, his body borne to the raging inferno to the accompaniment of the triumphant sounds of the full orchestra. And before cursing his faithless city and its 'degenerate people'[34] – Wagner's concept of 'degeneracy' was also to make a lasting impression on Hitler – Rienzi reveals the secret of his heroism: he can never surrender to the love of a mortal woman. Since his youth his passion has been directed towards a 'higher creature, his life devoted to the salvation of one shamefully degraded, scorned, dishonoured and abused'. So at the end, as he faces death, he cries: 'Be it known to all! My beloved is called Rome!'[35]

Rienzi's cry echoed on through the decades. For the new Rienzi too, who found his Fatherland in a similar state of humiliation in 1918, had no intention of marrying. It was a source of happiness that he had to deny himself, he said in 1930, because he had already chosen another bride – 'Germany! I am already married – to the German people!' All the more intensely, therefore, did he feel the agony of Wagner's hero. 'I see how the people suffer, tormented by the terms of the wretched Treaty of Versailles and ground under the heel of enemy troops.' 'I watch', he went on, as though picking up Rienzi's lament, 'while they are scorned and abused.' Finally: 'My heart belongs to my people. No, I cannot – may not – marry!'[36]

One of the most popular icons of the Führer, commissioned in 1938, shows him dressed as Wagner's 'last of the tribunes', bareheaded and resplendent in full armour.[37] Summoned by the echoing call of the trumpet, the people of Rome flock to pay homage to their new Messiah and break into a frenzy of rejoicing. Taking his cue from the cries of jubilation, the tribune makes his solemn appearance before the crowd and the cry goes up from a thousand throats: 'Hail Rienzi!'[38] Wagner's theatrical portrayal of the scene can, of course, lay no claim to historical authenticity. But it did make its mark on history. Its choreography of the serried ranks of triumphant marchers, taken from the stage of the theatre in Linz and transferred to the open-air arena in Nuremberg, provided a model for the Nazi Party rallies of the 1930s.

Hitler chose the Overture to *Rienzi* to open the Party spectacle. The long trumpet call, characterized by Wagner as 'awesome', rouses the nation from its slumber and summons it to action. Then follows Rienzi's prayer, the proud battle hymn and finally the triumphant chorus of the people, accompanied by trumpets and drums, reaching its culmination in the rousing rhythm of a victory march. Hitler had opened his rally with a condensed version of his philosophical programme in musical terms. But few noticed it.

On occasion he also concluded the rally with the same music. In 1935, for instance, the six-day festival was brought to its spectacular close with a solemn procession of the standard bearers to the sound of the Nibelungen March, followed by the Overture to *Rienzi*.[39] When one of his ministers tried to persuade him to replace this by now hackneyed piece with something more modern, Hitler dismissed the idea as unthinkable. 'This is not just a question of the music,' he snapped indignantly.[40] Wagner's overture had become a kind of official anthem of the Third Reich.

It was entirely possible, above all for a seventeen-year-old youth captivated by scenes of military ostentation, to regard Wagner's monumental 'grand opera' as one continuous mass demonstration, broken only by speeches or sentimental outbursts which provided pretexts for fresh and ever more extravagant displays of pomp and circumstance. The dominant feature was the marching. Rank after rank of flag-waving citizens surged on to the stage brandishing their weapons aloft, then filed out in no less impressive formation. No other opera offered such a jubilant celebration of the rhythm of marching feet. The ritual of alternating groups of the *Volk* and the white-clothed 'ambassadors of peace', the columns of Roman citizens and of the aristocrats, the shining emissaries of the towns and the soldiers in their resplendent armour – all gave a glittering façade of variety to the amorphous mass of Hitler's hordes. Hitler himself, who had pretensions to being an amateur stage designer, had helped to create the costumes and also the banners, which proudly proclaimed their Roman provenance. That the Germanic emblems of victory were crowned with

the image of the Roman eagle probably has its origin in his personal passion for the Roman tribune. And as Rienzi 'woke the *Volk* from its sleep',
so Hitler's rallying cry became 'Germany Awake!'

Banners held high, fluttering in the wind of exhilaration, were the symbol of Rienzi's 'seizure of power', and their dedication to the popular cause
was the ritual climax of the celebrations. Hitler too consecrated a host of
new banners which were held aloft at his rallies like a forest of crimson
flags – crimson, because they all had their origin in the sacred 'Blood Banner', which, like Wagner's Holy Grail or the Turin Shroud, was only rarely
displayed before an enthralled and expectant congregation. This relic of
Hitler's failed Putsch in 1923 was a flag claimed to have been soaked in the
blood of the martyrs killed in the fighting that had put an end to Hitler's
uprising; a mystical aura was said to pass from the contact of this hallowed
flag with all the other banners, a ritualistic act performed by the Führer
himself.

This banner still remained a political symbol for him as late as 1944,
when he declared that he would 'always serve as a proud standard bearer'
at the head of his people.[41] Maybe he was recalling his Rienzi, who had
vowed to avenge his brother's death at the hands of the reactionary nobility. 'I have plunged this hand into the blood that flowed from my brother's
heart and sworn an oath!' he cries to his enemies. 'Woe to him who sheds
the blood of my kinsman!'[42] That bloodstained banner now flew at the head
of Hitler's vassals.

The Freinberg, the hill outside Linz where he had first been vouchsafed
his vision of Rienzi, also had a special place in Hitler's plans. Here Hermann
Giesler, his personal architect, whom he had charged with preparing designs for a monumental rebuilding of the town, was to erect 'a residence
for his old age'[43] – a place he specifically compared with 'the clear lines of
the Emperor Frederick II's charming Castel del Monte',[44] from which he
could look out over his ideal town with its new opera house. When in
1943, shortly after the German defeat at Stalingrad, Hitler attended a performance in the old theatre, he was overcome by his nostalgic memories of
the place – maybe also haunted by the vision of a *Götterdämmerung* to come
– and asked to be left alone. 'He stood there absentmindedly for a while,'
wrote Speer.[45] Two years later, shortly before his death in the bunker, he
took out the wooden model of his new opera house and expressed his ad-
miration of Giesler's work.

The real-life Rienzi has gone down in history as a dreamer with a tendency to self-dramatization. Born Nicola di Lorenzo, son of an innkeeper,
in *circa* 1313, Cola di Rienzi excelled as a classical scholar but was less successful as a politician. His sense of history and love of display made him
popular among the people of Rome but he forfeited his power through his
delusions of grandeur. His vision of a coming 'Third Reich' that would
turn the world into a garden of paradise after his opponents had been elimi-

nated also caused displeasure, in particular to the Pope. Allowing his dreams of power to go to his head, he was brought to his knees by the forces ranged against him.

Hitler quickly recognized his own embodiment in the figure of the Roman tribune. 'This son of a small innkeeper', he once said, in the presence of Albert Speer, 'was only twenty-four when he persuaded the Romans to get rid of their corrupt senate by calling to their minds the glorious days of the Empire.'[46] Rienzi was in fact ten years older than Hitler made out, but his praise would no doubt have been even more enthusiastic if he had known Wagner's source, Lord Bulwer-Lytton's vast novel *Rienzi, the Last of the Tribunes*. For Bulwer-Lytton has his hero claim that there was royal blood in his veins: the Emperor Henry VII, who had tried in vain to restore the faded fortunes of the Hohenstaufen dynasty in Italy, was his father, he maintained, and he, as his son, was therefore the rightful ruler of Rome.

If the Ghibelline Rienzi stood in the Hohenstaufen line from Barbarossa to Konradin, protectors of the Holy Roman Empire who the legend said were only waiting to return and reclaim their rightful possession, then the Guelphs, the Papal party, those responsible for the downfall of the imperial line, were their enemies. The historical Rienzi could thus see his struggle for Rome as a new chapter in the centuries-old rivalry between Germania and Rome for world domination. Hanging over Hitler's bed during his time in Vienna was a motto that read:

> If Jew and Church will leave the state,
> That will make Germania great![47]

Identification with the historical character who vacillated between heroism and bombast, between a thirst for power and the quest for national salvation, came naturally to Wagner, archetypal man of the theatre. Rienzi, born five hundred years, to the month, before Wagner, was also a passionate visionary, 'like a flash of light to his depressed and degenerate people whom he felt called upon to rescue'. The historical Rienzi, Wagner went on in this letter to the tenor Joseph Tichatschek, creator of the role, 'was a young man of about twenty-eight'[48] – making the same error as Hitler. It was he himself who was twenty-eight, and at the time he had plans for a further work, *Die Sarazenin* ('The Saracen Woman'), from the world of the Hohenstaufen dynasty.[49] He had always felt called to summon up the great ages of the past.

Richard Wagner, born in 1813, the youngest of a large family living in the Jewish quarter of Leipzig, grew up in Dresden in the house of his stepfather, an actor and painter named Geyer, who put his sisters on the stage at an early age. An imaginative boy but deprived of the attention of his parents, he became self-taught. The cramped surroundings, coupled with a chronic shortage of money, quickly induced in him a desire to live on a grand scale, a desire encouraged by a legend current in the family. His mother Johanna, a baker's daughter, had once confided to her children that she had at one time been the protégée of 'a well-placed friend of the family . . . whom she later described as a prince at the court of Weimar', as Wagner wrote suggestively in his autobiography.[50] His implication was subsequently made explicit by Houston Stewart Chamberlain, who claimed that Wagner could trace his origins back to the twelfth century, since his mother was the natural daughter of Prince Constantin von Sachsen-Weimar, brother of Goethe's friend Karl August.[51] Neither Wagner nor his son-in-law Chamberlain suspected what Johanna was really trying to say, namely that she was not Constantin's daughter but his mistress decades before Richard was born.[52] The legend of Wagner's aristocratic heritage persisted in Bayreuth for decades and became part of the cult which Hitler himself later embraced.

In reality Wagner, who, like his idol Rienzi, felt aristocratic blood coursing through his veins, lived a quite different life. Small in stature since childhood, denied a proper education, from a poor family but full of extravagant wishes, he resolved to become a musician,[53] setting his heart on achieving success in the field of opera. His chosen scene for this success was to be not some provincial German town like those in which he eked out a living by conducting, but Paris, where, in the city of revolution, he hoped to sweep audiences off their feet with his own revolutionary opera Rienzi.

But he lacked the necessary support. Dependent on occasional work for his livelihood, and suffering, like his hero, 'from the discrepancy between the nobility of his thoughts and feelings and the crude vulgarity of his environment',[54] he was in danger of being swallowed up by the metropolis, 'a victim of the pain of being unknown', as Berlioz, who was also in Paris at the time, cuttingly put it.[55] His hopes were dashed and he left as poor as he came, in obedience to what Heine mockingly called 'the voice of reason and of his stomach'.[56] As he crossed the German border, there were tears in his eyes. 'Impecunious musician that I was,' he wrote, 'I pledged unswerving loyalty to my German Fatherland from that moment.'[57]

But at the same time he swore eternal vengeance on his enemies, those whose jealousy he believed had ruined his chances in Paris but whom he was not yet prepared to mention by name. They too had their place in Rienzi – as the nobili, illegitimate possessors of power and riches. Not only were they the ideal target for any and every revolutionary, but their malevolent and despicable ways made them the model of the Antichrist, traditional adversary of any Messiah. As the Devil has taken possession of the world and brought it to rack and ruin, so his representatives on earth, the nobility, appear in Wagner's opera as usurpers. They have driven out the divine rulers of Rome and divided the city up among themselves, plundering it and reducing the holy Roman Empire to the level of Sodom and Gomorrah.

'You strangle our brothers while they are yet little children and seek to dishonour our sisters!' cries Rienzi to the oppressors. 'Rome, once the Queen of the world, you have turned into a robbers' den, and you even desecrate the Church!'[58] Sucked dry by the tyrants, the city lies barren, sterile; 'the menfolk have been put to the sword, the women defiled'. Rape, indeed, was for Wagner the salient characteristic of the enemy. The opera opens with an attempt to violate Rienzi's sister and reaches its climax in a pantomime enacting the classical motif of the rape of Lucretia. In naturalistic mode Wagner dwells on the protracted struggle between the noble Roman virgin and the ruthless conqueror, a struggle between 'uncontrolled lust' on one side and 'pleas for mercy' on the other,[59] ending with the triumph of the abuser and the suicide of his victim.

This powerful scene is meant not only to show the corrupt oppressors in their true light and to justify Rienzi's rebellion, but also to make the people aware that his revolt is an act of vengeance for 'a thousand years of ignominy and shame'[60] – for a crime, in other words, that went back to the days of the Roman Empire.

Hence the curse that Rienzi pronounces on his eternal foe: 'Never shall his misdeeds be forgiven on earth. Death to his soul! No God shall save him!' What foe could Rienzi have had in mind, a foe who had disturbed the order of the world not only during Rienzi's lifetime but a long while earlier, even abrogating to himself the riches of Antiquity? The answer is hinted at by one of the invaders himself, who reveals that Rienzi 'detested their whole tribe'[61] – in other words, the tribune, acting as Wagner's mouthpiece, was thinking of the Jews. Wagner frequently speaks of the Jews as an 'alien tribe' which has visited untold disasters on the human race over the centuries. And one need only recall Ahasverus, the Wandering Jew, or his female counterpart Kundry, who sets out to seduce the young Parsifal. It had been the Jews, moreover, who, according first to Wagner's, then to Chamberlain's, paranoid conviction, had destroyed the empire of the Caesars with the help of the Christians, had undermined the medieval dynasty of the Hohenstaufens, had ruined Rienzi's Rome, and then finally, having taken over the whole German Empire, had slandered and intrigued against Wagner himself, condemning him to a pitiable existence and to total insignificance as a composer.

Further information on the nature of this 'tribe' is contained in Wagner's libretto for a comic opera called *Männerlist gegen Frauenlist* ('A Man's Guile versus a Woman's Guile'). The title comes from the Arabian Nights, but there seems no immediate reason why he should have chosen to transfer an Oriental burlesque to an almost contemporary Germany. The 'tribe' cruelly satirized in his story is a community 'such as I imagined would have been found among proud aristocratic French *émigrés* at the time of the Revolution'.[62] In his autobiography he gives the date of the work as the winter of 1836–7. In fact the text dates from June 1838,[63] that is, the same time as the prose sketch of *Rienzi*, with which it is linked. And his *'émigrés'* were not French aristocrats at all but members of the 'community' which only his supercilious disdain would describe as 'proud'. In short, he was referring to the Jews.

The names of such characters as 'Abendtau' and 'Perlmutter' in the text are Jewish. Jewish also is the extraordinary urge on the part of these noblemen to marry into aristocratic German families.[64] The whining lamentations of the *'émigrés'* were a stock feature of contemporary caricatures of the Jews. 'O unhappy man that I am!' moans Baron von Abendtau in Shylockian tones: 'O most miserable member of my line, which stretches back through time immemorial, a royal line for whose demise nature herself has to answer!'[65] Years later the concept of the 'demise' of a 'tribe' would reappear in Wagner's essay 'Music and the Jews'.[66]

Among the stock of anti-Semitic stereotypes in Wagner's description of Abendtau's young daughter is that feature traditionally associated with the Jews – their long nose. Wagner, who was himself afflicted in this respect, described Fräulein Abendtau's nose as 'somewhat like an elephant's trunk'.[67] On closer inspection she turns out to be like 'a hunchbacked monkey with the nose of a horse . . . which there would be no point in trying to improve'. She was a freak, 'a misshapen creature cursed with the accumulated ugliness of her ancestors'.[68] It was the good fortune of Julius, German through and through, a character modelled on Wagner's younger brother, that the sudden, unexpected appearance of the hero Richard, the bear trainer's son, saved him from becoming espoused to this 'devil in human form'.

Wagner's misleading remarks in *Mein Leben* disguised the fact that the comedy *Männerlist gegen Frauenlist* is a counterpart to the tragedy *Rienzi* in the message it conveys. As Rienzi dies at the hands of the accursed 'tribe' of the *nobili*, so Richard destroys the 'tribe' of repulsive, would-be 'aristocrats' seeking to marry into 'pure' German circles, by exposing them to ridicule.

For the success of *Rienzi* Wagner had banked on the support of the Jewish composer Meyerbeer. Maybe that is why he did not continue work on his now forgotten comedy. At the same time he may have wanted to conceal the real background to the work from the sponsor of his autobiography, King Ludwig II of Bavaria, who was well disposed towards the Jews. The work was consigned to a drawer and has only curiosity value today. The première of *Rienzi* in Dresden, on the other hand, which, ironically, Meyerbeer did much to promote, was the greatest operatic success of his life. 'This interesting young German composer', wrote Meyerbeer, 'deserved his success in every respect.'[69]

That success, accorded a work whose actual subject was not events in medieval Rome but the subjection of Germany and a vain attempt at liberation, was indeed overwhelming. Dresden was a city in which Italian tastes had traditionally prevailed. Carl Maria von Weber had already taken issue with the artificiality of this foreign opera and championed the cause of the 'natural' German tradition. Wagner now continued in Weber's line. Where once the spectacular works of Meyerbeer and Spontini had held sway, there now appeared a 'thoroughly German' composer, one, moreover, who impressed his German contemporaries by having survived unscathed his baptism of fire in the pandemonium of Paris.

Rienzi struck a raw nerve. Since the Paris revolution of 1830, the event that turned the seventeen-year-old Wagner into a revolutionary 'at a single stroke',[70] German intellectuals had begun to make common cause in a movement calling itself 'Young Germany', opposing the forces of reaction and pledging themselves to political revival and the ideal of human progress. One of their heroes was Rienzi, 'tribune of the people', and one of their youngest members was the wild-eyed Richard Wagner. It was something of a sensation that, with the support of Meyerbeer and Wolf von Lüttichau, the conservative administrator of the Dresden court theatre, it should have been here, in the sleepy, traditionally minded Kingdom of Saxony, that the young firebrand mounted his revolutionary work. No less extraordinary was the fact that shortly afterwards King Friedrich August appointed Wagner royal Saxon Kapellmeister, unaware that the proud, silver-braided Saxon uniform concealed a hotspur only waiting his moment to break out. In fact the eruption had already occurred.[71] 'The Dresdeners at the première of *Rienzi*', wrote an eye-witness, 'no longer behaved like Dresdeners.'[72] The awakening of the masses on the stage spread to the audience. 'From the opening sounds of the overture there was an absolute silence that lasted until the act was over; then frenzied applause burst out, becoming louder and culminating at the end of the fifth act, when the cheers became deafening.'

From one moment to the next the long-awaited revolt seemed to have broken out, bringing an otherwise so staid and respectable audience to their feet in the plush velvet surroundings of their opera house. Wagner's dream of spanning the divide between theatrical illusion and reality had come true. The royal family alone seemed not to have noticed that the frenzy running through the city was not the result of an opera but a foretaste of the political freedom to come.

The man most deeply affected by the success of *Rienzi* – 'which is driving the whole of Dresden wild', said Clara Schumann[73] – was the composer himself. Convinced that its effect could not be restricted to the tumultuous scenes that followed the performance, he declared his vision to have become reality. 'The whole city was united in the excitement of revolution,' he wrote to his sister. 'Victory! Victory! The day has dawned! Its radiance will shine on you all!'[74] His words were taken from the first scene of the opera, when the hero, bareheaded and in full armour, appears before the people to proclaim their freedom. Spokesman for Wagner himself, he directs his hatred of the *nobili* against the aristocrats in the audience as well as against the Jews. Unnoticed by most of those present, he had publicly branded that 'tribe' which had fought and raped and pillaged its ruinous way through history. Naturally it was a message expressed in coded form. But those attached to the Young German movement would grasp his meaning, especially since the work was composed in a style that bore the 'unmistakable marks of German-ness'.[75]

Wagner hoped that the success of *Rienzi* would giver Meyerbeer a shock. 'Meyerbeer has taken flight,' he wrote to a member of his family.[76] A friend had also told him, he added, that Meyerbeer's opera *Les Huguenots* had been 'totally eclipsed by his own work'.[77] He was irritated by suggestions that he had borrowed and copied from Meyerbeer in his music. 'Even if there really were something that could be called "Meyerbeerian,"' he wrote spitefully to Schumann, 'it would be a remarkably perverse quirk of nature if I were to borrow from a source whose very smell I find repulsive.'[78]

Although, with its disguised anti-Semitism and its call to revolution, *Rienzi* struck a chord at the time, it was a seven-day wonder. Opera houses subjected it to severe cuts, its attractive melodies were reduced to popular tunes and a few of the familiar motifs were made into bugle calls. The sound of the trumpets did not rouse the Germans from their slumbers once and for all but only for a brief moment in the theatre. Wagner himself, now a rebel drawing a salary from the state, had to wait until the end of the decade before taking up the fight against 'the arch-enemy of all things German' and sounding the signal that announced the real revolution.

Graf von Beust, the Saxon Minister of State, recalled that Wagner had once told him he had toyed with the idea of 'playing the part of the tribune of the people himself'.[79] Some sixty years later the same thought was to occur to Adolf Hitler, the passionate opera-goer. 'Like the hero of Wagner's opera', recorded Nicolaus von Below, Hitler's adjutant, 'the Führer too felt he had been called to save the German Fatherland.'[80]

3

DRESDEN BURNS

W agner knew that only a radical upheaval could free his German Fatherland from the grip of the aristocracy and the capitalist barons. In his characteristic euphuistic style he talks of the coming revolt as 'the irresistible onward march of the triumphant power of universal progress which will sweep away the detritus of the old order'[1] and leave mankind 'to witness with its own eyes the advent of a new world order'. These words, written in the revolutionary year of 1848, refer in the first instance to his plans for an opera called *Die hohe Braut* ('The Noble Lady'), the climax of which was to be the procession of the victorious rebel forces marching to the sound of the 'Marseillaise'.

Like Rienzi, Wagner's 'noble lady' was meant in the first instance to stir the Parisians into action. But the French opera-going public cold-shouldered this upstart from Leipzig with the same disdain they had shown towards his Roman tribune. His success in Dresden had left him with the reputation of being something of a revolutionary. 'His *Rienzi*', a critic wrote later, 'opened a new era in music, a music that throbbed with the spirit of 1848.'[2]

Wagner first felt the desire to become an active revolutionary when he was only seventeen. Fired by the success of the Paris revolution of July 1830, which led to the installation of Louis Philippe, the 'citizen king', the people of Leipzig flocked on to the streets 'in their thousands',[3] rampaging through the city, ransacking the villas of the wealthy bourgeoisie,[4] and after two days of rioting finally forcing the chief of police to resign. Confined to a tiresome discipline of music practice, conjuring up in his imagination the figure of General Lafayette, commander of the National Guard, as he marched through Paris,[5] the young Wagner could no longer stand by and watch but threw himself into the fray alongside his fellow-citizens.

'This day marked for me the beginning of history', he later wrote, 'and I naturally committed myself heart and soul to the revolution, turning my back on the world of art in order to take part directly in political events.' He threw himself into this activity like a man possessed, storming houses, destroying their contents and making a banner out of a red curtain. 'I was like a madman', he later admitted, 'dragged involuntarily into a welter of destruction.'[6]

Hardly had he recovered from this frenzy of devastation than he switched his allegiance to the other side, joining those who had pledged themselves to the protection of property, both private and public. This was a decision also influenced by the fact that his brother-in-law, the publisher Friedrich Brockhaus, had just been appointed deputy commander of the Leipzig Civil Guard. The function of this body was in effect the very opposite of its counterpart in Paris, but Wagner took pride in comparing the Leipzig militia with the French National Guard and calling Brockhaus 'a Saxon Lafayette'.[7] He did not appear to realize that his brother-in-law's sole concern was to protect the new machines in his printing works. Troops called upon to crush the rebellion were surprised to find themselves confronting not the marauding hordes they had expected but a 'fully armed civilian force'.[8]

A far more spectacular and momentous event was the revolt in Dresden a week later, in which, as Wagner reported in *Mein Leben*, 'real street battles took place'. The town hall and the police headquarters were stormed and everything that could be burned was thrown out of the windows onto the street below. Two great bonfires, with the insignia of the detested police state and bundles of banknotes, lit up the night sky as the church bells rang and the crowds rejoiced.

Wagner, who had grown up in Dresden, shared the celebrations from a distance and, changing sides once again, hailed the victorious revolution which had forced the King to abdicate in favour of the regent Friedrich August – the very man against whom Wagner himself would rebel nineteen years later. In 1830 he dedicated to Friedrich August a 'political overture' with the title *Friedrich und Freiheit* ('Frederick and Freedom'), in which the principal theme, emerging from a mood of gloom and oppression, works its way gradually upwards towards a joyful finale 'in which it finally reigns triumphant'.[9] This is the first attempt that Wagner made to express his revolutionary ideals in musical form. It is also the moment when fire, symbol of both destruction and purification, becomes a permanent weapon in his revolutionary arsenal. At the Wartburg Festival in 1817 – Wagner was just four years old at the time – it had been the lighting of a great bonfire that signalled the awakening of Germany, with smaller fires in the neighbourhood called 'Flames of Joy'. Maybe this was the inspiration for the pseudonym 'Flame of Joy'[10] that Wagner adopted as a music critic in the 1840s.[11]

For the poetic expression of their ideals the rebels turned to Schiller, poet laureate of the German freedom movement. His 'Ode to Joy', set to music by Beethoven, became the anthem of national revolt, and for Wagner himself the chorale that heralded the Bayreuth Festival. The 'divine spark of joy' of which Schiller sang was to light the fire of divine inspiration; 'ravished by the flame', we would enter the freedom of paradise, 'chanting the joyous message of redemption'.[12]

In Wagner's birthplace, where the 'Ode to Joy' had been written, a Schiller Society had been founded in 1840,[13] devoted less to furthering the cause of classical literature than cultivating the spirit of liberation that would accompany the coming revolution. The foundation of the Society, with its apparently harmless name, had been initiated by one Robert Blum, librarian at the Leipzig Stadttheater, who appeared equally harmless. But as librarian also of the Schiller Society, Blum was in fact quietly preparing the way for the revolution.

By organizing a series of Schiller celebrations, Blum set out to give the masses a foretaste of the revolution through being made aware of the poet's 'prophetic significance'. 'If only a single spark of truth were to send a flash into the mass of the common people,' wrote Blum, paraphrasing Schiller, 'what an inspiration it would be!' At the Society's first meeting, according to the *Leipziger Allgemeine Zeitung* at the time, Blum set the tone in his opening address, demanding 'that the celebration of Schiller be made a national event'. To conclude the proceedings, all those present joined in singing the 'Ode to Joy'. 'The occasion left a powerful impression,' concluded the paper.[14]

The Schiller Society, described by the Young German writer Heinrich Laube as a 'hotbed of radicals', was not the first front organization in Leipzig to promote the cause of rebellion. As early as 1828, in the wake of the Berlin literary club called 'Der Tunnel über der Spree' – later made famous by Fontane – a branch of the club had been established in Leipzig as a meeting-place for liberal writers and scholars to exchange views. They adopted their own secret language intelligible only to insiders,[15] disguising their real political meaning behind ostensibly harmless puns and plays on words. The place was a goldmine for political informers. Robert Blum was also active in the 'Tunnel', his work for the revolution and the club earning him honorary membership in 1845.

It is reasonable to assume that Wagner, all of whose political activities had an atmosphere of the conspiratorial about them, including the use of coded language, may have had contact with the 'Tunnel'. His music teacher Weinlig was a member, and his sister Rosalie, the most faithful supporter of his artistic ambitions, appeared there as a singer. Other members of his family also acted in various Leipzig theatres, so he might have even met Blum personally. But he makes no reference to him in his autobiography.

Blum was to reappear later in Wagner's life. He was regarded as the mind behind the freedom movement in Saxony, and it was he who in 1845 called the people to man the barricades – a time when Wagner was court Kapellmeister in Dresden. His skill as a fiery orator led him to be elected to the Frankfurt National Assembly in 1848, where he rose to become leader of the left-wing deputies. His career came to a premature end in October 1848 in Vienna, where he was arrested with a number of other rebels and summarily executed, in spite of being a member of the National Assembly.

The indignation provoked by Blum's death led to protests and demonstrations over the whole country. Wagner, who looked for 'the complete rebirth of art, of society and of religion in the wake of the victorious revolution',[16] had travelled in June 1848 to Vienna, where the insurrection seemed to be taking a more hopeful course. Now, the revolt crushed and Blum dead, he cast his reaction in literary form. Three days after Blum's death he made the prose draft of a work conceived at the time of the March rebellion, a work to be known in its final form as *Götterdämmerung*, the last part of *Der Ring des Nibelungen*. A few weeks later he began the task of turning the work into verse. At this moment the work bore the title *Siegfrieds Tod*, the foundation stone of the entire myth of the *Ring*.

In his capacity as royal Saxon Kapellmeister Wagner was also in a position to pursue the aims of Blum's Schiller Society – provided he disguised his intention as the 'Tunnel' club had done. Ignoring the protests of his orchestra, who feared reprisals, he included in his Palm Sunday concert of 1846 Beethoven's Ninth Symphony, with Schiller's 'Ode to Joy' in the last movement. He borrowed the score and parts from Leipzig[17] – in Dresden, a strictly monarchist capital, they had never been needed. He had long seen in the poem the poetic equivalent of his own urge to rebel. Now he hoped that Schiller's 'divine spark of joy' would rouse the passions of his audience as well. 'My realization of the emptiness of my existence, both as man and musician, suddenly changed in the presence of this symphony into a sense of exhilaration which left me sobbing and weeping,' he wrote later.[18]

In order to induce a suitable atmosphere of enthusiasm, he sent to the *Dresdner Anzeiger* in advance of the performance a programme note which drew attention to the deeper meaning of the work. Thus the first movement describes 'the struggle of the soul in its search for joy and happiness against the enemies that thrust themselves between us and our earthly bliss'. The conflict, says Wagner, is not resolved until the last movement, when victory, launched by Schiller's 'divine spark', is finally won. 'To the bold sounds of military music we seem to catch sight of a column of valiant youths marching towards us, ready to charge into battle and win a victory in which all men will embrace each other.'[19] It was no accident that in 1933, the year Hitler seized power, the Bayreuth Festival opened with a performance of Beethoven's revolutionary Ninth Symphony, as it had in 1872, when the foundation stone of the Bayreuth Festspielhaus had been laid.

The success of Wagner's performance in Dresden in 1846 was 'extraordinary and far in excess of anybody's expectations'.[20] One of those present was the sixteen-year-old Hans von Bülow, a passionate admirer of Wagner's who was immediately converted to the twin causes of Beethoven and the revolution. Wagner afterwards wrote in Bülow's album: 'If you are glowing with a love of pure art, you will surely come to feel the true flame within you.'[21] Gripped in the spell of Schiller's 'divine spark', art and social change had become one. Three years later history repeated itself when Wagner's Palm Sunday performance of Beethoven's Ninth in 1849, wildly applauded as a performance given in memory of Robert Blum, served as the musical prelude to the May uprising in Dresden.

One month later the old opera house in Dresden, where the concert had taken place, was burned down, while Wagner watched spellbound. Seeing him standing there, one of his fellow-rebels shouted to him: 'Herr Kapellmeister, the divine spark of joy has set off a fire and the rotten old building has gone up in smoke!'[22] 'He must have been one of those who heard that performance of the Ninth Symphony,' observed the Kapellmeister in question.

In *Mein Leben* Wagner refrained from recording anything about his emotions surrounding these events, but in the more intimate so-called *Annals* he refers to a sense of 'strange delight'[23] that came over him as he watched the destruction of the place where he worked. He may even have cherished a secret hope that the 'divine spark' might jump from the opera house to the rest of the town and set fire to the whole corrupt administration of the place.

If that had really happened, it would have been not only the revolutionary tribune in him that rejoiced but also the private citizen, dependent, as he was, on financial assistance from others. 'Even if the May catastrophe had not come,' wrote Ernest Newman, 'it is difficult for us today to conceive how Wagner could have continued to live much longer in Dresden, if only by reason of his debts.'[24] The luxurious conditions in which he lived, coupled with the French culinary delicacies that he shared with his friends, were the talk of the town, and he had run up debts that would have exceeded the combined salaries of a dozen Kapellmeisters. The interest alone made it impossible for him to survive. His privileged position as a servant of the court had been undermined and his dismissal was only a matter of time. True, since the resounding success of *Rienzi* – a success never repeated – he had enjoyed the King's grace and favour.[25] But he had forfeited this support by the aristocratic airs he gave himself, behaviour which could not be tolerated from a man in a subordinate position.

At the same time he had also shown a gift for ingratiating himself into court circles by composing festival overtures and the like to mark the dedication of a royal statue or to accompany an address of loyalty to His Majesty. Such occasional pieces would no doubt have also owed their existence to his eagerness to see his detested patron Wolf von Lüttichau removed from the scene. Lüttichau had originally given him 'a life appointment with a respectable salary and with the prospect of regular increments as time went on'.[26] But he remained Wagner's superior, provoking the resentment of the anti-authoritarian Kapellmeister, who acknowledged only one authority – that bestowed on him by his genius. Wagner, who, according to Princess Marie Wittgenstein,[27] subjected both the leaders of the revolutionary movement and the monarchs and rulers around him to his iron will, carried on his feud against Lüttichau by a variety of means – begging for loans, requesting leave of absence under false pretences, then thinking up reforms in the running of the theatre – all of which were aimed at undermining Lüttichau's authority and putting Wagner in supreme artistic control. The last straw for Lüttichau was when Wagner, aware of the imminence of the revolt, won over his musicians by offering them the prospect of a radical improvement in their social position if they would support him. Lüttichau had had enough. Bitterly resentful of his treatment at Wagner's hands, he dismissed him.[28]

The principal factor in Wagner's fall from grace, however, was his anti-monarchist stance. The Saxon royal family recalled only too painfully the effects of the French Revolution. Now Wagner proposed to offer them a compromise. 'Grandiose socialistic ideas were buzzing around in his head,' observed the actor and producer Eduard Devrient sceptically, ideas which were not confined to Germany alone. 'The fate of the whole of Europe is at stake,' he is reported to have cried, 'the fate of the whole of mankind!'[29] The condition he laid down was that the leadership of this great movement of popular liberation should be placed in the hands of 'a man sent by God'. What use to the people was the right of self-determination if not consecrated by the divine blessing of a Hohenstaufen emperor, a 'tribune of the people' or a messenger from the Holy Grail?

In April 1848 Wagner had completed his opera *Lohengrin*, a work that could be seen, in one respect, as a political manifesto demonstrating that only through the appearance of a man sent by God could the doomed German Fatherland be saved. But this very work, in which a saviour 'clad in shining silver armour'[30] arrives to proclaim the dominion of justice throughout the land, was removed from the repertory by the embittered Lüttichau – together with *Rienzi* – before its première could take place. The miraculous appearance of Lohengrin did not take place in Dresden. Yet the King of Saxony – like Ludwig and like Hitler – could have seen himself reincarnated in the figure of the Knight of the Swan.

In an address delivered in Dresden in June 1848 before the patriotic organization known as the 'Vaterlandsverein', Wagner urged the King to see his new opera in this light. The following day the text of the address appeared in the local paper. It was a paradoxical argument. Himself a servant of the court, he called for the overthrow of the oligarchy and its replacement by the sovereignty of the people, that sovereignty, ironically, to be embodied in the person of King Friedrich August II, whom he boldly called 'a man sent by Providence'.[31]

Three thousand listeners greeted Wagner's lecture with 'wild enthusiasm',[32] and in the days that followed, his ideas were keenly discussed throughout the city. 'How Can Republican Impulses be Reconciled with the Monarchy?' – such was the title of the lecture. It was a subject that exercised the mind of every honest citizen who welcomed the former but did not want to sacrifice the latter. In Wagner's rosy picture of communal bliss the removal of the aristocracy was to be followed by the abolition of the whole financial system, which would at a stroke 'release mankind from the Satanic grip of money'. It would be 'suffering mankind's great "war of liberation" against usury, profiteering, fraud and speculation' and thus – the taunt aimed at the Jews is unmistakable – 'the absolute emancipation of the human race and the pure fulfilment of the teachings of Christ'.[33]

Having cleared the ground by thus promising the Saxons 'a complete rebirth' and securing for himself both his freedom from Lüttichau and the settlement of his debts, Wagner was ready to unfurl his great vision of the future. A new generation will arise, he declared, 'sailing across the seas and establishing a new, young Germany wherever they land, giving birth to a new race of divine children. We shall make it German and glorious, with the sun shining down on a free and wonderful Germany from dawn to dusk.' And as an ultimate goal he envisaged the emergence of 'a happy, blessed humankind'[34] led by a people's monarch sent by God.

This patriotic proclamation of 1848 would be incomplete without the assurances which, leaving his unsuspecting friends unaware of his actions, he gave to the King. Like anyone driven by the purest of motives, he averred, he was 'repelled by the acts of violence, instinctive in origin but no less misguided for that, perpetrated by the masses'. It was not the rebellious *Volk*, ignorant of the true situation, who would ensure the creation of a state built on freedom but only 'the sublime power of the monarchy'. A hereditary monarchy, he continued, 'was the sole natural guarantor of freedom because the King united in himself the freedom of all'. Keeping up his pose of self-denial to the end, he signed himself 'in the profoundest humility' as His Majesty's 'most devoted subject'.[35] The King, who was well aware that a week earlier Wagner had abolished the status of subject, did not believe a word.

But Wagner took his revenge. In a piece of fiery demagoguery published anonymously in the revolutionary *Volksblätter* at Easter 1849, he showered contempt on his monarch, who was 'pretending to retain a cool and controlled demeanour while in fact sitting fearfully in his palace, trembling and with beating heart, anxiously awaiting the inevitable outbreak of the revolution'. In the same breath Wagner denounced the hated Lüttichau as a ' "lickspittle" set on engaging all his underhand tricks employed over the years to win him a pile of medals and titles for this and that service, in order to reassure the terrified little dukes and duchesses that all would be well'. All this was in vain, of course, since the days of the state in its current form were numbered. Only a gentle push, 'and the whole edifice would collapse without trace'.[36]

The closer the revolt approached, the more Wagner's eager anticipation gave way to a mood of destruction, which he interpreted in his article in the *Volksblätter* as a basic aspect of life itself. 'I destroy whatever exists,' he cries, 'and wherever I turn, new life springs out of the dead stones. . . . The seed has ripened and I am the reaper.'[37]

In 1849 he wrote a poem which also preached the violent end of the *ancien régime*. 'Let your torches burn brightly!' he cried to those who were manning the barricades. 'Let them reduce everything to dust and ashes in the service of Mammon!' And to make sure that the revolutionaries knew that one particular torch was reserved for the roofs of Jewish houses, he added: 'Never again shall they mockingly blaspheme against the living God.' According to legend, Ahasverus, the Wandering Jew, contemptuously turned his back on the Saviour, and in Wagner's *Parsifal* Kundry, the sinner, confesses that she once mocked Him. Reserving a flaming torch for the Children of Israel, Wagner urged the fireraisers to continue burning everything in sight until all incriminating promissory notes, bills of exchange and other documents were finally destroyed. 'Consign them to your flaming pyre!' he cried, relishing the thought of the carnage to come.[38]

A delight in the all-consuming power of fire remained with Wagner throughout his life. Whether he urged Bismarck to reduce Paris to dust and ashes,[39] or the Tsar to set fire to St Petersburg,[40] the attraction of the flames was always there. The new age would dawn as the embers of a dying civilization grew cold. His universal remedy 'to heal, that is, to destroy, the signs of the sickness that is all around us' was through 'healing by fire'.[41]

Wagner himself arranged for the necessary pitch torches and hand grenades to be prepared in the spring of 1849. In his biography of Hitler, Joachim Fest talks of Wagner's work as being 'an explosive mixture brewed in the laboratory of the nineteenth century'.[42] It is a description that matches equally well the months that led up to the Dresden uprising. The royal Kapellmeister did his utmost to be the one who lit the fuse under the powder keg.

Secret meetings of a few dozen of the conspirators were held in his rooms, when strategy was discussed, and the Russian agitator Bakunin advised on tactical matters. Wagner even implies that it was in his house that the actual date of the uprising was fixed. Seeing himself as 'the prophet of the Lord',[43] and thus above all trivial questions of detail, he set about his task, with the signal for the commencement of the battle – in the best operatic traditions – to be the torching of the royal palace.

Wagner later tried to make out that he had only been an innocent bystander at the time. In reality, as Ernest Newman recognized, 'he ranked with the others as a leader of the revolt'.[44] Two more of the ringleaders, both summarily dealt with after the insurrection was over, belonged to Wagner's circle of friends. One was August Röckel, whom Wagner himself had engaged as conductor at the Dresden court; the other was Mikhail Bakunin, who had taken rooms nearby under the pseudonym of Schwarz, the inventor of gunpowder.

After the rebellion had been crushed, however, Wagner disclaimed all responsibility. Röckel was sentenced to thirteen years in jail, largely due to Wagner. For claiming that he had done no more than report on events as they happened, Wagner thrust Röckel and Bakunin into the limelight as the main culprits. They were political activists, he emphasized, whereas he was a simple musician, one, moreover, who had still found time in the midst of the disturbances to plan new operatic ventures.

Some modern critics have taken Wagner at his word. 'There was not a single political work among Wagner's books in Dresden', wrote Martin Gregor-Dellin, 'from which he could have drawn his ideas. Everything came from Röckel.' Wagner had developed a certain 'curiosity' about the revolution but 'it was Röckel who inspired it'.[45] Similarly the discussions that took place in Wagner's garden on forming 'a people's militia'[46] were said to have been led not by him but by his protégé, who had written an authoritative pamphlet on the subject. Apparently only his contemporaries knew that Röckel had been made to act as the Master's 'faithful standard bearer'.[47] Röckel's later claim that Wagner had attached considerable importance to procuring weapons was also ignored. And although Röckel did publish a subversive weekly journal in which Wagner, anonymously, was able to print his revolutionary appeals, he only did so, according to Gregor-Dellin, 'in order to help Röckel and his family eke out a meagre existence',[48] since his political zeal, kindled by Wagner, had cost him his job.

As to the few hundred hand grenades that were prepared for the uprising, there is general agreement that Wagner and Röckel were equally involved. Scant credence was given to Röckel's later statement[49] that Wagner alone had been responsible for planning the cache, and it was regarded as Röckel's personal ill-fortune that at the time of his arrest he had in his pocket an incriminating note from Wagner containing practical instructions.[50] Bakunin, alias Dr Schwarz, a failed revolutionary who now hoped to make his mark in Dresden, was another figure used by Wagner to portray his own secret ambitions. A delight in the spectacle of fire, characteristic of Wagner's operas from *Rienzi* onwards, is described in *Mein Leben* as typical of the Russians, who have a childlike fascination for the flames, culminating in visions of 'a massive universal conflagration'.[51] For Bakunin, said Wagner, this conflagration was to end with the destruction of the whole of civilization, a destruction launched from the streets of Dresden by the 'great Russian pyrotechnician'.

Writing years later of these events, which cost the lives of hundreds, perhaps thousands, Wagner was by no means at his ease. As late as 1863, after having been granted immunity from prosecution by the King of Saxony, he still felt it necessary to engage a lawyer to look through the records in the Dresden town hall in case there were any incriminatory evidence against him.[52] He was mainly concerned about a document in which, according to Graf Beust, 'Wagner was said to have boasted about having set fire to the Prince's palace, though fortunately without any serious consequences.'[53] This was an act, maintained Beust, which could have resulted in Wagner, a servant of the state, being charged with treason and sentenced to death. The incriminating document was not found. But the charge was revived when a credible witness appeared and claimed to have seen the Kapellmeister urging the rebels to spray the Prince's palace and the royal palace with flammable liquid and set the buildings alight.[54]

The rebels refused. But the following day, 7 May 1849, Wagner was compensated by witnessing the destruction of the old opera house, which gave him 'a strange sense of satisfaction'. The suspicion was often vented that he was looking for an alternative use for the petrol and pitch torches originally intended for the royal palace. But nothing was ever proved. He would, of course, have had every reason to destroy a theatre that symbolized both the tradition of Italian opera, which he detested, and the *ancien régime*, whose time in Dresden was a long way from being over. Furthermore nobody, apart from Röckel, knew the layout of the theatre as well as he did. 'For years', he wrote in *Mein Leben*, 'it had been feared that this flimsy construction of wood and canvas, only planned to be a temporary structure, would fall victim to a fire.'[55] Wagner's description makes the building sound very different from the far from 'temporary' opera house built by the Baroque architect Matthäus Daniel Pöppelmann, whose sumptuous interior, as modern writers confirm, 'satisfied all the demands of an absolutist monarchy'.[56]

Yet there would seem to be no causal connection between the senseless destruction of this architectural jewel and the figure of Wagner, as he gazed down from the tower of the Kreuzkirche at the flames and the teeming masses below – unless, that is, he communicated his wish for a fire to Leo von Zychlinsky, a law student who had been present at meetings of the Wagnerian cabal, then become an adjutant with one of the battalions of the National Guard, and 'appears to have been ordered to pass on the command to set fire to the opera house'.[57]

It was a barbaric act, absurd from the military point of view, and it was not repeated. The fire, which could easily have spread to the nearby Zwinger palace, was quickly extinguished. Zychlinsky's name is mentioned in Wagner's diary on 5 May 1849, then again eleven years later in a secret despatch from Albin Leo von Seebach, Saxon ambassador in Paris, in which he connects Wagner, by then a famous composer, who was staying in Paris at the time, with the otherwise unknown figure of Zychlinsky. According to Seebach, Wagner assured him on oath that he was no longer in contact with the men of 1848; the only thing he could recall was that some six months earlier the painter Zychlinsky had had dinner with him.[58] Another who may have been the one who set fire to the Dresden opera house was Röckel. When, having served his prison sentence, Röckel renewed his association with his former comrade, the one-time Kapellmeister wrote him a confidential letter recalling their 'fire-raising days in Dresden'.[59] Evidently the chief 'fire-raiser' himself remembered more about his past than his memoirs reveal.

Wagner enjoyed activities in which he could keep himself out of sight. When problematical situations arose, he would let his friends bear the brunt of the crisis. In the Dresden uprising he was to be found neither in the ranks of the Civil Guard nor in the provisional government; he preferred to play the role of a theatrical producer, pulling the strings in the background like a puppet master. In this way he could exert the greatest influence on the course of the drama without exposing himself to personal risk. A number of eye-witnesses reported how he would be here, there and everywhere, hurrying up and down the staircase in the town hall where the revolutionary government was meeting, rushing from one barricade to another, then leaving the town to fetch reinforcements from the outskirts. The only place he would stay for any length of time, covered by revolutionary snipers and thus protected from attack by enemy forces, was the tower of the Kreuzkirche.

The overture to the revolution was itself a piece of Wagnerian theatre. After a meeting of the Vaterlandsverein the bell of the Annenkirche suddenly began to toll – to the amazement of Wagner, reminded that it had also been a church bell that summoned the people to arms in his *Rienzi*. In fact the bell was the signal for an attack on the armoury, where the crowd hoped to collect supplies of weapons. Instead they encountered a hail of cannonballs, and the first martyrs fell. Shocked at what she saw, the famous soprano Wilhelmine Schröder-Devrient, who had had a brilliant success as the heroine in *Rienzi*, 'shouted out of her window to the crowd to take their bloody revenge on the King and the government'.[60] Wagner, 'always in the thick of things',[61] was present to hear, 'with both delight and amazement', the singer's passionate outburst.[62] By chance he had just left the house of the tenor Joseph Tichatschek, where he had requisitioned Tichatschek's collection of sporting guns.

It may well have been Wagner, who was evidently responsible for supplying arms to the rebels, who gave the signal to attack the armoury. 'He spent the night in the tower, under the great bell,' said the daughter of one of the rebels. 'We have no difficulty in believing that he got to work on it occasionally.'[63] The *Neue Zeitschrift für Musik* also reported that it had been Kapellmeister Wagner in the tower of the Kreuzkirche who had given the signal to attack.[64] 'Many citizens of Dresden', reported the *Leipziger Zeitung* some days later, 'will still find their ears ringing to the deafening sound of the bells. A group of insurgents kept a constant look-out from the top of the Kreuzkirche and tolled the bell at any sign of danger.'[65] They even used special peals to communicate messages, like Morse code, so that the rebels knew what was happening.

Around eight o'clock on 9 May 'the great bell in the tower of the Kreuzkirche gave out a nine-fold boom: it was the signal to the last gallant defenders of the barricades to seek safety in flight. At nine o'clock the Saxon troops took possession of the town hall. The rising was at an end.'[66] The man responsible for this brilliant idea, according to Lieutenant-Colonel Waldersee, commander of the Prussian contingent, was none other than the former Kapellmeister, 'who himself tolled the bell'.[67] 'The bell rope was close to his hand,' added Ernest Newman.[68]

Another of Wagner's companions at the time of the May uprising was the architect Gottfried Semper, who had also taken part in Wagner's secret meetings. In contrast to Wagner, however, Semper, designer of the new court theatre in which the first performance of *Rienzi* had taken place, joined the Civil Guard as a sniper. But in his later account of the events Wagner only showered scorn on him. 'I was amused and surprised', he wrote in *Mein Leben*, 'to come across Semper in the town hall wearing full uniform.' When Semper pointed out that one of the barricades was very flimsily constructed, Wagner ironically suggested that he should seek the authorization of the appropriate military committee to bring the barricade in question up to the highest defensive standards, 'adopting the aesthetic criteria of a Michelangelo or a Leonardo da Vinci'.[69] Wagner's frivolous tone, which reduced what was in effect a civil war to the level of a schoolboy prank, was aimed at concealing the fact that Germany's most distinguished living architect, as Friedrich von Beust later confirmed, had personally supervised the construction of the barricades which were the scene of some of the bloodiest fighting.[70] Later, remembering their collaboration in Dresden, Wagner arranged for Semper to come to Munich, where, at King Ludwig's expense, he designed a gigantic Richard Wagner Theatre for the exclusive performance of the Master's works. He subsequently adopted the most original of Semper's ideas for the construction of his Festival Theatre in Bayreuth – characteristically without offering him a fee.

Hitler, devoted both to Wagner and to Bayreuth, appears to have been deeply impressed by the two men's cooperation. Turning up one day in 1909 at a hostel for the homeless in Meidlingen, the twenty-year-old Hitler struck up a friendship with a certain Reinhold Hanisch. 'He was particularly enthusiastic about architecture,' Hanisch later recalled, 'and one could listen to him talk about Semper for hours. Wagner's music, too, set his heart aglow.'[71]

The image was not idly chosen. When in 1933 Hanisch, himself an amateur artist like Hitler, suggested to a group of Party comrades that they present the Führer with a painting by Hanisch himself, he proposed Wagner and Semper as a subject. 'Hitler is devoted to both Richard Wagner and Gottfried Semper,' he explained. 'The two men were involved in the 1848 revolution in Dresden and sentenced *in absentia*.' If he were to receive this commission, Hanisch concluded, it would be a great source of pleasure for Hitler, 'who often used to queue for hours to find standing room at performances of Wagner's operas'.[72]

In the background of his painting Hanisch proposed to have the court theatre in flames – not, however, the old opera house in Dresden but Semper's building that had burned down in 1869. Hitler, who admired Semper's design for the Burgtheater in Vienna and wanted to incorporate Semper's sketches in the plans for his new theatre in Linz, also took an interest in Semper's project for the extension of the Heldenplatz in Vienna, the great ceremonial square in the centre of the city where on the occasion of the *Anschluss* in 1938 he enjoyed one of his greatest public triumphs.

Wagner, the failed demagogue, 'Hitler's unchallenged mentor', as Joachim Fest called him,[73] remained faithful to his revolutionary motto during the years of exile in Switzerland that followed his escape from Germany. That motto was 'Destruction'. His revolutionary aim was 'to crush and destroy everything that deserves to be crushed and destroyed. The only thing now necessary is destruction.'[74] His pupil was to pay good heed.

One day in 1925, returning from a visit to the Schiller Museum in Weimar, Hitler recalled his years as a boy in Vienna, when he had stood spellbound and listened to Wagner's operas 'more times than I can count'. 'For', as he explained to his Nazi companion Hans Severus Ziegler, an ardent Wagnerian, 'Wagner is not only an inspired artist but a true fighter, nay more – a revolutionary genius.'[75] By this Hitler meant that Wagner 'had the courage to throw himself personally into the struggle to eradicate the corrupt conditions that prevail in the field of politics, culture and art'. What Wagner had failed to achieve in Dresden he, Hitler, would bring to fruition in his own way. 'I have always felt attracted to this Dresden revolutionary,' he confessed to Ziegler, adding: 'He was a man who always remained true to himself, never wavering from what he had recognized to be the one and only correct path.'

Maybe it was not mere coincidence that Hitler's invasion of Austria took place exactly ninety years after the outbreak of the 1848 Revolution in Vienna. He had always regarded himself as the man called upon to fulfil the age-old dream of national revolution, the dream of the artistic revolutionary Richard Wagner. 'The goals for which our ancestors fought and died ninety years ago', he declared in Frankfurt in March 1938, 'can now be regarded as achieved.'[76]

After the débâcle in Dresden Wagner veiled his political plans in secrecy, disguising his real intentions, confiding only in those closest to him and relying on the mass effect of his operas, in which those with ears to hear could not fail to find his entire message. With a warrant out for his arrest, he spread the story that in fact everything had sprung from a serious misunderstanding: the truth was, he declared, that from the beginning his only concern had been 'to find a new basis for my artistic works in a totally new world'. Destroying things, he said in the dissembling tone of the typical traitor, had never held any attraction for him, and for that reason 'I distance myself from the revolution'.[77]

Similarly he sought to reassure Eduard Devrient, whom he had for years taken into his confidence over his plans for an insurrection and for the whole associated project of the *Ring*, that his activities had been completely harmless. He had been a 'mere onlooker', he later told Devrient, and had taken refuge 'in the most neutral place imaginable', namely in the tower of the Kreuzkirche, therefore 'without the slightest pangs of conscience' he could sincerely extend the hand of friendship to his former employers and offer to return to Dresden 'at some later date'.[78] But Devrient saw through him. Wagner could hardly expect him, he wrote in reply, 'to gloss over your extreme political views, which were at that time a constant source of friction between us'.[79]

Wagner's sudden attack of amnesia was the product, on the one hand, of a genuine fear that, like Röckel, he might end up in jail, and, on the other, of an illusory hope that the King might pardon him as a harmless hanger-on during the revolution and offer to reinstate him in his former well-paid job. In fact his brazen volte-face in political outlook affected only that one aspect of the revolution with which he had calculatedly identified himself, namely its egalitarian socialist message, which ran counter to his whole elitist personality. At the most he would only have ever accepted the 'communism' for which there was a general desire, and of which he himself also spoke, as a first step towards his vision of an artistic paradise on earth. But he would never have stomached an elected parliament.

In later life Wagner expressed only contempt for his one-time comrades-in-arms. At the time of the social unrest in 1872 in Vienna he advocated crushing the leaders 'like insects',[80] and in 1878 he told Cosima that he would have had 'no objection if the socialists were ground into the dust'.[81] This hatred had a philosophical basis: for Wagner was convinced that behind the world of the capitalists, as behind that of communism, there lurked the sinister presence of the Jews. Half a century later this hatred became the official doctrine of the German state.

4

STUDIES IN THE *RING*

~∞~

Deprived of his parents, as befitted a future hero, Hitler arrived in Vienna. But he was not, as legend had it, also deprived of funds. As the son of a civil servant, he was entitled to an orphan's allowance and also had the interest from his parents' investments. Yet in terms of a professional career his position was hopeless. He had been thirteen when his father, always partial to a drink, collapsed and died in his favourite tavern. Now that there was no longer anyone to abuse him and order him about like a dog, he had nothing and nobody left to fear. His mother, a downtrodden woman with the bright, cold eyes that he later recognized in Franz von Stuck's painting *Medusa*,[1] died of a protracted cancer when he was eighteen.

Apart from a little money Alois and Klara Hitler had left their son nothing that was of any use to him in the Austrian capital, and he himself had little of his own – just enough, in the event, to pay for meagre lodgings with a Czech woman in the Stumpergasse. Not to put too fine a point on it, he was a nobody; there was nothing he was fit for and precious little to hope for. But it was precisely this that qualified him for the mythological role he had felt himself called upon by fate to play since seeing *Rienzi* barely eighteen months earlier.

The hero who has been called by Providence to break the bonds of slavery has no need of certificates or qualifications or sponsors. His pockets are empty; instead, invisible to the outside world, the sword of justice hangs from his belt. Obeying only his inner calling, destined to plough his lonely furrow, with no parents to consider, he advances relentlessly towards his goal. It is no coincidence that Tristan, Parsifal, Walther von Stolzing and Tannhäuser all lost their parents in childhood. The two most Germanic heroes at the heart of *Der Ring des Nibelungen* are likewise forced to sacrifice the comforts of family life. Wotan, Siegmund's father, leaves his son only a wolf-skin, while his son, Siegfried, called 'Son of a Wolf,[2] does not even know his parents' names. Like the 'tribune of the people' from Linz, utterly free from commitments, they go out into the world at will, their gaze set not on material gain but on those deeds through which they will earn themselves the title of 'hero' – through victories over dragons and other monsters, bringing relief to a suffering humankind.

There was another reason why Hitler should have felt himself to be the incarnation of these imaginary characters – there was no place for him in the real world. Bugs made his room unbearable, and, having hardly any friends, he was forced to go for walks on his own. Worst of all, the Academy of Art in Vienna, where he had set his heart on studying, rejected his application with the humiliating comment that he was 'totally unsuited' for a career as a painter.

The authorities at the Academy had, however, failed to notice that the boy had an extraordinary talent for copying. Without reference to nature, he could convert postcard views into large pictures, true to scale and accurate in colour, which could be framed and hung on the wall. This ability, which he could exercise in oil, watercolour or pencil, ought to have earned him a place at the Academy; instead he was left to teach himself. Nevertheless his skill did enable him to make a passable living.

Nor were his powers of imitation limited to copying postcards – he had an uncanny talent for mimicking voices, sounds and gestures. He was a born imitator, both in a visual and in an aural context. Incapable of being an original artist, he reproduced, thanks to his remarkable memory, with the precision of a machine. Once learned, a date would stay in his memory for the rest of his life. He would make copies of copies, reproducing to whatever format was required.

There were many opportunities in Vienna to listen to the music which he needed to give purpose and direction to his life. Everyday life in the city, however, apart from visits to the parliament to listen to the debates, had little to offer him. So he concentrated on the evenings, sleeping until midday and using the remaining hours of daylight to prepare himself for what had become the central experience of his life-performances of the operas of Richard Wagner in the Hofoper. These preparations took the form of strolls in the woods, visits to museums and galleries, the study of libretti and painstaking attention to his appearance. Since, as he later declared, he knew entire scores by heart, he was able to give a scene-by-scene review of the work at the end of the performance, paying particular attention to the sets and the lighting.

The stage decor was his great passion, and he filled folder after folder with large-scale sketches of buildings, ground plans, façades and other architectural features, which were to form the basis of the sets for his vision of the society of the future. After he came to power, he lost no time in putting this vision into practice. The physical features of the Third Reich were those

Hitler designed in his imagination as he walked up and down the Ringstrasse in Vienna and stood night after night in the Hofoper, listening to Wagner.

One to hear the homesick young Hitler's views on art was his old friend from Linz, August Kubizek. Hitler's appearance filled Kubizek with astonishment. He wore 'an elegant top coat and a dark hat' and carried a 'walking stick with an ivory handle' – in short, he was dressed like a born theatre-goer. Hitler took his friend to the opera on the evening he arrived. 'After his miserable quarters in the Stumpergasse', wrote Kubizek, 'it was like being transported to a different planet.'[3]

Such were the extremes between which Hitler wandered. If a Wagner opera was being performed, the time spent waiting in his wretched room would quickly give way to the joy of standing in the auditorium. If there was no Wagner in the Hofoper, he would go to the Volksoper. Only when under the spell of the Master, wrote Kubizek, could he escape to that 'mystical world of dreams which he needed in order to counteract the tensions of his explosive nature'.[4] This was the world in which a sense of heightened awareness took the place of that drab day-to-day existence which only ignorance could call 'reality'.

Summarizing his impressions of his visit, Kubizek wrote:

> When Adolf listened to Wagner's music, he was transformed. All violence drained from him and he became quiet, congenial. His eye lost its restlessness and what had worried him throughout the day simply evaporated. The fate that weighed so heavily upon him was lifted from his shoulders and he no longer felt lonely and ostracized. A feeling of ecstasy came over him and he allowed himself to be transported into that mythical world which was more real to him than the mundane reality around him. Leaving his dank, musty room behind him, he was wafted back in time to the age of Teutonic mythology, that ideal world of which he never lost sight.[5]

The leading personality at the Hofoper during this time was Alfred Roller, whom he had already met in Linz at the time of his mother's death and whom he had hailed in 1906, on the occasion of his first visit to Vienna, as 'a master of stage design'.[6] A friend of his landlady's had approached Roller and asked him to put in a word for the promising young orphan. When Roller replied that the young man should call on him and bring some of his work with him, Hitler was delighted.[7] 'You should have seen him,' wrote his landlady gratefully to her friend. 'He took the letter in his hand and read it slowly, reverently, word by word, as though learning it by heart, with a happy smile on his face.'[8]

Hitler had already seen Roller's production of *Tristan und Isolde* and wanted to take up his invitation straightaway, but in the end he could not pluck up courage.[9] So instead of joining Roller's magic workshop, he eventually found himself studying with a schoolteacher not good enough even to gain his pupil a chance to qualify for a place at the Academy.

Roller, who taught whole generations to view the stage in a new perspective, never lost his place as Hitler's ideal designer. Throughout his life
he produced endless copies of Roller's sets, the one more monumental than
the other, finally coming to regard these sets as the sole reflection of a valid
social context. For one of Roller's most important aims was to overcome
the conflict between art and reality and to fuse the stage with the auditorium.

Like Wagner, who sought to reconcile the antitheses of words and music, performers and listeners, in his *Gesamtkunstwerk*, Roller designed a grandiose world which did not just portray the drama as a spectacle but created
a new world with a new, heightened reality. Where scenery had formerly
consisted of lifeless images painted on canvas, Roller evoked dreamlike
shapes in semi-darkness or sharp-edged shadows to announce impending
disaster, turning the stage into a single, all-encompassing area with mysterious lights and colours, its non-representational shapes creating an atmosphere that held the audience in thrall. The stage was no longer a place
where drama was enacted – it had itself become part of that drama.

Roller's companion in his radical transformation of the operatic stage
was Gustav Mahler. Like Roller, Mahler also subscribed to the ideal of the
Gesamtkunstwerk, in which the individual arts were subordinated to the
work of art as a composite whole. As a co-founder of the Viennese Secession, Roller was an opponent of academic classicism, while Mahler, as director and conductor, aimed to emancipate the large Wagnerian orchestra
from its sentimental romantic excesses. The combination of Wagner's tone-
painting and Roller's 'play of light'[10] was to transform the conventional
fairy-tale realism of opera, with its superficial displays of pomp and heroism, into a 'devotional festival drama', as Wagner's *Parsifal* was to be called.

The Vienna production of *Tristan und Isolde* in 1903, twenty years after
Wagner's death, marked the breakthrough. On to a stage with a minimum
of scenery Roller and Mahler released 'a huge wave of music, colour and
light', as one critic put it, 'creating a seductive midsummer night's dream
filled with stars and the heavy scent of blossom'.[11] This bold impressionis-
tic manner signalled 'the arrival of a new operatic style which will set the
tone for decades to come'.[12]

Hitler was also to play his part in this. In the course of his years in Vienna, he wrote in 1925, he saw all Wagner's operas 'time and again . . .
spending my last penny to be able to stand and listen'.[13] There was no
shortage of performances. When Kubizek visited him in June 1908, for example, the Hofoper put on *Der fliegende Holländer, Tannhäuser, Lohengrin,
Meistersinger*, the complete *Ring* and *Parsifal*.[14] Hitler was especially attracted
to *Tristan*. In the spring of 1913 he met a young apprentice called Rudolf
Häusler, whom he immediately took under his wing. 'In particular Hitler
introduced me to the works of Wagner', Häusler wrote later, 'and took me
for the first time to the opera' – *Tristan*, produced by Roller and Mahler,

with Anna Bahr-Mildenburg as Isolde. 'Hitler was in a state of considerable agitation', Häusler remembered, 'and pointed out the various leitmotifs to me throughout the performance.'[15]

Hitler is said to have seen *Tristan* thirty or forty times in Vienna.[16] It was above all the second act, the famous 'night of love', that gripped him. Roller's design, the castle courtyard dominated by trees, with the star-studded heavens giving way towards the end of the act to a pale ray of light on the horizon, recurs in Hitler's sketchbooks of the 1920s. It also reappears in the production notes for Bayreuth performances in the 1930s: for the second act the Führer is said to have demanded 'that there be a moon in the sky and a host of stars'.[17] In 1937 Benno von Arent took Roller's sets as the basis for a production instigated by Hitler, and as late as 1943 Furtwängler insisted that Roller's sets from the production of 1903 be used for a new production at the Vienna Staatsoper.[18] Since nothing happened in the theatre during the years of the Third Reich without Hitler's consent, we may assume that here too it was he who was responsible.

When, a few years after his emotional experience of *Tristan* in Vienna, Hitler was serving as a dispatch rider in the First World War, his piano reduction of the opera, 'long stretches of which I knew by heart', was his faithful companion. 'So familiar was I with the music', he told Ziegler, 'that I could hum or whistle all the most important sections in all three acts, often scene by scene, such as only someone can do who knows the work inside out. At every bar I could picture what was happening on the stage.'[19] The work filled his mind again during his time in Landsberg jail in 1924, and after his release his most pressing wish was to listen to his friend 'Putzi' Hanfstaengl playing the 'Liebestod' on the piano.[20] To the end *Tristan* remained for him, as it does for all devotees of Wagner, the Master's greatest work.[21]

But it was the Master's most monumental work, the *Ring* cycle, that was to leave the deepest marks on the young man from Linz. Like *Rienzi*, the four parts of the *Ring des Nibelungen* deal in coded mythological form with the history of Germany. For twenty-five years, transferring the abortive uprising against the aristocracy and the rule of money to mythological, prehistoric times, he had been turning over in his mind the subject of the failure of the revolution. A fourteen-hour marathon with a huge cast, a work claiming to span the whole of human experience, from the heavens above to the underworld below, the *Ring* matched Hitler's ideal conception of what the work of art should be. He once boasted to his secretary that he had seen parts of the tetralogy some 140 times.[22]

On his way to the Hofoper from the Stumpergasse or from the hostel where he later lived, he would picture 'the fantastic clouds and lighting effects' of Roller's *Ring*. Here, in a series of inspired designs and the brilliant interplay of light and shade, he discovered a world hitherto unknown to him. He was caught in a world of beauty, a world of monumentality and symmetry, a world encompassed by the power of music, sometimes *fortis-simo*, sometimes *pianissimo*, a rich orchestral texture from which arise the sounds of human voices issuing from the mouths of supernatural beings. Here were gods and demons, giants and dwarfs, lascivious nymphs and fire-breathing dragons, but also real people in prehistoric garb such as one only reads about in legends and fairy-tales. Spellbound by Roller's lights and by the swelling sounds coaxed from the orchestra by Felix Weingartner, Mahler's successor, he confronted these characters face to face, their obedient servant till the end of his days.

A matching philosophy for this new world was also available. Wherever in Vienna Wagner was played, anti-Semitism and the resurgence of the Germanic world were in attendance. Bodies such as the 'New Richard Wagner Society'[23] devoted themselves to cultivating the values of Teutonic culture and opposing Jewish infiltration, and when the Pan-German Party held their Bismarck celebrations not far from the Stumpergasse,[24] the mood was set by the Overture to *Rienzi* and the Pilgrims' Chorus from *Tannhäuser*. Hitler's visits to debates in the Viennese parliament had also given him samples of that pan-German, anti-Semitic ideology which was so closely associated with the Master's name. But it was only in the *Ring* that he found this ideology given full, vivid expression. The gulf that separated rich from poor, the contrast between his miserable living conditions and the dazzling splendour of the opera house, its boxes occupied by aristocrats and well-to-do citizens of dubious racial origins – the split that ran through his own existence was given its true context in the *Ring*. To whom does the world really belong? Who has gold and fair women – and why? The answers were in the *Ring*. From time immemorial, ran the explanation, there had been a bitter struggle over who should be heir to the world. Repulsive creatures from the dark underworld, filled with greed and lust for power, fought their way upwards to the light, where they were opposed by the gods and their heroic sons. A mighty battle ensues which decides the fate of the world – though it is not the outcome that the anxiously listening Hitler was hoping for. For the *Ring* ends in tragedy. Its heroes, scions of a divine race, perish, and Valhalla, where Wotan reigned, goes up in flames.

In one of the endless monologues with which he tried the patience of his staff in the 'Wolf's Lair', Hitler dwelt on the subject of the *Ring*. He loved art in general, he told them after the German defeat at the gates of Moscow in 1942, because 'it showed mankind the way forward'.[25] 'When I listen to Wagner', he went on, 'I seem to hear the rhythms of a pristine world.' The connection between these two sentences is not immediately clear, and a secretary has added a note to the effect that in the *Ring* 'Wagner had provided a mythological scenario for the life of the German people of which Hitler approved'. A note by a second secretary[26] states that by 'rhythms of a pristine world' Hitler meant the Prelude to *Rheingold*, in which Wagner describes the origin of all existence, starting with soft rolling tones in the bass, surging upwards louder and louder until triumphantly reaching the first light of sunrise on the waters of the Rhine. Pursuing the analogy further, Hitler said he could imagine 'that scientists might one day discover the parameters of the world through the relationships between the various wavelengths in the music of *Rheingold*'. That is to say, Wagner had revealed at the very beginning of the *Ring* those eternal verities which have later been confirmed by the findings of science and philosophy. Since, therefore, his works unveil the hidden laws of existence, 'the rhythms of a pristine world', he is in a position to 'show mankind the way forward'.

An eye for 'what ultimately holds the world together', however, as Goethe's Faust puts it, was not the only thing the young Hitler learned during his evenings at the Hofoper. He also began to understand the meaning of the world around him. The aimlessness of his day-to-day existence in alien surroundings was acquiring a deeper significance through the *Ring*, giving fresh meaning not only to his actual visits to the theatre but also to the intervals between performances. On his own realistic assessment of his position he saw himself as a nonentity in a society facing confusion and the threat of upheaval; Wagner now helped to resolve the uncertainty and distinguish between darkness and light. What could be successfully managed in the world of gods and earth spirits on the stage also had to be possible in the 'racial melting-pot' of Vienna.

After his triumphant re-occupation of the Rhineland in 1936 under the slogan 'Fortune Favours the Brave', Hitler was travelling one night through the Ruhr by train. Whether the sight of the glowing blast furnaces reminded him of the fires at Nibelheim in *Rheingold*, or whether he felt himself on the threshold of achieving that national unity of which he had dreamed in the days of *Rienzi*, he was seized by a sudden desire for music – the music of Wagner. His servants fetched his gramophone, and soon the scratchy sounds, first, of the Prelude to *Parsifal*, then of Siegfried's Funeral March, were heard from the loudspeaker – a kind of epitome of the *Ring*, combining the lament for the fallen hero with his defiant apotheosis, an accompaniment to the heights and depths of Hitler's own career as national hero.

'I first heard the *Ring* in Vienna,' he said, resuming his monologue in the train and thinking in all probability of Roller's production, conducted by Weingartner, which had its première in November 1910. 'And I remember, as though it were only yesterday, being infuriated at the sight of a group of jabbering Jews in caftans that I passed on my way home. No greater contrast can be imagined: the divine drama of a dying hero, and then these Jewish swine!'[27]

It was a traumatic experience that appears to have left its mark for decades to come. The question remains, however: Why should it have done? On the surface the two have nothing to do with each other: an operatic hero on the stage cannot be compared with a real man walking down the street. The world of the theatre, however realistic and gripping, stands in implacable antithesis to the world of everyday reality. But maybe it was precisely this, and not a chance encounter with what seemed an alien group of people, that so disturbed the young Hitler. For the endless evenings he spent in the opera house left no mark on his sordid day-to-day existence. When the curtain went down, the whole world of theatrical magic collapsed, leaving not only the Sephardic Jews to come to terms with their unhappy situation but also the would-be artist and postcard copier from the Stumpergasse and the men's hostel for the homeless, who eked out a living by selling his amateurish watercolours to dealers like Josef Feingold or framemakers like Samuel Morgenstern.

Refusing to acknowledge this antithesis between theatre and reality, he turned the extremes of his own experience into a new reality. As early as *Mein Kampf*, twelve years before that 'journey down the Rhine' in 1936, the polarization between the dying Germanic hero and 'those creatures with black locks and long caftans'[28] was firmly established in his mind. Casting himself in the role of theatrical designer, fascinated by contrasts of darkness and light, he painted a picture of a Fatherland betrayed, a Germany in whose coming transformation the Jews, with their 'foreign features' and their 'moral depravity', would have no part to play. Moreover, they spread an 'intellectual pestilence more infectious than the Black Death'. And when Hitler shone his spotlight on this source of disease, it revealed, 'like a maggot in a rotting carcass and dazzled by the sudden light, the little figure of a Jew'.[29] It sounded very dramatic. In fact it was all play-acting.

This theatrical posturing had become necessary because in reality no such antithesis existed. Hitler never tired of playing off the heroes of his mythological world against the dubious concept of 'world Jewry'. In one speech, one article after another he would maintain that this polarization was a reality and that he had experienced it for himself in Vienna – but not, as seems to have escaped his attention, in real life. For it is in the world of Wagner's *Ring* that we witness 'the transfiguration of the dying hero' and the sadistic conspiracy of the forces of the underworld which have brought about his downfall. The vision that dominated Hitler's mind from his nights at the Hofoper down to his death in the bunker was the result of a confusion. Although anti-Semitism was rife in Vienna at the time, and nationalist parties in the Austrian parliament laid responsibility for the city's ills at the door of the Jews, for Hitler reality was constituted by the underworld of dwarfs and demons in the myth of the Nibelungen. He strained with every nerve in his body to turn into reality the myth, the fiction, that was meant to help him understand that reality.

This, indeed, was precisely Wagner's purpose. In the traditional sense his *Ring* had nothing to do with art and theatre. 'I am not concerned to bring about a reconciliation with the contemptible world of the theatre,' he said after fleeing from Dresden, and turning over in his mind the project of the *Ring*, 'but to declare absolute, pitiless war. . . . It is not a question of convincing or persuading but of destroying.'[30] He had in his thoughts the theatre of the time, the blame for whose decline he laid principally at the door of the Jews. Opera in particular, a form of entertainment designed for the upper classes, symbolized for him a society ruled by rank and money. Money, synonym for 'the detested tribe of Israel', had tarnished everything, while the nobility, who had made life intolerable for him in Dresden, were still profiting from the situation.

After the bloody suppression of the March revolution in 1848, Wagner had considered what he called 'a new plan for an opera based on the Siegfried legend'.[31] Following the insurrection in Vienna that October he wrote the poem 'Siegfrieds Tod'.[32] But the tragic subject continued to exercise his mind until well into the days of the Second Reich, and the completed work was first given in 1876 as the final part of the *Ring* under the title *Götterdämmerung*. Although the previous events in the story had in the meantime expanded to fill three other operas – *Rheingold*, *Die Walküre* and *Siegfried* – the central theme remained constant, the theme of Siegfried, the revolutionary who stood for the Germany of the future. But his tragic death, and with it the death of the highest hopes of mankind, the extinction of the divine spark of Aryan ideals – that death had to be prevented at all costs.

What Wagner set out to present in his *Ring des Nibelungen* was not only a coded account of his experiences in the revolution but also the elevation of this account to the status of a higher mythological reality. Consequently he demanded that it should be performed not to a conventional audience but to a congregation of 'disciples of a new religion who support each other in our faith by the expression of mutual love', as he put it in 1849.[33] As the ancient Athenians attended their sacred dramatic ceremonies in order to recognize themselves in the great mythological characters before them on the stage, so the citizens of a liberated Germany should discover their own heroic portrait in the Nibelungen saga.

'I will establish an opera house on the banks of the Rhine,' prophesied Wagner from his exile in Zurich, where, 'over a space of four days',[34] in a 'spirit reminiscent of the age of classical Greek tragedy,'[35] the monumental work will be performed – and finally be put to the torch. 'At the end of the performance,' he promised, 'I shall take the score and throw myself on to Brünnhilde's funeral pyre.'[36] This would have been the closest Wagner came to fusing reality and theatrical illusion, for the fire that was to consume him and his work was smouldering in his own opera house.

Only through this unique spectacle, which, as in a collective vision that would convey to the German *Volk* a higher sense of self-awareness, Wagner continued, would the act of political liberation take hold in people's minds. With the *Ring* 'I am providing the men of the revolution with the explanation of that revolution in its noblest form',[37] he wrote in 1851. Only history can supply this explanation. Starting with the earliest murmurings of creation at the opening of *Rheingold*, the story passes through the golden age of Paradise to the moment when evil first appears with the theft of the Rhine gold, setting in motion an irresistible train of events. Primitive creatures fight for dominance until finally man appears, proclaiming the end of the age of greed and covetousness and the advent of freedom and love – a dazzling vision that sheds its transfiguring rays over the whole harrowing historical process.

Yet scarcely has this day of bliss dawned, joyfully greeted by Siegfried and Brünnhilde, than the powers of evil begin to hatch new plots to destroy this happiness. Shadows of treachery and betrayal fall over the idyllic scene, Hagen's murderous blade glistens in the rays of the setting sun, and as night falls, the sounds of Siegfried's Funeral March ring out. The mists rise again from the Rhine, as at the beginning, and the time has come to build the funeral pyre.

The rival forces in this global conflict do not only belong to the world's stock of indestructible myths: Wagner had experienced them for himself on the barricades of 1848–9. In *Siegfrieds Tod* he portrayed the representatives of good and evil as Burgundians, transferring the action to the world of the medieval German epic, the *Nibelungenlied*, then writing the earlier works one by one in order to explain the meaning of the story as a whole. Before Siegfried appears, the world knows only slavery: the fantastic creatures in *Rheingold* are not yet fully human. On their thrones high above the earth, reigning in beauty yet hard of heart, sit the gods, who consolidate their power, gained through crimes committed against creation itself, by their authority and by acts of violence.

A gulf separates them from their opposites, the Nibelungen, 'creatures of the dark and of death', hairy and ugly, crawling around on the bed of the Rhine and watching over the world's gold. The loathsome Alberich drives them on, a dwarf who, like Wotan, ruler of the gods, owes his power to crime. In these opposing figures Wagner portrayed the social conflict of 1848: the smug, selfish gods, who, without working themselves, enjoy the fruits of the earth, represent the aristocracy, while the repulsive dwarfs, avaricious yet fearful, stand for the money-grubbing Jews.

Although both sets of adversaries struggle for world domination – symbolized by the 'ring' of the title – the appearance of the freedom-loving hero finds them both on the same side of the barricades. Together, though by different means, they will extinguish the 'divine spark' of *joie de vivre* and universal love, represented by the heroes Siegmund and Siegfried, whose hearts are full of the joys of freedom and who sing of the glories of life. They own nothing but their 'own bodies',[38] and since they have no desire to rule over others, they refuse to let others rule over them. Their driving force is their joy in creation, at the heart of which lies their yearning for love. It is not long, however, before they inevitably arouse the resentment of the loveless gods and the hatred of the power-hungry inhabitants of the underworld.

Men blindly follow their urge for freedom, the argument goes on, clearing away the obstacles in their path one by one but in the end inevitably falling victim to their enemies – like Wagner in Dresden. Instead of founding a kingdom of love within which even the evil creatures of darkness can be absorbed and find redemption, the two reckless heroes, parted from their loved ones, are betrayed and slain. In the end the whole world is on fire and Wagner, the revolutionary resurrected in the characters he has created, would have dearly loved to be caught up in the flames. 'If only I could perish with Valhalla!' he cried after finishing the libretto of the work. 'My poem embraces the beginning and the end of the world.'[39] To the 'plenipotentiary of destruction', as he liked to call himself,[40] the *Ring* poem was 'the greatest ever written',[41] and at the same time, 'in its beauty and grandeur the most complete artistic expression of my entire *Weltanschauung*'. And since *Rienzi* the aim of that *Weltanschauung*[42] had been nothing less than that pursued by his heroes Siegmund and Siegfried – the overthrow of society and the triumph of the New Man.

This New Man was distinguished from the *ancien régime* and its slaves not only through a new, liberated consciousness but also by biological criteria. The race of heroes that sprang from Wotan's loins would have bodies stronger, healthier, more beautiful. 'Let the blood of the Wälsungen flourish!'[43] cries Siegmund, invoking the ideal of a eugenically pure race of Teutons. This post-revolutionary elite, in Wagner's expectation, would one day make his *Ring* a national icon. 'It is the most Aryan work of art imaginable,' he wrote to King Ludwig. 'No people on earth has ever had its origins and its national character demonstrated with such clarity.'[44]

In Richard Wagner, the 'most German' of all artists, the heroic Aryan *Volk* of the future had found its prophet. And in his Festspielhaus in Bayreuth, opened in 1876 and intended from the beginning to be devoted to performances of the *Ring*, they found a national shrine. Born out of the spirit of revolution – albeit a revolution that failed in the face of reality – it became itself a political reality. 'My artistic ideal stands and falls with the salvation of Germany,' he said in 1866. 'If Germany is not great, my art will remain but a dream. But if my dream is fulfilled, Germany will achieve that greatness for which it is predestined.'[45]

Hitler made this dream his own. Swept off his feet by the 'mighty sounds' of Wagner's orchestra and dazzled by the magical skill of Roller's productions, he now realized what life had hitherto denied him – a meaning that he could understand and a goal that he could attain. The stark contrasts revealed in the *Ring* he had witnessed every day in the streets of Vienna: on the one hand, the lights in the luxurious villas on the Ringstrasse, where the well-to-do held court, heedless of the hardships of their downtrodden people; on the other, the shadowy figures of the Jews shuffling along in the gloom – 'these tormentors of suffering mankind',[46] as Wagner had called them, who had a stranglehold over the people through their financial manipulations.

The role of the fearless hero who marches out to slay the Hydra seemed as though it were his of right. With no parents and no possessions, scorned as an artist and denied a share in the good life, his position seemed hopeless. In fact, it was this very lack of attachment which enabled him to grasp Wagner's vision as a divine command to turn Germany's 'pre-determined greatness' into a reality. Kubizek recalled that Hitler literally 'donned Wagner's personality and made it part of his own'.[47] He divided people into two classes – pro-Wagnerians and anti-Wagnerians, the latter made up of those sinister, dark-skinned creatures of the underworld who he believed were among Wagner's most implacable enemies and on whom he had waged war since his days in Linz. As the next Wagner performance drew near, wrote his fellow-fanatic, 'we found ourselves in the grip of the same emotions as the heroes on the stage, living out a proud life of fearless deeds before entering the realm of Valhalla and joining the ranks of its immortal denizens.'[48]

Had Hitler really understood Wagner? *Gesamtkunstwerk* is a complex concept, capable of manifold interpretations. Wagner himself constantly changed the text of his libretti, with contradictory endings, and also put out different interpretations at different times which made things even more complicated. Simple explanations, it seems, are out of place where the *Ring* is concerned. The ability to provide a detailed exegesis remains to the present day the touchstone of a critic's mastery of the material, both literary and musical, and there is no prominent producer who cannot count at least one failure among his productions. Modern interpretations at the Bayreuth Festival still show that Wagner's tetralogy seems to have a great deal to do with questions of power and the subtleties of psychology but virtually nothing with the *Weltanschauung* of Adolf Hitler.

Or, for that matter, with the *Weltanschauung* of Richard Wagner. All the progressive humanistic ideas that have been ascribed to Wagner and have found their way into interpretations of the *Ring* are based on conceptual misunderstandings. By 'democracy', for instance, Wagner means an authoritarian state governed by an elite. When he talks of 'socialism' he has in mind the art-loving masses whose lives find their culmination in attending the Bayreuth Festival. When he demands the destruction of capitalism – a particular hobbyhorse of his, according to Devrient[49] – the capitalists are also to be destroyed. And if he desires to see Christianity 'ennobled',[50] then only through an Aryan Jesus, whose command to mankind to show compassion is intended only for those of pure race. For those who nailed Him to the Cross there remained only perdition.

So could all the 'experts' have overlooked, or even deliberately ignored, what struck the attention of a twenty-year-old cultural and theatrical novice on the eve of the First World War? Could one, since the fall of the Third Reich, have possibly been mistaken about Wagner's chauvinism and intolerance, the racism and glorification of violence which were obvious to con-

temporary audiences? And is there in the *Ring* – as many modern Wagnerians are prepared to swear – not the slightest trace of anti-Semitism? A
man of Hitler's mentality could not but detect such features in the work, in
company with all the other recipients of its inflammatory message as they
watched it unfurl on the stage before them.

Many intellectuals saw things in the same light. For instance, when the
racist philosopher Arthur Gobineau, one of the precursors of Nazi racial
doctrine, saw the *Ring* in Berlin in the Master's company, he found it conveyed 'the ideal expression of all his ideas on race . . . on extinction and
survival', according to Cosima, Wagner's widow.[51] In the official Bayreuth
programme of 1924 Hans Alfred Grunsky wrote that 'an intense racial dislike' existed between Siegfried and the Nibelungen dwarfs, who exercised
'a pernicious influence on the rest of the world'. There is, however, a solution in sight, concluded Grunsky – 'though we would be well advised not
to explain in so many words what this solution involves'.[52]

As anti-Semitism was the driving force behind his *Weltanschauung*, so in
the *Ring* Wagner gave his *Weltanschauung* artistic form – a mirror in which
the Germans should see themselves reflected. The symbolic key to the enigmatic story, which starts in the primeval world and reaches forward to
historical times, lies in the 'ring' of the title. Forged from stolen gold, it
gave the man who possessed it total dominion over the world. Or, in the
words of Wellgunde, one of the Rhinemaidens, representative of a golden
age of innocence which came to an end with the theft of the Rhine gold:
'He who inherits the world will be he who fashions the ring from the gold,
and the ring will give him boundless power.'[53]

This secret, innocently revealed by the Rhinemaiden, comes into the
hands of the ugly dwarf Alberich, one of a hairy, hunchbacked race that
lives in the underworld 'like maggots in rotting flesh'.[54] With this repulsive image Wagner also has the Jews in mind, 'the race that destroys all
living things like crawling insects'.[55] Alberich picks up the Rhinemaiden's
words about 'inheriting the world' and grabs the gold, paying for his crime
with the repudiation of love. Indeed, he not only renounces love, the divine principle of creation, but curses it. According to Christian propaganda
the Jews cursed the Saviour. And as Alberich cries out in mocking laughter: 'Thus do I lay my curse on love!', so the world becomes shrouded in
darkness.[56]

The concept of 'inheriting the world' comes from St Paul's epistle to the
Romans, in which, according to Wagner, the right to become 'heir of the
world' is promised to 'Abraham and his seed'. It was a concept not chosen
in vain. Wagner made it mean that the Jews laid claim to rule the world.
The gold they have 'wrenched from the bowels of the earth' they use to
assert their power over the rest of mankind, turning it into money with
which to build banks and indulge in financial speculation.[57] This, said
Wagner, was what he had set out to convey in his *Ring des Nibelungen*. On

a visit to London in 1877, a year after the first performance of the *Ring*, he claimed to detect signs that the world of the Nibelungen had already become a reality. 'Alberich's dream has been fulfilled here – Nibelheim and world domination,' he said to Cosima.[58]

But it is also part of the message of the *Ring* that this world has no future. Born through crime, sustained by injustice, shot through with all conceivable vices, it is moving inexorably towards its doom. 'I have given a complete picture of the curse that besets avarice,' he told Cosima, 'together with the ruin to which it leads.'[59]

The curse of avarice, a specifically Jewish characteristic in Wagner's eyes, is enacted symbolically in the Nibelungen dwarfs and their compulsive pursuit of the ring. Their ruin, on the other hand, he predicted quite openly in the pamphlet 'Music and the Jews', published anonymously in the year after the Dresden revolt.[60] First settling his account with his Jewish rivals Meyerbeer and Mendelssohn, he arrived at a principle of universal application: the cultural decadence for which Alberich's crime was responsible was not final and irreversible; there was a way in which his race could be saved. 'Never forget', he cried to the serried ranks of Jewry, 'that only one thing can lift the curse that lies upon you, the way the curse was lifted from Ahasverus – by *annihilation!*'[61]

What curse does Wagner mean? According to Christian legend, Ahasverus, the Wandering Jew, was condemned by Jesus to a life of eternal restlessness. Christ's Crucifixion led to a curse on the entire people of Israel. And did not Judas, who betrayed Jesus, kill himself in his despair? But it was not the religious ignorance of those who wilfully refused to be baptized that provoked his fury; it was the stranglehold that he maintained they had over the affairs of the modern world, including the world of music. Wagner now made himself their bitterest enemy, a bitterness unmatched by any comparable figure in German history.

The Jews, says Wagner at the beginning of his pamphlet, will hold sway 'so long as money remains the power that eclipses all others in our lives'.[62] 'No one notices that these innocent-looking bits of paper – IOUs and the like – are thick with the blood of countless earlier generations.' Instead we make light of the situation, casting a veil over it in our well-intentioned way 'so as to make the sight of it less unpleasant'. Wagner's pamphlet was intended to put an end to all this. 'By revealing the true state of affairs,' he wrote, 'we must hope that we shall drive out this Satan from those hiding-places in which he has been able to survive under the cover of darkness.' In the *Ring* this Satan is the hairy, dark-skinned Alberich, who escapes from the murk of Nibelheim to admit some rays of half-light into the dawn of creation.

In an act of 'fearful violence'[63] Alberich bears the gold away. 'It will make me ruler over the whole world,' he boasts.[64] But things work out differently. Wotan steals the ring from him, whereupon, true to his nature,

Alberich utters another curse: the ring will bring a twofold death to whoever possesses it, first the slow, lingering death of insatiable greed,[65] then
the sudden death at the hand of the Grim Reaper. This is exactly what
Wagner meant when he spoke of the curse of avarice and the catastrophe
that will follow. Responsibility for this curse, uttered by Alberich in the
opera and claimed in his article to be the only way out of the situation,
rests firmly on Wagner's shoulders. And that he was the first writer to
have incited the 'destruction' of the Jews is a boast that nobody is likely to
challenge.

In the *Ring* the man charged with this task is Siegfried, the revolutionary
who puts an end to the world of Alberich and his curse. On the one hand,
he fulfils the curse by slaying the power-hungry Nibelung Mime with the
sword Nothung; on the other, he preaches a new philosophy of life, a life
of optimism and positive values which he contrasts with the obscenities of
the underworld, whose energies are exhausted in cupidity and greed. A
figure credited as early as Jakob Grimm's *German Mythology* with 'traces of
the superman',[66] Siegfried emerges as the man of the future, ready to in-
spire the world with the divine spark of joy. He needs neither god nor
teacher: Wotan he puts to flight, Mime he slays. At the same time he knows
neither fear nor envy, characteristics which soured the life of pre-revolu-
tionary man. He is consumed with the joy of nature and ultimately with
yearning for his beloved. 'The fate of the world rests on the divine simpli-
city and singularity of this one fearless individual.'[67]

After the 'dawn of creation' shattered by Alberich, a new day appears to
begin and a new man enters the scene. The Nibelung gold matters not to
him, so that the curse has no power over him, as Alberich angrily observes.[68]
Dominion over others holds no attraction for him; even death, the very
thought of which made the old world tremble, has lost its sting. United
with Brünnhilde, he lives on in her and in the race of heroes they engen-
der.

But Siegfried has long since lost his freedom. He knows nothing of his
history but history knows all about him. Even before he was born, Wotan
had assigned him his role in the world scheme of things. For Mime, who
raised him, Siegfried will have to slay the dragon, under whose belly the
Nibelung gold, together with the ring, lies as in a bank vault. For Wotan,
his forebear, from whom the heroic race of the Wälsungen sprang, he will
have to free the world both from the Nibelungen and – an original motif of
Wagner's – from Wotan himself, who has grown weary of life. Could this
idea – particularly effective in theatrical terms – have sprung from the
thought of the revolution in Dresden, when Wagner had urged the King to
abdicate and at the same time make himself the liberator of his people? It is
a shift of power foreshadowed in the *Ring*. Wotan relinquishes authority,
whereupon Siegfried, grasping the sword already stained with the blood
both of the Nibelungen and of the giant Fafner, breaks Wotan's spear into

splinters. As the one appointed to oversee the collapse of the old world, Siegfried, the new man, still seems unable to dispense with brutality.

Hardly has Wotan been disposed of than the scene changes to the rock on which Brünnhilde lies sleeping. Amidst the pulsating tones of the orchestra he wakens her with a kiss. Nothing, it seems, can now stand in the way of the perpetuation of their noble clan. But things work out differently. As Wagner, the rebel, had failed in Dresden, so Siegfried, the freedom fighter, now fails also. For Alberich, prince of darkness, consumed by hatred and a thirst for vengeance, is still alive. The evil principle, in the form of the curse that persists throughout the *Ring* legend, will still triumph as it did when the story began at the bottom of the Rhine. The new pawn in the power game is Hagen. Conceived in a loveless relationship with the sole purpose of regaining the ring, he is commanded to live by the precept of 'Hate those who are happy'[69] and to honour the slogan imprinted on the minds of all Nibelungen: 'We shall inherit the earth.'

Hagen, 'pale and ashen', like Ahasverus, thus becomes a traitor, like Judas, and murders his hunting companion Siegfried, who has the ring in his possession. With no chance of conquering Siegfried in open combat, Hagen gives him a magic potion – black magic is also one of the weapons in the armoury of the Antichrist – which causes him to forget his past. His consciousness thus disturbed, Siegfried becomes an easy prey and Hagen plunges his spear into his back. There follows the Funeral March, the martial thud of its repeated semiquaver rhythms sounding like an outburst of rage at the failure of the revolution and the end of a vision but also like an oath of vengeance that will be fulfilled some time in the future, perhaps only a very distant future. After Brünnhilde's immolation the Rhine bursts its banks and Hagen dives into the water in pursuit of the ring, but the Rhinemaidens hold it up in triumph and Hagen drowns, while Valhalla goes up in flames. 'When the gods are completely surrounded by the flames', reads Wagner's stage direction, 'the curtain falls.'[70]

In Hitler's imagination the curtain never fell. Even after he had become Reichskanzler, Speer reported, he would make detailed sketches for all the scenes in the four parts of the *Ring*, a task, Hitler added with satisfaction, 'on which he worked night after night for three weeks'.[71] The drama of political reality, it appears, took place for him against a background of changing sets for Wagner's operas.

DRAGON-SLAYER BY
PROFESSION

~∞~

In February 1883 Siegfried's Funeral March, angry lamentation over the
death of a dream, became Wagner's own funeral music. A nation's
mourning over the death of the 'most German' of its composers found expression in the triumphant celebration of a hero's sword. In every town
and city where the funeral cortège stopped on its way from Venice, where
he had died, back to Bayreuth, the same music was played – the collective
leitmotif of a grieving nation. Vienna too, for years under the Master's spell,
wore black. Church bells tolled, improvised meetings took place and the
piece was played at every concert, recalling how the blond hero met his
death at the hands of the black-haired Hagen.

In Vienna, where they had discovered in the composer of the *Ring* the
redeemer of Austria's racial chaos, the students held a special meeting in
the Sophiensaal. The subject was not music but politics. They felt themselves to be a threatened elite in their multi-ethnic society, and Wagner,
protagonist of an aggressive German-ness, had become their guardian angel. Not unexpectedly the occasion turned, according to the *Allgemeine
Zeitung*, into 'a fervent demonstration of nationalist German sentiment',[1]
which, in the eyes of Theodor Herzl, a student in Vienna at the time, meant
'an exhibition of anti-Semitism'.[2] The Austrian poet Hermann Bahr, then a
philosophy student, played a particularly prominent part in exploiting their
grief and turning it into a tirade against Wagner's enemies. Bahr and others were wildly applauded, and some even called for the reintroduction of
the yellow star that had been used in the Middle Ages.

Bahr, who years later became an influential supporter of the Bayreuth
cause, explained after the meeting that he had merely 'characterized Wagner
as a politician, specifically a pan-German politician', whereas Austria was
like Kundry, the sinner in *Parsifal*, 'anxiously waiting for her saviour'. The

time was ripe for a figure, acting in the name of Wagner, to free the country from cultural decadence and from infiltration by the Jews, preferably by re-uniting it with the German Reich. It should be made clear that this was the only way forward, declared Bahr and his companions. Indeed, Wagner himself, Bahr pointed out in his address from the black-draped platform, had come out openly at the time of the revolution in Dresden for 'the most noble of causes, a pan-German republic . . . without any petty attachment to the Saxon court'. This was a remark aimed at the unpopular Austro-Hungarian monarchy and its liberal policies, which could be removed only by a determined act of insurrection. Bahr ended his speech in the Sophiensaal by calling on all present to swear an oath 'not to rest until Richard Wagner's divine dream of a greater Germany has been fulfilled'.[3]

The meeting turned into a riot. The police moved in to silence the agitators and a member of the government threatened to bring the proceedings to a close. 'Then', wrote the *Neue Freie Presse*, 'Ritter von Schönerer mounted the platform to the frenzied applause of his supporters and addressed the assembly in thunderous tones, his words interspersed with cheers.' This was six years before Hitler was born.

Georg Ritter von Schönerer, landowner, anti-Semite, passionately devoted to Wagner, came from the same district as Hitler's family and is even said to have converted Hitler's father to his racial ideas. A man whose supporters wore on their watch-chain an anti-Semitic emblem depicting a Jew hanging from the gallows,[4] Schönerer has gone down in history as 'the most powerful and radical anti-Semite in Austria before Hitler'.[5] A year before his dramatic appearance in the Sophiensaal he had published his nationalistic views in his so-called 'Linz Programme', which proposed, first, the segregation of the Jews, then the removal of Jewish influence from all areas of public life.[6] At the same time as the Hofoper in Vienna was providing a perfect example of Jewish–German cooperation with its Mahler–Roller production of *Tristan und Isolde* – both men enthusiastic Wagnerians – Schönerer was distributing a postcard bearing a likeness of Wagner together with his dictum: 'The Jew is the evil genius of the decline of civilization.' It was to become a shibboleth in the years of the Third Reich. The card was signed 'Heil! Schönerer'.[7]

When Hitler found refuge in Vienna in 1908, politics in the city were under the influence of Schönerer, alongside whom was the figure of Karl Lueger, anti-Semitic major of Vienna and a man with a far more popular appeal. Both men stood in the shadow of Wagner.[8] The first performance in the capital of the complete *Ring* in 1879 was described by a Hofoper publication as 'a resounding success, made all the more overwhelming by the tide of national feeling that sweeps through it'. The critic Eduard Hanslick saw in it the sinister threat of a 'four-barrelled revolver'.[9]

Hitler found the *Weltanschauung* of the *Ring* reproduced in Schönerer's policies and felt 'a personal sympathy' for the man to whose politics his father and his companions had already committed themselves. He also considered Schönerer a more substantial thinker than Lueger[10] and soon became his faithful supporter,[11] not least because he found that the nationalistic views expressed by Schönerer in parliament corresponded to those associated with Bayreuth.

The question as to why Hitler became an anti-Semite is often met with the counter-question of whether, in this hate- and envy-ridden city with its domineering cock-sure politicians, there was any way he could have avoided it; hatred of the Jews was a matter of course and required no particular justification. This seems to be the only way one can explain why he justified his anti-Semitism 'by referring to a conviction, based on experience, that the Jews in general were a pernicious influence', as Konrad Heiden, an early biographer of Hitler, put it. 'Nowhere does he mention names, make specific allegations or refer to concrete cases where he has suffered at their hands.'[12]

Another writer on Hitler's years in Vienna, Brigitte Hamann, also failed to find any hint of conflict with his Jewish neighbours.[13] Dr Eduard Bloch, the Hitlers' family doctor, was Jewish, and well after he had become Chancellor we find Hitler expressing his gratitude to Bloch for looking after his ailing mother. He admired Gustav Mahler, a Jew, for his interpretations of Wagner, and he sold his sketches almost exclusively to Jewish dealers and collectors. Once he went with Kubizek to a private recital in the house of one Dr Rudolf Jahoda, a Jewish amateur musician in whose library he took a special interest. Even during his months in the men's hostel he counted a number of Jews among his friends, and the officer who decorated him with the Iron Cross during the First World War was also of the Judaic persuasion. None of these men appears to have given him the slightest reason to hate them, let alone to wish them dead.

There is, however, one remark of Hitler's, recorded by Helene Hanfstaengl, which seems to contradict this. His hatred of the Jews was a personal matter, he is said to have explained.[14] So did he have an unpleasant experience at their hands after all, or suffer an unforgivable slight which made him seek revenge? Frau Hanfstaengl probably understood Hitler's remark in a sense he did not intend. It was meant to refer not to some private affair, which would in any case have contradicted his confidence in his messianic mission, but to the simple fact that, since it was 'a personal matter', he could not discuss it. Although she belonged to the wider Bayreuth circle, Frau Hanfstaengl could hardly have believed that Hitler's rabid anti-Semitism was the result of his intellectual dependence on the ideas of Wagner.[15]

In fact his war against the Jews derived from a fundamental and wholly personal conviction which, seen in retrospect, constituted the *raison d'être* of his entire life. This paranoia was stimulated by his encounter with Wagner's 'dualistic artistic world', in Heiden's words, in which 'the noble and the base confront each other in an unmistakable political context'. This is what defined the kingdom of the man Heiden called in 1935 'the greatest mass agitator in the history of the world'.[16] 'In Hitler's kingdom the curse on the Nibelungen gold symbolizes subjection to usury; the dwarf Alberich represents inferior racial stock, i.e. the Jews; Siegfried and Hagen the schism in the German nation; and Wotan the tragic hero of the Teutonic race.'[17] Wagner, unequalled in his power to rouse the masses, had portrayed on the stage the heroic struggles to come, and Hitler, leaving reality behind and embracing the world of the theatre, had assumed his master's mantle.

The Hofoper in Vienna made things easy for him. The great Wagner heroine of the day was Anna Bahr-Mildenburg, once Mahler's mistress, then Hermann Bahr's wife; heroic tenors trained by Cosima hurled their triumphant cries of 'Nothung! Nothung!' into the auditorium, and the shouts of 'Heil!' resounded through the theatre as though in anticipation of the war that was to come.

The forces of opposition were also present. While Lueger ranted against Mahler, and Schönerer demanded that the growing Jewish influence on public life be halted,[18] the opera house offered an opportunity to witness these destructive creatures at work on the stage. The part of Mime, Alberich's brother, was taken by Hans Breuer, who turned the dwarf into a Jewish caricature that bore no resemblance to reality but was highly effective on the stage. There was in Bayreuth, under Cosima's patronage, a 'school' of such stylizations run by the producer Julius Kniese, a man known for his ruthless anti-Semitism,[19] who in 1883 had launched an attack on the conductor Hermann Levi for spreading his 'pernicious Jewish influence'.[20] Now he poured his hate into his characterization of the figure of Mime, making him the embodiment of all the detestable qualities of the Jewish race.

When Romain Rolland attended a performance of the *Ring* in Bayreuth, he described Breuer's portrayal of Mime as resembling something out of a horror film: 'Dirty, unkempt, a dishevelled wig making him look like an aged ape, red eyes, limping around with mincing gait on crooked legs, constantly making grimaces and indecent gestures'[21] which Wagner himself, according to Cosima's diary, had prescribed. When the Master gave an imitation of Mime's grotesque antics during rehearsals for the first Bayreuth Festival in 1876 it was like seeing 'the ugly little dwarf in person',[22] wrote Wagner's young friend and patron Wendelin Weissheimer. His jerky movements, according to the Bayreuth orthodoxy, conveyed the Jews' 'sinister greed' and 'frantic anxiety'.[23]

Mahler, Jewish conductor of the *Ring*, whom the *Alldeutsches Blatt* compared to Wagner's 'wicked magician Klingsor in *Parsifal*',[24] was in no doubt about whom Wagner had in his sights. When, as usual, the singer playing Mime began to mimic the Jews, Mahler was furious. 'This Jewish jabbering is the worst feature about him,' he said in 1898. 'Although I am certain that

Wagner intended Mime to be a parody of a Jew, he cannot in all conscience be allowed to exaggerate to such a degree as this.'[25]

But such exaggerations were part and parcel of anti-Semitism. The actual origins of Wagner's animosity are difficult to define but the development of his prejudice can be traced in that of his characters. Thus the race of the Nibelungen, who taught Hitler the meaning of terror, were not initially the repulsive creatures they appear in the action. As their features became distorted, so they became stereotypes that could be used for propaganda purposes. From one draft of the *Ring* to another their negative qualities grew – not, however, according to the logic of motivation but to that of the drama. Before Alberich and Mime revealed themselves as dangerous ogres, they had represented in Wagner's drafts the adversaries the hero needed in order to fight his way to the position of saviour of the world. For this, not rescue from the Nibelungen, was the hero's original mission. The 1851 draft of *Rheingold* still has no trace of Alberich's 'curse on love', which opens old wounds, and in *Siegfrieds Tod*, before it became *Götterdämmerung*, Brünnhilde was even able to promise the dwarfs release from their slavery. 'Hear my word!' she cries to them: 'I declare your slavery at an end. He who forged the ring . . . shall be as free as you!'[26]

The longer Wagner brooded over the *Ring*, the more his passion of 1848 cooled. Instead the underlying conflicts in the drama became more pronounced. The fallen hero, originally borne aloft by his bride to eternal life in Valhalla, dies in the final version unredeemed, leaving behind an angry audience driven by the insistent rhythms of the Funeral March to seek vengeance on the Nibelungen. But because of the hero's murder on the open stage, the underworld creatures can no longer look for mercy or for Brünnhilde's redemption. The only outcome for them is their destruction.

Indeed, comparing Wagner's sketches with his final score, one begins to suspect that the formal extremism of the work may have been not the result of his growing anti-Semitism but its cause. The dialectical principle of dramatic conflict, in which contrasts are magnified in the interest of dramatic tension, may have found its way into his racial prejudices and then, exacerbated by hatred and by resentment of his critics, turned into the horror story which we have as *Der Ring des Nibelungen*. The forces present on the stage and in the music that bring about the necessary dramatic intensity lead in the world of reality to catastrophic misinterpretations. It comes as no surprise if a gun, once loaded, goes off.

Was Wagner a victim of his own dramaturgy? If it is possible for a fanatical illusion to distort the psyche, alienating it from itself and making it intolerable to those around it, then Wagner is a terrifying example. Hitler, on the other hand, experienced no such self-alienation through the power of Wagner's music because he was not yet in possession of the identity which this power would have caused him to lose. Only his complete absorption into the Wagnerian world of devotion, terror and revenge established a firm, definable personality. By seeing Hitler purely in terms of his impact on history, one overlooks a vital consideration – his identification with the theatre. Here the *Ring* was paramount. In broad sweeps he divided the world into Wagnerian categories, creating a social order in which costume stood for function and greasepaint for character. For a real world between the superhuman and the subhuman there was no room left.

Similarly Hitler's speeches swarm with the heroes of Valhalla and the dwarfs of Nibelheim. Whether he was addressing a beer-hall meeting in Munich in the twenties or an assembly in the Kroll opera house in Berlin in the thirties, whenever he came to his stock themes, he spoke with the croaking voice of Alberich and Mime. The next moment he would launch into an aria in the ringing tones of a Heldentenor, until finally, overcome with emotion in his impersonation of the character before his eyes, his voice gave out altogether. He was invoking not human beings, creatures from the real world, but the legendary characters of the *Ring*. Fact gave way to fiction.

One of Hitler's favourite figures for such performances was Mime, the spiteful dwarf who hides his concupiscence behind a smokescreen of prattle. Volubly he persuades his adopted son Siegfried to capture the treasure for him, telling him he will then 'strike off his head'.[27] Likewise Hitler denounced his political enemies as assassins who disguised their real purpose, namely to gain power and riches, behind a torrent of words. In 1934 we find him raging against 'all those petty dwarfs' who blocked his path, only, like Mime, to be swept aside by 'the force of his genius': 'once roused from their slumbers', says this new Siegfried, 'the people will never again fall asleep.'[28] It was Mime too who plotted how to give Siegfried a drugged drink. 'Only a few drops and he will sink into oblivion. Then, with his own weapon, I shall easily remove him from the scene.'[29]

Mime knows that he can outwit the young Siegfried with his glib words but is frightened of the youth's untamed nature. 'A dwarf who has nothing but knowledge', reflected Hitler in his 'Wolf's Lair', 'will always be afraid of force.'[30] He claimed to have known the truth of this from his days in Vienna, when in conversation the Jews would try to confuse him with their glib patter and their inveterate lying. When he challenged them, 'they would quickly change the subject' and make it difficult 'to come to grips with the inborn hypocrisy of their race'.[31] Siegfried's dealings with Mime clearly had a firm place in Hitler's memory, as though his refuge in the hostel were the dwarf's cave.

Likewise the way the angry Siegfried wanted 'to take Mime by the scruff of the neck and dispose of him once for all'[32] left its mark on Hitler's mind. In 1942 we find him reflecting that 'the Jews were in the habit of confronting non-Jews with meaningless slogans and sayings. The more meaningless and obscure these sayings, the longer they would brood over them, getting further and further away from reality.' 'The worst thing', Hitler went on, 'was that they used to chuckle about the way they had hood-winked us.' These words sound like a commentary on the first act of *Siegfried*, in which Mime makes desperate efforts to keep the young hero in ignorance of his background. And Hitler's next sentence – 'If people had any idea of the hypocrisy of the Jews, they would have them all put to death'[33] – could summarize the second act. When Siegfried realizes Mime's true intentions, he slays him on the spot, exclaiming in self-justification: 'He tried to trap me: therefore I had to kill him!'[34] Only now is the dragon-slayer free to seek out his bride. And 'only after the terrible nightmare has passed', said Hitler, with the 'conquered Jews' in mind, 'will the spirit of carefree joy return to the world'.[35] 'Away with the nightmare!' cries Siegfried. 'I will set eyes on it no more!'[36]

The vision of the Jews as a 'nightmare' is one of Wagner's stock horror-images. As early as his revolutionary days in Dresden, when he had cast the King of Saxony in the role of hero, he had seen the world of the moneygrubbers as the King's most sinister adversary. With the success of the revolution, he told the 'Vaterlandsverein' in 1848, 'this nightmare will pass, together with everything associated with it . . . and the Christian message will be victorious'.[37] To which Hitler, who loathed the Church as much as his predecessor, added: 'What Christ began, I shall finish.'[38]

In his speeches Hitler concentrated on the concept of the Antichrist, whom Wagner vividly and savagely personified in the figure of Alberich. Unlike his cunning brother Mime, the braggart Alberich seeks power through violence and brutality. The curse that he lays on love gives him the right to claim 'to inherit the world' and subject it to his will with all the sadistic delight at his command. Cracking his whip, he mockingly drives his slaves to work and the women to be objects of his lust. 'Beware the creatures of the night,' he warns.[39] It is only a matter of time before he has transformed the entire world into a slave camp, in which generations of Nibelungen perpetuate their evil, impure race. This is the vision that Hitler set out to destroy, calling it 'the kingdom of Alberich',[40] which had already taken hold in Russia. Wagner's Alberich set out to destroy the noble line of Wotan by killing or subjugating the men and ruining the women by bastardiza-tion. The rebellious Jews in the East had already 'infected' the superior blood of the Teutons and eradicated the intellectuals. 'Since the Jewish dic-tatorship of the Bolsheviks seized power in Russia,' wrote Hitler, 'it has led to a submissive, mindless populace held in check by a regime of brutal-ity.' And as though he were the only one to have been made aware of the parallel, he invokes the terrible vision of *Rheingold*. As Alberich cries in jubilation, 'The whole world will be mine!',[41] so Hitler sees the dwarfs' evil empire, 'which so far has only taken root in Russia, extending to other countries as well'. To the end of his life he was haunted by the nightmare that the land of Siegfried might degenerate into the land of Alberich.

As Hitler had no difficulty in identifying the Russian Revolution and its bloody aftermath with the events of the *Ring*, so Alberich's theft of the gold and hoarding of the Nibelungen treasure offered him an equally compelling parallel to the financial and economic forces that dominated the contemporary world – a parallel which had also been in Wagner's mind. In Hitler's eyes the Jews alone held the power of money in their hands,[42] growing fat on the proceeds of moneylending without having to raise their little finger. This swindle was only possible, according to Hitler, because they had convinced the world of the validity of one single, central principle, namely that money is material power. Alberich performed the same trick when he commanded that the gold, properly a source of disinterested delight, devoid of intrinsic value, should be given metaphorical status in the form of a ring, symbol of unscrupulous self-interest. Coming thus by his trickery into the possession of money, he employs his Nibelungen brothers as slave labour, driving them with his whip to pile up the gold. One day, he says to himself, the inherent dynamism of the system will make him 'heir of the world', as the Jews, according to Hitler, will come to dominate the world and the noble German nation. 'I am the only one who understands the danger,' said the Führer to his secretary in 1944, 'and the only one who can avert it.'[43]

Hardly had he returned from the Flanders trenches in 1919 than Hitler began to reflect on the part played by the Jews in world affairs.[44] Support came in the form of one Gottfried Feder, an engineer who had founded an organization called 'German Fighters Against Enslavement to Usury', from which he gained an insight into the workings of international finance and venture capital,[45] discovering to his surprise how close this world was to the kingdom ruled by Alberich. Whether it be Russia or Wall Street, Alberich was always lurking round the corner. Not for nothing does he force Mime to make him the magic Tarnhelm, the helmet that renders its wearer invisible and able to change his form at will. Dwarf, dragon, ugly toad – all are Alberich in disguise. Feder's basic thesis was explained in 1932 by Theodor Heuss as the result of an obsession with 'getting away from gold', which attached excessive importance to the metal and led to a misinterpretation of its function as a measure of value. 'By breaking the link with gold', Heuss concluded, 'Feder thought he could break the link with the Jews.'[46]

Dispensing with gold as a symbol of power, achieved in the *Ring* by the eventual return of the ring to the Rhinemaidens, was to become a matter of dogma in the Third Reich. In 1940 Walther Funk, Minister of Economics, announced that in the new European order the German currency would not be tied to the gold standard but determined by the 'actual strength'[47] of the German Reich. In 1942 Hitler himself confirmed the success of his nation's economy by abolishing the Nibelungen treasure. 'Gold is beginning to lose its attraction,' he explained in a private address. Protests had come immediately from Jews all around the world, he went on, who saw their power threatened not only in Europe but also elsewhere: in America, where financial institutions were in the hands of the Jews, they were beginning to hoard gold in immense quantities, but he, Hitler, had established a new world 'in which the concept of gold is unknown'.[48] Had he perhaps the figure of Siegfried in mind, who, having discovered the treasure in the dragon's cave, simply left it there?[49]

The parallel between economics and the Wagnerian myth seemed to Hitler to be so close that he made one single crime, comparable to Alberich's theft of the gold, responsible for all the disasters that had befallen the world. In the course of a discussion with the economics expert Otto Wagener in the early 1930s he posed the central question of whether, as he put it in his laboured Wagnerian language, 'there was any way out of the labyrinth of this illusion, originally created by the Jews',[50] apart from Marxism. The answer, to Hitler, was obvious. Only by a grand act of atonement could such a monstrous crime be expiated.

In 1942, his armies deep in Alberich's territory, Hitler drew aside for a brief moment the curtain that veiled his real thoughts. 'The result of this war', he declared to the masses in the Berlin Sportpalast, 'will be the annihilation of world Jewry . . . and for at least a thousand years the most villainous demon of all time will be powerless to raise its head.'[51] Then he lowered the curtain again on Alberich, the poisonous figure to whom Wagner had assigned the role of arch-enemy of mankind.

Since the days of his visits to the Viennese opera Hitler had assigned himself the symbolic role of 'dragon-slayer' in the struggle as to who should 'inherit the world'. In the intervening years, a totally unheroic figure with little to show for his life and with scant prospects of improvement, he occupied himself in polishing his image. At the same time he set about manipulating the scene which would provide him, the hero designate, with the context for his entrance in the role of national saviour. To look for the man behind the mask, the 'real' Hitler beyond the stage, is a vain pursuit. 'I was mistaken', wrote his secretary after the war, 'in thinking I could uncover his "true face". It was simply impossible – he had so many faces.'[52]

The fact that Hitler both acted his role and provided the context for it must have made him irresistible. The hero he personified was sometimes Siegfried, sometimes Wotan. Finding himself one day in the early 1920s in the house of the Munich publisher Hanfstaengl, in whose studio Wagner too had had his photograph taken, Hitler came across a folder of photos of familiar scenes and characters from the world of the *Ring* – the Valkyries riding across the sky; the Norns weaving the rope of destiny; Hagen, the murderer, as a black shadow, his spear plunged into Siegfried's body; and the scene where Siegfried advances with his sword towards the dragon, moments before emerging from the fight victorious – for a while.

But there was another collection of reproductions from Hanfstaengl's studio that also caught Hitler's attention. These were paintings by Franz von Stuck, a follower of Böcklin's with an eye for striking effects, who became one of the Führer's favourite artists. Like Wagner before him and Hitler after him, Stuck painted mythological figures in stark contrasts of light and shade, his direct manner leading to a taut, concise meta-realism. Hermann Bahr described his paintings as exhibiting a 'mystical symbolism of primitive grandeur'[53] – a phrase that could as well be applied to the whole period of Hitler's life from Wahnfried to the death of the Third Reich in the Berlin bunker.

Hitler hung Stuck's painting *Sin* on his wall, and the staring eyes of Stuck's *Medusa*, he said, reminded him of his mother. But there was another work to which he may also have been particularly drawn – a painting which, remarkably, revealed his own features, mask-like, with black quiff and moustache, an expression of grim, determined heroism on his face and the clenched fist of the orator raised aloft. On this, Franz von Stuck's first oil painting, done in 1889, the grim features belong to Wotan, god of war, leading his ghostly pack in the hunt. If this mysterious painting, in which the young Hitler might have suddenly seen himself elevated to the mythological hierarchy, served to intensify his *Ring* fixation, then the god to whom he bore an uncanny resemblance could have provided him with his alias. For like Hitler, Wagner's Wotan also took the name of 'Wolf' as he wandered incognito through the world. In Stuck's picture[54] he is accompanied by the pack of wolves to which Jakob Grimm's *German Mythology* had already referred. Grimm's book – a favourite of Wagner's – also states that Wotan is accompanied by two ravens, called Hugin and Munin.[55] These were the nicknames given to Otto Dietrich and Ernst Hanfstaengl, Hitler's two closest followers in Munich.[56]

Hitler's ability to cast himself simultaneously in the roles both of the young Siegfried and of his grandfather Wotan derived from their function in the *Ring*, where the hero carries out the acts of redemption that the god has decreed. The biblical analogy with God the Father and God the Son, the Saviour, is also apparent. Untainted by Old Testament influence, Wotan shows the same favours to his Wälsungen – and to their racial incarnation, the Germans – as did Yaweh to the descendants of Abraham. Again and again Hitler emphasized the superior status of the blond-haired race which was properly entitled, in contrast to that other, dark-haired tribe, to call itself 'the chosen people'.

'This nation is not the creation of men', proclaimed Hitler in 1937 to his Aryan *Volk*, 'but of the God who reigns above us. It is He who formed our people and what we have become is in obedience to His will.'[57] Likewise it was Wotan's will that created the Wälsungen. And as the ruler of the gods controls the fate of his kinsfolk, so the Germans are governed by their national god, who has made them the instrument of his destiny, like Wotan with his sons. Their heroic mission to crush the satanic Alberich and his pursuit of riches matched that which Hitler, Wotan's mouthpiece, assigned to the German nation. But it was not from the lonely, brooding

Wotan, who abandoned himself to the flames of his castle, that Hitler drew the characteristics with which an excited public could identify, but his bright-eyed grandson Siegfried. Instead of musing darkly on his fate, like his forebear, the young hero strides out boldly into the world, contemptuous of the warnings pronounced by the Norns, which Wotan too had to heed. 'There is to be no more rise and fall in our nation,' declared Hitler, the new Siegfried, in 1935: 'I shall stop the stars in their orbit and change the laws of the gods.'[58] Such utterances were not the products of insane raving, still less of prophetic vision, as was widely conjectured – they were words taken from the mouth of an operatic character created eighty years earlier, the words of Siegfried, familiar to every opera singer, ecstatically declaimed like the pronouncements of an inscrutable oracle. It seemed like a word from on high. In fact it was a second-hand theatrical gesture.

The man who wears a mask is liable to lose control of the situation if others are not doing the same. Hitler's self-dramatizations, however, found themselves in a very favourable historical climate at the time he arrived in Germany from Austria. In May 1913 imperial Germany, due not least to the activities of Wagner and his son-in-law Houston Stewart Chamberlain, was highly receptive to the concept of the hero and the battle he was called upon to fight – though at that moment the man wearing the costume of Siegfried was Kaiser Wilhelm.

The stage for the struggle between the Germans, the 'people of God', and their inferior enemies was set and Hitler, enthusiastically greeting the outbreak of war in 1914, volunteered for the front with thousands of others. Never for a moment losing sight of his theatrical calling, he cultivated a spirit of inwardness by reading Schopenhauer and recalling memories of *Tristan*. He earned his military decorations as a dispatch rider, an activity outside the common run of events and away from the monotony of the trenches, allowing him scope for the imagination when he delivered his messages. He was at his ease passing on orders from others but had little inclination to give his own, so there was little reason to promote him. Although he declared as late as 1924 that he was always prepared to 'respect his superiors, not contradict anybody and guarantee blind obedience',[59] he seems to have drawn unwelcome attention to himself in the field and thus ruined any chance of promotion. 'Never', his company commander is said to have declared, 'will I make this madman a corporal!'[60] So he stayed a private throughout the war.

But he found his triumph in defeat. His secret religion, which had given his life in the dugout a higher meaning – this was, after all, Germany's war to end all wars – now pointed the way through the chaos. What Siegfried had suffered, the German army was now suffering. What others had called 'mad' turned out to be sober realism. With everything around him in ruins, the little Austrian private now found himself vindicated in a strange way: once again the heroic saviour had been overtaken by malign fate, as Wagner had foretold in *Götterdämmerung*.

Hitler was not the only one to recognize the mythological parallel. The defeated generals in the German High Command seized on it as a convenient excuse, presenting it as a disaster for which they themselves were not responsible. When General Ludendorff appeared before his officers to announce the capitulation, the situation carried a resonance. 'It made me think of Siegfried with Hagen's spear plunged into his back,' wrote one of the generals.[61] Like Ludendorff, who allied himself to Hitler's abortive coup five years later, Hindenburg, then Chief of the General Staff, also found himself thinking of the *Ring*. 'As Siegfried fell to Hagen's treachery,' he wrote, 'so our war-weary front collapsed, having tried in vain to derive fresh strength from the fountains of life in the Fatherland.'[62] When generals have such pretensions to be poets, it gives little cause for surprise to find a stage-struck private declaring that the world is his true scene.

As in Wagner, the fatal spear – soon to be replaced by the more graphic 'stab in the back' – had been thrown not by a visible enemy but by an unseen traitor from their own ranks. The German army, so ran the legend, had not been defeated in battle but betrayed from within: reinforcements had been held up, morale undermined and the disaster finally sealed by the November Revolution.

Initially there was a certain reluctance to identify the criminals by name. But a few years later one could read in *Mein Kampf* that 'corrupt parliamentarians . . . cunning murderers preparing the nation's downfall' had intrigued and agitated until 'at last the defiant Siegfried was forced to succumb to a vicious attack from behind'.[63] And the weapon used was forged by the modern-day heirs of the Nibelungen – the Jews. 'It was the Jews', declared Hitler at the beginning of the 1930s, 'who sharpened the dagger which the elected representatives of the people plunged into the back of the government and of the German soldiers fighting at the front.'[64]

A summary of what Wagner meant to post-war Germany was given by Foreign Minister Walther Rathenau, one of those Hitler called 'corrupt parliamentarians', and a Jew to boot, who was assassinated in 1922. 'It is hardly possible', wrote Rathenau, 'to overestimate the influence of Wagner on the previous generation – the influence not so much of his music as of the actions of his characters and of his ideas. . . . People looked for the noble phrase and the sweeping gesture, great moments from the historical past, with brandished swords and flying banners.'[65]

Hitler was also looking for this, like thousands of others, and the legend of the 'stab in the back', an image invented in order to blind the people to the truth of the situation, became a commonplace. Instead of the victorious 'Siegfried' they had hoped for, they were given 'Siegfried's Death', the title under which *Götterdämmerung* was first known. But whereas his contemporaries were crushed under the weight of the events they witnessed, Hitler recognized the role that fate had given him: he himself was the tragic saviour, the slain hero. And from his identification with Siegfried came his identification with Germany, Siegfried's murderers representing the arch-enemies of the nation. The private soldier from Linz, with no job but with a burning sense of mission, had survived the catastrophe, been spared the wounds and the poison gas attacks that others had suffered. All he needed was a stage – he would write the play himself.

The German defeat not only elevated the figure of Siegfried to national importance but gave his sword Nothung a special significance. Had not the German Reich been smashed into pieces like the sword of the Wälsungen hero Siegmund? And had not Siegfried, Siegmund's son, welded the frag-ments together to forge the all-conquering Nothung? It is Nothung that splits the anvil in two, slays the crafty dwarf Mime and pierces the heart of the giant Fafner. The sword, a symbol recalling for Wagner the 1848 Revo-lution, in which everything that runs counter to mankind's pursuit of free-dom had to be destroyed, symbolizes the awakening spirit of nationalism.[66] Like Nothung, a new Reich would arise from the shattered fragments and resume the struggle until victory was achieved. As the nationalistic jour-nal *Stahlhelm* put it in 1921: 'Though Siegfried fell to the treachery of his friend, and though the German army was betrayed,' old warriors still re-tained the proud confidence expressed in Wagner's *Ring*: 'We can forge the sword of Siegfried!'[67]

In 1924, six years after the end of the war, the Bayreuth Festival re-opened with a new production of the *Ring des Nibelungen* in an atmosphere of per-vasive nationalism. Its motto, taken from *Siegfried*, was: 'Nothung! Nothung! New and invigorated! I brought thee back to life!'[68] What took place on the stage had long been taking place in reality. Hitler openly admitted to Siegfried Wagner, the composer's son, that 'the spiritual sword with which we are fighting today was forged first by the Master, then by Chamber-lain.'[69] 'After all, the route to Berlin goes via Bayreuth,' said the new Siegfried to the old.

Years later, with the Führer firmly installed as the dragon-slayer who had demolished parliamentary government and eliminated the Nibelungen, the official radio celebrations to mark his forty-forth birthday opened with the cry from Siegfried's Forging Song: 'Nothung! Nothung! Fiery sword!'[70] Those who had hoped that the theatrical weapon, having been 're-forged', would now be returned to the cupboard from which it had been borrowed were in for a rude shock. Brandishing his steel, Wagner's hero cries exult-antly: 'Soon it will draw hot blood!'[71]

Nothing could have been more to Hitler's taste. There had been an occa-sion in Linz when he had envisaged building a memorial hall and crown-ing it with a statue of Siegfried, sword in hand.[72] And in the Vienna Hofoper he had listened night after night as Siegfried's crashing blows merged with his own political vision of a Germany rising like a phoenix from the ashes.

There will, he admitted, be 'hammer-blows to endure. But under these blows the iron that runs through the German people will be forged and made as tough as steel!' As though seeing the figure of the blond hero standing before him, flourishing his shining blade, he transfers the image of the newly created, unbreakable sword to Germany, 'the German people, the people destined to be the sword of God!'[73]

Hitler never lost sight of Siegfried, symbol of his mission to wield the 'sword of God' against the Antichrist. Every German triumph was greeted by Wagner's majestic ringing brass, every national setback was accompanied by the subdued resonance of the Wagner tubas. However fantastic his demands, the familiar music was always at hand, and however far he eventually fell, Siegfried's Funeral March was always waiting for him.

Hermann Rauschning, politician and writer, reported that one August morning in the 1930s, in Hitler's retreat at Berchtesgaden, the conversation turned to the defeat of the First World War, and in particular to that 'tragic frustration of all German victories', by the activities of traitors. Electrified, Hitler shouted out: 'We shall never give in, never!' 'Then,' Rauschning went on, 'as though struck by another thought, he added: "We could perish. But if we do, we shall take the world with us. Think of the Old High German poem 'Muspilli' – the world in flames." Then he hummed a phrase from *Götterdämmerung*.'[74] Five years after Rauschning published his memoirs in exile, Germany did indeed go up 'in flames'. But before this the hero of the tragedy had made sure he 'took a world with him' – the world of European Jewry.

6

THE FUTURE AS ART

W ith the Third Reich in flames and its Chancellor immured in his
bunker, making vain efforts to postpone the inevitable catastrophe,
and with it his own end, Hitler's only consolation was the past – his collection of Wagner scores and his gramophone, the plywood model of the reconstruction of Linz and the portrait of Frederick the Great. Goebbels too
brought consolation at times when he needed something to raise his spirits. He could no longer hold a book in his trembling hand, and Goebbels
would read to him from Carlyle's *The History of Friedrich II of Prussia, Called
Frederick the Great*.

Carlyle's biography portrays a hero of the kind Hitler saw himself to be
– an historical character presented as a superman on the stage of world
events. It also demonstrated how fate could intervene to rescue the threatened hero from catastrophe. This brought back memories to the Führer,
who, according to Goebbels, knew the work through and through.[1] Carlyle
himself was a hero also to the Germans, a man, wrote Houston Stewart
Chamberlain, 'who belonged to Bayreuth without having known it'.[2]

Wagner too had had a soft spot for Carlyle, whose praise of German
culture as a universal ideal, coupled with a contempt for the masses, was
much to his own liking. The Master was greatly entertained, wrote Cosima
in her diary, by Carlyle's scorn of democratic government and his contempt for the English, the majority of whom were what he called 'block-
heads'.[3] And since, in addition, Carlyle's views on liberty reflected a
decidedly elitist attitude, Wagner gratefully turned to him as an authority
for his own doctrines.

In 1871, the year of the German victory over France and the foundation
of the Second Reich, Wagner published the third volume of his collected
works, containing the writings of his revolutionary period. In his preface

he proceeds from a quotation taken from Carlyle which he used to demonstrate that his revolutionary views have now changed and at the same time to establish a link between the Schillerian utopia of 1848 and the new German Empire.

His stratagem was brilliantly successful. The passage from Carlyle, skilfully chosen, centred on a phenomenon of nature which had fascinated Wagner throughout his life and also linked Dresden and Sedan by the same image – the image of fire. Carlyle's theory, appropriated by Wagner from Carlyle's biography of Frederick the Great, gave an interpretation of history which Hitler could experience for himself by opening the steel doors of his bunker. The French Revolution, said Carlyle, marked the beginning of the self-immolation of a nation rotten with duplicity and deceit, an act that will plunge the world into anarchy for hundreds of years to come.[4] Everywhere the fire of rebellion had been kindled, the fire that Kapellmeister Wagner had once hailed by tolling the bell of the Kreuzkirche in Dresden.

For Carlyle, who saw history as a series of interconnected epochs, this was a cruel but inevitable part of the self-purging process of mankind. It could take a thousand years, he said, before the process was complete and the new epoch firmly established. But it might also be possible to accelerate this development and avert the threat of years of anarchy, and this was a task to which we should bend all our efforts.[5]

Wagner, who was in the habit of laying out his arguments in cryptic terms where questions of doctrine were concerned, used Carlyle as a spokesman for his views. Since his Dresden days, he asserted, he had pursued the aim of purgation, but, being at that time under the threat of arrest as one of the rebels, he did not want to tempt providence and instead transferred his message to the inoffensive realm of aesthetics, thus avoiding the need to talk about revolution and destruction. 'Nothing had been further from my mind', he now claimed in 1871, 'than to describe the new political order that would arise above the ruins of an old and discredited world.' 'In the mankind of the future the false peddlers of illusion will have become an extinct species.' The old Adam was dead.

This, said Wagner, was what he had meant in 1848, when, talking of 'the work of art', he had really meant 'a cleansed and purified society', with 'the destruction of decadent art' becoming the equivalent of 'the destruction of the world'. The heroes of the future, who would put an end to the present era of anarchy, would arise from out of the ranks of the German nation, which would thereby fulfil its pre-ordained destiny. He had come to realize, he wrote in conclusion, that his aesthetic ideals stood in the same relationship to the reality of existence as the German people to their 'self-purging world'.[6] In other words, the triumph of his music dramas over a mundane and colourless reality was the triumph that awaited the German nation, which would emerge from the destruction of a doom-laden world as the herald of a new mankind.

Did Hitler, we may wonder, know this preface of Wagner's? He certainly seems to have taken his lead from Carlyle's prophecy of 'a thousand years of anarchy' when he addressed a gathering of young army officers in the Berlin Sportpalast in 1942. 'If we had not been victorious in 1933,' he declared on that occasion, 'a new Genghis Khan would have attacked us in the form of international Jewry, which believed that the moment had arrived for it to establish its thousand-year kingdom.' If this terrifying prospect had not been averted, Hitler argued, 'the whole of Europe would have collapsed, leading to a chaos that would have lasted for two or three thousand years'.[7]

Hitler indeed knew the preface in question. His friend Kubizek reports that the young Adolf was already familiar with Wagner's theoretical writings during his time in Linz. He appears to have been particularly drawn to this third volume, which contains the revolutionary essays. Here the seventeen-year-old schoolboy read for himself that the German nation was predestined to give birth to the race of heroes that would put an end once for all to the anarchy that reigned in the world. That 'alter ego', as Kubizek recalled the occasion after they had been to see a performance of *Rienzi*, which seemed to take possession of him as he talked in 'grandiose language' about the future facing the country, spoke in the tones of the Roman tribune but the words were taken from Wagner's revolutionary vocabulary.

'Sometimes', wrote Kubizek, his friend would 'quote by heart from a letter or passage from Wagner or recite from one of his essays, such as "The Work of Art of the Future" or "Art and Revolution"'.[8] Both these essays, written during Wagner's exile in Switzerland, were included in the third volume of his collected works; the former in particular, with its coded call to revolt, would have gripped the impressionable young Hitler, who, having nothing else to do, set about attending to the reorganization of the country.

Wagner's confusing practice in these essays of combining utopia with reality, switching from aesthetic dreams to revolutionary violence and from the perfection of Classical Antiquity to the current afflictions of the German nation, like moving from one key to another, is a reflection of his intention to disguise the true significance of his dangerous thoughts. To Hitler it was a procedure that removed for all time the barrier between reality and imagination. As Kubizek put it: 'Wagner's world became far more real to him than the real world itself.'[9] The stage must become reality. 'What he planned when fifteen he put into practice when he was fifty.'[10]

Wagner's 'Work of Art of the Future', published in 1850 in Leipzig, is not, as the title suggests, an essay on aesthetics. Its centre of attention is the same as that which had concerned him a few months earlier in Dresden, namely the creation of a new society of free men and women and the bloody struggle to achieve it. By 'work of art' he meant a world radically transformed, a world filled with harmony and the creative spirit, the world as anticipated by his music dramas.

But hardly anyone noticed this. Possibly because modern readers felt uneasy at the thought of Wagner's violent past, they allowed themselves to be misled by his metaphorical masquerades and took his subsequent attempts to distance himself from his revolutionary past at face value. But one man, at least, saw through him, ignoring the subtleties of his Hegelian language and concentrating only on what retained the scent of revolution, violence and the awakening *Volk*. The layman discovered what the experts fail to notice.

If one strips 'The Work of Art of the Future' of its ideological trappings, ignores its convoluted dialectical arguments and turns first to its final conclusions, one is left with what Wagner wanted the reader to find – an explanation for the depressing state of the world, a finger pointed at those responsible, and encouragement to take them to task, coupled with the prospect of a glorious age to come. It sounded to the unemployed masses like a future that had already begun.

Complicated as Wagner's essay is, its underlying message is simple: man only becomes his true self when he has discovered his true nature. And that nature lies buried beneath the accumulated debris of civilization. Once one recognizes oneself as a creature of nature, one sees through the degradation of society and discovers one's true creative being. Before that, however, one must identify one's cultural lineage, from which one receives language and the world of one's emotions. Only as a member of his race can man function as a creative power. And only when he has learned to express the real nature of that race will he become a true artist.

The essence of a nation lies in its experience of a shared predicament and the yearning to be free of it – a society in which each individual is called upon to help liberate it from oppression. The artist will do this by making his nation aware of how it has been deceived and by confronting it with the awareness of its true destiny. The hero, embodied in a man like Rienzi, will play his part by rousing the people from their falsely induced lethargy to rise up against their oppressors. 'Together we will forge the bond of community that binds us one to the other,' he writes, as he flees from the doomed adventure in Dresden, 'and the fraternal kiss that seals this bond will be our "work of art of the future". Only when the people have cast off their chains and can recognize themselves as works of art will we become a happy band of brothers.'[11]

The community Wagner envisaged was that to which he himself belonged – not the Saxon *Volk*, whose predicament he had himself shared, but that of the Germans as a whole, the only truly creative race on God's earth. Theirs was the fate which found its fullest expression in him, the 'most German' of composers, and in his music dramas. It was not until the time of the complete *Ring des Nibelungen*, however, on which Wagner was working at the same time as his revolutionary essays, that he was able to demonstrate to his people how deeply German he was and how profoundly he shared their destiny.

Before giving himself over to the composition of the *Ring*, Wagner turned his attention to the earlier development of his ideal *Volk*, seeking the deeper causes of their tragedy. In 1848 he published an essay called 'The Wibelungen', a piece of high-flown pseudo-history which scholars circumspectly declined to discuss and which at the same time remained utterly unknown to the people for whose benefit it was written.

Wagner's historical fantasy links, in free association, the Hohenstaufen dynasty, which he calls 'Wibelungen', with Aeneas; Siegfried – slayer of the dragon – with the Jews – 'on whom we are still taking revenge in the name of Christ';[12] and the legendary treasure of the original Aryan monarch with the Holy Grail. In a fantastic twist of the imagination he transports the birthplace of Germanic culture to the Himalayas and sees its rebirth in the revolutionary age of nineteenth-century Germany.

Wagner had originally planned a drama on the subject of the Emperor Friedrich Barbarossa, explaining that recent events had made him reflect on the legend of 'the eagerly awaited reawakening of the Emperor',[13] who was expected to arise one day from his resting-place in the Kyffhäuser mountain or the Untersberg to lead the fight against the Antichrist – a metaphor for the uprising of the Germans against their foreign oppressors. On the basis of the phonetic similarity between the names Friedrich and Siegfried, Wagner fused them into a single entity. 'When, O great Friedrich, wilt thou return, thou noble Siegfried?' he cries at the end of 'The Wibelungen': 'When wilt thou slay the dragon that is tormenting mankind?'[14] The 'dragon' stands for the adversaries of the Wibelungen, the covetous tribe of the Nibelungen, that is, the Jews, while in the Emperor Friedrich Barbarossa, who would destroy the Nibelungen in his crusade to the Holy Land, he saw the reincarnation of Siegfried, the hero who from primeval times had fought against the powers of darkness, only to perish at the end through an act of betrayal. Such is the fate of the Wibelungen, the fate that threatens the revolutionaries of the future.

Separating 'The Wibelungen' and the 'Work of Art of the Future' are the abortive uprising in Dresden and Wagner's escape to Zurich. His old conception of the Teutonic race in the Himalayas, founder of ancient cultures, as having lost its heritage, symbolized by the treasure, to the treacherous Nibelungen did not produce the desired result. On the one hand, Barbarossa did not return to rescue his people, while, on the other, the *Volk*, the creative national community, had not ridden itself of the financial domination of the Jews.

But Wagner still held fast to his central ideas. Only in a people sharing a common paternity,[15] he wrote, could the individual find his true nature; and only through discovering the common fate that had hung over the

German *Volk* for thousands of years, ever since its power was unlawfully taken from it, could the individual draw the inevitable conclusion – namely that the people must be liberated from their state of servitude before their metaphysical identity as 'inheritors of the world' can be re-established. From the common birthright of the past shall emerge the 'work of art' – that is, the society – 'of the future'.

For this to happen, the people must first dispose of its enemies, prominent among them all those who live in 'heedless luxury' and do not share the sense of a common fate. Profligacy was to Wagner profoundly unnatural because, instead of stimulating activity, it has a corrosive and destructive effect. The extravagant life-style to which he was so addicted in his private life, as greedy for riches as his dwarf Alberich, is portrayed in 'The Work of Art of the Future' as a hell on earth: 'Insatiable, ruinous, agonizing, joyless, offensive – it deprives life of all happiness, all serenity, all joy.'[16]

The antithesis of the pure world of the German *Volk* is branded by Wagner as a domain ruled by egoism which 'sucks the life-blood of the people'. This vampire symbolizes the Jews. To free oneself from their clutches, says Wagner, the *Volk* need only follow their natural instincts. 'They only need to know what they do not want, and this will be made clear by their instinctive impulses', which, being determined by nature, are not open to dispute. It is this life-force alone which directs man to follow the path of necessity. Or, in his own contorted language: 'Man needs only the strength of his inner fate to turn that which he does not want into that which has no right to exist. If he destroys that which is only worthy to be destroyed, the true nature of the future will emerge of its own accord.'[17]

A vision of 'that which is only worthy to be destroyed' is revealed by the *Ring*. Siegfried, the German hero, following his natural instincts, turns what he does not want, namely Mime, into 'that which has no right to exist' and destroys the dragon who devours men and hoards gold as something 'which is only worthy to be destroyed'. He thereby inherits the world, gaining possession both of the ring and of his bride, with whom he will beget the heroic race of the future. Put in everyday language: Get rid of the Jews and the heroes will take over.

Always anxious that he might not be understood, and at the same time eager to be inscrutable, Wagner attached a corollary to his advice on the art of destruction. 'Only after the old religion of egoism has been destroyed root and branch can the new religion assume mastery over that life which also incorporates the conditions for the "art work of the future". This it will do of its own volition.'[18] The vocabulary of the savage also had its share of Wagnerian expressions.

The old religion to be eradicated was that of the Jews. As 'the work of art of the future' meant 'the society of the future', so in Wagner's essay 'Music and the Jews' music is only a pretext for a general anti-Semitic onslaught.

At the very beginning of the piece, originally published anonymously in 1850, Wagner makes clear that his views are not based on personal feelings and experiences but reflect the national instinct, the spontaneous reactions of a community that is 'involuntarily repelled' by this alien race.[19] Their unpleasant personality, he maintains, arouses in every German 'a reluctance to have anything to do with people who look like that'. Since such an assertion could hardly claim to be universally applicable in real life – his own dealings with the Jews generally proved profitable – Wagner adduced further arguments which go far beyond the bounds of taste. In accordance with his principle that a community is defined by its sharing of a common birthright and a common fate, the Jews could not but be seen to present, by definition, a totally different picture. Even if they tried, being born parasites, they could never join this community.

Indeed, are they human at all? Wagner was far from certain. Later he coined the strange phrase 'the demon of a degenerate mankind'[20] to characterize them, an expression that became commonplace in the days of the Third Reich. The rest of the horrible story followed inexorably. As these parasites lived by theft and robbery, Wagner's argument went on, so Jewish composers turned out to be plagiarists. Mendelssohn and Meyerbeer, his direct rivals yet men from whom he had gained a great deal, are accused of being mere 'parrots'.[21] Hitler was to 'parrot' the same sentiment: 'The Jews have no original music to show. Such art as they have produced is either pastiche or stolen from others,' he wrote in *Mein Kampf*.[22]

To move from these generalities to the 'murky gloom'[23] in which these 'demons' chose to live is to move into the world of the Nibelungen. When they speak, mocked Wagner, 'it is like a babble of hissing, screaming, humming and grunting';[24] their sentence construction is 'intolerably abstruse', while their religious chants are a repulsive mixture of 'chattering, yodelling and gargling which no caricature could exaggerate'[25] – with the exception, perhaps, of that produced by his own perverted imagination.

This caricature, indeed, has as little to do with real life as has 'Music and the Jews' itself. And Wagner's personal experiences also point in the opposite direction. From Heine he took the subject of the *Flying Dutchman* and the glittering irony of his Parisian writings; from Meyerbeer he borrowed both money and dramatic stage effects, subsequently dismissing the latter as mere 'show'; Mendelssohn taught him the subtleties of orchestration; he used his Paris friend Samuel Lehrs to collect information for him on the Hohenstaufens, and Jewish musicians like Karl Tausig, Hermann Levi and Joseph Rubinstein to perform his works – not to mention all the Jews who supported him financially, promoted his works or praised him as a critic. Jews flocked to performances of his operas and covenanted subscriptions to the Bayreuth Festival. The first to make him aware of this paradoxical situation was King Ludwig II, his own foremost patron.

It was not a real-life situation that Wagner was describing in his essay on the Jews but a phantom, a spectre that he could make responsible for all the ills in the world and at the same time use as a contrast to the image he sought to create of himself. Accustomed to exchanging fantasy for reality, he gave the Mimes and the Alberichs a prominent place in his life. Before they made their entry on the stage and then acquired representative status, they had spent a great deal of time lurking in the corners of Wagner's mind.

Only at the end of 'Music and the Jews' does Wagner show his full hand. As though talking of his Nibelungen, who in 1848 were crawling over the earth 'like worms in a rotting corpse', he accuses them, now openly called Jews, of falling on the lifeless body of Western culture like vultures: 'the rotting flesh will then decompose under the attack of these swarming creatures' and all that remains of our culture will be 'a worm-eaten cadaver'.[26] To this distasteful metaphor Wagner then appends his crushing verdict: the Jews must be made to understand that they have no right to exist and must therefore assist in the task of their own destruction;[27] then, thus purged, they will be able to return to the bosom of Mother Nature and be born again. But in this life there is little ground for hope. Their atonement can only mean their extirpation.

In Wagner's vicious essay the intensification of the conflict between Jewishness and Germanness as laid out in the *Ring des Nibelungen* virtually assumes the character of an incitement to action. 'Never forget', threatens Wagner, 'that only one thing can lift the curse that lies upon you, the way the curse was lifted from Ahasverus – by *annihilation!*'[28] This bald statement, breathtaking in its ruthlessness, marks a new, violent phase in the development of anti-Semitism in Germany. The most cold-blooded spokesman of this phase in the century to come knew every word of Wagner's essay. If, said Hitler at the Nazi Party rally in 1938, a Jew had managed somehow to infiltrate the Aryan culture of the Germans, then this was only because at some point 'a drop of Aryan blood must have found its way into the lineage of Ahasverus. . . . Otherwise, as a race, the great mass of the Jewish race is totally unproductive.'[29] The rest of mankind, Hitler implied, would have little difficulty in coming to terms with the demise of Jewry.

After re-issuing his pamphlet in 1869, this time under his own name and with a number of additional distasteful jibes, Wagner returned in his introduction to the third volume of his collected works to his notion of the Jews' 'self-destruction'. Gratified to have discovered in Carlyle an analogous reference to the 'self-immolation of a thousand years of anarchy', he made the quotation from Carlyle the centre of his argument, describing in colourful language the consequences that would follow this act of collective suicide: only when the Jews sank into the darkness of the night, he wrote, would the day of the Germans dawn.

The only historical model that Wagner would accept was the culture of the Greeks. 'Let us look back longingly to these favoured children of nature, the most beautiful race that ever walked the earth, and learn through our understanding of their innermost being how the "work of art of the future" will be constituted.' That 'innermost being' resided for Wagner in tragedy, a celebration fashioned out of drama and music which portrayed the fall of the hero and his deification in death.

The Greeks saw in tragedy, according to Wagner, 'a celebration of the recollection of their communal origins',[30] a devotional drama portraying their collective memory. In 'Art and Revolution', written before 'The Work of Art of the Future', he describes this collective experience as a solemn feast at which 'the strong, handsome, free man will celebrate the pains and joys of his love and finally accept with noble sublimity the ultimate sacrifice of his life',[31] a sacrifice he will make in the name of all. Now, however, after years of alienation, the time has arrived for this popular feast to be reborn on German soil – the process called by Nietzsche, with Wagner's music in mind, the 'birth of tragedy out of the spirit of music'. At this moment also Schiller's vision of the liberation of mankind from its chains will be fulfilled: the world will join him in his cry of 'Joy!' – the word that had sparked off the uprising in Dresden. 'Embrace one another, ye millions!' he will cry in the words of Schiller's ode, 'and these words will become the language of the work of art of the future.'[32]

But all this was still a long way off. It was not yet the *Volk* that reigned but still the vampires who oppressed them, and the concept of a sense of common deprivation, albeit endured, was not yet comprehended. Having failed as a political activist, Wagner developed a role for himself as spiritual leader. Instead of rebellion from the bell tower he took to revolutionary journalism, concealing a political message behind a smokescreen of apparently aesthetic arguments which found their way past the censor without difficulty. Yet the initiated could not fail to recognize the numerous hints and images by means of which he conveyed his coded call to arms. What the country needed was a collective display of strength.

The time had finally arrived, wrote the exiled prophet, for the Germans to become aware of their common birthright and 'draw on their inalienable rights for the power to resist and to rebel against their oppressors'. Only those prepared for action were true members of the *Volk*, 'for they alone feel this "sense of deprivation"'.[33] When Hitler read such words aloud to his friend Kubizek, he identified himself with Wagner's sentiments to such an extent that he was able to refer back to them a quarter of a century later. 'I can still understand', said the German Chancellor, 'why Wagner's destiny meant so much more to me than that of so many other great Germans. We are facing today the same need as Wagner for an unyielding struggle against hatred, envy and irrationality.'[34] Not for nothing did Hitler's Enabling Act of 1933, which marked the beginning of the all-out attack against those he saw as the enemies of the Reich, have the title 'Law to Abolish the Deprivation of *Volk* and Reich'.[35]

Wagner concluded the vision of his 'work of art of the future' not with political slogans but, in keeping with his concept of the artist as a helper in time of crisis, by appending a sketch for a drama of his own. This was *Wieland der Schmied* ('Wieland the Smith'), based on a legend 'of considerable relevance' to the Germans,[36] which he set about dramatizing 'in response to a sense of inner compulsion', a legend which itself deals with the 'deprivation' afflicting the people and the alleviation of that affliction.

In Wagner's dramatic sketch the legendary Germanic figure of Wieland is portrayed as an artisan who is captured by King Neiding, put in chains and forced into slavery. What he used to create out of pleasure in his craft he now has to produce under duress. To symbolize his broken will the King has his tendons cut. Then, condemned to live as a cripple and at the mercy of his captor's greed, he suddenly sees the way forward. 'Revenge!' he cries. 'Revenge on this Neiding, whose vile egoism has brought me to this miserable pass! If only I could destroy him, along with all his tribe!'[37]

Driven on by his desperate plight, Wieland forges a pair of wings on which to escape, though not before having wrought the revenge he craved. 'Borne aloft by the products of his hands,' wrote Wagner, 'he took aim and pierced the monster's heart with the barb.' It is the message of violence he preaches time and again, in an endless variety of forms. 'O thou one and glorious nation!' he proclaims at the end of his drama. 'Thine are the words of this work and thou thyself art this Wieland! Forge thine own wings and fly away!'

Before that, however, Wagner sought to forge his *Wieland* into a finished work of art. His sketch grew into a drama which he assembled with an eye to its performance in Paris. Ultimately designed to show the Germans the way to salvation, in the short term it could be made to help pay off his debts. The capital of revolution, which excited him as a European centre of opera as much as it repelled him as the bastion of Meyerbeer's triumphs, offered an appropriate setting for the presentation of those personal contradictions whose interplay he illustrated on the stage.

When at the end of 1849 Wagner wrote to his friend Theodor Uhlig in Dresden about what he called his 'completed plan' for an opera on the Wieland theme, he made it clear that it was not to be a conventional piece of stage entertainment but a work with a revolutionary message which the Parisians, who had had a successful revolution of their own the year before, would find to their taste. 'My aim is to make revolution wherever I go,' he declared, as though he were still manning the barricades. As the time of the society of the future had not yet come, one must 'crush and destroy everything that deserves to be crushed and destroyed'. His *Wieland* was to prepare the ground for the destruction to come. For, as he said to Uhlig, 'the first truly creative artists to follow in the wake of the destruction will be very different people from us'.[38]

Hitler, tucked away at the back of the house in the Stumpergasse, must have had similar feelings. His imagination fired by reading what most people found totally indigestible, he began to use the long intervals between Wagner performances in the opera house to write works of his own – 'work after work, chiefly dramas but also short stories', as Kubizek recalled. 'I knew that they were all derived from Wagner and set in the world of Germanic legend.'[39]

As an example of these literary efforts of Hitler's, Kubizek describes a sketch for a tragedy set in the Bavarian Alps during the period of the Christianization of the country. The native inhabitants plot to kill the Christian missionaries – a plan of which Hitler himself clearly approved. Kubizek remembered the key scene as having a gloomy setting of the kind found in the *Ring*; the natives in their bearskins are also borrowed from there and located in a landscape 'with a holy mountain in the background'. In the foreground, in the shadow of great oak trees, stands a sacrificial altar, where two mighty warriors are preparing to sacrifice a black bull, gripping it by the horns and pressing its head onto the stone. Behind them stands the solemn figure of the High Priest, wearing a brightly coloured robe. Under the gaze of bearded men, their spears held aloft, he brandishes the sacrificial sword.[40]

Whether this scene is indebted to Hitler's memories of his life in the village of Leonding or to Roller's production of *Götterdämmerung*, we cannot tell. It would appear, however, that the ritual sacrifice of the bull is an anticipation of the murders – not worked out by Hitler in the play, or maybe forgotten by Kubizek when he came to write his memoirs – in which the chthonic Germanic peoples were to triumph over the blandishments of Judaeo-Christianity. Schönerer's motto 'No Jews, No Rome!' merged with Hagen's cry to his warriors in *Götterdämmerung*: 'Slay strong bulls and let their blood flow for Wotan on the sacrificial altar!'[41] – as Roller's *Götterdämmerung* became the counterpart of the political slogans being hurled to and fro in the Vienna parliament.

Continuing with his own means what Wagner had begun, Hitler inevitably came across the unfinished *Wieland*. Already familiar with the subject matter as an enthusiastic reader of 'The Work of Art of the Future', he would have found the Wieland scenario in the same volume of Wagner's collected works that had aroused his thoughts of revolution. Moreover, by a strange coincidence, *Wieland* was to experience an unexpected revival. In 1908, to commemorate the twenty-fifth anniversary of Wagner's death, the legendary actor Josef Kainz, one-time friend of King Ludwig, gave a reading of the drama in the Vienna Burgtheater. The two young friends from Linz, who had also queued for tickets to hear Kainz in Goethe's *Faust*, would hardly have missed the occasion.

No sooner had the subject of Wieland the Smith gripped his imagination than Hitler was found by Kubizek one day sitting at the piano. In response to his friend's look of astonishment Hitler exclaimed, according to Kubizek:

'Gustl, I'm going to turn *Wieland* into an opera!' Hitler knew even less about playing the piano than about watercolours but he seemed determined to put together a kind of 'Overture', which turned out, not surprisingly, to be like something out of Wagner himself – 'a compilation of unrelated themes', Kubizek described it, preferring to draw a veil over its musical quality. Elsewhere, Kubizek records that where Wagner prescribes cow horns with which Hagen summons his vassals in *Götterdämmerung*, Hitler was obsessed with the idea of having Nordic lurs – which would have first had to be built.

This attempt by Hitler at a *Gesamtkunstwerk* – 'he also designed the sets and costumes, and did a chalk sketch of the hero with wings fastened to his back'[42] – was an abject failure, like all the other bizarre notions he had, completely ignorant, as he was, of how to put them into practice. So he looked in a different direction. If he could not demonstrate in the field of music that he was Wagner's chosen successor – no less than this, indeed, had he aimed to demonstrate by trying to set the Wieland libretto to music – then he would follow another path, namely that revealed in *Rienzi* and in Wagner's revolutionary writings. In a word, he would make himself the executor of Wagner's political estate.

He had already acquired the necessary equipment. As his polarized view of the world was based on the extremes of the *Ring*, so he centred his programme of action on the 'Work of Art of the Future'. With frightening resolution he derived his plan for world domination from convictions held in his youth, and his programme of human mass destruction from fantasies of late romantic origin. Joachim Fest was only one of those who have identified in him an intransigence that characterized his life from beginning to end, and since his days in Vienna, as he himself used to maintain, his outlook on the world had not changed one iota.[43] He also claimed that he owed his later successes to the fact that he 'never allowed weaklings to change his mind or dissuade him from what he knew to be the correct path'.[44] By talking of 'what he knew to be the correct path', he implies that his decisions were the products not of mere cogitation but of inspiration. The result was his sense of mission, of vocation, embodied in secret aims concealed even from his closest confidants. In consequence what passed as the Nazi ideology was full of ambiguities and obscurities. One thing, however, we can say for certain. From his early days Hitler had clear goals to which he stubbornly adhered to the end.[45]

Neutral observers had no difficulty in identifying the source of the *Weltanschauung* which found expression in the Third Reich. The Australian historian Stephen H. Roberts, for example, in his book *The House that Hitler Built*, was not slow to see through the enigma.[46] 'Everything that Hitler does', wrote Roberts, 'is Wagnerian – this is the leitmotif of the whole Hitler piece, . . . Hitler's spectacles are nothing more than an enlargement of this Wagnerian drop-scene, with the improvements offered by modern science.'[47]

Roberts, whose research was supported by the Nazi Party, found further confirmation of his view while staying in Munich during the Olympic Games year of 1936. 'In Munich in the early autumn of 1936,' he wrote, 'I saw coloured pictures of Hitler in the actual silver garments of the Knight of the Grail, but these were soon withdrawn. They gave the show away, they were too near the truth of Hitler's mentality.'[48] Two years later Peter Viereck published an analysis of National Socialism in the American journal *Common Sense*, in which he portrayed Wagner as the embodiment of the German *Volk*, a man waiting for a national leader, whose writings, unknown to the majority of people but of immense influence, could be regarded as the single most important source of the Nazi ideology.[49]

But rarely did Hitler speak of the source from which he drew his philosophy. We find casual remarks such as: 'Wagner's works are the embodiment of everything to which National Socialism aspires',[50] and: 'In order to understand what National Socialism is, one must read Wagner.'[51] But scarcely anyone seems to have wanted to grasp the point. Hitler's speeches, libretti of his self-staged theatrical performances, also bear the fruits of his earlier reading. The monotony of these interminable sermons, full of rousing, passionate outbursts, matched the immutable sameness of his message, a message reflecting a uniformity like that of the cheering masses assembled in front of him.

Hitler's rhetoric was, like Wagner's, that of the demagogue. Taking his lead from Schelling and Hegel, Wagner adopted a style founded on the technique of dialectical opposites, whose contradictions created ever-increasing tensions which led in turn to ever-higher syntheses. Hitler also interpreted reality in terms of antithesis, conflict and ultimate victory.

As Hitler, following the action of Wagner's *Ring*, saw mankind as divided into two classes, heroes and subhumans, perpetually at war with each other, so he interpreted the course of history as a process leading from disintegration to unity and the elimination of destructive conflict. A constructive inner dynamism drove life forward from a state of racial chaos to the achievement of a national community, from a multiplicity of petty states to the unity of the German Reich. At the same time the dialectic of this dynamism could also be made to serve the rhetorical interests of Hitler the orator.

One consequence of the theatrical principle that Hitler everywhere applied was inevitable and exhausting repetition and a related obduracy of mind. As Wagner had fused the separate arts into a single higher union through his *Gesamtkunstwerk*, and had thought to create by analogy a 'single community of brothers' out of a society torn apart by the malignant influence of the Jews, so Hitler offered numerous variations on the same theme, revealing polarities and sources of conflict and emerging with the symbol that provides the answers to the problems presented in the *Ring*, namely the sword. If contradictions arose, they were removed, absorbed into an allegedly 'higher synthesis'. If the voice of protest were heard, it would be silenced in the name of national unity, the ideal of universal concord. The Nazis' name for it was *Gleichschaltung*, 'conformity'. As in drama, one needed only to drive things to extremes, whip up resentments and passion until, at the moment of climax, a glowing sense of community descends on the scene, enveloping the individual.

Hitler interpreted the Germany of the Weimar Republic in the same way. The Jews, he argued, were responsible for provoking disunity in the country in which the individual had taken precedence over the community and the Babel of political parties had been allowed to prevail over the well-being of society. This inner disunity was matched by the disunity created from without in the shape of the detestable Treaty of Versailles. 'What has become of Germany?' he cried in 1929. 'In the space of ten years our hopes for the future have been dashed and we have been reduced to the level of miserable slaves!' This imminent collapse of the nation, however, like everything that falls apart from its inner contradictions, will give way to a 'higher unity', that of the 'new Reich which is to come'. 'What Richard Wagner promised the German nation as "the work of art of the future"', Hitler went on, 'we, as that new Reich, shall bequeath to the power and glory of that future.' And this can only be achieved through the dialectical struggle, opposition to the negative principle. 'What the Master found himself unable to stomach' – the allusion is to Wagner's 'instinctive repulsion' by the Jews – 'we, as fighters, will fight to a finish!'[52] Wagner called his autobiography *Mein Leben*; Hitler called his *Mein Kampf*.

Four years later, as though in fulfilment of his prophecy, the decaying republic fell into Hitler's hands like a rotten apple. The age of party squabbles and racial chaos seemed to have vanished like a bad dream. On 1 February 1933, setting the scene for his seizure of power, Hitler delivered an 'Appeal to the German Nation', in the course of which 'his whole body shook and trembled'. Overcome by his own oratory, he painted a lurid picture of a body politic riven by inner dissension and conflict that had ruined the Reich and was on the point of 'reducing the richest cultural centres in the world to rubble . . . through the subversive inroads of Bolshevism'. All he could offer to prevent this decimation, he said in conclusion, was 'the spiritual unity and strength of will of our people'.[53]

After coming to power the triumphant victor set the situation in his own historical and mythological perspective. 'In a state of disunity,' he said in March 1933, 'spiritually unsure of itself and thus powerless to act, the Germans became introspective,' able only to dream of a better future. 'Only after enduring years of intolerable deprivation and misery can they begin to yearn for a rebirth through art, for a new Reich, for a new life.'[54]

Wagner's name for the man who would be thus reborn, through the strength of his own will, was 'Wieland'. The desperation of his situation would lead him to build the wings on which he could fly to a radiant new future. Wieland as spokesman for the German *Volk*,[55] escaping from slavery as would the *Volk* in their turn – an image to which Hitler returned time and again. During all their years in the wilderness they retained their longing for a real community.

'Fate has laid upon us the burden of restoring the unity of the German *Volk* and lifting them out of their misery,' announced the man who had once had the idea of completing Wagner's *Wieland* drama himself. That implied, if one followed the legend, slaying one's oppressors. In January 1933 Hitler stated that if his National Socialist movement were to succeed in fulfilling its historic task, its 'predestined mission', it had no alternative but 'to adopt a stance of intolerance, eradicating everything that is gnawing at the roots of our nation. Then, and only then, will the path be open that leads onwards and upwards to the freedom of our country.'[56]

Waiting at the end of that path, Wagner had predicted, was a regenerated Greek Antiquity, with marble cities shimmering in the sunlight, built for an eternity, with sculptured figures of the gods and with Wagner's music dramas playing in huge cathedrals of art like ritual celebrations of a new religion. Phalanxes of fearless warriors would defend the distant frontiers of the new kingdom of 'Germania'. A *Volk* fashioned out of the stuff of eternity; a Reich on which the sun never sets; and a *Führer* who has already secured his immortality during his lifetime. '*Ein Volk, Ein Reich, Ein Führer*' – the Nazi refrain. And in the midst of all this, as he saw it in his dreams, stood a fifteen-year-old Wagnerian from Linz.

All the grandiose symbols with which Hitler surrounded himself – processional routes flanked by smoking columns, open fields packed with rhythmically swaying masses, the monumental sculptures of Arnold Breker and spectacular searchlight displays – were derived from the vocabulary of a self-taught man for whom the world was represented by the works of Richard Wagner. In a speech to munitions workers in Berlin in the middle of the war he declared: 'I want us to have the best and finest culture there is. I want the theatre and all other manifestations of culture to be for the benefit of the people'[57] – the culture, in other words, of Athens, home of the first *Gesamtkunstwerk* in history. And the culture of Germany after the war has been won.

On another occasion he said: 'When, in a thousand years' time, men walk over German soil and look at our buildings, I want them to contemplate these manifestations of our glorious German culture just as we today contemplate the wonders of Greece and Rome.'[58] To him the parallel was striking. 'Never', he said in 1937, 'has mankind been closer to Antiquity in its appearance or in its emotions than it is today.'[59]

At one point, indeed, he was on the point of going to see for himself 'the glory that was Greece'. The thought occurred to him and Goebbels in 1936 at the Bayreuth Festival, which Wagner had seen as the rebirth of Classical tragedy. In the event, however, although the Führer was 'utterly under

Wagner's spell',[60] as Goebbels put it, nothing came of the idea, probably because of Hitler's chronic fear of foreigners.

Yet, like Wagner before him, Hitler was firmly convinced that the descendants of Achilles, far from being foreigners, obviously belonged to the Germanic race, for how else could one explain their cultural energy? 'If we are asked about our ancestry', he once said, 'we need only to refer to the Greeks.'[61] We can go ever further, he went on, and 'adopt a totally new historical perspective by establishing our links with Greek Antiquity and the Roman Empire'.[62]

Wagner too liked to think in terms of historical perspectives. One striking example is Wahnfried, the Wagner family villa in Bayreuth where Hitler was a regular visitor from 1923 onwards. Wagner designed an allegorical composition above the entrance to the villa to express his concept of the 'work of art of the future' and the fusion of the Greek and the Germanic worlds. Four robed figures represent the evolution, past and future, of his vision for mankind, with the centre occupied by 'the Germanic national myth' embodied in the figure of Wotan, around whose bearded features the two ravens, Hugin and Munin, are flying; on either side of the god stand two female figures, one representing Greek tragedy, the other the music of Wagner, with the living symbol of the 'work of art of the future', Siegfried – both hero of legend and Wagner's own son – at their feet, holding his sword aloft.[63] That 'society of the future' was still in its infancy. But the time would come when it ruled the German Reich and, thanks to Siegfried's sword, the whole world.

7

A ROYAL FAILURE

~∞~

Hitler was not the first head of state to live his life in the shadow of
Richard Wagner. King Ludwig II of Bavaria, Wagner's patron, had
also set about transforming the world into a Wagnerian opera. What he
failed to achieve in the field of politics, in spite of his protégé's assistance, he realized in the realm of architecture. The fairy-tale castle of
Neuschwanstein, romantic mythology cast in stone, is an assemblage of
stage sets taken from the productions of the Munich opera. A fantastic
creation which it would almost be a shame to inhabit, its sole function was
to raise Wagner's visions above the mundane transience of the world of
the theatre and give them the cachet of immortality.

Ludwig had already brought Lohengrin, his favourite mythological character, to life by having the hero drawn across the lake clad in silver armour, his boat lit up by rays of electric light to the sounds of Wagner's
music. On the spot where the Knight of the Swan arrived he later erected
his castle, dedicated to Lohengrin and his companions Tannhäuser and
Parsifal.

At the heart of Neuschwanstein castle, whose rooms offer a promenade
through the world of Wagnerian mythology, lie two chambers dedicated
to art and religion: one has motifs from *Tannhäuser* and the Wartburg, the
other represents the Grail Temple in *Parsifal*, with a shining golden dome
beneath which the hero of the opera performs his task of redemption. The
finished building, as its architect proudly proclaimed, was 'a temple worthy of my divine friend'.[1]

Half a century later the newly elected Chancellor and his retinue, sur-
rounded by banners and swastikas, marched solemnly into the castle for a
Wagner memorial concert. First the 'guardian of the German Grail',[2] as the
Völkischer Beobachter called him, was made an honorary citizen of

Hohenschwangau. Then, taking his seat in the neighbouring hall, with its massive candelabras, he gave himself over to the music, 'leaning slightly forward' as he concentrated on the 'Liebestod' from *Tristan* and Hans Sachs' monologue from Act Three of the *Meistersinger*, 'abandoning himself to the sounds of the destiny of Germany'.

Recalling moments of divine inspiration in his own past, surrounded by the heroes who had lived in the Master's imagination and now filled his own, Hitler gave an address in which he declared himself to be Ludwig's heir. The King's architectural mission, he explained, had been 'the protest of genius against the mediocrity of parliamentary government'; he, Hitler, had fulfilled the King's dream by 'acting upon this protest and ending this pitiful regime once and for all'. As he left the candle-lit hall in the castle, shouts of 'Heil!' reached him from his vassals in the courtyard below.

In less hallowed halls, such as the Hofbräuhaus beer cellar in Munich, Hitler had many years earlier conducted this battle with his own weapons. When in 1929 Max Reinhardt, the famous producer, was invited to Munich, Hitler protested in the name of the local deities Ludwig and Richard. Reinhardt was a Jew. 'People are trying to impose Jewish art on us,'[3] he declared, an art which, as every reader of 'Music and the Jews' knows, will always be alien to us, an art produced by a people 'that has never had an art of its own and is in essence totally unproductive, seeing in art merely a commodity with which to make money. If Ludwig II or Wagner were to return to earth today,' he went on, warming to his theme and encouraged by bursts of applause from his listeners, 'I know whose side they would take. . . . Their verdict would be damning.'

How much better was the situation in the glorious days of King Ludwig, continued the preacher. The King called to his aid a man 'who rebelled against the commercializing spirit of his age. . . . But Munich betrayed him. The King in his enthusiasm and the musician in his incomparable genius wanted to present the city with a new opera house for Wagner's works, to be designed by Semper . . . but the city, in its senseless ignorance, refused.' As one who considered himself entitled to pronounce on matters of architecture, Hitler gave it as his opinion that the building might well have been the greatest the world had ever seen, 'a temple of German art'.

To the accompaniment of sustained applause, Hitler promised his audience in the Hofbräuhaus that he would 'take the rudder in his hand' and guide the ship of state along the course pioneered by King Ludwig and Wagner. 'The time will come', he cried, 'when German art will celebrate its resurrection, a national resurrection that will be felt by all the nation, a profound inner revolution.' And not only an 'inner' revolution but also the strength 'to match the great acts of spiritual liberation with public manifestations of the creative spirit'.[4] But before that could happen, Max Reinhardt and his ilk had to be removed from the scene.

The regeneration of the German spirit after years of decay, a subject to which Hitler also addressed himself on other occasions, was a process to which Wagner had also looked forward when Ludwig invited him to his Munich palace in 1864. Since the salvation of European culture could only proceed from German policies of the kind Wagner secretly hoped to be able to put into practice in Munich,[5] the fifty-year-old composer now placed himself under the care of the eighteen-year-old King. Ludwig, Wagner imagined, would not only finance the completion of the national drama *Der Ring des Nibelungen*, which would show the German nation the way forward, but also help to promote a revolution which, starting in Bavaria, would spread to the rest of Germany and eventually to the whole of Europe. Wagner was a man who wanted everything at once.

And Ludwig would have dearly given it to him. Wagner's dream of a new mankind had long been part and parcel of the King's vision of the world as opera. Brought up on strict Catholic and monarchist principles, Ludwig nevertheless described Wagner, a man with a boundless enthusiasm for heathen Antiquity, as 'the best tutor and mentor of my early youth'.[6] When only fifteen, reduced to tears by the story of the hero Lohengrin, Knight of the Swan, he devoured Wagner's prose writings 'with burning desire',[7] and 'The Work of Art of the Future', which also contains a section on homosexual love as found among the Greeks, became his favourite reading.

According to the Swiss scholar Verena Naegele, Wagner's philosophy was 'the driving force in the King's life from his youth onwards'.[8] Hardly had he succeeded to the throne than he used his new authority to put the results of his reading into practice. Disappointments were inevitable: the very promises with which he enticed his bankrupt idol to his court cost him millions, and with them his credibility. But the young king was not going to be deflected from his purpose, either by the intrigues of his courtiers or by the Master's debts. 'This is the fulfilment of my childhood dreams!' he declared.[9] Nothing else mattered.

This was what the Master expected. Although the fighting at the barricades of Dresden now lay fifteen years in the past, thoughts of 'the liberation of the people' and of a utopia in which he himself would reign had never left him. What had begun with the figure of Rienzi, and developed into the concept of a popular leader sent by God, was about to change into a vision of a German Saviour in the form of a dragon-slayer like Siegfried or his historical reincarnation, the Emperor Barbarossa. That the achievement of his vision was a goal only to be reached after a bloody battle went without saying.

There were, however, now fewer enemies to be overcome. To be sure Rienzi had waged war with equal determination against the power both of the aristocracy and of the financial barons. But the later Wagner, with an eye on his sponsors, left the aristocrats unharmed and concentrated his attacks on the arch-enemy, the Jews, who, as both an actual and a metaphysical force, were impregnable to popular insurgence. Kings could be toppled, castles put to the torch, but Jewry, the embodiment of evil, was unassailable, a phantom behind masks.

This phantom, Wagner complained, had also infiltrated the ranks of the revolutionaries and reduced what should have been a German war of liberation to a 'noisy declamation' of socialist slogans by self-seeking demagogues.[10] That they had 'so remarkably little success' – Wagner's way of describing the failure of the 1848 Revolution – was due, he claimed, to the fact that the democracy they had in mind was thoroughly 'un-German', and that the German freedom fighters had 'no wish to give their lives in the name of a national pseudo-democratic policy prescribed by the Jews of Prussia and Austria'.

Because the revolution had been infiltrated by the Jews, on whom, in Wagner's scheme of things, it should turn its attacks, the only way for it to achieve its goal was through the advent of a Messiah against whom even the enemy's most malicious machinations would be unavailing. Only a hero of untarnished purity could confront absolute evil, only a Son of God could overthrow the Antichrist.

In May 1864 Wagner found a candidate for the position of saviour. A handsome young king, in the resplendent glory of the Knight of the Swan, came into his life, displaying all the innocence that the delicate role required. At a stroke the debt-laden Wagner found himself raised by his unsuspecting patron to the eminence of personal confidant, whose every wish was to be instantly fulfilled. In the long nights in the 'Wolf's Lair' during the Second World War Hitler was to be heard praising the young king for coming to the aid of the 'long denigrated Master', who found in him 'a friend prepared to take his part on every occasion'.

Requests for funds from the King's privy purse became a daily occurrence as Wagner surrounded himself with servants and other accoutrements of prosperous living. But Ludwig paid no heed to his mentor's life style; his sole interest was the sublime aims to which Wagner devoted his life, a life that he, King of Bavaria, now proposed to share. It was his heartfelt desire, no less than Wagner's, to see the work of art of the future become a reality, and since his childhood he had longed to bring salvation to mankind, like Lohengrin. Indeed, he had already ordered the appropriate silver armour to be made.

The old revolutionary and the starry-eyed young monarch behaved like a love-struck couple, casting themselves in the role of gods pledged to an all-consuming worship of art, to the point of renouncing the pleasures of conjugal love. Alone together, to the accompaniment of music, they would spend 'ardent, passionate hours'[11] in the King's private apartments, while the copious correspondence that passed between them is a mixture of incoherent outpourings of emotion and high-flown formality,

philosophical profundity and trivial intrigue, like a romance in a sentimental magazine.

Yet the two men never lost sight of their practical goals. Ludwig, who
had no idea how to govern and had little to offer against the political uni-
fication of Germany which had been achieved at his expense, set out to
turn Wagner's ideas into reality and demonstrate the ideals of the 'music
of the future', far from the petty world of political argument, which he
detested. Wagner, for his part, could only concur in such plans. But by
'turning his ideas into reality' he meant something considerably more far-
reaching than his patron envisaged. The otherworldly Ludwig wove his
fantasies into the fabric of his life and would turn away, offended, if that
life did not follow the prescribed libretto. Wagner, however, knew this
discrepancy from personal experience and was certain that it could only
be resolved by force. The struggle was paramount; art would follow.

Ludwig now became for his mentor the catalyst by which his vision
would be made reality. 'This young man', he wrote to his friend Mathilde
Meier, 'is as much a son to me as ever a son was to his father. He is my
descendant, my future. My sole wish', he went on, 'is to make him the true
Messiah of the Germans.'[12] Pronouncements such as this, which fill the
effusive letters that passed between them, turned the young King's head.
'It is a secret that can only be revealed to my sweet friend in the hour of my
death', confided his self-appointed father, 'that he and only he is the maker
and creator of all that is ascribed to my name from now on. The sole justification for my existence is the glorious love that spreads its heavenly
warmth over me as though from God Himself, making fresh seeds grow
within me. . . . He is my new saviour, come to lead me to a new religion.'[13]

These honeyed words, chosen to reduce the love-sick Ludwig to a state
of helpless dependence, reveal not only Wagner's characteristic hypocrisy
but also his practical political intentions. Since he no longer had any illusions about his ability to influence the course of world events, he now
banked on his spokesman to give him what fate had denied him – power.

The *Ring* provided Wagner with a mythological model for a character
who performs the will of another. Wotan, laden with debts and compromised by a dubious mode of life, creates for himself a hero who of his own
volition carries out his, Wotan's, will. The god's initial aim, which he cannot achieve by his own efforts, is to conquer the Nibelungen and reclaim
the ring that will bring him world domination. Likewise the awakening
of Brünnhilde, an act which Wotan enables Siegfried to perform so that
they can perpetuate a race of heroes, corresponded, in political terms, to
Wagner's own purposes.

In the same letter in which he anoints his 'beloved King' as the new
saviour proclaiming a new religion, Wagner defines what he sees as the
function of the 'new redeemer'. Wotan – with whom he identifies himself
– now knows 'that he lives on in Siegfried'[14] and is therefore involved in

his actions. Having performed the noble deed of slaying Fafner, the hero can turn to awaken Brünnhilde, his bride. But for Wagner his bride is not a woman. 'Brünnhilde', he tells his King, 'is to him Germany!'[15]

Wagner's concern, unlike that of the day-dreamer Ludwig, was with action – more precisely, with the symbolic fight against the dragon by which the hero frees his captive bride. From their very first declarations of loyalty to each other – 'He loves me with the radiant intensity of a first love,' the Master cried joyfully[16] – Wagner had put high-flown ideas into his head about being one of a chosen few, ideas the young man had all too eagerly embraced and which Wagner had cultivated in a barrage of further emotional missives.

Julius Hey, Ludwig's singing teacher, reported that from the beginning his pupil had been 'consumed by an overwhelming desire to see that Wagner's artistic ideals reached their highest degree of fulfilment'.[17] At the same time the Master was at pains to persuade the King to extend his aesthetic enthusiasms to the field of politics. Of what use, he argued, were the finest festivals of opera and the handsomest of tenors as long as Germany was still waiting, like the sleeping Brünnhilde, for her deliverer? Even the theatres, where the people could at least dream of their future, had been defiled by the miserable products of a decadent Franco-Jewish clique. What profit was there in the finest of kings, was Wagner's underlying complaint, if he did not don the mantle of a man of action?

Wagner impressed on his disciple that he had been called to be not merely the ruler of the Bavarians but a 'prince destined to save the entire German people'[18] – which was Wagner's answer to the fundamental question: When will the Emperor Barbarossa return to the earth to slay the wicked dragon? For as Barbarossa was only an incarnation of Siegfried, hero of the *Ring*, so Ludwig should assume this role himself and 'have himself elected Kaiser by the German people'.[19]

'The King is fully aware of my political programme', he told August Röckel, fellow-revolutionary from his Dresden days, whom he had invited to Munich, 'and is passionately committed to seeing it put into practice. Believe me when I tell you that here is the saviour of the German people.'[20] But Wagner was not thinking of a Christian redeemer who would preach of the Son of God and the virtues of brotherly love; he had in mind a Germanic counterpart who would set about attacking raging dragons with his flashing sword. 'He is divine!' cried the prophet. 'As I am Wotan, so is he my Siegfried!'[21]

Henceforth Wagner bent all his efforts towards keeping his young companion on the proper path. In a series of political essays for which Ludwig himself had asked, he took care to disclaim any intention to provoke rebellion, only then, with his next breath, to enjoin upon him a revolutionary mission – to unite Germany and deliver her from her arch-enemy. As the dream of the Holy Roman Empire had been at the heart of Ludwig's romantic self-interpretation, so Wagner held it to be his particular and bounded duty to expose the King's malign enemies as trenchantly as he could. For as yet, noted the Master regretfully, his young charge had not the faintest idea of the true nature of his foes.

In diary jottings which the King ordered to be copied and passed to his ministers 'for immediate implementation of the proposals they contain',[22] Wagner called upon Ludwig 'to deliver the German nation'[23] from the racial disaster brought about by the rise of the Jews. They had swarmed over the decaying body of German culture like parasites, he said in 1865, in their efforts to 'make it assimilate to their own',[24] and were now pretending that the cultural booty they had thus gained belonged in fact to their own tradition. Indeed, they went even further, holding up their perverted image of the German psyche as though it were a reflection of the Germans themselves. This degenerate culture would totally confuse the unsuspecting Germans, and deprive them of their true heritage. 'There are grounds for fearing', Wagner warned, 'that in time the people will come to believe that this perverted image is indeed a true picture of themselves. If that happened, one of the finest races in mankind would be lost for ever.'[25]

Years later Wagner declared to his protesting monarch: 'I consider the Jewish race the born enemy of a pure human race and all its noble qualities. It is certain that they will prove to be the downfall of us Germans in particular. Maybe I am the last German to stand up for a true German culture against the all-powerful influence of these Jews.'[26]

As long as the final day of reckoning had not yet arrived, the Saxon Wotan set about stirring up lesser issues for his Bavarian Siegfried to deal with. Since his exclusive access to the King had made an enemy of the entire cabinet, and since, in retaliation, they were constantly looking to expose the vulnerable aspects of his behaviour, he put his mind to seeing how he could engineer their dismissal. In order to make his radical measures palatable to the King in the sleepy Bavarian capital, he transferred them from the realm of reality to the world of the *Ring*. Pfistermeister, secretary of the cabinet, was now attacked not in his own person but as 'Mime'; Julius von Hofmann, the treasurer, became 'Fafner', the dragon; while the archschemer appeared as 'Wotan', quietly watching from on high as the bold hero disposes of Mime and Fafner in the forest. 'Behold the brave warrior!' he cries. 'Give him your trust! He has forged the sword by his own efforts and now holds it in his hand! His feeling of revulsion will tell him when to act!'[27] Seeing the pallid reality of his courtly routine enlivened by the myth, Ludwig joyfully responded: 'With fresh courage and in a spirit of rejoicing I will confront the treacherous Mime and Fafner and overcome them. . . . I have nothing but contempt for the impotence of Mime and Fafner and shall consign the snivelling reptile to the nether regions!'[28]

A 'reptile' of a special kind was Ludwig von der Pfordten, appointed Prime Minister of Bavaria by the King in 1864. A thoroughgoing conservative, Pfordten had been Foreign Minister of Saxony in 1849 and Wagner had already crossed his path at that time. As a man with the ear of the King, he now became an object of Wagner's particular dislike and was assigned to the role of the sinister Hagen, who, as Siegfried's treacherous assassin, represents the destructive aspect of the Nibelungen world. Wagner now heaped on Pfordten's head the coals of fire he usually reserved for the Jews. Pfordten, says Wagner, is a cunning, ruthless politician who in reality despises the King and intrigues behind his back, inciting others to do the same, 'like a puppeteer pulling the strings behind the scene'.[29] These lackeys whispered in the King's ear each new rumour of Wagner's latest indiscretions – matters he would have preferred not to become public, such as his adulterous relationship with Cosima, wife of Hans von Bülow, orchestral director at the Munich court and personal musician to the King.[30]

In this way Wagner turned Pfordten into the embodiment of evil – into Hagen the schemer and Judas the betrayer. Admittedly Pfordten was not a member of the tribe of Israel, but Wagner, well informed about events in Leipzig, very likely knew of one Adelgunde Marx, daughter of a prominent banker in the town, who had married Pfordten in 1844.[31] A beneficiary of Jewish funds, he was branded by Wagner a 'Jewish consort', a man who had allowed himself to become contaminated by the unpleasant ways of Jewry. As it happened, the first round of the struggle between the two men went to Pfordten, who succeeded in 1865 in having Wagner banished from Munich. But ultimately the man with the greater hate in his belly won the day, succeeding in ousting the minister as a traitor the following year. Amid clouds of incense but also with not infrequent outbursts of rage 'in which he thumped the table with his fist',[32] the Master gradually trained his 'son' in the arts of the dragon-slayer. For a long while the young monarch remained unaware of what his ministers had quickly realized, namely that Wagner was blatantly using him as a means of furthering his own ambitions. The King's advisers had resigned themselves to the fact that he had plundered the royal treasury to the tune of millions, but the suspicion that he was also guilty of political machinations was regarded as going too far. Everything was said to have been done, after all, in the name of art.

Wagner himself saw things otherwise. Sometimes openly, sometimes cryptically, he revealed to those closest to him the nature of his true intentions. In a letter of July 1865, which would of itself have been sufficient to banish him from Bavaria once for all, he advises his old friend Röckel to refrain from political agitation for the moment because there was no prospect of it being successful 'without creating a great deal of unnecessary confusion'. While, on the one hand, deluging his benefactor with page after page of gratitude and homage, on the other he confided to Röckel that he must first allow his emotional relationship with Ludwig to run its course. 'Do not be over-hasty,' he advises Röckel; 'let us rather keep things non-committal for a while as far as this young hero is concerned.' It would fit in very well with his plans, Wagner goes on, if Ludwig retained his public image as a starry-eyed idealist – 'a future artistic friend of the art of the future', as he sarcastically calls him – because anyone who believed that their concern was with music had lost any significance as a political opponent. Precisely for this reason he was concerned to cultivate this misunderstanding. 'I like seeing him in the mask of Brutus . . . for behind this mask something quite remarkable will grow,'[33] namely Germany's future saviour, who, manipulated from a distance, will bring the whole German Reich under his wing and destroy her foes.

'Shall I tell you what I predicted to the King?' wrote Wagner again to Röckel three months later: 'Ten years of utter humiliation and oppression. This will be *his* time, the moment to become what he is destined to become, an inspired young monarch who will risk all in the name of German freedom.' And this, lest there be any doubt, meant only one thing – the fight against the dragon. 'The Germans have thick skins', he concluded, 'and fully half of them are already in the hands of the Jews. In Heaven's name understand what is at stake and what a struggle lies before us!'[34]

This struggle, later described by Cosima as a 'gruesome fight',[35] was a central tenet of Bayreuth dogma, as the hope for a Messiah who would wage this struggle was firmly embedded in the Wagnerian religion. The King of Bavaria, with his love of champagne and Lohengrin masquerades, proved thoroughly unsuitable for the task, even though it matched his own conception of his role as foisted upon him by Wagner. A tendency to megalomania was part of his image, a characteristic that was to have dire consequences for the survival of the mentally unstable young monarch. Wagner once boasted that he had the ability to induce clairvoyant powers in the young king, 'who could not otherwise comprehend the commonest aspects of everyday life. This convinces me that I am entitled to hope that, through the ineffable love that he has for me, I can persuade him to embark on the grandest and most far-reaching of policies.' This reflection brought Wagner back to thoughts of himself and of 'how he too might be called upon to make his mark on the future of Germany'. As he never tired of saying: 'If Germany is not great, my art remains but a dream.'[36]

But before gaining power in Germany, he had to gain it in Munich. Having received almost limitless sums of money from the King – for the year 1865 alone the total amounted to more than the combined annual salaries of over eighty Gymnasium directors[37] – he pressed for the establishment of two institutions by means of which he could extend his influence. At the same time the musical taste of Munich was to be brought into line with his own and that of its ruler.

First the city's conservatoire, regarded by Wagner as an establishment where false values were taught, must be closed, the entire staff dismissed and all those who took a contrary view relieved of any responsibility for the musical life of the city. After that Ludwig was to herald a new age by

founding a school of music in the Wagnerian spirit, at which selected disciples would teach composition according to the Master's principles. The
school's Director was to be his favourite conductor, Hans von Bülow, whose
wife Cosima was already pregnant with Wagner's daughter Isolde. 'First
and foremost', stated the conservatoire's spiritual progenitor, 'everything
will be organized from the top on authoritarian principles which permit of
no discussion. . . . The only ideas that will be found in this establishment
are Wagner's ideas.'[38]

Correspondingly, the only works to be performed in the new Festival
Theatre, where the students of the conservatoire would perform, would be
Wagner's. This was to be the jewel in the crown, a monumental palace in
which the whole Wagnerian enterprise was to find its consummation.[39]
The building, to be erected by the banks of the River Isar, would be designed by Semper, architect of the Dresden opera house and former fighter
on the barricades of 1849, and would dominate the city skyline, not by
accident putting the nearby parliament building in the shade. Combined
with a ceremonial central avenue linking the royal palace via a bridge to
the opera house, it was a grandiose project that anticipated the style of
town planning adopted by Hitler – who in fact later bitterly complained
that the Munich plan had never been carried through.

As Ludwig himself put it, Semper's opera house, compared with which
the court opera would look like a rehearsal studio, would be used exclusively for 'performances of the divine works of the one, unique figure dear-
est to me'. Munich would have become the centre of the Wagnerian world.
Overcome with delight at the prospect, Ludwig wrote to his 'dearly beloved Master': 'I can see the street before me, crowned by the magnificent
"architectural work of the future" for performances of "the work of art of
the future". The crowds will assemble to hear the *Ring*, to hear *Parsifal*!' At
that moment he recalled in his ecstasy that Schillerian vision of freedom
which had once inspired the insurgents in Dresden. 'All men shall become
brothers wherever thy gentle wings shall rest,' sang Schiller in his 'Ode to
Joy'.[40] But in this case the wings were to be Wagner's.

The reference to Schiller was not fortuitous. Barely had he and his retinue settled into his new villa in Munich than, in the King's name and at the
King's expense, Wagner invited his revolutionary friends of Dresden days
to join him. As well as Semper and August Röckel, Julius Froebel and
Friedrich Pecht arrived, fellow-members of the 'Monday Club', which had
planned the uprising. Now, in the strict Catholic capital of Bavaria, in the
shadow of the throne, Wagner assembled his subversive clique, also to be
joined by Hans von Bülow, who as a mere eighteen-year-old had been a
member of the patriotic 'Vaterlandsverein' in those Dresden days.

At a second attempt and under a changed set of circumstances Wagner
might have proved successful as a revolutionary – a revolution in the name
of art and with King Ludwig at its head. He could first have roused his

immediate circle to action, then captured the enthusiasm of the whole country. 'While Germany seems about to enter a long period of political hibernation under the surveillance of Prussia,' he wrote to the King in 1866, 'we can quietly set about preparing the homely hearth from which the German sun will again be able to draw its warmth.'[41] The image of the flame would have been a more obvious metaphor in the context of revolution. Apparently Wagner decided, wisely, not to invoke it.

But the second revolution was a failure before it began. The ruthlessness with which Wagner imposed his will, even to the extent of blackmailing his noble patron, soon cost him his position of power in Munich, while the King, who had always been interested more in playing theatrical roles than in power politics, proved incapable of doing what Wagner required of him. Instead of ostracizing the Jews, as he had been instructed to do, he sprang to their defence, saying that he found 'nothing more objectionable, nothing more distasteful', than hatred of the Jews.[42] He even went so far as to express to Wagner his astonishment 'that the Jews you find so repulsive, dear friend, still, against all the odds, retain their unshakeable attachment to you'.[43] And as though to drive home the message, he later insisted on the Jewish conductor Hermann Levi being appointed to conduct the first performance of *Parsifal*, making this a condition for putting his court orchestra at Wagner's disposal for the Bayreuth Festival.

Generally, however, Ludwig gave in to his mentor. The moment Wagner made a demand, the King hastened to meet it, soon finding himself at odds, in consequence, with his ministers, his family and not long afterwards with public opinion. Yet he never managed to escape from the Master's powerful claws. After their grandiose plans for a happier, more joyful world had come to naught, Ludwig continued to cling to his boyhood dream of turning Wagner's myths into reality. To counter the depressing political situation, which had cost him control, first, over his kingdom, then over his life, he embarked on a series of extravagant building projects with the sole purpose of restating the *Weltanschauung* which reality had demolished. As the lavish private performances in the Munich opera house were for his eyes alone, so his castles – which he scarcely managed to maintain – were only for his personal use. It was only natural that, having lost contact with the real world, he should want to take his private universe with him to the grave. After his death, he instructed, all his monuments to the world of Wagner's operas were to be blown up.[44]

From Wagner's break with Munich sprang his plan for Bayreuth. In 1866, ten years before the first Festival, he and the King had considered making the old imperial city of Nuremberg a second royal seat. 'Let us set about the salvation of Germany from here and leave the world of evil in ruins behind it,' wrote Ludwig.[45] To which the Master responded: 'This is the place from which we can launch the work of national deliverance . . . if we are not to lose the country for ever.'[46] Their plan was to establish in the Franconian capital those two institutions, the festival theatre and the conservatoire, whose creation had been thwarted in Munich. Decades later Wagner's heirs would make it the place from which to begin their search for a God-given leader who would make the Master's cosmic visions a reality.

In the eyes of Nietzsche, a Bayreuth enthusiast who offered his services to the cause of the Festival, Wagner often assumed this exalted role himself. In his *The Birth of Tragedy from the Spirit of Music*, in which he presents Wagner's works as models for a future society, Nietzsche proclaims the imminent 'rebirth of German mythology'.[47] And 'if we are looking for a leader to take us back to the land we abandoned long ago', then we shall find him in Bayreuth, where the spirit of Germany will be rekindled and the heroic deeds of the past displayed before our eyes.[48] 'The dragon will be slain, the wicked dwarfs destroyed and Brünnhilde awakened.'[49]

This is the same course that Wagner had urged on King Ludwig seven years earlier. But whereas Ludwig had resisted the anti-Semitic implication, Nietzsche welcomed it with open arms. In the enigmatic language characteristic of Bayreuth he wrote of the agony suffered by the Germans 'during their long years of degradation in distant lands, oppressed by a race of heinous dwarfs. Let this be understood.' It was understood. Wagner's unyielding views, first eagerly publicized, then bitterly attacked, by Nietzsche, set a new trend in Bayreuth. A political precept, born of envy, resentment and dramatic necessity, became raised to the status of dogma, and the next generation of Wagnerians, who called themselves 'Knights of the Grail', inclined less and less to metaphysical circumlocution and openly preached the radical social solution proposed by Wagner in his so-called 'regeneration writings'.

After Wagner's death in 1883 the tone in Bayreuth became harsher, as the political orientation, previously well concealed behind the aesthetic façade, thrust itself to the fore. Nietzsche foretold that this would happen. Future generations concerned to preserve the Wagnerian spirit would, he anticipated, appear worse than the present because they will be more 'open' generations, 'both in the bad sense and in the good', and their voices 'will shock and frighten us . . . as though the voice of some evil spirit, hitherto hidden out of sight, suddenly made itself heard'. Shrill and unnerving though the sound of this voice was, Nietzsche recognized it as heralding a new kingdom, a world in which a state of nature has been restored to mankind. Once this state has been achieved, there will no longer be any soil on which negative values such as lies and subversion can grow. 'A denial of nature', concludes Nietzsche, prophet of the Superman, 'can only mean confronting the void, longing for oblivion.'[50]

So what did Bayreuth mean to its founder? In the first place it signified the return of the Greek amphitheatre, the stage for the birth of human tragedy from the spirit of its music. But above all it meant, after years spent in developing a new style of performance and production, the realization of the 'work of art of the future' as demonstrated in model performances of the *Ring des Nibelungen*, by means of which to place before a politically conscious public the living history of its ancestors' liberation.

For Nietzsche Bayreuth represented 'the blessing bestowed on the dawn of the battle between the individual and the apparently invincible forces of necessity that confront him. . . . The individual can lead no finer life than by preparing for death and sacrifice in the struggle for justice and love.'[51] Those initiated into this world will recognize themselves in the deeds and the tragic death of the hero – an experience which Wagner maintained corresponded to a readiness for self-sacrifice which formed part of the German national character. 'We are not a nation of peace,' he proclaimed in 1873 on the anniversary of the Battle of Sedan; 'we are a nation of warriors, and we have a warrior culture.'[52]

The ceremonial opening of the Bayreuth Festival in 1876 was attended by a bevy of Germany's aristocrats, all tried and tested in conflict, who had emerged as victors from, and shared the spoils of, the Franco-Prussian War of 1870–1. At their head stood Kaiser Wilhelm I. The critic Martin Gregor-Dellin described the occasion as amounting almost to 'a convocation of the German Princes'.[53] King Ludwig, whose coffers still stayed open but who no longer had a say in matters, played only a minor role. The centre of Wagner's attention had switched to Berlin, from where the Kaiser – the 'Cartridge Prince' of 1848 – and Bismarck had defeated the French and unified the German nation.

A dream that Wagner had had in 1871 illustrated the shift in loyalty. Ludwig had already paid Wagner handsomely for the *Ring*, but, according to Cosima's diary, Wagner dreamed that Bismarck, acting on his behalf, 'had offered the scores of the *Ring* to the Kaiser with a request for an advance of 4000 talers'.[54] He was haunted by thoughts not only of the Hohenzollern king but of the imperial throne itself, symbol of divine authority. He also told Cosima that the figure of the Emperor Barbarossa still occupied his mind, 'the glorious Siegfried who would liberate Germany from the evil dragon'.[55] Bismarck, invested from time to time with Wagner's hopes for the future, politely declined to intervene.

On his death in 1883 Wagner left not only the Villa Wahnfried, his family home, and the Festspielhaus on the 'Green Hill' in Bayreuth, but also a journal devoted to the dissemination of his views. Founded in 1878, it survived for sixty years, by which time it had served its purpose. The original editor of the *Bayreuther Blätter*, as the journal was called, was to have been Nietzsche, at a time when he was still in the Wagnerian camp. The second number (1878), contained an essay written by Wagner in 1865 with the title 'What is German?', intended for the political edification of the King.

In this piece Wagner reiterates for the benefit of a wider public the views on the Jews as 'parasites' and the impending collapse of Western civilization which he had already expressed to the King himself. Indeed, from now until his death five years later he published in the *Blätter* one article after another to ensure that his opinions were handed down to posterity. In ever-blunter terms he demanded that the doom-laden culture of the Jews be brought to its pre-destined close and the vision of its antithesis, the 'work of art of the future', finally turned into reality. This and other unbridled outbursts of his last years seem so totally at odds with his sublime music that people have done their best to ignore them. But for the disciples of Bayreuth they were soon to acquire seminal importance.

The works in which Wagner laid down the tenets of his extreme 'religion' – for such it was – were later collected in volume ten of his collected works under the title of 'Regeneration Writings'. Here he stigmatized all the obstacles that stood in the way of the rebirth or 'regeneration' of the German nation. Paramount among these obstacles was Judaeo-Christianity,[56] which was responsible for the atrocities committed in the name of the Church and for the perversion of the Aryan figure of Jesus into a Jewish Messiah. Then there was the eating of meat – 'the consumption of mutilated parts of slaughtered domestic animals butchered out of all recognition'[57] – which had led to the decay of a vegetarian culture. Even more important, miscegenation had undermined the 'nobility' of the German blood,[58] since when the 'demon of decadence' has ruled, spreading its tentacles over the whole world.[59] In abstruse utterances such as these Hitler was to find the tenets to set at the foundation of his own 'religion'.

It was Wagner's determination that the Germans should bring the rule of this demon to an end. He had first envisaged 'the downfall of Ahasverus' in his pamphlet 'Music and the Jews'; now he called for direct action to bring that downfall about. 'It is easier for us Germans to achieve this grand solution to the problem of ridding the world of the Jews', he wrote in the *Bayreuther Blätter*, 'than for any other nation.' Whether this 'final solution' implied expulsion or eradication, Wagner left to his readers' imagination. At all events he placated their conscience by urging them 'to overcome any false sense of shame and not to shrink from the consequences of [their] beliefs'.[60] Not for nothing was his article headed: 'Know Thyself.'

This self-knowledge, equated by Wagner with the 'grand solution', was the prime pre-condition for the rebirth of the German nation and one of the cornerstones of the Wagnerian religion. In the pages of the *Bayreuther Blätter* Wagner and his disciples laid down what the music critic Hans Heinz Stuckenschmidt described in 1933 as 'the fundamental principles of National Socialist philosophy, politics and culture', adding that it was thanks to the Wagnerian journal 'that Bayreuth stands today under the emblem of the swastika'.[61] Thanks also to Hitler's secretiveness and, after 1945, Bayreuth's suppression of the fact in the interest of its own survival, this is a connection that has largely passed unnoticed. As recently as 1993 a doctoral dissertation supervised by the Wagner scholar Peter Wapnewski asserted that 'to see Wagner through the eyes of Hitler is historically unacceptable and morally indefensible, since there is no direct path that leads from Wagner to Hitler'.[62]

The expansion of the *Bayreuther Blätter* from a private house journal to an official publication reporting the proceedings of nationalistic bodies such as the 'Richard Wagner Association of German Women' and the 'Bayreuth Union of German Youth' runs parallel to the development of the Festival itself. What had begun as the private initiative of a determined composer, rewarding with a glorious musical experience those enthusiasts prepared to make the long journey to the sleepy Franconian town, became after Wagner's death a sacred shrine for popular patriotic movements of all kinds. The central figure guarding the shrine to which those eager for 'regeneration' flocked was now Cosima, incarnation of what the Master had preached.

Unyielding in her loyalty to the Master, Cosima now devoted herself to creating a cult whose acolytes she called 'Knights of the Grail' but whose slightest insubordination she punished with life-long banishment. Unlike her husband, who had to resort to theatrical displays and outbursts of rage in order to gain respect, Cosima, who had been brought up in Paris, exuded a dramatic dignity which had even her aristocratic friends bending the knee to her. The image of the 'Noble Lady', a role model for the female dignitaries of the Third Reich, Cosima brought to life the slogans of the Bayreuth movement. Where Wagner put people in mind of the agitated, gnome-like creatures from the stories of E.T.A. Hoffmann – let alone his own Mime – the tall, grave Cosima, with her light brown plaits, represented the epitome of a superior race. As Wagner demanded that his followers approach his works in a spirit of religious devotion, so Cosima, daughter of the Abbé Franz Liszt, showed how a restrained joy in art could be combined with spiritual dedication and the discipline of a religious order. Above all Cosima, who liked to be seen wearing a black veil, was anti-Semitic. ' "Cherchez le Juif!" might have been her device,' commented Ernest Newman.[63]

Canny diplomat that she was, Cosima knew that the struggle could not be carried on openly: any primitive display of resentment could have no place in the grounds of a temple. It was also essential, amongst a public liberal rather than conservative in disposition, to avoid arousing any suspicion of reactionary demagoguery. She feared no less than Wagner the Jewish press and its influence, even expecting, as she wrote in her diary, that one day an attempt on his life would come from that quarter. Hatred led to paranoia. As it was customary to avoid referring to the Devil, so now the name of the detested race was not mentioned. When we come across references to 'Phoenicians' or 'Dalmatians' in her correspondence we can be sure that she has returned to her favourite subject. Nietzsche, whom she had already singled out in her husband's lifetime as one of the heralds of the new religion, was also initiated into the linguistic conventions of the cult. When in his zeal he attacked the Jews by name, Cosima restrained him. 'I have a request to make of you,' she wrote to the young firebrand, like a governess, 'a request as from mother to son. Do not stir up a hornets' nest. Do you follow my meaning? Do not refer to the Jews by name, especially not *en passant*. Later, yes – if you are prepared to take up the fearful struggle. But not yet.'[64] So for the moment Nietzsche talked only of 'international hoarders of riches' or 'callous optimists'.[65]

The success of Cosima's struggle, which she relentlessly pursued until her death in 1930, also depended on the acceptance of Bayreuth as a religious centre. It was an unspoken article of faith that the Festival theatre was not a common or garden opera house but a holy temple. This made the 'Green Hill' a politically neutral area not subject to control. If the concept of 'Bayreuth' represented 'an act and a mission', as the music critic Oscar Bie put it in 1931, with the *Ring* not 'a conventional series of operas but a philosophy, a statement of faith, then Cosima can be seen as the high priestess, fulfilling her unique task in this religion of isolation.'[66]

This affirmation of its status as a religious community was intended to bring about not only the canonization of the Master and the elevation of his *Weltanschauung* to the standing of religious doctrine, but also the disguisement of his political aims, on the basis of which no state could ever be founded. The ambivalent nature of the Bayreuth ideology was revealed most clearly in Wagner's last opera, *Parsifal*. This 'devotional festival drama', as he called it, differed only in minor respects from other operatic works. It had also been bought for a large sum of money by King Ludwig and the publishing house of Schott. Yet on the Master's orders it was never to be performed in a public theatre. His explanation, that *Parsifal* was not a piece of theatre but a declaration of faith, and presented not a conventional action drama but a mystery play, was surreptitiously extended by Cosima to cover his entire oeuvre. *Parsifal*, however, which once upon a time was intended as the manual from which Ludwig would learn his role as saviour of the nation, remained at the heart of the mystery.

Apart from the financial advantages of the *Parsifal* monopoly, its sacralization also led to the exclusion of criticism. Sceptics were no longer welcome on the 'Green Hill'; those who wanted to argue could go to the tavern. The sacred temple itself, on the other hand, was shrouded in an aura of devotion, not to say worship, and the audiences that participated in the religious celebration regularly abandoned themselves 'to an hysterical, unnatural state of trance',[67] which reached its climax with the miraculous appearance of the white dove sent down by the Holy Ghost. After the final chord had died away, the curtain was raised again in order to allow the faithful a final glimpse of the Grail, held aloft like a magic icon.

On her marriage, Cosima, who had been raised a strict Catholic, had been persuaded by Wagner to convert to Protestantism; now she expected her adopted faith to assume Wagnerian features. On the first anniversary of her husband's death she demanded that the celebration of Holy Communion in the Bayreuth Stadtkirche be accompanied by the corresponding music from *Parsifal*.[68] When the consistory rejected her request, she protested directly to the Bavarian government, which merely replied that 'the Church has not seen fit to include the Master's noble melodies in the Protestant order of service'.[69] But that had been exactly what Cosima wanted to achieve.

The conception of *Parsifal* as a musical declaration of faith that was taboo for conventional opera houses also provoked the first political attack on Bayreuth. In the course of a debate in the Reichstag in 1901 on the extension of performing rights and copyrights, Cosima petitioned the deputies 'not to allow the holy mysteries of Christianity to be left at the mercy of common theatres'.[70] But to no avail. Her hopes for a 'Lex Cosima' thus frustrated, and with *Parsifal* having already been performed in New York in 1903, she returned to the attack in 1912, the year the copyright on all Wagner's works expired. With the support of her fanatical followers she submitted a further petition, which, through its emphasis on the religious nature of the work, became a sensational political declaration. 'It was during the years between Cosima's two *Parsifal* campaigns,' wrote the historian Michael Karbaum, 'with their clear political slant, which took the discussion far beyond matters concerning the Festival itself, that the nationalistic tendency of the Bayreuth circle was born.'[71]

Cosima's Bayreuth, according to Karbaum, whose book was only cleared for publication after Wolfgang Wagner had vetted the text,[72] 'saw itself increasingly as a political force and used the Festival merely as an aesthetic cover for its activities as a centre of reaction'.[73] The two *Parsifal* campaigns alone, for which the intervention of no less a figure than the Kaiser was solicited, showed what powerful allies Cosima could recruit. In the end the arguments in favour of granting Bayreuth special privileges did not carry the day but the whole public debate caused a great deal of excitement. The 'Bayreuth agitators', as Karbaum called them, 'made a considerable contribution to an ideological and organizational discipline of the kind usually associated only with military bodies.'[74]

Mahler, conductor at the Vienna State Opera, had been approached for his support as early as 1901, but to his regret, he wrote in his reply to Cosima, he 'could not see any way in which so just a cause could be successfully promoted'. Nevertheless, he concluded, 'I place myself at your complete disposal.'[75] As she sought to use Mahler for her own purposes while despising him as a Jew and never allowing him to conduct at Bayreuth, so she tried to influence the decisions of a parliament she would have dearly loved to abolish. 'Universal suffrage', she complained in one of her letters on behalf of *Parsifal*, 'is like an ulcer on the body of the nation, full of foul-smelling pus. Where shall we find a surgeon with the courage to perform the operation that is needed?'[76]

The proclamation of Ludwig's coronation as Parsifal had been premature. Since Wagner had dismissed him as a 'cretin', the search had been on for a new saviour, the 'surgeon' who would lance the ulcer and set the nation free. Like the hero of the 'devotional festival drama', he would have to be one who could crush the evil in the old world and push open the door to a new age in the life of the Wagnerian religion.

One such man now presented himself – Houston Stewart Chamberlain, an Englishman. Cosima had first met him five years after Wagner's death at a fund-raising meeting in Dresden. From the moment he introduced himself to her with the words 'I am not a Wagnerian but a Bayreuthian', he had won her heart. They had spent five hours together without interruption, Cosima recorded, 'and neither of us felt weary'.[77] Chamberlain became Cosima's alter ego. As Wagner's ideas came to life in her, so he converted into modern philosophical terms her authoritarian administration of the Wagnerian heritage. In a letter to Kaiser Wilhelm II he described the late Master as the 'centre' and the 'sun' in his life,[78] while Wagner's work struck at the 'life-giving nerve of a reborn Germany, a Germany which had been freed from the crushing embrace of the Jews'.[79]

Chamberlain shared with the Kaiser and with Cosima the conviction that Germany could be liberated only by storm. He therefore recommended to his imperial admirer that he should 'summon a meeting of the members of all the political parties in the Reichstag and blow the whole place sky-high with dynamite'.[80] Eleven years later, after the Kaiser's war, Chamberlain was to proclaim another Wagner fanatic to be the new Parsifal. This new custodian of the Grail was to demonstrate that he too knew how to use dynamite.

8

THE WITCH'S KITCHEN

In order to understand the Bayreuth cult one must first decipher its language. To take it literally is to play into the hands of tricksters. Not infrequently it says the opposite of what it means, with an apparently straightforward message concealing its meaning behind a veil of flowery rhetoric. We are in the world of dissembling, not of reason. To assume that this language is a path to understanding, a convenient vehicle of communication, is only to perpetuate the deception. The numerous letters, articles and other public statements that issued from the inner circle of Bayreuth devotees consist not of ideas that link people together, but of coded messages that keep them apart, separating those who think they understand, but are being deceived, from those who do understand and thus count themselves among the initiates.

Cosima's Bayreuth substituted sacred communion for profane communication. Wagner, a master of word-play, smuggled his subversive message into the longwinded prose of his essays as he wove his leitmotifs into his music, and the members of the Bayreuth circle continued to play the same game of intellectual hide-and-seek right down to the sermons of Adolf Hitler. A torrent of commonplace utterances, calculated to rouse the masses, Hitler's speeches often contain only passing references to substantive issues, a point being made by a change of facial expression or an unexpected gesture picked up by those in the know. In this way he would invoke 'the unfathomable wisdom of destiny' and the mission with which he had been charged, together with the fulfilment of prophecies that lie beyond the power of human language to express.

Rarely was anything said in Bayreuth about these clandestine matters, and then only in concealed allusions adapted to the occasion. When, for example, Houston Stewart Chamberlain was studying Wagner's prose works in preparation for his hagiography of the Master, he availed himself of such conventions. Wagner, he said, had written at length, albeit *sous entendu*,[1] to the King about the 'demoralizing influence of the Jews'. In obedience to the Bayreuth insistence on using mystifying circumlocutions, Chamberlain chose hardly to mention the key word 'Wagner' at all in his Wagnerian study *Foundations of the Nineteenth Century* – 'out of tact and prudence', as he explained.[2] The hallowed name of the Master is also studiously avoided in *Mein Kampf*.

That it was only permitted to reveal the true Bayreuth message through hints and allusions was also made clear by Hans von Wolzogen, editor-in-chief of the *Bayreuther Blätter*, who was responsible for censoring any overly uninhibited comments. Because Bayreuth played for high stakes, it held its cards close to its chest. It is not in our interests, Wolzogen reminded the racist agitator Ludwig Schemann in 1894, 'at this early stage, when we are only just embarking on our campaign, to make the broader public aware of exactly what we have in mind. We do not want the Jews and their friends to get wind of our plans and resort to counter-measures.'[3]

Schemann, whose activities the Master had encouraged during his lifetime, travelled the country conducting anti-Semitic rallies and making converts to the cause. Cosima let him know that in reality she and the others in the inner circle saw the *Bayreuther Blätter* as having something of a debasing influence, though she also conceded that, once such a Wagnerian community was in existence, 'it was only natural that one should wish to address it'. And there was no danger of betraying secrets because 'our language is known only to the initiated'.[4] Many were called but few were chosen.

Schemann was entitled to consider himself one of the chosen. Like many Wagnerians he had fallen under the spell of *Lohengrin* in his youth and had finally pledged his loyalty to the cult at the first Bayreuth Festival in 1876. A scholar of private means, he wrote regular contributions for the *Bayreuther Blätter*, then, in 1894, found ultimate fulfilment in the foundation of the Gobineau Society. Many years before this Cosima had urged him to translate Gobineau's main work, the four-volume *Essai sur l'inégalité des races humaines* (1853–5), which warned of a threat to the blood-stock of the Aryans through intermarriage with inferior races.

According to Cosima, Gobineau, whose name was scarcely known at the time, joined Wagner's circle and found himself amply compensated there for the 'general lack of interest' that his racial theories had aroused.[5] It was also thanks to Wagner that he became one of the intellectual authorities for the conception of a racially pure Aryan state. That Gobineau, like Chamberlain, owed his popularity to the Master was a fact quickly lost sight of.

The Gobineau Society, founded with Cosima's blessing, was far from being the only organization to warn against the threat to the Aryan bloodline. There was, for example, the 'Alldeutscher Verband', whose leader,

Heinrich Class, was to have a similar influence on Winifred Wagner's intellectual development as Ritter von Schönerer, leader of the Austrian branch of the 'Alldeutscher Verband', had on that of Adolf Hitler. Wolzogen introduced Schemann into the Bayreuth inner circle in 1877, a group from which numerous similar bodies later took their lead. 'At the heart of our great community, with its many and varied elements and interests,' wrote Wolzogen, 'I wish to see a secret inner cell, a religious order, an "inner Bayreuth", which should have as its prime purpose to muster the forces needed for a public campaign.'[6]

Cosima herself, the 'Noble Lady', had granted Schemann access to the inner sanctum and initiated him into the rule of the brotherhood. 'As a true Wagnerian committed to the cause',[7] she insisted, he must prove himself 'to be both inwardly and outwardly a tireless fighter for our aims, a warrior in the ranks of the heroes under the King, our Genius'.[8]

These warriors, as Cosima explained to her daughter Daniela, concerned themselves primarily with Wagner's *Weltanschauung*, not with his music, and it was this that distinguished them from rank-and-file Wagnerians. The true followers are those fired with a mission, 'as opposed to those who like to listen to "O Star of Eve". . . . True Wagnerians will be as few as listeners to his operas will be many.'[9] Hitler and Kubizek, the two young men from Linz, who were not content to be mere opera-goers but eagerly took up arms against Wagner's adversaries,[10] would certainly have included themselves among the elite who set out to fight for the fulfilment of the Master's ideas.

Schemann developed into one of the most active missionaries to follow Cosima's slogan 'Go out into the world'[11] and promote the interests of the 'Anti-Semitic Union', spreading Gobineau's racial theories through the country and recruiting new members for nationalistic organizations. After Schemann's death his daughter was proud to declare that 'the seeds Frau Wagner had sown achieved a rich and profitable harvest' in her father's hands.[12]

Among the numerous such organizations that sprang up in imperial Germany, with their rallies, their dedications of the flag and their rabble-rousing speeches, none had an appeal that came close to that of the Bayreuth sodality, whose aura of high culture had a particular appeal to the intellectual elite. In addition it had its own 'Grail Temple', the Festspielhaus, 'whose bells rang out to summon the German spirit to worship in the Master's house', as Hans von Wolzogen emotionally put it.[13]

Over and above this there were performances of opera which offered an irresistible invitation to each and every listener to discover himself. There was hardly a single evening when the audience was not transformed into an enthralled and awe-struck congregation, or when the individual did not feel himself transfigured as an otherworldly Siegfried or Parsifal. And if the occasional stage-struck visitor decided to plunge into the Master's prose works, he would find there the origin of all the subjects his national-istic followers later discussed until they were blue in the face. If one read Wagner himself, one could dispense with epigones.

The Bayreuth cult worked because it was controlled by the iron hand of the 'Noble Lady' and because her henchmen were held 'in a state of total subjection'.[14] As in a modern sect, all was concentrated on an inner core to which only the elect were granted access, competing for the favour of their mistress and despising those left aside. Bayreuth became the model of a political party, the product of a tradition of diverse secret societies, which had set itself the task, in an aura of religious charisma, of making Germany conform to Wagner's inspired *Weltanschauung*.

It had been common knowledge from the beginning that Wahnfried was the centre of a cult that sought new converts and where there were inde-fatigable fund-raisers. But it was not taken seriously. Critics spoke con-temptuously of the 'idolatry' they displayed towards a 'megalomaniac composer'. Writing at the turn of the century about 'the international broth-erhood of Wagnerians who behaved like an exclusive clique', a journalist called Ernst von Wolzogen accused them of 'acquiring their enthusiasm second-hand and reducing themselves to a state of self-inebriation by their worship of holy relics in an incense-laden atmosphere'. 'There was some-thing of the Dervish or Fakir about them,' Wolzogen concluded.[15] What outsiders saw as mass psychosis, of the kind that later took hold of an entire nation and filled it with 'second-hand enthusiasm', the members of the sect themselves felt as religious ecstasy, and their despised servility as monastic discipline.

The Wagner faithful watched the star rise above the 'Green Hill'. The Gospel had been proclaimed and those who had heard the call assembled to witness the arrival of the future. Their experience was summarized in the title of a popular book published shortly before the First World War: *The Consummation of the Aryan Mystery in Bayreuth*, by one Leopold von Schroeder, professor of Indology at the University of Vienna.[16] A friend of Chamberlain's and a passionate Wagnerian, who delivered a lecture at the university in 1913 to commemorate the centennial of the Master's birth, Schroeder declared that the Aryan peoples, scattered five thousand years ago, had now been finally reunited in order to celebrate their religious mysteries. The echoes of Wagner's 'Wibelungen' were unmistakable. 'Thanks to the Master', Schroeder continued – his two-volume *Aryan Reli-gion* (1914) deals with the same issues – 'Bayreuth had been made the ideal centre for all Aryan peoples . . . a hallowed spot where the miracles of the Holy Grail are revealed, where the dragon is slain by the sword of a pure, fearless hero, and where the radiant thought of salvation shines out like a beacon across the dark chasm of primeval thoughts.'[17]

In order to 'consummate' the Aryan religion, in reality only one, single 'pure and fearless hero' was needed, a hero who wielded a sword. The failure of Cosima's *Parsifal* petitions had shown how little influence Bayreuth had in a parliamentary Germany. Bayreuthians themselves found this in no way surprising: had not the Master himself unmasked the democratic principle as thoroughly 'un-German'? Help could only come, as the *Bayreuther Blätter* wrote in 1886, 'not through the processes of democracy, but through self-confident heroes and leaders who are their own vindication'.[18] Wahnfried had a contingent of such heroes and leaders available, well-disciplined, well-trained, committed to the destruction of democratic decadence and distinguished from a political party by the secrecy in which it veiled its real aims. 'The feature that differentiates Bayreuth from other similar coteries', wrote a critic in 1912, 'is the strictness and discipline of its organization, which underlies all the various Wagner societies both in Germany and abroad.'[19] Everyone was free to observe the annual rites performed on the 'Green Hill' but scarcely anyone knew what the show was all about. And as long as the hero had not yet been found who would put their secret ideas into practice, the Bayreuthians were well content. When he did arrive, he would find his weapon waiting for him in the Grail Temple.

'Wagner', wrote Ludwig Schemann, 'fashioned a two-edged sword out of German music'[20] – to which Cosima added that Bayreuth was not concerned to offer the nation merely a doctrine 'but also instructions on how to act'.[21] Cosima is not here giving the Master's aesthetic views a political twist which he did not intend, for he had never had anything else in mind. Rienzi, 'tribune of the people', had set out to free Rome from its oppressors as Wagner, also a 'tribune of the people', embarked on the liberation of Dresden. Having failed as a revolutionary and been banished from the political scene for his pains, he continued the battle through his writings – the battle with Germany's arch-enemy, the Jews.

Wolfgang Wagner sees the situation differently. To him his grandfather's writings express 'the very opposite of a fanatical anti-Semitism',[22] and he supports his view by quoting Wagner's own words, as recorded by Cosima: 'If I were to write about the Jews again, I would say that there is nothing to object to about them except that they arrived too soon.' But this overlooks that Wagner was referring not to his opinion as such but to the strategy of how to express his opinions. He gave a glimpse of how he really saw his programme for action in 1879, when he was discussing with Cosima the sudden rise in anti-Semitism. 'We were amused by the thought', she wrote, 'that his essay "Music and the Jews" really does seem to mark the beginning of the struggle.'[23]

Wagner's '*Kampf*', which Hitler was later to make his own, was obscured, on the one hand, by the hectic activities surrounding the Festival itself, and, on the other, by Cosima's withdrawn, nun-like behaviour after her husband's death. But many observers were too sharp-witted to allow the wool to be pulled over their eyes. In 1921, when Germany was a republic but when Hitler had already taken up his 'struggle', the Jewish novelist Jakob Wassermann published his autobiography under the title *My Road as German and Jew*. In the course of his story Wassermann lights on Bayreuth and the Wagnerians, urging those of democratic persuasion 'to expose the widespread anti-Semitic machinations, often tragic in their consequences, in which dyed-in-the-wool Wagnerians indulged in the 1870s and 1880s. In a curious state of mesmerization and agitation they were at pains to draw a veil over the disparity between Wagner the outspoken German' – Wassermann's cautious way of referring to Wagner's anti-Semitism – 'and Wagner the composer, with Bayreuth as the controlling "witch's kitchen" '.[24]

In charge of this 'witch's kitchen' was an Englishman. Of all promoters of the Wagnerian cause Houston Stewart Chamberlain was the most significant. Born in 1855, son of an admiral, Chamberlain grew up in France and became a Germanophile under the encouragement of his tutor. He had a considerable influence on Kaiser Wilhelm II and converted the nationalistically minded bourgeoisie to the 'prophet of Bayreuth', whose philosophy he popularized in his bestselling book *Foundations of the Nineteenth Century*.

Chamberlain had been chosen personally by the guardian of the Grail. From her first encounter with him in 1888 until his death in 1927 he was for Cosima the man who came immediately after Wagner. Nietzsche had dreamed of inheriting Wagner's estate, including his widow, but Chamberlain superseded him at a stroke. Before conquering the Reich and making himself the most-read, most-quoted predecessor of Hitler, he had already conquered Cosima. Her last thoughts, as she lay dying in Wahnfried, were not of her husband – they were of the man who had taken his place but whose death three years earlier had been kept from her. 'How is Houston?' she asked her daughter Eva, Chamberlain's widow. 'Tell him he is often in my thoughts.' Or on another occasion: 'Houston made you his bride and thereby gave me such joy.'[25] According to Eva's diary, her mother did not mention Wagner's name once during the last six months of her life; all her thoughts were of Chamberlain.

The Englishman, Bayreuth's 'Grey Eminence', underwent the same initiation into Wagner's world as King Ludwig before him and Adolf Hitler after him. A highly strung child, he was transported into a state of euphoria whenever he heard the sounds of Wagner's music. 'It had an electric effect on me,' he wrote in his autobiography; 'the moment I heard it, I jumped out of my seat.'[26] 'The sound of a leitmotif would send a thrill through my whole body like a call to arms', he recalled.[27] In order to be able to hear the striking leitmotif as often as he could – it was the so-called 'Sword motif' – he asked the village organist to teach him to play it. Described by Chamberlain as expressive of 'Wotan's sudden urge to see a hero conquer the world',[28] it makes its first appearance in *Rheingold*, when

Wotan has a vision of the future dragon-slayer – a vision as yet unexpressed but invoked by the triumphant motif, at the sound of which Wagner requires Wotan to flourish his sword aloft.

The message is clear: only by force can the domination of the world by the 'powers of darkness' be prevented. 'It would be no exaggeration', wrote Chamberlain, 'to say that in this handful of notes I discovered the character of the music of the entire *Ring* – its monumentality, the power of nature it conveyed. Day after day I hastened into the village to play the organ, always beginning with this motif, which I could never hear too often.'[29] The thought that went through Wotan's mind became the guiding principle of Chamberlain's life. And that thought needed a hero to turn it into reality; the world would be rescued from the clutches of the dragon not by thought alone but by the piercing blade of a sword.

The course of Chamberlain's life as a missionary for Wagner was thus pre-ordained. In 1879 he joined the subscribers to the Bayreuth Festival and offered his services to the *Bayreuther Blätter*. The moment in 1882 when he first set foot in the Festspielhaus he described as 'one of the greatest and most hallowed experiences of my life'.[30] From 1885 onwards he published a number of pamphlets on Wagner, crowning his work with a full-scale biography ten years later. It was not, however, his passionate attachment to Wagner's music that made him Wahnfried's ideal propagandist but his gift for converting Wagner's flowery and often abstruse articles into a more accessible language, supplemented with 'results of recent research'.

Thanks to Chamberlain, Wagner's 'regeneration' writings, with their Byzantine sentence constructions, were presented in a more acceptable form, acquiring pseudo-scientific dignity and a validity that extended to broad cultural circles. Even the Kaiser was accustomed to spice his remarks with the comment: 'Chamberlain is of the same mind.'[31] Bayreuth, moreover, was to become not merely 'a centre of good intentions' but 'a place of fulfilment . . . a school for action',[32] in which every pupil must believe 'in the ultimate victory of the will that is directed towards the achievement of high ideals'. And through this will the promise embodied in Siegfried's sword-motif will finally be fulfilled, for 'everyone who has been gripped by Wagner's work and vision knows that his day will dawn only for future generations'.[33]

Chamberlain set out to pave the way to this future. Bayreuth became his spiritual home as Cosima became his spiritual companion. They would appear together before the assembled devotees of Wahnfried, issuing directives and pronouncing sentences of excommunication. The 'Noble Lady', who still insisted on wearing a veil thirteen years after her husband's death, stood by the side of the tall, blond Englishman in shining riding-boots[34] and received the homage of the faithful. In this mediocre company[35] Chamberlain, who spoke excellent German, stood out like a sage. Intellectually superior to both Wolzogen and Schemann, and assuming the airs of a philosopher, he was the perfect counterpart to the cool, oracular Cosima. While she was responsible for the mystical aspects of the cult, he made himself responsible for translating them into intellectual terms.

It was probably as a result of their guise of solemnity and majesty that the purely personal aspect of the relationship between Chamberlain and Wahnfried, made permanent when Chamberlain married Eva and moved into the family villa, has received so little attention. Even the hint dropped by Richard du Moulin Eckart, Cosima's official biographer, that 'she grew more and more attached to him'[36] has remained unnoticed. Yet the extensive correspondence that passed between them after their first meeting in 1888 shows unmistakable signs of emotional attachment. There is much flirting between the lines in their philosophical missives. Two days after their long conversation in Dresden the thirty-year-old Chamberlain wrote wistfully, almost yearningly, to his 'esteemed *Meisterin*' – who, in her early fifties, was still a highly desirable woman: 'If only I could tell you everything that is in my heart! But I cannot. Yet at least we both have eyes.'[37]

To this Cosima confessed how attached she already felt to him, comparing his advances to her to the rising sun. 'I had the same feelings when I received your note,' she replied. 'It is so long since I received such sympathy that at the beginning my heart felt unsure. But now it shines into my soul like a ray of sunlight, bringing me joy and happiness.'[38] Words such as these, from the pen of an unapproachable High Priestess, who since her legendary adultery with Wagner had posed as a model of austere feminine propriety, left Chamberlain, who was married himself, feeling like a love-sick teenager. 'For days I was haunted by the thought of your profound loneliness,' he confessed to her: 'Even in my dreams I wept. Maybe I have no need to say such things. Maybe, as a woman, you feel things differently and do not pine like a man.'[39] Cosima's response came in the form of dreams whose meaning was not hard to guess. She told him, for instance, that, preparing for a reception she was supposed to give for the Kaiser, she completely forgot about her royal guest and lost herself in imaginary conversations with her new favourite, so that, when the time came, absolutely nothing was ready. This breach of etiquette, the nightmare of every society hostess, filled her with delight. 'It was a dream', she told him, 'that put me in a very good mood.'[40] On another occasion she wrote that while visiting a palm garden, she had suddenly been overcome with a 'passionate melancholy' while 'the scent of the silent palms had formed a union in my aching heart with the languishing sounds of distant music'.[41] To this he replied that her description of the palm trees 'had caused my heart strings to quiver'.[42]

The epistolary union of these two cult figures, concealed behind a smokescreen of metaphor which deceived even the editor of their correspondence, bore rich fruits. Chamberlain threw himself body and soul into the service of the common cause, and Cosima knew on whom she could impose the responsibility for Bayreuth's public image. There could, of course, be no question of an official union between them, any more than there was fifty years later between her daughter-in-law Winifred and Adolf Hitler. The Grail insisted that its widows kept faith with the blood-line of the Wagners. Incite him as she might to ever fresh outbursts of emotion, the myth of the austere, self-denying priestess had to be preserved.

Cosima remained unapproachable and her admirer, whom a friend once characterized as 'a man and a woman rolled into one',[43] contented himself with her affection, which fluctuated between veiled provocation and spinsterish severity. 'One of the most wonderful manifestations of your strength of character', Chamberlain wrote to her, 'is the way you mete out punishment where punishment is due.'[44] Barely less frustrated than he, she moved the inopportune liaison onto a harmless plane. 'I have been pondering over recent weeks', she told him, almost *en passant*, 'how best we can set about sowing the seed of pan-Germanism.'[45] One way was by persuading her frustrated suitor to secure a divorce from his childless marriage and become the husband of her daughter Eva, at forty almost an old maid and 'her mother's right hand', as she was known. So here too she acted as a stand-in for her mother, making it possible for the older couple to spend time in each other's company every day while planning the future of the Wagnerian empire.

Chamberlain achieved fame with his biography of Wagner – the contract for which was signed with the publisher Bruckmann in Wahnfried – which finally confirmed his credentials in Cosima's eyes as 'a true campaigner for the Bayreuth ideal and its fulfilment'. Henceforth, she went on in the *Bayreuther Blätter*, 'he will invest the power of his inspiration, the penetration of his eloquence and his all-embracing intellect in making the world aware of the nature of our cause'.[46]

Enthusiastically received by the press, Chamberlain's biography soon established itself as the Wagner Bible. A copy was to be found on Hitler's bookshelf in Landsberg prison in 1924.[47] Its motto – 'It is good to talk but better to keep silent' – made it clear that the most vital truths would not be stated but at the most adumbrated. The true meaning must be sensed, not arrived at by argument. Chamberlain's purpose, though not stated in so many words, was to present the Master's philosophy as guidelines for conduct in the future.

Chamberlain developed a particular skill in formulating provocative points in a way whose true meaning often became clear only on a second reading. Tortuous, self-conscious sentences like those in 'The Work of Art of the Future' alternate with pithy judgements disguised in a metaphorical form that reveals the author's underlying aggressive intentions. Proud of his unrestrained hatred of the Jews, and brandishing the sword of Siegfried as his chosen device, he describes Wagner now as 'the victorious commander in the second "Battle of the Nations" ',[48] now as 'the man for whom

Schiller had yearned, a man born out of his time, come like Agamemnon's son to purge the world'. His invocation of Orestes is not accidental. The man who has come to regenerate the world, like the son of the treacherously murdered Agamemnon, or the dramatist of the assassinated Siegfried, cannot shrink from extreme measures. 'Wagner too knew the force of hatred,' wrote Chamberlain, 'a hatred of an art that has been prostituted and turned into an industry.'[49] All the greater was his hatred of those responsible for this decadence.

In the final chapter of his biography of Wagner, entitled 'The Concept of Bayreuth', Chamberlain lowers his guard a little and explains how Wagner's art is to be interpreted in Darwinian terms. 'It is a symbol of our struggle,' he writes, 'a standard round which the faithful, ready for the fight, will rally. . . . Only in battle can the fighters become hardened.' And in case this challenge should pass unnoticed, Chamberlain emphasizes it with a quotation from Wagner himself. 'If it be admitted', said the Master, 'that my view is correct, then the man who has not the courage to risk his life in the struggle is lost.'[50] In other words, once one has identified the causes of the decline, one cannot help but pluck them out, in the interests of one's own survival. Hitler, during whose dictatorship Chamberlain's book went through ten editions, summarized the situation: 'It was first by the Master, then by Chamberlain, that the spiritual sword with which we fight today was forged.'

This 'spiritual sword' was at its sharpest in Chamberlain's main work, *Foundations of the Nineteenth Century*, first published in 1899. To build on the success of his Wagner biography, his publisher, Hugo Bruckmann, proposed a new work that should deal with the century then coming to an end, with the genius of Wagner set in its historical context. In 'The Wibelungen' Wagner had sited the birth of man's creative genius in the Himalayas, its earthly path ending, for the time being, in the symbolic depths of the legendary mountain of the Untersberg. Chamberlain now planned to trace the history of civilization – synonymous with German civilization – from its origins via the fateful intervention of the Jews down to the decisive moment in the nineteenth century when Wagner appeared, heralding the transformation from global disaster to a world of well-being and serenity.

Excited by Chamberlain's plan,[51] Cosima followed the course of his work with keen anticipation[52] and supplied him with ideas of her own. In the event the apotheosis she looked for did not materialize, and Wagner's name rarely occurred. Nevertheless Cosima called the book a 'landmark'. 'With admirable clarity', she wrote to the author, 'you have revealed all that is valuable and indispensable in our tradition . . . and are the first to have the courage to state what is the truth, namely that the Jews are a considerable factor in our present-day culture.'[53]

With the support of Bayreuth behind it, Chamberlain's *Foundations* achieved a success unmatched by that of any other philosophical work of the time, and it was soon enjoying the status of a modern classic. The various Wagner Societies, delighted to find the principles of Bayreuth restated in the book,[54] also put their weight behind it. It was reprinted no fewer than thirty times, including cheap editions and war-time reissues – hundreds of thousands of copies in all.

Chamberlain's bestseller claimed to provide scientific proof in support of Wagner's fantastic ideas. Kaiser Wilhelm II, who had already shown his support for *Parsifal* and ordered the trumpeters of his regiment of guards to sound a bugle-call at Wagner's graveside,[55] was so impressed that he sent the author a personal note of appreciation.[56] He also gave instructions that a copy should be put in the library of every school in Prussia, and it became recommended reading for his officers. In Berlin it was eagerly discussed in court circles for a long while, and a Catholic bishop even commended it to his priests. Cosima was highly satisfied. 'Your *Foundations*', she wrote to Chamberlain, 'is the most-read book today in all ranks of society.'[57]

Its popularity was also furthered by the praise of well-known writers such as Hermann Graf Keyserling, who called it 'a work of art',[58] or the Basle philosopher Karl Joël, for whom it was 'the most interesting book of the last decade'.[59] The *Neue Zürcher Zeitung* referred to the 'splendour' of the work, 'which gives the reader an incredible feeling of liberation', while the *Christliche Welt* found itself reminded of Wagner, 'like whom the author also has his leitmotifs – the race motif, the Germanic motif and the Jewish motif'.[60] It was a message that rang out loud and clear.

The Kaiser was fulsome in his praise, thanking the man he addressed as his 'friend' for 'having brought order to my confused thoughts and light into my darkness, and pointed out the paths that will lead to the salvation of the German nation and thereby of mankind itself'. And he concludes, in the effusive tones of a religious zealot: 'God has sent your book to the Germans, and you personally to me.'[61]

Twenty-two years later, in a New Year message, Chamberlain struck the same tone, calling down the divine blessing on Hitler, Wagner's heir: 'May God, Who has given him to us, preserve him for the salvation of the German *Volk* for many years to come.'[62] The urge to become the leader of the nation which Chamberlain aroused in Hitler was a characteristic that Wahnfried believed it had already discovered in Chamberlain himself. 'The reader of Chamberlain's book', said the *Bayreuther Blätter*, 'feels himself drawn to the spirit of a leader who is ideally predisposed to this calling.'[63]

By confining his spiritual father too often to the background, Chamberlain aroused the anger of Cosima's other son-in-law, Henry Thode, a respected art historian. Probably out of envy of the dominant position into which Chamberlain had worked himself, Thode accused him publicly of having brazenly copied from the Master's works.[64] The argument, which flared up in an instant and was watched by a bewildered Wagner public for over a year, arose from a misunderstanding. Chamberlain had in fact only been following the custom adopted in Bayreuth from the beginning, that Wagner's name should never be mentioned in connection with the 'Jewish question'. Since, however, Chamberlain, a man of action, was determined to 'stir up the hornets' nest', as Cosima had put it, he was only conforming to her wishes that the Master himself should be left out of the picture while still being present in spirit through quotations and subtle allusions which the initiated would immediately recognize but which Thode had apparently failed to see.

Thus in the introduction to his *Foundations* Chamberlain quotes the admonition 'Know Thyself'.[65] Any reader of Wagner would have known that this was not a reference to the Delphic oracle but to Wagner's anti-Semitic essay, where the chilling phrase 'the demon of decadence' first occurs.[66] Chamberlain was not plagiarizing Wagner but assimilating him.

Chamberlain's self-willed, eccentric theory of history was only meant as a prelude to action. Once one has stripped away all the fanciful fictions of Wagner's 'Wibelungen', with its talk of the creative Germanic race and its mortal enemy, the destructive tribe of the Jews, one is left with a straightforward message. This is, that for the Germanic race to rise above the chaos caused by miscegenation and enter into its rightful inheritance of the world of Classical Antiquity, it must be rescued from 'the claws of bestiality'.[67] Those who do not belong to our race must be 'mercilessly struck down',[68] 'their marauding vessels consigned to the deep',[69] 'the Phoenician race exterminated',[70] and it must be understood that these Jews, apparently so immutable, are the product of evolution and, like all things that evolve, will perish. 'This of itself brings them closer to us in human terms.'[71] Chamberlain, the Mephistopheles of Bayreuth, could hardly wait to see the emergence of the man of action who would 'inflame the hearts of millions'[72] before finally putting his torch to the pyre.

There was a pyre in Wahnfried as well. Since Chamberlain's biography of Wagner at the turn of the century Cosima's daughter Eva, on her mother's instructions, had been preserving the purity of the Master's image by quietly burning whatever did not accord with the official legend. Among the correspondence that fell victim to the flames of the symbolic '*autos-da-fé*', as the family called them,[73] was that between Wagner and Heine, Berlioz, Semper, Baudelaire and many other distinguished contemporaries. Even more tragic, in the year after Chamberlain's marriage into the Wagner family, Eva destroyed her mother's letters to Wagner and then, after Cosima's death, his letters to her[74] – all priceless documents the loss of which makes a complete reconstruction of his life impossible. Which was no doubt the intention.

While parts of the Wagner heritage were being senselessly destroyed, others were brought to the fore. Chamberlain, for example, took pains to establish Wagner's aristocratic descent from the house of Sachsen-Weimar, maintaining that his line 'could be followed back uninterruptedly to the twelfth century'.[75] This claim was then restated by other biographers, who circulated the story that the composer's grandfather had been Prince Constantin of Weimar. Wagner himself was said to have believed in this line of descent,[76] which Chamberlain went so far as to trace back to St Elisabeth.[77]

This claim, with its overtones of Lohengrin, was not Chamberlain's only contribution to the Wagner household. 'In 1908,' complained Cosima's daughter Daniela, wife of Henry Thode, 'our misery began – with Eva's marriage.'[78] Chamberlain had taken up residence in the Villa Wahnfried and immediately set about bringing everything under his own control. With the help of his utterly devoted wife, who enjoyed far-reaching powers of her own, he devoted himself, as Michael Karbaum put it, 'to the manipulation of the documents and autograph material in the Wahnfried archives, as well as to the running of the *Bayreuther Blätter* and public relations in general . . . a significant shift of power'.[79]

Chamberlain's 'seizure of power' also led to an intensification of the smouldering conflicts within the clan, whose wealth amounted in 1908 to more than four million marks.[80] First Daniela divorced Thode, then Isolde, Wagner's daughter, was banished from Bayreuth after a legal dispute over inheritance matters allegedly stirred up by Chamberlain. Whether that be so or not, it was in his interests to reduce the number of heirs to a minimum so as to control the affairs of Bayreuth together with Wagner's only son Siegfried. Indeed, did not Cosima think of him as her 'second son'? From then on Siegfried, whose homosexual tendencies laid him open to blackmail, was given responsibility for the artistic side of the Festival, with political and ideological matters in Chamberlain's hands. The two areas of activity were to come together again in the person of Hitler, heir to the legacy of both men.

Compared with the meek, gentle Siegfried, who died at sixty-one, shortly after his mother, the tall, energetic Englishman was a far more likely redeemer. With his great capacity for hate, for which the Wagnerians greatly admired him, and publicly lauded by the Kaiser himself as a man 'blessed by God',[81] he conducted himself as one 'who derived his authority from above'. He had the personality of a Führer before the real Führer arrived.[82]

But Chamberlain, like Wagner before him, faced the problem of how to translate his power into political terms. Influence was one thing, control was another. So what more natural than to seek to influence those who did have power? As Wagner thought he had found his instrument in King Ludwig of Bavaria, so did Chamberlain in Kaiser Wilhelm II. Like Ludwig an admirer of robust manliness and resilience, a man who liked to paint naval battles in oils, the Kaiser had also resolved to turn Wagner's Teutonic world into reality – not by building fairy-tale castles, to be sure, but through his annual yachting trips into the world of Wotan and Siegfried. On these voyages into Nordic waters, which Hitler was to repeat with warships, the Kaiser dreamed of past heroes and wrote Skaldic odes in a Wagnerian idiom.

For his first acquaintance with Chamberlain's *Weltanschauung* the Kaiser was indebted to his close friend Prince Eulenburg, a member of Schemann's Gobineau Society and a contributor to the *Bayreuther Blätter*. The two men met in 1901 and Chamberlain reported to Cosima that the meeting had given him 'a pleasant glimpse of Hohenzollern family life'.[83] He, for his part, captivated the Kaiser, whose yachting excursions took place 'under Chamberlain's spell'.[84]

The *Foundations* also opened the Kaiser's eyes to the glorious world of the Teutons and the Aryan race, and soon he developed a warm personal relationship with the Englishman. Like Wagner with the dreamer on the throne of Bavaria, so Chamberlain convinced the complex-ridden Kaiser of his divine mission, characterizing him as a man of action 'like Siegfried, who slew the dragon', a parallel which the Kaiser took to mean that 'the tribe of Judah must be eradicated from German soil once for all'.[85]

Wilhelm II interpreted the world according to Chamberlain's principles: the German nation, God's chosen people, was surrounded by inferior races consumed with envy, behind them the power of international Jewry. In the course of his Nordic voyages he had expressed his desire that a kind of cult be formed round Chamberlain[86] and his works, and Chamberlain's views found their way into statements by the Kaiser that aroused terrible forebodings of what was to come. 'There are too many Jews in my country,' he said in 1907. 'They must be got rid of.'[87] In 1929, then in exile, he demanded that the Jews be killed 'like mosquitoes'. It was no chance that one of the first to greet the Kaiser's accession in 1888 had been Ritter von Schönerer, Hitler's icon. 'Wilhelm', prophesied Schönerer, 'will free us from the Jewish yoke.'[88]

From having been cast in the role of dragon-slayer, the Kaiser suddenly found himself in 1914, as he said, 'with a sword in his hand'. What else could he do but wield it? The audience watching *Siegfried* at the Bayreuth Festival in July of that year felt the same way, sympathizing with the hero, who, held in the clutches of the spiteful Mime and bereft of friends or allies, was compelled to forge the magic sword Nothung. At the famous moment when he cried 'Nothung! Nothung! Fiery sword!', something incredible happened in the opera house. The audience sprang to its feet and a storm broke out. Siegfried's revolt against his foe took hold of the listeners. 'What a moment!' exclaimed one. 'The whole audience jumped up and the Festspielhaus was swept into a tempest in which the soul of the German people was carried aloft to the heavenly abode of its noble heroes.' Drama became heightened reality, the 'Green Hill', like the theatre of Classical Antiquity, had become a hallowed place of collective self-awareness, as Wagner had envisioned it. 'Young Siegfried had become Germany, forging its sword,' continued the same eye-witness. 'It was Germany that flourished its sword in the air, Germany that would be victorious in its struggle against a world of enemies.'[89]

The country flocked to the colours. Like Hitler among the crowds in the Odeonsplatz in Munich when war was declared that same year, millions of Germans fell under the spell of the mythological hero who strode out with flashing sword to meet the dragon. The Kaiser, centre of the nation's hopes, saw it as the fulfilment of Wagner's prophecies – what he had learned from Wagner's operas or from Chamberlain's *Foundations* was now taking place in a real war. 'This war is a struggle between two *Weltanschauungen*,' he used to say: 'on the one side, decency, justice, faith and loyalty, the virtues of a true Teutono-German humanity; on the other, materialism, greed, covetousness, deceit, treachery and ultimately murder.' In a word, all the characteristics of Wagner's Nibelungen. The two sides were irreconcilable, therefore, as in the *Ring*: 'one side must win, the other perish'.[90]

That a war necessarily entailed the downfall of one or other of the rival powers was hardly something that the Kaiser had been able to learn from recent history, but for Bayreuth it was a matter of course: the Kaiser's war on several fronts could not but spell final disaster. And both Cosima and Chamberlain were able to say that they were there. 'Two weeks ago', wrote Prince Hohenlohe to Cosima from the eastern front, 'I was in my beloved Bayreuth. Now I am in the midst of preparations for war . . . well aware that it has been shamelessly forced upon us and that we are fighting for our most treasured possessions.'[91]

Wahnfried also joined the war. As Wagner had written a patriotic ode in 1871 addressed to the German army before Paris, so in 1914 his son Siegfried composed a hymn of allegiance to the flag, while Cosima sent telegrams of congratulation to the German General Staff. The initial lightning victories seemed to confirm the Bayreuth doctrine of German racial superiority, while their experience of their adversaries revealed the sinister converse. France was throwing subhuman Negroes into the battle and on the eastern front German soldiers stood face to face with the enemies of German civilization. In the course of the Polish campaign Hohenlohe found himself in what he described as 'a district inhabited almost entirely by the most objectionable kinds of Jews. Field Marshal Hindenburg recently remarked that it seemed as though a Judas Iscariot were poking his head out of every window.'[92]

Bayreuth's participation in the Franco-Prussian War had been limited to the role of well-wishers, with the sack of Paris, which Wagner would have dearly loved to see, 'as a symbol of the final liberation of the world from the oppression of evil forces', as Cosima wrote in her diary.[93] In the Great War, however, Wahnfried was more active, in that the man who had put himself at the head of the Wagner propaganda machine now turned to promoting the war effort with patriotic appeals to the nation. Summoned by the Prussian Ministry of Culture to mobilize popular enthusiasm for the war on the home front, Chamberlain assured the Kaiser – 'a gracious patron of my work' – of his full support and raged against his native England for having betrayed the Aryan race.[94]

Chamberlain's wartime essays, which all carried a certificate of approval from Bayreuth, first appeared in journals and were then published in book form by Bruckmann. Responsibility for the war, he declared, lay with Great Britain. This nation of 'hypocrites, cheats and liars', as he called them,[95] had plotted with other countries 'to attack and destroy an industrious, peace-loving Germany that threatened no one'.[96] The war was nothing but 'a diabolical attack, a calculated act of plunder and murder'. Parallels with Alberich's treachery and Hagen's assassination of Siegfried came immediately to mind, as Chamberlain pointed out to the Kaiser. And in the background, naturally, lurked the Nibelungen.

'England has fallen into the hands of the Jews and the Americans,' Chamberlain went on. 'Nobody can therefore understand this war who does not share the German view that it is basically a struggle on the part of the Jews and their allies, the Americans, to rule the world.'[97] Britain, Aryan brothers to the Germans, has been led astray by these alien influences, poisoned and robbed of her birthright, finally 'to be delivered into the hands of Satan'.

So nothing had changed since Alberich stole the gold. As his fight 'to inherit the world' led to the death of Siegfried, so also was it responsible for the senseless slaughter of the trenches. The curse he had laid on love and racial purity was to be redeemed at Verdun.

But danger came from within as well as from without, warned Chamberlain, for the hypocrites who betrayed Germany and who deserved to be hanged as traitors[98] were sitting at the very heart of the Fatherland. In the Reichstag itself the deputies were only concerned to 'undermine the power of the people and create chaos'.[99] Chamberlain invented the legend of the 'stab in the back' long before the defeat came.

Chamberlain's re-interpretations of myth, turning an avoidable catastrophe into an ecstatic crusade, were enthusiastically received. Compulsory reading for every citizen, a prescribed text for use in Gymnasien and propaganda material for the front, they presented an image of the war which was to have an effect that lasted far beyond 1918. Hatred was the order of the day, while the concept of politics as the art of the possible was covered in ignominy – precisely because the goal was the impossible.

Honoured by the Kaiser with the sobriquet 'the new prophet',[100] Chamberlain supplied the magic philosophical tool for the metaphysical justification of the Great War. Even Thomas Mann joined in the general jubilation that followed the publication of his wartime essays, praising him for his commitment to the cause of his adopted homeland. Letters of appreciation arrived from a number of generals and from Admiral Tirpitz, 'father of the German navy'. The Kaiser awarded him the Iron Cross. Cosima, in a letter to Hohenlohe, wrote of her gratification that her 'son's works should be so widely read and meet with such universal approval'.[101]

In 1918 the disaster was complete. The proud military commanders surrendered, the Kaiser had fled, and the people, living largely on turnips, realized that defeat was a reality. It should also have spelled the end for the whole world of Wagner's Teutonic mythology and Chamberlain's arrogant racism because they had been proven to be false. But Bayreuth chose this very moment to demonstrate its indestructibility. Defeat and a world in flames followed the familiar pattern: not Siegfried but Hagen, leading the forces of darkness, had triumphed, and hot on the heels of the victorious fight with the dragon, that is, with the successes which nobody could deny, came treachery and murder. The principal culprits, Hindenburg and Ludendorff, penned a lamentation on the subject of the 'stab in the back'. Bayreuth provided the music.

To make explicit the pivotal point in Wagner's prophetic *Ring*, the Nibelungen hordes of the Jews were identified as bearing the major share of the guilt for the nation's defeat. The runaway Kaiser accepted this, so did the vanquished generals. And so did one Adolf Hitler, who, demobilized from the army in 1920, at once began to give talks on the secret mythological significance of the nation's collapse. Anti-Semitism and the 'stab in the back' theory were the main planks in his platform. The nation's wartime policies had, he said, all been geared to defeat, policies not 'pan-German' but pan-Judaic'.[102] And as to the liberal republic that had been formed after the 1918 revolution, he declared two years later that it was 'not German in its essence but . . . a Jewish body committed to the removal of the country's Aryan leaders'.[103] Democracy itself he described as 'the hole that had been shot by the Jews in the German heart'.

Chamberlain experienced for himself the tragedy of his beloved German *Volk*. During the war he was stricken by 'an irreversible, progressive paralysis'[104] which confined him to a wheelchair and to his bed, and, according to Cosima,[105] made him wish to die. Although weakened by illness herself, Cosima visited him almost every day and spent hours in conversation with him. Later, when he could barely move his lips, it was 'the beautiful voice of the "Noble Lady", who tended him like a mother and comforted him like a guardian angel',[106] that kept him alive.

The Bayreuth orthodoxy held that Chamberlain had died of no ordinary disease but from the sufferings of his Fatherland, which he had had to endure like a Saviour on the Cross of the German Ideal. In a later letter to Hitler he himself described his paralysis in terms of a parable. 'It was', he said, 'on the outbreak of the war, that moment when the Fatherland was dragged into the horrors of battle, that fateful day in August 1914, that this terrible sickness befell me.'[107]

As the post-war years of hunger and disintegration set in and the country was eventually torn apart, the paralysis gradually took complete control of the martyr's body. A cruel fate had befallen him, as it befell Wagner's Amfortas, King of the Grail, a wound that would not heal but allowed him to crave only one thing – to be united with his Redeemer. 'In the next few days', wrote his wife Eva to one of the 'Knights of the Grail', 'the last article of the war veteran Houston Stewart Chamberlain will be published. . . . It will sound to you like a prophet's despairing cry for help.'[108] Though the Reich was defeated, the Kaiser expelled, power usurped – in terms of the myth, the sword Nothung shattered – the *Ring* still offered hope that a hero would join the pieces together. Maybe a man would appear, moved by the prophet's 'despairing cry', to wield a bright new sword. Maybe, as Chamberlain foretold in 1916, lying in his living grave, it would be a 'man from the trenches' – 'that is where our redeemer will come from!'[109]

A LETHAL SUBJECT

R ight from the beginning a veil was drawn over the fact that in Hitler Bayreuth had found Wagner's legitimate heir. After the defeat of Germany in 1945 the very mention of such a connection was taboo. 'As far as Wolfgang is concerned, it is undesirable for such matters to be raised again,'[1] said Winifred Wagner à propos the appointment of her younger son to the Festspielhaus. According to the official line, Wahnfried had as little to do with the Reich Chancellery as Wagner with a mass murderer. Hitler's enthusiasm for Wagner served merely to legitimize what Wolfgang Wagner called 'his political mission';[2] it was not the fault of the Master that he came to embody the aesthetic values of the Third Reich but of those who 'misunderstood and misused him'. 'There are no skeletons in the Wahnfried cupboard,' declared Wolfgang.[3]

But matters were not that simple. When Wolfgang's sister Friedelind emigrated at the beginning of the war and revealed the extent of her family's association with the Führer, her mother hastily followed her to Switzerland, threatening in a theatrical gesture that if she did not stop spreading such gossip, 'orders will be given for you to be removed from the scene at the earliest opportunity'.[4] But Winifred herself, who claimed after the war to have 'borne the brunt of everything', was also to suffer the indignity of banishment. Despite maintaining that she had allowed herself to be made a scapegoat 'only so as to leave my two boys with a clean slate',[5] her pro-Hitler remarks proved too much for Wolfgang, who in 1975 forbade her to enter the Festspielhaus. Her elder son Wieland, who died in 1966 after having been accused by his mother of usufruct, embarked on his own campaign against 'traitors'. Anyone who could not hold his peace was punished.

Wieland Wagner, favoured by Hitler as director of Bayreuth, re-emerged in 1951, after a brief period of penitence, as the architect of a 'new' Bayreuth. He had no time for the 'old guard'. When the ex-Nazi Hans Severus Ziegler, an ardent Wagnerian and anti-Semite, reminisced about Hitler's close relationship with Bayreuth, Wieland accused him of 'having done the Festival a grave disservice . . . undermining my attempts to bury this lethal subject once for all'.[6] When Wieland's mother herself turned her back on the new direction he had taken by applying in April 1945 for political asylum in Switzerland, he had a wall erected between his garden and his mother's – a visible symbol of how radically he had cut himself off from the past.

Wahnfried's policy of suppressing the past worked. Friedelind, who returned to the bosom of the family after the war, was accused of heresy. Scholars who probed into Bayreuth's past had their work censored. When Wagner's great-grandchildren raised the question of Wahnfried's responsibility for the Holocaust, they were banished from the Festspielhaus. The extensive correspondence between Wahnfried and Hitler remained locked in the vaults and the vital letters of Chamberlain to Hitler were not quoted in official biographies, or, if so, then heavily doctored. Even Hitler's declaration to Siegfried, Wagner's son, that the sword of National Socialism had been forged by Wagner and Chamberlain has been changed in Wolfgang Wagner's highly selective memoirs to read that only 'Uncle Chamberlain' was involved.[7] The question of Wagner's responsibility was quietly dropped.

According to the present director of the Bayreuth Festival, whom his mother dubbed 'Wolf', his grandfather was a harmless operatic composer 'whose views existed uneasily alongside the philosophy of National Socialism'.[8] The much-vaunted antipathy of the Nazis to Wagner – 'a callous, empty claim',[9] Michael Karbaum calls it – was put forward by Wahnfried after the defeat of 1945 as an act of self-defence in the context of coming to terms with the past. As though Bayreuth, having supplied the country with the necessary nationalistic stimulants before the war, were now offering it a post-war potion of amnesia, it was agreed not to ask questions but to marvel at the theatre of regained innocence – a policy kept intact down to the present day.

Those who saw things in a different light, like Wolfgang's cousin Franz Wilhelm Beidler, son of Wagner's daughter Isolde, are long since dead. Forgotten also, drowned in the jubilation that attended the re-opening of the Festival in 1951, is Beidler's article 'Misgivings about Bayreuth', in which he wrote:

> The Festival, together with its compulsory philosophical trappings, was always a highly political occasion. What happened in 1933 was merely the fruition of the seeds which had been sown over the course of previous decades, particularly in Bayreuth. If there is anything that can be called a Nazi ideology or a Nazi temperament, then that ideology and that temperament owe a frightening debt to Bayreuth.[10]

Those who, like the writer Erich Kuby and the scholars Michael Karbaum and Hartmut Zelinsky, set out to examine Beidler's claims, were shouted down. When in 1968 Wolfgang Wagner declared: 'Bayreuth's political past has been confronted and the matter is now closed,'[11] he was greeted with applause. Not that he was so far from the truth. For the matter was indeed closed – not, however, because reason had prevailed but because Hitler, Bayreuth's saviour, had failed, bringing down his theatrical Third Reich with him and leaving the Bayreuth temple in ruins. Nobody has since shown any inclination to re-issue 'The Work of Art of the Future'.

But 'closed', in the real sense, Bayreuth's political history certainly was not. For that to happen, this history would first have to be brought into the open. Thanks to the smoke-screens put up by Wahnfried and its academic cronies, however, only fragments of the 'elective affinity' between the un-employed ex-private from Austria and the paralysed Anglo-German phi-losopher in Bayreuth ever reached the ears of the public. The scraps of information given from time to time by Winifred and her son Wolfgang – not to mention their obeisant biographers and chroniclers – also lead one to suspect that they too had only the vaguest notions about what really happened.

Wahnfried did, however, seek to satisfy public curiosity with a regular supply of anecdotes and assured its audiences that what had happened was purely private in nature. For Cosima herself the art of dissembling had become second nature, since Bayreuth's esoteric message had to be kept from the uninitiated. To be sure, after 1945 Wahnfried's secret no longer lay in the visionary ideals of Wagner's 'regeneration writings' – those ideals had collapsed in their confrontation with history. But a quite new secret had taken its place – that of the inseparable link between the racist mysteries of the religion of the Grail and the mass slaughters ordered by the new Messiah, together with the family relationship between the chil-dren left fatherless by Siegfried Wagner's death in 1930 and their favourite 'Uncle Wolf'. It was a terrible secret, one that in reality could never be laid to rest. Once made public, it did indeed turn the Bayreuth Festival into a 'lethal subject'.

The Bayreuth tradition had in its armoury one tried and tested weapon which they thought would finally dispose of the secret. Hitler, they now said, was in truth quite different: the brutal leader of the Nazi Party and inventor of industrialized genocide had not the slightest connection with that sensitive devotee of Wagner's music who presented himself as what Wolfgang Wagner described as 'an Austrian gentleman of the old school'.[12]

On top of this dichotomy between the outer and the inner realm, be-tween official interpretation and conspiratorial message, there now emerged a further distinction, one between Hitler the evil villain, about whom, after Auschwitz, as Wieland said, 'there is nothing more to say',[13] and Hitler the Wagner enthusiast 'who found in our family circle the peace and harmony that his own family had never given him', as Wolfgang wrote. It was therefore hardly surprising that he should have 'often and with great pleasure spoken about our grandfather's works and how they should be interpreted. . . . On occasion he even contributed his own ideas.'[14] But anyone who tries to publish more than the accounts of such idyllic family scenes that Wolfgang trots out in his memoirs is quickly made to realize that this would be to risk exposure to charges of breach of copyright and infringement of individual rights, as Wolfgang makes clear.[15] What at the time was confidential and restricted to the family circle round the fireside is still today kept under lock and key.

At the same time it must be remembered that this dichotomy of evil politician and Bayreuth lover was from the beginning part of the image that Hitler himself deliberately cultivated. He lived out these contradictions, moving to and fro between the external world of his public appearances and the internal realm of his divine mission, and defining himself in terms of these extremes, which rendered him insensible to contradiction. As a politician he knew he was unassailable, because he shrouded his goals in mystery; as an aficionado of the Wagner cult he resisted attempts to pin him down because he had always been concerned with the realization of the cult's ideals. He presented a façade of inscrutability, and did so to the end.

It was not, however, because of his insane ravings that his intentions escaped comprehension[16] but because, as befits the mythological image of the demon, he was able to switch identities. He was never like himself yet always remained the same. He slipped from the internal to the external mode of existence as circumstances required, from the role of acolyte in a secret religion to that of perpetrator of unspeakable crimes. In talking of Hitler, one is also talking of his counterpart; for every statement made about him there is a contrary statement. He will go down in history not as a man riddled with contradictions but as the incarnation of an ideology which nurtures within itself the irreconcilable extremes of the sublime and the terrible.

When the dramatist Carl Zuckmayer witnessed Hitler in 1923 at meetings in taverns and beer cellars, he was reminded of a 'howling dervish who chanted the same phrases over and over again, whipping up the emotions of the masses in the smoke-filled, beer-swilling atmosphere'.[17] Others recalled how he would strike the table with his whip, foaming at the mouth as he shouted at his henchmen to beat up those who did not display the requisite degree of enthusiasm. Nevertheless, as Zuckmayer, who fled the country in 1938, was forced to admit, 'such primitive, barbaric scenes were skilfully planned and staged, and had a frightening effect' – like Wagner's Siegfried, in fact, whose career also starts with acts of violence and chanted slogans.

Opposed to this frenzied one-man show, which would not have been out of place in a circus, was the other Hitler, the lone wolf, withdrawn, reflective, with shining blue eyes and a pleasant, deep-toned voice, a man of whose secret philosophy only his closest friends had the slightest inkling. This was the Hitler, for example, that Hermann Rauschning, President of the Danzig Senate, knew at the beginning of the 1930s, and whose words he later recalled in exile.

Rauschning, who in the course of a handful of meetings came to understand Hitler better than many who spent decades in his company, identified the secret of the Nazi elite as lying in the clandestine nature of National Socialist dogma, a body of doctrine accessible only to the chosen few, a select band like the medieval Teutonic Knights. Indeed, the hierarchical nature of the Party makes for a direct comparison with the military orders of the Middle Ages. 'The mass of the people, on the other hand,' wrote Rauschning, 'did not understand such parallels. They were like spectators of a sacred rite. The individual clings to what he can understand, to what concerns him personally; beyond this lies the world of rhythm and chanting and action in which one can rouse the masses to a state of frenzy.'[18]

Rauschning could not know that those Paladins that he took to be members of Hitler's inner circle – and who also took themselves to be such – were in fact kept at a considerable distance from the Führer's real secret. Occasionally, when there was no need to fear that he would be taken too literally, Hitler would lift the veil a little. 'For me Wagner is a god', he once confided to a journalist; 'his music is my religion. I go to his operas as others go to church.'[19] Christa Schroeder, Hitler's secretary, who recorded her reminiscences of her employer after the war, also emphasized the religious nature of his feeling for Wagner, whom he described as 'the rediscoverer of German culture through the spirit of music' and whose operas 'rang in his ears like a revelation from on high'.[20] Years earlier, living in the men's hostel in Vienna, he had confessed to his companion: 'Opera is the supreme religious rite.'[21]

But who, outside his adopted family in Bayreuth, knew what he really meant? How were the citizens of Leipzig to take him at the unveiling of the Wagner monument in 1934, when he spoke of the 'unhappy time through which the Master's will and desire had passed', and of the solemn pledge which, 'hardly able to speak for tears', he now gave that that 'will and desire' would be restored? Was he referring only to faithful performances of the operas? Who, apart from Wagner's daughter-in-law, who was also present, knew what Hitler, 'visibly moved',[22] really had in mind? On another occasion he talked of a 'longing for an ultimate unity to which Wagner had given symbolic form, revealing through one gigantic example how creative power can overcome apparently insuperable obstacles'.[23] What would his supporters have made of this?

The uninitiated might conclude that Hitler was referring to Wagner's notorious financial problems. Or had he in mind, what was familiar only to the Bayreuth circle, Wagner's struggle against his own personal enemy, later taken up by Chamberlain, the enemy he had cryptically declared to be at the same time the arch-enemy of the whole of mankind? Maybe Hitler was drawing attention to the passage in *Mein Kampf* where he declared himself called upon to engage in a 'mighty battle' against this seemingly invincible foe. The interpretations are legion, and he intended it to be so. Sublime or hair-raising – it was a decision not for his contemporaries but for history.

For all this, he was pleased to think that his achievements had not been inconsiderable. When he returned from the front in 1918, his future, insofar as he had one, seemed behind him. Pitched into a Reich stabbed in the back by Jews and torn apart by the Jewish November Revolution, he felt he had plumbed the depths. Wounded and decorated but with no job, he found himself in Munich, Wagner's city, which was now in the hands of the republican enemy. Nearing thirty, with no qualifications, no money and no family, he was back where he had been four years earlier, his hopes dashed.

There being little demand for copies of watercolour paintings in the post-war Bavarian capital, he stayed in his barracks, lived on his army pay and fed bread to the mice in his room, as he wrote. 'When I first met him,' recalled Captain Karl Mayr, the man who 'discovered' Hitler's political potential, 'he was like a tired stray dog looking for a master.'[24] He knew that what he needed was a respectable job with decent prospects, but what of any value had he to put into a letter of application? He decided that the war was in fact not over, continued to wear his uniform, did guard duty at the railway station and felt himself to be engaged in work of national importance. Wagner and Chamberlain had made him aware of the scale of the horrors that had been visited on his Fatherland, from betrayal through the revolution to the imminent downfall of European civilization. A man like Hitler, who went to the opera as others go to church, was able to experience all this in its higher significance in the *Ring des Nibelungen*.

His personal ruin was a fate shared by the nation. And if the Fatherland still retained a spark of hope for revenge and regeneration, as the myths taught, he too could still hope. 'We know', Wagner had declared in his essay 'Shall We Hope?', 'where our un-German barbarians are to be found – in our government, which knows everything except where to find the source of the people's power. Once this has been found, an irresistible need for action will follow, propelled by a sense of inner compulsion. Without this need, truth and virtue can have no proper foundation.'[25]

The concept of national tragedy, invoked by Wagner at the time of the Dresden uprising and used as a rallying-cry ever since, had now become for Hitler a reality. This Unknown Soldier, whose name was regularly misspelled in official documents and who, in an act of pitiful self-denial, put on a red armband and joined the mourners behind the coffin of the assassi-

nated Bavarian President Kurt Eisner, was only waiting for the right moment to be driven into action by the nation's tragic fate.

But for the present he had to survive the 'chaos' and make do with the
theatre as the herald of the future. In February 1919 he and his wartime
comrade Ernst Schmidt were instructed by the Second Demobilization
Company to test the gas masks. That same month, when Eisner was shot,
'releasing a short-lived wave of Jewish domination',[26] Hitler later recalled,
he and Schmidt were to be found unscrewing the filters in gas masks to
check that everything was in order. 'It was a boring job', Schmidt said,
'with whole mountains of the things to deal with.' Hitler used the three
marks per day that he earned to finance his double life. He went to the
opera, persuading his friend to go with him. 'We only bought the cheapest
tickets', reported Schmidt, 'but that did not matter. Right down to the last
note Hitler was lost in the music, blind and deaf to everything around
him.'[27] It was a characterization that did not apply only to Hitler the opera-
goer. He would habitually cut himself off from reality in order to concentrate on his inner world, where a higher form of existence, the fantasy of
'the work of art of the future', was celebrating its Saturnalia.

Hitler's transformation from gas mask tester to opera maniac left his
companion completely baffled. His friend Ernst ('Putzi') Hanfstaengl later
experienced the same phenomenon when Hitler was already leader of the
Nazi Party. 'Nervous and distraught', he was on one occasion in a state of
'near despair' on discovering political intrigue going on behind his back.
He sought consolation from Hanfstaengl, who sat down at the out-of-tune
old piano and began to play a Bach fugue. Hitler showed little interest.
When Hanfstaengl turned to the Prelude to *Die Meistersinger*, the whole
scene changed. This was the music Hitler wanted to hear. 'The next moment he sprang to his feet and strode up and down the room, conducting
with his arms and whistling the melody in a strangely piercing vibrato
with uncanny accuracy. He knew the whole Prelude from beginning to
end. When I had finished, there stood a radiant, totally transfigured Hitler
before me.'[28]

It was the archetype of his mass performances. Starting in a subdued,
hesitant manner, his voice would rise in a gradual crescendo, dwelling on
familiar leitmotifs, finally reaching a feverish climax, performer and conductor in one, oblivious to his surroundings. Then came the audience, who,
as well as the monotonous message of repetitive leitmotifs, experienced a
Gesamtkunstwerk of dramatic acting, Wagnerian *Sprechgesang* and all-
embracing stagecraft. As in the theatre, they broke out into cries of delight
and deafening applause at the end of each scene, until finally, after the
hero, dripping with sweat but utterly transformed, had left the platform,
they shouted and cheered, themselves bringing the evening to an ecstatic
and boisterous conclusion.

With no possessions and few talents, Hitler was to discover his true milieu in Munich, that grand forum for street-corner orators. By a process of theatrical self-projection he was able to take a crowd of people in the most mundane of circumstances and turn them into an hysterical operatic audience. They saw him no longer merely as a commonplace agitator standing in front of his jug of beer but as a spokesman for higher powers, the bearer of tidings sent by destiny, a visionary who at the end, surrounded by the cheering throng, seemed to have become an exhausted victim of the truth that he himself had preached. He was an emissary, carrying sublime messages to the common man. Outsiders saw in him a bizarre figure of ridicule; those in his spell were overcome by a sense of religious inspiration. Whatever they thought of his views, the citizens of Munich soon agreed that he gave value for money.

The fantastic talent that enabled Hitler to escape from the confinement of the barracks was nurtured by the philosophies of Bayreuth. Had he not been absolutely certain of the religious significance of these philosophies and allowed them to penetrate the deepest corners of his being, his unprepossessing appearance would in itself never have succeeded in winning over the masses. He convinced by means of his own passionate conviction, suddenly releasing the pent-up forces that had been building up over years of reading and pondering. The dam finally burst, sweeping all before it.

But the message alone, which he effortlessly reduced to its lowest level of comprehension, would not have sufficed to achieve the kind of mass delirium otherwise found only at meetings of religious sects or performances of Wagner. His success as a demagogue derived from the transference of the ways of the theatre to the world of everyday politics. Affecting the fascination that surrounded a Heldentenor, he launched into the history of his sufferings and his struggles, culminating in the symbolic representation of his tragic downfall, from which he was to arise defiantly into a new, larger-than-life reality. In the course of his performance he would be miraculously transformed from a stubborn little member of the Nazi Party with a hoarse voice into a high priest of racialism, the inspired lyrical prophet of a glorious future which only he could see. In the same way the plebeian crowd in the beer-cellar found themselves converted from a state of alcoholic intoxication to one of aesthetic exaltation, their bodies swaying to and fro to the sound of their raucous voices and their rhythmical clapping. With the appearance of Hitler, an invisible curtain went up and the beer-cellar, decked out with Nazi banners, turned into a Festspielhaus.

The message that Hitler preached, wrote Konrad Heiden, a journalist who fled Germany in 1933, never changed. 'It always came down to the same thing – that everything was to be blamed on the Jews.'[29] It was the old theme, repeated over and over by Wagner and Chamberlain, on which Hitler now wrote his own variations. As though following the ebb and flow of Wagner's musical phraseology, he composed speeches in striking contrasts and with sudden changes of tempo. 'He would begin on a nor-

mal level,' wrote an eye-witness, 'then embark on a gradual crescendo before reaching a climax, which he marked with a powerful final sentence'[30]
– sword blows such as those with which Wagner brought an act to a close.

Even before Hitler began his career as an orator the historian Karl Alexander von Müller referred to his sonorous voice, which he described as
'that of a natural tenor, which seemed to emerge of its own accord once he
had got into his stride'.[31] Hanfstaengl, who had gained his doctorate under
Müller, ascribed Hitler's particular secret to 'the extraordinary power of
his vocal cords and a remarkable head voice. He would play with his voice
as though it were an instrument.' In addition he had 'a whole gamut of
melodramatic touches at his command. He would employ a sensitive vibrato when speaking of the unjust fate that had befallen a wronged and
much-abused nation; in the next section he would predict an impending
storm, then overwhelm his audience with declarations of an immense power
and strength, concluding with a despairing sob.'[32] Siegfried's dying words
in *Götterdämmerung* show what Hanfstaengl was describing. It was these
vocal acrobatics, which included the so-called 'Bayreuth consonant-
spitting', far more than the actual content of his speeches, that gained
him an aura such as no other politician in post-war Germany could claim.
His rivals talked of the fate of the German nation; Hitler sang of it.

'People flocked to listen to Hitler as though they were going to the theatre,' wrote Hanfstaengl. 'It was something quite unique – a play called Hitler written by a dramatist called Hitler.'[33] So was it all just play-acting,
calculated wizardry, the actual substance of which was merely 'the violent
struggle against the Jews, when the opportunity arises',[34] as a police informer wrote in 1921?

Play-acting it was, and the actor was a man with no outstanding qualities who for that very reason was an ideal medium. Something spoke
through him. 'His ideas', observed his one-time comrade Gregor Strasser,
later to be murdered on Hitler's orders, 'come somehow from outside. He
himself cannot grasp them.'[35] After the war his life-long admirer Otto
Wagener attempted to explain the phenomenon with the help of a vocabulary borrowed from the Bayreuth Grail: 'Hitler was pure "word", speaking with a gleam in his eye and a radiant gaze. I absorbed it all – the eyes
and the *logos*, the essence, that he conveyed.'[36]

But the divine message came not from God but from his idol Richard
Wagner. The play he performed may well have been called Hitler but the
script and the staging came from Bayreuth. A piece of theatre, yes, but not
only. It was a question of turning theatre into reality. Wagner's
Weltanschauung, embodied in the drama, had to become political reality.
Wagner himself had searched for the transition from stage hero to ruling
monarch in the person of King Ludwig of Bavaria but had failed. Chamberlain, next in ideological succession, had looked to find a saviour in Kaiser Wilhelm II and had also been disillusioned. Now it was Hitler's turn to

act out his own melodramatic piece aimed at giving world-historical dimensions to Wagner's visions.

Hitler's one-man show, which the above-mentioned police informer described as a 'pogrom', with an incitement to 'robbery, plunder and murder', was designed as a prelude to action. Goebbels, fascinated by Hitler and his ideas, which had a 'profound, mystical effect on me, almost like a Gospel', wrote in his diary in 1926: 'With a shudder I walked with him past the edge of the abyss.'[37] Did Goebbels mean the abyss that opens up when play becomes earnest, theatre turns into reality? What if the sword forged in the orchestra pit at Bayreuth is used to kill real people?

Precisely that was the action which Bayreuth expected of the new Messiah. The Festival itself, indeed, founded in 1872 as a bulwark against the official emancipation of the Jews in 1869, according to Chamberlain, was expected to promote the ideological cause. 'Bayreuth', wrote the poet Hermann Bahr, 'represents a Will, a resolve, that reaches every corner of Germany, a Will that brings everybody within its orbit, empties him, then fills him again. Soon everyone will be a new man. No one can resist.'[38]

The Will in question was Wagner's will, formed since the days of the revolution in 1849, to change Germany by force. The fire-raiser's 'divine spark' had never been extinguished, for after his death the 'Knights of the Grail' had tended it. Cosima, the priestess, was only waiting for the advent of a 'Führer' who would realize that his people were being 'sucked dry by the Jews'[39] and take the necessary steps. Likewise Chamberlain had also demanded that 'thoughts must be turned into actions'.[40]

With the Revolution of 1918 Chamberlain's prophecy appeared to have been fulfilled and the 'German Empire of the Jewish Nation' feared by Cosima to have become a reality.[41] Siegfried Wagner observed sarcastically that the French revolutionaries Robespierre and Marat were actually called Rubinstein and Marx,[42] but there was no longer any need to reveal the identity of their German successors. The mortal enemy had left his visiting card; the only question was, who would now go forth, sword in hand, to meet him?

Cosima had originally looked to the ex-generals Hindenburg and Ludendorff for her answer;[43] Chamberlain, on the other hand, lying on his sick-bed, opted for the younger generation, from whom he hoped for relief from his own sufferings and those of his ailing country. The doors of the Festspielhaus had been officially closed since the outbreak of war and only opened on one occasion in 1921 for a 'patriotic memorial occasion in the spirit of the man who founded this place'.[44] Now it became a symbol of spiritual renewal, with Wagner's music, in Chamberlain's words, as 'a mystic herald of the Will',[45] rousing the nation from its slumbers with the magical sounds of the *Ring* and the *Meistersinger*. 'I feel a certain optimism,' wrote Chamberlain in 1918, 'for Germany is not poor in strong, determined men. If we can bring these men to the fore, the present chaos will be lifted from us overnight like a bad dream.'[46] Nobody in Bayreuth, of course, was prepared to show his true colours. Much as they detested the 'criminals' of the November Revolution and the 'traitors' who had signed the Treaty of Versailles, the Bayreuth elite did not want to draw attention to themselves. They kept in the background, pulling the strings from behind the scene. Siegfried, Wagner's sole son and heir, had learned in Wahnfried how to draw a line between inner commitment and public utterance. In his inner circle he made no attempt to disguise his contempt for the Jews, since, as the SA officer Kurt Lüdecke stated, he fully shared his father's anti-Semitism.[47] To outsiders, on the other hand, he pretended to hold liberal views, not least because the re-opening of the Festival in 1924 was heavily dependent on the Jews both as performers and as financial backers. The Jews had, after all, been traditionally well disposed towards Wagner.

By preserving this dual personality, the Wahnfried clique saved themselves from being unmasked and the Festspielhaus from being closed. After the war Winifred, Siegfried's widow, set the record straight about her overtly non-political husband. He was, she said, 'a thoroughly conscious patriot who had been deeply wounded by the defeat of 1918 and was desirous of making contact with others who were prepared to help rebuild the country'.[48] For this reason, noted his friend Franz Stassen, he had made a 'pact of friendship' with Hitler[49] and 'declared his support for the Führer's struggle'.[50] That Winifred, as many today maintain, was the only Wagner to have been a friend of Hitler's is contradicted by the facts. As Wolfgang later admitted, his mother 'had always taken it for granted that she and her husband were of one mind'.[51]

Since the 'new' Bayreuth, Siegfried Wagner has been considered as belonging to that part of the tradition which deserves to be preserved, unlike Cosima, Chamberlain and Winifred, whom one would have preferred to forget. But Siegfried was far from being a friend of the Weimar Republic. He envisaged Bayreuth as the cultural centre of a Germany restored to strength, for which he sought a director absorbed in the Master's teachings. The hallowed flame that had been guarded in the apparent privacy of Wahnfried would one day ignite the fire of national revolution. The man to light that fire was already waiting outside the door.

PIONEERS

How did Adolf Hitler come to find himself in the role of saviour of the nation – this insignificant little private who resisted a return to civilian life and preferred to do guard duty and check gas masks than go out into the world and earn a living? What predestined this inconspicuous ex-dispatch rider to become the bearer of a nation's hopes, and turn a self-taught intruder from a neighbouring country into the Messiah of the Gospel according to Bayreuth? How did Hitler become 'Hitler'?

Apparently because everything about him was pure theatre. He attached no importance to having an identity of his own – what mattered was his mask. And where there is one mask, there are many. 'He had great talent as an actor', observed his secretary, 'and was very good at impersonating people'[1] – not only other people, moreover, but also the image that he had formed of himself on the basis of his chosen ideals. This corresponded in turn to the role which had been waiting since Wagner's time for someone to fill. And precisely because Hitler himself did not represent anything, he could give himself over entirely to this role.

André François-Poncet, French ambassador in Berlin, identified three aspects of Hitler. The first was that of a 'naïve, rustic man . . . a face like thousands of other faces spread over the face of the earth'. The second was a mask, 'his jumbled complexion and vague globular eyes, lost in a dream, lent him an absent, faraway air, the troubled and troubling face of a medium or somnambulist'. The third François-Poncet described as 'his "storm and assault face" . . . the face of a lunatic', with eyes that 'dart lightning'.[2]

These three were perfectly combined only in his states of ecstasy, whether induced by music or carried away by his own rhetoric. In such moments he played the parts both of hero and sword, and when he also took over the role of producer, he turned the world into his own stage, on which the other actors were mere extras. 'We need a German sword again!' cried one man in rapture, at a demonstration in 1920, 'and this time it will not be called Nothung but the German Workers' Party, with Hitler as its point!'[3] Years later, at a party in General Ludendorff's house, someone dubbed him 'the young Siegfried', in spite of his black quiff and his poor posture.[4] Wherever Hitler was, there, it seemed, Bayreuth was also.

He did not enter the political arena of his own volition. He had to be pushed. To be sure, he had told Kubizek and his comrades in the barracks that he sensed that he would be summoned to become what Nietzsche had called 'an incarnation, a medium, an instrument of mighty powers',[5] but he lacked the necessary self-confidence to appear on the public stage. Had he shown himself in the war to be a natural leader of men, capable of giving orders, he would hardly have been condemned to remain a private soldier. Instead he showed himself to be experienced at carrying out orders, a reliable messenger honoured by the award of the Iron Cross.

And it was to an order that he owed his attendance at the University of Munich for lectures on history, his training in political oratory and his first visit to the Sterneckerbräu beer-hall, where his future party was rehearsing its coup. The order had come from Captain Karl Mayr of the German General Staff, who planned to employ Hitler's striking gifts as an orator in his programme of the 'anti-Bolshevik' re-education of the old imperial army. Mayr, later an opponent of Hitler who died in the concentration camp of Buchenwald in 1945, was the first in the long line of Hitler's political patrons.

The Soviet-style republic in Munich had been overthrown in May 1919. Mayr, charged with overseeing the re-indoctrination of the provisional army, appointed Hitler as an anti-Bolshevik teacher, while suspecting that he would soon be able to employ the ex-private on more important tasks. In September 1920 he wrote to Wolfgang Kapp, leader of the abortive coup in Berlin, that he had found a number of 'promising young men', among them a certain 'Herr Hitler, a first-class speaker. His Workers' Party could well become the core of a company of shock troops we hope to set up.'[6] Now revelling in the title of 'Education Officer', Hitler had been ordered the previous year to present himself at the Sterneckerbräu, where, as they had expected, he had joined in the discussions and shortly afterwards become a member of the German Workers' Party.

This decision, 'the most crucial in my life', Hitler later called it,[7] had been engineered by Mayr and others. Operating behind the scenes, Mayr had provided the little backroom party with a distinctive leader.[8] But Mayr too, he later claimed, had only done what his superior officers had ordered him to do, 'and it had been the express desire of General von Möhl, then Supreme Commander of the German Army, that this man Hitler should attend an interview with him'.[9] In this way, quite unexpectedly, Hitler's stock gradually rose until he became one of the leading lights in the as yet insignificant German Workers' Party.

Appointed in the summer of 1919 to carry out his 'educational' work in the transit camp of Lechfeld, Hitler quickly lighted on the subject that interested him above all others and that promptly brought him into conflict with one of his superior officers. A difference of opinion had arisen over 'whether one should express one's views bluntly and openly or in a veiled form'. As a declared Wagnerian, Hitler 'had expounded the Jewish question above all from the Germanic point of view', whereas the officer in charge advised that 'explicit references to that race which is alien to the German nation should as far as possible be avoided'.[10]

Neither Hitler nor Mayr, a man who, according to Ernst Röhm, later Chief of Staff of the SA, 'was well thought of in nationalist circles',[11] took any notice of this advice. Speaking in oblique terms was not their strong point: one should display one's colours openly. When Mayr, still firmly anti-Semitic at this time, received a letter enquiring what view the Social Democrat government under Friedrich Ebert took on the 'Jewish threat to the nation', he passed the letter to his new assistant to deal with.

The assistant, revelling in his newly discovered powers of oratory, replied like a propagandist for the Bayreuth cause. Like the author of 'Music and the Jews' he proceeds from an instinctive dislike of the Jews, 'which cannot be argued away'.[12] At the same time, he goes on, following the Master, one must move beyond mere feelings and come to realize as an objective reality that we are dealing with a race that has retained its peculiarities to a more pronounced degree than other peoples – Wagner had described it as 'a remarkable case of racial consistency'.[13] The most striking characteristic of the Jews, Hitler goes on, is their urge to make money and gain power: 'they prostrate themselves before kings and princes and at the same time suck out their blood like vampires' – language plucked from Wagner's 'regeneration' writings. Also taken from the Master is Hitler's claim that the power of money and the practice of usury constitute the 'most oppressive yoke' that torments the nation, 'which, dazzled by the golden opportunities dangled before its eyes, failed to recognize the tragic results that would ensue'.[14] This is pure Wagner, who, from the beginnings of the Ring down to the essay 'Know Thyself' at the end of his life, declared the curse of money to be the root of all evil, 'the demon that strangles man's sense of innocence'.

Wagner's 'terrible vision of a ghostly dictatorship of the Jews',[15] eagerly embraced by his pupil, inevitably led Hitler to look beyond occasional pogroms to a solution that went to the root of the problem. 'Our ultimate goal', he declared – this is twenty years before his invasion of Poland – 'must be the removal of the Jews.' And as Wagner had already made clear, this could only mean their removal from both place and time. 'Only when there is no corner in which they can find refuge, no hope for survival in the future, will their fate be sealed.'[16] Hitler will not have failed to be impressed by the fact that it was to the Germans that Wagner looked for the accomplishment of this 'grand solution'.

Wagner's regeneration, described by Hitler as a 'rebirth', could only be achieved, he continued, by 'total commitment on the part of patriotically minded men with a gift for leadership and a sense of unqualified responsibility'. They are words, written a few days after his first contact with the German Workers' Party, that could describe his own political career. That they corresponded almost down to the last detail to the principles that issued from Bayreuth is hardly surprising. And since they were inseparably linked with the heroic role for which he was now being groomed, it was all the more necessary that he should hold fast to these principles. These are the 'granite foundations' of which he wrote in *Mein Kampf*.

Having reached the age of thirty without making any noticeable mark on the world, with no prospects and even reluctant to accept his discharge from the army, Hitler now found himself entering a state of permanent mobilization which lifted him out of the ranks of anonymity to the status of 'a prominent leader of the anti-Semitic movement'.[17] The immense confidence he had in himself as a tribune of the people and as a dragon-slayer, which contrasted painfully with the actual conditions under which he was made to live, was about to justify itself. Hitherto it had been unable to find an outlet; now the gulf between ideal vision and personal inadequacy, between a glorious world of musical grandeur and the pitiful existence of a failed artist, began to close.

The force of Wagner's musical expression now started to penetrate his own voice, his quivering body, his public gestures. What had been negative now became triumphantly positive. Every entrance he made seemed to him like Lohengrin's arrival in Brabant, and every exit left him recalling Siegfried's and Brünnhilde's love duet at the end of *Siegfried*.[18]

Even at the lower end of the social scale, the world of the Munich beer-cellar, from which he had hitherto held aloof, his appearances were rapturously greeted with almost religious ardour. Not that he felt this to be his proper milieu. He was, after all, a messenger from another world who, though the preacher of a message of joy, like Wagner's Knights of the Grail, was bound to avoid answering troublesome questions – indeed, to avoid the common horde itself. Hitler was not a prophet to be touched. He came and went, leaving a community spellbound by his charisma.

From the days of his youth Hitler had felt that his proper social position was not in the world of tavern life but among the 'better classes' to be found in the theatre foyer, or in an aristocratic drawing-room, then in the Bayreuth Festspielhaus and ultimately in his own art gallery, the 'Haus der deutschen Kunst' in Munich. The 'workers' who gave their name to his party were not part of his ambience, and despite his rhetorical assurance to the contrary, he never felt himself constrained to represent their interests. True, they too profited from his political victories. But it was not they, the cheering masses at his rallies who were soon to become cannon fodder for his crusades, who were his main concern – it was an ideal, a dream of which no one other than readers of Wagner and Chamberlain could have any conception. As it was impossible to expect his proletarian cheer-leaders to have any idea of the meaning of 'The Work of Art of the Future', so was it pointless to explain to them what the 'grand solution' was about. In any case the theatrical excesses of his gestures pointed to what his words concealed.

The organizers of these occasions, a mixture of hysteria and brutality that repelled neutral observers, stayed in the background. As in Bayreuth the publicity machine was kept strictly separate from the spiritual realm, so no connection could be traced between Hitler's missionary activities and their organizers. As Cosima never tired of insisting, a subversive struggle depends for its success on secrecy. At the same time she communicated to those around her a sense of community that elevated them, as an elite group, far above the level of the common man.

The men behind Hitler belonged to a secret order that observed rituals like those of a Masonic lodge, used a symbolic language and threatened heretics with summary execution. Even its name, the 'Germanic Order',[19] had to be kept secret, and its members' vow of silence meant that little information about it reached the outside world. The name alone, however, made it clear that its values were those represented by the heroic warriors who abound in Wagner's *Ring* and Chamberlain's *Foundations of the Nineteenth Century*.

Founded in Leipzig in 1912, the Germanic Order, appropriately enough, decked out its propaganda material with motifs derived from Wagner. One of their broadsheets[20] shows Wotan and Brünnhilde, winged helmets on their heads, hastening to meet their invisible foe. A local branch of the order took the name 'Walvater', a synonym for Wotan known only to the few, while another group, later amalgamated with the Germanic Order, called itself the 'Wälsungen Order', after the race that sprang from Wotan. When the Walvater Order set out during the war to recruit men of German blood to its ranks, it appended to its name the appellation 'Lodge H.G.', which Wagnerian insiders had no difficulty in deciphering as 'Lodge of the Holy Grail'.

Induction into the Germanic Order followed a thoroughly Wagnerian pattern. 'The ceremony began with soft music played on a harmonium', according to a report dating from 1912,

and the brethren sang the Pilgrims' Chorus from *Tannhäuser*. Then the novices, blindfolded and in pilgrim's garb, were led into the room by the Grand Master. As the Bard lit the holy flame, the novices' blindfolds and habits were removed and the Grand Master held Wotan's spear aloft. Swords were crossed, and the oath was taken in antiphonal solemnity to the accompaniment of music from *Lohengrin*. Finally the new recruits were admitted to the inner chamber, where the holy flame was burning.[21]

The Order's basic doctrines were unashamedly derived from Wagner, issuing a challenge 'to fight the forces of the Devil and prevent the adulteration of Germanic blood by intermarriage with foreign races'.[22] The word 'Jewry' was avoided but the forces of the Devil were obviously Wagner's 'demon incarnate'. The ways of the enemy, declared the Grand Masters of the Lodge, had to be studied closely before a successful attack could be mounted that would totally eradicate them. The goal was not war but destruction. Quoting a prophecy from the Old Testament, a broadsheet published by the Order announced that the Children of Israel would one day be annihilated by a tribe of Nordic warriors,[23] while, to symbolize their crusade to extirpate the Jews and establish a Germanic Reich, they adopted the sign of the swastika.[24]

Grotesque as such rituals and mystifications may sound, designed to commit the individual to the achievement of the common goal, their implementation was a serious matter. Almost all the assassination attempts made on leading personalities of the Weimar Republic involved the Germanic Order or one of its cells. The racist ideals so passionately preached by Chamberlain were put into practice with the help of revolvers, hand grenades and cyanide sprays. Those who instigated the murder of Kurt Eisner, Matthias Erzberger and Walther Rathenau and organized the attacks on Scheidemann and Maximilian Harden saw themselves as agents of a religious cause; therefore their crimes, most of them directed at Jews, were not subject to the common moral law. With the conversion of the Order's dogma into a policy of terror came an intensification of the need for secrecy, 'since the Order had to protect itself against acts of revenge by the Jews'.[25]

The Munich lodge of the Order achieved particular notoriety. Founded in 1918, it built up a secret front against the influence of Jewry, calling itself 'Thule' – a name taken from a popular collection of heroic Nordic lays issued under this title by the reactionary publisher Eugen Diederichs. A particular feature of this collection was the inclusion of references to the poem of Wagner's *Ring*, which was rarely quoted in editions of the *Edda*. In return Diederichs received Cosima's blessing on his publication of the Master's letters to Hans von Bülow in 1916.

In this way the Thule Society[26] could claim to be merely a literary association interested in Teutonic sagas. For their emblem they adopted Siegfried's sword Nothung, and for their fraternal greeting the *Ring* formulae 'Sieg' and 'Heil'. Their meeting-rooms were hung with swastikas, and members were required to prove their Aryan descent over the previous three generations. This presented a particular problem for one Anton Graf Arco-Valley,[27] a Germanophile army officer who discovered to his embarrassment that he had a racially 'unacceptable' grandmother. To prove his credentials, and presumably also in accordance with the Order's plans, he thereupon shot and killed Kurt Eisner, Minister-President of Bavaria.

Cosima hailed him as a martyr; his victim she contemptuously dismissed as a 'Galician Semite'.[28]

The members of the Thule Society came largely from the Bavarian aristocracy and industrialists but also from the ranks of academics and artists. Their meetings were held in the elegant Vier Jahreszeiten hotel, the owner of which also belonged to the Order, and in which the leaders of the Nazi Party regularly stayed during the years of the Third Reich. In these sumptuous surroundings representatives of German high society came together after the war to plan a reign of terror under the emblem of the swastika. When the republic was proclaimed in November 1918, Rudolf von Sebottendorf, leader of the Thule Society, announced: 'The Jew is our mortal enemy. From today on we shall take action.'[29]

Supported by influential citizens and sheltered in the magnificence of the Vier Jahreszeiten, the Order offered the perfect platform for opponents of the Weimar Republic. It financed private militias which launched brutal attacks on Jews, founded subsidiary lodges which also met in the Vier Jahreszeiten, and gave its support to a terrorist group calling itself the 'Organization Consul', which carried out contract killings of Jewish politicians. The Order's oath of silence ensured that the names of the instigators of these attacks were never mentioned in court.

The first martyrs of the movement also came from the Thule Society. During the attack on the Räterepublik in Munich so-called 'Red Guards' stormed the headquarters of the Order, apparently well informed about its activities, took seven hostages and had them shot on 1 May, 1919. Among the victims were a Prince Thurn and Taxis and a Countess von Westarp, the latter a woman who had gained a reputation as a political organizer. These murders, which aroused far more anger than the massacres carried out by the Freikorps at the same time, marked the beginning of the death cult practised in right-wing circles, a cult that was to reach its climax with the glorification of Hitler's attempted coup of 1923.

As late as 1936 Hitler remembered the members of the Thule Society – 'the ten men and one woman who consciously embodied a new ideal', he called them, 'who never did anything to harm their opponents but lived for one vision alone, that of a new, purer, better society. They were savagely slaughtered in Munich.' And he added ominously, as though to justify in advance the barbarities he was to commit: 'We are well aware who is to be blamed – members of that breed which we hold responsible for the fratricide now ravaging our people, that is, our odious Jewish adversaries. . . . We acknowledge the challenge and we shall pick up the gauntlet.'[30]

The Order learned from the 'Red Revolution' that raiding parties operating covertly were in themselves not sufficient: the government could only be overthrown through control of the streets. The Kapp Putsch of 1920 had collapsed through a lack of popular support because, as the Thule plotters put it, the workers' minds had been 'poisoned with the Jewish ideas of communism and internationalism'.[31] As the soldiers were being re-oriented by Mayr's 'education officers', so the population at large had to have their minds cleared of unpatriotic, un-German thoughts and be made to understand their national duty. The aim was re-education, to be achieved by the creation of a party through which the necessary propaganda could be channelled.

One of the Thule brotherhood, a journalist called Karl Harrer, was charged with setting up a workers' debating society. Out of this grew the German Workers' Party, founded by Harrer and a 'genuine' worker by the name of Anton Drexler, which was pledged to the 'ennoblement of the German working class'.[32] In June 1919 a member of the Order had circulated a pamphlet announcing their intention to clear the ground for the arrival of 'the man who is destined to lead us'.[33] In the following September Captain Mayr, an associate of the Order, presented them with a suitable candidate.

Mayr's protégé gave the impression of being working class and was politically an unknown quantity. At the same time, however, he believed in the twin concepts of a ruling elite and a racially superior master race and energetically preached the anti-Semitic doctrines of the Thule Society as though he had been a member from the beginning. Approval of his activities came from all sides, attracting welcome financial contributions but also new members, among them Heinrich Himmler, Alfred Rosenberg, Hans Frank and Rudolf Hess – the last of whom organized supplies of arms. By some roundabout means Hitler even succeeded in gaining control of the Thule's journal *Völkischer Beobachter*, which enabled him to reach those who were reluctant to attend his infamous meetings.

Hitler's theatrical self-confidence, based on the 'granite foundations' of his *Weltanschauung*, was further boosted by the knowledge that he had behind him 'the most powerful secret organization in Germany'.[34] He felt a far closer affinity with the members of this organization, who, like him, lived a double life, going about their work by day and planning terrorist attacks by night, than with the uniformed louts who marched at his side or the crowds who prostrated themselves at his feet. He knew where he belonged. In the year he seized power his one-time sponsor Rudolf von Sebottendorf, a founder member of the Thule cult who drowned himself in the Bosphorus in 1945, wrote: 'It was to the Thule that Hitler first turned for help, and the Thule that first allied itself with Hitler.'[35]

As the Germanic Order shook the Weimar Republic with its political murders, so its protégé was to destroy it. And that he, a political mass murderer, was to shake the entire world was the achievement of a member of the Thule who gave his ideological fanaticism a practical orientation. The name of this man, who saw in the rising young demagogue the future 'Führer' and at the same time moulded him into an instrument for the destruction of the Jews, was Dietrich Eckart. 'Whenever Hitler mentioned the name Dietrich Eckart', wrote Christa Schroeder, Hitler's secretary, 'tears came into his eyes.'[36] Over twenty years older than his pupil, Eckart became Hitler's 'fatherly friend' and personified more completely than anyone else the *Weltanschauung* that they shared.

Eckart was a journalist and a poet but at the same time, according to Mayr, 'a raving anti-Semite'.[37] And a passionate Wagnerian. The contacts he had had with aristocratic circles since the days of Empire now proved profitable for the Order, and later for Hitler's party, enabling him to combine the popular will for change with a Bayreuthian anticipation of the Messiah to come. His life-style, too, reflected the twin-track strategy of anti-Semitism. To the public he was a 'dissolute poetaster'[38] who spent his days in beer-cellars and his evenings in a night club; to those in the Order, on the other hand, he had the status of a Grey Eminence, a man skilled at forging links with nationalist circles, a man one listened to. Taking Schopenhauer and Wagner as his models, writing doggerel in the style of the Meistersinger which brought him a certain popularity, Eckart proved to have a special feeling for men of extreme natures.

No one was to derive greater profit from Eckart's connection with Bayreuth and with Berlin court circles, with the German General Staff and with industrialists, than Hitler. Mayr may have discovered him and introduced him to the German Workers' Party but it was Eckart who turned him into the party leader who would eventually become dictator of the whole country. Like an impresario, he corrected Hitler's weaknesses and paved the way for his onward march, acting as a publicity agent for the leadership cult for which he had enlisted Hitler's support. And it was he who prepared Hitler for his anointment in Bayreuth.

Johanna Wolf, Christa Schroeder's colleague in the Berlin bunker during the last days of the war, had previously been Eckart's secretary. Hitler will not have forgotten the fact when he took his final leave of his staff. 'Never again', he confided to Fräulein Schroeder, 'did I find a friend with whom I was in such complete harmony, both in thoughts and in feelings.'[39] 'This is the man of the future,' said Eckart, pointing to Hitler. 'One day the whole world will be talking about him.'[40]

Hitler saw to it that people talked about Dietrich Eckart, mentioning him by name at the very end of *Mein Kampf* as though he were his last word on the subject.[41] He died in Berchtesgaden in 1923, not far from the Untersberg and Hitler's Berghof, a man whose name remained hallowed throughout the years of the Third Reich.

In the 'Brown House', Hitler's Party headquarters, a picture of Eckart hung above the Führer's table. School textbooks included his poems among the classics of German literature, and in the Reichstag debate on the Enabling Act in March 1933 Goering paid tribute to his memory.[42] Later that year Hitler unveiled a statue to him in his native town of Neumarkt, in the Upper Palatinate, while in Berlin an open-air theatre was named after him, where in 1939 ten thousand members of the Nazi Party were to receive their marching orders to the music of *Rienzi*.

Eckart's name continued to be invoked during the war. At the anniversary celebrations of the founding of the Nazi Party in 1943 Hitler declared that they owed to their great forebear the capacity 'not only to resist the pressure of the Jews but to utterly destroy them. The call to arms of our unforgettable, faithful old comrade Dietrich Eckart has become a fanfare to awaken us to the fate that would befall us should we fail to frustrate the diabolical plans of the murderous Jews.' At this moment, three weeks before Stalingrad, Hitler could still imply that everything was going according to plan, assuring his listeners that the battle will end 'not with the destruction of the Aryan race but with the eradication of European Jewry'.[43]

The link between Hitler's hint of a 'final solution' and Eckart's poem 'Call to Arms', with its familiar refrain 'Germany Awake!', can only be established with the help of Wagnerian mythology. Wotan calls himself the 'awakener',[44] and in the *Meistersinger* the cultural darkness that covers the land is seen as giving way to a new dawn. That dawn begins with the expulsion of Beckmesser, caricature of a Jew. 'Awake, the dawn is breaking!' sing the chorus, picking up the old Reformation hymn but having in their minds the Germany of the moment, which, as Wagner's Nuremberg leaves its fusty medieval traditions behind, shall rid itself of all its Beckmessers.

Alongside Wagner's chorale, with its double significance, Eckart now set his own radical interpretation: Germany must awake because 'Judas is out to capture the Reich'. 'Sound the alarm', runs his poem, 'and let the earth rise up at the sound of the avenging thunder. Woe to the nation that still slumbers! Germany Awake!'[45] Wagner's hymn, mobilizing the Germans against the peril of foreign domination, became in Eckart's hands a war chant for street-fighters, and the fate awaiting the disgraced plagiarist Beckmesser[46] is turned into a call for vengeance. Eckart was deadly serious – literally so. Right from the very first visit Hitler paid him in January 1920, he made no secret of his views. 'What I would most like', he said, 'is to pack the entire Jewish race into a train and drive them into the Red Sea.'[47]

This was the image in Hitler's mind when he talked of Eckart's 'fanfare'. Years later he reiterated to Goebbels how grateful he had been to his mentor, 'protagonist of a clear, intellectually superior anti-Semitism'.[48] In the line of such protagonists, leading from Wagner to Chamberlain, Eckart now took third place. The fourth, the man of action, would be the last – the remainder were just there to carry out orders.

Like Hitler, Eckart, 'one of the best-known figures in the Bayreuth circle',[49] as he was still described in 1939, had also experienced his spiritual awakening in the opera house. As a twenty-six-year-old journalist he had been sent to cover the Bayreuth Festival, and he remained loyal to the cause ever after. He wrote a collection of 'letters from Bayreuth', which he followed in 1895, the year after his initiation into the Wagner cult, with a political essay on *Tannhäuser*, in which he called on the people of his 'ill-used nation' to fight against treachery and deceit, like Wagner's Minnesinger, and above all to take steps against 'the common vermin that crawl out of those big sacks of money and pollute the whole atmosphere'.[50]

Eckart's next contribution to the Wagnerian world was an introduction to *Parsifal*, written in 1899. When, decades later, Hitler began to wax eloquent about Bayreuth, Wagner and Eckart,[51] it was usually in connection with Wagner's 'sacred festival drama', as Nicolaus von Below recalled. 'The atmosphere in Bayreuth is something wonderful,' Eckart said to Hitler ecstatically. Once, according to Hitler, Eckart related how they walked out to a field behind the Festspielhaus one morning 'in order to give themselves over to the magic of the Good Friday music'.[52] By referring to this key scene in *Parsifal* Eckart must surely have been thinking of the part in history his disciple was destined to play, for it is on the green sward before the Grail Castle that Parsifal, having delivered the kingdom from evil, is anointed as the new King of the Grail.

Like Chamberlain, Eckart set his hopes for the future of Germany on Kaiser Wilhelm II, who commissioned from him an historical drama to celebrate his daughter's wedding. For his hero, Eckart took the Hohenstaufen Emperor Henry VI, son of Barbarossa, 'a monarch driven by a mission to enhance the greatness of Germany'.[53] After the war he became a political journalist, taking his lead from Wagner's *Weltanschauung*. Convinced that the failure of his dramas was to be laid at the door of various Jewish critics who blamed Wagner for any and every undesirable development, he abandoned all disguise and attacked the enemy head-on in a weekly journal with the title *Auf gut deutsch*, or 'Put Bluntly', which he founded in 1918.

Eckart also reached a wide public with his broadsheets which, distributed in their hundreds of thousands, called on the workers of Munich to rise up against the Jews.[54] The enormous costs of his campaign were met partly from his own royalties, partly from benefactors like Kapp and Karl Mayr, and partly also, we may assume, from the fighting fund of the Thule Society. For it was only natural that this propagator of the 'stab-in-the-back' legend and prophet of a worldwide Jewish conspiracy[55] should find his way into the arms of the Thule clique. It was equally natural that his membership should be kept quiet.

Eckart's most important contribution to the Thule philosophy lay in the old Bayreuth tenet that salvation, when it arrived, would come in the form of a charismatic leader, a fusion of Siegfried with his sword and Parsifal with his spear. And since it was also assumed that he would emerge from the ranks of the working class, he would have the masses behind him to help guarantee the victory of the national revolution. After his disappointment with the Kaiser, Eckart pinned his hopes on the nationalistic Junker

Wolfgang Kapp,[56] whose abortive coup in Berlin he supported by suggesting, among other things, that all Jews should be put in a concentration camp – his word was 'protective custody'. In March 1920 Eckart and Hitler hastened to Berlin in the hope, perhaps, of salvaging something from the disaster. Kapp had left the country. But Eckart already knew whom he was going to propose to Ludendorff and other men of influence as the bright new hope of the nation.

Whereas Wagner, in his racist mythology, had consigned the Jews to the 'realm of the night and of death', leaving the heroic Wälsungen to inherit 'the kingdom of life-giving light', Eckart now hailed his disciple as 'a force . . . before which the night will recede'.[57] Exaggerated claims such as this were responsible for making Eckart 'the intellectual founder of the Führer myth in the Nazi Party', as Konrad Heiden put it.[58]

But there were years of work ahead. The prospective leader had to be rid of his provincial awkwardness and his Austrian accent; he needed a respectable wardrobe in place of his shabby army uniform – the legendary trenchcoat was an idea of Eckart's – and his bushy moustache, which accentuated his fleshy nose, had to be trimmed. Above all he had to learn, through regular visits to cafés and restaurants, how to conduct himself in high society. Eckart was also at pains to improve his abysmal grammar and teach him how to control his undisciplined volubility. In fact, his 'paternal friend' took care of everything.[59] Formerly, as an occasional playwright, Eckart used to create tragic heroes for the stage; now he was creating a national saviour for real life.

He also paid for Hitler's introduction into bourgeois conservative society. He once said: 'Whatever contributions found their way into Party coffers through Hitler are ultimately due to me,' adding: 'Where I got my own funds from is no business of the Social Democrats.'[60] It was also necessary to widen the future leader's cultural horizons. Eckart instructed him in the doctrines of Wagner and Chamberlain and took him to the theatre, where, among other things, he saw *Peer Gynt* in Eckart's own much-praised translation. Ibsen's drama remained one of Hitler's favourite plays throughout his life, his interest in the subject extending also to Grieg's incidental music and the later opera (1938) by Werner Egk.

Eckart introduced Hitler to the Viennese author Otto Weininger as a prime example of a writer who showed how to deal with the Jewish question. A Jew who was said to worship Wagner,[61] Weininger had written an anti-Semitic work called *Race and Character* which ascribed all the evil in the world to the Jews and to women. Leaning heavily on Wagner's 'Music and the Jews' and Chamberlain's *Foundations*, Weininger demonstrated the extent to which Wagner's philosophical views had found their way into his operas. In *Der fliegende Holländer* as in *Lohengrin* and *Parsifal*, 'the Jewish problem is clearly formulated', while Siegfried is represented as the embodiment of 'everything that stands for the opposite of things Jewish'.[62]

Weininger thereby created an unbearable dichotomy within himself, and in 1903 he took his own life in the house where Beethoven had died. 'Time and again', wrote Margarete Plewnia in her biography, Eckart would refer to the unhappy Weininger, 'who was torn apart by the conflict between his glimpses of a bright vision of the future and the dark reality of his Jewishness'.[63]

Hitler repeatedly took his lead from Eckart. 'Many of the Jews', he said in December 1941,

> are unaware of the destructive character of their existence. But those who live by the sword must perish by the sword, and they cannot escape their fate. .... Eckart once told me that only once in his life had he met a decent Jew, and that was Otto Weininger, who committed suicide when he realized that the Jews only lived on the decayed remains left by other peoples.[64]

Whether this was the real reason behind Weininger's suicide is uncertain, but Hitler seems to have taken it as a portent of the ultimate solution to the 'Jewish question'.[65]

Besides his intellectual stimulus Eckart established vital personal contacts for Hitler. Acting like the controller of a countrywide network, he introduced him to Berlin industrialists like Emil Gansser and, in Munich, Hans Ulrich Klintzsch, a member of the 'Organization Consul', a body implicated in a number of political assassinations in the 1920s, who went on to play a substantial part in the formation of the SA.[66] Eckart also arranged meetings for Hitler with the racist literary historian Adolf Bartels and the Nazi ideologue Alfred Rosenberg.

The costs of Hitler's activities, including those of his personal bodyguard and the Party newspaper, the *Völkischer Beobachter*, grew day by day, and Eckart was constantly called upon to find new ways of replenishing the Party coffers. He even succeeded in attracting funds from abroad. Through Warren C. Anderson,[67] an American dealer in tractors, he managed to get the great Henry Ford, a notorious Jew-hater who kept his activities secret for fear of a boycott of his products, to contribute to Nazi Party funds. Hitler never forgot these generous donations from the Ford empire.

In these ways Eckart, described by Hanfstaengl as an 'honest idealist with a childlike nature',[68] laid the social foundations for Hitler's rise. He was also a decisive influence on the development of Hitler's thinking. For long before he worked his way to the top of the Nazi Party Eckart had secured his acceptance into the exclusive, well-to-do circle of Wagner admirers. Here the insignificant, anonymous little demagogue from the world of the beer-cellar suddenly found himself treated like an adopted son – encouraged, pampered, adored.

In 1920 Eckart, who owned a right-wing publishing firm, persuaded two leading Munich publishers to throw in their lot with Hitler. One was Julius

Friedrich Lehmann, born in 1864, who had made his fortune through medical textbooks, racist brochures and official naval publications. An active member of the Thule, Lehmann became a supporter of the Pan-German League, then, convinced that the salvation of the country lay in Hitler's hands, joined the Nazis. He also ran a training camp for the Freikorps in his castle in Franconia. Lehmann, one of those involved in the abortive coup of 1923, was in addition the father-in-law of Hitler's comrade-in-arms Friedrich Weber, who commanded a detachment of the Freikorps and was later Hitler's cell mate in Landsberg prison.[69]

Lehmann's connection with Bayreuth can be traced back to the time before the First World War. In 1911 he published Leopold von Schroeder's *Consummation of the Aryan Mystery in Bayreuth* and later the same author's biographical sketch of Chamberlain; in 1917 he secured Schroeder's appointment as editor of the patriotic handbook *Deutschlands Erneuerung* ('The Renewal of Germany'). Heinrich Class, leader of the Pan-German League, was also one of the contributors to the *Monatszeitschrift für das deutsche Volk* ('Monthly Journal for the German Nation').

Of far greater importance for Hitler was the second of these two publishers, the firm run by the Bruckmanns, husband and wife, whose art books were extremely popular throughout the country. Hugo Bruckmann, born in 1863, was an old friend of Cosima Wagner's. He was the publisher of Chamberlain's biography of Wagner and of his *Grundlagen*, for which Cosima rewarded him with the permission to publish Wagner's autobiography *Mein Leben* in 1911. Although Bruckmann was an early member of the Nazi Party[70] and was given a state funeral at Hitler's behest on his death in 1941, it was his wife Elsa, a Romanian born in 1856, who acted as the firm's titular head in its dealings with the dangerous revolutionary Hitler, presumably in order to protect the firm's reputation.

Officially, therefore, it was Elsa Bruckmann who invited the political newcomer, now a man of thirty-three, to her magnificent villa in Munich's Karolinenplatz, showering on him the fulsome attention that Hanfstaengl found so out-of-place. She arranged parties for him and gave him not only money but expensive gifts. 'I no longer need the enclosed wristwatch,' she once wrote, inviting him to the house to select 'anything you might find useful'.[71] During the time he was barred from speaking in public, the firm's offices were made available for him to give private talks which made him a centre of attraction in well-to-do circles. The Bruckmanns went even further, introducing him to the powerful industrialist Emil Kirdorf, who quickly fell under the ambitious young politician's spell. 'I had signed a bill of exchange for the Party for 40,000 marks', Hitler later told his secretary, 'and the due date came closer and closer without there being the slightest chance that I could find the money. I even considered shooting myself. Then, four days before it became due, I told Frau Bruckmann of my embarrassing situation. She immediately

telephoned Geheimrat Kirdorf and told me to go and see him.'[72] Kirdorf
gave him the money.

It was, however, neither the young hero's social qualities nor, as was
rumoured, an old lady's secret passion that opened the door to all these
favours; it was what Hanfstaengl called 'a shared reverence for Wagner
and Bayreuth, coupled with the fact that Chamberlain, Wagner's son-in-
law and defender of the cause of the "Aryan spirit", was one of Bruckmann's
authors, that was the decisive factor in establishing this "ideological affinity"'.[73] Hanfstaengl, whose family was among the leading promoters of
the Munich Wagner cult and therefore welcomed Hitler in their midst, knew
only too well the nature of this affinity.

Having organized such and other contacts, Eckart would return to the
beer-halls and bars where he felt most at home. Or, if there was a warrant
out for his arrest on a charge of slander, as sometimes happened, he would
hide himself away in a farmhouse somewhere in the Berchtesgaden area.[74]
Towards the end of his life he was said to have realized how mistaken he
had been about his protégé, whose success, he now saw, had gone to his
head. He was particularly enraged, according to Hanfstaengl, by Hitler's
boast that he would clear up the situation in Berlin as Christ cleared the
moneylenders out of the temple. 'The raving of a megalomaniac', was
Eckart's reaction, 'somewhere between a Messiah complex and Neroism'.[75]

Whether Eckart meant this in the way that Hanfstaengl claimed to remember it in 1970, may be open to dispute. Driving the Jewish moneylenders out of the Germanic temple was, after all, one of his own main
claims, and it had long been no secret who, in the Wagner–Chamberlain
tradition of an Aryan Jesus, was the man chosen to do it. Was the 'cunning
fox' trying to provoke a rash retort? At all events, in the political testament,
in verse, that he wrote in November 1923 in his prison cell, Eckart em-
phatically reaffirmed his confidence in his temporarily silenced pupil. Even
in defeat, after all, Hitler remained his creature.

'O stupid Germans!' cried Eckart after the failed coup – 'showing their
gratitude to Hitler with blasphemies and by throwing themselves into the
arms of their Hebrew rulers!' 'Thank Heaven', he concluded bitterly, 'that
what Hitler planted was quickly dug up, so that he did not have to experience the shame of having liberated such a worthless rabble!'[76] Twenty-two
years later, as he faced his nemesis in the Berlin bunker, similar suspicions
seem to have crept into the mind of his pupil.

When Eckart died in 1923 he regarded both himself and his pupil as
political failures. He could not know that, following the mythological pattern, defeat through treachery and naked violence would be the guarantee
of a political rebirth. This seems to have been the interpretation put on
Hitler's disappearance from the scene by the Bayreuth circle. Support for
him was doubled, internal propaganda intensified, and letters were written to the press. Under the slogan 'Now more than ever!' work began on

his rehabilitation. The underground activities of the Nazi Party were subject to a strict vow of silence, so we can only assume that Wahnfried was responsible for engineering his successful comeback.

Another name inseparably linked with Hitler's meteoric rise and fall is that of Edwin Bechstein, of the famous family of piano manufacturers who had supplied Wagner with instruments since 1864. The cream of Berlin's musical life was to be found in the Bechstein villa – Franz Liszt, Cosima's father; Cosima's first husband Hans von Bülow, a friend of the firm's founder; and Karl Klindworth, who made piano reductions of Wagner's operas for the Master. Klindworth, born in 1830, was the oldest surviving champion of the Wagnerian cause and was still in close contact with Bayreuth.

In March 1920, Kapp's attempted Putsch over, Eckart visited the Bechstein villa, followed by an awkward, sinister-looking man in a trenchcoat who spoke dialect. Eckart introduced him as the future saviour of the nation, and soon the Bechsteins rivalled Wahnfried in their expectations of him. Since Hitler had firm roots in the Wagnerian ethos and was determined to turn it into reality, the Bechsteins convinced themselves that, as Edwin's wife Helene put it, they had found 'Germany's young Messiah'[77] and were prepared to risk their wealth, their contacts and their reputation in his support.

The most vital need was for him to be made presentable in conservative circles, a process that Eckart had already begun. As in the case of the Bruckmanns, the master of the house stayed in the background and left the task to his wife, who was less directly concerned with the running of the firm. Hitler, who preached openly against the Jews while secretly planning a *coup d'état*, was a potential terrorist and traitor, and as such of interest to the secret police, whereas a society dame such as Helene Bechstein could be active on behalf of her protégé without arousing suspicion. The wolf had to be domesticated and the sombre, grim-faced bachelor turned into a confident, relaxed gentleman. So earnestly did Frau Bechstein take her duties that she pretended to be his adoptive mother in order to be allowed to visit him in jail.

According to Winifred Wagner, Frau Bechstein 'fed and clothed him and instructed him in the basic forms of etiquette', of which, as a village boy, he was evidently ignorant. And, of course, she took him to the opera, where he sat in her box and looked down – in both senses – on those in the standing areas below. Having provided him with money, she also 'arranged receptions at which to introduce him to people of influence'.[78] The claim that Hitler was a self-made man is pure fiction. But he was ideally suited to the role for which he was being groomed, a role into which he slipped with ease as though it was his own real identity. To those who witnessed the transformation, above all the Bayreuth circle, it was like a miracle.

For the food that he was served on silver platters by liveried waiters in the Bechstein villa in Charlottenburg or in the Bayerischer Hof in Munich he had 'nothing but praise'.[79] Champagne flowed and he was even taught how to eat artichokes. In the bathroom, to his delight, he found he could regulate the temperature of the running hot water. Soon he was wearing a dinner jacket, starched shirts with cufflinks and patent leather boots, with a dog-whip of the kind carried by Wagner – this latter a personal gift from Frau Bechstein. The metamorphosis from army private to man of the world was quickly accomplished; indeed, it appears to have given the adoptive parents considerable pleasure, and wherever they went, he went too.

As Hanfstaengl saw it, Hitler was 'somewhat naïve' in his reaction to cultured society. Yet this was the secret of his success. He was like Siegfried, a young hero with no talents and little knowledge, yet who in the end succeeds in forging the sword. Or like Parsifal, Wagner's 'guileless fool', who does not even know his name but is the one chosen to deliver the country from evil. Hitler learned refined manners, gallant gestures and the thousand-and-one little forms of etiquette that endeared a man to polite society. As a skilled copier possessed of a prodigious memory, he took note of everything, and it was not long before he cut an elegant figure in the noblest circles of the land. The airs and graces of the 'old school' which he affected even impressed the young Wolfgang Wagner.

Helene Bechstein's efforts succeeded. With instruction in deportment and courses in elocution Hitler gradually worked his way up. By 1921, Goebbels wrote, the Bechsteins' villa had become 'Hitler's salon',[80] and later their house on the Obersalzberg mountain was amalgamated with Hitler's Berghof retreat, Bechstein assuming financial responsibility for the whole property. In the early 1920s he conferred in Charlottenburg with Bechstein, Eckart and Class over a proposal to extend the influence of their movement northwards,[81] and on another occasion with Count Yorck von Wartenburg over transferring the Party's headquarters to Berlin.[82] In 1933, on the point of assuming absolute power, he also used his patrons' villa to receive General von Hammerstein, emissary of Chancellor Kurt von Schleicher.[83]

There was no end to the Bechsteins' support. They provided him with money and valuable *objets d'art*, sent him, albeit too late, a car in which to escape after the November Putsch, and kept in close contact with him during his time in Landsberg prison, acting as intermediaries between him and the officials of his leaderless party. In return Helene Bechstein received the original manuscript of *Mein Kampf*, which Hitler had written in prison on paper provided by Wahnfried.

Nor was Hitler the Bechsteins' only adopted child. In a letter to him in Landsberg Winifred Wagner wrote, as a casual item of information: 'In Berlin we shall be staying with our common friends the B . . . ns. I do not need to tell you that you will be with us in spirit.'[84] The B . . . ns were more to Winifred than 'common friends' – Edwin Bechstein had in fact been her guardian. Officially, to be sure, responsibility for the education of the orphaned Winifred had been given to Karl Klindworth, but at the time of their first visit to Bayreuth he was a man of eighty-four and hardly capable of fulfilling such a role. Admittedly, Winifred spent most of her time in boarding-schools, but she needed a home with children of her own age, not one like a museum, dominated by aged relatives. The Bechsteins were rich, had experience of rearing children and subscribed to the strict Bayreuthian principles to which Klindworth expected his little 'Senta', as he called her, to be raised.[85] Wahnfried tried to hush the matter up but Du Moulin Eckart, Cosima's official biographer, states categorically that Winifred was taken to Berlin and brought up first by Klindworth, then in the house of Edwin Bechstein.[86]

Does this mean that the young woman who was later taken to Bayreuth in order to present a son and heir to Wagner's son Siegfried was brought up in the same house and in the same spirit as the man who was to find his way to Bayreuth in order to transmute the spirit of Wagner into political reality? The key role played by the Bechsteins was confirmed by Winifred's daughter Friedelind. 'Edwin Bechstein, the famous piano manufacturer,' she wrote, 'was my mother's guardian, and it was during a visit to him in Munich that she caught the Hitlerian fever.'[87] From that time onwards Wahnfried went into raptures over 'the saviour of the nation'.

11

AN OFFICIAL BLESSING

Wagner had the same significance for Hitler's personality as did Wahnfried for his career. As the inner workings of his consciousness took their bearings from the coordinates of Wagner's universe, so his political career followed the lines laid down by Bayreuth. It was neither the 'Brown House' in Munich nor the Reich Chancellery in Berlin that stood at the centre of his world but the Master's Villa Wahnfried and the Festspielhaus – something he suspected his enemies also knew. 'I trust you are aware of the fact', Friedelind Wagner overheard him say, 'that in the next war the first bomb will fall on the Festspielhaus and the second on Wahnfried.'[1]

There are contradictory versions of when and how Hitler first came into contact with Bayreuth. According to Winifred, the mistress of the house, the family first met him in Wahnfried on 1 October, 1923; up till then, she stated after 1945, he had been completely unknown to her.[2] Her daughter Friedelind, on the other hand, maintained that long before this her mother had 'caught the Hitlerian fever' at the Bechsteins and then brought it back with her to Bayreuth.[3]

Friedelind's account is confirmed by Bertha Geissmar, one-time secretary to the conductor Wilhelm Furtwängler, who was well acquainted with goings-on at Wahnfried. 'It must have been a great experience for Hitler', she wrote, 'to meet Wagner's attractive young daughter-in-law in the Bechsteins' house in Munich.'[4] As Ernst Hanfstaengl claimed that it was Dietrich Eckart[5] who first brought Hitler and the Wagners together, we can imagine the historical encounter taking place in the luxury of a drawing-room in the Bechsteins' villa, where Eckart introduced the champion of the Wagnerian religion to Winifred Williams, the Bechsteins' ward.

Exactly when the first meeting took place is also a matter of dispute. Whereas Wolfgang Wagner agrees with his mother that it was 1 October, 1923,[6] Hitler's photographer Heinrich Hoffmann and Friedelind Wagner both put it a good deal earlier, the former by one year, the latter by several. 'When Winifred joined the party in 1920 or 1921', wrote Friedelind from exile in the United States, 'she was one of the first few hundred to do so.'[7] Only after the party was re-founded in 1925 after having been proscribed 'did she receive a membership number in the eighty-thousands' – although it is hard to imagine that so prominent and self-confident a woman would join the party of a man described as a 'phenomenon' without having met him first. After all, Bayreuth itself was hardly unbiased.

In her statement to the de-Nazification court in 1946, in which she attempted to clear her name, Winifred claimed that she had only joined the Nazi Party in 1926 'in response to Hitler's urgings'. She admitted that there had been a local branch of the party in the town of Bayreuth but denied that any of the members of the Wagner family had ever joined.[8] It would in any case have been unnecessary, for Wahnfried was the source of the *Weltanschauung* that the Nazi Party was committed to disseminate. What Hitler believed, Wahnfried believed. 'All the aims of National Socialism', said the Führer to the local branch of the Party, 'are contained in the works of Wagner.'[9] And after the war Franz Beidler, a grandchild of Wagner's, wrote that if the Nazis did have an ideology, then 'it reflected to a frightening extent the *Weltanschauung* of Bayreuth'.[10]

That the name of Hitler had been known in Wahnfried at a time when hardly anyone had heard of a German Workers' Party is a fact corroborated by Winifred herself. According to Erich Ebermayer, her defence lawyer at the de-Nazification proceedings, the poet Michael Georg Conrad and the music critic Josef Stolzing-Czerny visited Wahnfried in the summer of 1919 and mentioned the foundation of a new national political party, together with the name of 'a charismatic firebrand called Adolf Hitler'; the Wagners had been interested 'but soon forgot the name'.[11]

This sounds improbable. Conrad and Stolzing-Czerny were highly thought of in Wahnfried. The former, born in 1846, a benefactor of up-and-coming young talents such as Thomas Mann and Siegfried Wagner, had been a friend of the Master's and active in the Wagnerian cause since the 1870s. In 1903 he wrote an offensive anti-Semitic article against the plan to perform *Parsifal* in New York and was given a fine. The Germans, wrote Conrad, should view Wagner as 'a man sent by God[12] . . . and themselves as a new-born nation infused with Wagner's spirit and art, and with an iron will to assume the leadership of the whole world.'[13] As 'a courageous defender of the Grail',[14] he was even awarded the town's silver medal for services to the community.

Stolzing-Czerny had similar credentials. An author published by Julius Lehmann, he had made his mark with a pamphlet in which he described

the path that led 'from an Aryan *Weltanschauung* to the rebirth of Germany';
he subsequently became editor-in-chief of the *Völkischer Beobachter* and was
appointed chairman of the Bavarian Press Association in 1933.[15]

It is highly unlikely that the local Bayreuth branch of the Nazi Party
could have been formed in November 1922 without the knowledge of the
Wagners, the most influential family in the town. In April 1924 Hitler wrote
to thank Siegfried for his part in securing a successful election result – 'a
result mainly due to the efforts of you and your wife'.[16] Whether the del-
egation sent by the Bayreuth Nazi Party to the first national party congress
in January 1923 included anyone from Wahnfried is not recorded. At all
events Winifred was not the only active sympathizer. Paul Bülow, writing
in the official chronicle *The Führer and Bayreuth* in 1936, stated: 'Siegfried
and Winifred Wagner, Houston Stewart and Eva Chamberlain and Daniela
Thode all declared fearlessly, openly and with genuine enthusiasm support for Adolf Hitler and acknowledged his outstanding qualities of leadership.'[17] This may well have appeared accurate in 1936, with the new
chancellor firmly established, but in 1923 no one could have known that.
Nor was elitist Bayreuth, its collective mind fully devoted at that time to
re-opening the Festival, the place where young talents of obscure origin
were discovered.

So what did Wahnfried see in this radical new politician who had found
his way to their door? Nothing beyond what they themselves had read
into him. The need for a national leader – the role that Hitler was soon to
assume with frightening realism – had been identified by Wagner, by Chamberlain and Cosima's 'Knights of the Grail', then by men like Eckart, Conrad
and Stolzing-Czerny long before Hitler appeared on the scene. All that
was left for him to do was to apply for the vacant position, and what had
started in mythology would become historical fact. Upper-class families
like the Bechsteins, the Bruckmanns and the Hanfstaengls were left to add
a final polish to his deportment, get him to leave his barrack-room ways
behind him, introduce him to high society and supply him with the necessary funds. By 1923 the finished product was ready to be delivered to
Wahnfried.

To judge from the ecstatic tones with which Wahnfried received him,
they really did believe that a new Messiah had come into their midst.
Carried away by their utopian vision, they believed what they wanted to
believe. The religious rapture that gripped both Chamberlain and
Winifred, the young mother, together with the two spinsterish aunts and
the homophile Siegfried, was utterly genuine, and, in Winifred's case,
had unmistakably erotic overtones. Her passion proved contagious and
the town of Bayreuth came to share it. Here was the saviour, the redeemer
all had been desperately looking for. Why ask where he had come from?
They anxiously sought to see in his blue eyes and delicate hands the superhuman qualities of the herald of their salvation, so that, mindful of

the story of Lohengrin, they might invest him with the attributes of a divine origin. In reality, they had to admit, he looked little like an Aryan hero.

Having nothing to offer but the role he had been practising for years to take over, Hitler did his utmost to live up to expectations. He avoided things 'human' in order to live up to the 'divine' qualities people saw in him. And he would only allow himself to be judged by one standard – that of his 'forerunner' Richard Wagner. As late as 1927, firmly established as the leader of his party and listening to nothing other than his 'inner voice', he was still concerned to receive the approval of his Bayreuth family. 'The time will come', he wrote to Winifred, 'when your pride in your friend's [that is, his own] achievements will be my gratitude for so much that at this moment I cannot repay.'[18] Wahnfried would indeed be proud of him. He was the chosen one, his coming predicted by his Master, 'the greatest prophet the German people have ever known'.[19] He was the embodiment of the ideal German invoked by Wagner in his operas, a blend of the heroic and the hallowed in whose hands the realization of the 'grand solution' lay. 'After all sense of false shame has been overcome', the Master had declared, 'we must not flinch from the final decision,'[20] the decision that will lead to the removal of the Jews from the face of the earth. But he, Adolf Hitler, had jettisoned this shame. He saw himself as a 'dragon-slayer'. And to demonstrate this, he now presented himself in the city of his dreams.

In Friedelind Wagner's recollection it was on a sunny May morning in 1923 that Hitler paid his first visit to Wahnfried. He was announced to Cosima, waiting on the first floor, as 'the saviour of the nation', a man Winifred had met in Munich.[21] But as it was not until the 1st of October that year that Hitler actually presented himself at the villa, it was assumed that Friedelind's account was unreliable. Her error can, however, be explained, for in reality Hitler had turned up earlier in Bayreuth.

In April 1923, after a visit to the Bechsteins' villa in Berlin, Hitler felt a sudden urge to go to Bayreuth. Since the owners of the house were away, he and his friend Ernst Hanfstaengl decided to have a look at the Festspielhaus. As they wandered among the dusty sets of *Der fliegende Holländer*, which had not been dismantled since the outbreak of war in 1914, Hanfstaengl noticed a peculiar change come over his companion. 'Listening attentively to every word I said', wrote Hanfstaengl, 'he pressed me to tell him everything I knew about Wagner's early years as Kapellmeister in Dresden.' Spellbound, he listened as Hanfstaengl talked about his great-grandfather Ferdinand Heine, designer of the first performance of *Rienzi*, who had been a friend of Wagner's, and also about those in his family who had painted portraits of the Master. Yesterday, wrote the baffled Hanfstaengl, Hitler had been an unpleasant, opinionated know-all, but today, 'a grateful listener who hung almost in awe and reverence on every word I uttered about his God'.[22]

Already at this stage in his life, the 'poor devil' from the Stumpergasse, who had painted watercolours for a Jewish clientele by day in order to be able to indulge his passion for the Nibelungen in the evenings, could look back on an extraordinary career. By dint of his oratory, his years of evening study and the patronage of some of the highest in the land, the mythomaniac had himself become a myth in which people believed as blindly as he himself believed in the Wälsungen. Not by virtue of his abilities or his accomplishments was he set on a pedestal but for the sake of the future in which these abilities and accomplishments would automatically find their place. What counted was not where he had come from but where he was going.

In order to reach the goal, unchanged since Wagner, of liberation from the Jewish yoke, his supporters smoothed his path so unobtrusively as to make it seem as though the hand of destiny were involved in everything. Similarly what was put down to his strength of will was in fact the result of meticulous planning. He was fitted with the image of a man who needed support, then helped to appear in public as a man who needed no help. Like Wagner's heroes, he was presented as one who started out with nothing and achieved everything.

His apparently irresistible rise to power – which ran curiously parallel to the course of post-war inflation – caused Hitler himself to talk of a miracle, and, feeling himself the incarnation of operatic values, he found no difficulty in offering an appropriate spectacle to his ostentation-loving audience. In July 1921, thanks largely to Eckart's support, he had become leader of the Nazi Party and in September 1923 had taken control of a small private army which various military units sponsored by the Thule Society had also joined. The question now therefore arose whether he was to be seen only as the head of a political movement or as the potential leader of the whole German nation. It was a question that he himself – indeed, the man to whom the masses flocked 'as to a redeemer'[23] – seems to have pondered.

In view of his nondescript career so far he might well have had doubts from time to time about the authenticity of his position, especially as others might have seemed more suitable for such a role. There was General Ludendorff, for example, bedecked with medals and a martyr of the 'stab-in-the-back' legend, who had moved to Munich in 1920 and turned his house into a national shrine. Or the lawyer Heinrich Class, leader of the nationalist Pan-German League, who had never ceased to instill in his supporters the slogan 'We await a Führer!'[24] – presumably meaning himself. Even Hitler, who was twenty years younger than Class, seems to have envisaged him in the role. In May 1922 he went so far as to declare that he himself was not the leader 'to rescue the sinking ship of state' because he 'needed a bigger man behind him'[25] – a remark taken to refer to Class.

But a year later it was no longer Class who would speak through Hitler but a far greater figure. 'We are all little John-like figures,' he declared in

1923, not so much with the Bible in mind as Richard Wagner, adding the mystifying words: 'I am waiting for the Christ figure!'[26] The John to whom he refers is not the Baptist of the New Testament but the legendary figure at the centre of Wagner's *Meistersinger*. 'Hans' is the diminutive of 'Johannes', the German John, and in the character of 'Hans from the River Pegnitz',[27] as he describes him in his libretto, Wagner saw the model for his national hero Hans Sachs. As the prophet in the Bible proclaimed the coming of the Son of God, so Wagner's Mastersinger announces the awakening of the oppressed nation and at the same time the triumph of the young Germanic hero Walther von Stolzing. Thus Hitler was not, as he made his public believe, waiting for the Christ of the Church but waiting for the Aryan redeemer who, in Wagner's scheme of things, would by his blood bring about 'the divine purgation' of the threatened race.[28] Wagner's redeemer was as far removed from the Jesus of the Gospels as National Socialism was from Christianity.

But who would emerge as the new saviour to drive the Jews out of the temple of the Fatherland and 'restore the blood of the noblest of nations'? Hitler, as theatrical producer, set the solemn scene for his entrance at the first Party rally in Munich in 1923, which was celebrated with all due ritual pomp and circumstance. Those who believed they were attending a political demonstration soon realized their error. It was a moment not for party programmes but for prophecies. Whoever expected concrete measures found themselves fobbed off with phrases about the future of the Aryan race. 'No one can describe the feverish air of expectancy that swept through the audience as the Führer entered the hall', wrote the historian Karl Alexander von Müller, 'caught in the white heat generated by the hypnotized masses! Through the middle of the waving flags and the cheering thousands the Man of Destiny, his right arm outstretched, marched resolutely to the podium, followed by his vassals.' At close quarters 'his pale, narrow features seemed to be clenched in an expression of frenetic rage, cold flames shot out of his protruding eyes, which glanced hastily from left to right as though in search of potential enemies to strike down' – in fact, an operatic hero setting out to slay dragons, urged on by tumultuous applause from the audience. 'Did he derive his enigmatic power from the masses', wondered Müller, 'or was it conveyed from him to them?'[29] The climax of this fusion of theatre and reality came with the dedication of the first *Rienzi* banners, designed by Hitler himself, which, with their swastika and their slogan 'Germany Awake!', were soon to set out on their triumphant march through the country.

Similar revolutionary religious assemblies were held the same year in Nuremberg, Coburg and Bayreuth, where the swastika was excitedly hailed by thousands upon thousands as the symbol of a new religion. A mixture of religious worship, sermons, parades and the dedication of party banners, these 'German rallies', as they were called, resembled the regeneration of those charismatic sects which practised baptism by the fire of the Holy Spirit. Like the recipients of divine inspiration, people stood in serried ranks waiting for the arrival of the Messiah who would liberate them 'from slavery and oppression'.[30] Hitler's cohorts too, parading through the cobbled streets with flags waving and music playing, proclaimed, in deliberate allusion to the origins of Christianity, 'that we seek national revolution with the swastika. And under this sign we shall be victorious!'[31]

This pseudo-religious tone, owing much to *Parsifal*, created an atmosphere in which the individual, certain of imminent deliverance, could surrender himself to a collective emotionalism. With equal sureness of touch Hitler also played on the emotions associated with the very opposite world, that symbolized by Siegfried's sword. It was like a change of scene on the stage, the mystical world of the Grail Castle, enveloped in the music of the spheres, suddenly giving way to the wild, rocky landscape of the *Ring* with the pounding rhythms of the Ride of the Valkyries. On the one side a mystical promise, on the other an appeal for strength of will and iron determination. 'The only thing that can rescue Germany', declared Hitler in May 1923, 'is the dictatorship of the nation's will. It is not our task to seek out the individual – the individual is either God-given or not given at all. Our task is to forge the sword the individual will need once he is there. Our task is to give the dictator, when he comes, a people that is ready for him. Germany Awake! The day is nigh!'[32]

Few of his listeners will have recognized in these last words the quotation from Wagner's *Meistersinger*. But none will have failed to realize that standing before them was a prophet, a man proclaiming the dawn of a new age, a new divine kingdom. After one such pseudo-religious occasion, recalled Karl Alexander von Müller, 'the stocky, red-faced little figure of Dietrich Eckart suddenly jumped on to a table and began to declaim at the top of his voice, gesticulating like a madman, his poem "Germany Awake!" He was a man out of his mind, a man turned into a maniac.'[33]

Throughout his demonstrations of 1923 Hitler had preached with the passion of a religious zealot of the sword that only the chosen one, the Messiah to come, would be able to wield. On 30th September that year he made his entry into the city 'in which the spiritual sword with which we fight today was forged'. Naturally only a man who knew this weapon would be able to handle it; in other words, only the man who had assimilated the spirit of Bayreuth could wear the sword; and that man would know that the sword was nothing other than this *Weltanschauung* of Bayreuth. It only received its true meaning when its razor-sharp blade forced reality to yield to its strength – when the talking stopped and the fighting began.

Long before Hitler appeared on the scene, Bayreuth had been the spiritual armoury in which the weapons needed for the struggle were stored. Back in 1901 Chamberlain had called it 'a symbol of the battle that would be waged by the Master's faithful followers'.[34] In 1914, the year Siegfried

Wagner was sent to the western front, Festival audiences had rejoiced at the cries of 'Nothung, Nothung!', while two years later the nationalist artist Franz Stassen designed a war emblem for the town in which the sword of the Wälsungen, 'new and rejuvenated',[35] proclaimed the German victories over the French dragon. And it was here that the young National Socialist movement had its first success,[36] when Hitler arrived with his blood-red flags, his waving banners, the stormtroopers with their batons, ex-servicemen's organizations, all greeted by thousands with shouts of 'Heil!' and showered with garlands of flowers – a *Meistersinger* parade of men and women singing and playing which older townsfolk still recall today. The 'drummer', as Hitler liked to call himself, had summoned his troops to parade in the town to the creator of the *Gesamtkunstwerk*, here, surrounded by his stalwart supporters, to stake his claim as a crusader for a cause in the only place where, under the constant gaze of the Master, he could receive blessing.

Whether he was merely the 'drummer' for a greater figure or was himself the awaited saviour was something he himself could not decide. However much he might feel himself to be that saviour, he needed an endorsement from on high. Only one man had the authority to recognize in Hitler the promised redeemer – the spiritual leader of the heirs to the Wagnerian kingdom, Houston Stewart Chamberlain. The Master's son-in-law and author of *Foundations of the Nineteenth Century*, which Hitler had read and digested as a young man,[37] Chamberlain alone had the power to declare this voluble leader of a small splinter party to be the redeemer of the Germanic race. 'During the first years after the defeat of 1918', wrote Winifred Wagner's friend Erich Ebermeyer, 'the inhabitants of Wahnfried were desperately looking for someone to rescue them.'[38] That someone was now standing at the gate.

In the quietness of the evening at the rally of 1923, as the party legend later described it, 'there occurred one of the most significant meetings in the history of Bayreuth – indeed, of the whole National Socialist movement – when Adolf Hitler shook hands with Houston Stewart Chamberlain . . . the moment when the prophet of the Third Reich felt that the destiny of Germany would find its joyful fulfilment in this simple man of the people'.[39] Less fulsomely Theodor Heuss, then a university lecturer in politics in Berlin, called Chamberlain an 'ageing figure' whose popularity was waning; the appearance of Hitler on the scene, according to Heuss, gave Chamberlain the satisfaction of seeing 'that his own earlier success in print was now being given a political dimension through action'. As Bayreuth had been looking for a new Siegfried and believed they had now found him, so the 'tribune of the people' saw himself as being offered the Bayreuth seal of approval. Whereas Hitler's anti-Semitism had hitherto been basically emotional in origin, concluded Heuss in 1932, 'he now found it formed part of a historical and philosophical context'.[40]

Heuss, who became the first President of the German Federal Republic after the Second World War, overlooked the fact that Hitler had long since secured this intellectual consolidation of his position. Besides that, Heuss was mistaken about the origins of Hitler's hatred of the Jews. He did, however, identify what linked the Austrian private and the Germanophile English philosopher. In contrast to the majority of people Chamberlain saw Jewry as presenting not a socio-political but a metaphysical problem, one which concerned not only the Germans but the whole of mankind. It was a question not of power and influence but of Being and Non-Being. There is no other way to explain how Chamberlain, a lover of Goethe, could have written those sinister words which anticipated the fateful actions of Hitler. 'With all the strength at my command', Chamberlain confessed to the theologian Alfred von Harnack, 'I hate the Jews and hate them and hate them!'[41] 'The Jews' very existence is an offence against the divine laws of life,' he declared, adding cryptically that they could only be 'purged' from an 'offence . . . they have committed without knowing it'.[42] Whether it is to be those who carry out this purgation, or the people in whose name they carry it out, who are to remain unconscious of it, Chamberlain deliberately leaves open. In their rabid detestation of this 'race of criminals' and their anticipation of its radical purgation the two men will have quickly found themselves to be of one mind when they met in the darkened room where the bedridden philosopher lay.

Not a word was breathed of what passed between them. From their subsequent correspondence, however, we may conclude that their conversation was dominated by the one subject that left them no peace. When Hitler later characterized Chamberlain as a man who, 'having cast off all the trappings of mortal life, lives only for his people, is concerned only for their future and desirous only of their liberation and redemption', he meant liberation from the real enemy, 'the arch-enemy of the Germans'. That enemy, wrote Hitler from Landsberg prison to his friend Siegfried Wagner, is 'Marxism and its promoters'.[43]

There is a second point in this letter at which Hitler deliberately avoids using the critical word which would undoubtedly have brought him to the attention of the censor. He had long kept away from the Villa Wahnfried, he said, 'out of fear, Herr Wagner, that I might arouse the hostility of those circles which were such a burden to your late lamented father, the Master of us all'. All the more grateful was he that Siegfried and Winifred 'had of their own volition assumed the mantle of defenders against the attacks that were sure to come'.[44]

The memory of the Master will have been omnipresent at the meeting between Chamberlain and Hitler. And perhaps not only his memory. Ten years later, now Reich Chancellor, Hitler found himself in Weimar, sitting opposite the eighty-seven-year-old Elisabeth Förster-Nietzsche, sister of the philosopher Friedrich Nietzsche. Elisabeth told of her delight at Hitler's 'wonderful, indeed phenomenal personality',[45] an impression which she was convinced would have been shared by her brother, the herald of the Superman; the Führer, she said, embodied the fulfilment of the vision of the future conveyed by the proclaimer of 'the will to power'.

Moved by Elisabeth's reception, Hitler told his friend Ziegler of a strange feeling that had come over him during this meeting in the Nietzsche Archive in Weimar. As he sat with her, he said, 'he seemed to see behind her all the important figures of that bygone era that she had ever known – even to hear them speak – among them the author of *Zarathustra*, before whose marble bust he had earlier stood in reverence and whose prophetic voice he now heard speaking to him through the mouth of his ageing sister'. The only comparable experience he had ever had, he added 'was when I sat with Houston Stewart Chamberlain'.[46]

That Hitler, caught up in the oppressive Wagnerian atmosphere that prevailed in the Chamberlain household, should have believed that he was hearing the voice of the Master seemed quite plausible to his biographer Joachim C. Fest. Chamberlain's words 'came like a call from Wagner himself to the man who only in flashes of the imagination grasped the reality of the position in which he now found himself'.[47] The significance of the occasion was intensified by the presence of Chamberlain's wife. Eva, totally committed to the Bayreuth ideology, acted as interpreter for her husband, who could barely speak and whose words she had to read from the movement of his lips. Born a Wagner, she shared her husband's extreme views on what Hitler called 'this profound problem which is utterly new to scholarship in this form and shows the history of the world in a completely different light'. The dogmatism of her views may well have served to raise the temperature of the discussion between the two men. Even as hard-bitten a witness as Goebbels was sufficiently disturbed by the radical nature of her opinions to observe that, 'though a refined and sensitive woman, she was somewhat harsh in her judgements'.[48] Hitler, on the other hand, who venerated in her the legacy of her father, found her company so stimulating that he continued to consult with her after becoming Chancellor.

The week following Hitler's visit to Chamberlain the forces of nationalism in Germany knew that their hour had come. From the lofty heights of the Holy Grail the ailing philosopher proclaimed the joyous message in which his personal emotions shaded imperceptibly into his vision of the national scene in the way that the Great War had found expression in his sickness. 'Since that fateful August day in 1914', he wrote in his open letter to Hitler, 'when I was struck down by this terrible disease, I had never experienced so long and refreshing a sleep – a sleep from which I would have had no need to awake.'[49] As guardian of the Wagnerian shrine, he was saying, he could now die in peace because the emergence of his promised successor marked the consummation of his own role – the role of John the Baptist.

Should anyone nevertheless doubt that this Munich firebrand really was the new custodian of the Bayreuth Grail and the new saviour of the nation, Chamberlain would set his mind at rest. 'You were described to me as a fanatic and an apostle of violence but you are nothing of the kind,' he wrote on 7 October 1923 to the man who a month later fired his revolver at the ceiling of the Bürgerbräu beer-cellar in Munich. 'Indeed, I would describe you as the very opposite of a fanatic. A fanatic turns people's heads, whereas you warm people's hearts.'

But the young party leader exuded not only what Winifred Wagner later called 'the power of love' but also the composure of the man blessed with charisma. 'The serenity you gave me', Chamberlain continued, 'is derived to a large degree from your eyes and your gestures. It is as though your eyes were hands, holding me in their grasp, while your hands have an expressiveness in their movements almost equal to that of your eyes.' It was a declaration of love in which Siegfried and Winifred Wagner, together with the Bechsteins, the Hanfstaengls and the Bruckmanns all joined. Those who saw Hitler merely as a hooligan did not know him; he only revealed his true nature to his intimates.

Great as was Chamberlain's fascination with Hitler's charisma, his energy impressed him still more. Here was a man not for the trivialities of everyday political life but for the exercise of universal power. 'There is a power that can construct a universe,' he wrote,

> and it is in this sense that I count you among the constructive forces in the world, not the destructive forces. . . . At a single stroke you have transformed the state of my soul, and the strongest proof of the vitality of the German nation is that it has given birth to a Hitler in its moment of utmost need. Hitler is not a chance gift from on high but the very incarnation of that transformation and that need.

The importance that Hitler attached to Chamberlain's homage was no secret to his followers. In 1934 a brochure published by the Bruckmann Verlag declared that Chamberlain's letter 'set the final seal on Hitler's divine mission . . . and by grasping the significance of his career in its entirety has ensured him the place of honour in the kingdom that is to come'.[50]

The last time that Chamberlain had waxed so lyrical was when he hailed Kaiser Wilhelm II as Germany's wartime saviour. Here now was a man who had not only the necessary hatred of the Antichrist but also the personal magnetism necessary to win over the masses; for only when the saviour had the whole people united behind him could the Jewish government of the Weimar Republic be removed. This made Hitler, in Chamberlain's eyes, 'the vital figure in the German counter-revolution'.[51] The first act of the new saviour, having proclaimed the revolution, would be to assume legitimate power and present himself to the people as the hero who would announce the advent of a new Aryan dawn, as Chamberlain had been the first to recognize. Here was the man for the kingdom, the power and the glory.

But first the temple had to be cleansed. In a second open letter, published in the *Grossdeutsche Zeitung* on New Year's Day 1924, this time addressed to Ernst Boepple, a member of the Thule Society, Chamberlain laid out in detail the characteristics and duties of the new leader, duties which must never be lost sight of. What first Hitler – one of the rare heroic figures 'bequeathed to us by God'[52] – then his faithful followers had felt was now confirmed by the highest authority, that of the Bayreuth 'Knights of the Grail'. Hitler was an heroic figure like Rienzi, like Siegfried, like Parsifal, an avenging angel like Lohengrin, sent by God to aid the people in their deprivation and need. From standing in the stalls he was about to step up on to the world stage.

'No one', resumed Chamberlain, 'can resist his fascinating gaze or the power of his words', since, as he had pointed out in the first open letter, 'they always go straight to the heart'. He 'roused the people's passions and forged new ideas' – forged the sword, in other words, that Siegfried had reassembled from the broken pieces and plunged into the heart of his foe. The only man equipped for this struggle was Hitler, 'who loves his German *Volk* with a fervent passion from which – not from any prejudice or base motive – his oft-deplored anti-Semitism flows'. He loves out of hatred. And those who love him must learn how to hate. Here already is the declaration that Hitler would make in his political last will and testament, that it had been only out of love and loyalty to the *Volk* that he had been led to make such shattering decisions. It is only his love for his Fatherland, writes Chamberlain, that makes Hitler follow his ideas fearlessly to their logical conclusion. To Chamberlain the most vital of these conclusions is that 'one cannot profess allegiance both to Jesus and to those who nailed Him to the Cross'.

This was a motif that had a history in Bayreuth. Wagner himself, though an atheist, took pleasure in invoking the name of Jesus when embarking on one of his diatribes against his 'born enemies'. A friend told of an argument that had broken out between the Master and his financial adviser Friedrich von Feustel, a Reichstag deputy for the National Liberal Party. Feustel said that he had no wish to subscribe to the theory that the Jews offered a threat to the country's future. Thereupon Wagner sprang up in a state of great indignation

and uttered one single sentence which said all he had to say on the subject. 'Children! Children! Have you forgotten Jesus Christ?!' He delivered these words with such an indescribable expression in his eyes and his voice that we were pierced to the quick. All of us, even Feustel, felt that the final word had been spoken on the subject and that there could be no demur.[53]

It also became Hitler's final word on the subject. What he referred to in a speech as everyone's duty 'to make a supreme effort to ensure that Germany herself does not suffer death on the Cross',[54] he later recorded in his testament as having been achieved. No common mortal, he reflected, had ever been called upon to fulfil such a task. But then, since his encounter with Chamberlain Hitler knew that he was no common mortal.

Chamberlain ensured that the appointment of the Messiah was inextricably linked with the solution of the Jewish problem. 'Hitler's greatest quality', he wrote on 1 January, 1924, 'is courage, which he possesses in abundance. In this respect he reminds us of Luther.' 'And to what do these two men owe their courage?' he asks, setting his Catholic protégé on a level with the Protestant reformer. To their 'religious seriousness', is his answer, and to the fact that they did not merely preach but confronted their communities with the existential choice – Either–Or. And because Hitler was filled with this 'religious seriousness', it was inconceivable 'that he should share our awareness of the lethal influence exerted by the Jews on the life of the German nation without taking the appropriate action'. In 1881 Wagner had conceded that 'it is certain that it will be we Germans above all who will perish at the hands of the Jews';[55] now, forty-two years on, his son-in-law envisaged a crucial turn of events brought about by the hero whose final testament, a further twenty-two years later, would record that the task had at last been accomplished.

The 'awareness' of which Chamberlain wrote was that of the Bayreuth circle and their fellow-conspirators. It was not shared by the average German anti-Semite. Indeed, without Wagner's polarizing *Weltanschauung* of the theft of the gold and the twilight of the gods, of the ruin brought about by miscegenation and of the salvation of the world, it would make no sense. It was not a question of 'to be or not to be' – many disliked the Jews, a number hated them and, driven by envy and insecurity, would have been glad to see the back of them. But no one thought seriously of genocide – that was in the realm of the unthinkable. They were cursed and abominated, but even the most vicious anti-Semite did not contemplate the gas chamber and the bullet in the neck.

It was Wagner's great metaphysical world epic of the battle against the Nibelungen, of treachery and assassination, of the defeat of the Aryan line and the rise of the power of Alberich, that first made the unthinkable concrete. The stage was set for the salvation of the world, and the sinister motif of collective destruction rose from a barely perceptible murmur in the depths of the orchestra through a long crescendo with ever more complex variations to an explosive climax of fanfares of brass and incessant drumbeats which exceed the threshold of pain. Chamberlain gave the initial downbeat. 'Once the threat to the German race has been recognized', he declared in his New Year message, 'counter-measures must immediately be taken. Everyone knows this but no one dares say so – no one dares to act on the conclusions to which these thoughts lead. No one, that is, except Adolf Hitler.'[56] Adolf Hitler read this and understood. He now knew what he had to do. It was already programmed.

To understand how Hitler sought to justify himself with the reference to 'decisions that had never before been demanded of a mortal human being', one must see his words in the context of the task that Chamberlain envisaged for him. It had been Chamberlain who forced Hitler to recognize where his thoughts were leading and who gave him his blessing as the chosen redeemer. It had been a task not for an ordinary mortal, Hitler intimated in 1945, but for 'a man sent from God'. Only he, being such a man, could defeat the Antichrist in a battle to end all battles. Having turned the scene over in his mind time and again, he acted out the drama while the eyes of the world were turned elsewhere. Even then it remained for him in the realm of the imagination; throughout his life he averted his gaze from the sight of dead bodies. Yet the fixed grimness of his features seemed to reflect the horrors which he refused to confront.

No less eerie is the thought that the crime of the century had its beginnings in a gloomy sick-room at No. 1 Wahnfriedstrasse in Bayreuth, a room stacked with Wagner memorabilia and medicine bottles. The dragon-slayer kept these terrible 'decisions' secret but he made no attempt to conceal from his confidants the role that Chamberlain had played. Joseph Goebbels, for instance, who visited the invalid in 1926, was fully aware of his importance for National Socialism and described in his diary the distressing scene as Chamberlain, 'a broken man, babbling, with tears in his eyes, grasped my hand and would not let me go'. Deeply moved, Goebbels described him as a 'pathfinder and pioneer, the father of our national spirit', reverentially taking his leave of him with the almost religious words: 'If we are on the point of despair, you will be there to help us.'[57] However, Goebbels can hardly have suspected at the time what Chamberlain really meant to Hitler.

Chamberlain died in 1927, his coffin borne to the grave by Hitler and his SA men. Neither he nor his wife Eva, on whose coffin lay a wreath from the Führer when she died fifteen years later, lived to see the fulfilment of their hopes. Siegfried Wagner died in 1930, a few months after his mother. Winifred, who had to come to terms with the death of her Führer and with the revelation of the Holocaust, survived, unrepentant, until 1980. The Wagner Festival resumed in 1951 as though nothing had happened. What really passed between the two men in Chamberlain's room on that evening of 30 September 1923 remained their secret. Even the consequences of Chamberlain's two letters presenting Hitler as the saviour of the nation can only be conjectured. The only thing we know for certain is that, as he wrote in his last testament, Hitler put his ideas into practice at the earliest possible moment, as Chamberlain had urged him to do.

At the time he met Chamberlain, Hitler was already a Wagnerian and a

convinced anti-Semite. But for these elements to combine to create the evil
monster that destroyed whole towns and villages and, had it not been
brought to a violent end, would have decimated an entire continent, there
had to be a higher will. He could only feel himself to be the leader of the
German nation if he had the courage to embark on the 'grand solution'.
The fulfilment of the dream that had hovered before his eyes since the
days of *Rienzi* in Linz depended on the fulfilment of Wagner's prophecy.
Only as a Messiah dare he become a mass murderer. Only in paroxysms of
love could he embark on anonymous blood-baths through which to dis-
gorge his hatred.

Neither neighbouring countries nor his own made any attempt to stop
him, for no one was prepared to lend credence to the terrifying prospects
that he held out in the sermons he delivered before the exultant masses. It
was mere play-acting, they said, ignoring the fact that the play had long
since started to turn into reality. They appeased their consciences by telling themselves that this ridiculous little demagogue, with his whining and
growling and sobbing, his ranting and raving, could not possibly mean
what he said in his absurd, uncontrollable ecstasy. When, with a sneer on
his lips, his eyes bulging, he conjured up the prospect of unimaginable
atrocities and began to talk of annihilating his enemies, it was dismissed as
the exaggeration typical of an election campaign.

So as people had smiled indulgently at Wagner, now they underesti-
mated Hitler. What took place at crowded party meetings was theatre, to
be sure, but the producer was the Master of Bayreuth, whose overwhelming, hypnotic dreams, which had long had a symbolic relevance to real life,
now began to invade that reality. Life and art would become one. Chamberlain's house, where Hitler had received the call, and Wahnfried, where
he was welcomed the following day, were like extensions of Wagner's great
Festspielhaus, where Wotan's children and Alberich's creatures of darkness fought out their struggle to the end.

The same evening Hitler was invited by the Bechsteins to an intimate
party in the Hotel Anker with Siegfried and Winifred.[58] The following
morning he went to the Villa Wahnfried, creeping reverentially on tiptoe
through the drawing-room left untouched since the Master's death, 'as
though he were viewing holy relics in a cathedral', Friedelind put it. Since
first hearing *Lohengrin*, he told Winifred, he had revered Wagner 'as the
greatest German who had ever lived'.[59] Winifred, fascinated by his blue
eyes, recognized at once that this man 'had been spellbound by Wagner
since his days in Linz'[60] and had now reached the goal of his boyhood
dreams. 'I was so deeply moved!' he later recalled in his 'Wolf's Lair', thinking back to this moment.[61]

The climax of the visit was to stand before Wagner's grave, a massive
granite block entwined with ivy. The simple stone slab had long been
a place of pilgrimage to those in the nationalist movement – the holy of

holies. Led through the tree-lined garden to the shady spot, he asked to be allowed to take the last few steps alone. 'For a long while he stood there silent and motionless,' reported Erich Ebermayer. 'When he turned round, there were tears in his eyes.'[62]

Back in the villa, Hitler vowed to solve the *Parsifal* question 'in the spirit of the Master', providing he succeeded in acquiring what he called 'the necessary influence over the country's destiny'.[63] According to Friedelind Wagner, he was quite open about the way he proposed to do this. 'He told my parents that his party was planning a *coup d'état* for the end of the year', she said, 'and that if it was successful, he would seize power immediately.'[64]

The previous evening Hitler had been pronounced 'Saviour of Germany' and, as he stood by the Master's grave, had recognized in the solid stone 'the granite foundation' of his *Weltanschauung*. Now he set out to assert himself as 'the man of action' of the Bayreuth religion. A few days later he declared it his aim 'to pave the way for the great German freedom movement'. 'In so doing', he explained, 'I will not rely on anyone else's help but solely on my own incomparable determination, with which and through which I shall emerge either as victor or as vanquished.'[65]

But behind this determination, as Chamberlain had convinced him, lay the force of destiny. Born out of the nation's grief, he was pre-ordained to become its saviour. It was not he who acted but providence that acted through him. The claim to infallibility inevitably followed – contradiction was blasphemy. His friends noted his increasingly Messiah-like behaviour.[66] Since he felt in his blood that he had been called to save his country, the choice lay between a blind acceptance of his inscrutable will and the threat of his eternal enmity. General von Lossow testified that in the spring of this momentous year of 1923 Hitler was still insisting 'that he was only preparing the way for the man who was to come. Now, however, he claimed that he himself was that man, and his followers hailed him as the German Messiah.'[67]

In the same way as Hitler was far from being a conventional party leader, so his movement was quite unlike a normal political faction. Where there was one party, there were many parties – but the Nazi Party made them all superfluous. Where there was one political opinion, there were contrary political opinions – but the Führer, incarnation of the will of the people, reduced them all to silence. 'We have been founded not so that we can take part in an election,' he told his electors, 'but so that we can intervene to rescue the country in the moment of its greatest deprivation. . . . That our movement is the source of our national salvation is something felt by millions. We have virtually created a new religious faith!'[68]

THE SAVIOUR BETRAYED

A s Hitler proclaimed not opinions but eternal verities, so his *Weltanschauung* appealed not to reason but to faith. And just such a faith, in Hitler himself and in the philosophy launched by Wagner and substantiated by Chamberlain, was what Siegfried Wagner craved.

Born in 1869, the Master's only son, Siegfried was an unsuccessful composer but an energetic partner in the organization of the Bayreuth Festival. Like his mother, Cosima, and the other 'Knights of the Grail', he was an implacable opponent of the Weimar Republic, waiting for the moment of truth so dramatically portrayed in his father's operas – such as the moment when the swan appears at the end of *Lohengrin*, or when Brünnhilde, the Valkyrie, rescues the unborn Siegfried. Miracles were the order of the day in the Festspielhaus.

Bayreuth too was waiting to be rescued. Its doors had been shut since the outbreak of war in 1914 and the country had become a 'pigsty', as Siegfried Wagner called it.[1] The only hope was for a revolution like that which his father had attempted in Dresden in 1849. 'Thank God for true German men!' he wrote to a friend before the Putsch of November 1923. 'Hitler is a splendid man, a genuine German. He will not fail us!'[2] In Siegfried's mind was the liberation movement launched by the one-time Royal Kapellmeister in Dresden and now led by the man who liked to announce himself over the telephone in Wahnfried as 'Kapellmeister Wolf'.[3]

Siegfried gave cautious support to those working to destroy the 'Jew-ridden republic'. In public lectures, when he would hold collections for the re-opening of the Festival, he would compare the cultural decadence of the Republic with the fall of Classical Antiquity. 'Surveying the present scene', he declared in the spring of 1923, 'one is involuntarily put in mind of the fate of Athens. The similarity between the Germans and the Athenians is striking.' Drawing a bold comparison, very much in the spirit of his father, between the performances of Aeschylus and Sophocles and those on the 'Green Hill' in Bayreuth, he maintained that political decline was followed by cultural decline, in Athens as in contemporary Germany, which without the Bayreuth Festival had become a cultural desert. And what was now facing Germany was the fate that had befallen classical Athens – 'It perished.'[4]

Then, leaving his cultural pessimism on one side, Siegfried gave musical expression to his hopes for radical change by composing a symphonic poem called *Glück* ('Happiness'), which had a programme reminiscent of Wagner's theatrical interpretation of Beethoven's Choral Symphony at the time of the May uprising: where in Schiller's ode the greatest of the divine gifts bequeathed to man was Joy, in Siegfried's tone poem it is Happiness. But it is only on those who are worthy of her, the moral continues, that the goddess Fortuna will bestow her blessing – not those who are obsessed with earthly riches and power or with fleeting pleasures but those who are prepared to plunge boldly into combat on their fiery steeds. 'We are taking up the fight,' cry the defiant warriors to the goddess in Siegfried's tone poem: 'the foe is seeking to rob us of our holiest possessions! But he shall not prevail!'[5]

In Wagner's *Ring* and *Parsifal* the holiest possessions are also stolen – the gold by the dwarf Alberich, the sacred spear by the magician Klingsor – until, their adversaries overcome, the shining heroes retrieve them. Interpreted to apply to the present day and to his composition, this meant for Siegfried that only the man who protected the shrine, and with it the doom-threatened Reich, was worthy to receive the divine gift, a gift bestowed by the goddess with jubilation and cries of 'Heil!' All this is underlined in the finale of Siegfried's work by a clarion call of trumpets to greet 'the deed of salvation' which brings ultimate 'happiness'. Hitler knew what that 'deed of salvation' was.

The leader of the Nazi Party will certainly have learned during his visit to Wahnfried on 1 October that Siegfried Wagner was to conduct the première of his symphonic poem the following month in the Nazi stronghold of Munich. As he was shortly to have a première of his own, using, not by chance, the same themes as Siegfried's composition, the two men might well have arranged to meet. Hitler's aim of revolution had been fixed in his mind for a long time, and according to Friedelind his friends in Bayreuth were party to his intentions.

Writing later from prison, Hitler told Siegfried that he had visited Chamberlain 'to bring him the best remedy for his suffering that the world has to offer'.[6] As 'the harbinger of the coming revolution' had received Chamberlain's blessing on his plan, the coincidence of the performance of Siegfried's work could well have seemed to him a sign from above, with music from the house of Wagner to launch the national rebellion, and his own 'act of salvation' finding its musical apotheosis in the fanfares of final victory.

So Hitler chose for his entry onto the stage of history the same day, 10 November, as Siegfried's first performance. After a night spent discussing strategy with his comrades, he planned to march on Munich the following morning[7] and, as though to fulfil his old vision of *Rienzi* days, set up a dictatorship. That in the event he advanced his operations by two days was due to the fact that his enemy Ritter von Kahr planned a rival demonstration which threatened to take the wind out of his sails. When on the evening of 8 November he discharged his revolver in the Bürgerbräu tavern as a theatrical gesture,[8] he knew that his Bayreuth supporters were nearby, for the next day was to see the final rehearsal of Siegfried's piece.

Hitler's attempted *coup d'état* has gone down in history like a scene from an operetta, an amateurish, ill-prepared adventure that ended in dismal failure. The leading character had indeed wanted to make history – not, however, history as farce but history as heroic legend. What he envisioned was a revolution of the masses orchestrated by Wagner. Like Rienzi, who led the people against the usurpers in the name of the Holy Spirit, or like Richard Wagner at the Dresden barricades, fanning the flames of revolt with Schiller's inflammatory message from Beethoven's Ninth Symphony, he saw himself borne aloft on a wave of patriotic sentiment and finally established on the throne that was waiting to be graced by the saviour of the nation.

Like the Messiah of the Scriptures, who came with the sword to sit in judgement over the people, so he too would 'wage war against that alien race which sucks our blood and drains us dry. We shall not rest until we have driven this breed from our Fatherland.'[9] Only then, as Wagner had demanded fifty years earlier, could he contemplate 'a rehabilitation of the entire German nation – even of the world'.[10] The Master's prophecies, like the biblical writing on the wall, would now come to pass.

The omens seemed favourable, and as Wahnfried too was awaiting the promised action, Hitler gave the signal, burst into the smoke-filled beer-cellar and shouted: 'The National Revolution has broken out!'[11] Writing somewhat prematurely in the *Völkischer Beobachter*, Joseph Stolzing-Czerny invoked the spirit of the *Meistersinger*: 'Germany is awakening from a feverish dream . . . and a new glorious era is shining through the clouds.'[12]

Five years after the end of the war Hitler emerged at the head of a national revolution in order to lead his country to a new dawn. Strangely enough, he used the same stratagem by which his mortal enemies, 'the criminals of the November revolution', had gained power. The 'Jewish revolution', as Hitler always called the establishment of the Weimar Republic, 'was brought about by a small but determined group of men who, like an assault unit, drove the lethargic majority before them.'[13] This was precisely what he himself now intended. He too would march at the head of the revolutionaries and soon the whole population would fall in behind his band of stormtroopers; then the storm of retaliation would break loose and the Reich would be reborn in its old glory.

Chamberlain had claimed miraculous powers for Hitler. Now, as though wanting to put Chamberlain's claims to the test, he broke into the Bürgerbräu meeting to display his charisma and steal the thunder of the speaker, Ritter von Kahr, whom eleven years later he ordered to be shot. By subtle manipulation and gentle blackmail, he argued, not by force of arms, he would win the ruling Munich triumvirate over to his side – Commissioner General Gustav von Kahr, General von Lossow and Hans von Seisser, Chief of Police. And his tactic seemed to work. His political opponents, pushed into a side room, capitulated, leaving the man of the moment, his Iron Cross proudly displayed on his black tail-coat, to revel in his strength 'with a kind of child-like delight'.[14]

It had also been like 'a child'[15] that he received Chamberlain's approval – an unchanging feature of his psyche that led him to believe not only in miracles but also in his ability to perform them. The symbol of this phenomenal gift, what the sword was to Siegfried, was his ever-present revolver. He had carried it with him from the very beginning of his political activity, hung it in the cloakroom when visiting friends, laid it ostentatiously on the table at meetings with his fellow-plotters, and took it out of its holster, to the children's amazement, on his midnight visits to Wahnfried.[16] Many times he toyed with the thought of shooting himself. But he was only to do so when the game was finally up.

That evening in the Bürgerbräu, wearing an expression of 'smug self-satisfaction', as Karl Alexander von Müller described it, Hitler delivered one of his characteristic frenzied speeches, 'a masterly performance that would have done credit to any actor'.[17] Never before, said Müller, son of a family long devoted to the Wagnerian cause, 'had I experienced how someone could transform the atmosphere in a hall in a matter of minutes, even seconds, changing the whole mood of the meeting with a few words, like turning over a glove. There was something of the magician about him.'[18]

What Müller could not know was that this was Hitler's maiden speech as the saviour of the nation. He had already demonstrated his strength by effortlessly disposing of Kahr and his colleagues in the Bavarian government. Now, holding his arms dramatically aloft, he cried in biblical tones:

> I am going to fulfil the vow I made to myself five years ago when I was a blind cripple in the military hospital: to know neither rest nor peace until the November criminals had been overthrown, until on the ruins of the wretched Germany of today there should have arisen once more a Germany of power and greatness, of freedom and splendour.[19]

Here was the new Jesus, it seemed. Thoughts like this must have gone through the mind of one of these present who, as the sentimental congregation in the beer-cellar struck up the German national anthem, is said to have whispered caustically to a policeman by his side: 'The only thing missing is the psychiatrist.'[20]

The aura of magic quickly evaporated. The Bavarian triumvirate gave way and agreed to join Hitler. The following day, 'banners waving and to the strains of *"Deutschland über alles"* '[21] but with no clear strategy in mind, Hitler's troops marched through the streets of Munich. They had either to mobilize the masses or abjectly surrender at the first road block – victory or ruin. At their head, looking more like desperadoes than national heroes, marched Hitler, leader of the Nazi Party, and Ludendorff, discredited Great War general of 'stab-in-the-back' fame. The latter, observed Müller in disbelief, 'was wearing an overcoat full of creases and a shabby felt hat'. As to those he was leading, 'they were like a disorganized rabble of civilians and ex-servicemen thrown together by pure coincidence'.[22]

There was no uprising, no revolution. It was all over in the twinkling of an eye. In front of the Feldherrnhalle memorial, which Hitler had often painted and where he had stood and cheered at the outbreak of war, the marchers were stopped by the police. Firing broke out and lasted, according to the police, some twenty or twenty-five seconds.[23] Müller heard from a distance 'a few shots' that sounded 'like an uncoordinated salvo'.[24] After thirty seconds at the most, said the official report, the demonstrators had been put to flight.

They left behind nineteen dead or dying. Hitler's theatrical Putsch, deprived of a director, had ended in a blood bath. Ludendorff had been arrested, Goering had been wounded and taken to a hospital in Innsbruck; others took refuge in the homes of Austrian comrades or, like Hans Frank, in Mussolini's Italy. Hitler had himself driven to Uffing on Lake Staffel, where his musical friends the Hanfstaengls had a villa. There, on 11 November, a few moments before the arrival of a car ordered by the Bechsteins for his escape, he was arrested.

He had wagered all and lost all. His reputation as a political strategist had been badly dented, and as the people at large had spurned his insurrection, nobody had any more desire to talk about new Messiahs. A failure once again, Hitler was only waiting to be shot.[25] Since his party was now proscribed and the *Völkischer Beobachter*, its propaganda journal, had ceased publication, the national liberation movement appeared to have run into the sand. 'The swastikas and the stormtroopers vanished,' wrote Stefan Zweig, who was to flee the country in 1938, 'and the name of Adolf Hitler fell into almost complete oblivion.'[26]

Like the 1849 uprising in Dresden, the attempted Putsch of 1923 in Munich had ended in disaster. Yet soon afterwards, as in Wagner's operas, the inevitable process of transformation began. Political observers hardly noticed but the leitmotif for a new work had already been heard. Hardly had the curtain fallen than it began hesitantly to rise again. As in Wagner's *Ring des Nibelungen*, the hero's downfall had been brought about by treachery. Following on the heels of his triumph in the Bürgerbräu, where his one-time opponents had made common cause with him, came the defection of his allies and finally an act of murder. Hitler himself had only escaped by the skin of his teeth when a bullet killed his friend Max Erwin von Scheubner-Richter, who had been marching arm in arm at his side. Long columns of protesters, among them many students, marched through the streets shouting 'Kahr is a Judas!' and 'Lossow is a Traitor!'[27]

The very fact of his failure turned Hitler into a true Messiah. Sitting in his cell in Landsberg, he could feel that what looked like final defeat in fact confirmed him in his Messianic role. As a redeemer he was indestructible. 'The first part of the national revolution is over,' stated a document circulated at the time among members of the Party.

> It has cleared the ground for our movement. Our beloved Führer Adolf Hitler has again shed his blood for the German *Volk*. No more heinous an act of treachery has ever been perpetrated in the history of the world than that now suffered by him and by the German people. Whether the weather be fair or foul, our patriotic troops are united by Hitler's blood and the blades held at the throats of our comrades by shameless traitors. The second part of the national revolution is about to begin.[28]

Only in the moment of failure was Chamberlain's prophecy to come true. Only the man who perishes can be born again.

Wahnfried was to play its part in this rebirth. On the fateful day Hitler's friends Siegfried and Winifred Wagner travelled to Munich, probably with other members of the family, primarily for the première of Siegfried's new tone poem but also for Hitler's revolutionary new work. According to the Wahnfried version of the story, the couple stayed with friends in the Widenmayerstrasse, where the family of Hitler's friend Scheubner-Richter also lived, 'but their minds were only on the concert, not on politics'.[29] On the evening of 8 November, when Hitler was planning his attack on the meeting in the Bürgerbräu, they took a stroll through the city and learned, on being stopped and told to show their papers, what had just been happening nearby. When Winifred was on her way to call on relatives the next day and found herself caught up in a crowd of people, she chanced to hear of the blood-bath at the Feldherrnhalle. Uncertain of what direction the riot might take, she hurried back to Bayreuth the same evening, leaving her husband, whose concert had been cancelled, to travel on to Innsbruck. Learning that the wounded Goering was being treated in the hospital there, Siegfried, according to Erich Ebermayer, made a spontaneous decision to visit him.[30] The Wagners are claimed by Ebermayer to have been ignorant of what was going on but in one way or another they discovered what had happened and sought to make themselves useful.

Siegfried, for instance, paid Goering's hospital bill. That, at least, is what

Friedelind claims – though her account of her parents' stay in Munich at this time differs from that given by Ebermayer in this and other respects. Her parents, she wrote, watched the column of demonstrators from their hotel window: Hitler and Ludendorff 'had marched down the middle of the street at the head of a detachment of stormtroopers wearing windbreakers and marching in step with the general, next to whose imperious presence Hitler cut a pathetically un-military figure. Then suddenly, as they approached the Feldherrnhalle, they were scattered by a burst of machine-gun fire.'[31] It is an account, especially as concerns Hitler's appearance and the salvo of bullets, that has the ring of authenticity.

Shocked by what they had seen, Friedelind went on, 'Winifred persuaded her husband to travel on to Innsbruck, where Goering was being tended in hospital by his Swedish wife'. It sounds entirely plausible that Siegfried Wagner gave the Goerings money and, as Friedelind says, also paid for them to stay in a hotel in Venice, since there were other occasions also when he helped them out.

Friedelind's story cannot account for the many coincidences, nor does it explain how her parents knew where the Goerings were hiding. It does, however, convincingly refute Winifred's statement that she only learned about the events from a distance. Friedelind knew that, on her mother's return from Munich, she had immediately given Nazi Party officials in Bayreuth a report on the failed coup. The only point in her doing this would have been to provide the local Party, disturbed by the course that events had taken yet strengthened by their sense of comradeship, with an eye-witness account of what had happened. On 17 December 1923, according to an official report, Daniela Thode, Siegfried's half-sister, also spoke to the Bayreuth Party about her experiences.[32]

Wahnfried had nailed its colours to the mast. A few days after Hitler had been put in jail, declaring him to be 'a disciple of Wagner's such as Bayreuth has never before seen',[33] Winifred took a sensational step. On 12 November she released to the press an open letter stating the family's position on the events in Munich, creating a furore heard far beyond the boundaries of Bayreuth. Written in typically Chamberlainesque style, it was probably the work of both Winifred and the highly respected Siegfried. By intervening directly in the affairs of the Weimar Republic, they invited comparison with the political activities of the one-time Dresden Kapellmeister – who had, however, preferred to remain anonymous. By coming out thus openly in favour of the defeated hero, Bayreuth was already preparing for his resurrection.

'The whole of Bayreuth knows that we have a friendly relationship with Adolf Hitler,' the letter begins. 'But it would be wrong to assume that we were therefore involved in his attempted coup. We happened to be in Munich at the time and were the first to return to Bayreuth. It is only natural that Hitler's supporters should have turned to us for an eye-witness account of the events that took place.'[34] Ignoring her husband's excursion to Innsbruck, Winifred took exception to what she called 'highly exaggerated rumours' that they had been about to be arrested for taking part in the revolt.[35] They had committed no offence, she insisted, but they still supported the cause of the man now languishing in jail.

'For years', the letter goes on, 'we have followed with the utmost interest and approval the constructive policies of Adolf Hitler. By devoting his life to the ideal of a pure and united Greater Germany he is offering thousands of despairing citizens the hope of seeing a new, noble Fatherland.' After praising his moral strength and purity, the letter reaches its Messianic climax in a declaration, suspiciously reminiscent of Chamberlain, that Hitler has embarked on the realization of his vision 'with the fervour and humility proper to a sacred mission'. This saviour, therefore, 'so absolutely committed to what is good and true, must fill the people with enthusiasm, must rouse in them a feeling of love and devotion, a willingness to sacrifice themselves for him'. Whereupon Winifred concludes with an outright declaration 'that we too are under the spell of this man, and that, as we stood side by side with him in times of happiness, so now we shall stand by him in his hour of need'.[36]

Had Wahnfried taken leave of its senses? Or, with the dragon-slayer now on the scene, did the Wagner clan perhaps choose deliberately to take leave of their senses? They drove themselves to the point of complete identification with an idol into which the chameleonic actor from Linz had likewise transformed himself. And what Hitler wanted, people did. Even Chamberlain, as the *Illustrierter Beobachter* wrote in its obituary in 1927, 'lent his name and his reputation to the local Party and supported the movement in its time of trial with great courage and loyalty'.[37]

Thanks to the consolidated efforts of the Wagner clan ten thousand signatures were collected from the citizens of Bayreuth[38] demanding their Führer's release. Siegfried too, who tried for understandable reasons to keep out of the limelight, worked for the restoration of the Party and its leader. As well as giving various sums to Goering,[39] he took money for Hitler from the Bayreuth donations fund and arranged for Winifred to pass on to Ludendorff a gift received from America.[40]

Everybody was working for the saviour's return. Winifred prepared Christmas parcels for the lonely inmate of Landsberg and cheered him up with what he called 'a touching sketch of her dear little ones'.[41] In a Christmas message to a friend, Siegfried wrote: 'We shall stay loyal to him, even if it lands us in jail.' To which he proudly added: 'But maybe Satan will be mistaken this time. If the grand German cause is really forced to submit, then I shall believe in Jehovah, God of vengeance and hatred. But Wahnfried will never yield. My wife is fighting like a lion for Hitler! Magnificent!'[42]

The authenticity of this letter has been questioned because it seems at variance with the popular image of Siegfried as cool and reserved. But there are numerous documented remarks which show that he made no secret of his anti-Semitism. And when, in the same letter, he goes on to lament that the defeat of Hitler's revolution has led to 'the glorification of treachery and perjury, with Jew and Jesuit walking arm in arm in order to destroy the soul of the German people', he is reviving an idea of his father's and of General Ludendorff's. Responsibility for crushing the revolt, the General had said, 'lay in the hands of the Jews and the Jesuits'.[43]

A genuine friendship grew between Hitler and Siegfried. Winifred told of an occasion when, 'out of pure affection', her husband had smiled at his protégé, a man twenty years his junior, laid his hands on his shoulders and cried: 'D'you know? I like you!'[44] Hitler never forgot Siegfried's support. 'Siegfried was one of those who stood by me when my fortunes were at their lowest ebb,' he said in 1942.[45]

The closeness of the ties between Hitler's National Socialism and Bayreuth became evident three months after the coup. Accompanied by Kurt Lüdecke, an SA leader and one of Hitler's fund-raisers, Siegfried and Winifred travelled to the United States to solicit donations towards the re-opening of the Bayreuth Festival and at the same time for the banned Nazi Party, which had continued to exist under a number of disguised names.

On 4 January 1924 Hitler had instructed Lüdecke to go to America and gain support for the liberation movement, especially financial support.[46] He had set his sights in particular on the automobile manufacturer Henry Ford – Hanfstaengl wrote that Ford seemed to be the only American in whom Hitler had any interest, seeing him as an anti-Semite and a possible contributor to the Party.[47] He had not forgotten the payments Dietrich Eckart had organized in 1921 via the American tractor dealer Warren C. Anderson.

Arriving in New York on 28 January 1924, the Wagners and Lüdecke planned their strategy. The Wagners, wrote Lüdecke, 'were here on a mission not very different from mine.'[48] Sitting together in the hotel lobby, Lüdecke went on, 'we talked less about music than about money and how we could involve Henry Ford in the Nazi movement'. Two days later all three travelled to Detroit, where the Wagners were invited to Ford's country estate. The lively conversation ranged from Bayreuth and the Master to the German political situation and finally, as planned, to Adolf Hitler. This led inevitably to the subject of the Jews, which they discussed at length. 'The philosophy and ideas of Ford and Hitler were very similar,' Winifred recalled.[49]

When they reached the question of financing the underground Nazi Party, Ford drew their attention to the money that had accrued 'from the sale of automobiles and trucks that he had already sent to Germany'. In reply Winifred pointed out that generous support was now more necessary than ever. Ford smiled and assured her that a man who had set out to rid Germany of the Jews could always reckon on his assistance. At this point Winifred brought Lüdecke into the picture, and Ford immediately agreed to a meeting with him.

While Siegfried prepared for his concert in Orchestra Hall in the evening – music by Wagner and Liszt's *Les Préludes*, with its fanfare of the war to come – his wife hastened to Lüdecke's box to tell him about the planned meeting. Even as he opened the door to her, Lüdecke 'could tell from her smile that she had been successful'. That he later claimed that his approach to Henry Ford had been in vain can probably be ascribed to his desire to protect the donor's identity, for the discovery that he had been subsidizing an anti-Jewish movement could well have led to a boycott of Ford's vehicles. Hitler too chose to keep Ford's donation secret. But in 1938 he made his own gesture of thanks by honouring Ford on his seventy-fifth birthday with the Grand Cross of the German Eagle, the highest order a foreigner could receive.

At the end of their fund-raising tour, which had been no less successful for the Bayreuth Festival, the Wagners and Lüdecke left by ship for Italy, where Siegfried and Winifred were introduced, probably by Lüdecke, to Mussolini. They chatted about the Rome of bygone ages and Winifred compared the Roman 'tribune of the people' with his counterpart in Munich. But she missed in Mussolini, she said, the 'power of love' that she found in Hitler's eyes.[50] Siegfried, on the other hand, detected a remarkable parallel, as he told the dictator, between his seizure of power and that of Wagner's hero Rienzi.

Back in Bayreuth, Siegfried and Winifred would not have been slow to tell the frail and ailing Cosima about the new acquaintance they had made, for Cosima had long been an enthusiastic admirer of Il Duce. 'Everything one hears about him', she wrote in 1923, 'speaks of *power*.'[51] Hitler also saw in the Italian dictator a political role model whose 'march on Rome' in October 1922 he interpreted as a challenge for his own 'march on Berlin', a march that would start in Munich.

As liaison officer between the Nazi Party and the Duce, Hitler had appointed the Machiavellian figure of Kurt Lüdecke, the fund-raiser, who was later to find himself an inmate of the concentration camp at Oranienburg. Hitler was especially fascinated by Mussolini's preparedness to use violence, wrote Lüdecke in his memoirs: 'His eyes grew thoughtful when he heard how the Blackshirts marched into Bolshevized towns and took possession.'[52] A report on Hitler ordered by General von Lossow, one of the 'traitors' of the Munich coup, summarized its findings by saying that Hitler saw himself to be 'the German Mussolini'.[53]

The heavy defeat that Hitler as national revolutionary had suffered in Munich was transformed the following spring into a triumph for Hitler as national martyr. For three months he was nowhere to be seen; then, before the eyes of the whole people, he suddenly, resplendently, arose from the dead. The trial for high treason of a man who had perpetrated an abortive *coup d'état* – three policemen had been killed – was turned by the accused into the trial of the real perpetrators of high treason in the central government in Berlin. Since the November Revolution of 1918 was an act of treason against the German people, argued Hitler, any attempt to remove the consequences of that illegal seizure of power could not itself be treasonable. His action, he went on, had been taken solely in the interest of the people, therefore the uprising so brutally crushed could claim a moral right before God and the world 'to represent the nation'.[54]

Had the revolution been successful, continued Hitler in the courtroom, as though addressing a Party meeting, 'the humiliated country would have participated in a miracle. Munich, Nuremberg, Bayreuth, indeed the entire land would have broken out into jubilation and rejoicing: the people would have been forced to realize that the country's misery could be brought to an end and that salvation could only be achieved through a rebellion which would sweep away the immoral government in Berlin.'[55] If that had been achieved, then he would have been in the same position as Mussolini in Italy, 'whose legality derived not from a seizure of power as such but from the gigantic process of purification that ensued. Thus would this treason be legalized, and thus would it be successful.'[56]

Who in the courtroom knew what Hitler meant by 'a gigantic process of purification'? What was this uncleanness that had to be dealt with? Did anyone suspect that they were dealing with a political metaphysician who was pursuing his pseudo-religious visions through the subtle manipulation of power politics? For indeed, at the heart of Hitler's peroration lay the 'gigantic process of purification' in its biblical form – deliverance from evil.

With these words Hitler transformed the old army canteen in which the trial was taking place into a courtroom representing the bar of history. At the same time he declared political events between the November Revolution of 1918 and his national revolution of 1923 to be stages in a process of salvation through which destiny was putting the German people to the test. In apocalyptic phrases that might have come from the mouth of a departing Wagnerian hero, culminating in the invocation of 'the eternal goddess of eternal justice', he sought to convert the fiasco of his attempted coup into a victory of epic dimensions. As the prisoner in the dock, his confidence growing with every word, took on the mantle of prophet, so the court, which had been convened in order to sentence a common criminal, found itself behaving like a reverent congregation. The sentence then handed down was so lenient that it seemed to have been passed not on a social fire-raiser but on the future leader of the German nation.

No one in the courtroom was under any illusion about the claims Hitler was making. Everyone present understood that, given the opportunity, he would follow the same path as Mussolini and legitimize his policy of violence by reference to the 'purification' that had to be carried out. Without him, all would be lost. Salvation was inevitable. The Great War, as Hitler interpreted it, had been a typical attempt to destroy the land of Luther and Goethe, both from without and within; the enemy's aim had been the destruction of Germany. 'So', he continued, as he prepared to start his nine-month sentence in a comfortable prison cell, 'the war was conducted as a war of annihilation, a racist war, with the intention, as Clemenceau made clear, of wiping 20 million Germans off the map'.[57]

Equally great as the threat from without, which had not come to an end with the war, was the threat from within, Hitler pointed out – 'though no progress can be made here as long as the enemy, that is, first the French, then the Jews, continue to plague us'. As Chamberlain, in his New Year message, had urged action rather than fine words, so his pupil considered it insufficient just to explain the situation. What was needed was 'propaganda for the destruction of Germany's destroyers', a dialectical formula to which he had recourse again in 1941, when he justified the Holocaust with the words: 'Those who destroy life expose themselves to their own destruction. That is just what is happening to them.'[58] Only when that point has been reached will the people rise up, will 'the wave of Marxism break' and the nation be healed from 'the racial tuberculosis that infects international Jewry'. At that moment, however, 'with fire in their bellies, the German people will regain their role in the history of the world'.

As Hitler's revolution sought its vindication in its racist aims, so he justified his right to lead this revolution by referring to his spiritual mentor. Actually, he conceded, neither his rank nor his status entitled him to the position of leader, but there seemed no point in trying to obtain some ministerial post or other for the mere sake of appearances. His real vision was a thousand times greater, he stated imperiously, namely to go down in history as 'the man who put an end to Marxism'. Filled with an overweening self-confidence in his power to rid the world of Marxism and of the Jews on whom it rests, he declared: 'This is my task, and after I have fulfilled it – as I surely shall – any thought of holding the title of minister will seem a triviality.' To carry through such a design one indeed needs to wear the halo of a Messiah.

Only when his task was completed, Hitler continued, would he have proved himself worthy of his great idol, the continuation of whose work he had planned from the beginning. Wagner too, the visionary of *Götterdämmerung* who warned the Germans of their impending doom, possessed neither rank nor title, having no need for such things. What he achieved through his own efforts far outshone any medals or decorations that others might bestow on him.

This was the genius with whom he identified himself, declared the prisoner, filled with the sense of his sacred mission. 'Standing by the grave of Richard Wagner for the first time', he told the court, 'I was filled with pride when I saw that here lay a man who had declined to have inscribed on his gravestone something like "Here lies the body of His Excellency Baron Richard von Wagner, Privy Councillor and Music Director." '[59] The memory of the moment stirred old emotions. For now he had revealed to the whole world that 'the greatest German who had ever lived' had died a plain man. And it was this discovery that raised him, Adolf Hitler, the Master's anointed successor, above all the assembled Privy Councillors, Excellencies and Barons who were now sitting in judgement over him. With scorn and contempt, he proclaimed, 'the eternal goddess of eternal justice' would simply tear up their verdict.

Towards the end of his statement Hitler asked a favour of the court, namely that the law requiring foreigners convicted of an offence to be deported, be not enforced in his case – not only on personal grounds, but also because such an act 'would subsequently be seen as a source of ignominy and shame for the German people'. 'Do not forget', he urged his judges, 'that almost all the greatest and best of our people have been made to suffer bitterly as refugees in foreign lands. Do not forget the words that Wagner spoke the first time he saw the Rhine.'[60]

In the heat of the moment Hitler forgot that Wagner had left Germany of his own free will so as to escape his debts and make a new life in Paris. But fortunately for Hitler nobody in the courtroom would have known much about Wagner's life, let alone about what he had said on the banks of the Rhine.

So what did Wagner say? On leaving France to return to Germany he wrote: 'Impecunious musician that I was, I saw the Rhine for the first time, and with tears in my eyes I pledged unswerving loyalty to my German Fatherland from that moment.'[61] Nobody would have noticed that the man in the dock, another impoverished artist with patriotic tears in his eyes, actually had himself in mind.

13

WAGNERIAN HERO: A SELF-PORTRAIT

The rebirth of National Socialism from the spirit of music – to adapt the Nietzschean phrase – took place in the Festspielhaus in Bayreuth. For ten years the building had stood deserted, the message unheard. The onward march of Hitler, to whom people had looked for a new Bayreuth in a new German Reich, had been temporarily stayed, but his friends in Bayreuth, thanks among other things to the generosity of Jewish-American benefactors, achieved their goal and the Wagnerian heroes took up residence again on the 'Green Hill'. The new leader may have been halted in his tracks and his movement reduced to silence, but in his place the curtain would rise again on the warriors of opera with drawn swords and raised spears, asserting their immutable claim to domination. The *Weltanschauung* of Bayreuth, which with Hitler's appearance on the scene had been brought out of the darkness of the opera house into the light of day and preached to the masses, had been forced to return to its starting-point.

The sword that had been struck out of Hitler's hand shone from the cover of the Festival programme in 1924 to symbolize the continuation of the struggle. Siegfried Wagner's friend Franz Stassen captioned his aggressive design with the cry 'Nothung! Nothung! New and invigorated! I brought thee back to life!'[1] It was a message directed no less to the pilgrims flocking to the Festspielhaus than to the Wagnerian Messiah languishing in jail and his outlawed party. But in effect there was no difference between the two. Both also shared the symbolic meaning of Stassen's design: on the right of the sword Aryan heroes gaze upwards towards the shining castle of the Holy Grail, while on the left, kept apart by the blade of the sword, the subhuman hordes with their emaciated bodies and drooping heads shuffle to their doom. It was there for all to see: the arm that wielded the sword had temporarily returned.

Bayreuth was the source not only of power but also of the eternal verities that the Master had preached in his visionary last writings. Everything that had happened since then he had already prophesied, together with that which was still to come so that the word should be fulfilled. As he had expressed his thoughts in coded form, like an oracle, so his heirs likewise disclosed their Nazi allegiance in cryptic terms. 'From 1878 onwards', stated the Festival programme book, 'Wagner saw everything coming to pass that with terrifying logic has indeed come to pass – world war, financial collapse, famine and the defeat of the Reich.'

Above all Wagner had pointed to the two directions from which these disasters would come. One is that which calls itself 'communist' – that crude and savage perversion of the Christian doctrine 'that screams with thinly-disguised greed "What is yours, is mine!"'; the other, characterized by an insatiable covetousness and a desire to spread its tentacles over oceans and continents as far as the eye can see, is international Jewry.[2]

'Who can save us?' comes the question. The answer, which the initiated will understand, is a reference to Wagner's own essay with the oracular title 'Know Thyself'. 'After we have overcome all false shame', wrote the Master, 'there remains for us Germans the ultimate knowledge, the grand solution – that there will be no Jews left.'[3] That moment has almost arrived, warns the Bayreuth programme, since the man to carry out the task has already announced himself. 'I came not to send peace but a sword!' he has proclaimed. 'Such was the Saviour's battle cry! . . . Only if we advance as Knights of the Grail into the great German war of liberation with such heroic sentiments in our breasts shall we wrench the sword Nothung from the tree, and no god in the world will be able to shatter it. Our strength will come from the spirit of Bayreuth.'[4]

This message, spoken by the voice of Wahnfried and couched in the imagery of Wagner, was at one with Hitler's own design, and the would-be warriors were already congregating in the Wagnerian shrine. For these were indeed outlawed Nazis who now flocked to Bayreuth to cheer Hitler's Führer, Wagner, instead of Hitler himself.[5] Instead of the swastika, which was soon to fly over the Festspielhaus, the imperial, anti-republican black–white–red flag was hoisted and 'all the adherents of the defeated Empire, with Ludendorff at their head, assembled at the Festspielhaus to demonstrate against the "Jewish republic"', as Franz Wilhelm Beidler recalled.[6]

Siegfried Wagner too knew that the hour had struck. By siding with the National Socialists he had put himself on a collision course with the Weimar Republic. Only if the saviour returned from prison to take control of the Festival as of the country could a new beginning be made in the spirit of 'the work of art of the future'. If he were ultimately to fail, there would be unimaginable consequences, one of which, in the words of the Festival's artistic director, Heinz Tietjen, would be 'a very real threat that the whole

Bayreuth Festival would simply collapse, since the music of Wagner was not to the liking of the previous government'.[7]

Siegfried's joy at the re-opening of the Festival was clouded by Hitler's defeat. It was too early for celebrations, though Siegfried lived in hope. Not until 1933, when the Führer and new Chancellor arrived in all his glory and his portrait was placed alongside that of the Master in the official Festival guide, could the real rebirth of Bayreuth be celebrated. As at the foundation ceremony in 1872, Beethoven's Ninth Symphony was played, conducted by Richard Strauss. And again, but this time flushed with victory, Hitler stood at the Master's grave, then laid a floral tribute on the unhappy Siegfried's last resting-place, with a black–white–red ribbon and his signature embroidered in gold.[8]

When Siegfried Wagner opened the first post-war Festival in 1924, all this had seemed barely thinkable. What had then been at stake was not aesthetic pleasure and the celebration of the revival of an elite institution but a demonstration of staying power. It was a question not of celebrating a musical occasion, said the director, but of seeing the performances as 'strengthening the German spirit'.[9] Those whose faith had begun to waver would find it restored to strength; those who had undergone baptism in the fire of rebellion would receive confirmation and pass from there to celebrate the Eucharist in the pure blood of *Parsifal*. 'I believe in one God and in a hundred thousand devils,' added Siegfried, 'but this time, as in the fairy tale, Hans will get the better of the devils.'[10] He knew that people would recognize the allusion.

Meanwhile Hitler sat in his cell and longed to be where others also longed him to be. In a letter to Siegfried he spoke of the 'great pain' he felt that summer. 'Since the age of thirteen', he wrote, 'I have never lost sight of my dream of attending the Festival. Unhappy fate has hitherto not considered me worthy or mature enough – it must be one of the two.'[11] When, in the middle of July, 'the Knights of the Grail, after long years of deprivation, hastened to Bayreuth to see the chalice revealed once more', as an anti-Semitic commentator put it, Hitler was marching in spirit at their side.

On the very first evening, a performance of Cosima's traditional pre-war production of *Die Meistersinger*, the presence of the Führer could be felt in the hall. Ten years earlier Siegfried's Forging Song had brought the audience to their feet, drowning the tenor's voice in cheers at the prospect of war. Now it was the words of Hans Sachs that had them applauding wildly, led by Hitler's companion Ludendorff. Attacks may threaten from hostile quarters without, but, as Sachs sings at the end of the opera, 'hallowed German art' will emerge victorious[12] – prophetic words which seemed to be fulfilled at that moment when the voice of National Socialism had been silenced in the country but seemed to be heard speaking to the faithful through Wagner's music at this very moment and in this very place. 'After Sachs' final words', wrote Rosa Eidam, a friend of Siegfried

Wagner's, 'the whole house rose to a man and stood during the final bars of the opera. Then, after minutes of tumultuous cheering and applause, they all broke into *"Deutschland, Deutschland über alles"*.'[13]

What Rosa Eidam described as an 'overwhelming, universal emotion' the critic of the *Frankfurter Zeitung* called a 'moving spectacle which reduced all true listeners to silence'. But the excitement only reached its climax when, after all the verses of *'Deutschland über alles'* had been sung, the solemn temple was turned into a meeting-hall where all manner of hitherto repressed emotions were given free rein. Defiant shouts of 'Heil!' came from members of the outlawed party, together with slogans hailing the imprisoned Führer, leaving the *Frankfurter Zeitung* correspondent both overwhelmed and perplexed.[14] Reality, as Wagner had foretold, had found its way into the theatre and there seen itself reflected as in a mirror. The audience had responded to Hans Sachs by singing their national anthem in praise of the Reich whose ideals had been preserved by art in times of difficulty. Thus, as an historian of the Party wrote in 1933, 'the Festival in Bayreuth was transformed into a gigantic demonstration of the newly awakened spirit of Germany'. For the first time Wagner's *Meistersinger*, stripped of its historical garb, appeared as the piece of didactic political drama that Wagner intended it to be.

The warning did not go unheeded. People who had previously thought of Bayreuth as an esoteric centre of art for art's sake now realized that it had become the bastion of an anti-Republican party and a breeding-ground for the most uncompromising anti-Semitism. Formerly interpreted for the music-loving public in aesthetic terms, Wagner's works were now beginning to reveal their contemporary relevance. 'The *Meistersinger* demonstration of 1924', wrote the *Völkischer Beobachter* in 1933, the year Hitler seized power, 'had the same effect on the new deities in Germany [a reference to the domination of the Jews] as the sound of Siegfried's horn-call on Alberich, the dwarf who steals the gold. It came like a thunderbolt to those who had hoped to keep Germany in their clutches for ever.'[15]

The combination of community singing and the bellowing of political slogans, which not only foreign members of the audience found distasteful, was instigated at the highest level. 'If we had the *Volk* on our side', said Cosima, giving her own interpretation of the *Meistersinger*, 'and could all join in the final line, then we would indeed have a true art!'[16] Only insiders recognized that she was following in the footsteps of her husband, who had used similar words after the first performance of the *Ring*. 'You see what we can do,' he cried to the jubilant crowds. 'Now it is up to you to will it. And if you will it, we shall have a true art!'[17] A few days later he added the word 'new'.[18] Not, therefore, theatre in an enclosed space, anxiously protecting itself against influences from the outside world, but theatre as a social symbol with a bearing on reality, challenging society to regenerate itself.

Just this was also in Cosima's mind. The ecstatic *Meistersinger* audience of 1924 was looking to build a bridge between the windowless confines of the theatre and the Germany outside, whose praises they never stopped singing. 'Not only on the stage was the Grail displayed,' wrote the aged Hans von Wolzogen; 'not only in the drama was the sword forged. All those inspired by the message should carry the Schillerian "divine spark" out into the darkness like a torch'[19] – a torch not to shed light, however, but to start a fire.

The story has it that Siegfried Wagner was annoyed by the outburst of political passion on the 'Green Hill'. It was admitted that he not only lent his name but also used Wagner's works and the Festival itself to protect the illegal Nazi Party;[20] but at the same time it was pointed out that he also made it clear that he would not tolerate such a misuse of the Festspielhaus in the future. Hitler also took this line, forbidding, after 1933, any use of the opera house for political purposes – after all, Wagner's works said all there was to be said.

Whether or not Siegfried's move to distance himself from the events of 1924 reflected his own convictions is hard to tell. It seems more likely that, using the ambivalent tactics characteristic of his father, he was concerned above all to appease those circles on whom he was dependent for the continued financing of the Festival. It was also a gesture towards the Weimar government, which he had already irritated by raising the old imperial flag, and towards the many Jewish performers, patrons and sympathetic journalists who found Hitler totally incompatible with the Master. Wagner and Cosima had already shown how to keep on good terms with people one despises, or positively hates, for the sake of their usefulness; and so long as their friend 'Wolf' was prepared to tolerate it, Siegfried and the 'fanatical' Winifred kept Jews among their domestic staff. Additionally, Hitler was always tolerant of Siegfried's political timidity and avoided the Festival in Bayreuth as long as his presence there might have compromised its integrity; until his triumphant emergence as Chancellor his presence was only evident in the programme and in the company of the family, never at the performances.

What looked like disloyalty on Siegfried's part presented no problem for Hitler. 'In personal terms he was my friend', he said in the 'Wolf's Lair' in 1942, 'but politically he was passive. He could not help it – the Jews would otherwise have ruined him.'[21] Hitler was referring here not to the devastating reviews of Siegfried's operas in the press but to that vulnerable aspect of his nature which Hitler himself later exploited against his own opponents. 'Siegfried Wagner had been through a serious crisis', he told Goebbels that same year, 'when he found himself compromised by his homosexuality and was made to marry in a hurry.'[22] Until the end of his days Siegfried lived in fear and trembling of being blackmailed by the press, which would have had a disastrous effect on the Festival. Winifred lamented to Goebbels that her husband was 'so listless', and Goebbels recorded how she wept 'because the son was not like the Master'.[23]

Meanwhile Wagner's real heir, whom Winifred worshipped, according to Goebbels, was in Landsberg prison, where he received regular reports about developments in Bayreuth from members of the family. They told him how his apostles had met at the Festival and felt his spirit come over them; a visit to Bayreuth, they said, should be made possible for all citizens – a kind of 'national pilgrimage'.[24] As his own philosophy had evolved from Wagner's works, so its fulfilment first manifested itself in the realm of sound – the sound of his voice, carrying a politico-religious message, whispering, urging, thundering, ranging over the whole gamut of musical dynamics, as though he were conducting an audience of millions.[25] But ten years earlier, in his comfortable prison cell, he could only enjoy these scenes of jubilation in his imagination and find consolation in listening to Wagner arias on his gramophone or dreaming of *Tristan*. Wherever one looked, the Master was present.

For the inner world that he had absorbed through the mystical Aryan choir in *Parsifal* or the heroic wrath of Wotan corresponded to the concepts of National Socialism, these concepts, like their musical model, expressing everything but saying nothing. What Hitler thought was what he heard in Wagner's music. What he felt embraced the extremes of Lohengrin's ecstatic arrival, on one hand, and Wotan's world-shattering departure, on the other, between the all-consuming flames of pagan destruction and the mystical magic of Good Friday. What he saw before him in Wagner's cosmic dramas merged naturally and with a logic of demonic power, conceptualized with magisterial authority, into the prophetic world of Wagner's philosophy. In the Bayreuth programme of 1924, which reads like a party manifesto in coded form, it is there for all to read: 'Richard Wagner is a guide to National Socialism.'[26]

It was not long before Hitler attracted the attention of cartoonists. On the front page of an issue of the satirical journal *Simplicissimus* the caricaturist Thomas Theodor Heine sketched a parody of his real-life defeat as an imaginary victory. Seated on his stallion, like Rienzi, Hitler rides victorious through the Brandenburg Gate leading President Ebert in chains; at his side rides the Emperor Barbarossa, while beneath a fluttering swastika a Jew is being killed by a Teutonic warrior, his eyes fixed on Hitler. When he was shown the caricature in Landsberg, he looked at it thoughtfully for a long time, then said: 'That can still happen, provided we remain firm.'[27] Heine, a Jew who fled Germany in 1933, had had a premonition of the Third Reich and its horrors.

In Landsberg Hitler began work on his own book at almost the same time as Bayreuth was preparing for the first post-war Festival. He once complained how reluctant the world had been to 'minister to the needs of a genius like Richard Wagner'[28] but he could make no such complaint about the way he was treated by Wahnfried. They served him like a prince, deluged him with parcels and set him various tasks, such as reviewing Wolzogen's latest essay or a libretto of Siegfried's – 'to be read as drama, like Richard Wagner's libretti, the meaning of which is made clear only through the music', as Winifred instructed.[29] Not for nothing has Winifred Wagner been called 'the driving force behind *Mein Kampf*'.[30]

As the young Cosima had played the role of 'carrier pigeon', conveying Wagner's thoughts and desires to King Ludwig in Munich, so now Winifred, with no official function in the Festival, adopted the role of innocent messenger acting in the name of the Wagner clan. Although Hitler had told Siegfried that he was not 'a man of the pen and wrote badly', and that he 'owed the German people actions rather than words',[31] Winifred sent him everything necessary for him to start writing. 'She bought untold quantities of typing paper, carbon paper, pencils, pens, ink and rubbers at the stationer's in the main street in Bayreuth,' wrote Friedelind. 'For the time he was in jail she supplied him with everything that a self-styled genius could require.'[32] The hope must have been that these services would have been gratefully acknowledged in the book when the time came. Wagner and Chamberlain, Hitler's predecessors, had both spiced their work with autobiographical material. The hero who seeks to move the world must raise his life to a world scale, for the trials that he has already undergone are those that still await mankind. The fact that the paper and other materials, which Hitler could have just as well got in Landsberg, came from Wagner's shrine in Bayreuth only served to underline the importance of his autobiographical exercise for his national mission. Herr Hitler would finally reveal himself as the saviour of the nation.

In his study *From Drummer Boy to Führer*, the historian Albrecht Tyrell set out to investigate how Hitler's conception of his role changed radically between 1919 and 1924, leading him in *Mein Kampf* 'to stake an ideological and political claim to world leadership'.[33] But Tyrell could find no satisfactory explanation. Without his commitment to Wagner, without the blessing of Chamberlain, without the fiasco of his attempted coup and without his resurrection as a Wagnerian hero in the pages of *Mein Kampf*, his change of persona cannot be understood. It cannot be explained in terms of his Austrian childhood, or his ecstatic response to the *Ring*, or the sudden revelation of reading Wagner's 'regeneration' writings. What caused him to feel that the future of the world had been laid in his hands? If he did not despair of himself and his ideals after his miserable attempt at revolution, then this was because those who represented his ideals did not despair of him. Bayreuth believed in him as he believed in Wagner. And if, after three months' meticulous work on his autobiography, he now presented himself as a man born again, although everyone was convinced, in this year when the Festival re-opened, that his political future lay behind him, then this was only because it was expected of him. He had been cast in the role of future leader of the nation and the life-story that he unfurled turned out, after a few adjustments, to be the early biography of that leader. Conceived as the new Messiah by the dying Chamberlain barely a year earlier, he now came to life in jail with the help of the typewriter.

Mein Kampf, stylistically so crude that one could be deceived into thinking that it was the work of a semi-literate, finally established the Hitler myth. People looked down their noses at the blunt, primitive statements of principle expounded by this strange creature who made such extravagant claims for himself, but they took notice of him. As a party leader he had been a flop, and the voice of the magnetic orator had been silenced, first by his imprisonment, then by being banned from speaking in public. But his book gave him an aura to which virtually no other politician of his age could aspire. This man, who wrote entirely about himself, could not simply be chased off the scene by the police or ridiculed out of existence by caricatures in *Simplicissimus*.

The success of the book proved him right. By the end of the Second World War some ten million copies had been distributed – though how many were actually read is a matter of debate. All the same, praise was showered on it from quarters as far apart as Elisabeth Förster-Nietzsche ('Hitler's wonderful book')[34] and the *émigré* Konrad Heiden. Almost against his will Heiden conceded in 1933 that it was 'an excellent book, full of perceptive observations and skilful formulations, albeit formless and endlessly repetitive . . . and, of course, thoroughly anti-Semitic'.[35]

For the general public, however, *Mein Kampf* – a copy of which Hitler ordered to be placed alongside Nietzsche's *Zarathustra* in the Tannenberg War Memorial where Hindenburg was buried – was like a new Bible. Hermann Rauschning spoke in 1938 of 'that remarkable book which has acquired the reputation of being a work of divine inspiration', although, as Rauschning well knew, 'it was held in no particular esteem by older party members. . . . Nobody took it seriously – indeed, nobody *could* take it seriously or follow its style.'[36] The most famous book of the National Socialist movement, of which Hitler proudly boasted in 1942 'that it had sold more copies than any book in the world apart from the Bible',[37] was also the least understood. After the war the ten million copies vanished without trace. So did their message.

Looking back during the Russian campaign at his time in Landsberg, when he had seen this campaign coming, Hitler reminisced in the 'Wolf's Lair': 'Had I not spent these months in jail, *Mein Kampf* would never have come to be written. During this time I became aware of the true significance of many things of which up till then I only had vague notions.'[38] The flattering image that he had cherished since his time in Linz, an image of himself as the longed-for 'tribune of the people', now took firm hold of him. Whatever had happened to him in the past, he now recognized, had been an inevitable stage in his rise to the status of hero, and whatever obstacles had been put in his way had only served to further his progress. What he had hitherto seen as the successive stages in a banal struggle for survival now appeared, from the summit he had reached, as actions which revealed the uniqueness of his role. A man becomes a hero only through action, and only through perpetual struggle, raised above the mundane preoccupation with mere survival, does his life acquire meaning. This too formed part of the vision whose consequences he later forced upon an entire nation.

The central experience of his thirty-five years, however, was in his eyes his struggle against the prime enemy of heroism – the Jews. This sly, cunning race was plotting the downfall of the Germanic peoples, and he himself had only narrowly escaped being caught up in the maelstrom of mass destruction and mass misery that had followed the war. First came the 'stab in the back', followed by the November Revolution and the advent of the Judaeo-Marxist Republic, which, working behind the scenes, had stifled his attempted insurrection at birth. The man who has realized that life is a struggle against evil is predestined to become a hero; the man who emerges victorious from this struggle, however, reveals himself as a saviour of mankind. The balancing act on the verge of survival that had constituted Hitler's pitiable existence up to then was of no moment; apart from his lurid career as a political leader there was nothing to claim attention. But presented as *Mein Kampf*, it evoked memories of the ancient heroic lay of the dragon-slayer in which everything could be interpreted in mythological terms.

All was now to be seen in terms of 'struggle' – struggle as the basic principle of life, already nominated as such by Wagner and adopted as his motto for the confrontation with Jewry. 'Understand here, in Heaven's name,' he had cried in 1865 to Röckel, his fellow-revolutionary, 'what is at stake, what a gigantic struggle lies ahead!'[39] Five years later he gave Cosima the task of explaining to Nietzsche, at that time intended for a lifelong career in the service of Wahnfried, what 'a terrible struggle' confronted them in their common crusade.[40]

Goebbels was only one of those who recognized that Hitler included himself among Wagner's crusaders. 'Many years had to elapse', wrote Goebbels in the *Völkischer Beobachter* in August 1933, 'before the nation as a whole found its way back to Wagner. At the time of his death his struggle had not yet been won.'[41] But Wagner's *Kampf* was that of *Mein Kampf*. The stimulus for Hitler's title came from the Jew-hater Chamberlain, who in a pivotal section of his *Foundations* called 'The Struggle' describes the fight between the 'creative Teutons' and the parasitic Jews for 'the heritage of the world'. As the book itself owed its existence to Bayreuth, so too may have its title. For the real subject of Hitler's autobiography is not his basically uneventful life but the racial struggle as expounded by Chamberlain and mirrored in Hitler's career.

This concept of struggle dominated Hitler's thoughts and actions till the end of his life. Even his later acts of aggression, excessive by any moral or military standards, seem like reruns of the old principle, the author claiming to be convinced that the struggle on which he had embarked – namely the Second World War – 'would end in the same way as that which I first fought out in myself'.[42] He was re-enacting the same drama that had received its first performance in 1926 as *Mein Kampf*. Still in February 1945 he is to be found telling the last meeting to commemorate the foundation of the Nazi Party that these 'difficult times' are merely 'a terrifying repetition on the world stage of that internal German struggle we have already been through' and consequently 'here too, in this very year, history will take a new turn'.[43] Reality mocked his posturing but for Hitler the last word lay with his myth; for as long as he lived – and, who knows, perhaps beyond the time of his heroic downfall – his role as saviour of the world had not yet been played out.

Mein Kampf spoke the words of the chosen saviour, a solitary knight, like that portrayed in Dürer's famous engraving, who follows his predestined path between Death and the Devil. With the encouragement of the Bayreuth myth factory the life of an unemployed nobody is transformed into the exploits of a Wagnerian hero who experienced in reality what otherwise only exists on the stage. In the same year as Hitler set himself symbolically alongside Siegmund and Siegfried, Bayreuth advanced a modern interpretation of the *Ring*. Wagner, said the Festival programme, was today more relevant than ever, for the 'rejecting of all foreign elements' that he had preached in his anti-Semitic writings 'was intimately linked with the Germanic spirit of his works'.[44] As the man in Landsberg cast the broken fragments of his life in the mould of the *Ring*, so Bayreuth declared the didactic drama of the Nibelungen to be a mythological anticipation of Hitler's mission.

In the same programme of 1924 Hans Alfred Grunsky, a friend of Chamberlain's, makes no bones about equating the Nibelungen with the Jews. Hatred and subversion, he writes, are characteristic of this underground people, for whose representatives the radiant Siegfried 'cannot but feel the most intense racial dislike'. The dwarf Mime is also depicted as one of these. Faced with such embodiments of 'the callous and ignoble pursuit of wealth and power', the Aryan god Wotan expounds his own rival values, 'setting heroism against greed, positive action against thirst for power'. Only a heroic man of action can rid the world from the curse of these 'nocturnal creatures'. The arrival of such a pure and glorious man, 'a free and fearless hero such as Wotan had yearned for', would consummate the work. 'In Siegfried Nordic man has created his ideal image, the most glorious embodiment of the heroic idea.' And as though wanting to link these abstract thoughts to the coming personification of Siegfried who would be greeted on the stage with cries of 'Heil!', Grunsky adds: 'A Siegfried understands only open and honest combat.'[45]

'Combat', 'struggle', was the goal that gave Hitler's planless life a surprising sense of direction, and it provided the title for the two volumes of
his autobiography, the first published in 1925, the second a year later. But
neither the sentimentalized biographical narrative of the first part nor the
longwinded history of the Nazi Party in the second constitutes the real
subject of the work. From the very first line the aim of the author is to
present the world as Wagnerian drama, with successive crises and a climax in catastrophe, and with himself cast in the role of hero. Confronted
by the prospect of destruction on a cosmic scale, leading from the collapse
of human civilization to the ultimate desolation of the entire universe, 'our
last hope of salvation lies in struggle, armed struggle'.[46]

This was the only way the young orphan from Linz, 'clutching an attaché
case full of clothes and linen' and growing up in the 'racial chaos' of Vienna, could assert himself as a redeemer of the world, in the expectation
that the 'twilight of the gods', the defeat of Wotan and his Wälsungen,
would be transformed into their triumph and their shining resurrection.
Once the irrevocable conflict between the gods of the Aryan race and the
misshapen 'creatures of night and death' had been identified, the political
reality in which Hitler found himself could be recognized as being a phase
in that conflict. To grasp this relationship and then to take up arms were to
Hitler one and the same. But only when, over and above this, it had become possible to mobilize the people in the struggle and show them their
part in the battle for survival as well as in the metaphysical tragedy would
victory finally be achieved. As hero he was the one chosen to lead his troops
with sword held aloft; at the same time, as a man of letters, author of an
autobiographical work of world history, he was entitled to see himself as a
producer who directs a performance of the old drama of the final battle
between the races but in a new production and with a surprising figure in
the principal role.

 It was in Vienna, writes Hitler, that his eyes were opened to the two
threats 'which I had hitherto scarcely even known by name, let alone the
meaning they had for the existence of the German people'. Penniless and
with no prospects, struggling to scrape a living, he experienced a sudden
flash of enlightenment that showed the whole population of Germans and
Austrians to be caught in the same parlous state. These two threats bore
the names Marxism and Jewry[47] – the forces responsible for the crisis which
Hitler too was now being forced to suffer in the name of the depressed
masses. He had willingly endured five years of hunger, since by devoting
his time to reading and occasional visits to the opera, which he had somehow managed to afford, he had been able to advance his political awareness 'as never before', in his words.

Under such circumstances, Hitler went on, the *Weltanschauung* developed which became 'the granite foundation of my actions at that time'.
Here those who accused him of a lack of realism, as for instance over his

abortive coup, found their subsequent justification, for Hitler's 'actions' were not logical responses to a given situation but followed his interpretation of reality as dictated by the 'granite foundation' of his beliefs. The knowledge he had acquired at the beginning of the century from intensive reading and from visits to the opera provided him with a blue-print of the society which, right down to his death in 1945, he never allowed to cast the slightest doubt on his vision of the future. 'I had little to add to the plan I made at that time', he wrote in 1924, full of ideological self-confidence, 'and nothing at all to change.'[48]

During his formative years in Vienna Hitler read anything and everything that could be pressed into service for his self-identification with Wagner. As well as the collected writings of the Master himself he absorbed the teachings of Houston Stewart Chamberlain as laid out in his *Foundations of the Nineteenth Century*. But when accused of having also studied the more extreme anti-Semitic writings of the time, he rejected the charge with the peremptory indignation of a man who has been caught out. The whole tenor of such publications, he said, coupled with 'their shallow and totally unscientific style of reasoning',[49] even made him doubt the validity of the whole anti-Semitic movement. Chamberlain's arguments, however, had a scientific basis, and it was a matter of regret that 'the members of the government were too conceited and too stupid to learn from them'.[50] The moment demanded, said Chamberlain, an unremitting struggle against the enemies of mankind. And once again it was Wagner who, having recognized the predicament in which the *Volk* found itself, emerged as the liberator of the nation.

'The *Volk* will achieve redemption', predicted Wagner in his 'Work of Art of the Future', 'by redeeming its own enemies' – which is to say, by reducing 'that which it does not want into that which has no right to exist', and by destroying 'that which is only worthy to be destroyed'.[51] First uttered by Wagner in the revolutionary year of 1849, then revived half a century later in a 'scientific' context by Chamberlain, it was a challenge that, a further twenty-five years on, became the battle-cry of *Mein Kampf* – 'The day of fulfilment is nigh, for the Messiah has come.'

Hitler's eyes had been opened not by his personal experiences but by the insights of his predecessors which had prepared him for these experiences. The *Volk*, however, who according to the Master should have risen up instinctively against the arch-enemy, had been kept in ignorance over the global struggle in which their future would be decided. They were suffering but did not know from what, feeling a sense of foreboding without suspecting that it was shared by all. If, Hitler argued further, Germany were to lose the war, it would only be because the people had been kept in ignorance of the real war in which they had been caught up for centuries. 'Not realizing the racial problem, and especially the threat posed by the Jews, was the main cause for the collapse of Germany,' wrote the prisoner in Landsberg.[52] It was not action that had been lacking but knowledge.

With little of interest to record about his own life, he now set about providing the missing foundation of knowledge which would enable the ignorant Germans to understand at last Wagner's message of 'Know Thyself'. As Wagner had challenged mankind to recognize the arch-enemy in its midst, 'the demonic harbinger of the downfall of civilization', so Hitler picked up the challenge and confronted the people with the facts.

His choice of a Wagnerian framework derived from his early experiences in Linz and Vienna. And since he saw himself as the heroic progeny of Wotan, the portrait he painted of his enemies might have been sketched while he was watching a performance in the Hofoper. His prime candidate for the role of archetypal Jew was Wagner's Mime, the cunning dwarf. Without mentioning him by name, Hitler painstakingly transfers all the repulsive characteristics with which Wagner had invested him to the race of demons who behave in normal life as normal people do. But – and this is what Mime reveals – they are only playing the hypocrite. They pretend to be respectable, even amiable citizens but are merely concealing their sordid selfishness, and no trick is too shabby for them to play in their pursuit of their secret aim.

Wagner's dwarf only rears the young Siegfried so that, when he is strong enough, he can capture the Nibelungen gold for him. Once Siegfried has slain the dragon who guards the treasure, Mime plans to drug him, then cut off his head with the sword Nothung. Pretending to be concerned with the youth's well-being, he tells him a pack of lies and assures him of his affection while in reality consumed with hate. For no one does the ugly dwarf hate more than the handsome warrior who has never learned the meaning of fear. Only after listening to the voice of nature does Siegfried recognize his foster-father's duplicity, and behind every flattering phrase he begins to hear the reverse. When, after the dragon has been slain, Mime seeks to kill the young hero, Wagner's stage direction enjoins him 'to adopt a gentle, tender tone' as he sings 'I am going to chop the boy's head off!' Mime's mendacity is now finally unmasked. Siegfried, made aware of the true situation, has no choice but, 'in an access of revulsion',[53] to strike the dwarf down. Here too it is the sense of tragic predicament that inspires the act of liberation. The man who refuses to allow himself to be entangled in the net of the creatures of the underworld must heed the voice of nature and 'destroy that which is only worthy to be destroyed'.

The vicious caricature of Mime, through which Wagner set out to make the racial characteristics of the Jew perversely explicit, was accepted by his disciple in Landsberg at face value. To him the 'unclean and shameless' Jews[54] lived in the filth and grime of the squalid Nibelungen hovels like those he had seen in performances of the *Ring* in Vienna, with the Bayreuth tenor Hans Breuer as Mime. Their language, like that of the stammering dwarf, was a mass of strange, distorted sounds, and equally perverse was the message it conveyed: Mime never ceases to emphasize what care he lavished on his foster-child but Hitler insists that the vaunted 'unself-ishness' of the Jews is only apparent.[55] Since their driving force is 'ruthless egoism', they have to resort more and more to deception in their dealings with others, while as 'masters in the art of lying', they engaged their elo-quence 'to disguise or at least conceal their real thoughts'.[56] Through dis-tasteful flattery they succeeded in worming their way into unsuspecting people's confidence, making out that they were the only ones to suffer injustice and then, when their exhausted listeners were on the point of giving up, 'embracing them and using them to their own ends'.[57] If they meet with resistance, like Mime with Siegfried, 'they loose a flood of lies and slanders until the nerves of their listeners snap'.[58]

Mime's ultimate goal to become 'master of the universe' through his pos-session of the gold[59] is shared by his brother Alberich, who also covets the world as his birthright. In Wagner's racial typography, followed by Hitler in *Mein Kampf*, Alberich is the sinister, demonic counterpart to his tragicomical brother. The fact that they are perpetually squabbling with each other over ownership of the booty also strikes Hitler as relevant: when attracted by the prospect of 'shared booty', he writes, 'a single colony of rats will fight each other wildly for a share of the reward'.[60] It was also Wagner's King Rat Alberich who led Hitler to identify another revolting species of Jew, one who indulges in open brutality. A moment in *Rheingold* dramatically illus-trates Hitler's point, when Wagner describes Alberich as a 'slimy toad'. If anyone touches him, reiterates Hitler, he finds himself 'holding soft slime' in his hand.[61] Such Alberichs also abuse 'innocent young blonde virgins',[62] laying hands on the noblest image of the Lord, namely the Aryan race – and for this offence they will be punished 'by being driven out of Paradise'.[63]

As Alberich plots to dispose of Siegfried, the new owner of the ring, so, according to Hitler, the 'Jewish world of international finance' has attempted to realize by underhand means its 'long-cherished plan' for the destruction of the German nation. In order to provoke a world war against the Reich, it resolved 'to forge a coalition, strengthened and encouraged by the thought of the marching millions at their backs, ready to pounce on the heroic Siegfried'.[64] As in the *Ring* Hagen plots the hero's downfall, so the murder-ing Jews of Hitler's imagination plan the dissolution of the Germanic race.[65] As Hagen prepares an amnesic potion for Siegfried before slaying him, so the inhabitants of Hitler's underworld seek 'to put their victims to sleep'.[66] Revelling in the spine-chilling imagery, he writes of a body politic 'through which flows an incessant stream of infectious organisms that penetrate to the furthest extremities, paralysing ever greater parts of the body'.[67]

Whilst Alberich succeeds in engineering Siegfried's murder from a dis-tance, he fails in his efforts to retrieve the ring and reduce the world to a slave colony. Here, Hitler concedes, matters are still not decided. As Alberich can use the Tarnhelm, the magic helmet, to assume whatever shape he pleases, so Hitler's Jew has donned the mask of Marxism, pretending to preach love among individuals and friendship among the nations in order to bring about, step by step, his conquest of the world.[68] This can only come about, however, if the Jews make a concerted attempt to 'wipe out' the world of Aryanism. With this aim in mind Karl Marx, a demon of the Nibelungen kingdom, building on the ideological foundations already provided by his race, has extracted the 'vital toxic substances' from the declining civilization 'in order to mix them in a concentrated solution, like a magician, and undermine the independent existence of free nations. All this is to be done in the interests of their race.' As Alberich wants to turn the world into a culture-less Nibelungen state, so Marxism 'delivers the world straight into the hands of the Jews'.[69]

As a prophet of doom, Hitler sees on the horizon flashes of the great revolution – the final revolution – to come. 'In gaining political power, the Jews will cast off the few pretences to which they still cling and a Jew-by-nation will become a Jew-by-blood, a tyrant.' While Alberich terrorizes his slaves with his whip, the Jewish terror will turn the whole human race into a world of serfs, 'forced into everlasting subjugation'.[70]

The fear that such a world would come to pass – the 'rule of Alberich', he later called it – filled Hitler's mind with a paranoid vision. 'If the Jews,' he meditated, 'with the help of their Marxist creed, succeeded in conquering the world, the culmination will be a danse macabre of the whole of mankind, and the planet, drained of human life, will follow its aimless orbit through the ether as it did millions of years ago.'[71]

Barely had the apocalyptic horseman divulged his scenario of the end of the world than he raised his visor and proclaimed himself the saviour for whom the world had been waiting. For the threatened 'twilight of the gods' could be prevented, providing one avoided the mistakes made by Wotan and the Wälsungen on the stage and treated the Nibelungen as they deserved to be treated. 'I believe I am following the will of the Creator,' declared the new redeemer; 'by keeping the Jews at bay, I am doing the Lord's work'.[72] This extraordinary self-possession, which exposed Hitler to the persistent charge of megalomania, corresponded not only to his sense of mission on behalf of Bayreuth but also to the polarization characteristic of his autobiography. If, as Mein Kampf insinuates, the Jews are really 'vampires'[73] who are sucking the precious blood of the Aryan race, the average politician would hardly be able to stem the flow. What was needed was a holy warrior, a man sent by God, possessed of the immeasurable strength of the Knights of the Grail, which would render the monster innocuous.

Because his enemies were in fact Nibelungen, Hitler had to become a Siegfried. Only a saviour sent from above could overcome the powers of the underworld. Hitler's psychopathic claims for himself only reflected the magnitude of the task he sought to set himself; a global challenge demanded a redeemer sent by destiny. 'The pestilence from which mankind must rid the earth – otherwise the earth could soon be rid of mankind – can only be eliminated by radical means',[74] as one has 'to fight poison gas with poison gas', in Hitler's words from *Mein Kampf*.[75] When one faces an 'Either–Or', any means justify the end.[76] If during the First World War one had had the foresight 'to subject a few tens of thousands of these menacing Hebrews to poison gas, one might have saved the lives of a million or more noble, honourable Germans'.[77] In the nick of time the man of destiny would appear and take the measures necessary to preserve the whole Aryan race from extinction. As this man, he, Hitler, had at this decisive moment therefore made the decision to 'enter the realm of politics'.[78]

In his own way, recognizable only to the initiated, this equation of divine calling with the politics of aggression also has its parallel in Wagner. In his 'Autobiographical Sketch' of 1843 Wagner talks of his early attempts to teach himself musical composition; he quickly realized that these efforts would not readily bear fruit but he persisted because 'it was these very difficulties that fascinated and challenged me, and I resolved to become a composer'.[79] This message of the self-made man who overcomes all obstacles in order to reach the top found its way from Wagner's autobiographical testimony into the world of Hitler's own self-justifying argument. He only entered 'the realm of politics' because the almost superhuman demands made by the 'Either–Or' compelled him to do so.

He remained, however, the man chosen by fate to be the saviour of the German nation, and by adopting the racial criteria underlying Wagner's *Ring*, he was able to present his less-than-heroic earlier career as the ideal training-ground for his future role as national hero. Deprived of his parents, like Siegmund the Wälsung, young Adolf had been pitched into the real world and made to undergo the bitter experience, like Wotan's son, of the people's tragic predicament.[80] This predicament, a sense of national grief, is a leitmotif of *Mein Kampf* as it is an obsession of Siegmund's, who, lamenting the fate that his enemies have prepared for him, is left to free himself with the help of his sword Nothung. Likewise Hitler talks of the 'deprivation and harsh reality' which threatened to engulf him.[81]

As Wotan steels his son through hardship before he considers him worthy to hold the sword of victory in his hand, so 'the wisdom of destiny' subjected the young Hitler to the trials of life in the 'racial chaos' of Vienna. But every time 'the goddess of deprivation took me in her clutches', he emotionally recalled, 'and threatened to crush me, my will to prevail grew stronger, and in the end it was my will that was victorious'.[82]

This goddess, not known to dictionaries of mythology, is another invention of the Master's. In 1849 he had written of 'a prolonged period of suffering that tormented us, burning our breasts and destroying our every desire. Light your torches in the flames of this suffering and let them tell the wrongdoers, "We heed your command, O cruel, inexorable goddess." '[83] As for Wagner, who saw the rebellion as born out of distress and oppression, so for his disciple all popular uprisings – 'volcanic eruptions of

human passions' – are provoked 'either by the cruel goddess of deprivation or by a blazing slogan hurled into the masses like a blazing torch'.[84]

Siegmund's sword is shattered before he himself, also a victim of this
tragic circumstance, is slain. Hitler, however, withstands the test. As the
embodiment of Siegmund's son Siegfried, he examines every source of grief
and anguish that threatens the serenity of his life and, with an instinct as
unerring as Wagner's, picks on the racial problem. Like Hitler, whose eyes
were opened when he first encountered the Jews in their kaftans and with
their black ringlets, Siegfried realizes that the source of his frustration is
the repulsive Mime and his deviance. 'Hateful and horrible, ugly and squat,
humpbacked and servile, with hanging ears and running noses' – such are
the terms he finds for him, finally crying out: 'Away with the detestable
creature. I cannot bear the sight of him any longer!'[85] All this leads him to
consider a radical solution. 'Let us put an end to them all!' he advocates.
When he discovers that 'that creature is not my real father',[86] it is as though
he is reborn. Similar thoughts went through the mind of the new Siegfried
as he revived memories of his nights at the Vienna opera. What he claimed
as his 'instinctive tolerance'[87] gave way, in the case of the Jews, to a full-
blooded Wagnerian feeling of revulsion which swept away the last ves-
tiges of any suspicion of tolerance or compassion. 'To my great delight and
satisfaction', he wrote, in a variation of Siegfried's exultant words, 'I now
knew once and for all that the Jews are not Germans.'[88]

The only question that remained was how to set about his task of destruction. Siegfried's answer was to take action. He reassembled the fragments of his father's sword and, after uncovering Mime's plot, wielded it
as it was intended to be wielded.[89] Hitler also summoned up the sword.
For the murder that Mime was planning to carry out, after drugging his
victim, was an act that Hitler saw surreptitiously taking place every day
on the international political scene. 'The Jews', he declared, like one who
had made a great discovery, 'are fighting unremittingly for domination of
the whole world. The only way to get rid of the hand that has us by the
throat is with the sword. The only force that can stand up against this world-
wide enslavement is the concerted resistance of a powerful national passion.' And as though remembering the blow with which Siegfried rid
himself of Mime, he adds: 'This cannot happen without blood-letting.'[90]

With a frightening coldness which anticipated the blood-letting that was
to take place twenty years later, Hitler provided the philosophy of the
massacre to come. 'Can one in fact eliminate ideas with the sword?' he
asks – giving the chilling answer that force alone will not suffice to destroy
an idea and its manifestations 'unless it takes the form of the complete
annihilation of all who hold that idea, down to the very last person and the
removal of all traces of that idea'.[91] The same solution is recommended in
Wagner's *Ring*. To kill Mime would not have been sufficient; in order to
cleanse the world of everything associated with the Nibelungen, all the

other creatures of the underworld must also be destroyed – and before a second Hagen emerges and attacks a new Siegfried. The sword is the only answer. And when this time comes, predicts the prisoner in Landsberg, 'that sword will proclaim and sustain a new philosophy of life'.[92]

The extermination of the Jews, the clear and unmistakable message of *Mein Kampf*, could not be stayed. Perhaps it was a message too clear to be understood, too drastic to be taken seriously. The Führer's autobiography, the most popular present for Christmas and birthdays during the years of the Third Reich, was published in its millions – but was it read in its millions? Or did it just stand on the shelf in every library, every home, every office? Did people refuse to pay heed to a call for bloodshed on a scale that amounted to genocide? The higher the wave grew, carrying all before it, the more urgent the question became of where it was leading. In retrospect it is undeniable that in a manner totally open and undisguised, *Mein Kampf* provided a timetable for action and did not shrink from naming the unmentionable destination. As it grew to become an unrivalled bestseller in the German language, people reassured themselves by telling each other that, as a guide to the politics of the twenties, it had long lost all claim to validity. And until the beginning of the war the autobiographer turned Reich Chancellor made no effort to disillusion them.

Bayreuth, on the other hand, had no illusions. As the Wahnfried clan may well have encouraged Hitler to write the book and is known to have supplied him with writing materials in jail, so they were kept informed of the stages in its publication. Contact between Wagner's heirs and the Munich publishers probably lay in the hands of Joseph Stolzing-Czerny, editor-in-chief of the *Völkischer Beobachter* and also responsible for editing Hitler's text. His correspondence with Eva Chamberlain shows how close the contact was between Wahnfried and the Nazi propaganda headquarters in Munich.

The intimacy of this contact was described by the historian Karl Alexander von Müller, who knew Hitler well. 'Perhaps I may take this opportunity', wrote Müller later in his memoirs, 'to record a few facts on what I heard about Hitler at this time from the Bruckmanns and which I have not seen published elsewhere'. Elsa Bruckmann, a thoroughly reliable witness, told him something quite extraordinary. 'She revealed to me', wrote Müller, 'that Houston Stewart Chamberlain and his wife Eva Wagner both corrected the proofs of Hitler's book, and even the aged Cosima read some of them. This story', Müller went on, fully aware of the enormity of what he was saying, 'is still vivid in my memory, especially because, given the excruciating style of the book, it seemed to me barely credible. But she repeated it more than once.'[93] So Hitler's promise, given in writing, to solve the Jewish question with the sword was delivered with the express blessing of Bayreuth.

BLOOD BROTHERHOOD

In order that that which was written should be fulfilled, Adolf Hitler, who in Vienna had had the temerity to call himself a writer,[1] had now, fifteen years later, really written a book. Also awaiting fulfilment at that time was the most pressing demand of the age – the final solution of 'the Jewish question'. Armed with the product of years of reading and with the encouragement of his Bayreuth sponsors, he had described the exceptional nature of his calling and his role as the future man of action. As he had written in *Mein Kampf*, his path 'from ineffectual citizen of the world to fanatical anti-Semite' had almost reached its end. Only one step remained.

Had he perhaps, in the flush of hubris that followed the confirmation of his mission by the highest authority, made a beginner's error? Had he not, intent on immediate action, followed the false example of Nietzsche, who in 1870, as Cosima charged, had prematurely launched the attack that announced the final struggle? Had it been wise to disclose the contents of his book, with all the attendant weakness of an overly zealous first work, before the stage had been set for the performance? Years later he acknowledged his impatience, admitting to the economist Otto Wagener that 'in politics one must never say in advance what one intends to do, except when there is no other way out. And even then one must only tell those who need to know, and only as much as they need to know.' When Wagener observed that in that case, he ought not have written *Mein Kampf* at all, Hitler agreed. 'I frequently regret it', he said, 'and would not do so today.' The world completely misunderstood his secret plans and aims, he added, 'but it taught me a lesson'.[2]

There was one aspect of his book that raised particular doubts about the wisdom of publishing it, though it was an aspect on which he stubbornly refused to budge, and that was the subject of public health. Putting up with the author's rabid anti-Semitism as the extreme expression of his envy and resentment, the reader can only regard Hitler's outburst against prostitution, syphilis and racial inter-marriage as the product of personal obsessions. They add nothing to his political claims to national leadership, and the unmistakable fascination with horror which comes over him in his discussion of the mating urge accords ill with the revelations of a would-be world redeemer.

As Hitler saw it, responsibility for what he had diagnosed in *Mein Kampf* as 'the infection of our sexual life'[3] had to be laid at the door of the Jews. As they had enslaved the world with Alberich's gold and ruined Aryan high culture by undermining its intellectual authority, so their most frightening attack was levelled at the future, at the very act of procreation. A threat hung not only over existing society but over those who give that society its radical identity – a community constituted by blood. For thousands of years Aryan society had been preserved by genetic tradition, but now it was facing imminent destruction by the forces of Jewry. 'The cardinal sin in the world today and the end of mankind as we know it', proclaimed the autobiographer in the tones of an Old Testament prophet, 'is the sin against blood and race.'[4]

With the cunning of Satan, says Hitler, the Jews have perverted the healthy urge to reproduction and made men the slaves of prostitutes. Instead of turning their minds to the procreation of the next generation, 'our young Teutons have allowed themselves to be drugged by the suffocating perfume of an unhealthy eroticism'[5] and, lost in the magic labyrinth of sin, have ended up by becoming victims of the 'Mammonization of the sexual urge'.[6] 'With the intention of adulterating all our future generations' the tempter has perfected the system of prostitution and worked himself into a position of 'callous and shameless controller of this whole obscene enterprise'.[7]

But in this 'hothouse of sexual fantasies and attractions'[8] there grows the poisonous plant of racial degeneration which, flourishing alongside the moral canker that holds the nation in its grasp, has been slowly destroying the body of the people, namely syphilis.[9] This, according to Hitler, is the worst disaster that can befall a society, and in order to counter the infection immense efforts and huge sacrifices will have to be made. 'Everything depends on solving this problem – either we shall have a future or we shall perish.'[10]

Hitler's readers may well have been aware of these dangers, if not of their causes, but the threat to the future that he sets at the centre of his prognosis lay beyond any rational comprehension. His concept of 'racial impurity', racial inter-marriage, with its medieval overtones of burning at the stake, was not confined to the begetting of 'bastards' but involved any sexual relations, even on a single occasion. The sin of this progressive degeneration is being committed every day before our very eyes. 'For hours the black-haired Jewish boy, an expression of evil lust on his face, will lie in wait for an unsuspecting maid, sullying her with his blood and thereby stealing her from her people.'[11] The Jews' aim of 'ruining the genetic foundations of the race at their mercy' was to be achieved by a biological process hitherto unknown to science, which the racial expert Julius Streicher later explained. 'At the moment of intercourse', wrote Streicher, 'the man's semen is absorbed, wholly or in part, into the woman's womb and passes into the blood. One single act of intercourse between an Aryan woman and a Jew is sufficient to pollute her blood for ever.'[12]

This theory of 'blood pollution' through multi-cultural sexual intercourse – a pathological theory that cries out for interpretation in psychiatric terms – remained the unshakeable foundation of Hitler's racial paranoia. It is the basis of all the anti-Jewish legislation passed during the years of the Third Reich, including the so-called Nuremberg Laws 'For the Protection of German Blood and German Honour', which prohibited not only marriage between Jews and Aryans but also any extramarital sexual relations between them, together with the employment of Aryan women under forty-five years of age in Jewish households – all this to preclude any threat to the purity of the nation's blood.

The Nuremberg Race Laws of 1935, the importance of which, said Hitler, 'would only be fully felt in centuries to come',[13] followed the lines laid down, sometimes in the most ludicrous of terms, in *Mein Kampf*. Thus: 'There is only one supremely divine human right, namely the right to ensure that blood remains pure.' The first duty of a race-state as envisaged by Hitler is 'to remove from marriage the ever-present threat of racial impurity', for the relationship between man and woman is most nobly sanctified 'by procreation of images of the Lord, not ugly monsters half-human, half-ape'.[14]

The mythical realm peopled by chosen men and women made in the image of God formed part of the imaginary 'regeneration' world created by Wagner and embodied on the stage in the figure of Parsifal. Paradoxically it was precisely Wagner's esoteric dogmas and his 'sacred festival drama' that inspired Hitler's preposterous verbiage on the subject of race. Chamberlain had talked of the 'racial chaos' produced by miscegenation,[15] and, even earlier than Wagner, Gobineau had complained of the absorption of Aryan blood by subhumans, which led Hitler to add that no one should talk about racial questions without first having read Gobineau and Chamberlain.[16] But it is in Wagner's later writings, and in *Parsifal*, their musical correlative, that the doctrine of blood as the holiest of values receives its full expression.

In Wagner's allegory of the Holy Grail Hitler found the prototype of a hero who went beyond Siegmund and Siegfried and pointed out the path that led 'in the spirit of the Almighty Creator'[17] to the redemption of the world. The hapless tribe of the Wälsungen had provided him with a mythological interpretation of his earlier career and also put the sword of victory in his hand, but ultimately they had fallen to the guile and trickery of more powerful forces. They had died the death of heroes but without having achieved the sought-for deliverance from evil. The *Ring des Nibelungen* ends tragically: the struggle to bring freedom to mankind leads to the apocalypse of *Götterdämmerung*.

Parsifal, by contrast, survives. He is the first hero to escape destruction, resisting Hagen-like intrigue and the pleasures of seduction through his purity and his strength of will. Under the banner of the Saviour he cuts through the web woven by the powers of wickedness so that in future the earth shall be inhabited only by those 'created in His own image'. As Hitler had earlier identified himself with Wagner's tragic heroes, so now he saw himself as the victorious Parsifal. And as his identification with the Wälsungen had shown him how to forge the sword and destroy his foes, there now opened up before him the prospect of a new beginning, the foundation of a new, racially pure sodality of Knights of the Grail, the transformation of a desolate world into a paradise on earth.

Such metaphysical speculations hardly lent themselves to treatment in the theatre. On the one hand, however dogmatically Wagner expressed himself in his theoretical writings, it was impossible to simply transfer, unchanged, the concept of race to the operatic stage; on the other, there was no way of characterizing some singers as Jews and others as Aryans. His revolutionary doctrine, the principal source of his work from *Rienzi* onwards, demanded constant transposition, poetic intensification and ultimately religious transfiguration. But in all his works, whether as writer or composer, the underlying conceit remains the immutable polarity between the creative principle of light and the destructive principle of darkness. Also at the heart of his work is the individual's awareness of his own tragic downfall, followed, beyond death and beyond the pangs of separation, by transfiguration. Above all, irresistible and omnipotent, here is a yearning for redemption, which, if not fulfilled by God or fate, must be achieved by the action of man himself. Wagner now creates just such a man, a hero who, with God or against Him, will overthrow reality and establish the kingdom of Heaven on earth, a kingdom ruled by love and by men who see themselves as images of God. *Pari passu* all images of Satan, those subversive living demons, rogues and murderers, will be herded by the hero into the abyss from which, as 'creatures of night and of death', they once escaped.

Human destiny decreed that all the Rienzis and Siegfrieds, all the Lohengrins and Tristans should perish at the hands of the forces of darkness – the envious, the covetous, the cunning, the domineering. If we except Walther von Stolzing in the *Meistersinger*, only one of these heroes emerges victorious and destroys his adversaries without himself being destroyed. Born an orphan who does not even know his own name, this Parsifal resists the temptations of the Devil, conquers the demon of sin and becomes the anointed king of a regenerated mankind.

The conception of a redeemer who overcomes the powers of evil had been in Wagner's mind since his days in Dresden when he had reflected on the possibility of a Christianity purged of all Jewish accretions. Its central figure, as he wrote in his 'Wibelungen' essay, was none other than Siegfried, the immortal dragon-slayer who, like Jesus, 'died, was mourned and eventually avenged, as we today are taking our revenge on the Jews'.[18] This was Wagner in the revolutionary year of 1848. In Jesus he saw the embodiment of Siegfried, and the glorious deed that led to the death of the one as of the other was their triumph over the forces of darkness, a triumph symbolized in the Siegfried saga by the recovery of the Nibelungen treasure. But the treasure, writes Wagner in 'The Wibelungen', which gives the hero power to rule the world, was lost, and the Church and the Jews together pluck the imperial crown from the head of the Hohenstaufen dynasty. Since that time the treasure has acquired a totally new meaning for the Germans: Siegfried's lost gold lived on in the form of the Holy Grail in which was preserved the blood of the Saviour on the Cross. 'The struggle to possess the Nibelungen treasure has thus given way to a striving to reach the Grail.'[19]

As the Germans, in honouring Jesus, were in fact honouring their hero Siegfried, Wagner continues, the latter assumed historical form as the Emperor Friedrich Barbarossa, who embarked on a crusade to the Holy Land in search of the lost Grail. When, at the end of his 'Wibelungen' sketch, Wagner cries: 'When, O great Friedrich, wilt thou return, thou noble Siegfried?', and expresses the hope that he will slay 'the dragon that is tormenting mankind', he is also thinking both of Christ, who will return to judge His murderers, and of Siegfried, who will come in the guise of Barbarossa to bring to a bloody end the Nibelungens' grip on the German Reich. Another name of this messianic hero is Parsifal – as pure as Christ, as heroic as Siegfried, searching, like Barbarossa, for the lost sacred relic.

But Parsifal avoided the vital mistake that was Christ's downfall – His boundless forbearance. Since it is not only oppressed mankind that is seeking deliverance from evil but the whole of nature, Wagner is convinced that, 'to adopt Darwinian terminology, it is only the strong who have been chosen for this act of salvation'.[20] Parsifal proves to have the strength to resist the temptation of miscegenation and to annihilate the 'false splendour' of his tempter, the magician Klingsor.[21] 'Parsifal', wrote a fascinated Cosima in her diary, 'is at once childlike, heroic and victorious, as pure as the driven snow and as tough as steel.' To which the Master added approvingly: 'They could not catch him as they caught Siegfried – he was too big for them.'[22]

Yet the opera appears to offer the very opposite of an ideology 'as tough as steel'. Even killing animals is regarded by the vegetarian community of the Knights of the Grail as a serious offence, and when Parsifal unwittingly kills a swan, he is severely reprimanded. Shedding an animal's blood is taboo in the brotherhood, and fighting is only permitted, as in the case of Lohengrin, Parsifal's son and messenger of the Grail in Wagner's earlier opera, in the defence of virtue against the powers of evil. But since Amfortas, King of the Grail, has infected his own blood as a result of his sin, the Grail community itself is in need of a redeemer. And it has been foretold that when this redeemer appears, he will be not a warrior but an innocent orphan who first needs to learn the nature of the act of redemption he has to carry out.

The 'guileless fool', bringer of salvation, 'learns through compassion'.[23] But it is a compassion that has nothing in common with the Christian commandment to love one's neighbour. As the prophecy, proclaimed by Christ's blood itself, has revealed to the ailing king, the compassion is not a self-justifying ethical principle but an aid to enlightenment. Only when the emotion has swelled his heart almost to breaking-point does the hero acquire the wisdom that enables him to carry out the act of redemption. What Wagner calls 'compassion', the virtue claimed to give Christianity superiority over Judaism, is in fact that awareness of a shared fate, a common sense of deprivation and oppression, about which he had written in his revolutionary days and out of which salvation comes. Only through this consciousness of compassion does Parsifal acquire the knowledge that enables him to carry out his task of salvation. As Wagner perceived the true self-awareness of the *Volk* to reside in the common predicament which both distinguishes it from its enemies and brings about their defeat, so at the crucial moment Parsifal is overcome not by compassion but by a fateful sense of existential anguish. And as Siegfried had his weapon in the sword Nothung, so Parsifal's all-conquering blade is the sacred spear of the Grail.

At the key moment in the drama when Kundry, the temptress, kisses him, Parsifal feels the tragedy of the Grail brotherhood – above all the agonies of the dying Amfortas, whose poisoned blood flows unchecked from his body – as though it were his own. 'He clutches his heart as though in response to a sudden flash of pain', says Wagner's stage direction, 'and stands motionless for a while, as though transfixed, feeling in his own veins the havoc that Amfortas' sinful blood has wrought in the Grail Castle.'[24] Instead of the warm, healing blood of the Saviour that brings the world the blessing of divine love, sinful blood rages through the Grail King's body and pours forth from the wound that will never close. Watching the spectacle, Parsifal shares the brotherhood's tragic grief and is enlightened. Thus armed, he resists the temptations of Kundry, who tries to adulterate his blood with her own poison.

Wagner's misleading use of the word 'compassion', which is hardly relevant to Parsifal's situation and only applies, if at all, to the Knights of the Grail, not to their enemies, struck one of the critics who attended the work's first performance in 1882. Writing in the *Preussische Kreuzzeitung*, Hermann

Messmer observed: 'Through compassion, compassion of a quite remarkable kind, Parsifal succeeds in redeeming Amfortas, himself ("the redeemer redeemed") and Kundry, and finally, through the Grail itself, on which a curse has lain all these years, he redeems the whole of mankind.'[25] The question as to what they are all to be redeemed and delivered from would in the Christian tradition receive the answer: 'From evil.' But Wagner wanted a more exact answer, and he therefore has the Holy Grail itself reveal the terrible curse that has been laid on mankind.

'Save me, redeem me from these sin-stained clutches!' cries a mystic voice in Parsifal's ears.[26] But it is a voice, coming from the blood of the Saviour, that calls not for compassion but for action, for relief by force from the weight of oppression. For by an act of abominable sacrilege the pure blood of the Son of God is guarded by a king whose own blood is polluted, a king whose divine image was stripped from him by a single sexual act with Kundry, the bride of hell, who at Klingsor's behest was also set to seduce Parsifal, the new Siegfried. But he, awakened to a realization of the blood ties that link him to the brotherhood, resists her and returns to the holy domains of the Grail with the spear that Klingsor had stolen from the dishonoured Amfortas. It is not Christian compassion that secures final triumph but the hero's steely determination to destroy whatever stands in his way. Only by feeling no compassion for the temptress and her lord could he preserve the holy vessel for posterity.

Now the miracle of creation can be re-enacted in the Grail Castle. No sooner does the blood from the spear mingle with that which wells up from the Grail, pure blood fusing with pure blood, than new life begins to grow and the Grail kingdom, the curse of infertility now lifted from it, will fill the tormented world with new images of the Divinity. The mystery of the Grail lies not in the dogmas of a mystic creed but in the reproduction of the Aryan race. It was not the compassion of the Bible that drove Wagner to present Parsifal as a genetic blueprint for the future, but fear of the threat to Germanic racial purity by the infusion of Jewish blood.

Shortly after Wagner had sent King Ludwig the prose sketch of the work, Hans von Bülow, his closest associate, revealed the Master's real motives. In an attempt to win over a Bavarian churchman to Wagner's conception, Bülow concentrated not on the apparent affinity of the sketch to Christian concepts such as compassion and the Eucharist but on more practical issues. 'Wagner's artistic tendencies', wrote Bülow in 1866, 'are for me and my friends entirely matters of the mind and heart, a kind of religion.' Bülow's talk of 'artistic tendencies' leads one to expect a statement of aesthetic principles but instead he simply justifies them as principles 'so genuinely German, anti-Jewish and anti-materialistic' that they merit the approval of all politically active Catholics.[27]

But this too was misleading. The Master, on the point of founding his own quasi-religion, hated the Catholic Church as much as his heroes Rienzi and Tannhäuser, both of whom had been excommunicated by the Pope. 'The Church of Rome', he once said to his wife, who had been raised in the strict Catholic tradition, 'is a universal pestilence.'[28] 'It is a scandal that it still exists.'[29] Instead of following the example of Jesus and taking up the struggle against the ancient Jewish faith with its moneychangers and its Pharisees, the Church supported the Jews in their assault on the Germanic peoples and helped them to establish a system of oppression based on terror and hypocrisy that had lasted for centuries. The Church, together with the total victory of Judaism which it had helped to bring about, was, concluded Wagner, 'the most terrible thing that had ever happened in history',[30] for it was the creation not of Christ's disciples, like those he had envisaged in his biblical scene *Das Liebesmahl der Apostel* ('The Love-Feast of the Apostles') back in 1843 as the victims of Jewish persecution, but of the Jews and their associates. 'They have desecrated Christianity – that is to say, they have accommodated it to the purposes of this world.'[31]

Such revelations were not meant for public ears. Only with the publication of Cosima's diaries, kept under lock and key until 1976, did the extent of Wagner's anti-Catholicism become known. Hints of it are to be found throughout his writings and in the authoritative pronouncements which Bülow scornfully dubbed 'encyclicals', but his vital utterances were left in cryptic form, their real meaning left for future generations to fathom.

Thus when Bernhard Förster, anti-Semitic husband of Nietzsche's sister Elisabeth, proposed to reveal Wagner's secret of the 'perverted form' of Christianity in the pages of the *Bayreuther Blätter*, the Master intervened.[32]

> If we reject the Church, the priesthood, indeed the whole historical phenomenon of Jesus Christ, then only for the sake of that Christ whom we wish to preserve in all His purity. What we must therefore ruthlessly eradicate is what harms and distorts this Saviour. And what is to be worshipped as a new ideal object of faith is a sublime, pure Redeemer cleansed of all Alexandrinian–Jewish–Roman–despotic accretions.

A picture of this ideal Jesus, free of Jewish and ecclesiastical associations, was given by Wagner in 1849 in a dramatic sketch, *Jesus von Nazareth*, in which the liberator drives the Jewish traders from the temple.

Thirty years later Wagner began work on the score of the opera in which the Son of God is omnipresent through His blood, miraculously preserved from the Crucifixion as the imperishable token of His presence. Whether Wagner had in mind the concept of transubstantiation or that of the resurrection of the flesh, is unclear. Certain, however, is that in the Holy Grail he has created and expressed in his music the most sacred symbol of the cult that has grown up around him, an icon of worship for all believers. In order to preserve the secret from profanation, he asked Bernhard Förster, who established a colony in Paraguay in 1886 based on Wagner's theories of 'pure blood', 'to retain a certain sobriety of language so as not to do the Jews' work for them'.[33]

It was also due to the Church, wrote Wagner in 1876 to King Ludwig – whom he liked to address in his letters as 'King of the Grail' – that this alien race dominated the Germans. Hoping to convert the young monarch to his Aryan–Christian gospel, he explained 'how the Jesuits have delivered our world into the hands of the Jews', as a result of which 'all has been lost'[34] – a thought that Wagner's son Siegfried repeated in all its absurdity after the failure of Hitler's *coup d'état* in 1923.[35] By this time a national cult had developed out of what in Wagner's own day was confined to a select band of disciples.

The 'sacred festival drama' of *Parsifal*, a devotional work originally not for performance in ordinary opera houses, became the principal vehicle for the propagation of the new religion. It was not a work that belonged in the theatre at all – reality itself was at issue and the doctrine of the coming regeneration was preached; the ceremony of *'lavacrum regenerationis'*,[36] baptism, the washing away of original sin, was transferred from the church to the Grail Temple in Bayreuth and the true meaning of transubstantiation conveyed by the blood-red glow issuing from the Grail chalice itself.

Parsifal, a pseudo-religious experience cast in ethereal music, mistakenly described by Wagner's father-in-law Franz Liszt as 'the purest Christian mysticism',[37] represents in fact the transition from Wagner's esoteric, fantastic racial blood theories to their public embrace. Its essence, said Wolzogen, a conduit for the Master's message, lay not in its subject but in its spirit: 'It is the same spirit that fills the pages of a number of essays written by Wagner during the same period, such as "Religion and Art" and "Heroism and Christianity". *Parsifal* cannot be separated from these writings.'[38] The 'spirit' of which Wolzogen writes is that which makes the restoration of paradise on earth dependent on the defeat of the 'demon of a suffering mankind' and the acknowledgement of the true 'blood of Jesus' as the most sacred symbol of the Aryan race.[39]

Since blood was seen not only as a metaphor but as a genetic reality, it became clear why the 'alien race' attacked it so determinedly as the source of Aryanism, seeking to adulterate it with its own juices or by open bloodshed, and finally to cause it to dry up altogether. Instead of witnessing the victory of the blood of the Wälsungen, as Siegmund had hoped, he and his son Siegfried both had to shed their blood before their time, while Wagner's other childless heroes also disappeared from the scene, laid low by treachery, by intrigue and by murder.

The epitome of all these hapless victims is Amfortas, who, bleeding from a malignant wound that will not heal, also has to suffer the agonies of his polluted blood, punishment for the original sin against racial purity. His torments embrace the sufferings of all Wagner's heroes from Rienzi to

Siegfried. Nor is it difficult to identify who is responsible for his fate – a member of that accursed race that has striven for thousands of years to adulterate the blood of pure humankind. Throughout its history, explained Wagner, the German nation had been 'defenceless against the invasion of the Jews',[40] unwittingly exposing itself to miscegenation and, since in any mixed marriage 'another little Jew will emerge', bringing about the downfall of our entire culture.[41] Portraying the sufferings of Amfortas as the sufferings of Germany, Wagner was convinced that he was the first to diagnose the causes of this decay of civilization. 'I have the feeling', he wrote to Ludwig in 1880, 'that I can do the world a great service by displaying to a sick and degenerate mankind the reason for its degeneracy and revealing its Redeemer Jesus Christ.'[42]

Salvation from racial debasement, in which Wagner also chose to see the origin of meat-eating, blood-letting and vivisection, can come only from the blood of the Saviour which has been preserved in its living purity in the Grail; whoever beholds it shall never die but enjoy the heritage of eternal life. But only the man who withstands the temptations of the world, the flesh and the Devil, and resists the enticement to racial impurity, 'can ensure the continued power of the Grail'.[43] Jesus, embodiment of the most sublime heroism, gave His body and His blood 'as the supreme sacrifice in order to bring salvation to a sinful world';[44] at the sacrament of the Eucharist His blood passes to the assembled congregation and lives on in them. Only through this mystical transfusion can the impure blood be cleansed.

The degradation of our blood, continues Wagner the preacher, has only come about through being mingled with the inferior blood of those he calls, in his ingrained hatred, 'those commercial managers of our society who were formerly cannibals'.[45] In other words, beneath a thin veneer of culture the Jews are cannibals. For Hitler, an avid reader of Wagner since his youth, who felt the Master to be 'a part of his own being',[46] such pathological passages from Wagner's 'regeneration' writings seem to have become second nature. In *Mein Kampf* Wagner's mutated anthropophagi continue to ply their racially destructive trade, deliberately pollute Aryan blood,[47] 'suck the blood of the helpless people like leeches',[48] and finally reveal themselves, having achieved a position of power, as cannibalistic 'Blood-Jews' intent on turning the world into a communist slaughterhouse.[49]

In *Parsifal* Wagner turns this spine-chilling world of blood and destruction into a Passion Play which ends with the salvation of the world. The common misunderstanding that sees the work as a didactic drama proclaiming the humanistic virtue of compassion – a conception that Wieland Wagner continued to publicize during his post-war regime[50] – had already been foreseen and rejected by Wagner himself, who pointed out that 'through the ever-present image of Christ on the Cross all is stark and brutal'.[51] The widespread thought that the Redeemer crucified by the Jews Himself belonged to the tribe of his crucifiers, and that His Father was the

God Jehovah, filled Wagner with alarm as 'one of the most frightening confusions in the history of the world'.[52]

The audience at the first performance of *Parsifal* in Bayreuth in 1882 knew full well that the glow from the electrically illuminated chalice did not come from Jewish blood. The nineteenth century, wrote the Viennese critic Max Kalbeck, had no more use for a 'Semitic Christian Saviour'; instead it was being offered a 'Germanic Christian Saviour'. 'The anti-Semitic worthies who have grown weary of brotherly love and an unwelcome degree of evangelical tolerance have good reason to be grateful to Wagner for giving us this new blond Christ.'[53] Many in the audience on the 'Green Hill' gazed in wonder at what they saw as a religious fairy-tale. Those who had ears to hear will have realized that here was the beginning of a new Christianity.

Had the saviour in *Parsifal* really revealed himself as an Aryan redeemer, as Kalbeck wrote? He was not so at the beginning but he became so. Born a 'guileless fool', a kind of human prototype before the Fall, he resists the temptations of Satan and is therefore able to free the Redeemer from 'guilt-stained hands'. But the man who rescues the Messiah, bringing 'redemption to the Redeemer', in Wagner's words, must needs be more powerful than this Redeemer himself; it is not Christ who reveals Himself as the true liberator of mankind but His reincarnation in Parsifal – not a man of compassion but a man of action. Exactly how this is to be interpreted is left in a haze of mysticism. Unproblematic as is the conquest of evil, whose power is neutralized by the purity of the hero, the concept of the salvation of the world by the 'redemption' of Christ's blood remains a mystery. How does one 'redeem' the blood, the genetic purity, that is languishing in 'guilt-stained hands'?

The answer, unwelcome to an all-male community, is: by procreation. Pure blood must be joined to pure blood to produce new life. As this presupposes, in biological terms, two opposed sexes, Wagner sets alongside the feminine vessel of the Grail a complementary masculine relic – the spear, at the point of which is a life-giving drop of the Saviour's blood, drawn from His side and collected in the sacred vessel.[54] At the beginning of the opera the two relics are exposed to great danger: while the Grail languishes in the guilt-ridden hands of Amfortas, Klingsor, the wicked magician, brandishes the spear at the knights, declaring it his aim to annihilate their whole race and seize the Grail.[55] 'Soon I shall watch over the Grail myself!' he boasts, mocking the male weakness of the Order.[56] He thus threatens the Saviour incarnate in the living blood, and thus the entire lineage of creative, God-like humanity, with ultimate extinction. As long as the two sexual symbols, Grail and spear – 'symbols of procreation', Wagner calls them[57] – remain apart, a pure humankind cannot reproduce; if, on the other hand, Klingsor gains possession of both sets of genes, the sacred spring is poisoned for ever.

Parsifal's path from fool to redeemer of the world resembles that which

Hitler imagined for his own mythical career, for, like the inmate of Landsberg prison, Parsifal too, who does not understand the suffering of the Grail King, has his eyes opened by his encounter with the alien race. In Klingsor's magic kingdom 'attractive young she-devils' seek, not without success, to seduce the errant knights. When *Mein Kampf* calls Vienna 'a hothouse of sexual titillation and fantasy',[58] Hitler's gaze may well have been made the sharper by the vision of Klingsor's *hortus deliciarum* and its temptresses. Even the sneering tone in which the sorcerer unmasks his sensual kingdom as a malicious trap recurs in Hitler's description of Vienna, for when Hitler talks of 'the coldly efficient, shameless manipulator of this immoral empire',[59] he is giving a perfect description of Parsifal's adversary in the magic garden. But all Klingsor's machinations – Wagner instructed that he should be dressed as a rabbi, and the tools of his magic decorated with snake motifs[60] – fail in the face of Parsifal's purity. And when he sends his most experienced sinner to tempt the hero – Kundry has already mocked the Saviour on the Cross, like the Wandering Jew[61] – Parsifal repels her advances when he realizes the purpose of her passion.

Instead of infecting himself with Kundry's evil blood, Parsifal becomes lost in a rapturous vision in which he sees before him the vessel glowing with the Saviour's blood. Pushing the demonic woman away, he shouts: 'Away from me, thou destroyer!'[62] Klingsor appears and hurls his spear at the incorruptible youth, as Hagen threw his lance at Siegfried. Parsifal catches the spear in mid-air, and as he makes the sign of the Cross with it, the magician's castle and the immoral pleasure garden disappear from view. Ahasverus has perished. Christ's death on the Cross, as Wagner put it in his 'Wibelungen', 'has been avenged by the downfall of the Jews'. Nor will Kundry survive her redemption at Parsifal's hands.

Wagner was at pains to emphasize that redemption from original sin and the solving of the great dilemma facing mankind were achieved not through the exercise of compassion but through the hero's recourse to action, specifically 'through the physical act of regaining the stolen lance'.[63] Like a living organ the weapon seeks a union with the holy vessel. Or, in Wagner's words: 'It is seized with yearning for the sacred balsam where it belongs.'[64] When the two finally come together, 'the purple glow of the Grail fusing with the glowing point of the spear',[65] the wound will heal and the death of the Saviour will be transformed into new life.

At the end of the opera a white dove, symbol of the spirit and of inexhaustible fertility, flutters down from the dome of the Grail Temple and hovers above Parsifal's head. The fanciful myth of the chaste hero who renounces the pleasures of the flesh for a celibate life in a monastic order was already refuted by Wagner himself at the time of *Lohengrin*. 'The king of the Templars', he wrote in 1845, 'is permitted a chaste wife so that his noble line may be perpetuated in its purity.'[66] The clearest proof of Parsifal's potency lies in the existence of his son Lohengrin, whose appearance in a boat drawn by a swan demonstrated before Wagner's astonished audiences, among whom were the two Grail fanatics Ludwig II and Adolf Hitler, the magic power of the mystic chalice.

As the union of the spear and the Grail, symbolizing the reproductive power of the Arian race, represents the climax of *Parsifal* on the stage, so the Bayreuth Festival, embodiment of the secret awareness of the meaning of redemption, became the centre of the cult of the Knights of the Grail. As in the days of Classical ritual mysteries cryptic obscenities were smuggled into the action, so now, with his symbolic *Parsifal*, Wagner founded a mystical cult for the Germany that was to come, including initiation ceremonies and blood sacrifices. When Leopold von Schroeder, a friend of Chamberlain's, spoke of 'the consummation of the Aryan religious play in Bayreuth', he was only following the conception that the Wagner cult had of itself. The 'Green Hill', which Cosima equated with the Grail mountain of Monsalvat, saw more performances of *Parsifal* than of all Wagner's other operas put together, except for the *Ring*. Its fascination, which invoked feelings of religious ecstasy even in those who were not fully initiated into its secrets, was connected with the unexpressed mystical message it concealed. Even those who did not grasp its meaning had the feeling that some sacred rite was being performed in the Grail Temple and the hypnotic music served to intensify the experience.

Eduard Hanslick, the leading Viennese music critic of the day, attributed the emotion felt by the first-night audience to the 'false pretensions' of the work to having 'a profound sacred significance'. 'With growing amazement', wrote Hanslick, 'I saw a halo above the head of the 'guileless fool' growing bigger and bigger as time went on, until finally Wagner literally made him turn into the Saviour of mankind. . . . Apparently he had in mind something akin to the Oberammergau Passion Play.'[67]

Another who realized that this was no mere innovative form of music theatre but a piece of propaganda on behalf of the Bayreuth faith was the pianist Elisabeth von Herzogenberg, a pupil of Brahms'. Thoroughgoing Wagnerians, she wrote in 1889, went to *Parsifal* 'as Catholics visit gravesides on Good Friday: it has become an act of worship which induces in them an unnatural state of ecstasy and hysteria'.

The Festspielhaus itself, unmasked by Elisabeth von Herzogenberg as the temple of an hypnotic cult, had an unpleasant odour about it, 'like a church that has never been ventilated, or like an abattoir in summer; a musty smell of stale incense, a fetid sensuousness of religious gestures fills the place, taking one's breath away'.[68] It is a description that reads like an anticipation of the spectacular rituals enacted by the Nazis amid flaming torches, fanatical processions and mass vows of allegiance to the Führer. The religious trappings of National Socialism were largely derived from the dramaturgy of the Bayreuth *Parsifal*. For 'blood' read 'Grail'. The community of the knights served as a model for the brigades of Blackshirts that were later to ply their murderous trade, and even the searchlight beams projected vertically into the night sky recalled the columns that flanked the shrine of the Grail Temple.

The congregation that gathered in Bayreuth to celebrate the launch of the 'final struggle' was not born in a Munich beer-cellar in 1919 but had been flocking to Cosima's Monsalvat since the 1880s. The doctrines that Wagner had expounded for the converts in the *Bayreuther Blätter* found their popular expression in *Parsifal*, a vehicle not of understanding but of faith. It was to be performed not before an audience but before a body of worshippers. The enactment of the Eucharist precluded applause. In 1879, three years before its première, Ludwig Schemann wrote in his first article for the *Blätter* of 'the inestimable importance of the work for the re-awakening of Germany',[69] while the critic Hans Herrig pronounced in his review of the first performance for the *Deutsches Tageblatt* that here 'Germanic civilization and Christianity are united to create a new development in our culture which excludes all foreign substance. A political policy on Christian–Germanic lines is profoundly indebted to Wagner for giving us this earnest of our hopes.'[70]

That this policy, with a new objective, was here being presented in the guise of religious worship escaped the attention of all but a few. But that in *Parsifal* one was witnessing the High Mass of a secret religion was something that hardly anyone could fail to realize. 'I was profoundly moved', said Angelo Neumann, the Jewish impresario who filled Wagner's empty coffers by performing the *Ring* all over the country, 'and felt as though I had been present at the celebration of a religious sacrament.'[71] Goebbels too was overwhelmed. Writing of a visit to Bayreuth in 1928, when he met Winifred Wagner and Eva Chamberlain – 'the sensitive widow of the great Wagnerian thinker', as Goebbels called her – he entered in his diary: 'Four hours of religious devotion. I am utterly dazed.'[72]

The Festival programme for that same year contained an article by the respected German scholar Professor Wolfgang Golther on the significance of Wagner's Grail for an awakening Germany.[73] 'The Holy Grail', wrote Golther, was 'the jewel of a deeply Germanic faith in the Saviour, a jewel jealously guarded by a trusty body of knights.'[74] 'The voices of the knights will ring out through the kingdom', cried the nationalist poet Friedrich Lienhard, 'with the Grail glowing in their midst.'[75]

What made Wagner's operatic hero so attractive to the Nazis was his openly messianic character. In contrast to the young Siegfried, when Parsifal performs the act of killing, he can not only claim, with a clear conscience, that it is in self-defence but also ennoble it by reference to his divine mission. Whereas the Wälsung Siegfried uses his sword as an instrument of violence, his successor destroys by gestures: with the spear he makes the sign of the Cross and Klingsor is banished; a mere glance from his eyes and the penitent sinner Kundry falls lifeless to the ground.[76]

However, the most decisive aspect of the figure of Parsifal for Hitler's mythological self-portrait in *Mein Kampf* was his function as King of the Grail. By resisting sexual temptation, he has earned the right to unveil the sacred mystery, thereby creating, after years of disease and impotence, the biological conditions for the procreation of the new, God-like human race. He thus joins the gallery of Wagnerian heroes from which Hitler recruited his role models. Parsifal too is a man of steel but at the same time a man of faith, one who cannot be deflected from his prescribed path. As calmly as he disposed of the realm of Satan, so he now, with sovereign self-confidence, assumes the role of King as though it had been created for him.

As to Parsifal's apotheosis in the final scene, to the accompaniment of choirs of angels and the music of the spheres, Hitler saw in it a prophetic vision of his own future as saviour of the world. After the blood has streamed from the lance as it comes close to the Grail, and the chalice, impatiently waiting to be touched, has begun to run over in shining waves, the new Grail King raises the holy relic before the kneeling congregation – 'as dusk gathers in the background and the light grows brighter from above'[77] – while heavenly voices proclaim the miracle of salvation and the dove bestows its blessing.

Houston Stewart Chamberlain, lying on his sick-bed in Bayreuth, was the first to recognize the new King of the Grail. As he felt himself to be the suffering Amfortas, paralysed as a result of the war inflicted on Germany by the Jews, so Chamberlain's young guest from Munich met all the qualifications one could require from a 'guileless fool'. Half-educated and with a brazen over-self-confidence, he appeared to fear nothing and to be prepared for anything, not least for the vital task of destroying Klingsor and his evil kingdom. This meeting with the leader of the Nazi Party was the fulfilment of all Chamberlain's dreams.

When Ludwig Roselius, nationalistic owner of the coffee manufacturers 'Kaffee Hag', visited the dying Chamberlain and told him of the young political aspirant, a transformation came over Chamberlain's face. Looking intently at Roselius with his blue eyes, he made as if to utter a name. The name, 'formed by the lips of a man in extreme pain, was "Parsifal" '.[78] Even this scene has its Wagnerian precedent. When the hero touches Amfortas' wound with the spear, the King's face lights up before he collapses on the ground in front of his young successor. Chamberlain saw his own role in just these terms: when the redeemer appeared, he could 'lie down and sleep in peace, with no need ever to wake again'.

Wagner himself had also dreamed of political fulfilment for his characters. Not only in his writings, where he fantasized about the return of the Emperor Barbarossa, and in his operas, in which one hero after another devotes his life to the superhuman task of delivering the world from evil, but also in his secret political aims he sought a way of entrusting his threatened nation to the care of a leader sent by God. He once had a dream, wrote Cosima in 1878, of standing in a crowd of people between two abysses which were suddenly transformed into a great hall. One man cried out: 'Only a ruler of genius can help us!' 'Richard realized that it was so,' said Cosima. 'And at this same moment it was as though a bridge had suddenly appeared and spanned the abyss.'[79] This abyss, which could be crossed only by an inspired leader, appears to be that which he had in mind when he complained in 1879 of the excessive influence of the Jews on German affairs. 'This is the real abyss that leads to hell,' he said to his wife; 'And who is there to save us from it?'[80]

Wagner's disciples would have known that a dragon-slayer would not be adequate for the task, if only because he himself was destined to perish in the abyss. To be sure, liberation had to be won with the sword. But for the creation of a new Reich a saviour was needed to destroy the arch-fiend and consolidate the future of the Aryan race. In Hitler, who had already proved himself to be a belligerent Siegfried, Wahnfried had also found its longed-for Parsifal. Here was the 'genius and ruler' it craved, the one who would bridge the 'abyss that leads to hell' into which the German nation was threatening to sink.

Hitler was released from Landsberg prison in December 1924. Two months later, with Winifred Wagner's help, he had re-established his party in Munich. But the Wahnfried clan's assistance was not restricted to clandestine financial donations to his cause – they even invited him to take up residence in the Villa Wahnfried.[81]

In 1925, the year he attended the Bayreuth Festival for the first time and saw the town laid out before him 'in shimmering beauty' – Winifred had already made sure that his prospects were 'Set Fair'[82] – Hitler discovered in the Festival programme an article on the figure of Parsifal which might as well have had himself as its subject. Written by Chamberlain's friend Hans Alfred Grunsky, the article spoke of 'an inspired genius who becomes an outstanding religious figure possessed of great strength of will, heroic spirit and an immense ability to impress – a man of whom great things are to be expected'. This hero – who is not mentioned by name –

> sees sin as the desecration of our divine essence and of all that is divine in the world . . . a man who has made it his life's work to share in human suffering for the good and join in the struggle against evil. . . . He will achieve his goal of salvation through the strength and purity of his will which, unperturbed by external events, will grasp its destiny at the appointed hour. . . . When the victory over evil comes to pass, moreover, he will be spared that inexorable tragic fate that befalls all Wagner's other heroes. . . . In the end what awaits him is not defeat but the achievement of his hallowed goal.[83]

Hitler, who would have had no difficulty in recognizing himself in this mirror, could well have found his interpretation of his historical role confirmed: in the opera Parsifal's goal was the salvation of the Holy Grail –

that goal now became Hitler's. Did he notice that this thinly disguised ode to the Führer had been printed twice – first in 1924, while he was in Landsberg, then again the following year, when the Bechsteins and the Wagners laid Bayreuth at his feet? At any rate the repetition suggested that it was intended to welcome the new redeemer.

A later Bayreuth programme carried another article, by the musicologist Alfred Lorenz, in which the Führer is disguised as the young Parsifal. The hero of Wagner's opera, wrote Lorenz in 1931, was not a Christian weakling but a man of iron will, capable, when necessary, even of cruelty.

> Siegfried's deeds are great, bold and ruthless but not the products of an iron will because he does not know how his enemy suffers. Only the hero who can empathize with suffering yet persist in the exercise of his strength has that will. . . . Because he can share the sufferings of the knights, Parsifal allows Kundry, their seducer, to continue to suffer, an action which defies mere rational interpretation.

Anybody who wants to understand Wagner's real meaning, says Lorenz, need only read his essays, above all 'Know Thyself' and 'Heroism and Christianity', to quickly see that all this is closely bound up with the 'regeneration' ideas of Wagner's last years, 'ideas which the German nation desperately needs to put into effect'. What the country requires is 'a man to regenerate the religion of the Grail', who, in contrast to Amfortas, whom Lorenz describes as 'the first servant of his people', will establish a completely new regime, founded on his own charisma and on the single-minded pursuit of regeneration.[84]

The heroic path that led from the historical Weimar Republic of the present to the ideal Reich that was to come,[85] a path that Hitler described as 'the greatest campaign to capture the minds of the people that there has ever been',[86] would have no need of Christianity. In spite of Parsifal's ostensible piety and the religious associations of his mission, Hitler shared Wagner's radical views on the Christian Church. For tactical reasons he held back in *Mein Kampf* from engaging in a premature confrontation with the ecclesiastical authorities, but in private he made no secret of his repugnance, often giving vent to his feelings in obscene comments. According to Christa Schroeder, his secretary, he 'savagely and sarcastically' dismissed the teachings of the Bible.[87] When she asked him if he intended to declare war on the Church, he replied that the ideal solution would be 'to let it die a natural death'. Like Wagner, who regarded Christianity as having been polluted by Jewish blood, and like Chamberlain, who saw it as shot through with Jewish elements, so Hitler declared Bolshevism to be Christianity's 'bastard son'[88] – both, therefore, 'Jewish excrescences'. For a thousand years Christianity, a kind of pre-Bolshevism, had prevented the Germanic world from flourishing and now, when it is on the point of dying, the Jews have returned with

their Bolshevism, an original form of Christianity.[89] Hitler even rejected without further ado Chamberlain's attempt to salvage at least the words of Christ
from the bankrupt stock of biblical material. 'Whether it be Old Testament
or New,' he said to Hermann Rauschning, 'or even the utterances of Jesus
alone, which is Chamberlain's idea, the whole thing is just one big Jewish
swindle. None of it matters. It will not give us our freedom.'[90]

Freedom, as Parsifal the saviour had taught, can only be gained by action. It is not enough to dispose of the magician Klingsor, source of all evil;
the Grail King Amfortas, who had brought the Jewish poison into the Christian castle of the Grail, had to be removed as well. 'Vital to our nation',
Hitler continued, 'is whether the people carry in their blood the enervating
faith of Judaeo-Christianity and its effeminate morality of compassion, or
whether they believe in a strong, heroic God.' The God in one's blood cor-
responds to the divine race in the Grail. All that remains is 'to destroy
Christianity in Germany root and branch.'[91] At the same time he consoled
the dying Amfortas, who in the final act of the opera prays for death and
release from his torment,[92] with the assurance that 'the time has now come
when the effects of the Christian poison are wearing off'.[93]

Hitler had no difficulty in reconciling his hatred of the Church with an
undisguised fascination for the lavish manifestations of its ritual. Many of
the dazzling features of his own processions and rallies, with the splendour of their uniforms and the chants of heavenly choirs, were drawn from
the practices of the Church, sometimes with Wagner's aid. But how, he
asked in 1941, could one possibly compare these false, deceitful practices
and unctuous displays of piety with the artistic magic conjured up by Bayreuth? 'In Bayreuth a Richard Wagner came down to earth, while in the
Church', he mocked, 'they just have the sound of hallelujahs and the sight
of rows of waving palms.'[94] With the Aryan Jesus' seizure of power in the
hallowed precincts of Bayreuth the old Church was to be healed once and
for all from the sufferings inflicted by the Jewish venom. Instead of waving fronds of palms, the nation was to flourish blood-red banners. From
1933 onwards Germany was governed by Parsifal.

When Hitler spoke of Christ, which he frequently did, he did not have in
mind the Good Shepherd, as most people thought. 'Christ was an Aryan,'[95]
he declared, with Wagner, and His life of salvation could not but end on
the Cross, because He lacked the necessary ruthlessness. Neither the purity of His life nor His humanistic teachings could bring about the salvation
for which the people were looking. 'My Christian feelings', he declared in
the year before receiving the blessing of Wahnfried, 'led me to a conception of my Lord and Saviour as a figure who, first alone, then with a handful of disciples, recognized these Jews for what they were and called upon
the world to resist them.' At the same time he admitted how profoundly
he had been moved by the image of Jesus 'grabbing a whip and driving the
money-changers – those slimy reptiles – out of the temple'.[96]

This Saviour driven by an urge to action was, of course, Hitler himself, and the world he experienced was the world he had created in response to his apocalyptic vision. As Parsifal, the Aryan Messiah, had seen through Klingsor's wiles in his glittering magic garden, so Hitler found in Berlin, hotbed of vice, the same Satanic power at work. 'When I came to Berlin a few weeks ago and looked at the Kurfürstendamm,' he told Hanfstaengl, 'the luxury, the perversion, the wanton display and the Jewish material-ism disgusted me so thoroughly that I was almost beside myself. I nearly imagined myself to be Jesus Christ when He came to His Father's temple and found it taken by the money-changers. I can well imagine how He felt when He seized a whip and scourged them out.'[97] As he said this, Hanf-staengl reported, he cracked his whip fiercely in the air.

But a few blows with the whip, a tool he always carried as part of his Messianic equipment, would solve nothing. Driving the Jews out only shifted the problem elsewhere. The ultimate solution was that exemplified by Parsifal. As Jesus, Hitler never tired of repeating, had had to die on the Cross for his courageous fight against the poison spread by the Jews,[98] so Parsifal, his Aryan reincarnation, penetrated the secret of the threat that hung over him and defended himself with the sacred spear. National Socialism, he promised at the Party's Christmas celebrations in 1928, would put Christ's ideals into practice, and the work that Christ had begun but not been able to complete, he, Adolf Hitler, would bring to a successful conclusion.[99]

In his infamous marathon speech to the Reichstag of the 'Grossdeutsches Reich' on 30 January 1939, to mark the sixth anniversary of his seizure of power, Hitler announced that he had accomplished his work in the 'tradi-tion of Christ'. In particular he referred to a theological motif from *Parsifal* which he used in order to integrate his policy of mass murder into the mythological tradition.

Opening his speech with talk of 'how much blood had been unnecessar-ily spilled in the cause of German unity' and 'how many millions of Ger-man men had been sent to a premature, agonizing death',[100] Hitler turned to consider whether the time had not come to stand the situation on its head: those responsible for these senseless sacrifices, for having crucified the German nation, as it were, 'could themselves sooner or later become the victims of some unimaginable disaster'.[101]

It was a fate that had been anticipated in the opera house when Klingsor's kingdom 'withered to dust' and vanished from the face of the earth, while Kundry, for her part, found salvation in the Grail Temple and was allowed to die gently at Parsifal's feet. The sin for which she had done penance went back to the time when she had mocked the suffering Saviour on the Cross and been punished by being cursed to wander through history in a series of changing incarnations, like a female Ahasverus. In the course of her wretched Odyssey she had appeared as the strangler of John the Baptist, as a warlike Valkyrie and finally as a temptress who adulterates the blood of the Knights of the Grail. Tragic symbol of her race, she is only liberated from her compulsive sinfulness by Parsifal the pure, albeit a liberation that also costs her her life. Not until her death is the downfall of the world of Ahasverus complete and the sin redeemed which the Jews had brought down on their heads when they mocked and crucified the Son of God.

This was the centuries-old mythological world, revived by Wagner and seen through to its end in the experience of his 'sacred festival drama', that Hitler now invoked in his address to the Reichstag. 'In the course of my struggle', he declared before the 885 deputies and an anxiously listening public throughout the world, 'it was first and foremost the Jews who laughed when I foretold that one day I would take over the running of the state and thus the control of the whole nation, thereby solving, among other things, the problem of the Jews.' Few will have had any memory of the 'laughter' which he alleged had greeted his prophecies; it had not been audible to the outside world but only within the legend of Ahasverus and to audiences who listened to its modern adaptation – *Parsifal*. It is in Wagner, too, that one finds the clearest prophecy of a solution to the Jewish problem, a 'grand solution' made crystal clear in the essay 'Know Thyself'.

How, in practical terms, the policy was to be put into effect was a question that Wagner had to leave open. His heir, speaking nine months before launching his policy of racial extermination, was able to make matters more explicit. 'The laughter that was heard at that time', said Hitler icily, 'will meanwhile have stuck in the gullets of all the Jews in Germany'[102] – a prediction of the extinction of the entire Jewish population of Europe. The fact that this terrible policy could only be embarked upon once war had broken out, beginning with the mass executions of Polish Jews,[103] was probably responsible for the fact that Hitler, who was normally very sure of himself in such matters, later post-dated his prophecy of 30 January to 1 September 1939, the date of the outbreak of war.

Wagner's devotional drama of Kundry, the laughing Circe, and Klingsor, the evil magician, of Amfortas, mortally wounded King of the Grail, and his resolute redeemer Parsifal, provided Hitler with a mythological universe from which he reinterpreted the reality around him. Chamberlain had taught him that such insights must be followed by corresponding actions, and one of his tasks as Messiah of the Bayreuth religion was the fulfilment of what was prophesied by *Parsifal* – that no sacred possession shall ever again be allowed to pass into 'guilt-stained hands' and no Aryan saviour shall ever again be mocked and crucified by his enemies.

He was already able to satisfy the first of these demands in his first year after seizing power. Standing by Wagner's graveside in 1923, he had vowed to carry out the Master's will to free *Parsifal* from the sordid clutches of the common run of opera houses and bring it back to Bayreuth. Now, ten years later, he announced the triumphant return of the 'devotional festival drama' to the Festspielhaus, in a production that corresponded to his conceptions. 'Hitler's great gift to Bayreuth, the return of *Parsifal*,' wrote Wolfgang Golther in 1933, 'has been linked to the condition that it be given a completely new production.'[104] Fifty years after Wagner's death the original production of 1882, which had survived almost unchanged until that moment, was to be replaced by one co-ordinated by Hitler, the new lord of the 'Green Hill'. The man who had only been able to afford to stand at the Vienna opera now felt ready to assume the mantle of authority. The *Parsifal* that would most closely match Hitler's desires would be one designed by the man who had moulded his taste a quarter of a century earlier – Alfred Roller. With Roller's help he now set out to relive his ecstatic experiences in the Hofoper by reproducing them in the hallowed precincts of Bayreuth. He had already conquered the Reich as a new Parsifal. Now he was to conquer Bayreuth with a new *Parsifal*.

On 22 July 1934, sitting in the royal box between the seventy-year-old Roller and Winifred Wagner, he watched the first performance of his new production, conducted by Richard Strauss and with the leading Wagnerian tenor Helge Roswaenge in the title role. It must have felt like the fulfilment of his wildest Wagnerian dreams.

But the sight of so much blood might also have aroused other thoughts in his mind, less uplifting thoughts – like that of the first systematic massacre of his career which had taken place barely a month before. His treacherous assassination of his own followers around the figure of the SA leader Ernst Röhm had been followed by the justification that 'the virulent poison of homosexuality had begun to spread its infection ever wider', leading to the creation of a 'conspiratorial cell' directed against the state.[105] Showing the steely qualities required of a redeemer, the new Parsifal gave orders to 'cauterize the abscesses that have left their foul mark on our society and burn away all the surplus flesh down to the bone'.[106]

The pain-racked Amfortas in *Parsifal*, who has sullied Aryan blood, also begs for such a radical solution. The poison that has infected his blood threatens to spread throughout the brotherhood and bring about its downfall. 'Here I lie!' he cries to his knights. 'Here is my open wound! Behold the poisoned blood that flows through my body! Draw your swords, ye heroes, and slay the suffering sinner! The Grail will then glow with life again.'[107] The mass execution of SA leaders was not the only bloody deed to take place during the period of the Führer's 'Parsifal reforms'. Hardly had he solemnly assured his friends in Wahnfried that only seventy-seven men had been executed[108] than he ordered a further bloody purge of his SS vassals.

On 25 July 1934, in the course of the première of *Rheingold*, news reached the Festspielhaus that the Austrian Chancellor, Engelbert Dollfuss, a sworn enemy of the Führer's, had been murdered by Hitler's men during an attempted coup. According to Hermann Rauschning, Hitler had the previous year coldly announced his intention of 'liquidating Dollfuss and his supporters as traitors'.[109]

The news of the brutal murder, however, in no way affected Hitler's enjoyment of the evening. 'Although his face could hardly disguise his delight', wrote Friedelind Wagner, 'he went to the restaurant as though nothing had happened and ordered a plate of liver dumplings.' 'I must stay here a while and show myself in public, otherwise people will think I had something to do with the business,' he said to Friedelind.[110]

The creation of a Grail religion also needed an unmistakable external symbol expressive of the universal claims being made by that religion. A shrine must be built to house the chalice which contains the sacred mystery of racial immortality. Inspired by Wagnerian visions, King Ludwig II had constructed a Grail Temple in the form of his castle of Neuschwanstein, in the Bavarian Alps, together with the 'hermit's hut' from the third act of *Parsifal*, where the hero, in the King's extravagant language, 'was anointed as the true King of the Grail and inherited a kingdom won through humility and the purging of all evil within himself'.[111] Ludwig's reveries led him to give instructions for the golden Throne Room to house a model of the interior of the Grail shrine but the scene as a whole bore no resemblance to Parsifal's Monsalvat.

A detailed description of how the remote fortress of Monsalvat was said to have looked is given in the medieval epic poem known as the 'Jüngerer Titurel' by Albrecht von Scharfenberg, and was reconstructed in the early nineteenth century by Goethe's friend, the art historian Sulpiz Boisserée. It was said to consist of 'a huge rotunda with a diameter of some 180 metres', surmounted by a forest of Gothic chapels and spires 'of fantastic proportions'.[112] In 1884 the painter Jakob von Steinle devoted a series of pictures to the Parsifal legend, in the centre of which stood the monumental rotunda of the Grail, its glow shining upwards to the heavens and illuminating a chalice and a white dove. Immediately Steinle had finished his cycle of paintings, the firm of Hanfstaengl in Munich, which made something of a speciality out of the mass production of Wagnerian icons, published the picture in a folder which Hitler, according to 'Putzi' Hanfstaengl, eagerly studied in the course of one of his visits to the family villa. Steinle's works may well have helped to stimulate Hitler's own architectural fantasies.

In 1925, the year Hitler first saw *Parsifal* in Bayreuth – in the 'Wolf's Lair' he was still to be heard praising 'the splendid voice and presence' of Carl Clewing in the title role[113] – he made his own sketch of the Grail Temple – a building of massive proportions with a portico of neo-Classical columns like the entrance to an opera house, and crowned by a lofty dome; in the piazza in front of the building groups of people are moving towards the entrance like families of ants. The interior may well have resembled the set of the Bayreuth production; Hitler even took over from Wagner the clerestory window through which the light shines down from the cupola and causes the Redeemer's blood to glow.[114]

When Hitler later set about building his New Germania in Berlin, he returned to his Grail design and made his domed shrine the focal point of his German – and later world – Empire. He instructed his chief architect, Albert Speer, to design a Grail temple on the old model, changing the proportions if necessary but keeping to the overall dimensions – a new Grail temple that would outshine all the other buildings in the world. Large enough to accommodate St Peter's in Rome several times over, a congregation of 150,000 souls would gather here in a service of Aryan worship, while the light from a window at the top of the 290-metre-high dome would shine down on the devotional scene below. Instead of the dove and the holy chalice, the scene was dominated by a thirty-metre-high eagle clasping the globe between its claws. 'Hitler believed', wrote Speer, 'that, as the centuries passed, his giant auditorium would become a sacred shrine. At the heart of the whole plan was the conception of a religious cult . . . a means of validating his *Weltanschauung* for all time.'[115]

The plan remained in the realm of fantasy. The funds to build the temple, which Hitler, a lover of superlatives, said would be 'the most expensive building in the world',[116] were not available. All that was left was the fine plaster model and the hope that, after victory had finally been won, it might still be possible for it to become a reality.

Even without 'Germania' and its cathedral the German nation had been converted to the Hitlerite religion. The stages along Hitler's triumphant path in the year since his appointment as Chancellor – the Enabling Act in March, the Jewish boycott in April, the burning of the books in May, the Party Rally of Victory in September and the laying of the foundation stone of the 'Haus der deutschen Kunst' in Munich in October, down to the massacre of Röhm and his men, and now to Roller's *Parsifal* in Bayreuth – all these were for him not just political events but like the Stations of the Cross, a journey at the end of which waited the downfall of Satan and the dawn of a new Germanic civilization. 'As the hero sacrifices his life so as to live on in the Pantheon of history,' he proclaimed at the opening of the Party rally in 1933, 'so a truly great movement must see in the truth of its ideology and in the truthfulness of its actions the talisman that will lead it triumphantly from a fleeting present to an immortal future.'[117]

Immortality, however – this was the message of Wagner's *Parsifal* – can be bestowed only by the Grail, the eternal source of the imperishable heritage of the Aryan race. The man who passed on to the future the pure message of the blood that he had inherited from his forebears would share in the eternal life of his people; and he who had grasped the mystery of the doctrine of the Grail was lifted above the fleeting vanities and trivialities of everyday existence. Indeed, he could count himself among the privileged few who formed the link that united the true Saviour with the Hohenstaufen

emperors and thence with the racial leader, Adolf Hitler. 'By devoting ourselves to the preservation of the blood with which destiny has entrusted
us,' Hitler concluded, as though addressing the Knights in Monsalvat, 'we
shall be helping to protect other peoples from diseases that spread from
one race to another and from one people to another.' In taking up the fight
against the poison of Bolshevism, 'our new Germany, as so often in its
history, is fulfilling a truly European mission'.[118]

Even when, six years later, this triumphal march revealed itself to be a
crusade that led not to the Grail Temple but to the concentration camp,
Hitler continued to cling to his concept of a divine mission, and with it to
the belief that both the origins and the ultimate aims of that mission lay in
the mystical depths of his inner Monsalvat. As befitting the sanctity of his
mission, he confined himself, even in the presence of close friends, to hints
and allusions. 'He only betrayed little secrets, and even then only parts of
them,' wrote Max Domarus.

> Important secrets he generally kept to himself and made no bones about it,
> even to those of his staff who were closest to him. He would weave a web of
> mystery about his thoughts and break off the conversation with the same
> kind of explanation as Christ used to give His disciples: 'I have yet many
> things to say unto you but ye cannot bear them now.'[119]

The doctrine of blood and race at the heart of Hitler's concept of regeneration is barely comprehensible and in the last analysis intolerable. What
he had convinced himself of, thanks to the authority of Wagner and the
pseudo-scholarship of Chamberlain, turned out to be a ponderous doctrine that could offer no answer to the real questions of the day. Instead of
solving the problems facing society, it created a mass of new ones, culminating in that which issued in one of the most unspeakable tragedies in the
history of the world. Those who allowed themselves to be seduced by his
racial theories were following not the dictates of reason, let alone of experience, but solely their love for the Führer. The question of where he had
acquired his wisdom was disregarded. The dilemma of the Nazi ideology
lay precisely in its derivative character. It offered premonition, supposi-
tion, not knowledge. And when, as in the case of its racial theories, it stated
as a scientific fact what was in fact nothing but hair-raising speculation, it
entered the realm of the preposterous.

The racial doctrine of the Third Reich, the central pillar of its political
ideology, ascribed to experience what contradicted experience and propa-
gated a faith which owed its power of conviction solely to the fact that it
was shared by the Führer. Jewish citizens had no more in common with
the 'Jew' of the Nazi imagination than had non-Jewish citizens – a glance
in the mirror would usually suffice – with the 'Aryan' of Scandinavian
origin. But Hitler talked of hardly anything else, and by repeating what he

said, one automatically enjoyed the protection of his truth. The question remains, whether he himself, Adolf Hitler, sole guardian of the true faith, believed what he said, and whether he said everything he thought. Maybe he left the most vital things unsaid. What his inner truth consisted of nobody knew – that much those around him quickly grasped. If, as many sensed but dared not say, his dogmatic utterances concerned only the outer trappings – a metaphor of his true meaning, so to speak – and left the heart of the message untouched, what did this heart consist of, and what was he concealing in his innermost being? Why, indeed, did he find it necessary to conceal this vital knowledge from his Aryan nation of heroes at all?

Hitler was not the kind of politician who announces a programme and then justifies his actions to the people, but a redeemer figure from an esoteric cult who had assumed the task of ridding the world of the Jews. He embodied not the masses who cheered him but the policies he had determined to carry out; his responsibility was not to the men and women who believed in him but to the secret ideals embedded in his faith. And since the Germans were for him only a means to an end, namely the establishment of a world of pure blood, they needed to know no more than was necessary to create the requisite conditions.

Strictly speaking they did not need to know anything. They only needed to believe. That was another reason why Hitler spoke almost entirely in mythological images, which he then decked out with facts and figures in order to relate his vision to the present day. Current situations were put into old settings and every new problem solved in terms of familiar figures and legends of the past. The perfect racial role model, used by Hitler in an endless variety of forms, sometimes mentioned by name, sometimes invoked as an ideal, was Siegfried. Whenever the subject turned to the blond-haired, blue-eyed Teutonic race – in any case a minority in the country – the attractive figure of the dragon-slayer was invoked. At the same time it will not have escaped people's memory that, for lack of caution and racial awareness, the heroic Siegfried was brought down by the treachery of the creatures of the underworld.

Parsifal, on the other hand, the victor, was less well suited to the role of national symbol. The myth and message of the Grail resisted any attempt at popularization. The figure of a 'guileless fool' who denies himself the pleasures of the flesh in favour of 'redeeming' a bleeding vessel with the touch of a spear seemed rather to belong to some bizarre fairy-tale.

Yet Wagner's mystery play was one of the most important paradigms of the Third Reich, with an authority that penetrated both the ideal faith and the external rituals of the Nazi state. And Hitler, the statesman who represented the secret Bayreuth cult by keeping silent about it, saw in his new Reich that realm of the Knights of the Grail which had only to be liberated from the curse on its blood to be transformed into God's kingdom on earth. Blood and race, purification and procreation – this is the message of *Parsifal*.

It cannot be talked about but only expressed in sublime symbols and embodied in strict rituals. A goal that cannot be defined in ordinary words clamours for a prophetic language; and a future that can only be attained through unspeakable horrors is best left shrouded in the mists of uncertainty.

'The man who sees National Socialism as nothing but a political movement', said Hitler, 'knows hardly the first thing about it. It is more even than a religion – it is the collective will of a new race of men.'[120] Nobody thought to ask just what he meant. Evidently he was nursing a secret in which he unwaveringly believed; and everyone shared his belief in this secret though hardly anyone apart from him knew what it was. After he had brought his life to a miserable end, the message was put around that there had never been a secret, so there had been nothing for people to believe. But it was just such unspoken features of Hitler's mission that imprinted on the Third Reich that mixture of sorcery and terror that really did make it more than 'a political movement' – or, indeed, than any known form of human association.

Hitler was well aware of the conflict between secret mission and public utterance. His problem was, to what extent could he disclose his innermost thoughts and feelings without sacrificing the aura of uniqueness that surrounded him? Did not the profound knowledge he had derived from Wagner, coupled with the terrifying commission laid upon him by Chamberlain, represent a confidential religious secret, which, if once made public, might give rise to dangerous misunderstandings, not to speak of the retaliatory measures it might provoke? By making ceaseless calls on his people to 'have faith', Hitler was in fact demanding that they exercise a voluntary intellectual self-restraint. Once enunciated, the principles of his primitive racial doctrine had the authority of dogma and had to be obeyed; reflection was out of the question, and even to ask what exactly was to be understood by the ever-recurring reference to 'blood' almost amounted to blasphemy. 'By provoking discussion of racial issues', Hitler confided to Otto Wagener at the beginning of the 1930s, 'we would only cause more divisions among the people. . . . On a number of occasions I therefore forbade any debate or discussion of racial doctrines or racial problems. . . . For the leaders of the National Socialist movement knowledge about the significance of blood is a key and a signpost; for the general public it is poison!'[121]

But how can something be poison and at the same time the heart of a doctrine of salvation? How can one leave in ignorance the very people for whose benefit, allegedly, the whole campaign of redemption has been mounted? Hitler himself left no doubt about the precedence of the principle of regeneration, and came to regard this as the most important achievement of his social revolution. 'If I were to assess my life's work,' he pontificated to Himmler in 1941, 'the first thing I would have to emphasize is that I have succeeded, in the face of a complete lack of understanding on the part of the outside world, in installing the concept of race at the heart of our national life.'

As his second most important achievement, in the spirit of Wagner's 'Work of Art of the Future', Hitler cites his moves 'to make German culture the foundation of German domination'.[122] But before these two achievements can be set on permanent and logical foundations one particular step must be taken, namely to eliminate the Jews. 'If we can once eradicate these vermin,' he had said the previous day – it was the time of the German advance on Moscow – 'we shall be doing something for mankind, the significance of which our men out there can as yet have no conception.'[123] In other words, these men were killing and dying without knowing why.

The Führer's henchmen were also celebrating without knowing why. When he raised his baton, they all cheered, believing in his infallibility because he told them to do so. And as his successes seemed to prove him right, his ends justified all his means. People sensed that they simply had to believe him – but could they be sure that their senses were not deceiving them? Why did they have to devote themselves to the cause just because sermon after sermon passionately said so? 'The great secret of our movement', ranted the Nazi fanatic Gregor Strasser in 1927, 'is our surrender, mind and body, to the ideal of National Socialism, our burning faith in the triumph of our doctrine of emancipation and salvation, and our profound devotion to our beloved Führer, who will lead his troops to victory in the coming fight for freedom.' Strasser then went on to rave about the 'steely tone' and 'brutal determination' with which the Führer 'addresses these things, declaring war on them, merciless war to the point of total destruction'.[124]

About the nature of these 'things' Strasser had nothing to say. Seven years later, along with Röhm and his supporters, he became a victim of his own Führer's 'brutal determination' and was murdered. Vague the nature of Hitler's secret intentions may have been but there was no escaping the violence of the consequences. Hans Frank, later Governor-General of Poland, one of those condemned to death at the Nuremberg Trials in 1946, compared his allegiance to Germany to 'religious worship', adding that 'if Christ were to come again, it would be as a German', and that 'the Germans were God's chosen instrument for the destruction of evil. . . . We are fighting in the name of God against the Jews and against evil. May God protect us!'[125]

Hitler, however, who may have encouraged Frank to invoke the blessing of the Almighty, did not believe in God but happily confessed himself a pagan. So what was the true state of affairs? Frank, who had taken part in Hitler's abortive coup in 1923, thought he knew; so did Strasser. But both seem to have overlooked, like millions of their fellows, that there was in fact nothing to know. For Hitler they were all willing and submissive lackeys. 'I can do without pledges of allegiance,' he said in 1931; 'they are meaningless to me. What I want is discipline.'[126] Not knowledge, not even faith – all he required was obedience and self-denial. What mattered was the actions that had to be taken – the thinking could be left to the Führer.

The larger the Nazi movement grew, the less it served the Führer's needs as a Party. The masses that swarmed round him like bees round a honeypot contradicted his image of an elite corps of devoted followers. Likewise the importunate Party bosses in their custom-made suits offended his ascetic band of crusaders who followed their Saviour into the final battle. What needed to be done, if the whole enterprise was to have any meaning, could not be accomplished by the man in the street, and certainly not by millions of them. What was needed was a select group of sworn disciples – in effect a medieval military order, who possessed both the requisite strength and a necessary sense of submission born, in this case, not of blind obedience but of love for the Führer.

As Hitler's movement had started as a conspiratorial cell, so now, its brown uniform having since become the basic earthy colour of the whole country, it returned to being a closed community with a secret agenda. This made it possible for the old aim of destroying the 'Jewish' Weimar Republic to be extended to cover the entire world, with the salvation of Germany seen as a prelude to the liberation of the planet. In this too Wagner's *Parsifal* afforded a model: for within the sacred precincts of Monsalvat, united in their religious fervour and their iron determination, lived that community of chosen knights who were ready at any time to shed their blood and also, with a clear conscience, the blood of others. They were prepared to sacrifice their lives in the sure knowledge that they would be born again in the welling blood of the Holy Grail. Such mystical visions could not be communicated to, let alone fulfilled by, the great Moloch of a Nazi Party.

Hardly had the leaders of the Party divided up political power among themselves than that power became an embarrassment for the man who had given it to them. It had been no accident that in 1933, with the Brownshirts in the full flush of victory, the family in Wahnfried had been among the first to whom Hitler promised to found a new party – 'I no longer like the old one,'[127] he said. For decades the elite of Bayreuth had been pursuing their own secret aims – never had they needed to make common cause with the common people. Wagner's closed community, its 'heralds of the Grail' preaching the message throughout the country, had achieved more than whole armies of common-or-garden Party members.

The notorious Bayreuth Festival programme of 1925, with its coded references to Hitler, also contains a statement of Bayreuth's vision of an ideal party, one very different from the Nazi rowdies of the day. 'What is so wonderful about this elite, aristocratic community', wrote Hans Alfred Grunsky, is that alongside its spiritual mysticism, its urge to the other-worldly and its union with God, growing spontaneously out of these sacred qualities, there exists a driving will to perform selfless acts of heroism in this life, an urge to do the Saviour's work and to fight the good fight. These Knights of the Grail are no mere reformers – they are crusaders fighting for goodness and justice. Through them the Master has portrayed the ideal life of an inspired religious community.[128]

The Bayreuth Wagner cult, with Chamberlain at its head, saw itself in just such terms, and this was to be the model for the new party that would claim their full allegiance. In the last analysis what was at stake was not a secular political aim but a metaphysical commitment.

The new Parsifal, gripped by the sacred conviction of his mission, was well aware that saints could not give him power. At the same time his gangs of loud-mouthed hooligans, with hordes of submissive vassals trailing along behind them with dog-like obedience – 'slaves waiting for orders',[129] he called them, according to Wolfgang Wagner – were hardly calculated to provide an appropriate response to the Master's challenge. The only answer was the model provided by Parsifal – Hitler would have to found an order in which the consciousness of his sublime mission was linked to a preparedness to put it into bloody practice. At the time of the Röhm Putsch he announced to his assembled Gauleiters that their most pressing task was to train a cadre of men both able and willing, in blind obedience, to put the government's measures into effect. 'The Party, as a military order, must create the conditions of stability necessary for the future of the country and therefore be utterly committed.'[130] As the smug Party bosses hardly conformed to Hitler's notions of what constituted a select band of heroes, so a mass party could never form a loyal order of individual warriors. For what mattered in such an order was not the right attitude of mind but purity of blood and nobility of race and body. One did not join an order, one was called to its service. What the Führer told his Gauleiters was really intended for quite different ears.

'The idea of a state built on the principles of a medieval Order,' Hitler told the avid Wagnerian Hans Severus Ziegler in 1925, the year of his first *Parsifal* in Bayreuth, 'fanciful though it may seem, is one that for years has struck me as thoroughly feasible.'[131] Maybe it crossed his mind at his first *Rienzi* in Linz in 1906, when the tribune summons his 'Knights of the Holy Spirit' – or perhaps later, in 1914, at the first Munich performance of *Parsifal* on Wagner's birthday in the year the First World War broke out. Or maybe it was later still – 1924, the year the Bayreuth Festival programme carried the article envisaging the creation of a party of Knights of the Grail. The vision of such a party had also been before his eyes since he first saw *Lohengrin*, with its band of knights in shining armour 'called to the service of the Grail' and pledged to 'lay its adversaries low with the sword'.[132]

And he had watched the German troops, with banners waving and the sun glinting on their weapons, as they cheered Lohengrin, their new leader, before marching off to the eastern front.

After listening one day in 1936 to his favourite gramophone recording of the Prelude to *Parsifal* – that conducted by Karl Muck – Hitler declared: 'I intend to found my religion on *Parsifal*.' As Wagner's music combines the gravity of formal chant with the ethereal tones of a mystical vision, so Hitler's religious order of the future was to blend heroic discipline with sanctity and dedication. His goal, he said in the same year, after the occupation of the Rhineland, was 'religious worship in solemn mode, devoid of any pretence of humility. . . . One can only serve God in the guise of a hero.'[133]

Rarely did Hitler openly discuss what his new *Parsifal* religion was intended to convey, not least because of a lack of suitable listeners. Except to those with a thorough knowledge of Wagner the esoteric nature of his vision remained ultimately unintelligible, a frightening utopia remote from all reality. One of the few whom he admitted into his sanctum – and who published their discussions even before the outbreak of the war – was Hermann Rauschning. Although Rauschning, then President of the Danzig Senate, attributes many more statements to the Führer in his *Conversations with Hitler*[134] than he can have possibly heard, he must have been an ideal person with whom to discuss Wagner. An eloquent Classical scholar, he had also studied music in Munich, where he got to know the Wagner epigones, and had also attended the Bayreuth Festival. Whenever Hitler met a connoisseur of Wagner, he abandoned his inhibitions and talked freely, so it was this shared love of the Master, we may assume, that led to Rauschning, a member of the Party, being admitted into the private recesses of Hitler's mind. It is hardly possible that what Rauschning subsequently recorded is merely the product of his imagination – it resembles too closely the secret doctrines of the Bayreuth inner circle.

He was completely disillusioned about the Party, Hitler told his friend and colleague: 'These men are simply incapable of understanding higher thoughts – indeed, all they know are the official tenets of National Socialism that they were once made to learn by heart. The old guard must therefore simply be got rid of.' Once that had happened, 'the Party would give birth to a new, original form of secular priesthood that would rule the state'. By this, Rauschning believed, Hitler meant nothing less than 'the foundation of a new religion of mankind, indeed, the creation of a new mankind itself'.[135]

Herein lay the mystical secret of the Parsifal cult. As the hero who overcomes the enemies of the sacred order and of a pure humanity, Wagner's 'guileless fool' becomes both High Priest of the Grail Temple and King of the Grail community. As secular ruler he governs the Knights in the castle of Monsalvat; as redeemer he enacts the symbolic union of spear and chalice and opens the way to a new generation of pure blood. These superhuman acts of redemption are accomplished on the stage in the course of a few hours – in reality it will be aeons before they will have come to pass. Not even a lifetime will suffice to destroy Klingsor's kingdom of evil and achieve the ultimate 'redemption of the redeemer'. This is no doubt also the reason why, in the course of his conversations with the Führer, Rauschning became aware of the 'growing impatience' with which he moved on to the subject that was his principal concern – that of 'the creative statesman and law-maker, the pioneering artist and architect, the prophet and the founder of religions'.[136]

'I will let you into a secret,' said Hitler to Rauschning on another occasion: 'I intend to found an Order.'[137] Like other things, it was to be in the image of Wagner. 'Nobody knows any more what Wagner really is,' he complained. 'I mean not just the music but his whole revolutionary cultural doctrine. . . . He is the greatest prophet the German nation has ever had.' It had been either by chance or by an act of providence that he, Hitler, had first come across Wagner, discovering with almost hysterical excitement that every word the Master had written sounded a chord in the depths of his own subconscious being.

From this, according to Rauschning, Hitler passed to the subject that was familiar to every National Socialist but was never discussed in connection with Wagner. 'The problem is', said Hitler, 'how can we put a stop to racial degeneracy?' Could it be done by bringing pressure to bear on the mass of the people? Rather, said the Führer, by taking one's lead from *Parsifal* 'and creating a select band who understand what is at stake, comparable to the Order of the Knights of the Grail who guarded the pure blood'.[138]

With the mention of this fateful word Hitler broached an interpretation of Wagner which, a secret doctrine of the Bayreuth circle, was virtually unknown elsewhere and at the same time – something Rauschning could not know either – was at the heart of Hitler's *Weltanschauung*. 'You must learn to interpret *Parsifal* quite differently from the way it is usually interpreted – by boneheads like Wolzogen, for example,' Hitler continued, distancing himself from Wolzogen's view of the work as a study in compassion.

> For behind the pseudo-Christian trivialities of its plot, with its Good Friday mumbo-jumbo, this profound work has a different and far more vital meaning. It is not the Christian–Schopenhauerian religion of compassion that is here being worshipped but the pure, noble blood which the brotherhood of initiates has vowed to preserve in its purity and to worship in its sanctity.

Such was the hidden meaning of Wagner's *Parsifal* as Hitler, the executor of Wagner's intellectual and spiritual estate, saw it.

But he had not finished. As he expounded to Rauschning:

The King is condemned to eternal suffering, the consequence of his adulteration of the pure blood, and an unknowing but pure youth is exposed to the temptations of Klingsor's magic garden of carnal pleasures and the attractions of a degenerate civilization; at the same time he is invited to join the select order of knights pledged to protect this pure blood, the secret of life.

It was a temptation as familiar to Wagner's listeners as to the readers of *Mein Kampf*. In Rauschning's recollection Hitler avoided mentioning the Jews by name but his meaning was unmistakable – only no one could have foreseen at this time the unimaginable lengths to which he would go after the outbreak of war to put his blood philosophy into effect. 'We are all suffering from the sickness of mixed, infected blood. How can we purge ourselves and atone for our condition?'[139]

Hitler's answer, couched in terms calculated to justify the mass murders that were to follow, sounded at the time of his conversations with Rauschning like mythological word-painting. 'Those who are sick must be left to die,' he said. 'The everlasting life granted by the Grail is only for the noble breed that is really pure.' Here Hitler himself drew Rauschning's attention to the fact that he was thoroughly familiar with Wagner's trains of thought, and that if one removed the extravagances of Wagner's poetic language, 'one would see that only in the tensions of an eternal struggle can a chosen race be born and renewal achieved'. That in talking of this 'struggle' Hitler did not mean, as Rauschning thought, the general Darwinian struggle for the survival of the fittest but the metaphysical confrontation with the Jews – the struggle he had glorified with the Messianic title *Mein Kampf* – was something he concealed from his guest.

He did, however, explain how he envisaged his new secret Grail order. 'In remote, isolated castles', he said, 'a new generation will grow up in whose presence the world will shudder. A bold, imperious, violent, cruel generation – that is what I want.' Not that the birth of this generation of Spartan warriors was to be an end in itself – they were to use their power and resilience 'to root out the effects of thousands of years of human domestication'. Through a process of natural selection the young 'will achieve the status of free men, the measure of all things, standing in the centre of creation, man made in the image of God, the proud image of a cult'.

There came a time when Hitler seems to have feared that he might have told the attentive Rauschning too much. 'He said', noted the man from Danzig, 'that there were stages in the development of affairs about which not even he was free to talk, and he abruptly broke off the conversation. Besides that, he regarded such matters as his own secret, which should only be disclosed after his death.'[140] What 'stages' could he have meant? That conquest of the world, perhaps, which would precede the universal 'work of art of the future'? Or the cryptic utterance whose secret he really did only wish to see revealed after his death, when his last will and testament was opened?

At this moment the thought of a Greater Germany presented as a work of art, like that of the extermination of millions of innocent people, still lay in the future. But now, at the beginning of his chancellorship, feeling no inhibitions about giving his imagination free rein in Rauschning's company, he was prepared to state his aim. This was his goal – nothing else. He therefore had no time to lose. The task he had been set, and of which Rauschning had no inkling, exceeded his powers and his life-span. 'I have too little time, too little time!' he lamented, adding: 'People barely know the first thing about me. Not even my closest Party colleagues have any idea what is going through my mind and what I must establish, at least in its fundamentals.' Rauschning recorded sensing in the Führer 'a febrile anxiety that he might not live to achieve his goal'.[141]

His anxiety was well founded. His attempt to translate Wagner's sacred festival drama into the reality of the twentieth century, and to transform the world into a theatre for the demonstration of Wagner's doctrines of regeneration, failed. Failure also attended his far less ambitious plan for realizing the dreams he had had in Vienna of seeing his productions performed in Bayreuth. After three years his version of *Parsifal*, prepared with Roller's help, was consigned to the warehouse. Another failure was the project for a gigantic Grail Temple in Berlin as a cult centre of the world; his plan to surmount the Festival theatre in Bayreuth with a monumental dome was abandoned at the beginning of the war. And his hopes of making *Parsifal* the climax of the worldwide events to celebrate the victorious outcome of that war expired, at the latest, in the Berlin bunker.

Only in one respect did Hitler come close – perilously close – to achieving his aim – that aspect of his insane fantasy of blood and purification which he hid in mystical obscurity until the very end. The indelible mark that Wagner's *Parsifal* has left on history is the Holocaust.

15

LIFE UNDER THE MASTERSINGERS

The irresistible rise of Adolf Hitler resembled a career in the theatre. Beginning as Wagnerian hero, he succeeded by dint of skilful acting and energetic support from outside in turning the country into his faithful audience, then, having been appointed director, transforming it into the theatre that matched his requirements. Thanks to Hitler, wrote Goebbels in 1933, politics began to turn into 'a people's drama'.[1] Germany became a Wagnerian opera. According to the designs of Hitler, as stage producer, the framework would be provided by the towns and cities, which would be made the object of a gigantic reconstruction programme. Prosaic functional buildings would give way to sublime temples which even as ruins would retain their grandeur, with campaniles looking down on ceremonial squares, and railway stations as Pantheons of travel throughout the world. 'His projects for monumental buildings were to be stage sets for his productions of world events,' wrote Albert Speer, Hitler's chief architect. 'Theatre was the vein that ran through his entire life.'[2]

The old name of Hitler's new theatre was 'Work of Art of the Future'. Wagner had taught him that music drama, as opposed to opera as a conventional form of entertainment, represented a higher reality which, as in Greek Antiquity, did not remain confined to the stage but penetrated the everyday life of the people. In Classical tragedy the Athenians saw themselves reflected in a mirror: the hero's life is told through his deeds and sufferings, his death leads to a rebirth in the hearts of the faithful, and his blood, tragically shed, courses for ever through the veins of the people. As the hero's mortality merges into the eternal life of the race, so everyday existence, seen as a drama in which man is inextricably caught up, takes on the features of a cosmic tragedy. Each individual rediscovers himself in the god-like hero, and the once faceless crowd, welded into a homogeneous community by a power from without, receives in moments of celebration its sense of collective identity.

In the Nazi calendar of events, as memorable as they were terrible, 9 November, date of the fiasco of Hitler's attempted coup in Munich, was the equivalent of Good Friday. On this most sacred of days[3] Hitler remembered his comrades who had given their lives for the salvation of the Fatherland, coupled with the temporary eclipse of his movement, seen as a paradigm of the mystical cycle of death and rebirth. The annual ritual, which has been compared to a Passion play[4] and owes a good deal to Wagner's Good Friday opera *Parsifal*, consisted of a ceremonial march of the veterans from the Bürgerbräu beer-hall to the monument of the Feldherrnhalle, scene of the shooting on that fateful day. The dominant symbol of the event, which aroused the sympathy not only of the citizens of Munich, birthplace of the movement, but of the whole country, was blood. Those killed in the Putsch were proclaimed martyrs; in 1935 their bodies were exhumed and the coffins brought back to the spot where the men had fallen.

Likewise in the final act of *Parsifal* the knights carry the body of Titurel into the hall of the Grail, chanting: 'The coffin bears the body of the hero and his divine power.' They place it in front of the table on which the Grail stands. When they open it, 'all utter a great cry of lamentation'.[5] Now, as in Bayreuth, the November martyrs lay in state in the Feldherrnhalle, which was draped in black flags, while the procession moved slowly closer from the Bürgerbräu, at its head those decorated with the so-called 'Blood Order' that Hitler had instituted and a group carrying the 'Blood Banner'. Marching past 240 pylons on which stood bowls of fire, each pylon inscribed with the name of one of the martyrs in the history of the Party – each name was called out in turn as the column of marchers moved past – the procession arrived at the shrine. A sixteen-gun artillery salute was fired and the names of the sixteen men killed in the Putsch were read out. Further salvoes followed, church bells rang and the procession made its way to the newly built 'Temples of Remembrance' in the Königsplatz, where the bodies were finally to be laid to rest. Again, one by one, their names were called out, like saints, and each time came the ringing answer from the boys of the Hitler Youth: 'Here!' The blood of the martyrs was thus shown to live on in the next generation, and the death of the few had brought new life to the many. 'For us they are not dead,' declared Hitler in the Königsplatz on 9 November 1935. 'These temples are not graves but eternal watch-towers. The sentries are guarding our Fatherland and keeping watch for our people.'[6]

But those who would have no rest until the blood of the fallen was avenged met again later in front of the Feldherrnhalle, torches held aloft, drums solemnly beating – a secret Order, inspired by blood, staked out its place in the future as detachments of black-shirted SS men, among them the feared death's-head units, vowed allegiance to the Führer.

In the mystical centre of these celebrations of the events of 1924 stood the 'Blood Banner'. As Hitler embodied the new Parsifal, King of the Grail, so this macabre relic, dipped in the blood of the martyrs, represented the Grail itself. As the magic vessel in Monsalvat was replenished once every year by the dove from Heaven, so 'the holy relic of the National Socialist movement', as Baldur von Schirach called it,[7] was displayed twice a year. And as Wagner's Grail, which held the blood of the crucified Christ, brought renewed strength to the knights, so the aura that surrounded the sacred banner of the fallen martyrs spread to all the new banners of the Party.

Only one man was allowed to carry the symbol of salvation – the veteran Party member Grimminger. And only the Führer, with his magic touch, could release the energy latent in the flag. 'The purest faith spreads from the Grail to the brotherhood of the Knights,' in Lohengrin's words. 'Those who are chosen to serve the Grail are filled with strength from above.'[8] The blood of the fallen comrades is transformed into the life-giving substance of the new generation – but also into that vow of vengeance uttered by Rienzi as he plunged his hand into the blood that streamed from his brother's heart: 'Woe to him who spills a kindred blood!'[9]

Hatred and vindictiveness robbed Hitler's theatrical religiosity of its last traces of humanity. Even the mass emotionalism generated by his public meetings, in which the barriers of individuality were swept away, left no room for reconciliation with the 'enemy'. Faith and hatred were inseparable – blood as symbol of racial continuity and blood to be shed in battle had a common origin.

This consecration of blood-red banners and standards was from the very beginning the climax of Hitler's mass meetings. At the first Nazi Party rally in Munich in 1923, launched to the strains of Wagner's overture to *Rienzi*,[10] the flags bearing the 'Germany Awake!' slogan designed by Hitler himself were raised to the status of sacred symbols. 'Like a wall of steel', reported the *Völkischer Beobachter*, 'more than two brigades of the best German blood marched through the streets of Munich, bearing the swastika that will become the symbol of a Germany reborn.'[11] For those doomed to die in Hitler's ritual drama, it became more than a symbol.

'The history of the German nation', declared Hitler at the first Party rally, 'must not record . . . that we forgot everything and cravenly forgave all our enemies. Rather it must report that all these scoundrels were called to account and a judgement pronounced on them that was remembered for centuries.'[12] He never retracted a word of his brutal prophecy – indeed, on the most solemn dates in the Nazi year, the march to the Feldherrnhalle and the Party rally, he was at pains to repeat it, using a variety of metaphors. This unshakeable hatred made Hitler a demon even to the most faithful of his followers – a human being impervious to anything humane. 'He was a demon possessed by delusions about the *Volk*,' wrote Otto Dietrich, for many years head of Hitler's press office.[13]

At the Party rally in 1935 Dietrich could still be found enthusiastically embracing Hitler's concept of 'a closed circle of initiates devoted to the interests of the *Volk*'.[14] Later, however, he wrote of the 'unnatural and unreal concept of the nation' that had grown out of Hitler's delusions about the *Volk*; it was this concept, said Dietrich, that explained

> the inhuman atrocities from which he did not shrink. This unrealistic, almost transcendental vision of the nation propounded in Hitler's Nuremberg speeches, which talked in terms of the thousands of years that stretched out before his mind as he devotedly worshipped at the shrine of Wagner's *Götterdämmerung* in Bayreuth, may well shed light on the deepest recesses of his personality.[15]

The nation 'as it was' – as opposed to the transcendental 'nation of blood' – was indeed only the raw material which the Führer set out to mould according to his ideal. And since he had found this ideal not in the world of reality but in the works of Wagner, he had to adapt that reality to the ideal setting that he had experienced in the darkness of the opera house. His most spectacular demonstration of this intensified reality, which descended on the masses like the dove on the Grail, was the National Party Rally. The sole organizer and stage manager of the occasion, he had arranged the content and sequence of the events down to the last detail – the parades, the processions, the meetings, the night-time spectacles, in which the individual was submerged in the mass marching and singing of the thousands, yet at the same time, through his identification with the Führer, could feel himself to be at the centre of attention.

The marathon event, 'which for ten days brought to the city the atmosphere of the Olympic Games in an earlier age', as Hitler described it,[16] also came to resemble Wagner's original conception of the 'work of art of the future', as identified by the Master in Classical Antiquity. When, he wrote in exile in 1849, the Greek citizen made his way to the theatre with 'all his urges centred on his rebirth through the ideal expression of art; when massed voices rang out loud and clear in chorus; and when, in the role of the architect, he raised a fine roof above the harmoniously disposed columns, laid out, one by one, the broad semicircular rows of the amphitheatre and designed the rational proportions of the stage' – then, says Wagner in 'Art and Revolution', the world was ready 'to bring forth the supreme work of art, namely Drama'.[17]

In his early days, as Kapellmeister in Dresden, Wagner had dreamed of the rebirth of Antiquity, while the Greek national drama of Aeschylus and Sophocles found its reincarnation in his *Gesamtkunstwerk*. Hitler's Nuremberg *Gesamtkunstwerk*, in which all the arts, from architecture to literature and from music to dance, had their part to play, also followed this romanticization of Classical Antiquity. While Wagner wrote in 1867 in his essay 'German Art and German Politics' about the 'state of degeneracy into which art had fallen',[18] and the Third Reich issued a formal declaration of war against 'degenerate art', Hitler saw his mass demonstrations as having helped to bring the Classical aspect of Wagner's ideal closer to contemporary experience: 'Never, either in appearance or in its sentient being, has mankind been closer to Antiquity than it is today,' he said in 1937 in his Munich art gallery, the 'Haus der deutschen Kunst'. 'A new breed of radiant beauty is set to appear.'[19]

The ritual celebration of this coming breed took place each year in Nuremberg. An old imperial city not far from Bayreuth, Nuremberg embodied a tradition that was German through and through. It had been the first free city to convert to the Lutheran faith and had for centuries succeeded in preventing Jews from settling within its walls – a fact not irrelevant for Wagner when, locating it symbolically in 'the centre of Germany', as he called it, he came to compose his *Meistersinger von Nürnberg*. Nor did Hitler forget, when choosing to make it the scene of his annual Party festival, that it was also the city of the artist Albrecht Dürer and the poet Hans Sachs.

The first of these festivals, in 1927 – the so-called 'Rally of Awakening' – was attended by 160,000 Party members; by 1933, the 'Rally of Victory', there were 400,000. Five years later 950,000 crowded into the stadium, and expecting even more in the future, Hitler ordered it to be expanded to take at least two million.[20] His ideal plan would have been to assemble the entire population in the city to witness the 'work of art of the future' – preferably the whole year round. But his dream of a monumental dramatic production with a cast not of thousands but of millions found its fulfilment only on 1 September 1939, when it was not, as usual at this time, the bells that rang out to greet the Party rally but the guns that marked the beginning of the Second World War. And for this special moment, Hitler later said, the Party rallies had done 'valuable preparatory work'.[21]

Wagner's dream that the *Volk* would one day flock to his Festspielhaus on the 'Green Hill' in Bayreuth as though to a national shrine was fulfilled by Hitler in Nuremberg. Here, as a sign to the astounded masses, he also planned to erect 'the greatest arena, the most gigantic conference hall and the most colossal stadium in the world'.[22] He never disguised that what was being celebrated here was the dream of Richard Wagner – the massed ranks of the 'most-German Germans' to be found, vowing to dedicate themselves to art and beauty. There was no rally without the Triumphal March of Rienzi, tribune of the people, no opening ceremony without the *Meistersinger von Nürnberg*. What Wagner had envisioned for his 'theatre of the future', in which the whole people should see a reflection of itself, Hitler intended to bring to fruition in the city of the Mastersingers. 'Those places', he said in 1920 in his address 'Why Are We Anti-Semitic?', which Wagner once needed to be darkened so as to create the highest possible degree of reverence and solemnity for the performance of the works he called sacred and devotional – these places, centres of national religious worship, should afford the ultimate degree of inspiration and moral uplift, a release from all misery and wretchedness but at the same time from all the foul and base aspects of life with which we are confronted.[23]

Wagner's vision, revisited by Hitler, provided the liturgy for the Party rallies.

The congress of 1933 opened with the Prelude to the *Meistersinger*. Addressing the 'League of German Culture', the Führer announced a further fulfilment of Wagner's hopes: in future, he said, following the demand made in 'Music and the Jews', non-Aryans would be forbidden to take part in the cultural life of the nation.[24] Goebbels joined in the chorus by pointing out that the Master had branded these un-artistic non-Aryans 'demons of decadence'[25] – words of encouragement to those who had come to Nuremberg to stand on picket lines in front of Jewish stores.

At the Party rally of 1934, held under the slogan 'Unity and Strength', Hitler returned in one of his customary outbursts of rage and hatred to Wagner's perverse theory that Jewish intellectuals had been worming their way into European cultural circles since the Middle Ages, causing intellectual confusion and plundering Classical culture – a concept basic to the *Meistersinger*. 'Only a pure race can produce high culture,' said Hitler.[26]

The rally of 1935, the 'Rally of Freedom', preceded the enactment of the infamous Nuremberg Race Laws. It might equally well have been called the 'Rally of Richard Wagner', for the entire week was dominated by the Master's music and the Master's ideas. As Hitler, greeted by peals of bells from all the churches in the city, entered the city hall to be presented with a replica of the imperial sword, choirs sang the 'Awake'-chorale from the *Meistersinger*. In the evening, at the Führer's request, there was a gala performance of the opera under Wilhelm Furtwängler, Germany's leading conductor, with a star cast from Bayreuth. Sitting between Winifred Wagner and the anti-Semitic Gauleiter of Franconia, Julius Streicher, Hitler watched the young Aryan hero get the better of his Jewish adversary. 'I must warmly congratulate you on a splendid performance of our national folk opera,' he said to Furtwängler afterwards.[27]

The following day the great festival, held in an arena like a larger-than-life version of the meadow in the opera where the townsfolk congregate, reached its 'sacred climax'[28] with the ceremony of Remembrance of the Dead and Dedication of the Banners. To the accompaniment of hymns that recalled the Lutheran chorales in the opera, the Führer marched down the broad central aisle in the arena, a guard of honour of SA and SS men on either side, towards the memorial for the fallen heroes, behind him the crimson relic of the November martyrs. He stood in silence for a while in front of the memorial and the banners were lowered. Then he turned on his heel and marched back the way he had come, this time to the rousing strains of the Badenweiler March. This piece was another of those exclusively associated with the Führer's public appearances, like the leitmotif that accompanies Siegfried throughout the *Ring*. While the bloodstained banner kept alive the memory of the attempted coup in which Hitler almost lost his life, the Badenweiler March, composed at the beginning of the First World War, evoked memories of the heroic battles of that war, which he had also survived. In the choreography of Hitler's operatic tattoos the banner and the march became inalienable leitmotifs of the hero.

The following days of the rally were dominated by the complementary motif of anti-Semitism. Hitler bitterly complained that the Jews were planning an 'underground attack' and the 'infiltration of racial poison'[29] in order, as the Nazi ideologue Alfred Rosenberg put it, 'to bring about the systematic subversion of the German blood for which they had such hatred'.[30] To put an end once for all to the 'racial destruction being carried out by the Jews'[31] – Goering's words – an 'Act for the Protection of German Blood and German Honour' was passed, which, as well as forbidding inter-marriage, dealt with such matters as the employment of domestic servants and the flying of flags. After a week of strenuous assertion of Teutonic values the rally was brought to a close with the Nibelungen March and the overture to *Rienzi*.[32] To the participants it was as though they had been witnessing the foundation of a new religion, at its head the God of an invincible Germany and with Adolf Hitler as His prophet.[33] No less effective than the way Wagner's heroes made their entrance on the stage were the techniques used by Hitler to stage-manage his public appearances. The eminence of his historic mission found expression, for instance, in the immense distance that he maintained between himself and the assembled crowds and marchers, while the long aisles down which he marched to the podium between the serried ranks of his uniformed guards symbolized his arduous life, his lonely trek to reach this culminating heroic moment. His favourite hour was the dusk, when the setting sun cast its last rays on the forest of banners. Twilight settled over the arena and searchlights lit up the sky from every corner.

The scene was set. A fanfare of brass announced the arrival of the Führer, and from the furthest point of the stadium, packed with over 100,000 of his faithful followers, emerged a single small figure. Striding briskly down the aisle, he made his way to the platform, where he stood erect until complete silence had settled over the crowd. Then, as in one of Roller's productions of Wagner, a parade of 25,000 blood-red banners, representing local Party organizations from over the whole country, streamed into the arena, searchlights picking out the golden eagles that crowned their standards, while the Führer saluted them in turn.[34]

This explosion of colour was followed by a mystic vision – the search-

lights suddenly directed their beams into the sky, the columns of light transforming the arena into the shrine in the Bayreuth production of *Parsifal*, in
which a 'dome of light'[35] was created above the darkened room by a circle
of vertical beams. Even a rough-and-ready character like Robert Ley, head
of the Labour Front, who committed suicide during the Nuremberg Trials
in 1945, was deeply moved by the spectacle, referring in oracular language
to 'the hallowed hour when an immense dome formed above our heads,
stretching as far as the eye could see'.[36]

Then, on behalf of the silent, dumbfounded mass of Party officials present,
a chorus of five hundred schoolboys from an elite Party school took a
sacred oath.[37] These young 'Knights of the Grail', educated according to the
two ideals of unconditional service to the German race and an uncompromising hatred of the Jews, had long been familiar with the mystical talk of
blood and race that belonged to Hitler's religion. In their school was a
special room in which were displayed plaques bedecked with flags and
bearing the names of the 'blood witnesses' who had taken the oath; at the
end of the room stood the figure of a naked hero.[38] 'In my schools', said
Hitler, founder of this and other such institutions, 'the image shall be displayed, as an ideal figure of worship, of the body beautiful made in the
image of God, man as master of his own fate.'[39] At the Party rallies, surrounded by a sea of blood-red standards, this 'figure of worship' was present,
not as an ideal vision but as a creature of flesh and blood, caught in the
glare of the searchlights which only a few years later were to rake the night
sky above the burning city of Nuremberg in search of allied bombers.

What the prophet had not foreseen was that a mere ten years after the
'Rally of Freedom' the city of the Mastersingers would be lying in ruins, the
once-proud arenas desolate and overgrown, and that at the Nuremberg Trials those of Hitler's vassals who had not taken their own lives would be
convicted of heinous crimes. The destruction of European Jewry, however,
he had foreseen. In November 1941, in the 'Wolf's Lair', when his advance
on Moscow had become bogged down in mud and ice, and the Gestapo,
after the systematic shooting of hundreds of thousands of Jews, reported
helplessly that 'this kind of action offers no solution to the Jewish problem',[40]
Hitler embarked on a long monologue on the fulfilment of his vision. 'With
the end of the war', he declared, 'the heavens will come crashing down, and
with them the Jews.'[41] As the angels who sinned against the Lord were cast
into the abyss, so the Jews – this, he calculated, must be the meaning of the
biblical comparison – will be condemned to perish, after having dared to lay
hands on the Aryan race, a people created in the image of God.

In the list of crimes to be laid at the door of the Jews as the foundation of
his judgement that the Jews must be put to death, Hitler names the customary 'egoism', an 'unimaginable deceitfulness' and the quality characteristic of the dwarf Mime – 'a propensity to conceal what they are really
thinking. . . . They lie with a shamelessness that is breathtaking.' Among

other aspects of their culpability Hitler includes the Jews' approach to culture. 'They have no understanding of art and no cultivated emotions,' was his verdict, 'no real composer, no philosopher, no art – nothing, absolutely nothing.' The thought of his great Party rallies crossed his mind. 'For four hundred years, down to 1838,' he mused, 'Nuremberg had had no Jews. The result was the city's dominant position in the country's cultural life.' The work in which this 'historical truth' is most firmly embedded, and which portrays the triumph of German art as linked to the expulsion from the country of these 'cultural robbers', is Wagner's opera *Die Meistersinger von Nürnberg*. When Hitler looks to enjoy the downfall of these 'liars, cheats and plagiarists', it is as though he had in mind Sixtus Beckmesser, the Jewish parody of the Marker in the *Meistersinger*, who is unmasked as a 'liar, cheat and plagiarist' and sent packing by the Masters. 'I have always maintained', declared Hitler, 'that the Jews are the stupidest wretches there are. The moment one withdraws one's support from them, their whole edifice collapses and – another thing that Wagner's opera teaches us – suddenly there is nothing left.'[42]

He had seen Wagner's comic opera a hundred times, he claimed. His friend 'Putzi' Hanfstaengl would drive away his depression by playing him the Prelude on the piano, maintaining that the contrapuntal interweaving of the various themes in the piece corresponded to the way Hitler constructed his speeches.[43] He once surprised Otto Dietrich with an extempore Wagner performance. 'He was extremely musical', wrote Dietrich after the war, 'and I found with amazement that, for example, he was able to whistle or hum all the themes in Wagner's *Meistersinger* from memory.'[44] Describing himself to the English journalist Ward Price in 1939 as 'one of the most musical people in the world',[45] Hitler, who had never learnt to play an instrument, found rich pickings for his whistling skills in the motifs and melodies of Wagner's Nuremberg opera.

He also took pleasure in quoting from Wagner's libretto. In 1934, at the ceremony to mark the beginning of work on the first German autobahn, he summoned the workers in the well-known call from the third act: '*Fanget an!*' – 'Commence!'[46] – words engraved on a stone commemorating the lifting of the first sod near Munich.[47] Again, when inaugurating his 'Haus der deutschen Kunst' in Munich in 1938, built as a bulwark against the 'decadent' art of the Jews, he quoted words spoken in the opera by Hans Sachs. Referring to the 'noble Germanic works of art which will leave their influence not on decades but on centuries', he invoked 'the charming moment when Sachs says: "Here a child is born." '[48] Hitler is alluding here to the key moment in the third act when Walther's Prize Song is blessed by Sachs to the accompaniment of a solemn pseudo-Lutheran chorale.[49] Art, Wagner is saying, as Hitler cunningly weaves it into his own words, belongs to the living body of the *Volk*, which, by virtue of being 'blessed', is distinguished from all other races.

But the most popular item in the *Meistersinger* was the chorale '*Wach auf*' ('Awake!'), whose words were those with which the historical Hans Sachs had greeted Luther and the Reformation. It was a phrase, moreover, that had rung out through the country since the days of Dietrich Eckart as a Nazi call to arms, and featured on every blood-red Nazi standard. The *Meistersinger* became one of the works most closely associated with the Third Reich, consolidating the racial message and the nation's claim to physical and spiritual well-being. 'The sound of the great "*Wach auf*" chorale', wrote Goebbels in Bayreuth in 1932, 'sends shivers down one's spine. . . . The time has come for us to take power.'[50] And as late as December 1942, at the re-opening of the Staatsoper in Berlin with a performance of the *Meistersinger*, the whole house, led by Hitler himself, rose to its feet when the chorale began,[51] as the proscribed Nazi Party had once done in the Bayreuth Festspielhaus in 1924. The singer Rudolf Bockelmann, who regularly sang the role of Sachs, said that at this point in the opera the audience would invariably break into applause and 'shouts of jubilation',[52] stamping and cheering, carried away by Wagner and the Führer alike.

In Hitler's plans for the future the true awakening was to follow the final victory. 'When this war is finally over', he said to Berlin munitions workers in 1940, 'a great period of reconstruction will set in, a great cry of "Awake!" will be heard throughout the land and out of all this work that great German Reich will emerge of which a great poet once dreamed.'[53] He was thinking of the poet of the 'Awake!'-chorale – though few, if any, of his audience would have recognized this.

The historic so-called 'Day of Potsdam' in 1933, which gave a preview of the theatricality that was to characterize the ten years of Hitler's rule, was among the first events to be organized in that operatic style intended to set the 'stamp of eternity' on all such occasions. The chosen date, 21 March, marked the beginning of spring, the time when Wagner's heroes, from Siegmund to Walther von Stolzing, felt a new fertility surge through their bodies. In *Parsifal* too the magic of Good Friday was devoted to the joys of a reborn nature. On the same symbolic day the formal opening of the Reichstag took place among the tombs of the Kings of Prussia, swathed in swastikas, in the Garrison Church in Potsdam, the monarchs reborn in the figure of the new Führer. 'Every moment in the ceremony,' wrote the historian Joachim C. Fest, 'every step taken, had been meticulously planned in advance by Goebbels and approved by Hitler.'[54]

One member of the audience in the Staatsoper that evening was Curt von Westernhagen, biographer of Wagner, who was inspired by the performance to write a book called *Richard Wagner's Struggle Against Foreign Spiritual Domination*. 'This book has its origins', wrote Westernhagen,

> in that splendid performance of the *Meistersinger* conducted by Furtwängler on the 'Day of Potsdam', one of those rare moments in the life of a nation

when a great historical event and a great artistic experience coincide. This coincidence was like an image of the German national psyche, in which the urge to action is combined with the faculty of profound contemplation.[55]

It had been Hitler's intention to demonstrate precisely this. For that art and the act of liberation belong together, and that only in the wake of victory over the enemy can a new popular culture arise, was what Hitler interpreted as the message of Wagner's opera.

The Bayreuth Festival of 1933, held under the slogan 'Awake! The dawn is breaking!',[56] also opened with the *Meistersinger*. This time it fell to Goebbels, Hitler's mouthpiece, to explain why it should be just this work that was crowned as the supreme expression of the Third Reich. 'There is no other work', declared Goebbels in a radio talk during the interval of the transmission from Bayreuth,

> that is so close to the spirit of our time and so faithfully reflects the tensions of our intellectual and spiritual life as Wagner's *Meistersinger*. How often in bygone years has its inspiring chorus 'Awake! The dawn is breaking!' swelled the hearts of the people as a tangible symbol of the rejuvenation of the German nation after the political and spiritual paralysis in which the events of November 1918 had left it![57]

The clearest reason for this, according to Goebbels, was that, of all German operas, *Meistersinger* stood out as the 'most German' – 'the epitome of German civilization, embodying everything that helps to make up the German soul and German cultural awareness'. Carried away by the occasion and by the opportunity 'to address the entire German nation and the cultural world far beyond its boundaries', Goebbels envisaged the whole country now brought under the spell of the Master: 'Many decades had to pass before the whole *Volk* found its way back to Wagner.'[58]

Four years later Goebbels returned to the subject of the *Meistersinger* and spoke openly of matters he had omitted from his radio talk. 'Richard Wagner', he wrote in the *Völkischer Beobachter* in 1937,

> taught us what a Jew is. Let us pay heed to him – we who have at last freed ourselves through the words and deeds of Adolf Hitler from slavery at the hands of a subhuman race. Wagner tells us all we need to know, both through his writings and through his music, every note of which breathes the purest German spirit![59]

The essence of this 'purest German spirit' was to be found in the old imperial city of Nuremberg itself. Here was embedded and preserved the 'people's art' of Albrecht Dürer and Hans Sachs as well as the memory of the symbols of the Holy Roman Empire which, before their removal to Vienna, had for centuries been kept in the city. In the very year that he seized power Hitler hastened to link himself to this tradition, arranging that in the course of the Party rally he should be formally presented in the town hall with Dürer's famous engraving *The Knight, Death and the Devil*, prototype of the bold knight in full armour who sets out, threatened by Death and tempted by Satan, to reach his promised goal. The following year the imperial insignia of Charlemagne – reproductions of crown, orb and sceptre that had been commissioned by Kaiser Wilhelm II – were brought to the Franconian capital, and at the 'Rally of Freedom' in 1935 the Führer was presented with a replica of the old imperial sword. Replicas of the Austrian crown jewels followed three years later. The climax of these symbolical historical transactions, however, came in the year of the *Anschluss*, the German annexation of Austria, when the imperial regalia themselves were removed from Vienna and taken to the city of the Nazi rallies. Crown, sceptre, sword, and the holy lance brought to life again in *Parsifal*, were installed in St Catherine's, the Mastersingers' church. As in the opera, the hero restored the stolen treasure to its hallowed home.

The struggle through which Wagner had set out to liberate the German nation from the Jews – or from 'foreign spiritual domination', as Westernhagen had put it in the title of his book – had also manifested itself in Nuremberg. Before it had become possible, as a result of Hitler's race laws, 'to bring Wagner's philosophical ideals concerning the universal campaign against the Jews to their triumphant fulfilment',[60] as an official publication of 1938 put it, a bitter argument had broken out in Nuremberg over the new ideology.

After Jews had returned to settle in Nuremberg in the middle of the nineteenth century, a synagogue was built on the banks of the river Pegnitz and consecrated in 1874.[61] Designed in the Moorish style – Klingsor's magic garden in *Parsifal* was also described as 'Moorish' – the synagogue aroused the anger of nationalistically minded citizens, especially as its shadow intruded into the nearby Hans-Sachs-Platz. It was therefore decided to erect a statue of Sachs next to the synagogue, which was unveiled in the same year with great pomp and circumstance, the Mastersinger poet being hailed as a 'prophet of the new German Reich' – the newly founded Reich of Bismarck, that is.[62] Wagner, who had long identified himself with his operatic hero and liked to sign himself as 'Sachs', offered to donate the takings from the first Nuremberg performance of the *Meistersinger* towards the cost of the monument, for he, too, as he wrote, was deeply offended by the decision 'to build a synagogue in the most explicitly Oriental style' on that particular site.[63]

When Wagner visited Nuremberg in 1877 with his family, Cosima recorded in her diary that his cheerful *Meistersinger*-mood was abruptly disturbed by the sight of the synagogue in the Hans-Sachs-Platz, finding it 'insultingly gaudy and vulgar'.[64] Here again it was to be Hitler who fulfilled Wagner's secret wish. In August 1938 the offending building was demolished in the course of a grand Party celebration. The order had been given by Julius Streicher, who shouted out the *Meistersinger* command: 'Commence!'[65] But razing just one synagogue to the ground was not enough for Hitler. At the Party rally the following month he remonstrated with Streicher for allowing other synagogues still to survive in Nuremberg.[66] Streicher, however, was soon able to report to his Führer that his wishes had been carried out. In the night of 9 November 1938, exactly fifteen years after Hitler's abortive coup, all the synagogues in Germany were put to the torch. Travelling on the autobahn from Munich that evening, Baldur von Schirach reported seeing 'a great glow from the flames in Nuremberg'.[67]

It had been some hundred years earlier that Wagner, returning from taking the waters in the Bohemian resort of Marienbad, had first set his sights on the Franconian capital. While in Marienbad in the summer of 1845, he had lighted on the idea of making the cobbler-cum-poet, 'the last representative of the creative artistic energies of the people', as he described him,[68] the central figure in an opera in which the authentic creative genius of German culture should triumph over all dishonest attempts to imitate it. In his autobiographical 'Communication to my Friends' of 1851 he talked of 'a quickly written sketch' for such a work, a sketch that followed for the most part the course of a little-known opera by Albert Lortzing called *Hans Sachs*, which he took over and adapted to his own purposes.

Besides the plot of Lortzing's innocent little comedy, the text of which he probably came across through his brother-in-law, the publisher Friedrich Brockhaus, the circumstances of its first performance may also have served to stimulate Wagner's interest. Lortzing composed his opera to commemorate the 400th anniversary of the invention of printing, which was to be marked in 1840 by a great celebration in Leipzig, Wagner's birthplace. Forty thousand people were said to have been present, using the occasion to demonstrate 'for freedom, the constitution and national unity'.[69] The motto that Lortzing inscribed at the head of his score might as well have served for Wagner's *Meistersinger*. 'When I came to understand the emotions within me', declares Lortzing's hero, describing the secret of folk-poetry and folk-art, 'I discovered the sources of my music – the bliss of love and the Fatherland!'[70]

Twenty-five years after Lortzing's popular piece, with its final chorus 'Long live the Fatherland!', Wagner started work on his *Meistersinger*. He felt himself to be the new Hans Sachs,[71] who would prepare the way for the national triumph of the coming saviour, King Ludwig II of Bavaria. 'Anyone with a true heart', he wrote to Ludwig, 'can feel what lies behind my *Meistersinger*, which I planned at a grim time when the Germans were being betrayed, and which I now offer to the only German prince who understands me, and with me the spirit of Germany. Here – take my hand! We shall win the day!'[72] What 'lay behind' Wagner's ostensibly so genial, so artless work was his intention to 'use it to reveal to the German public an image of its own true nature, an image hitherto conveyed only inadequately and ineptly'.[73]

But there was also an antithesis to this image, the enemy of this 'true nature' which seeks to prevent its creative development – an antithesis which for Wagner, in reality as in art, could mean only one thing – the Jews, whom from the very beginning he had made responsible both for the 'degeneration' of art and for the suppression of his own works. Nobody could conceive how much his *Meistersinger* meant to him, he wrote to Ludwig: 'It is a work in which I look down my nose with contempt at my foolish foes,' having just equated Hans Sachs' opponents with the Jewish music critic Hanslick. 'My work preserves the noblest features of popular art and I am building from the ruins a new world of German glory'[74] in the chosen city of Nuremberg, ideal scene for the 'work of art of the future'. The Franconian capital, indeed, had become 'the Archimedean point from which we can move the whole listless world of the degenerate German spirit'.[75]

In a series of diary entries Wagner provided the King – who sponsored the completion of the work and its first performance in 1868 – with information on the ideological background, since it was Ludwig, when all was said and done, who was to help him establish the 'new world of German glory'. 'The greatest danger we face', he told the King, 'is that the German princes are no longer capable of understanding the German people and its true spirit.'[76] This assertion found its way into the opera itself. In his final monologue in praise of the German Masters Hans Sachs himself warns of the threat to true German values when, 'led astray by displays of foreign pomp and by flimsy attractions alien to our nature, the German princes cease to understand their peoples'.[77] The sense of national consciousness, Wagner is saying, is becoming confused, dissipated, and the natural link to a God-given ruler has been broken. Confused by a smoke-screen of false ideology, the prince and his subjects become separated from each other and set themselves up in rival camps. The danger of rebellion looms and chaos threatens.

Wagner had no doubt as to who was to blame for this state of confusion and ensured that Ludwig was made aware who was behind the insidious forces responsible for the disintegration of the Holy Roman Empire. These forces were anything but German, Wagner says, for 'German' – '*deutsch*' – means nothing other than 'clear' – '*deutlich*' – 'and what is clear is what is familiar, congenial, that which is passed on from generation to generation'.[78]

Since the Thirty Years War, Wagner continued, the German princes had virtually lost all sense of what this spirit meant, for at that moment a fateful development for the nation was taking place, 'that strange phenomenon of the penetration of German culture and the German psyche by the most alien of influences – that of the Jews'.[79] Furthermore this invasion of the German mind and spirit, an invasion of parasites that attacked the German body and undermined its health, was only possible because the German princes had ceased to understand the spirit of the German people and had thereby exposed it to the predations of these vampires. Since that time there has been a serious danger that the German psyche – 'one of the finest manifestations of the human spirit ever known' – might be lost to the world for ever.[80] In its place, revelling in its victory, we have the parasitic hordes of Jewry. Not only do they attack every aspect of public life, but also, according to Wagner's abstruse reasoning, 'the essence of the German spirit, its profound musical emotions, are presented to the people today in a form distorted by the Jews'.[81]

This antithesis of true creative emotion and its distortion by the intervention of the Jews lies at the heart of *Die Meistersinger von Nürnberg*. But it is not only the future of art that is at stake – the future of the whole human race hangs in the balance. As in almost all Wagner's works, the central question is who will win the bride. If mankind is beset on all sides by 'false ideology', to whom does it fall to perpetuate the blood-line? The Germanic bride of the future, christened Eva, the first mother, here the daughter of Pogner the goldsmith, is the prize in the song contest, the winner of which will be offered her hand. Only two competitors enter the lists. One is the young knight Walther von Stolzing, German through and through, the last in a long line of aristocrats, who sings of the heroic deeds of his great ancestors. In an early version of the opera he was called Konrad, after the last of the Hohenstaufen emperors.[82]

Walther's rival is Sixtus Beckmesser, the town clerk, whom Wagner has endowed with all the repulsive characteristics familiar to Wagnerians from the world of the Nibelungen, in order to brand him, both visually and vocally, as a 'musical Jew'. The intention was not lost on Wagner's contemporaries. In Vienna, for instance, the opera was satirically dubbed 'The Meistersinger, or Music and the Jews'.[83] In an early prose sketch Wagner had called the town clerk 'Hanslich', after the Vienna music critic Eduard Hanslick, who was listed in the official Nazi *Dictionary of Music* (1941) as a 'Jewish half-breed'.[84] Hitler justified his censorship of the press in 1933 by drawing attention to 'false verdicts on the music of Richard Wagner',[85] and later, because of what he alleged to be the 'rejection of so many artists of genius in the organs of the press',[86] ordered Goebbels to ban all critical reviews of artistic activity. All this went back to Hanslick, Wagner's detested Beckmesser.

In Lortzing's opera the poet and dramatist Hans Sachs is the principal character. In Wagner, however, Sachs assumes the role of herald of the future, a John the Baptist figure who announces the coming of the Messiah, assists him in composing his Prize Song and lays a deadly trap for his cunning but ludicrous opponent. Sachs settles the comic contest between the handsome, blue-blooded young knight and the elderly poetaster of dubious descent – not, of course, that Wagner openly reveals anything about Beckmesser's ancestry – and adds his own words of wisdom to the occasion, for a victory won for art is also a victory won for blood. In his famous 'Wahn'-monologue in Act Three he interprets all bloodshed, from a street brawl to the final destruction of the world, as due to blood from like sources being prevented from reproducing. As, in Sachs' chosen image, 'the glow-worm will not find its mate',[87] so society will be plunged into confusion, people will lash out at each other in their distraction – 'and if human folly and delusion so will', reflects Sachs in Wagner's stilted pseudo-Old German, 'blows must rain down and put out the flames with cudgels, clubs and bludgeons'.[88] Such was Wagner's first version of Sachs' meditation, written in 1862.

The street riot, one of the high points in the opera, was provoked by the behaviour of the troublesome Beckmesser, who acted as a 'fermenting agent of decomposition', as the historian Theodor Mommsen characterized the Jews. Beckmesser foments unrest in Nuremberg, unsettles the burghers, disturbs the peace. In his final aria, in which he draws the lesson of both the song contest and the street fighting, Sachs utters an express warning about foreign infiltrators. It will hardly be a coincidence that he uses for this warning the words of Alberich when he proclaims the domination of the Nibelungen in *Rheingold*: 'Beware! Beware the army of the creatures of the night!'[89] 'Beware!' cries the cobbler to the assembled populace: 'We are at the mercy of evil forces!' And he goes on to paint a picture of a Germany that has been caught unawares by foreign duplicity and lost its way. Yet even if the Holy Roman Empire were to perish at the hands of these foreign forces, 'We still shall have our Holy German Art to cherish!'[90] It was in this art, as Wagner the revolutionary had already declared, that true nature, pure human values and the eternal message of blood were revealed. Kingdoms may perish but the inner essence of the master race, created in the image of God, will last for ever. It is precisely the sacred nature of German art, its 'holiness', that reveals this truth.

In Beckmesser Wagner has created a grotesque figure to embody everything that negates this. Some critics have taken a different view. Writing in the Bayreuth Festival programme for 1996, Dieter Borchmeyer expressed the opinion that, on closer examination, 'nothing is left to justify the hypothesis that Beckmesser is meant to be a caricature of a Jew'.[91] Yet his whole presence in the opera is predicated on the crime that he commits against true art. This is precisely the destructive role that Wagner ascribed to the Jews. Before our very eyes Beckmesser acts out on the stage, as we anxiously watch, the way in which Wagner envisaged that race of men which causes instinctive revulsion among the public. Wagner also maintained that race exuded 'a foreign air', an aura which the philosopher Schopenhauer, also a prominent Jew-hater, called '*foetor-Judaicus*' – a stench, said Schopenhauer, strong enough to 'chloroform' the senses of the people around them.[92]

For the same reason Siegfried's instinctive dislike of the ugly dwarf Mime recurs in Walther's spontaneous reaction to the disgruntled Beckmesser. He sees Beckmesser looking down impudently at him, as Siegfried had looked at his foster-father, wishing he could 'grab him by the throat and finally put an end to him'. Walther, Siegfried's successor in the tradition of Wagner's petulant heroes, now waxes furious over the behaviour of his rival, who woos Eva 'in his screeching, whining voice', and he feels the urge 'to plunge straight in with his sword'. Brandishing his weapon he cries: 'I will soon put an end to the wretch!'[93]

As Mime covets the gold, so Beckmesser reveals that his aim is to win Eva, 'the goldsmith's most priceless possession'.[94] As early as his prose sketch of 1861 Wagner drew attention to the grotesque, Nibelungen-like features of the ugly suitor; he also prescribed that the part be taken by a singer whose voice had 'a shrill, screeching timbre which could be driven to extremes'. Actually, he added, as far as Beckmesser was concerned, real singing – a characteristic of the Aryan race – was hardly required, 'merely a forceful, staccato manner of delivery'.[95]

Walther, the shining hero with a lyrical tenor voice, is reminded by Beckmesser's voice of 'a chorus of cawing crows' which, like Alberich's horde of Nibelungen, fill the world with howling and caterwauling. When the pedantic Marker Beckmesser goes so far as to set himself up as the judge of the quality of Walther's song, the knight responds by comparing him to a cruel, destructive winter which, 'consumed by envy and resentment, lurks in a thorn bush, waiting only to see how it can ruin the joyful singing of the coming spring', to quote Wagner's libretto.[96] Walther's comparison of the Marker's chair to a thorn bush reminded Thomas Mann of the anti-Semitic story of 'The Jew in the Thorn Bush' from the Grimms' fairy-tales.[97] Wagner too may well have had this story in mind, for at the end the same fate threatens Beckmesser as befell the Jew.[98] 'His song is a mass of nonsense,' declare the assembled Masters. To which the people cry: 'He will get his deserts! Soon he will be for the gallows – we can already picture him hanging there!'[99]

In the Grimms' tale the Jew is hanged because, according to the superstition attaching to his race, he is a thief. Beckmesser is also portrayed as a thief. Because, according to the doctrine laid down by Wagner in his essay 'Music and the Jews', Beckmesser is incapable of original creative activity, he has to equip himself for the song contest by 'borrowing' from Sachs, the people's poet. Well aware that Beckmesser will scarcely be able to make any use of it, Sachs gives him a poem of Walther's. As had already happened with his Nibelungen, the further Wagner got into the composition of the work, the more prominent the negative features of Beckmesser's character became, so that what had started as a laughable suitor for the hand of Eva gradually developed into a contemptible scoundrel. In the first draft of 1845 Beckmesser picks up Walther's poem from the table 'rather in a state of confusion than with deliberate intent', as Glasenapp put it in his biography of Wagner.[100] In a later version Sachs openly offers Beckmesser the poem on his own initiative. In the final version[101] Beckmesser hastily stuffs the sheet of paper into his pocket and only produces it after Sachs asks the humiliating question: 'Did you take it?'[102]

Nor is it only Beckmesser's character that becomes increasingly more depraved. His performance of the song he has stolen grows more and more grotesque with each new attempt. In the early versions he is described as singing the poem 'to a totally ridiculous melody'.[103] Following Wagner's theory that only a thoroughly German artist can draw out the music that is latent in the words, Beckmesser becomes like Meyerbeer, in whose empty, meretricious works a poor text has even poorer music foisted upon it. Only a genuine composer can achieve a true union of the two; Meyerbeer, says Wagner, produces only distortion. And when Beckmesser suffers the fiasco of trying to sing Walther's Prize Song, Sachs accuses him of 'garbling' it.[104]

Whereas, to start with, the display of Beckmesser's ineptitude was restricted to the music, from 1861 onwards Wagner also portrayed him as making a parody of Walther's words. Devoid of any feeling for the German language, he concocts a few stanzas of pure gibberish, leaving the impression that Wagner is out to emphasize how alien a figure he is. Walther's attractive Prize Song is perverted and distorted out of all recognition – a misshapen monstrosity that came to typify for Hitler all 'degenerate art'. But not only does Beckmesser distort the words he has stolen, he also unwittingly turns them into a confession of his shameless guilt. As Mime's apparently friendly words are realized by the observant Siegfried to conceal the dwarf's true murderous intent, so Beckmesser's plagiarism returns to haunt him. To the assembled citizens of Nuremberg his musical parody spells his downfall – a symbolic verdict of death.

It is the same image of death as awaits the Jew in the folk-tale of the brothers Grimm, where theft leads to the gallows. Also in this line stands the figure of Meyerbeer, who, with Hanslick, went to make up the composite Jew-figure represented by Beckmesser and viciously attacked by Schumann. Schumann wrote a devastating review of Meyerbeer's popular opera *Les Huguenots* in 1836, which, in terms that in a number of respects anticipated the formulations of Wagner, he concluded by wishing that Meyerbeer could simply be removed from the scene. 'It is easy', wrote Schumann, 'to identify Mozart, Rossini and other composers in Meyerbeer's music. What is peculiar to him, however, is that persistent, nagging, unpleasant rhythm that runs through almost all the themes in the opera. . . . Vulgarity, distortion, perversity, immorality' – such qualities run through the whole work, a piece not of music but of 'un-music'. Summing up his distaste, Schumann writes: 'Nothing worse than this can be imagined, unless one were to turn the stage into a gallows. Then the cry of terror from the mouth of a tormented talent would be followed by the hope that things would soon get better.'[105] Stripped of its romantic self-indulgence, this means exactly the same as the last sentence in Wagner's 'Music and the Jews' – that only Ahasverus' death can redeem us all.

It was a view shared by Hitler. He first put forward his racist interpretation of Wagner's *Meistersinger* in the pages of *Mein Kampf*. Wagner, said Hitler, portrayed his Beckmesser as a pedantic town clerk; but in the First World War 'almost every clerk was a Jew and almost every Jew a clerk'[106] – which, as he well knew, was an out-and-out lie, but which fitted the requirements of the situation. The manner in which Beckmesser, the uninspired dullard, lays hands on the jewel of Walther's poetic imagination serves to reveal the nature of the entire race of polluters and destroyers: 'What the Jews have produced in the field of art is either parody or plagiary.'[107] Even the words of Hans Sachs, that craftsmanship is not to be despised, especially in times when Germany is under threat from foreign influences, are set out in *Mein Kampf* as though they were the fruits of Hitler's own ruminations. 'The inner Jewification of the nation', he pronounced, 'can be measured by the lack of respect, not to say the contempt, that people show towards craftsmanship. This is not a German trait.' In the libretto of *Meistersinger* Wagner uses the epithet 'foreign' to denote what is un-German, but the disciple knew that his Master was only following an operatic convention. 'It was the infiltration of what some called foreign influences,' wrote Hitler, 'but were in fact of Jewish origin, that brought about a change from a respect for craftsmanship to a certain scorn of it.'[108] As Sachs himself put it: 'Let us have no contempt for the Masters!'[109]

In no other work of Wagner's is the merciless message so completely hidden behind boisterous humour and displays of popular jollity. Even Beckmesser, a public laughing-stock, is allowed to escape and mingle with the crowd. He evaporates, so to speak, in the glow that surrounds Hans Sachs, herald of the new Germany, disappearing without trace among the flags and banners, trumpets and drums of the brightly dressed citizens.[110] It was a scene that anticipated the Nazi saturnalia later to be performed in the same setting. But behind all this ostentatious glitter, behind the scent of lilac wafted through the evening streets as the moon shines between the steep-gabled roofs onto the cobbled roads below – the kind of scene painted by Spitzweg – there lurks a deep-rooted hatred of all things foreign which can break out at any moment into fights and scuffles. Or, in the case of the Nuremberg town clerk, into heartless mockery.

The gallows, which are only hinted at in the *Meistersinger*, were in Hitler's 'Mastersinger state' also kept in the background, concealed behind the familiar trappings of everyday life and moments of festive celebration. Initially those Jews who survived were, like Beckmesser, not killed but ostracized until they either made their way into exile or were transported to Eastern Europe. As in the *Meistersinger*, the cries of the vilified were drowned by the deafening music of the marching columns, while writers were banned, 'decadent' art confiscated and destroyed, those in the 'Beckmesser' category branded and outlawed. While he was engaged in conducting his pompous rallies and clearing the way for the triumph of Wagner's and Sachs' 'Holy German Art', Hitler did not want to be disturbed.

Hans Sachs, facing the encroachment of foreign elements, tried to console the public by pointing out that while the Reich might temporarily be lost, art would come to the rescue. But this did not satisfy Hitler. He wanted both the Reich and art. When, as the Third Reich was literally going up in smoke, his staff grew indignant over how much time their Commander-in-Chief was spending on planning new cultural centres and poring over models of art galleries and the sets of Bayreuth productions, while Germany's cities and museums and opera houses were being razed to the ground, they must have forgotten the message of the *Meistersinger*: 'Let the Holy Roman Empire perish! / We still shall have our Holy German art to cherish!'[111]

Hitler wanted to go down in history not just as a lover of art but as an 'administrator' of art, a man who brought things about. Visits to the opera issued a challenge to his theatrical imagination. Before setting about changing reality, he intervened in matters of operatic production. 'When I had occasion to talk with Adolf Hitler in private', said Heinz Tietjen, Director General of the Prussian State Theatres and a friend of Winifred Wagner's, 'I was always amazed how well he knew the scores of Wagner's operas. Once he came up to me afterwards and said that the oboe had not been quite satisfactory. I had to admit that he was right.'[112] He would often criticize performances, impressing people by the extent of his knowledge and insisting that the only proper interpretation was that vouchsafed to him by the composer himself. On one occasion, at a performance of *Lohengrin* in Weimar, he asked the conductor to come to his box after the first act and pointed out to him 'that Elsa's ladies-in-waiting had stood much too far apart on the wide stage, and that in his view it would be better if they were grouped more closely around Elsa'. 'The Führer was absolutely right,' said Hans Severus Ziegler, who was with Hitler at the time, 'as he was indeed on dozens of other occasions.'[113]

'Particularly in moments of crisis', wrote Ziegler, the man responsible for the infamous exhibition of 'Degenerate Music' in 1936, 'Hitler needed to pay frequent visits to the opera.' There is only one interpretation that can be put on this, namely that if events on the political stage went contrary to his wishes, he could always fall back on the operatic stage to change the situation in the way he required.

Thus one evening in August 1932, feeling particularly frustrated after Hindenburg's refusal to hand over power as he had demanded, Hitler suddenly felt the urge to listen to a Wagner opera. Walking with Ziegler near his retreat in the Bavarian Alps, Hitler suggested that they drive to the Prinzregententheater in Munich, where the Wagner Festival was being held. At that moment the full moon appeared from behind the mountains and cast its light over the meadows. 'Hitler suddenly stopped', wrote Ziegler, and said: ' "Ziegler, what is the proper colour for moonlight? Think of the *Meistersinger*, end of Act Two. What kind of light must the lighting director use?" "White light," I replied. "White light, of course!" he exclaimed. "But sometimes you find greenish or bluish light being used, which is totally wrong – romantic kitsch." '[114]

The Prinzregententheater, where Hitler and Ziegler shortly afterwards found themselves, was close to Hitler's Munich apartment. Indeed, when he moved into the elegant nine-room flat at 16 Prinzregentenplatz, the proximity of the opera house would have been much in his mind. No less important were the Wagnerian associations of the apartment itself. Here, according to Hartmut Zelinsky,[115] Isolde Beidler, Wagner's eldest daughter, had lived with her family after being banished from Bayreuth. Since 1929, when Hitler moved in, a monumental bust of the Master stood there, and until her suicide in 1931 it was also the domicile of Hitler's niece Eli Raubal, whom 'Uncle Alf', as she called him, was at great pains to make into a Wagnerian soprano.[116]

On the opposite side of the square the Master himself reigned. Built in 1901, the Prinzregententheater, with its sunken orchestra pit, like the Festspielhaus, performed his works in productions faithful to the Bayreuth tradition – much to the annoyance of Cosima, who compared the director, Hans von Possart, and the conductor, Hermann Levi, both of Jewish descent, with the Nibelungen dwarfs Alberich and Mime, who were out to lay their greedy hands on the treasure.[117] The construction of the opera house did in fact follow ideas put forward by Wagner himself, who had wanted to build a monumental theatre nearby to plans by Semper. This is where Hitler saw his first performances of Wagner in Munich, for almost all the Master's works were performed at the annual festival there. Above the entrance, to his satisfaction, he discovered the inscription 'To German Art', and if needs be, he could make his way to the adjoining Wagner memorial, there to say his prayers. When, for financial reasons, the theatre was forced to close a few weeks after the *Meistersinger* he had seen, Hitler put its re-opening on his list of matters to be attended to immediately he came to power.

That re-opening came in April 1933 with a performance of the 'regeneration' opera *Parsifal*, followed, from then to the end of August, by all Wagner's other works. On 9 November 1933 – the Nazi Good Friday – there was an event to commemorate the martyrs who had lost their lives in the abortive coup ten years earlier, and the following year the theatre was handed over to the 'Strength Through Joy' organization as a 'Leisure Centre for the German Workers'. It may well have been at the Führer's request that on the evening of a meeting in honour of Dietrich Eckart, a selection of excerpts from Eckart's forgotten drama *Heinrich der Hohenstaufe* was performed there; an equally unknown play, *Friedrich Friesen*, by an early patron of Hitler's, Josef Stolzing-Czerny, was also revived, and in an evening of literary readings the famous Thule collection of the publisher Eugen Diederichs was exhibited to the accompaniment of recitations from the *Edda*.

Events such as these turned the Prinzregententheater into the Party's own theatre, which, as well as Wagner's operas, also put on some of the Shrovetide plays of Hans Sachs. But it was not to last. In 1936 Winifred Wagner persuaded her friend Wolf to give instructions that only those works of Wagner should be performed in the theatre which were not at that moment being given in Bayreuth.[118] From then on its fortunes declined: its repertoire grew smaller and smaller, until finally, in 1939, it closed its doors. So as Salzburg productions of Wagner too had fallen into disfavour – Goebbels talked scornfully in 1938 of 'Viennese kitsch'[119] – from 1939 onwards the Master's own festival in Bayreuth had no competition anywhere in the world.

Legend has it that from the moment he made his first appearance in Wahnfried in 1923, Hitler set out to misuse the Bayreuth Festival for his own purposes, and, as the final stage of his abuse, ordered that 'Wartime Festivals' should take place from 1940 onwards, which, like the performances in the Prinzregententheater, were to be attended by a hand-picked audience. 'When the war broke out', Winifred maintained before the de-Nazification tribunal in 1946, 'I wanted to close the Festspielhaus, but Hitler gave instructions that so-called "Wartime Festivals" should be held there.'[120]

In reality Hitler had from the very beginning only accepted the position that was offered to him. He had come to Wahnfried as a saviour, therefore all doors were open to him. He had absolute control, proposing and rejecting at will. As 'Uncle Wolf', moreover, appointed successor to 'Uncle Chamberlain' – as Wolfgang Wagner still called him in 1994[121] – he belonged to the family. The mistress of the house worshipped him, while 'for Wagner's four grandchildren', reported Otto Dietrich, Hitler's press chief, 'whom he had known from childhood, he had developed paternal feelings since the death of their father Siegfried. In fact', Dietrich added, 'Wahnfried was virtually the only family circle of which Hitler ever felt part.'[122]

By 1933, at the latest, the Wagner Festival in Bayreuth had become the Hitler Festival. In the bookshops *Mein Kampf* outsold *Mein Leben*, and if for any reason the Führer was delayed by affairs of state and unable to reach the theatre in time, the performance was held back until he arrived. Then, when he had taken his place at her side, Winifred motioned to the conductor to begin.[123] After every performance the details of the singing, the orchestral playing and the production in general were discussed into the small hours, with Hitler always having the last word.

Winifred Wagner was held as unshakeably in the dictator's spell as was Elsa in that of Lohengrin, messenger of the Grail. The handful of letters from her to 'my dear, dear friend and Führer' that have survived exude such an excited, breathless tone that one could be forgiven for thinking they could have come from an infatuated schoolgirl rather than from Richard Wagner's daughter-in-law. When in 1934 Hitler sent her a portrait of himself, she replied that she 'was beside herself with joy and gratitude, and you must accept these stuttering thoughts in place of a proper letter. . . . This wonderful gift will bestow on my humble abode the blessing of your eternal presence.' She concludes with a quotation from Beethoven's *Fidelio*: 'Accept my everlasting gratitude, thou giver of such ineffable joy!'[124]

By 1942 Hitler had long made the Bayreuth Festival his own. He decided not only the works to be performed but also the composition of the audiences – war wounded, veterans and those decorated with the Iron Cross, nurses and munitions workers. When Winifred wrote to him in the course of this year, it was as though she were carrying out the orders of a superior officer. 'The fact that this summer we shall again be able, in obedience to your command, to open the doors of the Festspielhaus, fills us with pride and gratitude,' she wrote. Naturally the choice of works to be performed 'lies entirely in your hands'. Hoping to receive his decision soon, she sent him best wishes from her sons Wieland and Wolfgang and their wives, and signed herself as 'ever grateful and faithful'.[125] Whatever credence one may attach to 'the considerable cooling of relations between my mother and Adolf Hitler'[126] which Wolfgang Wagner, the present director of the Festival, claims took place in the course of the war, it is hardly confirmed by her letters. Both Winifred and Wolfgang made New Year 1945 the occasion to send the Führer – by registered mail[127] – good wishes on behalf of the Villa Wahnfried.

If in fact there was any 'cooling off' in relations between Hitler and Bayreuth, then it came from the Führer's side. *Götterdämmerung* in 1940 was his last visit to the Festival;[128] after that Wahnfried had to do without its Führer. Not that he had in any way lost confidence in the enterprise and in his place in it – this, after all, was the source of his identity. But he was now in a position to fulfil his plans in reality. He exchanged the role of stage manager of theatrical performances and Party rallies for that of commander of the theatre of war. And because, waging the battle to end all battles against the demon threatening the world, he was fulfilling Wagner's prophecies in the military arena, he felt closer to the Master in the 'Wolf's Lair' than round the fireside in Wahnfried. Wherever Hitler was, there was Bayreuth. By going to war against 'the enemy of pure mankind', he was realizing his idol's visions far more faithfully than through any theatrical production, which would only conjure up the crisis to whose 'final solution' he had pledged himself. Even before the conditions were ripe for converting Wagner's ideas into political reality, he had slipped into the Master's ideological role and elevated what were existential characteristics to the status of non-negotiable articles of belief.

Thus it was chiefly due to Wagner that Hitler became a vegetarian,[129] urging on his entourage a diet which Wagner himself, a lover of steaks, persistently failed to observe. Because Wagner surrounded himself with dogs – his resting-place in the garden of Wahnfried was surrounded by little gravestones in their memory – Hitler had to do the same. Because the Master spoke out in favour of animal welfare and vehemently opposed experiments on animals, Hitler, according to Otto Dietrich, was 'almost passionate in his defence of the rights of animals and his opposition to vivisection'.[130] Whatever he took over from his icon, he made, by virtue of his position, into a universal law. His Nazi state, which had no objection to experiments on human beings, outlawed experiments on animals. The man who had learned in *Parsifal* to share the pain of suffering creatures, and therefore despised hunting, declared open season at the beginning of the war on those human beings for whom he had no compassion. From the sentimental, patriotic tear that Wagner had shed by the Rhine, to his pathological fear of a Jewish world conspiracy, almost everywhere behind Hitler's public utterances lurks the figure of the Master, starting as a dark shadow, then emerging in the glare of torchlight processions and parades or the flames of burning synagogues.

Otto Dietrich seemed to sense some kind of link between the two men as he was sitting one evening with Hitler and a group of friends round the fireside in the Berghof. As the others listened attentively to the Führer in the light of the glowing logs, Dietrich noticed the shadows and reflections cast on the walls by the flickering flames, and how 'the mermaids in Böcklin's painting *The Play of the Waves* looked down from the wall on the assembled company, while in the darkness of the room the bronze bust of Richard Wagner seemed to come to life'.[131]

Hitler not only achieved his own self-fulfilment in the wake of Wagner but also tried to carry out the Master's wishes, some trivial, some important. His plan to surmount the Bayreuth Festspielhaus with a giant dome, for instance, with which both Wieland and Wolfgang Wagner were very much in favour, originated with Wagner himself. In 1872, the year the foundation stone of the opera house was laid, he made it clear that what was to be erected was only temporary: 'This building provides only an outline of the conception. We deliver it into the hands of the nation to be executed as a monumental structure.'[132]

In contrast to the Bayreuth Acropolis, which was never built, a project of Houston Stewart Chamberlain's did materialize, thanks to Hitler. 'There is only one way', wrote Chamberlain to Wolzogen, 'to instil Wagner's noble ideas, aspirations and achievements in the soul of the nation, and that is by sending hundreds and thousands of teachers to Bayreuth.'[133] So there arose in the shadow of the Festspielhaus a 'German Teachers' Academy', described by Hans Schemm, Bavarian Minister of Culture and a friend of Wahnfried, as an adornment to the town 'in which Richard Wagner and Houston Stewart Chamberlain lived and worked, two of the greatest preceptors of the German nation in the highest philosophical sense'.[134]

When, in June 1940, after the fall of France, Hitler drove through the streets of Paris, he seems to have cherished a secret intention to transform the ignominy that Wagner had suffered here exactly one hundred years earlier into a triumph. According to his own highly coloured account of those days, Wagner was forced to submit to Jewish exploitation for a mere pittance, at the same time being paid a derisory sum for the libretto of his *Fliegender Holländer*. Now he, Hitler, could march through the French capital as the master of that grand opera house of which the poor composer could only have dreamed.

Indeed, as though he could hardly wait to avenge the wrongs that had been done to his idol, Hitler had barely arrived in the city when he ordered his chauffeur to drive him to the Opéra, scene of Meyerbeer's spectacular successes and of the boos and whistles that had greeted *Tannhäuser* in 1861. Strutting down the aisle, the new owner delivered disparaging judgement on what he saw. 'The impressive façade', he complained later, 'leads one to expect something remarkable.' But when he saw the mediocre stage settings, distinguished only by the brightness of their colours, it struck him how much the once proud Paris Opéra had deteriorated.[135] As though sent by fate in the role of Wagner's avenging angel, he deliberately chose *Der fliegende Holländer*, which Paris had rejected at the time, to crown the victory celebrations.[136] Ostensibly as a gesture of tact towards the Paris population, Hitler cancelled a parade and an operatic gala performance that had been planned but this did not prevent him from preceding a performance of *Tristan und Isolde* under Herbert von Karajan the following year with the Nazi 'Horst-Wessel-Song'.[137] His supreme expression of scorn took the form of a sketch he made, after France had fallen, for a new opera house in Munich worthy of the works of the Master. It would have filled the Paris Opéra three times over.

What Hitler undoubtedly regarded as his greatest service to the Bayreuth cause was to open the Festival to the people at large. 'The wartime Festival of 1942', he said, 'gave me the opportunity to meet Wagner's wish that men and women chosen from the *Volk* should be enabled to attend the Festival free of charge.'[138] As early as 1939, however, as the Festival programme for that year proudly stated, he had taken steps to see that this wish of Wagner's was fulfilled. That year ten thousand tickets were distributed free 'to those deemed worthy of the chance to edify themselves through the experience of German art and culture. If Adolf Hitler himself were not so grateful an admirer of Wagner, he would never have found ways, time and again, of making it possible for thousands of his fellow-citizens to share "the miracle that is Bayreuth".'[139]

Hitler's main reason for opening up the Festival in 1933 to a new audience drawn from the *Volk* was to fill the seats left by the withdrawal of foreign visitors. Daniela Thode complained to Goebbels that they were facing a disastrous situation: whereas in the past the performances had been 98 per cent sold out, that year sales were only 50 per cent.[140] Hitler met the deficit by buying up whole blocks of unsold tickets until, from 1940 onwards, he had assumed virtual personal control of the Festival.[141] The only work he allowed to be performed in 1943 and 1944 was *Die Meistersinger*.

'The choice of *Die Meistersinger* for the wartime Festival of 1943', wrote the forty-six-year-old Winifred Wagner in a preface to the official brochure to accompany the performance,

> has a profound symbolic significance. It is a work that reveals to us in the most impressive form the creative German mind in its popular manifestation. In the figure of the Nuremberg cobbler and people's poet Hans Sachs the Master has given us an immortal embodiment of the German spirit. In the struggle that we are at present waging on behalf of Western civilization against the destructive world conspiracy being plotted in plutocratic and Bolshevist circles, that national spirit will infuse our soldiers with an unconquerable will to prevail and with a fanatical faith in the ultimate victory of our arms.[142]

Goebbels himself could not have put it better.

Over thirty thousand soldiers, nurses and armaments workers, all engaged on one front or another in the fight against the Jewish world conspiracy, came to Bayreuth to watch the display of street brawling and popular festivities in Nuremberg and found themselves nostalgically recalling the distant days of triumphant Party parades and rallies. From 1935 onwards Hitler had insisted that in all the opera houses in the country the final scene of the *Meistersinger*, with the whole people assembled on the festive meadow, should be decked out with flags and banners to make it resemble the field where the Nuremberg rallies took place – symbolically restoring reality to that theatre which had been its point of departure. The crowds of singing and dancing citizens were supplemented by members of the SS, who also, in full uniform and wearing steel helmets, sounded the fanfares that signalled the intermissions.[143]

At the performances themselves, many attended by soldiers brought straight from the sick bay, there developed a kind of national euphoria, with cheers and emotional outbursts, the like of which had not been seen since the beginning of the war. 'I openly confess', wrote a lance-corporal from Königsberg, 'that at the sound of the chorale "Awake!" the tears ran down my cheeks like a child. And I know from talking to my comrades that I was not the only one to be affected in this way.'[144]

The Festival programme also made sure that the ideological significance of Wagner's opera was not lost on its new audiences. 'German to the core,' the soldiers were told, before being sent back to the front the next day, 'this work was from the day of its first performance subjected to the most vicious and underhand attacks on the part of the Jews and their lackeys', a natural consequence of 'this rootless race's hatred of anything indigenous and racially pure'. The object of such attacks on Germany's noblest artists was to promote the interests of 'the many Jews who have infiltrated the musical life of Europe' – Beckmesser-figures, in other words, who have been shown up for what they are – 'and at the same time to destroy the man who, in all he said and did, stood out as the greatest enemy of the Jews, the man who tore off the mask that concealed the true nature of these parasites on the cultural life of the nation – Richard Wagner'.[145]

Any who might have had doubts about this, in the face of what was happening in Eastern Europe, could now console themselves with the thought, as they sat in the Bayreuth Festspielhaus, caught up in the intoxicating atmosphere of patriotism and pride generated by the conducting of Wilhelm Furtwängler, that the threatened destruction of the German spirit had rebounded on its originators. 'As a modest token of my gratitude', wrote an infantryman from Strasbourg to the director of the Festspielhaus, 'I vow to sacrifice all to ensure that the enemies of German culture shall receive their true deserts and never succeed in undermining the spirit and the achievements of the German masters.'[146] Any who had had the audacity to speak out against the *Meistersinger* and the 'German spirit' need not be surprised if the same treatment were now meted out to them – and on a far more massive scale.

Hitler himself, promoter of these wartime festivals, was kept regularly informed about the performances, and assumed as late as December 1944 that the critical state of the war would have no effect on what went on in Bayreuth. 'You will be surprised to learn', wrote Tietjen to Winifred Wagner at the end of 1944, 'that when the Führer asked whether the Festival could be held in Bayreuth in July 1945, I was able to reply unhesitatingly Yes. Commands from the Führer were as unnecessary as they had been in the past.'[147]

BARBAROSSA RETURNS; AHASVERUS PERISHES

Hitler's attack on 'the political system of the Soviet Union, seat of Judaeo-Bolshevism', which is traditionally but mistakenly divided into two separate parts – the Russian campaign and the Holocaust – neither served the interests of his nation nor corresponded to any rational, comprehensible political aim. And no less irrational than the policy was its execution. After only a few months, with the extent of the military losses kept secret and the policy of the rigorous extermination of the Jews equally so,[1] the parlous situation of the country was patent, the outcome blindingly obvious at the latest since the disastrous invasion of the Soviet Union.

The whole gory spectacle of a fight to the finish between an 'Aryan' race of creators and a Semitic race of destroyers reflected neither a tendency of the age nor the German national character, nor was its instigator even fulfilling a secret wish which he maintained had existed throughout the whole of German history. Hitler was carrying out a task in which he believed because he believed in those who had set him that task. He did not adapt himself to the political realities, because in moments of doubt they did not interest him; instead, as far as he could, he adapted the political realities to his own ideas. He saw himself not as a politician who, within a given framework, pursues certain goals with skill and diligence, but as an instrument of Providence charged to destroy this framework and replace it with a new one.

There was nothing that he was required to acknowledge or accept in advance – no laws or limits, no moral values. Such things belonged to a world that was doomed to destruction; his task was merely to set his seal on this destruction and assimilate elements of irrefutable reality into a higher system revealed only to him. Hitler did not want this reality, or this history, or this Western civilization with its poisoned roots. He did not want it because he had been told not to want it. 'As to his attitude towards the

Marxists,' Chamberlain had said prophetically in 1924, 'Hitler knows only one thing – total annihilation.'[2]

Hitler was merely an agent. It was not he who had decided that this world was ripe for collapse but those on whom he based his life. 'I have an unshakeable feeling and an utter conviction that nothing untoward can happen to me,' he said in the year before his seizure of power, 'because I know that I have been summoned by Destiny to carry out my task.'[3] Four years later he declared that he was following 'with the sureness of a sleep-walker the path that fate had laid out' for him. Even after the disaster of Stalingrad he was still to be found insisting that he had 'a right to believe that fate has called me to fulfil my role'. And in the very last radio address he gave to the country, in January 1945, he repeated: 'Only he who gave me this task can release me from it.'

The nature of this task, a subject to which Hitler returned time and again, was certainly not to pursue a set of political aims, that is, to arrange the political and social realities of the time in the interests of the nation whose Chancellor he was. Reality meant for him the task of transforming the world into a Wagnerian drama, part of which involved a hatred of those said to have tried to prevent this even in Wagner's own day, yet who at the same time were part of this drama. 'Hatred of the Jews was the guiding force of Hitler's life,' wrote Albert Speer after the war. 'Indeed, today it almost seems to me as though everything else was totally incidental to this overriding obsession.'[4]

This obsession was the heart of the Wagnerian heritage. Likewise the self-confidence with which Hitler confused, intimidated and terrorized the world came from Wagner's imperatorial claim to be superior to reality. Hitler did not just represent such a claim, based on knowledge drawn from reading the works of Wagner and seeing his operas on the stage – he *was* that claim. His energy was generated by the tension between his own grandiose pretensions as the preacher of an aesthetic and racial doctrine and the destructive, world-threatening power of his enemies. Hatred was his life's blood. But hatred is not a state or condition – it is ceaseless activity, aimed at the destruction of the object of that hatred. 'With all the strength at my command', Chamberlain had written about the Jews, 'I hate them and hate them and hate them!'[5] And nothing other than this obsession was the task which found its fulfilment in and through Hitler.

By hailing the Nazi leader as the only man with the courage to draw the natural consequence from his knowledge of the deadly influence of the Jews and turn it into action,[6] Chamberlain had already programmed Hitler's course. He had become an instrument, a mask from which a hidden voice came. As long as he pursued this task – this much he knew – Providence would guide his steps.

Not for nothing had he chosen the Christian concept of Divine Providence. He saw himself as the Saviour who resumes the struggle against the Jews which had been lost two thousand years earlier. But this time he would secure a victorious outcome. 'The forces we are releasing today', he predicted in 1923, 'will issue in an even bigger explosion than the Great War. The battle will be fought out on German soil for the entire world. There are only two possibilities: either we shall be the victors or we shall be sacrificial lambs!'[7]

Hitler never spoke openly about the man who had laid this charge on him. When he mentioned the name of Wagner he meant either a personal musical preference or the great German cultural revolution. That Wagner was the centre of his existence both set the parameters of his experience and represented the source of his self-confidence and the real object of his love, a love indistinguishable from the self-love which he always denied. All this he kept to himself like a holy relic. In this way the Bayreuth circle prevented the Master's doctrines from being desecrated before the time for their revelation arrived. Hitler had only to follow his words. But the words were crying out to be converted into actions, and Hitler's name for the law according to which this conversion was programmed to take place, the entelechy that would one day cause this metaphysical time-bomb to explode, was 'Providence'. He could equally well have called it 'Wagner' – but then nobody would have understood. So he called it 'Providence' – and people thought, at least, that they understood.

Providence implied the self-fulfilling power of fate that drove the genius that was Wagner. But it also embodied a concrete reality that Hitler himself had experienced, namely that by looking at the world through the Master's eyes, one could prophesy everything. Every set of circumstances that he had known, from Leonding to Munich, could be seen as a metaphor for events in society which, on a monumental plane, unfolded according to the same principles. To follow Providence also meant for Hitler to foretell what will and must come. A man called to become an instrument of Providence has an eye that looks into the future and a will that, with the 'sureness of a sleepwalker', puts into effect what the eye has seen. When he rediscovered in the real world what he had seen in his young days in the theatre in Linz and the Hofoper in Vienna, from Rienzi's triumph to Alberich's downfall, he could not but recognize the hand of Providence at work. With his experience of the martyrdom of Siegfried's victorious army, 'stabbed in the back', another prophecy found fulfilment. And that, as Hagen makes to grab the ring after murdering Siegfried, the Jews were now intent on grasping power for themselves gave no cause for surprise. It was all written in the stars.

As they had nailed the body of Christ, reincarnation of Siegfried, to the Cross, so now the Jews were seeking to drag the Aryan German nation, body and soul, into their clutches. 'In November 1918', said Hitler, who believed that, thanks to Wagner, he had come to understand all the laws of history, 'the forces of Marxism attacked and destroyed the old Reich in a wretched revolution.'[8] But the blood that was shed, preserved in the Grail chalice at Bayreuth, returned to life new and rejuvenated. The Saviour came. The seizure of power by the Antichrist, intended to wipe out the Aryan race and thus put an end to the forces of creation, ended as the prophecy said it would. 'We National Socialists', proclaimed Hitler in 1937, 'have totally and utterly destroyed the enemy in Germany – spiritually, ideologically and in reality.'[9]

Also foreseeable was that Hitler's career would be repeated on a world scale. The play was familiar but it was being performed in a different theatre. 'The enemies I see before me', said Hitler, as his troops froze to death in the Russian countryside, 'are the enemies that have been known to us for over twenty years. . . . As we showed no mercy towards our foes in our struggle for power, so now we shall be equally merciless in the fight to preserve our nation.'[10]

Hitler's adversaries were the Jews, who, he was convinced, had seized power not only in Germany but also in Russia, where the 1917 Revolution had set an example for the November Revolution in Germany. Disguising themselves as seekers after humanity and peace, liberty and fraternity, the revolutionaries in the east had overthrown and destroyed the ruling Aryan class and assumed control themselves. What went under the name of revolution, said Hitler, was in fact nothing other than the bloody usurpation of power by an alien race which had subjugated another people, not in open combat but by treachery, deceit and incitement to violence. And as happened a year later in Germany, he concluded, only a handful of Jews were needed to establish 'the rule of Alberich'[11] over the helpless Russian giant.

As Hitler saw it, the Russian Revolution was not an act of self-liberation on the part of an oppressed class but the first step by the Jews to secure world domination; feeding the unsuspecting masses with lies about their true purpose, they planned to extend their campaign first to neighbouring countries, then over the entire globe. And the man with the courage to take up the struggle would have to avail himself of the same means and lie, deceive, break treaties, assassinate former friends – anything and everything necessary to defeat the enemy with his own weapons.

In Hitler's eyes the Judaeo-Bolshevik revolution in Russia was only able to succeed because no one there was familiar with the 'scientific knowledge' that had come out of the Bayreuth School. He, Hitler, wiser for this experience, had been able to banish the spectre of the 'Jewish Weimar Republic'. His attempted Putsch in 1923 – an honest revolution in the name of humanity, in contrast to the underhand trickery resorted to by the Jews – represented a first revolt against the power-hungry Alberich's attempt to swallow up the German Reich. That attempt could not but fail because, like Siegfried, he had attacked the enemy head-on, an enemy that ruled by deception and betrayal. His success, only a few years later, in reducing the Weimar Republic to an empty shell was due to what he had learned from the martyrdom of his comrades in front of the Feldherrnhalle.

In the same year, 1941, as he dispatched his troops to the eastern front to finally settle his account with European Jewry, Hitler drew the historical parallels in the course of a speech that he delivered on the anniversary of the Putsch. In his familiar oracular style he declared to his comrades in the Löwenbräu beer-cellar in Munich that, as after the defeat of the First World War and the despicable revolution that followed, so now also 'the search for those ultimately responsible for these events leads to those who have always profited from conflicts between nations – the Jews'.[12] This too was a proposition well known to Wagnerians. 'It is an inevitable outcome of Jewish culture', wrote the Master in 'Know Thyself', eight years before Hitler was born, 'that in the last analysis the Jews always find themselves facing the need to wage war.'[13] For his part, Hitler claimed to have traced the activities of these international warmongers over many years 'and to be the first in the history of our nation to have scientifically and systematically settled the problem for all time'.

Credit for making the country aware of this remarkable advance in scientific knowledge belonged to National Socialism, Hitler continued. Facing the reality of half-a-million casualties on the Russian front – dead, wounded and missing[14] – he invoked his familiar confidence in ultimate victory. 'We have already recognized this danger to be the driving force in our internal struggle, and after a long and arduous battle we have finally emerged victorious. Now it is an external struggle that we face, a struggle against the instigators of a world-wide conspiracy to destroy the German people and the German Reich.' Seen in this light, Hitler's attack on Russia, which began with the callous breaking of a non-aggression pact and immediately led to the suspension of all the principles of civilized human conduct, was an act of self-defence. It was not, in a concrete sense, a preventive war, as though Hitler had pre-empted a planned attack by Stalin; but in a metaphysical sense it could be seen as such, because Germany, as Bayreuth interpreted the situation, had long suffered from being in the clutches of international Jewry. Putting the situation in these terms, Hitler was able to reassure his old guard that his risky military strategy – after only a few months his armies had already suffered losses of some fifteen per cent – corresponded in reality to the necessary dictates of fate to ensure the survival of the Aryan race.

He had also foreseen, Hitler went on,

> that one day Germany would be attacked by the power in which this Jewish spirit holds the greatest measure of control, namely the Soviet Union, which has become the Jews' most faithful servant. The age has confirmed what we National Socialists have maintained for many years – that Russia is a country in which the entire intelligentsia was slaughtered, leaving a mass of unintelligent, proletarian subhumans – a race of slaves under the domination of a huge organization of Jewish commissars.[15]

Twenty years earlier, on 4 August 1921, as the charismatic leader of a minor political party, he had invited all and sundry to a mass meeting in Munich to save the country from the threat of Soviet Russia. 'Barely three years have passed', his election poster read, 'since the Jewish apostles of the new Russian state promised that the revolution would create a paradise on earth. Instead the country has become a desert. We can no longer disguise the fact that the largest agricultural country in the world has become the biggest human graveyard in the world.' He therefore called on his audience to 'liberate the dying country of Russia by getting rid of its present oppressors. Charitable contributions given to Russia today find their way not into the hands of the Russian workers but into the pockets of their exploiters, the Jewish commissars.'[16] Support for these views came from Alfred Rosenberg, the Nazi ideologue and admirer of Chamberlain's who was appointed in 1941 to be Minister for the Occupied Eastern Territories. On 6 June 1941 Hitler ordered the 'commissars', one and all, to be shot – or, as the order put it in the chilling language of the day, to be 'immediately and totally disposed of by a bullet in the neck'.[17]

Externally the Soviet Union looked like a state with which a treaty of friendship could be signed. But internally it continued to promote Judaism by other means; its priests in officers' uniforms had therefore to be annihilated and its ritualistic meeting-places – Hitler called Stalingrad the 'shrine' of Communism,[18] and Leningrad 'an ideological fortress'[19] – razed to the ground.

Settling scores with the bastion of the Antichrist, on which the whole future of the planet depended, was not an operation that could be carried out as a normal 'armed confrontation' but had the character of a crusade. It would not be ordinary soldiers who perpetrated the murderous acts but police battalions and the black-shirted thugs with the death's-head emblem on their caps. This was not a situation in which, as in the conventions of war, the victor simply imposed his will on the vanquished, but one where, as Wagner had demanded, what was fit only for destruction should be destroyed. And as the Judaeo-Bolshevik Alberichs of this world camouflaged themselves as liberators advancing under the banner of the class struggle, so Hitler turned his policy of genocide into a pre-emptive strike. The slaughter of innocent men, women, children and the elderly was described as 'the execution of looters' or 'the elimination of partisans', while the gassing of the deprived, the humiliated, the poorest of the poor and those 'racial enemies' long condemned to a death in life was defined as 'transportation' or 'resettlement'.

It was not only *Lebensraum* and subjugation that were at stake; there was the whole question of 'who would inherit the world'. Only one side could inherit it; the other side must needs perish. The Jews, though scattered throughout the world and held responsible for stirring up hatred against the Germans wherever they went, had established their first sizeable bridgehead in Russia, so that their destruction would mean not only the destruction of the Jewish race and the Jewish ideology but also the defeat of a territorial power. 'Stalin wanted to enjoy the heritage of an impoverished Europe,' Hitler had said before his attack on the Soviet Union[20] – not, however, in order to bring it to a new peak of achievement but eventually to turn it into one gigantic slave-factory.

It was to prevent this happening that Destiny had called on him, as Hitler saw it, that he might both put a stop to the Bolshevization of the world and turn the tables on its perpetrators, wiping them from the face of the earth, lancing the boils they had left, fumigating the nests of the parasites, relieving the world of the bloodsucking vampires and sterilizing the parts they had infected. This done, he would claim the land as liberated *Lebensraum* for the resurgent Aryan peoples. The rigours of a Bolshevik winter would give way to the joys of a Germanic spring, and where hell used to be they would create a Garden of Eden.[21] Hitler had dreamed of such a moment in *Mein Kampf*. Now, in the year of his seizure of power, the dream returned. 'Bolshevism is ruining Russia. One day we shall inherit it all.'[22]

That day, which he would greet by marching with his glittering hordes on to the stage that had long been prepared for him, came nearer with each year that he consolidated his power and increased his military might. As the ruling caste had in any case already been extinguished, the only question was: who would take over the leadership of the slaves – the Jewish Bolsheviks, who had urged them on to world domination, or the Aryan race, who would offer them the opportunity to become part of a high culture devoted to the cultivation of a monumental beauty? This participation would not, of course, be equivalent to that of human beings – rather, they would be like the serfs in Classical Greece,[23] living robots, but at the same time enjoying an existence justified by 'the work of art of the future', in the creation of which, however ignorant of their fortune, they would be entitled to share.

As early as 1936, the year the Classical spirit was invoked with the Olympic Games in Berlin, Hermann Röchling, director of the largest iron and steel works in the Saarland, sent a confidential memorandum to Hitler in which he expressed his concern about preparations being made for war and for the conduct of such a war. 'Since, through its anti-Semitism,' wrote Röchling, 'Germany has declared its most determined opposition to the Jews who have taken control in Russia, as well as to world Jewry, the most influential forerunner of Bolshevism, the threat of war in the east is becoming ever greater.'[24]

This memorandum from Röchling, who later visited Hitler in his 'Wolf's Lair' in 1942 for discussions on the progress of the war,[25] seems to have influenced a confidential note of Hitler's in which, three years before his first advance eastwards – the campaign of slaughter, preparatory to his invasion of the Soviet Union, which went under the cynical name of the 'Polish Operation' – the Führer clearly saw himself as an instrument of Destiny. He did not intend, he wrote in his note, 'to prophesy exactly when the untenable situation in Europe would erupt into a crisis'. He did, however, wish to record his conviction 'that such a crisis could not and would not be averted, and that it is Germany's duty to protect itself against this disaster with all the means at its disposal. A number of consequences flow from this obligation, consequences that include some of the harshest trials the German *Volk* has ever had to endure.' These are no doubt the trials which he described in his 'testament' of 1945 as being of a severity 'to which no mortal man has ever before been subjected'.

The memorandum of 1936 shows Hitler as being fully aware of the steps he had to take in his capacity of Man of Destiny. 'The victory of Bolshevism over Germany', he recorded, 'will lead to the ultimate extinction of the German *Volk*.' In order to avoid this unimaginable catastrophe, which would pose a threat to the whole of Europe 'such as mankind has not known since the time when the cities of Classical Antiquity collapsed', decisions would have to be taken of a nature so drastic that it lay beyond the scope of historical experience. Lest there be any doubt: 'Compared with the need to avert this danger, all other considerations are insignificant.' He followed this with two demands: first, 'that the German army must be ready for war in four years', and second, 'that the German economy must be ready for war in four years'.[26]

The recipients of the memorandum would hardly have been surprised. Nor would they have been in any doubt that the state of readiness of the army and of the economy had as its sole purpose the removal of the Judaeo-Bolshevik threat, heedless of the political, economic and moral factors which Hitler had classed as 'insignificant'.

At the Party congress in September 1937 Hitler again conjured up the spectre of a gigantic danger facing the world, the greatest since Classical times.[27] These repeated references to Antiquity, which his mass audiences in the Nuremberg Kongresshalle would have hardly understood, were in the best traditions of Bayreuth. Wagner himself had identified the fall of Classical Greece as marking the decisive break in the development of mankind and linked the renaissance of the earliest glories of Western culture with the 'work of art of the future'. Friedrich Nietzsche, from 1869 a devotee of Wagner's philosophy, also connected the decline of Classical culture with the emergence of the 'Jewish spirit' and saw the only road to revival as that embodied in the ritual worship of Wagner's music dramas. Classical tragedy, and with it Athenian society, would be reborn in Germany out of the spirit of Wagner's *Gesamtkunstwerk*.[28] That all cultural decadence was the result of infiltration by Jewish elements was then raised to the status of dogma by Houston Stewart Chamberlain. 'Like a flood', declared Chamberlain, 'foreign blood poured into an almost totally deserted Rome, and the Romans forthwith ceased to exist.' But thereupon, thanks to Christianity, 'a single, minute cell gave birth to a force that eventually spanned the world'.[29]

The consequences of this blood pollution, namely 'racial chaos' and 'cultural decadence', were also in Hitler's mind when, at the spectacular Nuremberg rally of 1937, he spoke of the 'turmoil' that was in danger of devastating the whole world. 'As it was two thousand years ago', he said,

> the infection is being spread today by the canker-worm of Jewry, which can be seen at work in the Judaeo-Bolshevik rulers in Moscow. If I deliberately call this 'the Jewish problem', it is because it is there that the Jewish minority has succeeded not only in driving the former leaders of the country and of society out of their positions but has summarily disposed of them.[30]

The Jews were now trying to do the same with the leaders of Germany, Hitler went on. When Wilhelm Gustloff, a local Nazi official, was assassinated in Switzerland in 1936 by a Jew, Hitler pronounced a solemn oath over his coffin: 'Our comrade has been laid low by that power which is waging a fanatical struggle not only against our German nation but against every free, independent and sovereign people. We have understood the challenge! We shall take it up!'[31]

In the propaganda war that preceded the processes of extermination, recourse was had to a vocabulary which, like the whole complex of anti-Semitic activities, must have had a strangely antiquated ring about it for the Germans of the 1930s. Wagner's *bons mots*, taken out and dusted down for the occasion, were solemnly recited on state radio like quotations from a medieval homily. In levelling the three standard charges against the Jews in a speech delivered to the Party in 1937 – that they were 'the sons of chaos', 'the agents of decomposition' and 'the demons of human decadence'[32] – Goebbels was only calling on the vocabulary of three of the Nazis' spiritual forebears. The reference to 'chaos' took him back to Chamberlain, and the 'demons of decadence' are Wagner's, while 'decomposition' was an image suggested by the historian Theodor Mommsen.

Mommsen was a liberal – a fact which Goebbels did not allow to worry him – and had spoken out vehemently against anti-Semitism. But his dangerous metaphor of fermentation and decomposition, when applied to the Jews, put new weapons into the hands of his opponents. Later to be awarded the Nobel Prize for Literature, Mommsen had written that 'as the Jews had once acted as an element of decomposition in the Roman state, so in Germany they furthered the decomposition of the tribes'.[33] He meant this in a positive sense, as a contribution to the creation of a unified German Reich. But the anti-Semites found in his chemical image of decay a seemingly scientific argument which had fateful consequences in the Third Reich.

Rarely did Hitler express his Wagnerian view of the world, with its abstruse premises and its terrible consequences, so clearly as in his speech of February 1939 to his assembled army commanders in the Kroll Opera House in Berlin, preparing them for the world war that was soon to come. The main aim of his speech, he said, 'was to discuss the basic tenets of National Socialism in the presence of my high-ranking officers in a way not possible, for understandable reasons, in public'.[34] In reality, he told them, 'National Socialism' was only a convenient term chosen for tactical reasons; it did not denote a party or a political programme in the conventional sense but an ideology, a way of looking at the world. And the vital thing here, emphasized Hitler, was to realize that 'National Socialism' – a mere name, in itself of no importance – represented 'one of the most revolutionary, most epoch-shattering revelations experienced by man – the revelation of the significance of blood for the future of mankind'. The ethnic *Volk*, the people, the foundation of human existence, is 'a living substance of flesh and blood', not an abstract concept under which millions of individual citizens can be subsumed but a single, unified organism, its characteristics determined by the characteristics of its blood.

This 'substance' is, however, not represented, as one might expect, in biological terms, as some kind of macro-organism that has to fight for survival in a Darwinian struggle between species, but – to the amazement of the rows of military experts sitting in front of him – as a mystical vision such as Wagner had embodied in his Grail. 'This substance', said the man who was preparing to send the world up in flames, 'is the Eternal and the Indestructible, what is and what is to come. All else will perish.' The goals of a state built in the knowledge of this holy Grail-substance thereby assume the dimensions of infinity.

For this reason, the Führer continued, reaching the heart of his message, the next great war – which, in practice, he declares at this very moment – will not be a fight over territories or philosophies but a war that goes to the 'substance' itself – creative Aryan blood versus racial pollution. 'The next war', he prophesied, 'will be a war of ideologies, that is, an open war between peoples and races.'

The assembled military strategists before him sat there dumbfounded. At the drop of a hat he had transformed their role from one of 'pursuing political aims by other means', a role dependent on political assessment, into the prosecution of a kind of religious war conducted not in keeping with the Hague Conventions but according to the will of the divine entity identified by Hitler as the 'substance' of the community held together by the forces of blood – a war waged in the name of eugenics.

Taken aback by this revolutionary new interpretation of war as the celebration of a religion of blood, the officers said nothing. They had committed themselves to a crusade before the first shot was fired. Only after his stroke of tactical genius did Hitler reveal the aim of the coming war. 'I have undertaken', he said, 'to solve the German question – that is, to solve the Germans' problem of *Lebensraum*.' This was another cunning move, this time one that checkmated the 'know-alls in uniform', as the one-time private dubbed the cream of the military he was addressing. The craftiness of his move lay in the fact that he avoided the expected mention of a threat from the east which would make a pre-emptive strike necessary, since he would in any case have been unable to convince the experts of the wisdom of such a move.

So instead of broaching the tiresome Jewish problem, which would have been likely to cause uneasiness among his listeners, he turned to the question of *Lebensraum*, 'living space'. This was an area in which the generals felt at home: fighting over areas of land was their business and the concept of territorial gains was familiar. But Hitler's very next words gave the lie to the impression of conventionality. He was reading from a different script. He was not concerned with 'space' in the abstract, he said, but with that which the Jews had annexed as the base from which they had set out to dominate Germany and the world. Since the removal of its ruling class, he argued, this territory had had no proper master, and the usurpers, born liars and swindlers, would be unable to withstand a frontal attack by the army of Siegfried. This time, moreover, care would be taken to ensure that there was no 'stab in the back'.

The vast area that stretched from a 'Judaized' Poland to the eastern extremities of Asia was crying out to be colonized, Hitler went on. If one removed 'the agent of decomposition' that had infected the whole of the East, all that remained would be a mass of helpless peoples, Helots who could be used for the construction of a new state. The German question, for Hitler, was not 'We need more space in order to be able to flourish' but 'We must solve the Judaeo-Bolshevik problem before the future of German blood, and thus the genetic future of mankind, can be secured.' These immense territories in the East would pass into the hands of the Aryan race as its rightful heritage, as pre-ordained by Destiny. All that was needed was the courage to set out on the quest to take possession of these abandoned lands.

Before that point was reached, however, there were a number of uncertainties to be confronted and hardships to be endured which Hitler could not keep from his submissive followers, albeit without going into detail. 'Be fully aware', he said firmly, with an arrogance that left no doubt that nobody else's opinions were called for, 'that this intention will dominate my whole existence until the end of my days. And be sure that if I consider that the moment for action has come, I shall immediately take that action.' He followed this up with a threat that reduced the officers to the rank of foot-soldiers fit only to carry out orders – which is what they had in fact long become by their passive acquiescence. 'I shall not shrink from taking the most drastic measures', he thundered, 'because I am convinced that this is a question that has to be settled one way or the other, and because I am not prepared to say "O well, let's just leave it to those who come after us."'

Every man present must have realized that Hitler was not talking about war. Officers did not see war as 'the most drastic measure'; nor was Hitler, to them, the man who had to emphasize that he would not shrink from such measures. Moreover, every regimental commander must have known that he personally would have to pledge to Hitler his preparedness to carry out these measures – the Führer would hardly carry them out himself. To make sure they fully grasped the situation, he repeated that they must see him not just as the Commander-in-Chief of the German Armed Forces but 'as your supreme ideological leader, whom you are pledged to follow through thick and thin, for better or for worse'.

The one-time Austrian private in the imperial German army seemed out to make the most of the discomfiture of his former superiors. 'For better or for worse' was nothing short of an abrogation of their authority. But they chose to hold their peace. Bravery in the face of the enemy was one thing – bravery in front of one's senior officer was something else. Crowning his address, Hitler issued a direct challenge: 'I need to put my faith in you as an elite detachment of the ideological forces that are guiding the fate of our German nation.'

Hitler's audience of army officers had listened in silence as he talked of things from which all but he himself would shrink. At least, they consoled themselves, he had not once let fall the word 'Jew'. In conclusion, skilfully weaving all his motifs together, he once again invoked 'the eternal substance, the substance of flesh and blood, the German nation to which we have all pledged ourselves'.[35] It was at this moment, and not only when the shootings began, that the German army became an accomplice to genocide.

Hitler planned the Grand Extermination not because he enjoyed exterminating but because he was the anointed saviour of his people. It was his responsibility alone to take up the struggle against the Jewish Antichrist and remove the serpent from the face of the earth. Only then would the age of the new man dawn, his divine origin reflected in the great monuments of his art. Hitler's emergence as the redeemer of the Germans had heralded a new age which would find fulfilment only after passing through the vale of tears and witnessing the overthrow of its adversaries. At the moment he came to power, the moment when his torch-bearing columns, proudly singing, marched through the Brandenburg Gate, he had considered a radical innovation that would have made the year 1933 mark the beginning of a new epoch. 'When I assumed power', he reflected in the winter of 1941, 'I had to make a momentous decision. Should we keep the old calendar, or should we regard the new world order as denoting the beginning of a new calendar? The year 1933, I said to myself, marks nothing less than the renewal of a millennial tradition.'[36]

In order to make this Thousand-Year Reich a reality, it was first necessary to fulfil the main condition, namely the extinction of the Arch-fiend,
embodied in the Jewish race and its domination of Russia. 'It will be a
salvation for the whole of Europe', Hitler declared in November 1941, 'when
this threat has passed. . . . We can be in no doubt that at this moment the
future of Europe is being decided for the next thousand years.'[37] When in
the first year of his chancellorship he felt it necessary to justify his first
campaign against the Jews, he pointed to his visionary goal and assured
an astonished King of Sweden 'that in a thousand years' time the world
will thank me for the measures I have taken against the Jews'.[38]

The old utopia of the Thousand-Year Reich that Rienzi had already tried
to achieve in the fourteenth century[39] was inseparably linked with the idea
of the 'final battle' against the Antichrist. Only a resurgent saviour in a
new form could overcome the enemy. Thus in many religious tracts
the path to everlasting peace is portrayed as leading through massacre
and terror:[40] a new army of crusaders, the soothsayers foretold, led by the
legendary Emperor Friedrich Barbarossa, would launch a blood-bath
against the Jews[41] as 'an indispensable purification of the world' on the eve
of the advent of the Thousand-Year Reich.[42] One sixteenth-century source
even announced the spot where this apocalyptic event would occur – at
the foot of the Untersberg mountain, between Salzburg and Berchtesgaden,
where Barbarossa slumbered. 'Here, near Reichenhall,' ran the prediction
in the chapbook of 1523, 'all the people will be strangled and slain in great
wrath, the fields will be strewn with the bodies of men and animals as far
as the eye can see, some clubbed to death, some shot, some trampled un-
derfoot, with blood flowing up to the ankles.' Then the Emperor and his
heroes will emerge from out of the Untersberg 'and help to root out the
unbelievers, the unrepentant and the Godless'.[43]

The crusader in the Untersberg had fascinated Wagner from his revolutionary days. His friend, the actor Eduard Devrient, recorded in his diary
that in 1848 Wagner had read him an historical essay in which he revealed
'his great enthusiasm for the concept of world domination as found in early
legends and sagas, with the figure of the Emperor Barbarossa arising in all
his power and splendour as the mightiest embodiment of that concept'.[44]
In his essay – it was in fact Wagner's phantasmagorial sketch 'The Wibelungen' – the Hohenstaufen Barbarossa, who was drowned on crusade
in 1190, returns to fulfil the hopes of the nation, setting 'the noble principle
of world domination' at the heart of his mission.[45]

The conception that filled Barbarossa's mind in Wagner's interpretation
went even further than the dreams of omnipotence cherished by Hitler, an
enthusiastic reader of 'The Wibelungen'. 'The Germans', wrote Wagner,
'are the custodians of the oldest royal lineage in the world. It derives from
a son of God known to his immediate kinsfolk as Siegfried but to the other
peoples of the world as Christ.' In other words, on the grounds of heredity

and blood alone, the reigning German prince stood in direct line of descent from the Aryan Messiah. His task was to deliver the Germanic world from evil. As in Barbarossa's day the holy places had been seized by the infidels, so the Emperor had answered the call to save the Holy Sepulchre. 'He felt an irresistible urge to go to Asia, the cradle of civilization. From wondrous legends he learned of a glorious land in the depths of Asia, in distant India, where he hoped to find the Holy Grail.'[46] It was a plan that Hitler also had in his mind – first to destroy the Russian Antichrist, then to advance with his armies on India.

Hardly had Barbarossa and his knights reached the frontiers of the Holy Land than, as Wagner described it, 'he unleashed a savage attack against the Saracens, leaving the country at his mercy'. But before he could take possession of his inheritance, he vanished from the scene and now sits, as the legend has it, in a dark mountain – some say the Kyffhäuser, others the Untersberg[47] – where, surrounded by his heroes, he awaits the final battle. When he rises again from the grave, says Wagner, the destruction of Satan will be sealed, 'for at his side will hang the sword that once slew the dragon'. And because, in effect, he only told the whole familiar tale in order to provide his fellow conspirators with a mythological framework for their revolution, he concluded with a call to arms. 'When, O great Friedrich, wilt thou return, thou noble Siegfried, and slay the dragon that is tormenting mankind?'[48]

Wagner himself had earlier made his own attempt to relive this historical moment. In 1846 he planned an opera on the subject of Barbarossa, returning to it two years later but never completing it – in the event Siegfried took the place of the Hohenstaufen Emperor. In 1869, the year he re-issued his anti-Semitic pamphlet 'Music and the Jews', another idea occurred to him for a work on Barbarossa. And as late as 1871, the year of the Franco-Prussian War and the foundation of the Second Reich, Barbarossa was still on his mind – 'a man of sublime, barbaric grandeur and divine naïveté',[49] Wagner called him, by which he meant not so much the Emperor's artless conceit that he could rule the world as that noble innocence which also characterizes his national saviours Siegfried and Parsifal. Not, however, that his thoughts were only aesthetic in nature when he reflected on the 'barbaric' possibilities of the notion of world domination. Sitting in Wahnfried with Cosima and Heinrich von Stein, his son Siegfried's tutor, in 1879, he toyed with the idea 'that we ought to take possession of the earth's cultural riches in a series of determined assaults'. On which Stein remarked in surprise: 'Wagner makes actions out of ideas.'[50]

And Hitler turned these ideas into reality. In *Mein Kampf* he had dreamed of picking up 'where things had left off six hundred years earlier'. In 1328 King Ludwig IV of Bavaria had had to go to Rome to be crowned German Emperor, and twenty years later Rienzi became leader of the Roman people in order to re-establish the grandeur of the Caesars – he too, according to legend, a late descendant of the Hohenstaufens. But the future of the new Reich did not lie in Rome, said Hitler. 'We shall put an end to this eternal German pilgrimage to southern and western Europe and turn people's eyes to the east.'[51] (Wagner had written in 'The Wibelungen': 'Friedrich turned his gaze to the Orient.')[52] Hitler was obsessed with the image of an armed crusade under fluttering banners, returning time and again to the comparison between his own aggressive military campaigns and the crusading excursions of the Middle Ages. 'Other generations have learned about heroic exploits,' he said in 1935; 'we have lived out this legend and marched in step with the advancing columns.'[53]

In 1942, with his hitherto unchecked advance being forced back from the Russian steppes, Hitler addressed an audience of ten thousand officer cadets in the Berlin Sportpalast and drew a historical parallel. 'In the past', he reminded them, 'German Emperors and knights rode these same paths on horseback and reached Palestine, the Promised Land. What we are doing now is not unique in history. Our forebears did exactly the same!'[54]

With the reference to Palestine, Hitler, without mentioning him by name, brought the Emperor Barbarossa back into the picture, the hero for whose return Wagner had longed a hundred years earlier to deal with the situation once and for all. Wagner's longing had taken a grip on Hitler. Under the nickname of 'Wolf' he had taken refuge with Dietrich Eckart on the Obersalzberg, near Berchtesgaden, where later, with the help of Winifred Wagner and Helene Bechstein, he made his own home. Not only did this bring him close to that field where Barbarossa's apocalyptic battle would be waged to establish his kingdom of peace – blood would be 'flowing up to the ankles', the chapbook had said – but he also directly overlooked the mountain in which the Emperor had been waiting for 750 years to make his return.[55] Hitler's 'Berghof' lay directly opposite this legendary scene. The 'Great Hall', where his guests assembled round the fireside to listen to his monologues, was equipped with a giant panorama window – said to have been the largest in the world – which could be lowered so as to give the impression that the mountain massif belonged to Hitler's interior architecture.[56]

Hitler's visitors were impressed. Heinrich Hoffmann, his personal photographer, was only one of those to remark on the majestic view and on the significance of its association with the saga of Barbarossa.[57] 'It is not a matter of chance,' the Führer said; 'it is a reflection of my mission.'[58] When, at the beginning of 1941, the moment arrived for what the Commander-in-Chief later called 'the greatest deployment of military forces that the world has ever seen',[59] he seemed also to have in his mind the mythological dimension of his undertaking associated with the Hohenstaufen Emperor in the Untersberg and his bloody battle.

One afternoon in February 1941, said Hermann Giesler, Hitler's architect, Hitler summoned his generals to the Berghof for a discussion of strategy and tactics. When they had finished, Giesler, who was waiting on one side, noticed that they went across to the great window that looked out on to the Untersberg. Going over to Giesler, Fritz Todt, Hitler's Minister of Armaments Production, who had been present at the briefing, pointed at the scene and said in a low voice: 'You know about the decision – Russia. Things will be hard. But look at the Führer, calm and composed. And in the background is the Untersberg. You know the story – for a thousand years the hopes of Germany have been linked with this mountain. – Is that not strange?'

'As we sat round the fire that evening', Giesler went on, 'Adolf Hitler was silent and withdrawn. At around midnight he asked Bormann something. Then suddenly, taking me completely aback, those mighty chords from Liszt's *Les Préludes* boomed out across the hall, which was lit only by the flickering flames from the hearth.'[60] These chords, the so-called 'Russian Fanfare', were later played as an introduction to radio bulletins of news from the eastern front. Hitler had found his musical leitmotif even before the curtain rose on his drama.

The title of that world-shattering drama had also long been chosen. In his 'Order No. 21' of 18 December 1940 Hitler gave his historic battle – whose importance he played down as a 'short, sharp campaign' – the name 'Operation Barbarossa'.[61] This was to be the moment when the conqueror of the Antichrist awoke from his slumber in the Untersberg. 'When Barbarossa arises', said the prophet of the Berghof on 3 February 1941, 'the world will hold its breath.'[62]

Hitler also had a suitable mythological image on hand to apply to the victims of Barbarossa's conquest. His secretary Christa Schroeder tells how, on 'one of the afternoons when he regularly had coffee in our room', he stressed that the attack on Russia had been 'the hardest decision he had ever had to make, first and foremost because we know so little about Russia'. The country had something sinister about it, he said, 'like the ghostly ship in Wagner's *Fliegender Holländer*'.[63] On the one hand the allusion to Wagner, which he is also said to have made to one of his adjutants, expressed his phantom-like vision of the Russian colossus, an abstruse, composite vision which had little in common with reality. On the other hand it is a simile that strikes at the heart of his thinking. For Wagner the Flying Dutchman was simply a manifestation of the phenomenon of the Wandering Jew[64] – 'the Ahasverus of the ocean'[65] – a man on whom, as on the crew of his vessel, the Devil has laid a curse, a man who cannot die, yet yearns for 'final destruction'. In a fate like Alberich's, the ghostly mariner is condemned 'to travel the seas for ever in search of treasure', as Wagner put it.[66] His despairing cry for redemption is echoed by the sailors, as they shout from the bowels of the ship: 'Eternal destruction, take us to thy bosom!'[67] The man who had shouldered the task of redeeming the world must have heard their cry ringing in his ears. What they craved, they were soon to be granted. We are in the realm of the Theatre of the Absurd, which dragged millions into the maelstrom of death.

'There was not the slightest military necessity for an attack on the Soviet Union,' wrote the historian Eberhard Jäckel.[68] Stalin had other problems than to embark on a military adventure against a well-armed, self-confident opponent steeled in the art of the Blitzkrieg. In addition there were various Friendship Treaties, Non-Aggression Pacts and Frontier Agreements in force which had been recently concluded; Poland had been brutally parcelled up and Hitler was already engaged in fighting another enemy. On pragmatic grounds, therefore, military operations were senseless, which meant that the thought of a preventive war, as the historian Roland Foerster put it, 'was, in the authoritative opinion of an overwhelming majority of historians, both at home and abroad', simply absurd.[69] Hitler opened up his eastern front not because there was an objective reason for doing so – he himself admitted in 1940 'that the Russians would not attack in a hundred years'[70] – but because, in the words of Joachim Fest, 'it had always been his aim to do so, and because any other course would have been just to take the long way round'.[71]

'Operation Barbarossa' became Hitler's provisional goal in life, a campaign of destruction which was intended to enable him to reach his real, ultimate goal – the achievement of the Wagnerian world of the 'work of art of the future'. Nicolaus von Below, his Air Force adjutant, had an opportunity of studying the Führer's trains of thought in the year war broke out. One summer evening in the Berghof, before the attack on Poland, Hitler met with his advisors. Gazing out at the looming mass of the Untersberg, recalled Below, 'he seemed to be lost in thought as to how best to put his political plans into practice'. Then, accompanied by Albert Speer and Below, he strode up and down the hall, 'allowing his thoughts free rein' – which he did all the more freely because he felt that in Speer he had found a kindred spirit. 'It was clear from the way he was talking', said Below, 'that he was looking to create as quickly as possible a basis for the peacetime work that needed to be done.'

He went on to sketch the outlines of the vision that he had had before his eyes since the very beginning of his political career. The basis for this 'peace-time work' – the creation of a Europe fit to receive a future race of heroes – was to be, said Below, 'a Greater Germany, acknowledged and unchallenged among the nations of Europe and the world'. Below had the impression 'that the territorial question was in fact not paramount, even though Hitler did indulge from time to time in exaggerated speculations about expanding towards the east. His overriding concern was really to destroy "Jewish Bolshevism", the greatest threat to Germany and Europe.'[72] In fact, Hitler had confided to Speer as early as the summer of 1939 that he was planning 'Operation Barbarossa'. And in August 1940, also in the Berghof, he returned to the subject of the Judaeo-Bolsheviks, this time in the presence of his Army adjutant Gerhard Engel, who heard him say: 'If only we could eradicate them.'[73]

Hitler had now finally turned himself into the German Siegfried who sets out to kill 'the dragon that is tormenting mankind'. And he knew that he was the Messiah sent by Chamberlain, the Messiah pledged to hear the plea of despair coming from the Dutchman's ghostly ship: 'Eternal destruction, take us to thy bosom!'

The destruction in question did not begin with the construction of gas chambers. Nor did it only take place with the mass executions behind the lines. The advancing columns of fire – three million men, 3500 tanks and 2700 aircraft on a front 1600 kilometres wide[74] – caused devastation and massive casualties from the very first day. The millions caught up in the hostilities died a lingering death, exposed to disease and starvation and herded into labour camps. Jewish men, women and children were systematically exterminated by four specially formed task forces, which, from the day of the invasion,[75] operated with terrifying efficiency, often with the cooperation of their unsuspecting victims. According to the statistics drawn up by Andreas Hillgruber, Task Force A (behind the northern sector of the eastern front) executed 136,421 Jews up to 25 November 1941 (1064 Communists, 56 partisans, 653 mentally ill, 44 Poles, 28 prisoners-of-war, 5 gypsies, 1 Armenian) – by 1 February 1942 the figure had risen to 229,052; by 14 November 1941 Task Force B (behind Army Group Centre) had disposed of 45,467 victims; Task Force C (behind Army Group South) had executed 95,600 by the beginning of December; and Task Force D (the southernmost sector of the eastern front) disposed of 92,000 Jews by 8 April 1942. In a second wave of slaughter between August and November 1942, covering the Ukraine, the rest of southern Russia and the area round Bialystok, a further 363,211 Jews were shot. This gives a total of over 824,000 by November 1942.[76]

These executions of defenceless civilians 'generally took place in remote spots in forests or marshy areas so as not to attract the attention of the local population'. Having been taken to the open pits where their bodies were afterwards to be dumped, 'they were forced to strip, men, women and children, and wait to be murdered. Having been ordered to move to the side of the pit in small groups, they were then shot – usually with a revolver or a semi-automatic weapon, sometimes by machine-gun.'[77] A Gestapo woman reported from Smolensk that infants were killed by a bullet through the neck.[78]

The establishment of extermination camps from 1942 onwards took matters a significant step further. Until then the murderers had had to go to their victims – now the victims were taken to their murderers, dragged in from all parts of Nazi-occupied Europe or, as in the case of half a million Hungarian Jews, from areas occupied in 1944 specifically for this purpose.[79] Over a period of three years three million Jews were transported to the six death camps on Polish territory. The centres worked quickly and efficiently: 'a man would step off a train in the morning, and in the evening his corpse was burned and his clothes packed away for shipment to Germany.'[80]

The victims were kept in ignorance of their fate. Kurt Gerstein, a senior SS officer, later described the process of gassing by diesel exhaust fumes. 'In a corner of the entrance to the gas chambers', said Gerstein, 'stood a strapping SS man who called out reassuringly: "Nothing is going to happen to you! All you have to do is breathe in deeply when you're in the chamber. That expands your lungs and protects you against epidemics and diseases." '[81]

The gas chamber in Auschwitz operated with cyanide gas. 'Everything was simple and straightforward,' according to Eugen Kogon. 'It looked like a shower room, which is what the victims were told it was. In the room where they took off their clothes there was a notice on the wall in the principal European languages telling them to fold their clothes tidily and tie their shoes together to prevent them from getting lost. After the shower, concluded the notice, a cup of hot coffee would be provided.'[82] As soon as the doors were shut, the deadly gas came out of the showers. The record for one single day, according to Kogon, was 34,000 bodies.

The majority of the gas chambers were camouflaged as showers. In Treblinka the victims were told that a large building housing several gas chambers on both sides of a corridor was a synagogue. On the front wall of the building there was a Star of David beneath the gable, while at the entrance hung a heavy dark curtain taken from a synagogue. On the curtain was the inscription, in Hebrew: 'This is the gate through which the just shall pass.'[83]

The whole system was built on lies. As the victims, after being humiliated and abused, were lied to even in the moment of their death, so the population at large, who would ultimately have to pay for the whole murderous system of the extermination camps, were fobbed off with hints and evasions. True, they had agreed to put up with the fact that Hitler was a virulent anti-Semite; but at the same time they had loved him because, steeping himself in the dramatic world of Wagner's operas, he played the role of redeemer, albeit concealing from them that the redeemer's decisive act of redemption consisted of the 'final solution'. Their Führer did not offer them the opportunity to reveal themselves as the murderous anti-Semites which a number of historians see the Germans to be. He did not trust them to display the inhuman cruelty necessary for such atrocities.

On a number of occasions before the war Hitler had attempted to rouse the German 'popular instinct' which Wagner had so effectively invoked in his 'Music and the Jews'. But the great boycott of Jewish shops, for instance, that he had instituted immediately after coming to power had met only with displeasure and been silently dropped. A second such attempt during the Nuremberg Party rally of 1933, when the baton-wielding columns marched straight from the arena to the Jewish stores in the town, only spoiled the citizens' enjoyment of the festive occasion. Various means of intimidation were employed but the average citizen had no prejudice against the Jews and was very willing to patronize their shops.[84]

Nor had the situation changed five years later, at the time of the so-called 'Kristallnacht', a pogrom called to commemorate the martyrs of Hitler's abortive coup of 1923. Orders were given for a general campaign of murder and arson against Jews and Jewish property. But it was in the event the stormtroopers who carried out the orders – many 'Aryans' were hardly less confused by the events than their Jewish neighbours. 'The brutal measures taken against the Jews', stated a confidential report at the time, 'have caused great indignation among the populace over these acts of vandalism ... but at the same time the people feel an increasing sense of intimidation.'[85] Another contemporary account was forced to concede that the acts of wanton destruction 'had aroused considerable sympathy for the Jews in town and countryside alike'.[86]

On the day the Jews were made to wear the yellow star, the Berliners tried hard to hide their embarrassment, lowering their gaze in order to avoid giving their Jewish neighbours the impression of being stared at.[87] Franz Neumann, a German working for the American OSS, reported as late as 1944 that 'despite the ceaseless propaganda to which the German people have been subjected over many years, there has not been a single spontaneous anti-Jewish act by anybody outside the Nazi Party. ... Paradoxical as it may sound, it is my own personal conviction that the Germans are the least anti-Semitic of all peoples.'[88]

Hitler appears to have shared Neumann's opinion. If the Germans had really had such a passionate hatred of the Jews, he would not have had to shout himself hoarse for the past twenty years. Maybe they were not free from a certain resentment springing from envy, superstition, or even a degree of xenophobia, but the Bayreuth policy of a radical solution was quite alien to them. Hitler was interested not in a simple, nationalistic anti-Semitism but a 'scientifically-based', fully developed concept based on the 'pernicious influence' of Jewry and the inescapable consequences to be drawn from it. If, as one sent on a divine mission, Hitler ceaselessly preached hatred towards the Jews, then it was not in order to tell the Germans what they were eager to hear but, on the contrary, because he knew that they were uncertain of themselves where racial matters were concerned. Before Hitler the question of one's attitude towards the Jews was not on the agenda, and in 1918, as he himself admitted, there had hardly been a 'Jewish question'.[89] The evil seeds of Nazi indoctrination took root not so much in the people as in the ranks of the Nazi Party itself: the Brownshirts and Blackshirts would have torn themselves into little pieces for their Führer – which is just what they did, when he demanded it, to his enemies. It was not 'the Germans' as such who were Hitler's obedient servants but only those who allowed him to turn them into such submissive agents.

When Hitler launched his eastern campaign of murder and terror, which had to be made palatable to the people as a kind of armed Party rally with march-pasts, fanfares and the rumbling of artillery, nothing was said about the ultimate aim being wholesale destruction. On a number of occasions he made oblique references to it in prophetic language but refrained from going into detail, since he could hardly have counted on general approval for his actions.[90] So the Germans, who were said to want nothing more desperately than to be rid of their arch-enemy, were denied all knowledge of the 'final solution'. And Hitler, for his part, to whom the Germans had always been unreliable allies in ideological questions, constantly complained that their attitude was too soft. 'Today', he observed in 1942, 'our fellow-citizens are lamenting the fate of the Jews who are being transported to the east – the very same Jews who stabbed the German nation in the back.' And he mocked those who shed 'crocodile tears' over every such Jew.[91]

The reason for this flabby, 'unscientific' attitude lay, according to Hitler, in a basic weakness of character. 'Beneath the surface', he explained,

> anti-Semitism is far more pronounced among the British and the Americans than among the Germans, who in spite of all their unpleasant experiences persist in clinging to their sentimental image of 'the decent Jew'. And there is a tradition to this. It was, after all, a German dramatist, Lessing, who idealized the figure of the Jew in his play *Nathan the Wise*.[92]

This had annoyed Wagner as well. At a recent performance of *Nathan the Wise*, he told his wife in December 1881 in Wahnfried, a Jew in the audience had stood up at the words 'Christ was also a Jew!' and shouted 'Bravo!' 'Wagner thought very ill of Lessing for this tasteless line,' wrote Cosima in her diary. The conversation then turned to the fire that had gutted the Ringtheater in Vienna ten days earlier, when over four hundred people had been burned to death. Wagner was especially fascinated by the thought of Jews being in the theatre – 'probably four hundred of them unbaptized and five hundred baptized', he sneered. Then a particularly gruesome thought occurred to him. 'In a jocular tone', wrote Cosima, 'he said all the Jews should be herded together in a performance of *Nathan* and burned.'[93]

Hitler never breathed a word about his plans for the greatest *auto-da-fé* in human history. As in Wagner's *Götterdämmerung*, the purifying flames were to reach out and embrace a doom-laden world. But in place of the Aryan heroes and gods who are consumed by fire in the *Ring*, it was now to be the turn of the other side. Hitler had been building his funeral pyre for over twenty years. Although he may have kept stubbornly silent over the Holocaust production he was planning for the world stage, on occasion he pictured himself as an actor – a shaman who is rehearsing the grand exorcism.

According to his elocution coach, Paul Devrient, 'Hitler breathed very jerkily, almost explosively, rather like a man giving orders. As a result of this faulty voice-production his tone became more and more forced, and the combined effect of strained neck muscles and vocal cords was a discoloration of the face, making it increasingly purple and blotchy.'[94] When his voice began to fail, he attempted to compensate by using exaggerated gestures, 'moving hectically from one side to another, rolling his eyes and gesticulating wildly. At other times, as though fleeing from the Furies, he would leap up and down on the platform, hold his head in both hands and sway violently from side to side.'[95] Or he would thrust his head and body backwards and forwards, as though performing a voodoo dance. In the course of his 'fiery discourses', as Devrient described these anti-Semitic tirades, he would mimic a Jew's nose or a Jew's ears with grotesque gestures, 'like a cabaret artist'. His audience, swept off its feet by this St Vitus' Dance, 'went wild, screaming and shrieking in their rage and fury. He had them eating out of his hand. "The Jew is our ruin!" he shouted, first waving his clenched fists threateningly in the air, then plunging them down into an imaginary pit below.'[96] It was the pantomime of the 'final solution'.

With the help of a strategy of obfuscation and cryptic camouflage, tried and tested since the time of Wagner's Bayreuth, Hitler deceived both the *Volk* whose future he had set out to fashion and the *Volk* that he had robbed of its future. He even deceived those who still today take his words at face value. Had he not graciously agreed in October 1939, a month before the invasion of Poland, that the Jews should live in self-governing ghettos, 'even with their own police force', so that there would be no need for them to wear 'a distinguishing badge'?[97] Had he not tried in February 1941, as though deeply moved by their plight, to find a humane solution to the problem of how they should be resettled? His adjutant Gerhard Engel heard him remark that he would approach the French and ask them to arrange for the Jews to be accommodated on the island of Madagascar. When the astonished Bormann asked how he planned to transport so many millions, especially in wartime, Hitler replied that they would have to work something out. 'The best thing would be to make the whole "Strength Through Joy" fleet available,' he said.[98] Those who did not know Hitler the Jew-hater and his mission in life will have failed to catch the tone of icy contempt in his voice as he uttered these words. In fact they concealed all his murderous intentions.[99]

Camouflage was not the only thought in Hitler's mind. He was also following the sectarian custom of conveying all confidential information to outsiders in coded form. Bayreuth, thanks above all to Wagner's penchant for talking in riddles, had honed this custom to a fine art, while the division of the message into two parts – general appeals and esoteric pronouncements – mirrored the separation of the world into common people and initiates. As Cosima's 'Knights of the Grail', arming themselves for the fight against the 'hornets' nest' of the Jews,[100] were sworn to silence over Bay-reuth's true aims, so Hitler's henchmen, like Himmler, were caught up in a cynical web of duplicity and deception.[101] Even the personnel of the mur-der units themselves resorted to euphemisms such as 'special treatment', 'cleaning up' and 'dealing with partisans', and developed a private lan-guage that pretended to be using code names as part of the wartime cam-ouflage measures imposed by the army.

When in 1943, in Poznań, Himmler was in the course of revealing to an audience of Gauleiters and other Party officials the secret task of his mur-derous Blackshirts, he suddenly noticed that the door to the adjacent kitchen was ajar. He broke off abruptly and angrily ordered the door to be shut. Then he continued in a whisper, giving instructions that nobody outside the room must learn what he had just said. He and his SS men, he con-cluded, would carry out their terrible task 'and take their secret with them to the grave'.[102]

The SS was a secret organization long before it was empowered to em-bark on its real role. Founded as Hitler's personal bodyguard of Blackshirts, it quickly took over the function of the Blood-Order of Knights in Wagner's *Parsifal*, an elite band pledged to protect the King of the Grail, stamp out evil in the world and beget the divine humanity of the future. 'A new kind of religious sect', as SS-Hauptsturmführer Dieter Wisliceny described them,[103] the brutal new Grail fraternity saw the world not in political terms but according to the secret doctrines of their faith. In the centre of the Or-der, which mounted guard over Hitler's blood-red banner, stood, in true Wagnerian style, the concept of the pure blood which is threatened with adulteration by the Jews. For their Monsalvat Himmler had chosen the Wewelsburg, near Paderborn, where he planned to build a 'quasi-religious cult centre'[104] which, with its hallowed burial place, its rotunda of columns and its dome, should recall the Grail Temple in *Parsifal*. The principal task of the blackshirted guardians of the Grail, which, under Himmler's leader-ship, spread terror throughout the land as they developed into a body of savage shock troops promoting the ideology of the Führer, consisted in 'turning the racial madness of the Nazi regime into bloodcurdling real-ity'.[105] What had started on the stage of the Festspielhaus in Bayreuth as a solemn procession of knights dressed as Templars had fifty years later gone down in history as the embodiment of Satanic forces intent on the destruc-tion of mankind.

Yet these nightmarish forces, emissaries from the world of *Götter-dämmerung*, were only carrying out the stage directions prescribed by Hitler. Everything about the SS, from their prescribed height, their uni-forms and their parades down to their sinister rituals and symbols, corre-sponded to the theatrical principles laid down by the man they had vowed to serve, and brought about a state of total intimidation well before the apparatus of mass murder was set in motion. Wherever the jackboot and the revolver ruled, life itself seemed threatened and the stars no longer seemed to be moving in their courses. The fabric of social life was torn and truth was defined as what the rule of terror ordained it to be. To the accompaniment of marching feet and the sounds of military music the actors of the Nazi ideology strode on to the stage and embarked on their work of destruction.

The man appointed to bring to life Hitler's dream of an order of Grail knights charged with the defence of Aryan blood was a pallid, lifeless creature, like a puppet exposed to the light of day, a spent shell-case stuffed with foreign matter. 'Himmler was utterly subservient to Hitler in intellectual matters,' said Otto Dietrich.[106] An early convert to the racial theories of Wagner and Chamberlain, Himmler found in the Bayreuth Messiah his lord and master. He earned his spurs as 'the Führer's servant'[107] and spoke proudly, having launched his campaign of terror, of 'the difficult task that the Führer has set me . . . a task for which I alone will shoulder responsibility'.[108] And as though echoing Chamberlain's injunction to Hitler to think his thoughts through to their natural conclusion and accept the consequences without flinching, Himmler repeated in his speech in Poznań that the responsibility that he and his SS men had assumed for dealing with the Jewish question was 'a responsibility for action, not merely for an idea'.[109]

But Himmler was also convinced that the execution of such a policy was beyond the power of the Germans: one could not tell them about it, still less expect them to participate in it. Mocking their weakness, he sneered: 'To judge from the number of applications for exemption on the part of threatened Jews, and from the number of different opinions in Germany, I am tempted to conclude that there are more respectable Jews left than there are Jews altogether.'[110] A few days earlier he had scoffed at 'all those worthy Germans, eighty million of them, each of whom has a respectable Jew in tow'.[111] But the real action required, for which, though being carried out above their heads, they must all answer, consisted, in Himmler's ice-cold words, 'in wiping the Jews from the face of the earth'.[112] As Hitler did not want to claim credit prematurely for this world-shattering achievement, his henchman made it clear at the beginning of the massacre that 'the Führer himself must under no circumstances be associated with the operation. I myself accept complete responsibility.'[113]

In contrast to Hitler, his intellectual mentor Wagner has so far been spared the consequences of this ominous association. He may have proposed the downfall of Ahasverus as the best way of achieving the salvation of Jewry, and hinted at a 'grand solution' that would lead to the disappearance of all Jews; maybe he was the originator, in the *Ring*, of those bizarre caricatures which Hitler foisted on to the public as true images of the Jews, and maybe *Parsifal* gives dramatic and musical credibility to an obsession with 'pure blood'; furthermore, as a leading composer and theoretician of the day, he may by his open incitements to racial hatred have sanctified primitive feelings of envy and resentment, creating a circle of conspiratorial anti-Semites which became the model for Hitler's Nazi Party. But in spite of all this there is still a reluctance to recognize the step that leads from thought to action, from 'thinking thoughts through to their natural conclusion' to 'accepting the consequences without flinching'.

Even an admission that there had been a 'Hitler's Wagner', a figure claimed to be a totally unpolitical composer and man of the theatre who had been perverted by the Nazis for propaganda purposes, has been only grudgingly forthcoming in the post-war era – while the possibility that the man who plunged Europe into disaster was 'Wagner's Hitler' lay beyond the realm of the thinkable. Equally unthinkable hitherto was the idea that Hitler's hatred of the Jews had nothing to do with the individuals classified as such – for in reality he barely knew them, besides which his dealings with a number of them were known to be anything but unfavourable. His campaign to exterminate the Jews was part of his love for Wagner. He had to hate the Jews because he loved the man who hated them. There was no time for a learning process, no opportunity to compromise or adapt to present reality, because Wagner's work was concluded, immutable for all time.

A number of Hitler's contemporaries were under no illusions about his mythological identity. 'He was not simply fascinated with Wagner's music,' wrote André François-Poncet, French ambassador to Berlin in the 1930s, 'but he also believed Wagner a prophet, the prophet of National Socialism. He "lived" Wagner's work, he believed himself to be a Wagnerian hero; he was Lohengrin, Siegfried, Walther von Stolzing, and especially Parsifal, who cured the bleeding wound in the side of Amfortas and restored its magic virtue to the Holy Grail.'[114] By the same token objective observers could trace back to Wagner the phenomena through which the Führer constantly commanded the world's attention – the Master's *Weltanschauung* and music dramas, his megalomania and the ruthlessness with which he destroyed those he imagined to be his enemies. Not only was Hitler a Wagnerian in respect of Wagner's music but his whole *Weltanschauung* – from his love of display and theatrical effect to the creation of monumental works of architecture – rested on the foundations established by the Master.[115] An anti-Wagner minority found all this repulsive but, as the political commentator Sebastian Haffner saw for himself, it exercised a strong attraction on the majority.

Hitler's followers built on the same foundations. Wagner's shadow can still be felt hovering over the anti-Semitic sentiments expressed by the hideous Himmler. 'Anti-Semitism is like de-lousing,' said Himmler in 1943, light-heartedly: 'De-lousing is not a question of ideology – it is a matter of cleanliness.'[116] Wagner too indulged in a similar crude and tasteless humour. In 1878, talking to Ernst Schmeitzner, publisher of the *Bayreuther Blätter*, he compared the Jews to household pests, and added: 'There are fleas and there are bugs. All right – they are there. But we fumigate them. And the people who don't are dirty pigs!'[117]

. Right to the end of his life Hitler kept all knowledge of his mass fumigations from the German people. Even in his last radio address, delivered on 30 January 1945, the twelfth anniversary of his seizure of power, he said not a word about the genocide that was still going on. Indeed, reflecting on the German losses in the field, he turned the real situation on its head and reported that the tens and hundreds of thousands of German soldiers on the eastern front who had been 'struck down by a tragic fate' had been 'victims of an international Jewish conspiracy'.[118]

But Hitler's truth had from the beginning been a perverted truth. It was not reality that counted but the stage directions that instructed how that reality should be enacted. In Hitler's production the world became a stage on which an apocalyptic final battle was to be fought out between the creative Aryan race, which Wagner had formerly called the 'Wälsungen', and the destructive tribe of 'Nibelungen', the 'forces of darkness and death'. This was the drama that had to be presented and its outcome decided, culminating in an apotheosis of Wagner's *Gesamtkunstwerk*. And over the millions of dead bodies would ring out the triumphant strains of Schiller's 'Ode to Joy'.

Only by enabling his suffering people to rise again victorious from this battle, Hitler believed, could he give their existence metaphysical meaning. 'Only when this mighty world drama is over,' he proclaimed in his final speech to the nation, 'and the bells of peace ring out, will the world recognize what the German people owe to this spiritual rebirth' – in other words, what they owe to the role that he, Hitler, had assigned to them. 'It is nothing less than the survival of their whole existence on this planet.'

Yet Hitler too, himself barely less great, in his own eyes, than the 'great prophetic genius' whose auguries he had been called upon to fulfil, had left his own indelible mark on history. As an anointed saviour, he told Hermann Rauschning, he wanted

to devote himself to the highest and noblest of all tasks – that of proclaiming the new faith which would stand as the culmination of his life's work. For if the era of Christianity is to make way for Hitler's Thousand-Year Reich, it will not be in response to some external political demand but the result of the proclamation of that new doctrine of salvation for which mankind is waiting.[119]

Hitler had set his sights high. At the end he had reduced a continent to rubble and almost completely exterminated the Jews of Europe. But to him, as he looked back on his fifty-six years, at one end the Linz opera house, at the other the Berlin bunker, this was part and parcel of the grand world tragedy which, called '*Götterdämmerung*' by his idol, left the promise of the hero's rebirth. 'On this day when I am addressing you, however,' concluded the Führer, his eyes fixed on his own immortality,

> there is something else about which I wish to leave no doubt. In the face of a hostile environment I chose my path and followed it through from humble beginnings as an unknown figure to a successful and triumphant end. Often given up for dead, constantly the victim of those who wanted me dead – in the end I have emerged as the victor![120]

To the extent that we fail to see through his theatrical world, he could claim to be right.

NOTES

~~~

Where German sources are available in English translation, details have been added to the Bibliography.

Chapter 1 *Ein Heldenleben*

1 Adolf Hitler, *Hitlers Tischgespräche im Führerhauptquartier*, ed. Henry Picker, Stuttgart 1976, p. 94 (Hitler in the 'Wolf's Lair', 25–6 January 1942).

2 Guido Knopp, *Hitler. Eine Bilanz*, Berlin 1995, p. 249 (Hitler in October 1941).

3 Richard Wagner, *Das Braune Buch. Tagebuchaufzeichnungen 1865 bis 1882*, ed. Joachim Bergfeld, Munich 1988, p. 86. (Wagner on 11 September 1865: 'I am the most German man. I am the German spirit.')

4 König Ludwig II/Richard Wagner, *Briefwechsel*, 4 vols, ed. Wittelsbacher Ausgleichsfonds and Winifred Wagner, rev. Otto Strobel, Karlsruhe 1936–7, vol. 3, p. 230. (From a letter of Wagner's of 22 February 1881: 'I consider the Jewish race to be the arch-enemy of pure mankind and of all that is noble.')

5 Eberhard Jäckel, *Hitlers Herrschaft. Vollzug einer Weltanschauung*, Stuttgart 1986, p. 122 (Hitler on 2 April 1945).

6 Adolf Hitler, *Reden und Proklamationen 1932–1945*, 2 vols, ed. Max Domarus, Würzburg 1962–3, vol. 1 (Hitler's testament of 29 April 1945).

7 Knopp, *Hitler*, p. 163. (Hitler in 1941: 'Anyone entering the Reich Chancellery must feel that he is entering the presence of the Lord of the Universe.')

8 Uwe Bahnsen and James P. O'Donnell, *Die Katakombe. Das Ende in der Reichskanzlei*, Bergisch Gladbach 1981, p. 22. (Hauptsturmführer Helmut Neermann, a member of Hitler's staff in the bunker: 'In this underground concrete prison one felt as though one had been buried alive in a God-forsaken mortuary.')

9 Richard Wagner, *Dichtungen und Schriften*, 10 vols, ed. Dieter Borchmeyer, Frankfurt 1983, vol. 2, p. 274 (from 'Der Nibelungen-Mythus', a dramatic sketch of 1848).

10   Bahnsen and O'Donnell, *Die Katakombe*, p. 37
11   Ibid., p. 67. (Albert Speer: 'The drama that came to an end in that miserable Berlin bunker had its origin in Hitler's decision to conduct the war from the concrete catacombs that he had ordered to be built for the purpose – one of his many bizarre decisions, as well as being obviously and palpably wrong.')
12   Joseph Goebbels, *Tagebücher 1945*, Hamburg 1977, p. 211 (entry of 12 March 1945).
13   Ibid., p. 414. (Entry of 28 March 1945: 'At times he seems to be living in the clouds. But then, he has often descended from the clouds like a *deus ex machina*.')
14   Bahnsen and O'Donnell, *Die Katakombe*, p. 107. (Speer: 'Today I believe that at the core of his being, the centre of his temperament and his emotions, Hitler was hollow and empty.')
15   Joachim C. Fest, *Hitler. Eine Biographie*, Berlin 1973, p. 684. (Hitler in 1936, contrasting the 'glorious ritual death of the hero Siegfried' with the 'Jewish scum' in Vienna.)
16   Hitler, *Reden und Proklamationen*, vol. 2, pp. 2236f. (Hitler's testament: 'Centuries will pass before, one way or another, the seed will germinate and the world can experience a shining new dawn.')
17   Goebbels, *Tagebücher 1945*, p. 540. (Addendum to Hitler's testament of 29 April 1945: '. . . in the frenzied atmosphere of betrayal that surrounds the Führer in these critical days of the war'.)
18   Hermann Giesler, *Ein anderer Hitler*, Leoni am Starnberger See 1977, p. 402.
19   Nicolaus von Below, *Als Hitlers Adjutant 1937–1945*, Mainz 1980, p. 398. ('He talked of taking his own life.')
20   Hitler, *Reden und Proklamationen*, vol. 2, p. 2245 (statement by Hans Baur, Hitler's chief pilot).
21   Ibid.
22   Cosima Wagner, *Die Tagebücher*, 4 vols, ed. Martin Gregor-Dellin and Dietrich Mack, Munich 1982, vol. 2, p. 722. (Wagner on 4 September 1873 to the Frenchman Édouard Schuré: 'To be German and to want to be German means experiencing a yearning that cannot be fulfilled in Romance countries.')
23   Hitler, *Reden und Proklamationen*, vol. 2, p. 2237.
24   Goebbels, *Tagebücher 1945*, p. 448 (31 March, 1945).
25   Ibid., p. 450 (31 January 1945).
26   Ibid., p. 239 (14 March 1945).
27   Bahnsen and O'Donnell, *Die Katakombe*, p. 42.
28   Hitler, *Reden und Proklamationen*, vol. 1, p. 9. ('[H]is shoulders began to droop and his tendency to stoop, always present, became more pronounced.')
29   Fest, *Hitler*, p. 1000. (Entry made by Goebbels. According to Fest, the news of Roosevelt's death on 12 April 1945 'was greeted in the bunker with wild enthusiasm.')
30   Bahnsen and O'Donnell, *Die Katakombe*, p. 53 (according to SS-Oberscharführer Rochus Misch, who worked in the telephone exchange in the bunker).
31   Brigitte Hamann, *Hitlers Wien. Lehrjahre eines Diktators*, Munich 1996, p. 11.
32   Adolf Hitler, *Monologe im Führerhauptquartier 1941–1944. Die Aufzeichnungen Heinrich Heims*, ed. Werner Jochmann, Munich 1982, p. 153 (17 December 1941).
33   Among the scores, according to Wieland Wagner, were the manuscript scores of *Die Feen*, *Das Liebesverbot* and *Rienzi*, the orchestral sketch of *Der fliegende Holländer*, fair copies of the scores of *Die Walküre* and *Das Rheingold* and fair copies of the orchestral sketch of the prelude and first act of *Götterdämmerung*.

Winifred Wagner's list, as given by Speer, differs from that quoted by her son in respect of the last item: 'Copy of the orchestral sketch of *Götterdämmerung*, made by Wagner, Hans Richter and various copyists' (Albert Speer, *Spandauer Tagebücher*, Berlin 1975, p. 157).

34 Hans Jürgen Syberberg in *Zeit Magazin*, 30 April 1976. ('Sold by the Wittelsbachs for 800,000 Reichsmarks. They then added: "under duress, instigated by Bayreuth." Icebergs beneath the surface, concealed by Winifred Wagner's words.')

35 Speer, *Spandauer Tagebücher*, p. 157. ('He was particularly excited by the orchestral sketch of *Götterdämmerung*, which he showed his guests page by page, providing an expert running commentary on the work as he did so.')

36 Hans Jürgen Syberberg, 'Winifred Wagner und die Geschichte des Hauses Wahnfried 1914–1975', film interview with Winifred Wagner 1975.

37 Hans Severus Ziegler, *Adolf Hitler aus dem Erleben dargestellt*, Göttingen 1964, p. 132.

38 Goebbels, *Tagebücher 1945*, p. 410 (28 March 1945, under which date Goebbels also records that 'the Führer was furious at the news of this treachery' – referring to the German collapse on the western front).

39 Hartmut Zelinsky, *Richard Wagner. Ein Deutsches Thema. Eine Dokumentation zur Wirkungsgeschichte Richard Wagners 1876–1976*, new edn Berlin 1983, p. 169. (Letter from Chamberlain to Hitler, 7 October 1923. Zelinsky's work, first published in 1976, contains the most important collection of documents concerning the relationship between National Socialism and Bayreuth.)

40 Theodor Heuss, *Hitlers Weg*, ed. Eberhard Jäckel, Tübingen 1968, p. 28.

41 Wolfgang Wagner, *Lebens-Akte. Autobiographie*, Munich 1994, p. 46 (a documentation of the ways in which the Bayreuth tradition continues to manipulate the facts of history).

42 Zelinsky, *Richard Wagner*, p. 170 (Chamberlain's pamphlet of 1 January 1924).

43 Winfried Schüler, *Der Bayreuther Kreis von seiner Entstehung bis zum Ausgang der Wilhelminischer Ära*, Münster 1971, p. 126. (Hitler's delight is described in a letter of 17 October 1923 from Josef Stolzing-Czerny to Eva Chamberlain.)

44 Gerhard Boldt, *Die letzten Tage der Reichskanzlei*, Hamburg 1947, p. 80. ('[A]n incessant rumble of gunfire set in on 28 April 1945.')

45 Hitler, *Reden und Proklamationen*, vol. 2, p. 2239.

46 Richard Wagner, *Gesammelte Schriften und Dichtungen*, 10 vols, ed. Richard Wagner, Leipzig 1871–83, vol. 5, p. 85. ('Remember – only one thing can release you from the curse that has been laid on you – the salvation that came to Ahasverus, namely, destruction!' – the final words of 'Das Judentum in der Musik.')

47 Hitler, *Reden und Proklamationen*, vol. 2, p. 2237.

48 Wagner, *Gesammelte Schriften und Dichtungen*, vol. 2, p. 274. (In his 'Nibelungen-Mythus' Wagner calls the underworld the 'bosom of night and of death' from which the Nibelungen emerge.)

49 Hitler, *Reden und Proklamationen*, vol. 2, pp. 2236 f.

50 Goebbels, *Tagebücher 1945*, p. 404 (28 March 1945: 'A doom-laden atmosphere has settled over the Führer's military advisers').

51 Bahnsen and O'Donnell, *Die Katakombe*, p. 273.

52 Franz Liszt/Richard Wagner, *Briefwechsel*, ed. Hanjo Kesting, Frankfurt 1988, p. 267. (Letter from Wagner to Liszt on 11 February 1853 in which he draws an analogy between his *Ring* and the downfall of the Jews. 'Would that I could perish in the flames of Valhalla! Take heed of my words – they embrace both

the creation and the destruction of the world! I shall soon set about composing the work for the Jews of Frankfurt and Leipzig – it is designed entirely with them in mind!')

53   Below, *Als Hitlers Adjutant*, p. 409. ('That day, the 12th of April, had one more unforgettable experience for me. Speer had arranged a farewell concert by the Berlin Philharmonic Orchestra for the afternoon, at which we heard the closing scene of Wagner's *Götterdämmerung*.')

54   'Hitlers Höllenfahrt' in *Der Spiegel*, 10 April 1995.

55   Fest, *Hitler*, p. 1021.

56   Bahnsen and O'Donnell, *Die Katakombe*, p. 269. ('After Blondi had been killed, Sergeant Tornow shot the five puppies that had been born in March, together with the dogs belonging to Eva Braun and Hitler's secretary Gerda Christian, and finally Hitler's own.')

57   Fest, *Hitler*, p. 993.

58   Hitler, *Reden und Proklamationen*, vol. 2, p. 2227. (According to Domarus, Hitler declared that the war was lost and announced his intention to commit suicide. General Eckhard Christian left an account of the dramatic events of that day, 22 April. 'The following day, however,' Domarus continued, 'Hitler had recovered from his depression. Maybe it was only the final trial he had to undergo – the onslaught of fate.')

59   Christa Schroeder, *Er war mein Chef. Aus dem Nachlass der Sekretärin von Adolf Hitler*, ed. Anton Joachimsthaler, Munich 1985, p. 134. (In conversation with Heinrich Hoffmann on 12 March 1944 in Berchtesgaden Hitler discussed the sketches and paintings he had done in his pre-Nazi days: 'You must never forget that all the ideas and architectural plans I make today go back to what I taught myself in those early years when I was burning the midnight oil.')

60   *Götterdämmerung*, act 3, scene 3.

61   Hans Mayer, *Richard Wagner in Bayreuth: 1876–1976*, Frankfurt 1978, p. 125. (Letter from Heinz Tietjen to Winifred Wagner, 17 December 1944: 'You will be surprised to learn that when the Führer asked whether the Festival could be held in Bayreuth in July 1945, I was able to reply unhesitatingly Yes. Commands from the Führer were as unnecessary as they had been in the past.')

62   Michael Karbaum, *Studien zur Geschichte der Bayreuther Festspiele 1876–1976*, 2 vols, Regensburg 1976, vol. 1, p. 91. ('On 13 January 1945 Wieland Wagner informed Otto Strobel, director of the research centre, that, judging this to be a unique opportunity, he had approached the Führer about the project and asked him for a decision – for in view of the immense difficulties involved there was no chance of carrying it through without his express approval.' According to Wieland's widow, Gertrud Wagner, this meeting took place some time in 1944. Karbaum's book is the most important collection of documents relating to the history of the Bayreuth Festival.)

63   Syberberg, 'Winifred Wagner.'

64   Gertrud Wagner in conversation with the author, 1996.

65   Syberberg in *Zeit Magazin* (see n. 34).

66   Karbaum, *Studien zur Geschichte*, vol. 2, p. 69. (Hans Conrad, 'Der Führer und Bayreuth', in *Bayerische Ostmark*, special supplement, 25–6 July 1936.)

67   Gertrud Wagner in 1996. Wieland's widow disputes the version of events given by Winifred and Wolfgang Wagner, according to which Wieland visited Hitler in the bunker in April 1945 and requested the release of the scores. 'Wieland spoke only once to Hitler about the manuscripts, and that was in 1944 at a

dinner in the Reich Chancellery to which my husband and myself, together
with Wieland's sister Verena and her husband Bodo Lafferentz, had been invited. Hitler, whose left arm was trembling, never stopped stroking his dog
Blondi, I recall. The Führer rejected Wieland's request. The following year my
husband and Bodo Lafferntz made a second attempt to see Hitler in Berlin but
the autobahn was choked, and with their wood-burning automobile they had
to give up in despair. When Wolfgang says that they managed to contact Hitler's adjutant, he is mistaken. They did not even get to Berlin.' Wolfgang
Wagner's account is given in his *Lebens-Akte*, p. 118: 'On 6 April Wieland and
Bodo Lafferentz travelled to Berlin to try to persuade Hitler to return the Wagner
manuscripts to Bayreuth which he had been given as a fiftieth birthday present
by the Confederation of German Industrialists, and which were held in the
bunker beneath the Chancellery. They did not get to see the Führer himself
but only his adjutant, who told them that the manuscripts were nowhere safer
than in the vaults of the bunker.'

68 Anton Joachimsthaler, *Korrektur einer Biographie. Adolf Hitler 1908–1920*, Munich 1989, p. 262. ('On 23 April 1945 Schaub flew from Berlin to Munich on
the Führer's orders and destroyed the contents, first of the steel safe in his
apartment at Prinzregentenplatz 16, then of his study in the Berghof in
Berchtesgaden.')

69 Hitler, *Reden und Proklamationen*, vol. 2, p. 2227 (report by General Eckhard
Christian at 20.45 on 22 April 1945).

70 Bahnsen and O'Donnell, *Die Katakombe*, p. 198 (statement by SS-Oberscharführer
Rochus Misch).

71 Ibid., p. 160 (Hitler to Hans Baur).

72 Ibid., p. 198 (SS-Oberscharführer Rochus Misch, who managed the telephone
exchange in the bunker).

73 Wolfgang Wagner, *Lebens-Akte*, p. 127.

74 Houston Stewart Chamberlain, *Richard Wagner*, Munich 1901, p. 4.

75 Ibid., p. 501.

76 Ibid., p. 505.

77 Ibid., p. 161. ('Wagner is a German in the exclusive sense of the word and at
the same time a universal genius in the image of Jesus Christ.' One of the strata-
gems practised by Bayreuth was to preach compassion and world redemption
while specifically excluding the Jews.)

78 Ibid., p. 216.

79 Ibid., p. 224.

80 Ibid., p. 61.

81 Ibid., p. 120.

82 *Tristan und Isolde*, act 3, scene 1.

83 Hitler, *Reden und Proklamationen*, vol. 2, p. 2234. ('Goebbels had summoned
Gauamtsleiter Walter Wagner, an official registrar, to perform the ceremony.')

84 Ibid., p. 2240.

85 Hugh Trevor-Roper in the *Frankfurter Allgemeine Zeitung*, 14 September 1988.
(He even planned and announced the precise moment at which he would die,
as one of his doctors, Dr Ernst Günther Schenck, recalled. 'After visiting Hitler,' wrote Schenck, 'Professor Werner Haase told me that Hitler had decided
to take his own life at three o'clock that afternoon – an announcement so formal and matter-of-fact that I could not get it out of my mind. . . . It was his last
official act' [Ernst Günther Schenck, *Das Notlazarett unter der Reichskanzlei. Ein*

Arzt erlebt Hitlers Ende in Berlin, Neuried 1995].)
86 Bahnsen and O'Donnell, *Die Katakombe*, p. 296.
87 Christa Schroeder, *Er war mein Chef*, p. 189.

‚Chapter 2 The Last of the Tribunes

1 Thomas Mann, *Das essayistische Werk. Politische Schriften und Reden*, 3 vols, ed. Hans Bürgin, Frankfurt 1968, vol. 3, p. 53. The article 'Bruder Hitler' first appeared in 1939 in Paris.
2 Thomas Mann, *Wagner und unsere Zeit. Aufsätze, Betrachtungen, Briefe*, ed. Erika Mann, Frankfurt 1983, p. 16. (From 'Versuch über das Theater', 1908, in which Mann addresses the transition from art to religion. 'Symbolism and ritual – only one step further, barely a step, and we find ourselves at the point where drama becomes ritual, worship – theatre at its peak, namely the Green Hill in Bayreuth, theatre that bears the name 'Parsifal'. . . . If one thinks out these thoughts to their natural conclusion, there seems no reason why, at some point in the future, the theatre should not inherit the banner of religion and become a religious temple.')
3 Ibid., p. 31 ('Betrachtungen eines Unpolitischen', 1918).
4 Ibid., p. 37.
5 Ibid., p. 31.
6 Rupert Hacker (ed.), *Ludwig II von Bayern in Augenzeugenberichten*, Munich 1972, p. 33. (The fifteen-year-old Crown Prince saw *Parsifal* for the first time on 2 February 1861. His biographer Gottfried von Böhm records that he 'quickly learned the libretto by heart, together with those of all Wagner's other operas, and read his prose works with passionate enthusiasm'.)
7 Adolf Hitler, *Mein Kampf*, 763rd–767th impression, Munich 1942, p. 15 – one of the few explicit references to Wagner in the work. There is only one reference in the index.
8 Joachim C. Fest, *Hitler. Eine Biographie*, Frankfurt 1973, p. 38.
9 Werner Maser, *Adolf Hitler. Legende, Mythos, Wirklichkeit*, Munich 1974, p. 67. (An assessment of his former pupil by Professor Eduard Huemer during the Putsch trial of 1924: 'Hitler certainly had talent, albeit of a one-sided nature, but only marginally kept himself under control.')
10 Adolf Hitler, *Sämtliche Aufzeichnungen 1905–1924*, ed. Eberhard Jäckel and Axel Kuhn, Stuttgart 1980, p. 1233 (letter of 5 May 1924 to Siegfried Wagner in Wahnfried, written from Landsberg prison).
11 *Mein Kampf*, p. 15.
12 Mann, *Wagner und unsere Zeit*, p. 30. (Letter of 14 September 1911 to Julius Bab: '. . . this snuff-taking gnome from Saxony with enormous talent and a despicable character.')
13 John Toland, *Adolf Hitler*, London 1997, p. 21 (postcard of 7 May 1906 to August Kubizek). [Translation modified – Translator's Note.]
14 Adolf Hitler, *Monologe im Führerhauptquartier 1941–1944. Die Aufzeichnungen Heinrich Heims*, ed. Werner Jochmann, Munich 1982, p. 288 (20–1 February 1942; just before this Hitler said that 'the world ought to do everything possible to meet the demands of a genius like Richard Wagner').
15 Walter C. Langer, *The Mind of Adolf Hitler. The Secret Wartime Report*, New York 1972, p. 92. (Hitler to the American journalist Frederick Oechsner: 'For me

Wagner is a god, and his music is my religion. I go to his operas as others go to church.') [Translation modified – Translator's Note.]

16 August Kubizek, *Adolf Hitler. Mein Jugendfreund*, Graz 1953, p. 138.
17 *Mein Kampf*, p. 14.
18 Kubizek, *Adolf Hitler*, p. 140.
19 Beatrice and Helmut Heiber (eds), *Die Rückseite des Hakenkreuzes. Absonderliches aus den Akten des Dritten Reiches*, Munich 1993, p. 72. (Letter of 21 July 1939, in which Kubizek writes that in 'those glowing days of our youth . . . Bayreuth shone out time and again as a brilliant star in the firmament of German art.')
20 Kubizek, *Adolf Hitler*, p. 141.
21 Albert Speer, *Spandauer Tagebücher*, Berlin 1975, p. 136 (on the occasion of the Bayreuth Festival of 1938).
22 Adolf Hitler, *Hitlers Tischgespräche im Führerhauptquartier*, ed. Henry Picker, Stuttgart 1976, p. 53.
23 Ibid., p. 95.
24 Kubizek, *Adolf Hitler*, p. 341.
25 Ibid., p. 142. (Before saying goodbye to his friend, Hitler gave him a tour of Wahnfried as though the house belonged to him. 'As young Wieland opened the rooms for me one by one, Hitler explained their significance. First he took me through the old part of the building. . . . In the music room stood the grand piano at which the Master had composed – it was open, a symbolic gesture which moved me to the quick.' Ibid., p. 342.)
26 Otto Wagener, *Hitler aus nächster Nähe. Aufzeichnungen eines Vertrauten 1929–1932*, ed. Henry A. Turner, Kiel 1987, p. 352.
27 Guido Knopp, *Hitler. Eine Bilanz*, Berlin 1995, p. 117.
28 Otto Strasser, *Mein Kampf*, Frankfurt 1969, p. 98.
29 *Rienzi*, act 2.
30 Fest, *Hitler*, p. 546.
31 *Rienzi*, act 2.
32 Wagener, *Hitler aus nächster Nähe*, p. 353.
33 *Rienzi*, act 2.
34 *Rienzi*, act 3. In the last words that he utters before plunging into the flames, Rienzi pronounces a curse on the city of Rome.
35 *Rienzi*, act 5.
36 Wagener, *Hitler aus nächster Nähe*, p. 99. (As well as vowing never to marry, Hitler pledged himself to celibacy. 'If I am to succeed in becoming a hero to the German people, then the people shall never be encumbered with any child of mine. What would Siegfried Wagner have become if, as well as being his father's son, he had not also been heir to Bayreuth and had at his side his mother Cosima and his equally impressive consort Winifred?')
37 *Rienzi*, act 1.
38 Ibid.
39 *Reichstagung in Nürnberg 1935. Der Parteitag der Freiheit*, ed. Hanns Kerrl, Berlin 1936, p. 418.
40 Speer, *Spandauer Tagebücher*, p. 136. (Robert Ley, organizational head of the Nazi Party, commissioned various new pieces, but, having listened to them, Hitler decided to remain with *Rienzi*, his favourite.)
41 Adolf Hitler, *Reden und Proklamationen 1932–1945*, 2 vols, ed. Max Domarus, Würzburg 1962–3, vol. 2, p. 2139 (Hitler to a meeting of Nazi leaders in the 'Wolf's Lair' on 4 August 1944).

42 *Rienzi*, act 1.

43 Hermann Giesler, *Ein anderer Hitler. Bericht seines Architekten*, Leoni am Starnberger See 1977, p. 99. ('I used to clamber over these rocks when I was a boy,' said Hitler, referring to the Freinberg in Linz. 'Build me a house there for my old age!')

44 Ibid., p. 406.

45 Speer, *Spandauer Tagebücher*, p. 255.

46 Ibid., p. 136.

47 Fest, *Hitler*, p. 65.

48 Richard Wagner, *Sämtliche Briefe*, ed. G. Strobel, W. Wolf, H. J. Bauer and J. Forner, Leipzig 1967–, vol. 1, p. 507 (letter of 6 or 7 September 1841).

49 *Die Sarazenin*, opera in five acts, conceived in 1841. The central character was to be Manfred, son of the Hohenstaufen Emperor Friedrich II.

50 Richard Wagner, *Mein Leben*, 2 vols, ed. Eike Middell, Leipzig 1986, vol. 1, p. 16.

51 Ernest Newman, *The Life of Richard Wagner*, 4 vols, London 1933–47, vol. 2, p. 614 (letter from Chamberlain to Hellmunth, 12 December 1913).

52 *Goethe-Jahrbuch*, vol. 106, ed. Karl-Heinz Hahn, Weimar 1989, p. 250 (information given by Volker L. Sigismund in his article 'Ein unbehauster Prinz – Constantin von Sachsen-Weimar 1758–1793', p. 269).

53 Wagner, *Sämtliche Briefe*, vol. 1, p. 97. (Wagner's well-known remark, modified by Hitler, occurs in his 'Autobiographische Skizze'.)

54 Carl Friedrich Glasenapp (ed.), *Wagner-Enzyklopädie*, vol. 2, Leipzig 1891, p. 103.

55 Herbert Barth, Dietrich Mack and Egon Voss (eds), *Richard Wagner. Leben und Werk in zeitgenössischen Bildern und Dokumenten*, Munich 1982, p. 303 (from Berlioz's fifth letter on his first journey through Germany).

56 Heinrich Heine, *Werke*, vol. 3, Frankfurt 1978, p. 504 (from part two of 'Lutezia').

57 Wagner, *Sämtliche Briefe*, vol. 1, p. 112 (the final sentence of the 'Autobiographische Skizze', which left a lasting impression on Hitler).

58 *Rienzi*, act 1.

59 Ibid., act 2.

60 Ibid., act 3.

61 Ibid., act 1.

62 Wagner, *Mein Leben*, vol. 1, p. 159.

63 John Deathridge, Martin Geck and Egon Voss (eds), *Wagner–Werk–Verzeichnis*, Mainz 1986, p. 163.

64 Richard Wagner, *Dichtungen und Schriften*, 10 vols, ed. Dieter Borchmeyer, Frankfurt 1983, vol. 1, p. 103. (Planned as a comic opera in two acts, the work has as its full title 'Man's Cunning Greater than Woman's Cunning, or The Happy Family of Bears'.).

65 Ibid., p. 110.

66 Richard Wagner, *Gesammelte Schriften und Dichtungen*, 10 vols, ed. Richard Wagner, Leipzig 1871–83, vol. 5, pp. 74 and 85.

67 Wagner, *Dichtungen und Schriften*, vol. 1, p. 117.

68 Ibid., p. 129.

69 Barth et al. (eds), *Richard Wagner, Leben und Werk*, p. 299 (letter of 18 March 1841 from Meyerbeer to Wolf von Lüttichau, General Administrator).

70 Wagner, *Sämtliche Briefe*, vol. 1, p. 98.

71 Eckart Kröplin, *Richard Wagner. Theatralisches Leben und lebendiges Theater*, Leip-

zig 1989, p. 15 (Heinrich Dorn in the *Neue Zeitschrift für Musik*, 1837).

72 Barth et al. (eds), *Richard Wagner. Leben und Werk*, p. 301 (letter from Ferdinand Heine, costume designer, set designer of *Rienzi* and great-grandfather of Hitler's friend Ernst Hanfstaengl).

73 Clara Schumann, *Tagebücher*, vol. 2, ed. Gerd Nauhaus, Leipzig 1987, p. 257. (Entry by Clara in February 1843: 'On the 12th I finally saw two acts of the great *Rienzi*, which is driving the whole of Dresden wild. . . . My own feeling was one of dislike.')

74 Richard Wagner, *Familienbriefe 1832–1874*, ed. C.F. Glasenapp, Berlin 1907, p. 75 (letter of 21 October 1842 to Eduard and Cäcilie Avenarius).

75 Wagner, *Sämtliche Briefe*, vol. 2, p. 182 (letter of 30 November 1842 to Samuel Schmidt, in which he acknowledges working in this style).

76 *Familienbriefe*, p. 81 (letter of 6 November 1842 to Eduard and Cäcilie Avenarius).

77 Barth et al. (eds), *Richard Wagner. Leben und Werk*, p. 302.

78 Wagner, *Sämtliche Briefe*, vol. 2, p. 223 (letter of 25 February 1843, in which he also says that mentioning him in the same breath as Meyerbeer is tantamount to pronouncing 'a sentence of death on my creative power').

79 Erich Haenel and Eugen Kalckschmidt (eds), *Das alte Dresden. Bilder und Dokumente aus zwei Jahrhunderten*, Bindlach 1995, p. 384 (a quotation from Beust's memoirs published under the title *Aus drei Vierteljahrhunderten*).

80 Nicolaus von Below, *Als Hitlers Adjutant 1937–1945*, Mainz 1980, p. 76. (Below adds: 'At the same time he did not deny the qualities that made him a musician.')

Chapter 3 Dresden Burns

1 Richard Wagner, *Sämtliche Briefe*, ed. G. Strobel, W. Wolf, H.-J. Bauer and J. Forner, Leipzig 1967–, vol. 2, p. 586 (letter of 4 January 1848 to Johann Kittl, to whom he had sold his libretto).

2 Eckart Kröplin, *Richard Wagner. Theatralisches Leben und lebendiges Theater*, p. 53 (*Leipziger Reibeisen*, 24 July 1849).

3 Lutz Heydick, *Leipzig: Historischer Führer zu Stadt und Land*, Leipzig n.d., p. 57.

4 Hans-Ulrich Wehler, *Deutsche Gesellschaftsgeschichte*, 2 vols, Munich 1987, vol. 2, p. 352.

5 Richard Wagner, *Mein Leben*, 2 vols, ed. Eike Middell, Leipzig 1986, vol. 1, p. 49.

6 Ibid., p. 51.

7 Ibid., p. 53.

8 Heydick, *Leipzig*, p. 58.

9 Wagner, *Mein Leben*, vol. 1, p. 50.

10 Jörg von Uthmann, *Attentat. Mord mit gutem Gewissen*, Berlin 1996, p. 70.

11 Hans-Joachim Bauer, *Richard-Wagner-Lexikon*, Bergisch Gladbach 1988, p. 168. ('Flame of Joy' was his pseudonym for the articles he wrote for August Lewald's weekly *Europa*.)

12 Schiller, *Sämtliche Werke*, vol. 1, ed. Gerhard Fricke and Herbert G. Göpfert, Munich 1958, p. 135.

13 Heinz Schirmag, *Albert Lortzing. Glanz und Elend eines Künstlerlebens*, Berlin 1995, p. 170.

14 Ibid., p. 174.

15 Ibid., p. 107.
16 Eduard Hanslick, *Aus meinem Leben*, 2 vols, vol. 1, Berlin 1894, p. 134.
17 Richard Wagner, *Dichtungen und Schriften*, 10 vols, ed. Dieter Borchmeyer, Frankfurt 1983, vol. 9, p. 13 ('Review of the Performance of Beethoven's Ninth Symphony in Dresden in 1846').
18 Ibid., p. 14.
19 Ibid., p. 26.
20 Heinrich Reimann, *Hans von Bülow. Sein Leben und sein Wirken*, vol. 1: *Aus Hans von Bülows Lehrzeit*, Berlin n.d., p. 125.
21 Ibid., p. 127.
22 Wagner, *Mein Leben*, vol. 1, p. 459.
23 Richard Wagner, *Das Braune Buch. Tagebuchaufzeichnungen 1865 bis 1882*, ed. Joachim Bergfeld, Munich 1988, p. 115.
24 Ernest Newman, *The Life of Richard Wagner*, 4 vols, London 1933–47, vol. 2, p. 100.
25 Eckart Kröplin, *Richard Wagner*, p. 52 (*Kleine Musikzeitung*, 20 May 1849).
26 Wagner, *Sämtliche Briefe*, vol. 2, p. 232 (letter to Samuel Lehrs, 7 April 1843).
27 Werner Otto (ed.), *Richard Wagner. Ein Lebens- und Charakterbild in Dokumenten und zeitgenössischen Darstellungen*, Berlin 1990, p. 179. (In the autumn of 1856 Princess Marie Wittgenstein, daughter of Liszt's mistress and one-time idol of Wagner's, wrote that 'his, Wagner's, belief in himself and his revolutionary mission had reached the point of supreme exaltation. Not even a Mohammed or a Jan van Leyden could feel a more intense conviction of being a prophet of the Lord. . . . He was no longer satisfied with being a reformer of the opera but saw his art as a kind of religion' [Marie Fürstin zu Hohenlohe, *Erinnerungen an Richard Wagner*, Weimar 1938].)
28 Eduard Devrient, *Aus seinen Tagebüchern, Berlin–Dahlem 1836–1852*, ed. Rolf Kabel, Weimar 1964, p. 465. (Entry of 26 January 1849: 'Then he said that he could not understand how I could think so highly of Richard Wagner – he hated him intensely.')
29 Ibid., p. 451 (entry of 21 October 1848).
30 *Lohengrin*, act 1, scene 3. ('The barque, drawn by the swan, reaches the shore in the centre background; in it, leaning on his sword, stands Lohengrin in shining silver armour, his helmet on his head, his shield on his back and a small golden horn at his side' – the prototype of the German Messiah.)
31 Richard Wagner, *Sämtliche Schriften und Dichtungen*, 16 vols, Leipzig 1911–14, vol. 12, p. 225 ('Wie verhalten sich republikanische Bestrebungen dem Königtume gegenüber?', talk given to the Vaterlandsverein on 14 June 1848).
32 Newman, *The Life of Richard Wagner*, vol. 2, p. 11.
33 Wagner, *Sämtliche Schriften und Dichtungen*, vol. 12, p. 221.
34 Ibid., p. 222.
35 Letter from Wagner to King Friedrich August II of Saxony, 21 June 1848, personally delivered by Eduard Devrient.
36 Wagner, *Sämtliche Schriften und Dichtungen*, vol. 12, p. 243 ('Die Revolution', 1849).
37 Ibid., p. 246.
38 Ibid., p. 358 ('Die Not', 1849).
39 Cosima Wagner, *Die Tagebücher*, 4 vols, ed. Martin Gregor-Dellin and Dietrich Mack, Munich 1982, vol. 1, p. 272. (Entry of 18 August 1870: 'R. said he hoped that Paris, this "kept woman of the world", would go up in flames. . . . A Paris

in flames would symbolize the liberation of the world from everything evil. ... R. feels like writing to Bismarck to ask him to raze Paris to the ground.')

40 Newman, *The Life of Richard Wagner*, vol. 4, p. 599. (Remark made in 1880 to Paul von Joukowski, designer of *Parsifal*. The destruction of Leningrad was also one of Hitler's war aims.)

41 Wagner, *Sämtliche Briefe*, vol. 3, p. 452. Referring to the revolution, which will restore a sense of reality to the world, Wagner writes: 'Our redeemer will quickly destroy everything that stands in our way' (p. 461).

42 Joachim C. Fest, *Fremdheit und Nähe. Von der Gegenwart des Gewesenen*, Stuttgart 1996, p. 297. (Fest's address 'Um einen Wagner von aussen bittend' appeared in the *Frankfurter Allgemeine Zeitung*, on 5 June 1995. He concludes: 'It is time, I think, to consider Wagner from an external perspective, something that has not been done for a long time. Moreover this should involve not just one discipline but involve politics, social sciences, cultural history and the history of ideology.')

43 Otto (ed.), *Richard Wagner. Ein Lebens- und Charakterbild*, p. 178 (Marie Wittgenstein, later Princess Hohenlohe).

44 Newman, *The Life of Richard Wagner*, vol. 2, p. 95.

45 Martin Gregor-Dellin, *Richard Wagner. Sein Leben, Sein Werk, sein Jahrhundert*, Munich 1980, p. 201.

46 Ibid., p. 249.

47 Günter Jaeckel (ed.), *Dresden zwischen Wiener Kongress und Maiaufstand*, Berlin 1989, p. 245. (Julius Schladebach, conductor of the Dresden choir: 'Wagner, at the time the all-powerful protégé of the artistic director's. ... Röckel is a worthy pianist but not an effective conductor. ... He probably owes his appointment, renewed from year to year, to the influence of Wagner, with whose cause he has identified himself and who can apparently use him as a loyal standard bearer.')

48 Gregor-Dellin, *Richard Wagner*, p. 249.

49 Woldemar Lippert, *Richard Wagners Verbannung und Rückkehr 1849–1862*, Dresden 1927, p. 215.

50 Ibid., p. 18.

51 Wagner, *Mein Leben*, vol. 1, p. 440.

52 Lippert, *Richard Wagners Verbannung*, p. 185 (letter of 20 February 1863 to Franz Adolf Schmidt, a Dresden attorney).

53 Erich Haenel and Eugen Kalckschmidt (eds), *Das alte Dresden. Bilder und Dokumente aus zwei Jahrhunderten*, Bindlach 1995, p. 387 (report by Count Friedrich Ferdinand Beust, the decisive voice in Saxon politics from 1849 onwards).

54 Newman, *The Life of Richard Wagner*, vol. 2, p. 75. (Letter from Schwender to Köchly, 14 June 1849. Schwender, who died in Dresden as a respected businessman in 1901, frequently maintained that Wagner acted as one of the leaders of the revolutionaries.)

55 Wagner, *Mein Leben*, vol. 1, p. 458.

56 Hermann Heckmann, *Matthäus Daniel Pöppelmann und die Barockkunst in Dresden*, Stuttgart 1986, p. 106.

57 Lippert, *Richard Wagners Verbannung*, p. 239.

58 Ibid., p. 152 (letter from Albin Leo von Seebach to Count Beust, 1 July 1860).

59 König Ludwig II/Richard Wagner, *Briefwechsel*, 4 vols, ed. Wittelsbacher Ausgleichsfonds and Winifred Wagner, rev. Otto Strobel, Karlsruhe 1936–7,

vol. 4, p. 177 (letter from Wagner to Röckel, 29 January 1867).

60   Haenel and Kalckschmidt (eds), *Das alte Dresden*, p. 363.
61   Wagner, *Sämtliche Briefe*, vol. 3, p. 532 (letter to Röckel's brother Eduard, 15 March 1851).
62   Wagner, *Mein Leben*, vol. 1, p. 449.
63   Newman, *The Life of Richard Wagner*, vol. 2, p. 80 (statement by the daughter of Alexander Müller, who was in close contact with Wagner in Zurich).
64   Ibid., p. 85 (*Neue Zeitschrift für Musik*, 21 June 1849).
65   Eckart Kröplin, *Richard Wagner*, p. 52 (*Leipziger Zeitung*, 20 May 1849).
66   Newman, *The Life of Richard Wagner*, vol. 2, p. 93.
67   Ernst Kreowski and Eduard Fuchs, *Richard Wagner in der Karikatur*, Berlin 1907, p. 41. ('Wagner keeps a look-out from the tower of the Kreuzkirche, carried away by the pealing of the bells, which, according to the report of Lieutenant Count Waldersee, commander of the Prussian auxiliaries in the city between the 4th and the 9th of May, he is said to have rung.')
68   Newman, *The Life of Richard Wagner*, vol. 2, p. 80.
69   Wagner, *Mein Leben*, vol. 1, p. 453.
70   Haenel and Kalckschmidt (eds), *Das alte Dresden*, p. 384.
71   Werner Maser, *Der Sturm auf die Republik*, Stuttgart 1973, p. 71 (handwritten memoir by Reinhold Hanisch, 'Meine Begegnung mit Hitler').
72   Ibid., p. 477.
73   Fest, *Fremdheit und Nähe*, p. 290.
74   Wagner, *Sämtliche Briefe*, vol. 3, p. 197 (letter to Theodor Uhlig, 27 December 1849).
75   Hans Severus Ziegler, *Adolf Hitler aus dem Erleben dargestellt*, Göttingen 1964, p. 125.
76   Brigitte Hamann, *Hitlers Wien. Lehrjahre eines Diktators*, Munich 1996, p. 162.
77   Wagner, *Sämtliche Briefe*, vol. 2, p. 653 (letter to Minna Wagner, 14 May 1849).
78   Ibid., p. 662 (letter from Wagner to Eduard Devrient, 17 May 1849).
79   Ibid., p. 669. (Devrient records that he spent the entire day drafting his reply to Wagner, having received from friends 'incontrovertible evidence of his involvement in leading the revolt'.)
80   Cosima Wagner, *Tagebücher*, vol. 1, p. 540 (27 June 1872).
81   Ibid., vol. 3, p. 105 (entry of 3 June 1878).

Chapter 4   Studies in the *Ring*

1   Robert G.L. Waite, *The Psychopathic God. Adolf Hitler*, New York 1977, p. 7.
2   Wagner, *Siegfried*, act 2, scene 3.
3   August Kubizek, *Adolf Hitler. Mein Jugendfreund*, Graz 1953, p. 188.
4   Ibid., p. 233. ('The opportunity to listen to Wagner was for Hitler not what one would call simply a visit to the opera but an occasion to indulge himself in that extraordinary state which Wagner's music invoked in him – a state of utter oblivion to his surroundings, hovering in a mystical world of dreams which he needed in order to counteract the tensions of his explosive nature.')
5   Ibid., p. 237.
6   Werner Maser, *Adolf Hitler. Legende, Mythos, Wirklichkeit*, Munich 1974, p. 84.
7   Brigitte Hamann, *Hitlers Wien. Lehrjahre eines Diktators*, Munich 1996, p. 60.
8   Ibid., p. 61.

9   Ibid., p. 88.
10   Karl-Josef Müller, *Mahler. Leben, Werke, Dokumente*, Mainz 1988, p. 538 (Oscar Bie, 1910).
11   Ibid., p. 254.
12   Siegrid Wiesmann (ed.), *Gustav Mahler in Wien*, Stuttgart 1976, p. 86.
13   Hans Severus Ziegler, *Adolf Hitler aus dem Erleben dargestellt*, Göttingen 1964, p. 125.
14   Hamann, *Hitlers Wien*, p. 89.
15   Ibid., p. 567.
16   Joachim C. Fest, *Hitler. Eine Biographie*, Frankfurt 1973, p. 1049. (Fest cites the American writer W.A. Jenks, who calculated that Wagner was without question the most often-played operatic composer in Vienna during Hitler's years there. In the Hofoper alone at least 426 evenings were devoted to his works.)
17   Friedelind Wagner, *Nacht über Bayreuth. Die Geschichte der Enkelin Richard Wagners*, Cologne 1994, p. 223. (The first edition appeared in America in 1944 under the title *Heritage of Fire*; as *Nacht über Bayreuth* it was first published in Switzerland in 1945.)
18   Oswald Georg Bauer, *Richard Wagner. Die Bühnenwerke von der Uraufführung bis heute*, Frankfurt/Berlin/Vienna 1982, p. 139. (This was the performance of *Tristan* in the Staatsoper on New Year's Day 1943, produced for the first time by Furtwängler.)
19   Ziegler, *Adolf Hitler aus dem Erleben dargestellt*, p. 70. ('Proof of the intensity with which he had studied *Tristan* came when I saw his stage designs, executed in watercolour, which Benno von Arent, the state designer, showed me in his villa by the Kleiner Wannsee.')
20   Adolf Hitler, *Sämtliche Aufzeichnungen 1905–1924*, ed. Eberhard Jäckel and Axel Kuhn, Stuttgart 1980, p. 1060. (Letter written 10 January 1924 in Landsberg prison to Herr Vogel: 'I constantly dream of *Tristan* and similar works.')
21   Hans-Jürgen Eitner, *Hitler. Ein Psychogramm*, Berlin 1994, p. 86 (from the conversation of 24–5 January 1942).
22   Albert Zoller (ed.), *Hitler privat. Erlebnisbericht seiner Geheimsekretärin*, Düsseldorf 1949, p. 47. ('The sounds of Wagner's music resounded through his head like a divine revelation,' said Christa Schroeder, one of Hitler's secretaries. Zoller's book is based on the records he compiled at the time of Schroeder's interrogation by the US 7th Army after the war.)
23   Hamann, *Hitlers Wien*, p. 344. (The declared aim of the organization was 'to get rid of all false and Jewish elements in German art' – this was also the vision first proclaimed by Wagner in his 'Das Judentum in der Musik' in 1850, a vision that was to reach its fulfilment with the total liberation of mankind from the presence of the Jews.)
24   Ibid., p. 364.
25   Adolf Hitler, *Hitlers Tischgespräche im Führerhauptquartier*, ed. Henry Picker, Stuttgart 1976, p. 95.
26   Adolf Hitler, *Monologe im Führerhauptquartier 1941–1944. Die Aufzeichnungen Heinrich Heims*, ed. Werner Jochmann, Munich 1982, p. 234.
27   Fest, *Hitler*, p. 683.
28   Adolf Hitler, *Mein Kampf*, 763rd–767th impression, Munich 1942, p. 59.
29   Ibid., p. 61.
30   Richard Wagner, *Sämtliche Briefe*, ed. G. Strobel, W. Wolf, H.-J. Bauer and J. Forner, Leipzig 1967–, vol. 3, p. 166. (Letter to Uhlig at the end of November

1849. Wagner follows up his talk of 'extirpation' with the no less radical demand: 'Let us concentrate our minds on young people and leave the old to rot – they are beyond hope.')

31 Karl-Heinz Kröplin, *Richard Wagner 1813–1883. Eine Chronik*, Leipzig 1983, p. 61. (According to Eduard Devrient, Wagner mentioned this plan on 1 April 1848.)

32 Ibid., p. 63.

33 Wagner, *Sämtliche Briefe*, vol. 3, p. 166 (letter to Uhlig at the end of November 1849).

34 Ibid., vol. 4, p. 176. (Letter to Uhlig, 12 November 1851: 'The next revolution will inevitably bring the entire world of the theatre crashing down . . . I will then extract from the ruins what I need . . . I will establish an opera house on the banks of the Rhine and invite people to attend a great festival of drama; after a year's preparation I shall then perform my entire work over a space of four days.')

35 Richard Wagner, *Mein Leben*, 2 vols, ed. Eike Middell, Leipzig 1986, vol. 1, p. 394. (His idea came from reading Gustav Droysen's *Didaskalien*, an appendix to the works of Aeschylus.)

36 Richard Wagner, *Familienbriefe 1832–1874*, ed. C.F. Glasenapp, Berlin 1907, p. 211. (Letter to his niece Clara Brockhaus, 12 March 1854. Wagner returned time and again to the vision of fire in connection with his *Nibelungen*. After the first Bayreuth Festival of 1876 he talked more than once about burning down the Festspielhaus, together with all the sets and costumes in it.)

37 Wagner, *Sämtliche Briefe*, vol. 4, p. 176. (Letter to Uhlig, 12 November 1851: 'Future audiences will understand me – today's audience cannot.')

38 *Götterdämmerung*, act 1, scene 2.

39 Franz Liszt/Richard Wagner, *Briefwechsel*, ed. Hanjo Kesting, Munich 1988, p. 267. ('Pay good heed to my new work,' said Wagner, referring to the destruction of Valhalla; 'it deals with the beginning and end of the world.')

40 Cosima Wagner, *Die Tagebücher*, 4 vols, ed. Martin Gregor-Dellin and Dietrich Mack, Munich 1982, vol. 3, p. 624. (Entry of 21 November 1880: 'R. says of himself, "I am the plenipotentiary of destruction" – this vision is constantly before his eyes.')

41 Wagner, *Sämtliche Briefe*, vol. 5, p. 118 (letter to Uhlig, 18 November 1852, signed 'Alberich – Your Prince of the Nibelungen').

42 Ibid., vol. 4, p. 385 (to Uhlig, shortly before finishing the poem in 1852).

43 *Die Walküre*, act 1, scene 3.

44 Udo Bermbach (ed.), *In den Trümmern der eignen Welt. Richard Wagners 'Ring des Nibelungen'*, Berlin/Hamburg 1989, p. 205 (letter from Wagner to Ludwig II, 17 May 1881, quoted from Hartmut Zelinsky 'Die deutsche Losung Siegfried').

45 Richard Wagner, *Briefe*, ed. Hanjo Kesting, Munich 1983, p. 530 (letter to Constantin Frantz, 19 March 1866).

46 Richard Wagner, *Sämtliche Schriften und Dichtungen*, 16 vols, Leipzig 1911–14, vol. 10, p. 274 ('Erkenne dich selbst').

47 Kubizek, *Adolf Hitler*, p. 101.

48 Ibid., p. 102.

49 Paul Devrient, *Mein Schüler Hitler. Das Tagebuch seines Lehrers Paul Devrient*, ed. Werner Maser, Pfaffenhofen 1975. (Diary entry of 2 December 1848: 'the subject turned to that of the state, where he inevitably mounted his hobby-

horse – the destruction of world finance'.)

50   Richard Wagner, *Briefe 1830–1883*, ed. Werner Otto, Berlin 1986, p. 427 (letter to Ernst von Weber, 14 August 1879).
51   Arthur Gobineau, *Ein Erinnerungsbild aus Wahnfried (von Cosima Wagner)*, Stuttgart 1907, p. 24. (Cosima's obituary in the *Bayreuther Blätter* for 1882 was reprinted by Ludwig Schemann.)
52   Official Bayreuth Festival programme of 1924 – *Bayreuther Festspielführer 1924*, ed. Karl Grunsky, Bayreuth 1924, p. 105 (Hans Alfred Grunsky, 'Der Ring des Nibelungen').
53   *Das Rheingold*, Prelude and act 1.
54   Richard Wagner, *Dichtungen und Schriften*, ed. Dieter Borchmeyer, vol. 2, Frankfurt 1983, p. 274. ('Der Nibelungen-Mythos', 1848: 'in constant, restless activity they burrow around in the entrails of the earth like worms in a corpse.')
55   Richard Wagner, *Gesammelte Schriften und Dichtungen*, 10 vols, ed. Richard Wagner, Leipzig 1871–83, vol. 5, p. 84 ('Das Judentum in der Musik').
56   *Das Rheingold*, Prelude and act 1.
57   Wagner, *Sämtliche Schriften und Dichtungen*, vol. 10, p. 268. ('Gold is seen as the demon that strangles the innocence of mankind . . .')
58   Cosima Wagner, *Tagebücher*, vol. 2, p. 1052 (entry of 25 May 1877).
59   Ibid., vol. 4, p. 692. (Entry of 15 February 1881: 'R. expressed his pleasure at having given in his *Ring* a complete picture of the curse of avarice and the destruction to which it leads.' Shortly before this he had drawn a strange parallel between his *Tannhäuser* and the death of Mendelssohn, saying, according to Cosima, that 'the impression made by the work might have stifled him, since he died shortly after'.)
60   Wagner, *Gesammelte Schriften und Dichtungen*, vol. 5, p. 66.
61   Ibid., p. 85.
62   Ibid., p. 68.
63   *Das Rheingold*, scene 2.
64   Ibid., scene 3.
65   Ibid., scene 4.
66   Jakob Grimm, *Deutsche Mythologie*, 3 vols, repr. Frankfurt 1981, vol. 1, p. 308. ('Such is the prominence given to Siegfried in the heroic lays that one is entitled to cast one's net wide . . . his whole nature bears unmistakable marks of the superman. . . . He unites the Frankish Wälsungen and the Burgundian Gibichungs, who from then on are called Nibelungen.')
67   König Ludwig II/Richard Wagner, *Briefwechsel*, 4 vols, ed. Wittelsbacher Ausgleichsfonds and Winifred Wagner, rev. Otto Strobel, Karlsruhe 1936–7, vol. 2, p. 258 (letter from Wagner, 24 February 1869).
68   *Götterdämmerung*, act 2, scene 1.
69   Ibid.
70   Ibid., act 3, scene 3.
71   Hamann, *Hitlers Wien*, p. 97.

Chapter 5 Dragon-Slayer by Profession

1   Hartmut Zelinsky, *Richard Wagner. Ein deutsches Thema. Eine Dokumentation zur Wirkungsgeschichte Richard Wagners 1876–1976*, new edn Berlin 1983, p. 50.
2   Ibid., p. 51. (Theodor Herzl on 7 March 1883 to the 'Albia' student society, one

of the organizers of the meeting: 'As an inactive member of the society, I apply to be released from my membership of it.')

3 Ibid., p. 51. (Letter from Bahr to his father, 13 March 1883. Bahr was sent down as a result of his provocative speech.)

4 Joachim C. Fest, *Hitler. Eine Biographie*, Frankfurt 1973, p. 66.

5 Marlis Steinert, *Hitler*, Munich 1994, p. 43.

6 Peter G. Pulzer, *The Rise of Political Antisemitism in Germany and Austria*, New York/London/Sydney 1964, p. 153. (The manifesto was issued in 1881. In 1885 the following sentence was added: 'For the implementation of these reforms it is essential to put an end to Jewish influence in all fields of public life.' [My translation from the German – Translator's Note.]

7 Marcel Prawy, *'Nun sei bedankt. . .'. Mein Richard-Wagner-Buch*, Munich 1983, p. 58. ('Hitler was one of the few who had really read Wagner's writings and was apparently impressed by their pseudo-scientific manner.')

8 Fest, *Hitler*, p. 65. ('Politically middle-class nationalist circles in Vienna were deeply impressed by Schönerer and Karl Lueger at the turn of the century; dominant in that striking area between politics and art, on the other hand, was the figure of Richard Wagner.')

9 Anniversary exhibition catalogue *100 Jahre Wiener Oper am Ring*, Vienna 1969, p. 59.

10 Adolf Hitler, *Mein Kampf*, 763rd–767th impression, Munich 1942, p. 107.

11 Fest, *Hitler*, p. 65.

12 Konrad Heiden, *Adolf Hitler*, 2 vols, Zurich 1936, vol. 1, p. 26.

13 Brigitte Hamann, *Hitlers Wien. Lehrjahre eines Diktators*, Munich 1996, p. 498.

14 John Toland, *Adolf Hitler*, London 1997, p. 46 (information provided by Helene Hanfstaengl in 1971).

15 Heiden, *Adolf Hitler*, vol. 1, p. 342. ('Hitler's intellectual enslavement to Wagner is highly revealing. As a person, Wagner was a characterless chameleon.')

16 Ibid., p. 6.

17 Ibid., p. 343.

18 Karl-Josef Müller, *Mahler. Leben, Werke, Dokumente*, Mainz 1988, p. 179. (Speech in the Austrian Chamber of Deputies, 28 April 1887: '. . . and this must be done very soon, before the people, at the mercy of their Semitic exploiters, are forced to take measures to defend themselves.')

19 Winfried Schüler, *Der Bayreuther Kreis von seiner Entstehung bis zum Ausgang der Wilhelminischen Ära*, Münster 1971, p. 128. (Cosima Wagner to the Jew-baiter Kniese: 'I regard your participation in our work not only as a great achievement in itself but as one of its foundations.')

20 Frithjof Haas, *Zwischen Brahms und Wagner. Der Dirigent Hermann Levi*, Zurich 1995, p. 282. (Kniese, who worked as Levi's assistant in 1883, 'sowed the seeds of violent controversy' and insisted that Levi's powers be restricted, 'so as to neutralize his harmful Jewish influence'.)

21 *Sinn und Form*, 1955, reprint Nördlingen 1988, p. 52. (In 'Four Days in Bayreuth', his impressions of his visit to the Bayreuth Festival in 1896, Romain Rolland wrote of Hans Breuer's characterization of Mime in *Siegfried*: 'I can still see him preparing the poison for Siegfried, cracking the eggs, wiping them clean with his finger, then drying himself on a rag.')

22 Wendelin Weissheimer, *Erlebnisse mit Richard Wagner, Franz Liszt und vielen anderen Zeitgenossen nebst ihren Briefen*, Stuttgart 1898, p. 119. ('Wagner excelled in this role. Bowing and scraping, he produced a screeching falsetto which

sent shivers down my spine; at the same time he pulled such grimaces that it was as though the ugly dwarf were there in person.')

23 Hans Bélart, *Gesangsdramatische Wagnerkunst (nach Richard Wagners Tradition)*, Dresden 1915, p. 131.
24 Hamann, *Hitlers Wien*, p. 92.
25 Herbert Killian, *Gustav Mahler in den Erinnerungen von Natalie Bauer-Lechner*, Hamburg 1984, p. 122.
26 Richard Wagner, *Dichtungen und Schriften*, 10 vols, ed. Dieter Borchmeyer, Frankfurt 1983, vol. 2, p. 289.
27 *Siegfried*, act 2, scene 3.
28 Fest, *Hitler*, p. 632.
29 *Siegfried*, act 1, scene 3.
30 Adolf Hitler, *Monologe im Führerhauptquartier 1941–1944. Die Aufzeichnungen Heinrich Heims*, ed. Werner Jochmann, p. 280 (statement of 17 February 1942).
31 Heiden, *Adolf Hitler*, vol. 1, p. 25.
32 *Siegfried*, act 1, scene 1.
33 Hitler, *Monologe*, p. 263 (3–4 February 1942).
34 *Siegfried*, act 2, scene 3.
35 Hitler, *Monologe*, p. 263 (3–4 February 1942).
36 *Siegfried*, act 2, scene 2.
37 Richard Wagner, *Sämtliche Schriften und Dichtungen*, 16 vols, ed. Richard Sternfeld Leipzig 1911–14, vol. 12, p. 221 ('Wie verhalten sich republikanische Bestrebungen dem Königtume gegenüber?').
38 Guido Knopp, *Hitler. Eine Bilanz*, Berlin 1995, p. 31.
39 *Das Rheingold*, scene 3.
40 Adolf Hitler, *Reden, Schriften, Anordnungen. Februar 1925 bis Januar 1933*, 3 vols, ed. Clems Vollnhals et al., Munich 1992–4, vol. 3, p. 124. (Article 'Politik der Woche' in the *Illustrierter Beobachter*, 30 March 1929, which, as well as talking of 'parliamentary dwarfs', 'Marxist poisons' and 'the dictatorship of gold', ends with the threat of a '*Götterdämmerung*' for those who promote left-wing ideas: 'The hour will come when the red flames will consume the reds themselves.')
41 *Das Rheingold*, scene 3.
42 Otto Wagener, *Hitler aus nächster Nähe. Aufzeichnungen eines Vertrauten 1929–1932*, ed. Henry A. Turner, Kiel 1987, p. 319.
43 Christa Schroeder, *Er war mein Chef. Aus dem Nachlass der Sekretärin von Adolf Hitler*, ed. Anton Joachimsthaler, Munich 1985, p. 149. (After the attempt on his life on 20 July 1944 Hitler said over afternoon tea: 'The criminals who tried to get rid of me have no idea what the effect would have been on the German people. They do not know the plans of our enemies who are set on destroying Germany so that it can never rise again.')
44 Konrad Heiden, *Geschichte des Nationalsozialismus. Die Karriere einer Idee*, Berlin 1933, p. 20.
45 Fest, *Hitler*, p. 165.
46 Theodor Heuss, *Hitlers Weg*, ed. Eberhard Jäckel, Tübingen 1968, p. 90.
47 Ralph Giordano, *Wenn Hitler den Krieg gewonnen hätte. Die Pläne der Nazis nach dem Endsieg*, Hamburg 1989.
48 Adolf Hitler, *Hitlers Tischgespräche im Führerhauptquartier*, ed. Henry Picker, Stuttgart 1976, p. 499 (address to young army officers on 30 May 1942).
49 *Götterdämmerung*, act 1, scene 2.
50 Wagener, *Hitler aus nächster Nähe*, p. 323 (Hitler, after England had given up

the gold standard in September 1931).

51 Adolf Hitler, *Reden und Proklamationen 1932–1945*, 2 vols, ed. Max Domarus, Würzburg 1962–3, vol. 2, p. 1829. (Speech on 30 January 1942 in the Berlin Sportpalast. That the destruction of the Jews was to run parallel with military operations was made clear by a particularly sinister sentence: 'The more extensive these battles become, the wider will become the scope of anti-Semitism – let the Jews be in no doubt about that.')

52 Christa Schroeder, *Er war mein Chef*, p. 9.

53 Eva Mendgen, *Franz von Stuck 1863–1928*, Cologne 1994, p. 17.

54 Ibid., p. 16. (The ghostly painting is here entitled '*The Wild Hunt* – My first oil painting'.)

55 Jakob Grimm, *Deutsche Mythologie*, vol. 1, Frankfurt 1981, p. 341.

56 Heiden, *Adolf Hitler*, vol. 1, p. 341.

57 Hitler, *Reden und Proklamationen*, vol. 1, p. 712. (Speech on 31 July 1937 in Breslau at a celebration of the German Sängerbund, allegedly attended by half a million people. By 'God', Domarus adds, Hitler meant a 'special God devoted to the interests of Germany'.)

58 Carl J. Burckhardt, *Briefe 1908–1974*, Frankfurt 1986, p. 157 (letter to Max Huber, 7 November 1935, in which Burckhardt calls Hitler's words 'blasphemous').

59 Heiden, *Adolf Hitler*, vol. 1, p. 34 (words used at his trial following the abortive Putsch).

60 Ibid., p. 34.

61 Udo Bermbach and Dieter Borchmeyer (eds), *Richard Wagner – 'Der Ring des Nibelungen'. Ansichten eines Mythos*, Stuttgart 1995, p. 165 (in Herfried Münkler, 'Die Nibelungen in der Weimarer Republik').

62 Ibid.

63 Ibid.

64 Wagener, *Hitler aus nächster Nähe*, p. 363.

65 Hartmut Zelinsky, *Sieg oder Untergang: Sieg und Untergang. Kaiser Wilhelm II, die Werk-Idee Richard Wagners und der 'Weltkampf'*, Munich 1990, p. 91. (Walther Rathenau, *Schriften aus Kriegs- und Nachkriegszeit*, Berlin 1929, p. 171. Wagner's omnipresence: 'There is always someone present – Lohengrin, Walther, Siegfried, Wotan – who can do everything and destroy everything, who can redeem virtuous suffering, punish vice and bring general salvation in spectacular manner, with fanfares, lighting effects and tableaux.' Rathenau was murdered on 24 July 1922 for being a Jew.)

66 Wagner, *Sämtliche Schriften und Dichtungen*, vol. 12, p. 360.

67 Bermbach and Borchmeyer (eds), *Wagner – 'Der Ring des Nibelungen'*, p. 166.

68 Lutz Köpnick, *Nothungs Modernität. Wagners 'Ring' und die Poesie der Macht im neunzehnten Jahrhundert*, Munich 1994, p. 170. ('These new productions were nothing other than appeals to old comrades to take up arms.')

69 Michael Karbaum, *Studien zur Geschichte der Bayreuther Festspiele (1876–1976)*, 2 vols, Regensburg 1976, vol. 2, p. 66 (letter to Siegfried Wagner, 5 May 1924).

70 Köpnick, *Nothungs Modernität*, p. 178.

71 *Siegfried*, act 1, scene 3.

72 August Kubizek, *Adolf Hitler. Mein Jugendfreund*, Graz 1953, p. 125.

73 Wagener, *Hitler aus nächster Nähe*, p. 251.

74 Hermann Rauschning, *Gespräche mit Hitler*, Vienna 1973, p. 11.

Chapter 6 The Future as Art

1   Joseph Goebbels, *Tagebücher 1945*, Hamburg 1977, p. 58.
2   Houston Stewart Chamberlain, *Richard Wagner*, Munich 1901, p. 496.
3   Cosima Wagner, *Die Tagebücher*, 4 vols, ed. Martin Gregor-Dellin and Dietrich Mack, Munich 1982, vol. 4, p. 899.
4   Richard Wagner, *Gesammelte Schriften und Dichtungen*, 10 vols, ed. Richard Wagner, Leipzig 1871–83, vol. 3, p. 1.
5   Ibid., p. 2.
6   Ibid., p. 7.
7   Adolf Hitler, *Hitlers Tischgespräche im Führerhauptquartier*, ed. Henry Picker, Stuttgart 1976 (Hitler's address to young army officers on 30 May 1942).
8   August Kubizek, *Adolf Hitler. Mein Jugendfreund*, Graz 1953, p. 101. (Kubizek, who said he did not understand much of these speeches, always looked forward to their conclusion, which was always the same: 'As you see, what happened to Wagner has also happened to me.')
9   Ibid., p. 238.
10 Ibid., p. 120. ('. . . as with his project for the new bridge over the Danube, the details were very accurate, as though the interval between the plan and its execution were to be measured in weeks, not in decades.')
11 Wagner, *Gesammelte Schriften und Dichtungen*, vol. 3, p. 50.
12 Ibid., vol. 2, p. 144.
13 Ibid., p. 115.
14 Ibid., p. 155. (In the final version the 'Wibelungen' ended as follows: 'There he sits, in the Kyffhäuser mountain, Friedrich Barbarossa, surrounded with the Nibelung treasure and at his side the sword that once slayed the cruel dragon.' The first version of 1848, on the other hand, ended differently: 'When, O great Friedrich, wilt thou return, thou noble Siegfried? When wilt thou slay the dragon that is tormenting mankind?' To which Barbarossa replies: 'Two ravens are circling above my mountain, having grown fat on the riches of the German Reich. One attacks from the south-east, the other from the north-east. Drive them away and the treasure is yours! But leave me in peace in my mountain!' [*Sämtliche Schriften und Dichtungen*, 16 vols, Leipzig 1911–14, vol. 12, p. 227]. Thus for Wagner's Barbarossa too the threat came from the east.)
15 Wagner, *Gesammelte Schriften und Dichtungen*, vol. 3, p. 131.
16 Ibid., p. 49.
17 Ibid., pp. 53f. (All attempts at reform, says Wagner, are useless as long as the enemies of Germany are sucking out the nation's life-blood and, themselves impotent, are destroying the nation's powers of reproduction. The only solution is to destroy what has to be destroyed.)
18 Ibid., p. 123.
19 Ibid., vol. 5, p. 67.
20 Wagner, *Sämtliche Schriften und Dichtungen*, vol. 10, p. 272 ('Erkenne dich selbst').
21 Wagner, *Gesammelte Schriften und Dichtungen*, vol. 5, p. 75. (As the Jews knew no sense of a common fate, said Wagner, their art had no 'necessity' about it and was only a 'superficial luxury'. They merely copied what great geniuses had done, with a closeness which gave them the character of parrots.)
22 Adolf Hitler, *Mein Kampf*, 763rd–767th impression, Munich 1942, p. 332. ('No,

the Jews have no cultural strength of their own, therefore their intellect will always be destructive, not constructive.')

23 Wagner, *Gesammelte Schriften und Dichtungen*, vol. 5, p. 69.

24 Ibid., p. 71.

25 Ibid., p. 76.

26 Ibid., p. 84.

27 Ibid., p. 85.

28 Ibid.

29 Peter Adam, *Kunst im Dritten Reich*, Hamburg 1992, p. 11.

30 Wagner, *Gesammelte Schriften und Dichtungen*, vol. 3, p. 131.

31 Ibid., p. 35.

32 Ibid., p. 96.

33 Ibid., p. 174.

34 Hartmut Zelinksy, *Richard Wagner. Ein deutsches Thema. Eine Dokumentation zur Wirkungsgeschichte Richard Wagners 1876–1976*, Berlin 1983, p. 215.

35 Joachim C. Fest, *Hitler. Eine Biographie*, Frankfurt 1973, p. 215.

36 Wagner, *Gesammelte Schriften und Dichtungen*, vol. 3, p. 175.

37 Ibid., p. 176.

38 Richard Wagner, *Sämtliche Briefe*, ed. G. Strobel, W. Wolf, H.-J. Bauer and J. Forner, vol. 3, p. 194. (Letter to Uhlig 27 December 1849. Already at this time Wagner wanted to found a journal called 'Für Kunst und Leben' to publicize his revolutionary ideas (p. 169) – a kind of predecessor of the *Bayreuther Blätter*. 'Each volume of such a journal', he said in 1849, 'should contain a cannonball aimed at some dilapidated tower or other; once that has been knocked down, the next cannonball should be aimed at another tower, and so on, until the ammunition is used up.')

39 Kubizek, *Adolf Hitler*, p. 240.

40 Ibid., p. 196.

41 *Götterdämmerung*, act 2, scene 3.

42 Kubizek, *Adolf Hitler*, p. 245.

43 Fest, *Hitler*, p. 229. ('No intellectual or artistic event that took place after the turn of the century, no book or idea made any impression on him – no personal experience or process of development is reflected in it. There he stands, motionless, petrified – the person he always was.')

44 Adolf Hitler, *Reden und Proklamationen 1932–1945*, 2 vols, ed. Max Domarus, Würzburg 1962–3, vol. 1, p. 24. (Speech delivered in Nuremberg on 14 September 1936, in which Hitler declares his unshakeable determination to 'follow under all circumstances the path of necessity that has once been revealed'. Domarus adds: 'Hitler's goals were firmly set in his mind from 1919 onwards.')

45 Ibid., p. 620. ('In effect what was known as the ideology of National Socialism amounted to nothing other than faith in Adolf Hitler.')

46 Stephen H. Roberts, *The House that Hitler Built*, London 1937.

47 Ibid., p. 9.

48 Ibid., p. 10, footnote.

49 Heinz-Klaus Metzger and Rainer Riehm (eds), *Richard Wagner. Wie antisemitisch darf ein Künstler sein? Musikkonzepte 5*, p. 16. (Peter Viereck, in this essay, 'Hitler and Wagner' [1939], describes how, although Wagner's tirades, published in the *Bayreuther Blätter*, were barely known to the masses, his ideas reached wider circles after his death in 1883 via his popularizers. The popularizers of his ideas and those of his close friend Gobineau constituted what was known

as the 'Wagner Circle' – his widow Cosima, his son-in-law Houston Stewart Chamberlain and their friends Alfred Rosenberg and Dietrich Eckart. In a reply sent to the editor of *Common Sense* in 1940, Thomas Mann wrote that he had to disappoint those who assumed that, as a long-committed admirer of Wagner's music, he would take exception to the essay. On the contrary, he highly approved of it and considered it an admirable piece of work. Mann added that he found Nazi elements not only in Wagner's questionable writings but also in his music, which was equally questionable, albeit on a more elevated plane. Ibid., p. 32.)

50 Michael Karbaum, *Studien zur Geschichte der Bayreuther Festspiele (1876–1976)*, 2 vols, Regensburg 1976, vol. 2, p. 69.
51 Marcel Prawy, *'Nun sei bedankt . . .'. Mein Richard-Wagner-Buch*, Munich 1983, p. 47.
52 Adolf Hitler, *Reden, Schriften, Anordnungen. Februar 1925 bis Januar 1933*, 3 vols, ed. Clems Vollnhals et al., Munich 1992–4, vol. 3, p. 528. (Speech delivered in Munich, 7 December 1929, before 7,000 people. The title of the speech given on the posters was 'The Final Blow! Victory is Ours!')
53 Fest, *Hitler*, p. 534.
54 Ibid., p. 525.
55 Wagner, *Gesammelte Schriften und Dichtungen*, vol. 3, p. 177.
56 Hitler, *Reden und Proklamationen*, vol. 1, p. 175 (speech delivered in Detmold, 4 January 1933).
57 Ibid., vol. 2, p. 1628 (speech delivered 10 December 1940).
58 Hans Severus Ziegler, *Adolf Hitler aus dem Erleben dargestellt*, Göttingen 1964, p. 123.
59 Adam, *Kunst im Dritten Reich*, p. 21.
60 Joseph Goebbels, *Die Tagebücher von Joseph Goebbels. Sämtliche Fragmente*, 4 vols, ed. Eike Fröhlich, Munich 1987, vol. 1, p. 648 (entries on 27 and 28 July 1936).
61 Hitler, *Hitlers Tischgespräche*, p. 85 (18 January 1942).
62 Ibid., p. 463 (26 July 1942).
63 Peter Wapnewski, *Der traurige Gott. Richard Wagner in seinen Helden*, Munich 1978, p. 299. (Letter from Wagner to Ludwig II written 1 October 1874. Wapnewski observes that this view of the future shows once again with what breathtaking naïveté Wahnfried identified the fate of the house of Wagner with events on the world stage.)

Chapter 7 A Royal Failure

1 Gerhard Hojer (ed.), *König-Ludwig-II-Museum Herrenchiemsee* (catalogue), Munich 1986, p. 32 (Ludwig to Wagner, 13 May 1868).
2 *Völkischer Beobachter*, no. 227, 15 August 1933.
3 Adolf Hitler, *Reden, Schriften, Anordnungen, Februar 1925 bis Januar 1933*, 3 vols, ed. Clems Vollnhals et al., Munich 1992–4, vol. 3, p. 129 (speech given at a Nazi Party meeting in Munich, 3 April 1929).
4 Ibid., p. 153.
5 Richard Wagner, *Gesammelte Schriften und Dichtungen*, 10 vols, ed. Richard Wagner, Leipzig 1871–83, vol. 8, p. 349 ('Deutsche Kunst und deutsche Politik').
6 Rupert Hacker (ed.), *Ludwig II von Bayern in Augenzeugenberichten*, Munich 1972, p. 65. (Letter from Ludwig to Wagner 5 May 1864: 'Without knowing it, you

have been my sole source of joy since my earliest youth, my best teacher and tutor, one who speaks to my heart like none other.' Hitler could have used similar words.)

7 Ibid., p. 33.
8 Verena Naegele, *Parsifals Mission. Der Einfluss Richard Wagners auf Ludwig II und seine Politik*. Cologne 1995, p. 9.
9 Hacker (ed.), *Ludwig II von Bayern in Augenzeugenberichten*, p. 87.
10 König Ludwig II/Richard Wagner, *Briefwechsel*, 4 vols, ed. Wittelsbacher Ausgleichsfonds and Winifred Wagner, rev. Otto Strobel, Karlsruhe 1936–7, vol. 4, p. 28 (diary jottings of Wagner's for Ludwig, 25 September 1865).
11 Ibid., vol. 1, p. 165 (letter from Wagner, 26 August 1865).
12 Richard Wagner/Mathilde Maier, *Richard Wagner an Mathilde Maier (1862–1878)*, ed. Hans Scholz, Leipzig 1930, p. 208 (letter from Wagner, 30 March 1865).
13 König Ludwig II/Richard Wagner, *Briefwechsel*, vol. 1, p. 30 (letter from Wagner, 6 November 1864).
14 Ibid., p. 31 (letter from Wagner, 6 November 1864).
15 Ibid., p. 187. (Letter from Wagner, 23 September 1865. Wagner continues: 'I sing of the awakening of this bride – a grave, solemn song, yet intimate and heartfelt. It is the sweet song of the German spirit.')
16 Hacker (ed.), *Ludwig von Bayern in Augenzeugenberichten*, p. 64.
17 Ibid., p. 67 (report from Julius Hey after an audience with the King on 13 May 1864).
18 Naegele, *Parsifals Mission*, p. 140.
19 Friedrich Herzfeld, *Königsfreundschaft. Ludwig II und Richard Wagner*, Leipzig 1939, p. 134.
20 Naegele, *Parsifals Mission*, p. 136.
21 Ibid., p. 114.
22 Ibid., p. 136.
23 König Ludwig II/Richard Wagner, *Briefwechsel*, vol. 4, p. 11 (diary entry of Wagner's for Ludwig, 15 September 1865).
24 Ibid., p. 19. (Diary entry of Wagner's for Ludwig, 21 September 1865: 'Nature is created in such a way that wherever a parasite sees its advantage, there it will settle. A dying body will attract these maggots, which will ultimately destroy the host and assimilate with it. This is precisely the role of the Jews in modern European culture.')
25 Ibid., p. 21. (Diary entry of Wagner's for Ludwig, 22 September 1864. Wagner goes on: 'It is our task to find out how to preserve it from being destroyed in this shameful way, and therefore we must first of all be clear in our minds about what constitutes the German spirit.')
26 Ibid., vol. 3, p. 230 (letter from Wagner, 22 November 1881).
27 Ibid., vol. 1, p. 224 (letter from Wagner, 25 November 1865).
28 Naegele, *Parsifals Mission*, p. 350.
29 König Ludwig II/Richard Wagner, *Briefwechsel*, vol. 1, p. 277 (letter from Wagner, 8 January 1866).
30 Eduard Stemplinger, *Richard Wagner in München 1864–1870. Legende und Wirklichkeit*, Munich 1933, p. 118.
31 Adelgunde von der Pfordten (b. 1823), mother of three sons and two daughters, suffered a fatal accident in 1873. Her husband died in 1880.
32 Ernest Newman, *The Life of Richard Wagner*, 4 vols, London 1933–47, vol. 4, p. 81.

33 König Ludwig II/Richard Wagner, *Briefwechsel*, vol. 4, p. 68 (letter from Wagner to Röckel, 15 July 1865).

34 Ibid., p. 99 (letter from Wagner to Röckel, 26 October 1865).

35 Dieter Borchmeyer and Jörg Salaquarda (eds), *Nietzsche und Wagner. Stationen einer epochalen Begegnung*, 2 vols, Frankfurt 1994, vol. 1, p. 52. (Letter from Cosima to Nietzsche, 6 February 1870. It is significant that the editors made no comment on this key aspect of Bayreuth policies.)

36 König Ludwig II/Richard Wagner, *Briefwechsel*, vol. 4, p. 134 (letter from Wagner to Constantin Frantz, 19 March 1866).

37 Naegele, *Parsifals Mission*, p. 217. (A Gymnasium director earned 2200 guilders a year; in 1865 Wagner received a total of 179,600 guilders from the King.)

38 Ibid., p. 178.

39 Ibid., p. 181.

40 Ibid., p. 187 (Ludwig to Wagner, 16 September 1865).

41 Andrea Mork, *Richard Wagner als politischer Schriftsteller. Weltanschauung und Wirkungsgeschichte*, Frankfurt 1990, p. 81.

42 König Ludwig II/Richard Wagner, *Briefwechsel*, vol. 3, p. 226. ('. . . all men are basically brothers, in spite of their denominational differences.' As early as 1866 the King had made it clear that, like his father, he supported the emancipation of the Jews.)

43 Ibid., p. 231 (letter from Ludwig to Wagner, 24 January 1882).

44 Dieter Borchmeyer (ed.), *Wege des Mythos in der Moderne. Richard Wagner 'Der Ring des Nibelungen'*, Munich 1987, p. 173 (Hermann Bauer, 'Wagner, der Mythos und die Schlösser Ludwigs II').

45 Eckart Kröplin, *Richard Wagner. Theatralisches Leben und lebendiges Theater*, Leipzig 1989, p. 158. (On 30 November 1866 he sent Wagner his poem 'To Hans Sachs', whom he lauded for 'kindling flames from the ashes with his breath'. He signed the poem 'Walther von Stolzing'.)

46 König Ludwig II/Richard Wagner, *Briefwechsel*, vol. 2, p. 110 (letter from Wagner, 11 December 1866).

47 Friedrich Nietzsche, *Sämtliche Werke*, 15 vols, ed. Giogio Colli and Mazzino Montinari, Munich 1980, vol. 1, p. 147.

48 Ibid., p. 149. ('So convinced are we of the pure, powerful heart of the German character that we dare to expect that it will expel any foreign elements that have been forced upon it' – a passage that recalls Wagner's warning in the *Meistersinger* of the infiltration of foreign elements into the German spirit.)

49 Ibid., p. 154.

50 Ibid., p. 507 ('Richard Wagner in Bayreuth').

51 Ibid., p. 451.

52 Cosima Wagner, *Die Tagebücher*, 4 vols, ed. Martin Gregor-Dellin and Dietrich Mack, Munich 1982, vol. 2, p. 720. (2 September 1873: 'All we have, added Wagner, is our army, our military service – our discipline and all our virtues reveal themselves in time of war.' On the other hand Wagner showed little interest in contemporary culture.)

53 Martin Gregor-Dellin, *Richard Wagner. Sein Leben, sein Werk, sein Jahrhundert*, Munich 1980, p. 720. (Looking back, Wagner was of the opinion that 'no artist had ever been honoured in this way'.)

54 Cosima Wagner, *Die Tagebücher*, vol. 1, p. 426 (entry of 11 August 1871).

55 Ibid., p. 458. (Entry of 12 November 1871: 'While correcting his "Wibelungen" R. said that he still thought repeatedly about Friedrich Barbarossa.')

56 Richard Wagner, *Sämtliche Schriften und Dichtungen*, 16 vols, Leipzig 1911–14, vol. 10, p. 232. (Wagner in 'Religion und Kunst': 'It will be sufficient for our purposes to trace the decay of the Christian religion to the participation of Jewry in the formation of Christian dogma.')
57 Ibid., p. 233.
58 Ibid., p. 283 ('Heldentum und Christentum').
59 Ibid., p. 231 ('Religion und Kunst').
60 Ibid., p. 274.
61 Hartmut Zelinsky, *Richard Wagner. Ein deutsches Thema. Eine Dokumentation zur Wirkungsgeschichte Richard Wagners 1876–1976*, new edn Berlin 1983, p. 207. (Stuckenschmidt's article 'Bayreuth' appeared in the journal *Anbruch* in January 1933.)
62 Dieter David Scholz, *Richard Wagners Antisemitismus*, Würzburg 1993, p. 196.
63 Newman, *The Life of Richard Wagner*, vol. 3, p. 284.
64 Borchmeyer and Salaquarda (eds), *Nietzsche und Wagner*, vol. 1, p. 52 (letter of 6 February 1870).
65 Joachim Köhler, *Friedrich Nietzsche und Cosima Wagner. Die Schule der Unterwerfung*, Berlin 1996 (English trans.: New Haven/London 1998), deals with the beginnings of the Bayreuth cult and Nietzsche's repressed anti-Semitism.
66 Oscar Bie (ed.), *Richard Wagner und Bayreuth*, Zurich 1931, p. 4.
67 Köhler, *Friedrich Nietzsche und Cosima Wagner*, p. 181.
68 *Parsifal*, act 1.
69 Richard du Moulin Eckart, *Die Herrin von Bayreuth*, Berlin 1931, p. 35.
70 Cosima Wagner, *Das zweite Leben. Briefe und Aufzeichnungen 1883–1930*, ed. Dietrich Mack, Munich 1980, p. 570 (letter to Bodo von dem Knesebeck, 10 January 1901).
71 Michael Karbaum, *Studien zur Geschichte der Bayreuther Festspiele (1876–1976)*, 2 vols, Regensburg 1976, vol. 1, p. 55.
72 Ibid., p. 6.
73 Ibid., p. 55.
74 Ibid., p. 56.
75 Cosima Wagner, *Das zweite Leben*, p. 850.
76 Ibid., p. 570 (letter to Bodo von dem Knesebeck, 10 January 1901).
77 Max Millenkovich-Morold, *Cosima Wagner. Ein Lebensbild*, Leipzig 1937, p. 409.
78 Houston Stewart Chamberlain, *Lebenswege meines Denkens*, Munich 1919, p. 160. ('The sun of my life is and always has been Richard Wagner.')
79 Zelinsky, *Richard Wagner*, p. 111 (letter from Chamberlain to Kaiser Wilhelm II, 1 January 1912).
80 Hartmut Zelinsky, *Sieg oder Untergang. Sieg und Untergang. Kaiser Wilhelm II, die Werk-Idee Richard Wagners und der 'Weltkampf'*, Munich 1990, p. 108 (letter from Chamberlain to Kaiser Wilhelm II, 1 January 1912).

Chapter 8 The Witch's Kitchen

1 Houston Stewart Chamberlain, *Richard Wagner*, Munich 1901, p. 224.
2 Winfried Schüler, *Der Bayreuther Kreis von seiner Entstehung bis zum Ausgang der Wilhelminischen Ära*, Münster 1971, p. 118.
3 Andrea Mork, *Richard Wagner als politischer Schriftsteller. Weltanschauung und Wirkungsgeschichte*, Frankfurt 1990, p, 165.

4   Cosima Wagner/Ludwig Schemann, *Cosima Wagner. Briefe an Ludwig Schemann*, ed. Bertha Schemann, Regensburg 1937, p. 37 (letter from Cosima, 8 January 1887).

5   Arthur Gobineau, *Ein Erinnerungsbild aus Wahnfried (von Cosima Wagner)*, Stuttgart 1907, p. 9.

6   Schüler, *Der Bayreuther Kreis* (letter from Wolzogen to Schemann, 1 July 1877).

7   Cosima Wagner/Ludwig Schemann, *Cosima Wagner. Briefe an Ludwig Schemann*, p. 26 (letter from Cosima, December 1881).

8   Ibid., p. 12 (letter from Cosima, 16 June 1881).

9   Cosima Wagner/Daniela von Bülow, *Cosima Wagner. Briefe an ihre Tochter Daniela von Bülow 1866–1885*, ed. Max Freiherr von Waldberg, Stuttgart 1933, p. 187. (Letter from Cosima, 4 April 1881: ' "Wagnerian" – the word can be used in the way that other words are used to describe a party . . . it is applied to those who are prepared to follow the Master everywhere and seek to realize the Wagnerian idea.' Those who will not subject themselves to this idea – 'will not swear by every word the Master said and wrote', as the critic Paul Lindau put it – will attract the hostility of the Bayreuth circle. 'Characteristic of their polemical manner', said Lindau, 'is not that they seek to clarify opinions but that they set out to destroy any views other than their own' [Paul Lindau, *Nüchterne Briefe aus Bayreuth*, Breslau 1880, p. 16].)

10   August Kubizek, *Adolf Hitler. Mein Jugendfreund*, Graz 1953, p. 102.

11   Cosima Wagner, *Das zweite Leben. Briefe und Aufzeichnungen 1883–1930*, ed. Dietrich Mack, Munich 1980, p. 465 (obituary of Anton Seidl, 1898).

12   Cosima Wagner/Ludwig Schemann, *Cosima Wagner. Briefe an Ludwig Schemann*, p. 84.

13   Mork, *Richard Wagner als politischer Schriftsteller*, p. 160 (*Bayreuther Blätter*, 1885).

14   Michael Karbaum, *Studien zur Geschichte der Bayreuther Festspiele (1876–1976)*, 2 vols, Regensburg 1976, vol. 1, p. 37.

15   Houston Stewart Chamberlain, *Die Grundlagen des Neunzehnten Jahrhunderts. Kritische Urteile*, Munich 1901, p. 92 (Wolzogen in *Das Literarische Echo*, 1 February 1900).

16   Leopold von Schroeder, *Die Vollendung des arischen Mysteriums in Bayreuth*, Munich 1911.

17   Schüler, *Der Bayreuther Kreis*, p. 219.

18   Ibid., p. 244.

19   Karbaum, *Studien zur Geschichte der Bayreuther Festspiele*, vol. 2, p. 51 (Paul Bekker, 'Bayreuth und seine Leute', p. 1912).

20   Klaus Umbach (ed.), *Richard Wagner. Ein deutsches Ärgernis*, Hamburg 1982, p. 163 (Schemann in his address on Wagner's artistic aims and his significance for German national culture, 1877).

21   Cosima Wagner/Ludwig Schemann, *Cosima Wagner. Briefe an Ludwig Schemann*, p. 24. (Letter from Cosima, 29 October 1881: 'Fortunately what issues from Bayreuth is not merely a doctrine but also instructions on how to put this doctrine into practice in every conceivable field. In the same way our Saviour sacrificed Himself so that His disciples should proclaim His message.')

22   Wolfgang Wagner, *Lebens-Akte. Autobiographie*, Munich 1994, p. 38.

23   Cosima Wagner, *Die Tagebücher*, 4 vols, ed. Martin Gregor-Dellin and Dietrich Mack, Munich 1982, vol. 3, p. 424. (Letter from Cosima, 11 October 1879. She noted: 'R. is in favour of their total expulsion.')

24   Udo Bermbach (ed.), *In den Trümmern den eignen Welt. Richard Wagners 'Ring*

des Nibelungen', Berlin 1989, p. 245 (Jakob Wassermann, *Mein Weg als Deutscher und Jude*, Berlin 1921, p. 117). [The reference is to the scene 'Hexenküche' in Goethe's *Faust* – Translator's Note.]

25   Cosima Wagner, *Das zweite Leben*, p. 766 (note by Eva Chamberlain, 30 March 1930, two days before Cosima's death).
26   Houston Stewart Chamberlain, *Lebenswege meines Denkens*, Munich 1919, p. 196.
27   Ibid., p. 197.
28   Ibid., p. 204.
29   Ibid., p. 205.
30   Ibid., p. 241.
31   Cosima Wagner/Houston Stewart Chamberlain, *Briefwechsel*, ed. Paul Pretzsch, Leipzig 1934, p. 627. (Letter from Cosima, 15 February 1902: 'In the course of the audience we had with His Majesty the Kaiser said repeatedly: 'Chamberlain is of the same mind.')
32   Chamberlain, *Lebenswege*, p. 242. (See note 21 above. Cosima too talks of Bayreuth as a 'school for action'.)
33   Ibid., p. 163.
34   George R. Marek, *Cosima Wagner*, Bayreuth 1981, p. 350.
35   Robert Hartford (ed.), *Bayreuth: The Early Years. An Account of the Early Decades of the Wagner Festival as Seen by the Celebrated Visitors and Participants*, Cambridge/London/New York/New Rochelle/Melbourne/Sydney 1980, p. 219.
36   Richard du Moulin Eckart, *Die Herrin von Bayreuth*, Berlin 1931, p. 839. (Du Moulin Eckart dedicated his biography of Cosima to Chamberlain.)
37   Cosima Wagner/Houston Stewart Chamberlain, *Briefwechsel*, p. 15 (Chamberlain: 14 June 1888).
38   Ibid., p. 22 (Cosima: 17 September 1888).
39   Ibid., p. 19 (Chamberlain: 29 July 1888).
40   Ibid., p. 29 (Cosima: 23 October 1888).
41   Ibid., p. 141 (Cosima: 2 February 1890).
42   Ibid., p. 142 (Chamberlain: 4 February 1890).
43   Ibid., p. 486 (Chamberlain: 25 September 1896).
44   Ibid., p. 255 (Chamberlain: 30 November 1891).
45   Ibid., p. 507 (Cosima: 12 March 1897).
46   Cosima Wagner, *Das zweite Leben*, p. 422 (Cosima to the president of the Richard Wagner Society, 31 July 1896).
47   John Toland, *Adolf Hitler*, Bergisch Gladbach 1977, p. 182.
48   Chamberlain, *Richard Wagner*, p. 35 ('Wagner, this most German of all artists').
49   Ibid., p. 62.
50   Ibid., p. 504.
51   Cosima Wagner/Houston Stewart Chamberlain, *Briefwechsel*, p. 445 (Cosima: 22 February 1896).
52   Ibid., p. 500 (Chamberlain: 1 January 1897).
53   Ibid., p. 569 (Cosima: 25 May 1899).
54   Cosima Wagner, *Das zweite Leben*, p. 487 (Cosima to Glasenapp, 15 November 1899).
55   Erich Kloss, *Wagnertum in Vergangenheit und Gegenwart*, Berlin 1909, p. 123.
56   Cosima Wagner/Houston Stewart Chamberlain, *Briefwechsel*, p. 607 (Chamberlain: 5 February 1901).
57   Ibid., p. 627 (Cosima: 15 February 1902).

58 Claus-Ekkehard Bärsch, *Erlösung und Vernichtung. Dr. phil. Joseph Goebbels*, Munich 1987, p. 344. (Kayserling: 'There has hardly been a book published in recent times that so fully meets the criteria of a work of art.')

59 Chamberlain, *Die Grundlagen des Neunzehnten Jahrhunderts. Kritische Urteile*, p. 64. (Joël in the *Allgemeine Schweizer Zeitung* called it 'a burst of fresh strength in a declining nation'.)

60 Ibid., p. 75.

61 Bärsch, *Erlösung und Vernichtung*, p. 359. (Letter from Kaiser Wilhelm II to Chamberlain, 31 December 1901: 'The feeling that one is fighting for a noble and divine cause brings a guarantee of victory.')

62 Hartmut Zelinsky, *Richard Wagner. Ein deutsches Thema. Eine Dokumentation zur Wirkungsgeschichte Richard Wagners 1876–1976*, Berlin 1983, p. 170 (letter from Chamberlain to Hitler, 1 January 1924).

63 Chamberlain, *Die Grundlagen des Neunzehnten Jahrhunderts. Kritische Urteile*, p. 54 (Wolfgang Golther in the *Bayreuther Blätter*, 1900).

64 Schüler, *Der Bayreuther Kreis*, p. 117. (Henry Thode in the *Literarisches Zentralblatt*, 10 March 1900: 'Chamberlain owes the recognition of these problems to Wagner.')

65 Houston Stewart Chamberlain, *Die Grundlagen des Neunzehnten Jahrhunderts*, 2 vols, 28th impression, Munich 1942, vol. 1, p. 5.

66 Richard Wagner, *Sämtliche Schriften und Dichtungen*, 16 vols, Leipzig 1911–14, vol. 10, p. 272.

67 Chamberlain, *Die Grundlagen*, vol. 1, p. 550.

68 Ibid., vol. 2, p. 859.

69 Ibid., p. 864.

70 Ibid., vol. 1, p. 28 ('Had the Phoenicians' – 'Semites' to Chamberlain – 'not been destroyed, and had their last capital city not been wiped off the face of the earth, leaving no trace, mankind would never have experienced this nineteenth century of ours.' Hitler too planned to raze the capital cities of Jewish Bolshevism to the ground and wipe out their populations.)

71 Ibid., p. 406.

72 Ibid., p. 294.

73 Carl Maria Cornelius, *Peter Cornelius*, 2 vols, Regensburg 1925, vol. 2, p. 250. (Those whose letters were destroyed except for a few isolated pages, and sometimes completely, wrote Cosima to Carl Maria Cornelius, included Pusinelli, Röckel, Heine, Berlioz, Herwegh, Otto and Mathilde Wesendonk, Semper, Gasperini, Baudelaire, Bülow, Nietzsche, Gobineau, Stein and Peter Cornelius. The Nazi burning of the books in 1933 had its sinister precedent.)

74 Marek, *Cosima Wagner*, p. 72.

75 Ernest Newman, *The Life of Richard Wagner*, 4 vols, London 1933–47, vol. 2, p. 614.

76 Friedrich Herzfeld, *Königsfreundschaft. Ludwig II und Richard Wagner*, Leipzig 1939, p. 53.

77 Wolfgang Wagner, *Lebens-Akte*, p. 52.

78 Cosima Wagner, *Die Tagebücher*, vol. 1, p. 8.

79 Karbaum, *Studien zur Geschichte der Bayreuther Festspiele*, vol. 2, p. 53.

80 *Wagners Werk und Wirkung. Festspielnachrichten Beiträge 1957–1982*, p. 83 (Herbert Conrad, 'Der Beidler-Konflikt').

81 *Bayreuther Festspielführer 1928*, ed. Paul Pretzsch, Bayreuth 1928, p. 217.

82 *Bayreuther Festspielführer 1924*, ed. Karl Grunsky, Bayreuth 1924, p. 91.

83   Cosima Wagner/Houston Stewart Chamberlain, *Briefwechsel*, p. 620 (Chamberlain: 31 October 1901).
84   Birgit Marschall, *Reisen und Regieren. Die Nordlandfahrten Kaiser Wilhelm II*, Hamburg 1991, p. 77.
85   Hartmut Zelinsky, *Sieg oder Untergang. Sieg und Untergang. Kaiser Wilhelm II, die Werk-Idee Richard Wagners und der 'Weltkampf'*, Munich 1990, p. 5 (Kaiser Wilhelm II to Field Marshal August von Mackensen, 2 December 1919).
86   Marschall, *Reisen und Regieren*, p. 79.
87   John C.G. Röhl, 'Wilhelm II: "Das Beste wäre Gas!" ', in *Die Zeit*, 25 November 1994, p. 15. (Remark made to Sir Edward Grey. In a letter of 15 August 1929 to Poultney Bigelow the Kaiser wrote: 'Jews and mosquitoes are a nuisance that humanity must get rid of in some way or other. I believe the best would be gas!')
88   Ibid., p. 14.
89   Richard Voss, *Aus einem phantastischen Leben*, Stuttgart 1923, p. 366.
90   Zelinsky, *Sieg oder Untergang*, p. 16 (Kaiser Wilhelm II, 15 January 1917).
91   Cosima Wagner/Fürst Ernst zu Hohenlohe-Langenburg, *Briefwechsel*, ed. Ernst Fürst zu Hohenlohe, Stuttgart 1937, p. 332 (Hohenlohe: 9 August 1914).
92   Ibid., p. 337 (Hohenlohe: 16 December 1914).
93   Cosima Wagner, *Die Tagebücher*, vol. 1, p. 272 (18 August 1870).
94   Cosima Wagner/Fürst Ernst zu Hohenlohe-Langenburg, *Briefwechsel*, p. 334 (Hohenlohe on Chamberlain's war essays, 11 October 1914).
95   Houston Stewart Chamberlain, *Kriegsaufsätze*, Munich 1916, p. 67.
96   Ibid., p. 76.
97   Zelinsky, *Sieg oder Untergang*, p. 16.
98   Chamberlain, *Kriegsaufsätze*, p. 59.
99   Ibid., p. 39.
100   Sigurd von Ilsemann, *Der Kaiser in Holland*, Munich 1967, p. 191.
101   Cosima Wagner, *Das zweite Leben*, p. 730 (Cosima to Hohenlohe, New Year's Day 1915).
102   Ernst Deuerlein (ed.), *Der Aufstieg der NSDAP in Augenzeugenberichten*, Munich 1974, p. 114 (Hitler at a meeting on 17 April 1920).
103   Ibid., p. 167 (Hitler at a meeting in Munich on 12 April 1922).
104   Max Millenkovich-Morold, *Cosima Wagner. Ein Lebensbild*, Leipzig 1937, p. 46.
105   Cosima Wagner, *Das zweite Leben*, p. 761 (21 May 1929).
106   Du Moulin Eckart, *Die Herrin von Bayreuth*, p. 888.
107   Zelinsky, *Richard Wagner*, p. 169 (Chamberlain to Hitler, 7 October 1923).
108   Voss, *Aus einem phantastischen Leben*, p. 364 (Eva Chamberlain to Voss).
109   Cosima Wagner/Fürst Ernst zu Hohenlohe-Langenburg, *Briefwechsel*, p. 353. (Chamberlain to Hohenlohe, 3 August 1916: 'How right you are about "the man from the trenches". It was a revelation – that is where our redeemer will come from!')

Chapter 9 A Lethal Subject

1   Hans Jürgen Syberberg, 'Winifred Wagner und die Geschichte des Hauses Wahnfried 1914–1975', film interview with Winifred Wagner 1975.
2   Wolfgang Wagner, *Lebens-Akte. Autobiographie*, Munich 1994.

3 Ibid., p. 49.
4 Friedelind Wagner, *Nacht über Bayreuth. Die Geschichte der Enkelin Richard Wagners*, Cologne 1944, p. 333. (Winifred in Zurich in February 1940: 'If you do not consent, we shall have you brought back by force.')
5 Syberberg, 'Winifred Wagner'.
6 Andrea Mork, *Richard Wagner als politischer Schriftsteller. Weltanschauung und Wirkungsgeschichte*, Frankfurt 1990, p. 243 (letter on the occasion of the publication of Ziegler's memoirs, *Adolf Hitler aus dem Erleben dargestellt*, Göttingen 1964).
7 Wolfgang Wagner, *Lebens-Akte*, p. 46. ('Hitler later said of Chamberlain, Wahnfried's private ideologue, that he forged the sword with which the Nazis had gone into battle. To Siegfried Wagner Hitler said: "I was filled with pride and joy when I witnessed the victory of the people in that very town in which, first by the Master, then by Chamberlain, the spiritual sword was forged with which we are fighting today"' [Michael Karbaum, *Studien zur Geschichte der Bayreuther Festspiele (1876–1976)*, 2 vols, Regensburg 1976, vol. 1, p. 66].)
8 Wolfgang Wagner, *Lebens-Akte*, p. 52.
9 Karbaum, *Studien zur Geschichte der Bayreuther Festspiele*, vol. 2, p. 8.
10 Ibid., p. 127. (Beidler in *Das literarische Deutschland*, 20 August 1951. Beidler compared the Third Reich with 'a twilight, not of the gods but of a bunch of gangsters, a theatrical illusion projected on to the screen of reality.... From the very beginning Bayreuth has been not a centre of artistic activity but rather a place of ideological worship, starting-point for a philosophical mission launched by the Anglo-Saxon sorcerer Houston Stewart Chamberlain, who surrounded himself with a host of little sorcerers, of minor and minimal significance.')
11 *Frankfurter Rundschau*, 24 June 1968 (remark made in the course of a rehearsal of the Festival orchestra).
12 Wolfgang Wagner, *Lebens-Akte*, p. 74. ('He always behaved with the utmost decorum towards my mother, bowing to her and kissing her hand.')
13 Mork, *Richard Wagner als politischer Schriftsteller*, p. 243.
14 Wolfgang Wagner, *Lebens-Akte*, p. 76.
15 Ibid., p. 102. (Wolfgang's annoyance is directed against Michael Karbaum's work, based on documentary evidence supplied by the then archivist Gertrud Strobel on her own authority, 'without reference either to me or my mother'.)
16 Ernst Deuerlein (ed.), *Der Aufstieg der NSDAP in Augenzeugenberichten*, Munich 1974, p. 23.
17 Ibid., p. 190.
18 Hermann Rauschning, *Die Revolution des Nihilismus. Kulisse und Wirklichkeit im Dritten Reich*, Zurich 1938, p. 39.
19 Walter C. Langer, *The Mind of Adolf Hitler. The Secret Wartime Report*, New York 1972, p. 92. [Translation modified – Translator's Note.] (The journalist in question, the American Frederick Oechsner, wrote an an article, 'Portable Lair: The Führer's Headquarters', in *Collier's* magazine, no. 110, 1942, and later the same year the book *This is the Enemy*. Oechsner described how he watched Hitler listening to Wagner with contorted expressions of both joy and pain gripping his features; brow furrowed, eyes closed, lips pressed tightly together.)
20 Albert Zoller, *Hitler privat. Erlebnisbericht seiner Geheimsekretärin*, Düsseldorf 1949, p. 57.
21 Brigitte Hamann, *Hitlers Wien. Lehrjahre eines Diktators*, Munich 1996, p. 243.

(Hanisch: 'Hitler was enthusiastic about Wagner and said on occasion that opera was the best form of religious worship.')

22 Adolf Hitler, *Reden und Proklamationen 1932–1945*, 2 vols, ed. Max Domarus, Würzburg 1962–3, vol. 1, p. 369.

23 Herbert Barth (ed.), *Der Festspielhügel. Richard Wagners Werk in Bayreuth 1876–1976*, Munich 1976 (*Völkischer Beobachter*, 14 July 1936).

24 John Toland, *Adolf Hitler*, London 1997, p. 83 ('I was Hitler's Boss', *Current History*, November 1941, p. 194).

25 Richard Wagner, *Sämtliche Schriften und Dichtungen*, 16 vols, Leipzig 1911–14, vol. 10, p. 136.

26 Adolf Hitler, *Mein Kampf*, 763rd–767th impression, Munich 1942, p. 226. ('. . . a short-lived Jewish domination, the goal that the instigators of the revolution always had before their eyes.')

27 Anton Joachimsthaler, *Korrektur einer Biographie. Adolf Hitler 1908–1920*, Munich 1989, p. 194.

28 Ernst Hanfstaengl, *Zwischen Weissem und Braunem Haus. Memoiren eines politischen Aussenseiters*, Munich 1970, p. 55.

29 Konrad Heiden, *Adolf Hitler*, 2 vols, Zurich 1936, vol. 1, p. 101.

30 Deuerlein (ed.), *Der Aufstieg der NSDAP in Augenzeugenberichten*, p. 259 (report in the *Hamburger Nachrichten* of a speech by Hitler in Hamburg on 1 May 1926).

31 Karl Alexander von Müller, *Erinnerungen*, vol. 2: *Mars und Venus. Erinnerungen 1914–1919*, Stuttgart 1954, p. 338.

32 Hanfstaengl, *Zwischen Weissem und Braunem Haus*, p. 84.

33 Ibid., p. 95. ('The firm conviction that his listeners took away with them was that with him they were embarking on a new and happier future.')

34 Deuerlein (ed.), *Der Aufstieg der NSDAP in Augenzeugenberichten*, p. 137.

35 Otto Wagener, *Hitler aus nächster Nähe. Aufzeichnungen eines Vertrauten 1929–1932*, ed. Henry A. Turner, Kiel 1987, p. 25.

36 Ibid., p. xi. (As he was writing his memoirs, noted Henry A. Turner, his editor, Wagener felt himself to be 'the custodian of the Holy Grail, that is to say, of the new Gospel preached by Adolf Hitler but maliciously distorted by so-called followers'.)

37 Deuerlein (ed.), *Der Aufstieg der NSDAP in Augenzeugenberichten*, p. 262. (At the second national Party rally in Weimar on 3–4 July 1926 Goebbels said: 'I thank Fate for having given us this man.')

38 Nike Wagner, *Über Wagner*, Stuttgart 1996, p. 252.

39 Cosima Wagner, *Das zweite Leben. Briefe und Aufzeichnungen 1883–1930*, ed. Dietrich Mack, Munich 1980, p. 319 (letter from Cosima to Hohenlohe, 22 December 1892).

40 Houston Stewart Chamberlain, *Die Grundlagen des Neunzehnten Jahrhunderts*, 2 vols, 28th impression, Munich 1942, vol. 1, p. 584.

41 Richard du Moulin Eckart, *Die Herrin von Bayreuth*, Berlin 1931, p. 443.

42 Cosima Wagner/Fürst Ernst zu Hohenlohe-Langenburg, *Briefwechsel*, ed. Ernst Fürst zu Hohenlohe, Stuttgart 1937, p. 368 (letter from Cosima, 14 February 1918).

43 Cosima Wagner, *Das zweite Leben*, p. 747 (letter from Cosima, 11 September 1919).

44 *Bayreuther Festspielführer 1924*, ed. Karl Grunsky, Bayreuth 1924, p. 272.

45 Winfried Schüler, *Der Bayreuther Kreis von seiner Entstehung bis zum Ausgang der Wilhelminischen Ära*, Münster 1971, p. 226 (*Bayreuther Blätter*, 1910).

46   Cosima Wagner, *Das zweite Leben*, p. 871.
47   James and Suzanne Pool, *Who Financed Hitler. The Secret Funding of Hitler's Rise to Power 1919–1933*, London 1979, p. 120. ('Lüdecke said that Siegfried fully subscribed to his father's written opinion that the Jew is the "plastic demon of decay"'.)
48   Syberberg, 'Winifred Wagner'.
49   Hartmut Zelinsky, *Richard Wagner. Ein deutsches Thema. Eine Dokumentation zur Wirkungsgeschichte Richard Wagners 1876–1976*, Frankfurt 1976, new edn Berlin 1983, p. 279.
50   Ibid., p. 213 (Paul Bülow, 'Adolf Hitler und der Bayreuther Kulturkreis').
51   Wolfgang Wagner, *Lebens-Akte*, p. 46.

Chapter 10 Pioneers

1   Christa Schroeder, *Er war mein Chef. Aus dem Nachlass der Sekretärin von Adolf Hitler*, ed. Anton Joachimsthaler, Munich 1985, p. 82.
2   André François-Poncet, *The Fateful Years: Memoirs of a French Ambassador in Berlin 1931–1938*, London 1949, pp. 289–90.
3   Albrecht Tyrell, *Vom 'Trommler' zum 'Führer'. Der Wandel von Hitlers Selbstverständnis zwischen 1919 und 1924*, Munich 1975, p. 40 (meeting of the Party on 26 October 1920).
4   Konrad Heiden, *Adolf Hitler*, 2 vols, Zurich 1936, vol. 1, p. 116.
5   Friedrich Nietzsche, *Sämtliche Werke*, 15 vols, ed. Giorgio Colli and Mazzino Montinari, Munich 1980, vol. 6, p. 339 ('Ecce Homo').
6   Anton Joachimsthaler, *Korrektur einer Biographie. Adolf Hitler 1908–1920*, Munich 1989, p. 229 (letter from Karl Mayr to Wolfgang Kapp, 24 September 1920).
7   Ernst Deuerlein (ed.), *Der Aufstieg der NSDAP in Augenzeugenberichten*, Munich 1974, p. 97.
8   Kurt Gossweiler, *Kapital, Reichswehr und NSDAP 1919–1924*, Cologne 1982, p. 554 (letter from Mayr to Kapp, 24 September 1920).
9   Joachimsthaler, *Korrektur eine Biographie*, p. 229.
10   Ibid., p. 247 (report by Lieutenant Bendt, 25 August 1919).
11   Deuerlein (ed.), *Der Aufstieg der NSDAP in Augenzeugenberichten*, p. 89 (Ernst Röhm in 1928 on the 'ambitious' Mayr, 'who today occupies a leading position in Marxist circles').
12   Ibid., p. 91 (essay commissioned by Mayr, 16 September 1919).
13   Richard Wagner, *Sämtliche Schriften und Dichtungen*, 16 vols, Leipzig 1911–14, vol. 10, p. 271 ('Erkenne dich selbst').
14   Deuerlein (ed.), *Der Aufstieg der NSDAP in Augenzeugenberichten*, p. 93.
15   Wagner, *Sämtliche Schriften und Dichtungen*, vol. 10, p. 268 ('Erkenne dich selbst'). ('The Nibelung's ring, symbolizing the wealth of the stock exchange, completes the frightening image of the sinister rulers of the world.')
16   Ibid., p. 274 ('Erkenne dich selbst').
17   Deuerlein (ed.), *Der Aufstieg der NSDAP in Augenzeugenberichten*, p. 130.
18   *Siegfried*, act 3, scene 3.
19   Martin Sabrow, *Der Rathenaumord: Rekonstruktion einer Verschwörung gegen die Republik in Weimar*, Munich 1994, p. 45. ('The Germanic Order did not operate in the twilight zone between camouflage and calculated publicity but completely clandestinely. So unclear is the nature of its activities, as deduced from

available sources, that its very existence has been questioned. It did exist, however, with a membership of some 1,500, most of them men of influence. Its guiding principle was to counteract the alleged influence of the Jews on the German nation.')

20   Karlheinz Weissmann, *Schwarze Fahnen, Runenzeichen. Die Entwicklung der politischen Symbolik der deutschen Rechten zwischen 1890 und 1945*, Cologne/Düsseldorf 1991 (illustrations).

21   Manuscript in the Bundesarchiv Koblenz, NS26/852.

22   Sabrow, *Der Rathenaumord*, p. 45.

23   Weissmann, *Schwarze Fahnen*.

24   Ibid., p. 70. (The Order had used the swastika since 1912. The following year it appeared on the cover of a book, *Die deutsche Kulturbewegung im Jahre 1913*, published by Diederichs in Jena.)

25   Sabrow, *Der Rathenaumord*, p. 46.

26   Richard Bauer et al. (eds), *München – Hauptstadt der Bewegung. Bayerns Metropole und der Nationalsozialismus*, Munich 1993, p. 54.

27   Robert G.L. Waite, *The Psychopathic God. Adolf Hitler*, New York 1977, p. 205.

28   Cosima Wagner, *Das zweite Leben. Briefe und Aufzeichnungen 1883–1930*, ed. Dietrich Mack, Munich 1980, p. 744 (letter from Cosima to Hohenlohe, 27 February 1919).

29   Gossweiler, *Kapital*, p. 143. (At a meeting of the 'Thule' on 9 November 1918, immediately after the collapse of the monarchy, Sebottendorf announced: 'In place of our blood-related princes we are now ruled by our arch-enemy – Jewry.')

30   Adolf Hitler, *Reden und Proklamationen 1932–1945*, 2 vols, ed. Max Domarus, Würzburg 1962–3, vol. 1, p. 574 (address delivered at the side of the coffin of the 'martyr' Wilhelm Gustloff on 12 February 1936).

31   James and Suzanne Pool, *Who Financed Hitler. The Secret Funding of Hitler's Rise to Power 1919–1933*, London 1979, p. 8.

32   Gossweiler, *Kapital*, p. 149. (On 5 January 1919 guidelines were issued based on the principle 'The German Workers' Party seeks the ennoblement of the German working class'.)

33   Ibid., p. 205. (A 'Thule' pamphlet of June 1919 reads: 'When the ground has been prepared, he will appear. Such is our faith.')

34   Pool and Pool, *Who Financed Hitler*, p. 7.

35   Gossweiler, *Kapital*, p. 146.

36   Christa Schroeder, *Er war mein Chef. Aus dem Nachlass der Sekretärin von Adolf Hitler*, ed. Anton Joachimsthaler, Munich 1985, p. 65.

37   Gossweiler, *Kapital*, p. 554. (Letter from Mayr to Kapp, 24 September 1920: '. . . a thoroughly German man, albeit a raving anti-Semite'.)

38   Heinz-Klaus Metzger and Rainer Riehn (eds), *Richard Wagner. Wie antisemitisch darf ein Künstler sein? Musikkonzepte 5*, Munich 1981, p. 17.

39   Christa Schroeder, *Er war mein Chef*, p. 65.

40   Albert Zoller, *Hitler privat. Erlebnisbericht seiner Geheimsekretärin*, Düsseldorf 1949, p. 117. ('One may well wonder how Hitler gained access after the war to those circles which would normally have been closed to a mere private. Anyway, in 1920, he made the acquaintance of the poet Eckart.')

41   Adolf Hitler, *Mein Kampf*, 763rd–767th impression, Munich 1942, p. 781.

42   Joachim C. Fest, *Hitler. Eine Biographie*, Frankfurt 1973, p. 558.

43   Hitler, *Reden und Proklamationen*, vol. 2, p. 1990 (speech on 24 February 1943).

44 *Siegfried*, act 3, scene 1.

45 Hermann Kretzschmann (ed.), *Bausteine zum Dritten Reich. Lehr- und Lesebuch des Reichsarbeitsdienstes*, Leipzig 1933, p. 587.

46 *Meistersinger*, act 3, scene 5.

47 Deuerlein (ed.), *Der Aufstieg der NSDAP in Augenzeugenberichten*, p. 104.

48 Joseph Goebbels, *Die Tagebücher von Joseph Goebbels. Sämtliche Fragmente*, 4 vols, ed. Eike Fröhlich, Munich 1987, vol. 2, p. 289. (Entry of 13 May 1943, in which Goebbels quotes Hitler as saying: 'The nations of today thus have no alternative but to annihilate the Jews.')

49 Metzger and Riehn (eds), *Richard Wagner. Wie antisemitisch darf ein Künstler sein?*, p. 17.

50 Margarete Plewnia, *Auf dem Weg zu Hitler. Der 'völkische' Publizist Dietrich Eckart*, Bremen 1970, p. 14.

51 Nicolaus von Below, *Als Hitlers Adjutant 1937–1945*, Mainz 1980, p. 22. ('I had previously no idea how close Hitler's relationship to music was. He waxed enthusiastic about Wagner, Bayreuth and Dietrich Eckart.')

52 Adolf Hitler, *Monologe im Führerhauptquartier 1941–1944. Die Aufzeichnungen Heinrich Heims*, ed. Werner Jochmann, Munich 1982, p. 308 (28 February–1 March 1942).

53 Plewnia, *Auf dem Weg*, p. 25.

54 Ibid., p. 31 (pamphlet of 6 April 1919, stating that the masses should be relieved of their Jewish leaders).

55 Ibid., p. 37. (A few weeks after Eckart's death his unfinished work on Bolshevism, entitled 'Bolshevism from Moses to Lenin. A Conversation between Myself and Adolf Hitler', was published. Although the authenticity of Hitler's words is dubious, they follow closely the doctrines of Chamberlain, which were basic both for Hitler and for Eckart. 'One can only understand the Jews', Hitler is recorded as saying, 'when one knows what their aim is – namely, beyond domination of the world to its destruction. . . . If one does not resist them, they will end up by destroying the world.')

56 Gossweiler, *Kapital*, p. 554 (letter from Mayr to Kapp, 24 September 1920).

57 Ibid., p. 317 (poem written for Hitler's birthday in 1923).

58 Heiden, *Adolf Hitler*, vol. 1, p. 58.

59 Christa Schroeder, *Er war mein Chef*, p. 65. (Hitler said that his friendship 'was one of the most beautiful things he had experienced in his twenties'.)

60 Heiden, *Adolf Hitler*, vol. 1, p. 250 (*Völkischer Beobachter*, 1922).

61 Hans Kohn, *Karl Kraus, Arthur Schnitzler, Otto Weininger. Aus dem jüdischen Wien der Jahrhundertwende*, Tübingen 1962, p. 30.

62 Otto Weininger, *Geschlecht und Charakter. Eine prinzipielle Untersuchung*, Vienna 1905, p. 600.

63 Plewnia, *Auf dem Weg*, p. 44.

64 Adolf Hitler, *Hitlers Tischgespräche im Führerhauptquartier*, ed. Henry A. Picker, Stuttgart 1976, p. 79 (statement of 1 December 1941).

65 George L. Mosse, *Towards the Final Solution. A History of European Racism*, London 1978, p. 110. ('Adolf Hitler knew Weininger's book and used it to bolster his own hatred of the Jews.')

66 Bauer et al. (eds), *München – Hauptstadt der Bewegung*, p. 56.

67 Pool and Pool, *Who Financed Hitler*, p. 74.

68 Ernst Hanfstaengl, *Zwischen Weissem und Braunem Haus. Memoiren eines politischen Aussenseiters*, Munich 1970, p. 105.

69 John Dornberg, *The Putsch that Failed. Munich 1923: Hitler's Rehearsal for Power*, London 1982, pp. 2, 312–13.
70 Bäuer et al. (eds), *München – Hauptstadt der Bewegung*, p. 123.
71 Ibid., p. 123.
72 Christa Schroeder, *Er war mein Chef*, p. 67.
73 Hanfstaengl, *Zwischen Weissem und Braunem Haus*, p. 48.
74 Kretzschmann (ed.), *Bausteine zum Dritten Reich*, p. 588.
75 Hanfstaengl, *Zwischen Weissem und Braunem Haus*, p. 109.
76 Kretzschmann (ed.), *Bausteine zum Dritten Reich*, p. 589.
77 John Toland, *Adolf Hitler*, London 1997, p. 101.
78 Friedelind Wagner, *Nacht über Bayreuth. Die Geschichte der Enkelin Richard Wagners*, Cologne 1994, p. 20.
79 Hanfstaengl, *Zwischen Weissem und Braunem Haus*, p. 49. (There are differing opinions about the source of Hitler's whip. According to Baldur von Schirach [*Ich glaubte an Hitler*, Hamburg 1967, p. 66] it was a gift from Helene Bechstein. Frau Bruckmann, on the other hand, maintained that it was she who had given it to Hitler. Schirach had his own answer: 'On closer examination it emerged that Hitler had not merely two but three such whips.')
80 Joseph Wulf, *Musik im Dritten Reich. Eine Dokumentation*, Berlin 1989, p. 91 (entry in Goebbels' diary, 28 November 1925).
81 Gossweiler, *Kapital*, p. 247.
82 Heiden, *Adolf Hitler*, vol. 1, p. 130.
83 Pool and Pool, *Who Financed Hitler*, p. 486.
84 Toland, *Adolf Hitler* (illustrations after p. 300).
85 Margarete Klinkerfuss, *Aufklänge aus vergangener Zeit*, Urach 1948, p. 229.
86 Richard du Moulin Eckart, *Cosima Wagner. Ein Lebens- und Charakterbild*, 2 vols, Berlin 1929, vol. 2, p. 882.
87 Friedelind Wagner, *Nacht über Bayreuth*, p. 20.

Chapter 11 An Official Blessing

1 Friedelind Wagner, *Nacht über Bayreuth. Die Geschichte der Enkelin Richard Wagners*, Cologne 1994, p. 159. ('One of Hitler's favourite remarks.')
2 Erich Ebermayer, *Magisches Bayreuth. Legende und Wirklichkeit*, Stuttgart 1951, p. 173.
3 Friedelind Wanger, *Nacht über Bayreuth*, p. 20.
4 Berta Geissmar, *Taktstock und Schaftstiefel. Erinnerungen an Wilhelm Furtwängler*, Cologne 1996, p. 239. (The original edition appeared under the title *The Baton and the Jackboot*, London 1944; the first German edition was published the following year in Zurich.)
5 Ernst Hanfstaengl, *Zwischen Weissem und Braunem Haus. Memoiren eines politischen Aussenseiters*, Munich 1970, p. 77.
6 Wolfgang Wagner, *Lebens-Akte. Autobiographie*, Munich 1994, p. 45.
7 Friedelind Wagner, *Nacht über Bayreuth*, p. 51.
8 Michael Karbaum, *Studien zur Geschichte der Bayreuther Festspiele (1876–1976)*, 2 vols, Regensburg 1976, vol. 2, p. 114.
9 Ibid., p. 69 (July 1925, when he also said: 'There is no more glorious expression of the German spirit than the works of the Master himself').
10 Ibid., p. 127 ('Bedenken gegen Bayreuth').

11 Ebermayer, *Magisches Bayreuth*, p. 172.

12 Michael Georg Conrad, *Wagners Geist und Kunst in Bayreuth*, Munich 1906, p. 8.

13 Ibid., p. 99. (Putting his views in a nutshell, Conrad said: 'Either for Bayreuth or against it! There is no middle course!')

14 *Bayreuther Festspielführer 1927*, ed. Paul Pretzsch, Bayreuth 1927, p. 21.

15 Peter-Karl Schuster (ed.), *Nationalsozialismus und Entartete Kunst*, Munich 1987, p. 270.

16 Karbaum, *Studien zur Geschichte der Bayreuther Festspiele*, vol. 2, p. 66 (letter from Hitler, 5 May 1924).

17 Ibid., p. 68.

18 Ibid., p. 67.

19 Joachim C. Fest, *Fremdheit und Nähe. Von der Gegenwart des Gewesenen*, Stuttgart 1996, p. 228 ('Um ein Wagner von aussen bittend').

20 Richard Wagner, *Sämtliche Schriften und Dichtungen*, 16 vols, Leipzig 1911–14, vol. 10, p. 274.

21 Friedelind Wagner, *Nacht über Bayreuth*, p. 14.

22 Hanfstaengl, *Zwischen Weissem und Braunem Haus*, p. 77.

23 Joachim C. Fest, *Hitler. Eine Biographie*, Frankfurt 1973, p. 223.

24 John Toland, *Adolf Hitler*, London 1997, p. 104. [Toland's translation modified – Translator's Note.]

25 Kurt Gossweiler, *Kapital, Reichswehr und NSDAP 1919–1924*, Cologne 1982, p. 316 (Max Maurenbrecher, editor-in-chief of the Pan-German League's *Deutsche Zeitung*, on a conversation he had had with Hitler in May 1922).

26 Albrecht Tyrell, *Vom 'Trommler' zum 'Führer'. Der Wandel von Hitlers Selbstverständnis zwischen 1919 und 1924*, Munich 1975, p. 272 (Hitler to Georg Schott in *Das Volksbuch vom Hitler*, Munich 1924, p. 53).

27 *Meistersinger*, act 3, scene 1.

28 Carl Friedrich Glasenapp (ed), *Wagner-Enzyklopädie*, vol. 2, Leipzig 1891, p. 311 (under 'Jesus').

29 Karl Alexander von Müller, *Erinnerungen*, vol. 3: *Im Wandel einer Welt*, ed. Otto Alexander von Müller, Munich 1966, p. 144.

30 Ernst Deuerlein (ed.), *Der Aufstieg der NSDAP in Augenzeugenberichten*, Munich 1974, p. 181 (the police authority for Nuremberg-Fürth on the rally of 1–2 September 1923).

31 Richard Bauer et al. (eds), *München – Hauptstadt der Bewegung. Bayerns Metropole und der Nationalsozialismus*, Munich 1993, p. 82 (Captain Adolf Heiss on the aims of the Kampfbund).

32 Tyrell, *Vom 'Trommler' zum 'Führer'*, p. 157 (May 1923).

33 Karl Alexander von Müller, *Erinnerungen*, vol. 3, p. 149.

34 Houston Stewart Chamberlain, *Richard Wagner*, Munich 1901, p. 504. (Chamberlain even quotes Nietzsche, who had long fallen out with Bayreuth, because he had been the first to take up cudgels on Wagner's behalf. ['For us Bayreuth symbolizes the dawn of the day of battle!'])

35 Jordi Mota und Maria Infiesta, *Das Werk Richard Wagners im Spiegel der Kunst*, Tübingen 1995, plate 105. (Stassen's design seems to have impressed Hitler, who said of the swastika that 'the old symbol of the Germanic peoples in Germany became the new and rejuvenated symbol of the Third Reich' [Baldur von Schirach, *Ich glaubte an Hitler*, Hamburg 1967, p. 315].)

36 Karbaum, *Studien zur Geschichte der Bayreuther Festspiele*, vol. 2, p. 68.

37 Friedelind Wagner, *Nacht über Bayreuth*, p. 68.

38 Ebermayer, *Magisches Bayreuth*, p. 170.

39 Karbaum, *Studien zur Geschichte der Bayreuther Festspiele*, vol. 2, p. 68 (Hans Conrad, 'Der Führer und Bayreuth', 1936).

40 Theodor Heuss, *Hitlers Weg*, ed. Eberhard Jäckel, Tübingen 1968, p. 27.

41 Erich Kuby, *Richard Wagner & Co. Zum 150. Geburtstag des Meisters*, Hamburg 1968, p. 148. ('You tell me that the worse the Jew, the greater must be our love. But I cannot understand how I can love all these vulgar and shameful features, all these despicable qualities that besmirch and pollute everything that I value and cherish, all these things that in the last analysis will utterly ruin and destroy the values of the noble old Europe that we esteem – how can I love all this? With all the strength at my command I hate the Jews and hate them and hate them!' Even Hitler could not have surpassed this – he could only put it into practice.)

42 Houston Stewart Chamberlain, *Die Grundlagen des Neunzehnten Jahrhunderts*, 2 vols, 28th impression, Munich 1992, vol. 2, p. 443. ('The Jews' very existence is an offence against the divine laws of life . . . the whole tribe needs to be purged – but not from an offence they have deliberately committed but from one they have committed without knowing it.')

43 Adolf Hitler, *Sämtliche Aufzeichnungen 1905–1924*, ed. Eberhard Jäckel and Axel Kuhn, Stuttgart 1980, p. 1231 (Hitler to Siegfried Wagner, 5 May 1924).

44 Ibid., p. 1232.

45 H.F. Peters, *Zarathustras Schwester. Fritz und Lieschen Nietzsche – ein deutsches Trauerspiel*, Munich 1983, p. 298. (On 17 February 1933 they even met at a performance of *Tristan* in Weimar.)

46 Hans Severus Ziegler, *Adolf Hitler aus dem Erleben dargestellt*, Göttingen 1964, p. 12.

47 Fest, *Hitler*, p. 259.

48 Joseph Goebbels, *Die Tagebücher von Joseph Goebbels. Sämtliche Fragmente*, 4 vols, ed. Eike Fröhlich, Munich 1987, vol. 2, p. 450 (entry made in Wahnfried, 24 July 1933).

49 Hartmut Zelinsky, *Richard Wagner. Ein deutsches Thema. Eine Dokumentation zur Wirkungsgeschichte Richard Wagners 1876–1976*, Frankfurt 1976, new edn Berlin 1983, p. 169 (letter from Chamberlain to Hitler, 7 October 1923).

50 Georg Schott (ed.), *Houston Stewart Chamberlain. Der Seher des Dritten Reiches*, Munich 1934, p. 6.

51 Konrad Heiden, *Adolf Hitler*, 2 vols, Zurich 1936, vol. 1, p. 114.

52 Zelinsky, *Richard Wagner*, p. 170.

53 *Bayreuther Festspielführer 1924*, ed. Karl Grunsky, Bayreuth 1924, p. 230 (Friedrich von Schoen, 'Eine Erinnerung an Richard Wagner').

54 Hartmut Zelinsky, *Sieg oder Untergang: Sieg und Untergang. Kaiser Wilhelm II, die Werk-Idee Richard Wagners und der 'Weltkampf'*, Munich 1990, p. 12.

55 König Ludwig II/Richard Wagner, *Briefwechsel*, 4 vols, ed. Wittelsbacher Ausgleichsfonds and Winifred Wagner, rev. Otto Strobel, Karlsruhe 1936–7, vol. 3, p. 230 (letter from Wagner, 22 November 1881).

56 Zelinsky, *Richard Wagner*, p. 170.

57 Karbaum, *Studien zur Geschichte der Bayreuther Festspiele*, vol. 2, p. 67 (diary entry of 8 May 1926).

58 Winfried Schüler, *Der Bayreuther Kreis von seiner Entstehung bis zum Ausgang der Wilhelminischen Ära*, Münster 1971, p. 85 (from a conversation between the

author and Winifred Wagner, 21 June 1961).

59 Friedelind Wagner, *Nacht über Bayreuth*, p. 20.
60 Hans-Jürgen Syberberg, 'Winifred Wagner und die Geschichte des Hauses Wahnfried 1914–1975', film interview with Winifred Wagner 1975.
61 Adolf Hitler, *Monologe im Führerhauptquartier 1941–1944. Die Aufzeichnungen Heinrich Heims*, ed. Werner Jochmann, Munich 1982, p. 224 (24–5 January 1942).
62 Ebermayer, *Magisches Bayreuth*, p. 174.
63 Ziegler, *Adolf Hitler*, p. 154.
64 Friedelind Wagner, *Nacht über Bayreuth*, p. 20.
65 Tyrell, *Vom 'Trommler' zum 'Führer'*, p. 162.
66 Ibid., p. 163
67 Albrecht Tyrell, *'Führer befiehl . . .': Selbstzeugnisse aus der Kampfzeit der NSDAP*, Düsseldorf 1969, p. 56 (statement made by General von Lossow at Hitler's trial, 10 April 1924).
68 Fest, *Hitler*, p. 253 (in Ernst Boepple, *Adolf Hitlers Reden*, Munich 1933, p. 87).

Chapter 12 The Saviour Betrayed

1 Friedelind Wagner, *Nacht über Bayreuth. Die Geschichte der Enkelin Richard Wagners*, Cologne 1994, p. 27. ('Germany has become a pigsty.')
2 Michael Karbaum, *Studien zur Geschichte der Bayreuther Festspiele (1876–1976)*, 2 vols, Regensburg 1976, vol. 2, p. 65 (letter to Alexander Spring before 9 November 1923).
3 Hans-Jürgen Syberberg, 'Winifred Wagner und die Geschichte des Hauses Wahnfried 1914–1975', film interview with Winifred Wagner 1975.
4 Peter P. Pachl, *Siegfried Wagner. Genie im Schatten*, Munich 1988, p. 325.
5 Ibid., p. 327.
6 Adolf Hitler, *Sämtliche Aufzeichnungen 1905–1924*, ed. Eberhard Jäckel and Axel Kuhn, Stuttgart 1980, p. 1232 (letter from Hitler to Siegfried Wagner, 5 May 1924).
7 Joachim C. Fest, *Hitler. Eine Biographie*, Frankfurt 1973, p. 20.
8 Ernst Deuerlein (ed.), *Der Aufstieg der NSDAP in Augenzeugenberichten*, Munich 1974, p. 193 (report by Karl Alexander von Müller).
9 Ibid., p. 126 (statement made 18 October 1920).
10 Richard du Moulin Eckart, *Wahnfried*, Leipzig 1925, p. 37.
11 Deuerlein (ed.), *Der Aufstieg der NSDAP in Augenzeugenberichten*, p. 193 (as note 8).
12 John Dornberg, *The Putsch that Failed. Munich 1923: Hitler's Rehearsal for Power*, London 1982, p. 122. ('To Paula Schlier, a young typist at the *Völkischer Beobachter*, the atmosphere was "electrifying, disturbingly tense"' [ibid., p. 122].)
13 Deuerlein (ed.), *Der Aufstieg der NSDAP in Augenzeugenberichten*, p. 157 (statement made in Munich, 25 October 1922).
14 Ibid., p. 196 (Karl Alexander von Müller).
15 Winfried Schüler, *Der Bayreuther Kreis von seiner Entstehung bis zum Ausgang der Wilhelminischen Ära*, Münster 1971, p. 127 (letter from Josef Stolzing-Czerny to Eva Chamberlain, 17 October 1923, telling her that Hitler had been 'as delighted as a child' to see Chamberlain's 'letter of approval' of 7 October 1923).
16 Friedelind Wagner, *Nacht über Bayreuth*, p. 52. ('However late it was, he never failed to come into the children's room and tell us bloodcurdling stories about

his adventures. Sitting on our pillows in the semi-darkness, the four of us listened in awe, shivers running up and down our spines. He showed us the revolver he wore – against the law, of course: a tiny weapon which fitted easily into his hand but carried twenty bullets.')

17 Karl Alexander von Müller, *Erinnerungen*, vol. 3: *Im Wandel einer Welt*, ed. Otto Alexander von Müller, Munich 1966, pp. 162–3. ('One listener not converted by Hitler's speech was the man next to Müller, Dr. Max von Grüber, professor of "racial hygiene" at Munich University. Himself an ardent nationalist, he was not impressed by this first close look at Hitler. "Face and head: bad race, mongrel. Low, receding forehead, ugly nose, broad cheekbones, small eyes, dark hair"' [John Toland, *Adolf Hitler*, London 1997, p. 944].)

18 Karl Alexander von Müller, *Erinnerungen*, vol. 3, p. 163.

19 Toland, *Adolf Hitler*, p. 158.

20 Ibid., p. 159.

21 Deuerlein (ed.), *Der Aufstieg der NSDAP in Augenzeugenberichten*, p. 200 (report by Paula Schlier).

22 Karl Alexander von Müller, *Erinnerungen*, vol. 3, p. 166.

23 Deuerlein (ed.), *Der Aufstieg der NSDAP in Augenzeugenberichten*, p. 199 (report by Police Inspector Michel Freiherr von Godin).

24 Karl Alexander von Müller, *Erinnerungen*, vol. 3, p. 167.

25 Fest, *Hitler*, p. 274.

26 Deuerlein (ed.), *Der Aufstieg der NSDAP in Augenzeugenberichten*, p. 202 (Stefan Zweig, *Die Welt von Gestern. Erinnerungen eines Europäers*, Stockholm 1942).

27 Karl Alexander von Müller, *Erinnerungen*, vol. 3, p. 168.

28 Bavarian Central State Archives, General Commissariat, p. 575.

29 Erich Ebermayer, *Magisches Bayreuth. Legende und Wirklichkeit*, Stuttgart 1951, p. 176.

30 Ibid., p. 177.

31 Friedelind Wagner, *Nacht über Bayreuth*, p. 28.

32 Karbaum, *Studien zur Geschichte der Bayreuther Festspiele*, vol. 2, p. 68 (Hans Conrad, 'Der Führer und Bayreuth', 1936).

33 Berndt W. Wessling (ed.), *Bayreuth im Dritten Reich*, Weinheim 1983, p. 187. (Siegfried Scheffler, 'Herrschaft und Dienst. Winifred Wagner über Bayreuths Zukunft', 1933. Winifred said that Hitler recognized in Wagner 'the educational, life-giving force that Germany needed for its development, the personification of struggle and of self-liberation'.)

34 Hartmut Zelinsky, *Richard Wagner. Ein deutsches Thema. Eine Dokumentation zur Wirkungsgeschichte Richard Wagners 1876–1976*, Frankfurt 1976, new edn Berlin 1983, p. 169 (open letter from Winifred Wagner, 14 November 1923).

35 Ebermayer, *Magisches Bayreuth*, p. 178.

36 Zelinsky, *Richard Wagner*, p. 169.

37 Ibid., p. 217.

38 Karbaum, *Studien zur Geschichte der Bayreuther Festspiele*, vol. 2, p. 68.

39 Otto Wagener, *Hitler aus nächster Nähe. Aufzeichnungen eines Vertrauten 1929–1932*, ed. Henry A. Turner, Kiel 1987, p. 230.

40 Frederic Spotts, *Bayreuth. A History of the Wagner Festival*, New Haven 1994, p. 139.

41 Hitler, *Sämtliche Aufzeichnungen*, p. 1233 (letter from Hitler to Siegfried Wagner, 5 May 1924).

42 Karbaum, *Studien zur Geschichte der Bayreuther Festspiele*, vol. 2, p. 65 (letter

from Siegfried Wagner to Rosa Eidam, an old supporter of Wagner's, Christmas 1923).

43 Karl Alexander von Müller, *Erinnerungen*, vol. 3, p. 180.

44 Hans Severus Ziegler, *Adolf Hitler aus dem Erleben dargestellt*, Göttingen 1964, p. 157. ('If Siegfried was later somewhat withdrawn, Hitler understood perfectly well why, since politically one had to proceed with the utmost caution. There was no question, unaffected and sensitive as he was, of his being politically weak or reluctant to commit himself.')

45 Adolf Hitler, *Monologe im Führerhauptquartier 1941–1944. Die Aufzeichnungen Heinrich Heims*, ed. Werner Jochmann, Munich 1982, p. 224. (In the 'Wolf's Lair', 24–5 January 1942: 'I love Wahnfried and these people!')

46 Hitler, *Sämtliche Aufzeichnungen*, p. 1059. (Letter from Hitler to Lüdecke, 4 January 1924: 'Thanking you most sincerely for representing the interests of the movement in Italy. . . .')

47 Ernst Hanfstaengl, *Zwischen Weissem und Braunem Haus. Memoiren eines politischen Aussenseiters*, Munich 1970, p. 46.

48 James and Suzanne Pool, *Who Financed Hitler. The Secret Funding of Hitler's Rise to Power 1919–1933*, London 1979, p. 120.

49 Ibid., p. 126.

50 Pachl, *Siegfried Wagner*, p. 336.

51 Cosima Wagner, *Das zweite Leben. Briefe und Aufzeichnungen 1883–1930*, ed. Dietrich Mack, Munich 1980, p. 750 (letter from Cosima to Hohenlohe, July 1923).

52 Toland, *Adolf Hitler*, p. 119.

53 Fest, *Hitler*, p. 276 ('. . . and his followers hailed him as the German Messiah').

54 Deuerlein (ed), *Der Aufstieg der NSDAP in Augenzeugenberichten*, p. 207 (statement by Hitler on 26 February 1924, the first day of the proceedings).

55 Ibid., p. 214 (statement by Hitler, 28 February 1924).

56 Hitler, *Sämtliche Aufzeichnungen*, p. 1199 (Hitler's final speech, 27 March 1924).

57 Ibid., p. 1208.

58 Adolf Hitler, *Hitlers Tischgespräche im Führerhauptquartier*, ed. Henry Picker, Stuttgart 1976, p. 78 (1 December 1942).

59 Hitler, *Sämtliche Aufzeichnungen*, p. 1210. (Hitler's final speech, 27 March 1924. His remark that he saw his task as lying in 'the destruction of Marxism' – that is to say, of Jewry – was made just before his visit to Wagner's grave in the garden of Wahnfried.)

60 Ibid., p. 1215 (Hitler's final speech).

61 Richard Wagner, *Sämtliche Briefe*, ed. G. Strobel, W. Wolf, H.-J. Bauer and J. Forner, Leipzig 1967–, vol. 1, p. 192. (The 'Autobiographische Skizze', first published in the *Zeitung für die elegante Welt*, 1 and 8 February 1843. Wagner, recently returned from Paris, wanted to draw attention to himself in his native Germany.)

Chapter 13 Wagnerian Hero: A Self-Portrait

1 *Bayreuther Festspielführer 1924*, ed. Karl Grunsky, Bayreuth 1924.

2 Ibid., p. 237 (Hans Schüler, 'Die Politik der Liebe').

3 Richard Wagner, *Sämtliche Schriften und Dichtungen*, 16 vols, Leipzig 1911–14, vol. 10, p. 274 ('Erkenne dich selbst').

4 *Bayreuther Festspielführer 1924*, p. 239 (Hans Schüler, 'Die Politik der Liebe').

5 Michael Karbaum, *Studien zur Geschichte der Bayreuther Festspiele (1876–1976)*, 2 vols, Regensburg 1976, vol. 2, p. 69 (Hans Conrad, 'Der Führer und Bayreuth', 1936).

6 Ibid., p. 127 (Franz Wilhelm Beidler, 'Bedenken gegen Bayreuth', 1951).

7 Ibid., p. 111 ('Heinz Tietjen, address on the occasion of the Appeal to the Prussian State Theatres', 30 January 1936).

8 Adolf Hitler, *Reden und Proklamationen 1932–1945*, 2 vols, ed. Max Domarus, Würzburg 1962–3, vol. 2, p. 291 (*Völkischer Beobachter*, 31 July 1933).

9 Peter P. Pachl, *Siegfried Wagner. Genie im Schatten*, Munich 1988, p. 337. ('It is not a time for festivals but I regard the occasion as one for "strengthening the German spirit". I know only one sin – the sin against the spirit.' But as his audience well knew, that spirit now rested on Hitler's shoulders, and it had been sinned against when he had been betrayed and imprisoned.)

10 Ibid., p. 337.

11 Karbaum, *Studien zur Geschichte der Bayreuther Festspiele*, vol. 2, p. 66 (letter from Hitler to Siegfried Wagner, 5 May 1924).

12 *Meistersinger*, act 3, scene 5.

13 Rosa Eidam, *Bayreuther Festspielzeiten 1883–1924. Persönliche Erinnerungen*, Ansbach 1925, p. 31.

14 Andreas Mork, *Richard Wagner als politischer Schriftsteller. Weltanschauung und Wirkungsgeschichte*, Frankfurt 1990, p. 254 (*Frankfurter Zeitung*, 3 August 1924).

15 Karbaum, *Studien zur Geschichte der Bayreuther Festspiele*, vol. 2, p. 91 (E. Müller, 'Zur Abwehr der gegen Richard Wagner angezettelten Lügenhetze', 1933).

16 *Bayreuther Festspielführer 1933*, ed. Otto Strobel, Bayreuth 1933, p. 182 (Karl-Alfons Meyer, 'Ein Meistersinger-Problem').

17 Martin Gregor-Dellin, *Richard Wagner. Sein Leben, sein Werk, sein Jahrhundert*, Munich 1980, p. 722.

18 Werner Otto (ed.), *Richard Wagner. Ein Lebens- und Charakterbild in Dokumenten und zeitgenössischen Darstellungen*, Berlin 1990, p. 558 (Max Kalbeck, *Das Bühnenfestspiel zu Bayreuth*, Breslau 1877).

19 *Bayreuther Festspielführer 1925*, ed. Karl Grunsky, Bayreuth 1925, p. 6.

20 Karbaum, *Studien zur Geschichte der Bayreuther Festspiele*, vol. 1, p. 70.

21 Adolf Hitler, *Hitlers Tischgespräche im Führerhauptquartier*, ed. Henry Picker, Stuttgart 1976, p. 116.

22 Joseph Goebbels, *Die Tagebücher von Joseph Goebbels. Sämtliche Fragmente*, 4 vols, ed. Eike Fröhlich, Munich 1987, vol. 2, p. 408 (entry of 30 May 1942).

23 Karbaum, *Studien zur Geschichte der Bayreuther Festspiele*, vol. 2, p. 67. (On 9 May 1926 Goebbels noted: 'Wagner's *Tannhäuser* aroused my youth.')

24 Albert Zoller, *Hitler privat. Erlebnisbericht seiner Geheimsekretärin*, Düsseldorf 1949, p. 57.

25 Ernst Deuerlein (ed.), *Der Aufstieg der NSDAP in Augenzeugenberichten*, Munich 1974, p. 363 (from the American journalist H.R. Knickerbocker's description of the scene at a Nazi rally).

26 *Bayreuther Festspielführer 1924*, p. 175 (the final sentence of an article by Erwin Geck, 'Richard Wagner und der Staat').

27 Ernst Hanfstaengl, *Zwischen Weissem und Braunem Haus. Memoiren eines politischen Aussenseiters*, Munich 1970, p. 158.

28 Adolf Hitler, *Monologe im Führerhauptquartier 1941–1944. Die Aufzeichnungen Heinrich Heims*, ed. Werner Jochmann, Munich 1982, p. 288 (20–1 February 1942).

29 John Toland, *Adolf Hitler*, London 1997, plates following p. 300 (letter from Winifred Wagner to Hitler, 9 December 1923). [My translation of the original German letter – Translator's Note.]

30 Pachl, *Siegfried Wagner*, p. 391.

31 Karbaum, *Studien zur Geschichte der Bayreuther Festspiele (1876–1976)*, vol. 2, p. 65 (letter from Hitler to Siegfried Wagner, 5 May 1924).

32 Pachl, *Siegfried Wagner*, p. 336. ('It was on her paper, with her ink and her pens, that he wrote the first volume of *Mein Kampf*' – Friedelind Wagner.)

33 Albrecht Tyrell, *Vom 'Trommler' zum 'Führer'. Der Wandel von Hitlers Selbstverständnis zwischen 1919 und 1924*, Munich 1975, p. 165.

34 H.F. Peters, *Zarathustras Schwester. Fritz und Lieschen Nietzsche – ein deutsches Trauerspiel*, Munich 1983, p. 301. (Hitler struck Elisabeth Nietzsche as a man whose influence was religious rather than political. 'Fritz would have been delighted with him,' she wrote in a letter of 31 October 1935.)

35 Konrad Heiden, *Geschichte des Nationalsozialismus. Die Karriere einer Idee*, Berlin 1933, p. 64.

36 Hermann Rauschning, *Die Revolution des Nihilismus. Kulisse und Wirklichkeit im Dritten Reich*, Zurich 1938, p. 39.

37 Hitler, *Tischgespräche*, p. 409 (4 July 1942).

38 *Monologe*, p. 262 (3–4 February 1942).

39 König Ludwig II/Richard Wagner, *Briefwechsel*, 4 vols, ed. Wittelsbacher Ausgleichsfonds and Winifred Wagner, rev. Otto Strobel, Karlsruhe 1936–7, vol. 4, p. 99 (letter from Wagner to Röckel, 26 October 1865).

40 Dieter Borchmeyer and Jörg Salaquarda (eds), *Nietzsche und Wagner. Stationen einer epochalen Begegnung*, 2 vols, Frankfurt 1994, vol. 1, p. 52 (letter from Cosima to Nietzsche, 6 February 1870).

41 Karbaum, *Studien zur Geschichte der Bayreuther Festspiele*, vol. 2, p. 91 (Goebbels, 'Richard Wagner und das Kunstempfinden unserer Zeit' in the *Völkischer Beobachter*, 8 August 1933).

42 Hitler, *Reden und Proklamationen*, vol. 2, p. 1603.

43 Ibid., p. 2205 (proclamation on the anniversary of the foundation of the Party, 24 February 1945).

44 *Bayreuther Festspielführer 1934*, ed. Otto Strobel, Bayreuth 1934, p. 124 (Karl Grunsky, 'Wege zu Wagner').

45 *Bayreuther Festspielführer 1924*, p. 99 (Hans Alfred Grunsky, 'Der Ring des Nibelungen').

46 Adolf Hitler, *Mein Kampf*, 763rd–767th impression, Munich 1942, p. 68.

47 Ibid., p. 20.

48 Ibid., p. 21.

49 Ibid., p. 59.

50 Ibid., p. 296.

51 Richard Wagner, *Gesammelte Schriften und Dichtungen*, 10 vols, ed. Richard Wagner, Leipzig 1871–83, vol. 3, pp. 53f.

52 Hitler, *Mein Kampf*, p. 359.

53 *Siegfried*, act 2, scene 3.

54 Hitler, *Mein Kampf*, p. 61.

55 Ibid., p. 330.

56 Ibid., p. 68.

57 Ibid., p. 345.

58 Ibid., p. 45.

59 *Siegfried*, act 1, scene 3.
60 Hitler, *Mein Kampf*, p. 331.
61 Ibid., p. 67. ('Whenever one grasped hold of one of these apostles, one found oneself holding soft slime which trickled out in rivulets between one's fingers, then the next moment flowed together again in a lump.')
62 Ibid., p. 630.
63 Ibid., p. 421.
64 Ibid., p. 163.
65 Ibid., p. 346.
66 Ibid.
67 Ibid., p. 169.
68 Ibid., p. 413.
69 Ibid., p. 420.
70 Ibid., p. 358.
71 Ibid., p. 69.
72 Ibid., p. 70.
73 Ibid., p. 358. ('After the death of its victim the vampire itself dies sooner or later.')
74 Ibid., p. 40.
75 Ibid., p. 46. ('. . . to fight poison gas with poison gas. More sensitive natures have to be told that it is a matter of life or death.')
76 Ibid., p. 225. ('There is no question of settling on a compromise with the Jews – it is a matter of "Either–Or." ' In other words, only one of the two races will survive. 'For my part, I resolved to enter the realm of politics.')
77 Ibid., p. 772. (Hitler suggested that it would have been sufficient to gas 'twelve or fifteen thousand of these Hebrew poisoners of our people'.)
78 Ibid., p. 225.
79 Richard Wagner, *Sämtliche Briefe*, ed. G. Strobel, W. Wolf, H.-J. Bauer and J. Forner, Leipzig 1967–, vol. 1, p. 97.
80 *Die Walküre*, act 1, scene 2. (Further references by Siegmund to 'the people's tragic predicament' occur later in the work.)
81 Hitler, *Mein Kampf*, p. 16.
82 Ibid., p. 20.
83 Wagner, *Sämtliche Schriften und Dichtungen*, vol. 12, p. 360 ('Die Not').
84 Hitler, *Mein Kampf*, p. 116.
85 *Siegfried*, act 2, scene 2.
86 Ibid. ('How happy I feel that he is not my father . . . the day has become bright and cheerful since the ugly creature left me, and I shall never see him again!')
87 Hitler, *Mein Kampf*, p. 56.
88 Ibid., p. 66.
89 *Siegfried*, act 1, scene 3.
90 Hitler, *Mein Kampf*, p. 738.
91 Ibid., p. 186.
92 Ibid., p. 189. (As Karbaum quotes [*Studien zur Geschichte der Bayreuther Festspiele*, vol. 2, p. 66]: 'The sword, both source and symbol of a new spiritual doctrine, is the same sword as that forged in Bayreuth, the sword with which we fight today.')
93 Karl Alexander von Müller, *Erinnerungen*, vol. 3: *Im Wandel einer Welt*, ed. Otto Alexander von Müller, Munich 1966, p. 305.

Chapter 14 Blood Brotherhood

1   Anton Joachimsthaler, *Korrektur einer Biographie. Adolf Hitler 1908–1920*, Munich 1989, plates following p. 64. (In his registration card from the late summer of 1909 Hitler is described as 'Writer'.)
2   Otto Wagener, *Hitler aus nächster Nähe. Aufzeichnungen eines Vertrauten 1929–1932*, ed. Henry A. Turner, Kiel 1987, p. 415.
3   Adolf Hitler, *Mein Kampf*, 763rd–767th impression, Munich 1942, p. 271.
4   Ibid., p. 272.
5   Ibid., p. 278.
6   Ibid., p. 270.
7   Ibid., p. 64.
8   Ibid., p. 278.
9   Ibid., p. 269.
10 Ibid., p. 274.
11 Ibid., p. 357.
12 Léon Poliakov and Joseph Wulf, *Das Dritte Reich und seine Denker*, Frankfurt/ Berlin 1983, p. 424. (Streicher in *Deutsche Volksgesundheit aus Blut und Boden*, Nuremberg 1935, p. 1: 'We now know why the Jew is at such pains to employ all the tricks of seduction at his disposal to dishonour German girls at as early an age as possible. It is to prevent them from ever having German children!')
13 Adolf Hitler, *Reden und Proklamationen 1932–1945*, 2 vols, ed. Max Domarus, Würzburg 1962–3, vol. 1, p. 538 (Hitler's 'final appeal' of 15 September 1935).
14 Hitler, *Mein Kampf*, p. 444.
15 Houston Stewart Chamberlain, *Die Grundlagen des Neunzehnten Jahrhunderts*, 2 vols, 28th impression, Munich 1992, vol. 1, p. 441.
16 Wagener, *Hitler aus nächster Nähe*, p. 341.
17 Hitler, *Mein Kampf*, p. 70.
18 Richard Wagner, *Gesammelte Schriften und Dichtungen*, 10 vols, ed. Richard Wagner, Leipzig 1871–83, vol. 2, p. 151.
19 Ibid.
20 Cosima Wagner, *Die Tagebücher*, 4 vols, ed. Martin Gregor-Dellin and Dietrich Mack, Munich 1982, vol. 3, p. 40 (entry of 24 January 1878).
21 *Parsifal*, act 2.
22 Cosima Wagner, *Tagebücher*, vol. 3, p. 68 (entry of 23 March 1878).
23 *Parsifal*, act 1.
24 Ibid.
25 Susanna Grossmann-Vendrey (ed.), *Bayreuth in der deutschen Presse*, vol. 2: *Die Uraufführung des Parsifal (1882)*, Regensburg 1977, p. 57 (Hermann Messner, 'Richard Wagners *Parsifal*,' 1882).
26 *Parsifal*, act 2.
27 Marie von Bülow, *Hans von Bülows Leben dargestellt aus seinen Briefen*, Leipzig 1921, p. 203 (letter of 12 February 1866).
28 Cosima Wagner, *Tagebücher*, vol. 3, p. 225 (entry of 11 November 1878).
29 Ibid., p. 224 (entry of 10 November 1878).
30 Ibid., p. 490 (entry of 10 February 1880).
31 Ibid., vol. 4, p. 687 (entry of 10 February 1881).
32 Carl Friedrich Glasenapp, *Das Leben Richard Wagners*, 6 vols, Leipzig 1904–11, vol. 6, p. 298.

33 Ibid., p. 299.

34 König Ludwig II/Richard Wagner, *Briefwechsel*, 4 vols, ed. Wittelsbacher Ausgleichsfonds and Winifred Wagner, rev. Otto Strobel, Karlsruhe 1936–7, vol. 3, p. 74 (letter from Wagner, 26 January 1876).

35 Michael Karbaum, *Studien zur Geschichte der Bayreuther Festspiele (1876–1976)*, 2 vols, Regensburg 1976, vol. 2, p. 65. (Christmas letter of 1923 to Rosa Eidam: 'Jew and Jesuit are walking arm in arm in their campaign to root out the German spirit.')

36 Ludwig Feuerbach, *Das Wesen des Christentums*, Stuttgart 1969, p. 354. (Feuerbach, who was much admired by Wagner, called holy water *'lavacrum regenerationis'* because it 'purges man from the uncleanliness of original sin, exorcizes the devils that reside in him and reconciles him with God' [edition Leipzig 1849].)

37 Wagner, *Parsifal*, programme for a performance given by the Bavarian State Opera in 1995, p. 46 (letter from Liszt to Carolyne von Sayn-Wittgenstein, 29 October 1872).

38 Hans von Wolzogen, *Bayreuth*, Leipzig n.d., p. 42.

39 Richard Wagner, *Sämtliche Schriften und Dichtungen*, 16 vols, Leipzig 1911–14, vol. 10, p. 274 ('Erkenne dich selbst').

40 Ibid., p. 270.

41 Ibid., p. 280.

42 Richard Wagner, *Briefe*, ed. Hanjo Kesting, Munich 1988, p. 615 (letter from Wagner to Ludwig, 31 March 1880).

43 Richard Wagner, *Dichtungen und Schriften*, 10 vols, ed. Dieter Borchmeyer, Frankfurt 1983, vol. 4, p. 333 (first prose sketch of *Parsifal*, 27–30 August 1865).

44 Wagner, *Sämtliche Schriften und Dichtungen*, vol. 10, p. 230 ('Religion und Kunst').

45 Ibid., p. 284 ('Heldentum und Christentum').

46 August Kubizek, *Adolf Hitler. Mein Jugendfreund*, Graz 1953, p. 101.

47 Hitler, *Mein Kampf*, p. 314.

48 Ibid., p. 339.

49 Ibid., p. 358.

50 Hans-Joachim Bauer, *Richard-Wagner-Lexikon*, Bergisch Gladbach 1988, p. 348 (Wieland Wagner's 'Parsifal cross' as a psychological symbol).

51 Glasenapp, *Das Leben Richard Wagners*, vol. 4, p. 311.

52 Programme quoted in note 37, p. 60.

53 Grossmann-Vendrey (ed.), *Bayreuth in der deutschen Presse*, vol. 2, p. 183 (Max Kalbeck, 'Das Bühnenweihfestspiel in Bayreuth', *Wiener Allgemeine Zeitung* 1882).

54 Richard Wagner, *Das Braune Buch. Tagebuchaufzeichnungen 1865 bis 1882*, ed. Joachim Bergfeld, Munich 1988, p. 75 (entry of 2 September, 1865).

55 Wagner, *Dichtungen und Schriften*, vol. 4, p. 365. (Second draft, 1877. Klingsor: 'I shall destroy his race.')

56 *Parsifal*, act 2.

57 Ibid., act 1.

58 Hitler, *Mein Kampf*, p. 278.

59 Ibid., p. 64.

60 Marc A. Weiner, *Richard Wagner and the Anti-Semitic Imagination*, Lincoln, NB 1995, p. 248.

61 Wagner, *Das Braune Buch*, p. 62 (entry of 29 August 1865).

62 *Parsifal*, act 2.

63 Glasenapp, *Das Leben Richard Wagners*, vol. 5, p. 334. ('He felt transported above the principal problem at the centre of the subject since the moment when he suddenly realized that what was at issue was not the problematic question of compassion directed at Amfortas but the physical action involved in regaining the stolen spear'.)

64 Wagner, *Dichtungen und Schriften*, vol. 4, p. 379 (sketch of 23 February 1877).

65 Wagner, *Sämtliche Werke*, vol. 30, ed. Martin Geck and Egon Voss, Mainz 1970, p. 154 (references to the first and second performances, 26 and 27 July 1882).

66 Michael von Soden (ed.), *Richard Wagner, Lohengrin*, Frankfurt 1980, p. 156 (prose sketch made in Marienbad in 1845).

67 Attila Csampai and Dietmar Holland (eds), *Richard Wagner, Parsifal*, Reinbek 1984, p. 138.

68 Bayerische Akademie der Schönen Künste (ed.), *Adolf von Hildebrand und seine Welt*, Munich 1962, p. 327 (letter from Elisabeth von Herzogenberg to Hildebrand, 7 August 1889).

69 Grossmann-Vendrey (ed.), *Bayreuth in der deutschen Presse*, vol. 2, p. 17 (Ludwig Schemann, 'Die Bedeutung des Parsifal für unsere Zeit und unser Leben' in *Bayreuther Blätter*, 1879).

70 Ibid., p. 59 (Hans Herrig, 'Richard Wagners Parsifal', in *Deutsches Tageblatt*, 26 July 1882).

71 Angelo Neumann, *Erinnerungen an Richard Wagner*, Leipzig 1907, p. 238.

72 Joseph Goebbels, *Tagebücher 1924–1925*, 2 vols, ed. Ralf Georg Reuth, Munich 1992, vol. 1, p. 311 (entry of 10 August 1928).

73 Karbaum, *Studien zur Geschichte der Bayreuther Festspiele*, vol. 2, p. 95 (letter to Eva Chamberlain, 11 September 1933).

74 *Bayreuther Festspielführer 1928*, ed. Paul Pretzsch, Bayreuth 1928, p. 82 (Wolfgang Golther, 'Der Gral in Gedichten des Mittelalters').

75 *Bayreuther Festspielführer 1927*, ed. Paul Pretzsch, Bayreuth 1927, p. 60 (Paul Bülow, 'Das Kunstwerk Richard Wagners in der Auffassung Friedrich Lienhards').

76 *Parsifal*, act 3.

77 Ibid.

78 Udo Bermbach (ed.), *In den Trümmern der eignen Welt. Richard Wagners 'Ring des Nibelungen'*, Berlin/Hamburg 1989, p. 224 (Hartmut Zelinsky, 'Die deutsche Losung Siegfried').

79 Cosima Wagner, *Tagebücher*, vol. 3, p. 239 (entry of 25 November 1878).

80 Ibid., p. 339. (Entry of 30 April 1879: 'And who is there to save us from it? Constantin Frantz in Blasewitz and me in Bayreuth. Ach!')

81 Karbaum, *Studien zur Geschichte der Bayreuther Festspiele*, vol. 2, p. 68. (Hans Conrad, 'Der Führer und Bayreuth', 1936: 'In 1924 Wahnfried confirmed its loyalty to Hitler by offering to make the villa his home after release from jail in December.')

82 Adolf Hitler, *Monologe im Führerhauptquartier 1941–1944. Die Aufzeichnungen Heinrich Heims*, ed. Werner Jochmann, Munich 1982, p. 259 (3–4 February 1942).

83 *Bayreuther Festspielführer 1925*, ed. Karl Grunsky, Bayreuth 1925, p. 138 (Hans Alfred Grunsky, 'Parsifal').

84 *Bayreuther Festspielführer 1931*, Bayreuth 1931, p. 105 (Alfred Lorenz, 'Das Heldische in Richard Wagners *Parsifal*').

85 Hitler, *Mein Kampf*, p. 487. ('That above all is why we need to set against the petty-minded leaders of our present republic the vision of an ideal Reich.')

86   Hitler, *Reden und Proklamationen*, vol. 1, p. 546 (speech in the Kroll Opera House, 8 October 1935).

87   Albert Zoller, *Hitler privat. Erlebnisbericht seiner Geheimsekretärin*, Düsseldorf 1949, p. 188.

88   Hitler, *Monologe*, p. 41. (11–12 July 1941: 'The hardest blow that mankind has had to bear is Christianity. Bolshevism is the bastard son of Christianity. Both are monsters created by the Jews.')

89   Ibid., p. 99 (21 October 1941).

90   Hermann Rauschning, *Gespräche mit Hitler*, Vienna 1973, p. 50.

91   Ibid.

92   *Parsifal*, act 3.

93   Alfred Rosenberg, *Das politische Tagebuch Alfred Rosenbergs aus den Jahren 1934– 5 und 1939–40*, ed. Hans-Günther Seraphim, Göttingen 1956, p. 32. (Entry of June 1934: 'He insisted more than once, with a smile, that he had always been a heathen, and that the time had now come for the poisonous influence of Christianity to be destroyed once and for all.')

94   Hitler, *Monologe*, p. 150. (Entry of 13 December 1941. Wagner repeatedly returned to this theme. 'He also raved about Jesus being a Jew,' wrote Cosima in her diary for 27 November 1878, 'adding that only when all the churches have perished will we come into the presence of the Saviour from whom the Jews separate us.')

95   Ibid., p. 150 (entry of 13 December 1941).

96   Claus Ekkehard Bärsch, *Erlösung und Vernichtung. Dr. phil. Joseph Goebbels*, Munich 1987, p. 400 (speech of 12 April 1922, reprinted in the *Völkischer Beobachter*, no. 31).

97   Walter C. Langer, *The Mind of Adolf Hitler. The Secret Wartime Report*, New York 1972, p. 35.

98   Bärsch, *Erlösung und Vernichtung*, p. 401 (as note 96).

99   Joachim C. Fest, *Hitler. Eine Biographie*, Frankfurt 1973, p. 354 (speech at the Christmas celebrations of the Nazi Party, 18 December 1926).

100 Hitler, *Reden und Proklamationen*, vol. 2, p. 1047.

101 Ibid., p. 1057.

102 Ibid., p. 1058.

103 Wolfgang Benz (ed.), *Dimension des Völkermords. Die Zahl der jüdischen Opfer des Nationalsozialismus*, ed. Wolfgang Benz, Munich 1996, p. 419. ('The killing of Polish Jews started only a few days after the invasion of Poland. . . . In Biala Podlaska, for instance, the SS murdered some 600 Polish-Jewish prisoners.')

104 Karbaum, *Studien zur Geschichte der Bayreuther Festspiele*, p. 95. (Wolfgang Golther to Eva Chamberlain, 20 December 1933. Roller's appointment was due entirely to Hitler: 'After his seizure of power the Führer summoned Roller to Bayreuth and charged him with a new production of *Parsifal* [Manfred Wagner, *Alfred Roller und seine Zeit*, Salzburg 1996].)

105 Hitler, *Reden und Proklamationen*, vol. 1, p. 415 (speech before the Reichstag, 13 July 1934, during which Hitler was flanked by SS men).

106 Ibid., p. 421.

107 *Parsifal*, act 3.

108 Friedelind Wagner, *Nacht über Bayreuth. Die Geschichte der Enkelin Richard Wagners*, Cologne 1994, p. 158. ('Everyone in the Festspielhaus was furious about the blood-bath.')

109 Rauschning, *Gespräche mit Hitler*, p. 86.

110 Friedelind Wagner, *Nacht über Bayreuth*, p. 160.
111 Reinhold Baumstark and Michael Koch (eds), *Der Gral. Artusromantik in der Kunst des 19. Jahrhunderts*, Cologne 1995, p. 71 (Michael Petzet, 'Die Gralswelt König Ludwigs II').
112 Ibid., p. 145.
113 Hitler, *Monologe*, p. 308. (28 February – 1 March 1942: 'Actually I did not want to go there, because it would have only made things more difficult for Siegfried Wagner, since he was to a certain extent in the hands of the Jews.')
114 Dawn Ades, Tim Benton, David Elliott and Iain Boyd Whyte (eds), *Art and Power. Europe under the Dictators 1930–1945*, London 1995, p. 282.
115 Hermann Giesler (ed.), *Ein anderer Hitler. Bericht seines Architekten*, Leoni am Starnberger See 1977, p. 324.
116 Frankfurter Kunstverein (ed.), *Kunst im Dritten Reich. Dokumente der Unterwerfung*, Frankfurt 1974, p. 64.
117 Hitler, *Reden und Proklamationen*, vol. 1, p. 297 (proclamation by Hitler in Nuremberg, 1 September 1933).
118 Ibid., p. 299 (Hitler's final speech to the Party congress of 3 September 1933).
119 Ibid., p. 744. (The biblical quotation is from St John's Gospel 16: 12.)
120 Fest, *Hitler*, p. 734.
121 Wagener, *Hitler aus nächster Nähe*, p. 349.
122 Hitler, *Monologe*, p. 101 (21–2 October 1941).
123 Ibid., p. 99 (21 October 1941).
124 Albrecht Tyrell, *'Führer befiehl . . .': Selbstzeugnisse aus der 'Kampfzeit' der NSDAP*, Düsseldorf 1969, p. 163 (Gregor Strasser in *Der Nationale Sozialist für Sachsen*, 9 January 1927).
125 Fest, *Hitler*, p. 1096 (entry in Frank's diary, 10 February 1937).
126 Baldur von Schirach, *Ich glaubte an Hitler*, Hamburg 1967, p. 92. ('I resent any restriction on this belief in my infallibility. This is the disease I suffer from and it has to be accepted.')
127 Friedelind Wagner, *Nacht über Bayreuth*, p. 128.
128 *Bayreuther Festspielführer 1925*, p. 150 (as note 83).
129 Wolfgang Wagner, *Lebens-Akte. Autobiographie*, Munich 1994, p. 76. ('. . . the time was ripe for founding a rival party. In the same breath he admitted that he had very few upright and efficient people in his own staff.')
130 Fest, *Hitler*, p. 625 (address to his Gauleiters, 2 February 1934).
131 Hans Severus Ziegler, *Adolf Hitler aus dem Erleben dargestellt*, Göttingen 1964, p. 48.
132 *Lohengrin*, act 3, scene 2.
133 Fest, *Hitler*, p. 683 (statement following the occupation of the Rhineland in 1936).
134 Rauschning, *Gespräche mit Hitler* (Rauschning's book is based on some thirteen meetings that he had with Hitler between 1932 and 1934, cf. *Die Zeit*, 19 July 1985).
135 Ibid., p. 236.
136 Ibid.
137 Ibid., p. 233.
138 Ibid., p. 216.
139 Ibid.
140 Ibid., p. 237.
141 Ibid., p. 229.

Chapter 15 Life under the Mastersingers

1   Wolfgang Michalka (ed.), *Deutsche Geschichte 1933–1945. Dokumente zur Innen- und Aussenpolitik*, Frankfurt 1993, p. 81. (Goebbels on 8 May 1933: 'At a moment when politics has become a people's drama, when the world is collapsing around us, when old values are fading and new values rising, this is no time for artists to be saying that all this does not concern them.')

2   Guido Knopp, *Hitler. Eine Bilanz*, Berlin 1995, p. 156. (Speer: 'Theatre was the vein that ran through his entire life, right down to the culminating moment when his own people were being destroyed.')

3   Klaus Vondung, *Magie und Manipulation*, Göttingen 1971, p. 83.

4   Ibid.

5   *Parsifal*, act 3.

6   Vondung, *Magie und Manipulation*, p. 167.

7   Baldur von Schirach, *Ich glaubte an Hitler*, Hamburg 1967, p. 37. ('Hitler dedicated the standards and banners of newly created units of stormtroopers by touching the new standard with the "blood flag". For us young people it was an act of religious worship.')

8   *Lohengrin*, act 3, scene 3.

9   *Rienzi*, act 1, scene 2.

10   Hamilton T. Burden, *The Nuremberg Rallies 1923–1933*, London 1969. (Burden notes that even at this first Party rally the music of Wagner was played, as it increasingly became at later rallies.)

11   Ibid. (*Völkischer Beobachter*, 31 January 1923). [All quotations from Burden are my own translations of the original German sources – Translator's Note.]

12   Ibid. (speech on 29 January 1923).

13   Otto Dietrich, *Zwölf Jahre mit Hitler*, Munich 1955, p. 23.

14   Hans Kerrl (ed.), *Reichstagung in Nürnberg 1935. Der Parteitag der Freiheit*, Berlin 1936, p. 24. (Dietrich: 'The Party is the sacred Order of the German people – knights honoured for their services to politics.')

15   Dietrich, *Zwölf Jahre mit Hitler*, p. 27.

16   Burden, *The Nuremberg Rallies*.

17   Richard Wagner, *Gesammelte Schriften und Dichtungen*, 10 vols, ed. Richard Wagner, vol. 3, p. 11 ('Die Kunst und die Revolution').

18   Ibid., vol. 8, p. 336. (Wagner refers to 'the decadence to which German drama, in particular, has fallen victim'. Klaus Backes points out in *Hitler und die bildenden Künste*, Cologne 1988, p. 48 that the concept of 'decadent art' was in fact coined by Wagner.)

19   Peter-Klaus Schuster (ed.), *Nationalsozialismus und 'entartete Kunst'*, Munich 1988, p. 250.

20   Burden, *The Nuremberg Rallies*.

21   Adolf Hitler, *Hitlers Tischgespräche im Führerhauptquartier*, ed. Henry Picker, Stuttgart 1976, p. 425. (6 July 1942: 'The rally was not only a remarkable event in the life of the Nazi Party but also contributed in a number of respects to the preparations being made for war.')

22   Dietrich, *Zwölf Jahre mit Hitler*, p. 173.

23   Adolf Hitler, *Sämtliche Aufzeichnungen, 1905–1924*, ed. Eberhard Jäckel and Axel Kuhn, Stuttgart 1980, p. 197 (speech in the Hofbräuhaus, 13 August 1920).

24   Burden, *The Nuremberg Rallies*.

25 Ibid., p. 104 (Goebbels, 'Die Rassenfrage und Weltpropaganda', 1933).

26 Ibid., p. 119.

27 Berndt W. Wessling, *Furtwängler. Eine kritische Biographie*, Stuttgart 1985, p. 23.

28 Vondung, *Magie und Manipulation*, p. 82.

29 Kerrl (ed.), *Reichstagung in Nürnberg 1935*, p. 71.

30 Ibid., p. 103.

31 Ibid., p. 360. (Goering: 'The swastika has become a holy symbol for us . . . a symbol of the struggle against the Jews as destroyers of the Aryan race. It therefore goes without saying that when in future this flag shall be flown throughout the country, no Jew may be allowed to hoist it.')

32 Ibid., p. 418. ('Then the sounds of the overture to Wagner's *Rienzi* rang out and Rudolf Hess marched to the podium. Finally the Führer himself rose to deliver his powerful final address.')

33 Burden, *The Nuremberg Rallies*. (The *New York Times* reported that the whole occasion became increasingly like a religious celebration.)

34 Ibid. (*New York Times*, 12 September 1936).

35 Albert Speer, *Erinnerungen*, Frankfurt/Berlin/Vienna 1969, p. 71. ('The sight far outstripped what I had imagined,' wrote Speer later. 'The 130 clearly defined rays, set at intervals of 12 metres round the stadium, were visible up to a height of 6 kilometres and more, forming a shining canopy. The impression was of a huge area in which the rays of light seemed like gigantic pillars supporting the outer walls. . . . This dome of light must have been the first "luminous architecture" of its kind.')

36 Vondung, *Magie und Manipulation*, p. 82.

37 H.-Dieter Arntz, *Ordensburg Vogelsang 1934–1945. Erziehung zur politischen Führung im Dritten Reich*, Euskirchen 1986, p. 124. ('A strikingly anti-Semitic feeling dominated these institutions.' 'Racial Doctrine' was the first subject on the curriculum, followed by 'Art and Culture'.)

38 Ibid., p. 127. (An illustration shows a 'devotional room' at the end of which stood a naked figure, as on an altar, greeting his worshippers in the pose of one risen from the dead.)

39 Hermann Rauschning, *Gespräche mit Hitler*, Vienna 1973, p. 237. (According to Hitler, the figure 'was to prepare the country's youth for its coming manhood through the display of a beautiful body'.)

40 Janusz Piekalkiewicz, *Die Schlacht um Moskau. Die erfrorene Offensive*, Bergisch Gladbach 1981, p. 156. (Report of 3 November 1941: 'Even though a total of some 75,000 Jews have been killed in this way, it is already clear that these methods will not bring about a solution to the Jewish problem.')

41 Adolf Hitler, *Monologe im Führerhauptquartier 1941–1944. Die Aufzeichnungen Heinrich Heims*, ed. Werner Jochmann, Munich 1982, p. 130 (5 November 1941).

42 Ibid., p. 131 (5 November 1941).

43 Erich Hanfstaengl, *Zwischen Weissem und Braunem Haus. Memoiren eines politischen Aussenseiters*, Munich 1970, p. 56. ('I would even claim that there are definite parallels between the form of the prelude to the *Meistersinger* and Hitler's speeches. There was the same use of leitmotifs, the same decorative features, the same counterpoint and then the powerful climax, with the triumphant sound of brass, beloved of Wagner and Liszt.')

44 Dietrich, *Zwölf Jahre mit Hitler*, p. 165. (Hitler seems to have kept count not only of the performances of the *Meistersinger* that he saw but also of his meet-

ings with individual singers. He told Wilhelm Rode, for example, that he had seen him as Hans Sachs 43 times [Alan Jefferson, *Elisabeth Schwarzkopf*, London 1996, p. 30]. After a performance of Richard Strauss' opera *Friedenstag* on 24 July 1938 Hans Hotter was introduced to the Führer, who greeted him, somewhat unexpectedly, with 'Grüss Sie Gott, Herr Hotter!' and went on, to Hotter's considerable surprise: 'On 29 June 1932 I heard you in the recital room of the Bayerischer Hof hotel at a concert for young singers. You sang Sachs' two monologues from the *Meistersinger*' [Hans Hotter, '*Der Mai war mir gewogen . . .*': *Erinnerungen*, Munich 1996, p. 128].)

45 Adolf Hitler, *Reden und Proklamationen 1932–1945*, 2 vols, ed. Max Domarus, Würzburg 1962–3, vol. 1, p. 20. ('Hitler claimed to have heard Wagner's *Meistersinger* a hundred times.')

46 Ibid., p. 31 (21 March 1934 at a construction site on the new autobahn between Munich and Salzburg).

47 Dietrich, *Zwölf Jahre mit Hitler*, p. 209.

48 Hitler, *Reden und Proklamationen*, vol. 1, p. 779. (Speech on the opening of the 'Haus der deutschen Kunst', 22 January 1938: 'There are architectural achievements here which bear the stamp of immortality.')

49 Marc A. Weiner, *Richard Wagner and the Anti-Semitic Imagination*, Lincoln, NB 1995, p. 132.

50 Joseph Goebbels, *Die Tagebücher von Joseph Goebbels. Sämtliche Fragmente*, 4 vols, ed. Eike Fröhlich, Munich 1987, vol. 2, p. 213. (Entry made in Bayreuth, 1 August 1932: 'The gigantic figure of Wagner looms so large above the dwarfs of today that it is almost an insult to his genius to mention them in the same breath.')

51 Wessling, *Furtwängler*, p. 353.

52 Ibid., p. 24. ('The enthusiasm was beyond compare,' said the singer Rudolf Bockelmann.)

53 Hitler, *Reden und Proklamationen*, vol. 2, p. 1633 (10 December 1940).

54 Joachim C. Fest, *Hitler. Eine Biographie*, Frankfurt 1973, p. 555.

55 Berndt W. Wessling (ed.), *Bayreuth im Dritten Reich: Richard Wagners politisches Erbe. Eine Dokumentation*, Weinheim 1983, p. 240.

56 *Bayreuther Festspielführer 1933*, ed. Otto Strobel, Bayreuth 1933, p. 7 (Hans von Wolzogen, 'Ein Wagnerspruch zum Wagnerjahr').

57 Attila Csampai and Dietmar Holland (eds), *Richard Wagner, Die Meistersinger von Nürnberg*, Reinbek 1981, p. 194 (Goebbels, 'Richard Wagner und das Kunstempfinden unserer Zeit', 1933).

58 Ibid., p. 198.

59 Wessling (ed.), *Bayreuth im Dritten Reich*, p. 13 (*Völkischer Beobachter*, 24 July 1937).

60 *Neue Zeitschrift für Musik*, September 1983, p. 16. ('Musik im Nationalsozialismus'. Hartmut Zelinsky, 'Das erschreckende "Erwachen" und wie man Wagner von Hitler befreit'.)

61 Harold Hammer-Schenk, *Synagogen in Deutschland*, Hamburg 1981, p. 227.

62 Germanisches Nationalmuseum (ed.), *Die Meistersinger und Richard Wagner. Die Rezeptionsgeschichte einer Oper von 1868 bis heute*, Nuremberg, 1981, p. 81 (Adolf Westermayer, 'Hans Sachs, der Vorkämpfer der neuen Zeit' – address on the occasion of the unveiling of the Hans Sachs Monument in Nuremberg, 1874).

63 Richard Wagner, *Sämtliche Schriften und Dichtungen*, 16 vols, Leipzig 19911–14,

vol. 10, p. 120 ('Wollen wir hoffen?' 1879).

64   Cosima Wagner, *Die Tagebücher*, 4 vols, ed. Martin Gregor-Dellin and Dietrich Mack, Munich 1982, vol. 2, p. 1062 (entry of 22 July 1877).

65   Udo Bermbach (ed.), *In den Trümmern der eignen Welt. Richard Wagners 'Ring des Nibelungen'*, Berlin/Hamburg 1989, p. 249. (Hartmut Zelinsky, 'Die deutsche Losung Siegfried'. Looking back in 1939 Richard Wilhelm Stock described the synagogue as 'provocative and impertinent, like the Jews themselves . . . in a bombastic Oriental style'.)

66   Hitler, *Reden und Proklamationen*, vol. 1, p. 971 (Gauleiter Otto Hellmuth, 10 September 1938).

67   Schirach, *Ich glaubte an Hitler*, p. 245.

68   Wagner, *Gesammelte Schriften und Dichtungen*, vol. 4, p. 284 ('Ein Mitteilung an meine Freunde', 1851).

69   Heinz Schirmag, *Albert Lortzing. Glanz und Elend eines Künstlerlebens*, Berlin 1995, p. 163.

70   Ibid., p. 169.

71   Ulrich Müller, Franz Hundsnurscher and Cornelius Sommer (eds), *Richard Wagner 1883–1983. Die Rezeption im 19. und 20. Jahrhundert, Gesammelte Beiträge des Salzburger Symposions*, Salzburg 1984, p. 111. (Gerhard J. Winkler, 'Hans Sachs und Palestrina': 'The persistence with which Wagner signs his letters as Sachs at this time, as well as having the initiated address him as Sachs and incorporating his own Saxon origins into his story, shows that he liked to regard himself as the third in the trinity of which the other two were John the Baptist and Hans Sachs.')

72   Germanisches Nationalmuseum (ed.), *Die Meistersinger und Richard Wagner*, p. 65 (letter from Wagner to Ludwig II, 25 October 1866).

73   *Bayreuther Festspielführer 1927*, ed. Paul Pretzsch, Bayreuth 1927, p. 46.

74   König Ludwig II/Richard Wagner, *Briefwechsel*, 4 vols, ed. Wittelsbacher Ausgleichsfonds and Winifred Wagner, rev. Otto Strobel, Karlsruhe 1936–7, vol. 2, p. 102 (letter from Wagner, 5 September 1866).

75   Ibid., p. 103 (letter from Wagner, 22 November 1866).

76   Ibid., vol. 4, p. 8 (diary entry of Wagner's, 15 September 1865).

77   *Meistersinger*, act 3, scene 5.

78   König Ludwig II/Richard Wagner, *Briefwechsel*, vol. 4, p. 14 (diary entry of Wagner's, 18 September 1865).

79   Ibid., p. 19 (diary entry of Wagner's, 21 September 1865).

80   Ibid., p. 21 (diary entry of Wagner's, 22 September 1865).

81   Ibid., p. 20 (diary entry of Wagner's, 21 September 1865: 'Jewish manufacturers of plays and pieces of music dominate our theatres and Jewish critics supply reviews of our artistic productions.' This was only possible, wrote Wagner the following day, because the German princes did not understand their people, 'a lack of understanding exploited by the Jews'.)

82   Michael von Saden (ed.), *Richard Wagner, Die Meistersinger von Nürnberg*, Frankfurt 1983, p. 163.

83   Ernst Kreowski and Eduard Fuchs, *Richard Wagner in der Karikatur*, Berlin 1907, p. 54. (The phrase was coined by Franz Bittong.)

84   Ernst Bücken, *Wörterbuch der Musik*, Leipzig 1941, p. 173. ('Hanslick, Eduard, 1825–1904 . . . critic immortalized by Wagner as the despicable Beckmesser in the *Meistersinger*.')

85   Fest, *Hitler*, p. 157.

86   Dietrich, *Zwölf Jahre mit Hitler*, p. 157.
87   *Meistersinger*, act 3, scene 1.
88   Richard Wagner, *Die Meistersinger von Nürnberg. Faksimile der Reinschrift des Textbuches von 1862*, ed. Egon Voss, Mainz 1983, p. 16.
89   *Rheingold*, scene 3.
90   *Meistersinger*, act 3, scene 5.
91   *Bayreuther Festspielführer 1996*, ed. Wolfgang Wagner, Bayreuth 1996, p. 89. (Dieter Borchmeyer, 'Beckmesser – der Jude im Dorn?' Borchmeyer concludes: 'At all events, admission to the innermost sanctum of his art is denied to anti-Semites.')
92   Arthur Schopenhauer, *Sämtliche Werke*, vol. 3, ed. Wolfgang Löhneysen, Frankfurt 1986, p. 775. ('Über die Grundlage der Moral'. Schopenhauer attacks the Jews and vivisection with equal vehemence. Compassion towards both human beings and animals is so rare in Europe, 'above all because of the *"foetor Judiacus"* that permeates everything.')
93   *Meistersinger*, act 2, scenes 5 and 6.
94   Ibid., act 3, scene 3.
95   Richard Wagner, *Briefe 1830–1883*, ed. Werner Otto, Berlin 1986, p. 309 (letter from Wagner to the singer Gustav Hölzel, 22 January 1868).
96   *Meistersinger*, act 1, scene 3.
97   Thomas Mann, *Wagner und unsere Zeit. Aufsätze, Betrachtungen, Briefe*, ed. Erika Mann, Frankfurt 1986, p. 168. (Letter from Mann to the stage designer Emil Preetorius, who had worked in Bayreuth since 1933. Mann also observes: 'There is a great deal of "Hitler" in Wagner.')
98   *Kinder- und Hausmärchen der Brüder Grimm*, vol. 2 (1814), ed. Peter Dettmering, Lindau 1985, p. 98.
99   *Meistersinger*, act 3, scene 5.
100 Carl Friedrich Glasenapp, *Das Leben Richard Wagners*, 6 vols, Leipzig 1904–11, vol. 2, p. 453.
101 Richard Wagner, *Sämtliche Schriften und Dichtungen*, 16 vols, Leipzig 1911–14, vol. 9, p. 353 (first sketch of the *Meistersinger* act 3, 16 July 1845 in Marienbad).
102 *Meistersinger*, act 3, scene 3.
103 Csampai and Holland (eds), *Wagner, Die Meistersinger von Nürnberg*, p. 176 (second prose draft, November 1861).
104 *Meistersinger*, act 3, scene 5. ('I tell you, gentlemen, it is a fine song – but you can see at a glance that our friend Beckmesser has distorted it.' For a facsimile of the original version of Beckmesser's parody of the Prize Song see Otto Strobel in the *Bayreuther Festspielführer 1933*, p. 153.)
105 Robert Schumann, *Schriften über Musik und Musiker*, ed. Josef Häusler, Stuttgart 1982, p. 132 ('Fragmente aus Leipzig', 1836–7).
106 Adolf Hitler, *Mein Kampf*, 763rd–767th impression, Munich 1942, p. 211.
107 Ibid., p. 332.
108 Ibid., p. 349.
109 *Meistersinger*, act 3, scene 5.
110 Ibid. ('The scene is an open meadow, with the town of Nuremberg in the distant background.')
111 Ibid.
112 Michael Karbaum, *Studien zur Geschichte der Bayreuther Festspiele (1876–1976)*, 2 vols, Regensburg 1976, vol. 2, p. 111. (Tietjen to a general meeting of the artists on 30 January 1936. 'When I pointed this out to Richard Strauss,' Tietjen

added, 'Strauss replied: "I didn't notice that."' Strauss conducted *Parsifal* in Bayreuth in 1933 and 1934.)

113 Hans Severus Ziegler, *Adolf Hitler aus dem Erleben dargestellt*, Göttingen 1964, p. 57.

114 Ibid., p. 64.

115 Manfred Treml and Josef Kirmeier (eds), *Geschichte und Kultur der Juden in Bayern*, Munich 1988, p. 423 (Hartmut Zelinsky, 'Der Dirigent Hermann Levi').

116 Fest, *Hitler*, p. 447.

117 Cosima Wagner/Fürst Ernst zu Hohenlohe-Langenburg, *Briefwechsel*, ed. Ernst Fürst zu Hohenlohe, Stuttgart 1937 p. 65. (Letter from Cosima, September 1893: 'I put forward the idea for a monumental national theatre at the point where the Main flows into the Rhine. But the stupid Mime and Alberich [Levi and Possart in Munich] intervened and made out that the grand project, which I never abandoned, was a merely speculative enterprise. Here we have a prime example of how the Jewish monsters treat the German spirit.')

118 Klaus Jürgen Seidel (ed.), *Das Prinzregenten-Theater in München*, Nuremberg 1984, p. 29.

119 Goebbels, *Tagebücher. Sämtliche Fragmente*, vol. 3, p. 489. (Entry of 24 July 1938: 'That is real Viennese kitsch. But I shall soon get rid of it, using all the means available to me.' The following day he wrote: 'Villa Wahnfried – the Führer is already here. . . . I tell him about the Salzburg Festival. No more Wagner there.')

120 Karbaum, *Studien zur Geschichte der Bayreuther Festspiele*, vol. 2, p. 116 (statement to the De-Nazification Tribunal, 1946).

121 Wolfgang Wagner, *Lebens-Akte. Autobiographie*, Munich 1994, p. 63. ('After the death of my Uncle Chamberlain in 1927 I inherited his hen-house, together with the surrounding fence, because my Aunt Eva no longer had any interest in keeping it up.')

122 Dietrich, *Zwölf Jahre mit Hitler*, p. 166. ('Already before the war the eldest daughter, Friedelind, had been a source of great disappointment to him. She left everything behind and went abroad, taking up a hostile attitude towards him.')

123 Wessling (ed.), *Bayreuth im Dritten Reich*, p. 189 (*Manchester Guardian*, 15 August 1933, 'Featuring Hitler').

124 Beatrice and Helmut Heiber (eds), *Die Rückseite des Hakenkreuzes. Absonderliches aus den Akten des Dritten Reiches*, Munich 1993, p. 14 (letter from Winifred to Hitler, 26 December 1934).

125 Nike Wagner, *Über Wagner*, Stuttgart 1996, p. 278 (letter from Winifred to Hitler, 12 February 1942).

126 Wolfgang Wagner, *Lebens-Akte*, p. 104. ('The outbreak of war, the wound I sustained right at the beginning and the order that "wartime festivals" were to take place . . . brought about a marked deterioration in my mother's relationship to Hitler, with the result that she no longer spoke directly to him and became alienated from him.')

127 Heiber and Heiber (eds), *Die Rückseite des Hakenkreuzes*, p. 117. (There was considerable annoyance in the Berlin Chancellery at the end of 1944 when it was discovered that two letters addressed personally to Hitler from Bayreuth, with the sender's address, 'Haus Wahnfried', on the back, had found their way into the normal mail and been opened. The offending clerks were called to account.)

128 Frederic Spotts, *Bayreuth. A History of the Wagner Festival*, New Haven 1994, p. 198. (Spotts claims that Hitler paid his last visit to Winifred in Wahnfried in 1944.)
129 Robert G.L. Waite, *The Psychopathic God. Adolf Hitler*, New York 1977, p. 26.
130 Dietrich, *Zwölf Jahre mit Hitler*, p. 220. ('He felt compassion for animals, considering them capable of thought.')
131 Ibid., p. 229.
132 Richard Wagner, *Bayreuther Briefe (1871–1883)*, ed. Carl Friedrich Glasenapp, Leipzig 1912, p. 78 (letter from Wagner, 12 April 1872).
133 Karbaum, *Studien zur Geschichte der Bayreuther Festspiele*, vol. 2, p. 50. (Chamberlain to Wolzogen, 2 December 1891: 'Promoting the interests of the people was, as you know, my friend, always my ideal.')
134 Andreas Mork, *Richard Wagner als politischer Schriftsteller. Weltanschauung und Wirkungsgeschichte*, Frankfurt 1990, p. 218.
135 Hitler, *Hitlers Tischgespräche*, p. 466. (26 July 1942, on his visit to Paris on 23 June 1940: 'Weimar is in a totally different league.')
136 Ziegler, *Adolf Hitler*, p. 90. ('. . . he asked me whether it might be possible to put together a cast from the Weimar theatre for a performance of *Der fliegende Holländer* in Paris.')
137 Jefferson, *Elisabeth Schwarzkopf*, p. 40. (The performance took place in May 1941, with Germaine Lubin, the Bayreuth Isolde, as Senta.)
138 Hitler, *Monologe*, p. 225 (24–5 January 1943: 'The ten days I spent in Bayreuth were always my happiest time, and I am already looking forward to returning there for the first time.')
139 *Richard-Wagner-Festspiele Bayreuth 1941*, Berlin 1941, p. 13 (Hans Lebede, 'Bayreuth').
140 Karbaum, *Studien zur Geschichte der Bayreuther Festspiele*, vol. 2, p. 86 (Daniela Thode's notes for a meeting with Goebbels in 1933).
141 Spotts, *Bayreuth*, p. 189.
142 Richard Wilhelm Stock, *Richard Wagner und seine Meistersinger*, Nuremberg 1943, p. 11.
143 Spotts, *Bayreuth*, p. 194.
144 Stock, *Richard Wagner und seine Meistersinger*, p. 190.
145 Ibid., p. 105.
146 Ibid., p. 201.
147 Karbaum, *Studien zur Geschichte der Bayreuther Festspiele*, p. 109 (letter from Heinz Tietjen to Winifred Wagner, 17 December 1944).

Chapter 16 Barbarossa Returns; Ahasverus Perishes

1 Eberhard Jäckel, *Das deutsche Jahrhundert. Eine historische Bilanz*, Stuttgart 1996, p. 206. ('Immediately the war started, he ordered the Jews in Poland – and after 1941 with particular ruthlessness in the Soviet Union – to be systematically shot.')
2 Hartmut Zelinsky, *Richard Wagner. Ein deutsches Thema. Eine Dokumentation zur Wirkungsgeschichte Richard Wagners 1876–1976*, Frankfurt 1976, new edn Berlin 1983, p. 170 (letter from Chamberlain to Hitler, New Year's Day 1924).
3 Hans-Jürgen Eitner, *Hitler. Ein Psychoprogramm*, Berlin 1994, p. 161. (Hitler made many references to the subject of Destiny: cf. 7 September 1932, 14 March

1936, 24 February 1943, 30 January 1945, etc.)

4   Brigitte Hamann, *Hitlers Wien. Lehrjahre eines Diktators*, Munich 1996, p. 501.

5   Erich Kuby, *Richard Wagner & Co. Zum 150. Geburtstag des Meisters*, Hamburg 1963, p. 148.

6   Zelinsky, *Richard Wagner*, p. 170 (letter from Chamberlain to Hitler, New Year's Day 1924).

7   Joachim C. Fest, *Hitler. Eine Biographie*, Frankfurt 1973, p. 219.

8   Adolf Hitler, *Reden und Proklamationen 1932–1945*, 2 vols, ed. Max Domarus, Würzburg 1962–3, vol. 1, p. 130 (23 August 1932).

9   Ibid., vol. 2, p. 731 (final address to the Party congress, 13 September 1937).

10 Ibid., p. 1810 (speech before the Reichstag on 11 December 1941, when he declared war on America).

11 Adolf Hitler, *Reden, Schriften, Anordnungen. Februar 1925 bis Januar 1933*, 3 vols, ed. Clems Vollnhals et al., Munich 1992–4, vol. 3, p. 124. (Article in the *Illustrierter Beobachter*, 30 March 1929: 'It seems to be possible for the Jews to extend the rule of Alberich from Russia, the only place where it is thoroughly established, to other countries.')

12 Hitler, *Reden und Proklamationen*, vol. 2, p. 1772 (speech in the Löwenbräukeller, 8 November 1941).

13 Richard Wagner, *Sämtliche Schriften und Dichtungen*, 16 vols, Leipzig 1911–14, vol. 10, p. 266 ('Erkenne dich selbst').

14 Janus Pikalkiewicz, *Die Schlacht um Moskau. Die erfrorene Offensive*, Bergisch Gladbach 1981, p. 286. ('German casualties between 22 June 1941 and October 1941 amounted to 564,727 – 119,464 of them dead and 24,793 missing. In the winter campaign from 11 December 1941 to 31 March 1942 total losses were 332,743.')

15 Hitler, *Reden und Proklamationen*, vol. 2, p. 1773 (as note 12).

16 Konrad Heiden, *Adolf Hitler*, 2 vols, Zurich 1936, vol. 2, plate V.

17 Gerd Ueberschär and Wolfram Wette (eds), *Der deutsche Überfall auf die Sowjetunion. 'Unternehmen Barbarossa' 1941*, Frankfurt 1991, p. 259 ('Instructions for the Treatment of Political Commissars: Units must understand that any display of mercy or regard for international conventions as far as these elements are concerned is totally wrong.')

18 Gerhard Engel, *Heeresadjutant bei Hitler 1938–1943. Aufzeichnungen des Majors Engel*, ed. Hildegard von Kotze, Stuttgart 1974, p. 130. (Entry of 10 October 1942: 'Stalingrad must be torn apart, then communism will be deprived of its holy icon.')

19 Ibid., p. 93. (Entry of 17 January 1941. After talking about Operation Barbarossa, Hitler referred to the coming 'destruction of the ideological centre of Leningrad'.)

20 Eberhard Jäckel, *Hitlers Herrschaft. Vollzug einer Weltanschauung*, Stuttgart 1986, p. 87.

21 Ueberschär and Wette (eds), *Der deutsche Überfall auf die Sowjetunion*, p. 63. (Hitler to Rosenberg, Göring and others, 16 July 1941: 'We must turn the newly gained eastern territories into a Garden of Eden . . . colonies, on the other hand, are a matter of only subsidiary importance.')

22 Eberhard Jäckel, *Hitlers Herrschaft*, p. 69 (6 July 1933 to a meeting of provincial governors).

23 Eugen Kogon, *Der SS-Staat. Das System der deutschen Konzentrationslager*, Munich 1988, p. 42. (An SS Leader at a Party school, autumn 1937: 'We who are

training the future leaders of our country are looking for a modern state on the pattern of the Greek city-states . . . resting on a broad economic basis of serfs.')

24 Wolfgang Michalka (ed.), *Deutsche Geschichte 1933–1945. Dokumente zur Innen- und Aussenpolitik*, Frankfurt 1993, p. 109 (memorandum from Röchling to Hitler on preparations for war and its conduct, 17 August 1936).

25 Adolf Hitler, *Hitlers Tischgespräche im Führerhauptquartier*, ed. Henry A. Picker, Stuttgart 1976, p. 311. (On 18 May 1942 the Führer 'discussed the transport problem in Russia with Röchling', described by Picker as 'an industrialist impressive in his reserve and in the clarity of his vision'.)

26 Michalka (ed.), *Deutsche Geschichte 1933–1945*, p. 110 (Hitler's secret memorandum on the Four-Year Plan, August 1936).

27 Hitler, *Reden und Proklamationen*, vol. 2, p. 728 (final address to the Party congress in Nuremberg, 13 September 1937).

28 Friedrich Nietzsche, *Sämtliche Werke. Kritische Studienausgabe*, 15 vols, ed. Giorgio Colli and Mazzino Montinari, Munich 1980, vol. 1, p. 131. ('Let no one try to denigrate our faith in the imminent rebirth of Greek Antiquity, for in this alone lies our hope for the purification and the renewal of the German spirit through the magic power of music.')

29 Houston Stewart Chamberlain, *Die Grundlagen des Neunzehnten Jahrhunderts*, 2 vols, 28th impression, Munich 1942, vol. 1, p. 332.

30 Hitler, *Reden und Proklamationen*, vol. 1, p. 728 (as note 27).

31 Ibid., p. 575. (Hitler, 12 February 1936: 'Our dead have all come to life again.')

32 Josef Ackermann, *Heinrich Himmler als Ideologe*, Göttingen 1970, p. 162. ('We see before us the enemies of the world, the destroyers of cultures, the sons of chaos, the incarnation of evil, the agent of decomposition, the demons who will bring mankind to ruin.')

33 Wanda Kampmann, *Deutsche und Juden. Die Geschichte der Juden in Deutschland vom Mittelalter bis zum Beginn des Ersten Weltkriegs*, Frankfurt 1979, p. 268. (In his *Römische Geschichte*, vol. 2, p. 550 Mommsen writes: 'In Antiquity also the Jews acted as an effective agent of cosmopolitanism and national decomposition.')

34 Jost Dülffer, Jochen Thies and Josef Henke, *Hitlers Städte. Baupolitik im Dritten Reich*, Cologne 1978, p. 290 (speech by Hitler in the Kroll Opera House in Berlin, 10 February 1939).

35 Ibid., p. 312 (as note 34).

36 Adolf Hitler, *Monologe im Führerhauptquartier 1941–1944. Aufzeichnungen Heinrich Heims*, ed. Werner Jochmann, Munich 1982, p. 155. (17–18 December 1941: 'The concept of the Reich had been almost completely eradicated.')

37 Hitler, *Reden und Proklamationen*, vol. 2, p. 1779. (Speech in the Löwenbräukeller, 8 November 1941. On 10 May 1940 Hitler had already said: 'The struggle that has commenced today will decide the fate of the German people for the next thousand years.')

38 Franz von Papen, *Der Wahrheit eine Gasse*, Munich 1952, p. 322.

39 Norman Cohn, *The Pursuit of the Millennium. Revolutionary Millenarians and Mystical Anarchists of the Middle Ages*, London 1970, p. 110.

40 Ibid., p. 120.

41 Ibid., p. 78. ('In the compendium of Antichrist-lore which Adso of Montier-en-Der produced in the tenth century and which remained the stock authority throughout the Middle Ages, Antichrist [is] a Jew of the tribe of Dan.')

42 Ibid., p. 122.

43   Leander Petzoldt (ed.), *Historische Sagen*, vol. 2: *Ritter, Räuber und geistliche Herren*, Munich 1977, p. 20 (the legend of the Emperor Barbarossa and the Untersberg).

44   Eduard Devrient, *Aus seinen Tagebüchern. Berlin–Dahlem 1836–1852*, Weimar 1964, p. 470 (entry of 22 February 1849).

45   Richard Wagner, *Gesammelte Schriften und Dichtungen*, 10 vols, ed. Richard Wagner, Leipzig 1871–83, vol. 2, p. 146.

46   Ibid., p. 150.

47   Friedrich Weigend, Bodo M. Baumunck and Thomas Brune, *Keine Ruhe im Kyffhäuser. Das Nachleben der Staufer*, Stuttgart 1978, p. 31.

48   Wagner, *Sämtliche Schriften und Dichtungen*, vol. 12, p. 227.

49   Cosima Wagner, *Die Tagebücher*, 4 vols, ed. Martin Gregor-Dellin and Dietrich Mack, Munich 1982, vol. 1, p. 458. (Entry of 12 November 1871: ' "How extraordinary", said Richard, "that this German Reich of ours, the most incomprehensible thing there is, will probably go on to outlive all other monarchies." ')

50   Heinrich von Stein, *Idee und Welt. Das Werk des Philosophen und Dichters*, ed. Günter Ralfs, Stuttgart 1940, p. 85 (letter from Stein to Paul Simon, 21 October 1879).

51   Adolf Hitler, *Mein Kampf*, 763rd–767th impression, Munich 1942, p. 742. ('We National Socialists have deliberately drawn a line under the foreign policies of the pre-war era and are starting again where things left off six centuries ago.')

52   Wagner, *Gesammelte Schriften und Dichtungen*, vol. 2, p. 150 ('Die Wibelungen').

53   Hitler, *Reden und Proklamationen*, vol. 1, p. 554 (speech in the Bürgerbräukeller, 8 November 1935).

54   Ibid., vol. 2, p. 1842 (speech to officer cadets in the Berlin Sportpalast, 13 February 1942).

55   Hanns Bächtold-Stäubli (ed.), *Handwörterbuch des deutschen Aberglaubens*, vol. 8, Berlin 1987, p. 1483. ('The Untersberg is one of the mountains in which famous national heroes are buried. . . . According to the legend these Emperors, in particular Barbarossa, will emerge from the mountain and launch the final battle against the Antichrist.')

56   Neue Gesellschaft für Bildende Kunst (ed.), *Inszenierung der Macht. Ästhetische Faszination im Faschismus*, Berlin 1987, p. 152.

57   Heinrich Hoffmann, *Hitler Was My Friend*, London 1955, p. 185.

58   Fest, *Hitler*, p. 714. ('With some emotion Hitler regarded it as a portent that his private residence should be situated right opposite this mountain.')

59   Hitler, *Reden und Proklamationen*, vol. 2, p. 1731 (Hitler's 'Proclamation to the German People' on 22 June 1941, the day he launched Operation Barbarossa).

60   Hermann Giesler, *Ein anderer Hitler. Bericht seines Architekten*, Leoni am Starnberger See 1977, p. 422.

61   Michalka (ed.), *Deutsche Geschichte 1933–1945*, p. 197. ('Instruction No. 21, 18 December 1940: "The German army must be prepared, even before the conclusion of the war against England, to embark on a successful Blitzkrieg against Soviet Russia." ')

62   Hitler, *Reden und Proklamationen*, vol. 2, p. 1664 (3 February 1941).

63   Christa Schroeder, *Er war mein Chef. Aus dem Nachlass der Sekretärin von Adolf Hitler*, ed. Anton Joachimsthaler, Munich 1985, p. 113.

64   Richard Wagner, *Dichtungen und Schriften*, 10 vols, ed. Dieter Borchmeyer, Frankfurt 1983, vol. 4, p. 238. ('Eine Mitteilung an meine Freunde', 1851: 'This

purposeless, joyless, unhappy wanderer through a stale, useless life had no prospect of redemption on earth. All that remained for him was to long for death, the only source of hope left to him.')

65 Richard Wagner, *Sämtliche Briefe*, ed. G. Strobel, W. Wolf, H.-J. Bauer and J. Forner, Leipzig 1967–, vol. 1, p. 109. ('Autobiographische Skizze', 1843. Here Hitler could have found the expression 'the Ahasverus of the ocean', together with Wagner's oath of loyalty to his fatherland.)

66 Wagner, *Dichtungen und Schriften*, vol. 2, p. 41. (Wagner gives an account here of the Overture to *Der fliegende Holländer*, 1852.)

67 *Der fliegende Holländer*, act 1.

68 Eberhard Jäckel, *Das deutsche Jahrhundert*, p. 200.

69 Roland G. Foerster (ed.), *'Unternehmen Barbarossa'. Zum historischen Ort der deutsch–sowjetischen Beziehungen von 1933 bis 1941*, Munich 1993, p. 10.

70 Rolf-Dieter Müller, *Hitlers Ostkrieg und die deutsche Siedlungspolitik. Die Zusammenarbeit von Wehrmacht, Wirtschaft und SS*, Frankfurt 1991, p. 21 (Hitler on 29 February 1940).

71 Joachim C. Fest, *Fremdheit und Nähe. Von der Gegenwart des Gewesenen*, Stuttgart 1996, p. 133.

72 Nicolaus von Below, *Als Hitlers Adjutant 1937–1945*, Mainz 1980, p. 6.

73 Engel, *Heeresadjutant bei Hitler*, p. 86. (Entry by Gerhard Engel, 10 August 1940: 'Once one has really taken hold of this giant, it will collapse more quickly than the world thinks. If only we could destroy it!')

74 Piekalkiewicz, *Die Schlacht um Moskau*, p. 74.

75 Foerster (ed.), *'Unternehmen Barbarossa'*, p. 20. (Jäckel: 'Hitlers doppeltes Kernstück'. In *Der Architekt der 'Endlösung'. Hitler und die Vernichtung der europäischen Juden*, Paderborn 1996, Richard Breitman shows convincingly that Hitler and Himmler deliberately planned the destruction of the Jews as early as 1939, while referring to it only obliquely, in coded form. By taking these references at face value, and failing to measure them against the actions that were being taken at the time, one would be falling into the trap that the murderers had set.)

76 Andreas Hillgruber, *Die Zerstörung Europas. Beiträge zur Weltkriegsepoche 1914 bis 1945*, Berlin 1988, p. 322.

77 Wolfgang Benz (ed.), *Dimensionen des Völkermords*, Munich 1996, p. 538. (Benz [p. 17] assesses the number as between 5.29 million and slightly over 6 million.)

78 George Lilienthal, *'Der Lebensborn e. V.'. Ein Instrument nationalsozialistischer Rassenpolitik*, Reinbek 1993, p. 68.

79 Benz (ed.), *Dimensionen des Völkermords*, p. 351.

80 Raul Hilberg, *The Destruction of the European Jews*, London/Chicago 1961, p. 555.

81 Ackermann, *Heinrich Himmler*, p. 169.

82 Kogon, *Der SS-Staat*, p. 185.

83 Raul Hilberg, *The Destruction of the European Jews*, revised and definitive edn, 3 vols, New York 1985, vol. 1, ch. IX. (Hilberg reports that the construction of a further gas chamber was under discussion in the Reich Chancellery, Hitler's private office.)

84 Hamilton T. Burden, *The Nuremberg Rallies 1923–1933*, London 1969.

85 Michalka (ed.), *Deutsche Geschichte 1933–1945*, p. 100 (German reports of the Sopade, vol. 5, 1938, p. 1205).

86   Ibid., p. 103 (from the monthly report of the Local Administrator of Lower Bavaria and the Upper Palatinate, 8 December 1938).

87   As described by the American newspaper correspondent Howard K. Smith. Sebastian Haffner, *Anmerkungen zu Hitler*, Munich 1978, p. 175 wrote: 'The mass of the Germans felt pity for the Jews and showed their shame and resentment – but that was as far as they went.')

88   *Der Spiegel*, 20 May, 1996, p. 55.

89   Albrecht Tyrell, *'Führer befiehl . . .': Selbstzeugnisse aus der 'Kampfzeit' der NSDAP*, Düsseldorf 1969, p. 209. (Hitler in 1928: 'The idea of anti-Semitism is gaining ground. What was scarcely known ten years ago is now before our eyes. The Jewish question has been brought to the fore and will not go away. We intend to make it an international question and will not cease our efforts until it is finally solved. We are confident that we shall live to see that day.')

90   Haffner, *Anmerkungen zu Hitler*, p. 175.

91   Hitler, *Hitlers Tischgespräche*, p. 305 (15 May 1942).

92   Ibid., p. 456 (24 July 1942).

93   Cosima Wagner, *Tagebücher*, vol. 4, p. 852 (entry of 18 December 1881).

94   Paul Devrient, *Mein Schüler Hitler. Das Tagebuch seines Lehrers Paul Devrient*, ed. Werner Maser, Pfaffenhofen 1975, p. 26.

95   Ibid., p. 127.

96   Ibid., p. 152.

97   Engel, *Heeresadjutant bei Hitler*, p. 65 (entry of 4 October 1939).

98   Ibid., p. 94 (entry of 2 February 1941).

99   Hitler, *Reden und Proklamationen*, vol. 2, p. 1885. (Jäckel also was of the opinion that Hitler never seriously intended to put the Madagascar plan into effect [*Hitlers Herrschaft*, p. 99].)

100   Dieter Borchmeyer and Jörg Salaquarda (eds), *Nietzsche und Wagner. Stationen einer epochalen Begegnung*, 2 vols, Frankfurt 1994, vol. 1, p. 52 (letter from Cosima Wagner to Nietzsche, 6 February 1870, telling him 'to avoid stirring up a hornets' nest . . . if you are later prepared to take up the cruel struggle, then with God's blessing').

101   Fest, *Fremdheit und Nähe*, p. 154 ('Die andere Utopie. Eine Studie über Heinrich Himmler').

102   Ibid., p. 155.

103   Heinz Höhne, *Der Orden unter dem Totenkopf. Die Geschichte der SS*, Gütersloh 1967, p. 7.

104   Ralph Giordano, *Wenn Hitler den Krieg gewonnen hätte. Die Pläne der Nazis nach dem Endsieg*, Hamburg 1989, p. 287. Illustration in Karl Hüser, *'Wewelsburg 1933–1945'. Eine Dokumentation*, ed. Kreis Paderborn, Paderborn 1987, p. 243.

105   Höhne, *Der Orden unter dem Totenkopf*, p. 9.

106   Otto Dietrich, *Zwölf Jahre mit Hitler*, Munich 1955, p. 259.

107   Kogon, *Der SS-Staat*, p. 50.

108   Michael Ley, *Genozid und Heilserwartung. Zum nationalsozialistischen Mord am europäischen Judentum*, Vienna 1993, p. 7 (letter from Himmler to Gottlob Berger, his Chief of Staff, 28 July 1942).

109   Heinrich Himmler, *Geheimreden 1933–1945*, ed. Bradley F. Smith and Agnes F. Peterson, Berlin 1974, p. 170. (Address to senior Party officials in Posen, 6 October 1943: 'You now understand the situation and will keep it to yourselves. At some time in the distant future we may consider telling the masses more about it.' According to Himmler that would only happen generations

ahead, 'for we, all of us here, have borne the responsibility [both for the practice and for the theory] on our own shoulders for the sake of the people, and will take our secret with us to the grave.')

110 Ibid., p. 169. (Same occasion as note 109: 'There are more millions of people in the country who have their own famous "decent" Jew than there are Jews themselves. I only mention this because you will know from your experience in your own parts of the country many honourable National Socialist citizens each of whom knows a "decent" Jew.')

111 Michalka (ed.), *Deutsche Geschichte 1933–1945*, p. 278. (Speech by Himmler, 4 October 1943: 'The others, obviously, are pigs but this Jew is a fine man.')

112 As note 110.

113 Hitler, *Reden und Proklamationen*, vol. 2, p. 1400.

114 André François-Poncet, *The Fateful Years. Memoirs of a French Ambassador in Berlin 1931–1938*, London 1949, p. 293.

115 Sebastian Haffner writes about this situation in *Germany: Jekyll and Hyde*, London 1940.

116 Himmler, *Geheimreden*, p. 200.

117 Nietzsche, *Sämtliche Werke*, vol. 15, p. 85. (Conversation between Wagner and Ernst Schmeitzner, May 1878. Schmeitzner later reported that Wagner indulged in a series of offensive remarks about the Jews 'to which Cosima and Wolzogen paid close attention, even to the lengths of writing them down and preserving them for future use'.)

118 Hitler, *Reden und Proklamationen*, vol. 2, p. 2195 (radio address given from the Reich Chancellery, 30 January 1945).

119 Hermann Rauschning, *Gespräche mit Hitler*, Vienna 1973, p. 266.

120 Hitler, *Reden und Proklamationen*, vol. 2, p. 2197.

BIBLIOGRAPHY

Primary Sources: Letters, Diaries, Memoirs

Wagner

Liszt, Franz/Richard Wagner, *Briefwechsel*, ed. Hanjo Kesting, Munich 1988.

[König] Ludwig II/Richard Wagner, *Briefwechsel*, 4 vols, ed. Wittelsbacher Ausgleichsfonds and Winifred Wagner, rev. Otto Strobel, Karlsruhe 1936–7.

Wagner, Richard, *Bayreuther Briefe (1871–1883)*, ed. Carl Friedich Glasenapp, Leipzig 1912.

Wagner, Richard, *Das Braune Buch. Tagebuchaufzeichnungen 1865 bis 1882*, ed. Joachim Bergfeld, Munich 1988.

Wagner, Richard, *Briefe*, ed. Hanjo Kesting, Munich 1983.

Wagner, Richard, *Briefe*, ed. Hans-Joachim Bauer, Stuttgart 1995.

Wagner, Richard, *Briefe 1830–1883*, ed. Werner Otto, Berlin 1986.

Wagner, Richard, *Briefe in zwei Bänden*, ed. Wilhelm Altmann, Leipzig n.d.

Wagner, Richard, *The Burrell Collection: Letters of Richard Wagner*, ed. John N. Burk, New York 1950.

Wagner, Richard, *Dichtungen und Schriften*, 10 vols, ed. Dieter Borchmeyer, Frankfurt 1983.

Wagner, Richard, *Familienbriefe 1832–1874*, ed. Carl Friedrich Glasenapp, Berlin 1907.

Wagner, Richard, *Fünfzehn Briefe Richard Wagners mit Erinnerungen und Erläuterungen von Eliza Wille, geb. Sloman*, Munich 1935.

Wagner, Richard, *Gesammelte Schriften und Dichtungen*, 10 vols, ed. Richard Wagner, Leipzig 1871–83.

Wagner, Richard, *Mein Leben*, 2 vols, ed. Eike Middell, Leipzig 1986: English trans.: *My Life*, London 1963.

Wagner, Richard, *Nachgelassene Schriften und Dichtungen*, Leipzig 1895.

Wagner, Richard, *Sämtliche Briefe*, ed. G. Strobel, W. Wolf, H.-J. Bauer and J. Forner, Leipzig 1967–.

Wagner, Richard, *Sämtliche Schriften und Dichtungen*, 16 vols, Leipzig 1911–14.

Wagner, Richard, *Skizzen und Entwürfe zur Ring-Dichtung*, ed. Otto Strobel, Munich 1930.

Wagner, Richard/Hans von Bülow, *Briefe an Hans von Bülow*, ed. Daniela Thode, Jena 1916.

Wagner, Richard/Mathilde Maier, *Richard Wagner an Mathilde Maier (1862–1878)*, ed. Hans Scholz, Leipzig 1830.

Wagner, Richard/Mathilde Wesendonk, *Tagebuchblätter und Briefe 1853–1871*, ed. Wolfgang Golther, Berlin 1904.

Hitler

Hitler, Adolf, *Hitlers Briefe und Notizen*, ed. Werner Maser, Düsseldorf 1988.

Hitler, Adolf, *Hitlers Tischgespräche im Führerhauptquartier*, ed. Henry Picker, Stuttgart 1976.

Hitler, Adolf, *Hitlers Zweites Buch*, ed. Gerhard L. Weinberg, Stuttgart 1961.

Hitler, Adolf, *Mein Kampf*, 763rd–767th impression, Munich 1942 (1st edn: vol. 1, 1925; vol. 2, 1926); English trans.: *Mein Kampf*, London 1992.

Hitler, Adolf, *Monologe im Führerhauptquartier 1941–1944. Die Aufzeichnungen Heinrich Heims*, ed. Werner Jochmann, Munich 1982.

Hitler, Adolf, *Reden und Proklamationen 1932–1945*, 2 vols, ed. Max Domarus, Würzburg 1962–3.

Hitler, Adolf, *Reden, Schriften, Anordnungen. Februar 1925 bis Januar 1933*, 3 vols, ed. Clems Vollnhals et al., Munich 1992–4.

Hitler, Adolf, *Sämtliche Aufzeichnungen 1905–1924*, ed. Eberhard Jäckel and Axel Kuhn, Stuttgart 1980.

Further Sources and Secondary Literature

(An extensive bibliography for the periods of the Weimar Republic and the Third Reich is given in Helen Kehr and Janet Langmaid (eds), *The Nazi Era 1919–1945: A Select Bibliography*, London 1982.)

Abshagen, Karl Heinz, *Schuld und Verhängnis. Ein Vierteljahrhundert in Augenzeugenberichten*, Stuttgart 1961.

Ackermann, Joseph, *Heinrich Himmler als Ideologe*, Göttingen 1970.

Adam, Peter, *Kunst im Dritten Reich*, Hamburg 1992.

Ades, Dawn, Tim Benton, David Elliott and Iain Boyd Whyte (eds), *Art and Power. Europe under the Dictators 1930–1945*, London 1995.

Adorno, Theodor W., *Versuch über Wagner*, Munich 1964.

Aly, Götz, '*Endlösung*'. *Die Völkerverschiebung und der Mord an den europäischen Juden*, Frankfurt 1995.

Arntz, H.-Dieter, *Ordensburg Vogelsang 1934–1945. Erziehung zur politischen Führung im Dritten Reich*, Euskirchen 1986.

Augstein, Rudolf et al., *Historikerstreit. Die Dokumentation der Kontroverse um die Einzigartigkeit der nationalsozialistischen Judenvernichtung, 69.–73. Tausend*, Munich 1995.

Bahnsen, Uwe und James P. O'Donnell, *Die Katakombe. Das Ende in der Reichskanzlei*, Bergisch Gladbach 1981.

Bärsch, Claus-Ekkehard, *Erlösung und Vernichtung. Dr. phil. Joseph Goebbels*, Munich 1987.

Barth, Herbert, *Bayreuther Dramaturgie. Der Ring des Nibelungen*, Stuttgart 1980.

Barth, Herbert (ed.), *Der Festspielhügel. Richard Wagners Werk in Bayreuth 1876–1976*, Munich 1976.

Barth, Herbert, Dietrich Mack and Egon Voss (eds), *Richard Wagner. Leben und Werk in zeitgenössischen Bildern und Dokumenten*, Munich 1982.

Bauer, Oswald Georg, *Richard Wagner. Die Bühnenwerke von der Uraufführung bis heute*, Frankfurt/Berlin/Vienna 1982.

Bauer, Richard et al. (eds.), *München – 'Hauptstadt der Bewegung'. Bayerns Metropole und der Nationalsozialismus*, Munich 1993.

Baumstark, Reinhold and Michael Koch (eds), *Der Gral. Artusromantik in der Kunst des 19. Jahrhunderts*, Cologne 1995.

Bayerische Akademie der Schönen Künste (ed.), *Adolf von Hildebrand und seine Welt. Briefe und Erinnerungen*, Munich 1962.

Bélart, Hans, *Gesangsdramatische Wagnerkunst (nach Richard Wagners Tradition)*, Dresden 1915.

Below, Nicolaus von, *Als Hitlers Adjutant 1937–1945*, Mainz 1980.

Benz, Wolfgang (ed.), *Dimensionen des Völkermords. Die Zahl der jüdischen Opfer des Nationalsozialismus*, Munich 1996.

Bermbach, Udo (ed.), *In den Trümmern der eignen Welt. Richard Wagners 'Ring des Nibelungen'*, Berlin/Hamburg 1989.

Bermbach, Udo and Dieter Borchmeyer (eds), *Richard Wagner – 'Der Ring des Nibelungen'. Ansichten eines Mythos*, Stuttgart 1995.

Bie, Oscar (ed.), *Richard Wagner und Bayreuth*, Zurich 1931.

Blasius, Dirk and Dan Diner (eds), *Zerbrochene Geschichte. Leben und Selbstverständnis der Juden in Deutschland*, Frankfurt 1991.

Boldt, Gerhard, *Die letzten Tage der Reichskanzlei*, Hamburg 1947.

Borchmeyer, Dieter, *Das Theater Richard Wagners*, Stuttgart 1982.

Borchmeyer, Dieter (ed.), *Wege des Mythos in der Moderne. Richard Wagner 'Der Ring des Nibelungen'*, Munich 1987.

Borchmeyer, Dieter and Jörg Salaquarda (eds), *Nietzsche und Wagner. Stationen einer epochalen Begegnung*, 2 vols, Frankfurt 1994.

Bracher, Karl-Dietrich, Wolfgang Sauer and Gerhard Schultz, *Die nationalsozialistische Machtergreifung*, Cologne 1962.

Breitman, Richard, *Der Architekt der 'Endlösung'. Himmler und die Vernichtung der europäischen Juden*, Paderborn 1996.

Bronnenmeyer, Walter, *Vom Tempel zur Werkstatt. Geschichte der Bayreuther Festspiele*, Bayreuth 1970.

Broszat, Martin, *Der Staat Hitlers. Grundlegung und Entwicklung seiner inneren Verfassung*, Munich 1969.

Bullock, Alan, *Hitler: A Study in Tyranny*, London 1964.

Bülow, Hans von, *Briefe und Schriften*, 8 vols, ed. Marie von Bülow, Leipzig 1895–1908.

Burbridge, P. and R. Sutton (eds), *The Wagner Companion*, London 1979.

Burckhardt, C.J., *Briefe 1908–1974*, Frankfurt 1986.

Burden, Hamilton T., *The Nuremberg Rallies 1923–1933*, London 1969.

Cecil, R., *The Myth of the Master Race. Alfred Rosenberg and Nazi Ideology*, London 1972.

Chamberlain, Houston Stewart, *Arische Weltanschauung*, Munich 1916.

Chamberlain, Houston Stewart, *Die Grundlagen des Neunzehnten Jahrhunderts*, 2 vols, 28th impression, Munich 1942; English trans.: *Foundations of the Nineteenth Century*, London 1911.

Chamberlain, Houston Stewart, *Die Grundlagen des Neunzehnten Jahrhunderts. Kritische Urteile*, Munich 1901.

Chamberlain, Houston Stewart, *Kriegsaufsätze*, Munich 1914.

Chamberlain, Houston Stewart, *Lebenswege meines Denkens*, Munich 1919.

Chamberlain, Houston Stewart, *Politische Ideale*, Munich 1915.

Chamberlain, Houston Stewart, *Richard Wagner*, Munich 1901; English trans.: *Richard Wagner*, London 1897.

Chamberlain, Houston Stewart, *Der Wille zum Sieg*, Munich 1917.

Cohn, Norman, *The Pursuit of the Millennium. Revolutionary Millenarians and Mystical Anarchists of the Middle Ages*, London 1970.

Cohn, Norman, *Warrant for Genocide. The Myth of the Jewish World Conspiracy*, London 1967.

Conrad, Michael Georg, *Wagners Geist und Kunst in Bayreuth*, Munich 1906.

Cornelius, Carl Maria, *Peter Cornelius*, 2 vols, Regensburg 1925.

Csampai, Attila and Dietmar Holland (eds), *Richard Wagner, Der fliegende Holländer*, Reinbek 1982.

Csampai, Attila and Dietmar Holland (eds), *Richard Wagner, Die Meistersinger von Nürnberg*, Reinbek 1981.

Csampai, Attila and Dietmar Holland (eds), *Richard Wagner, Parsifal*, Reinbek 1984.

Dahlhaus, Carl, *Wagners Konzeption des musikalischen Dramas*, Regensburg 1971.

Dahlhaus, Carl and John Deathridge, *Wagner*, Stuttgart 1994.

Daim, Wilfried, *Der Mann, der Hitler die Ideen gab. Jörg Lanz von Liebenfels*, Vienna 1994.

Deathridge, John, *Wagner's Rienzi. A Reappraisal Based on a Study of the Sketches and Drafts*, Oxford 1977.

Deathridge, John, Martin Gech and Egon Voss (eds), *Wagner–Werk–Verzeichnis*, Mainz 1986.

Deuerlein, Ernst (ed.), *Der Aufstieg der NSDAP in Augenzeugenberichten*, Munich 1974.

Devrient, Eduard, *Aus seinen Tagebüchern. Berlin–Dahlem 1836–1852*, ed. Rolf Kabel, Weimar 1964.

Devrient, Paul, *Mein Schüler Hitler. Das Tagebuch seines Lehrers Paul Devrient*, ed. Werner Maser, Pfaffenhofen 1975.

Dietrich, Otto, *Zwölf Jahre mit Hitler*, Munich 1955.

Donington, Robert, *Wagner's 'Ring' and its Symbols*, London 1974.

Dornberg, John, *The Putsch that Failed. Munich 1923. Hitler's Rehearsal for Power*, London 1982.

Drüner, Ulrich (ed.), *Parsifal*, Taufkirchen 1990.

Dülffer, Jost, Jochen Thies and Josef Henke, *Hitlers Städte. Baupolitik im Dritten Reich*, Cologne 1978.

Du Moulin Eckart, Richard, *Cosima Wagner. Ein Lebens- und Charakterbild*, 2 vols, Berlin 1929.

Du Moulin Eckart, Richard, *Hans von Bülow*, Munich 1921.

Du Moulin Eckart, Richard, *Die Herrin von Bayreuth*, Berlin 1931.

Du Moulin Eckart, Richard, *Wahnfried*, Leipzig 1925.

Ebermayer, Erich, *Magisches Bayreuth. Legende und Wirklichkeit*, Stuttgart 1951.

Eckart, Dietrich, *Der Bolschewismus von Moses bis Lenin. Zwiegespräch zwischen Adolf

Hitler und mir, Munich 1925.

Eichner, Walter (ed.), *Weltdiskussion um Bayreuth. Ein Querschnitt durch die ersten Festspiele nach dem Kriege*, Bayreuth 1952.

Eidam, Rosa, *Bayreuther Festspielzeiten 1883–1924. Persönliche Erinnerungen*, Ansbach 1925.

Eitner, Hans-Jürgen, *Hitler. Ein Psychogramm*, Berlin 1994.

Engel, Gerhard, *Heeresadjutant bei Hitler 1938–1943. Aufzeichnungen des Majors Engel*, ed. Hildegard von Kotze, Stuttgart 1974.

Ezer, David, 'Das Judentum in dem "Ring"', *Opera*, 3, March 1995.

Felix, D., *Walther Rathenau and the Weimar Republic*, Baltimore 1971.

Fest, Joachim, C., *Fremdheit und Nähe. Von der Gegenwart des Gewesenen*, Stuttgart 1996.

Fest, Joachim C., *Hitler. Eine Biographie*, Frankfurt 1973; English trans.: *Hitler. A Biography*, London 1974.

Field, G.C., *Evangelist of Race: The German Vision of Houston Stewart Chamberlain*, New York 1981.

Foerster, Roland G. (ed.), *'Unternehmen Barbarossa'. Zum historischen Ort der deutsch–sowjetischen Beziehungen von 1933 bis 1941*, Munich 1993.

Förster-Nietzsche, Elisabeth, *Wagner und Nietzsche zur Zeit ihrer Freundschaft*, Munich 1915.

François-Poncet, André, *The Fateful Years. Memoirs of a French Ambassador in Berlin 1931–1938*, London 1949.

Frank, Hans, *Im Angesicht des Galgens*, ed. Oswald Schloffer, Munich 1953.

Franke, Rainer, *Richard Wagners Zürcher Kunstschriften*, Dissertation, Hamburg 1983.

Frankfurter Kunstverein (ed.), *Kunst im Dritten Reich. Dokumente der Unterwerfung*, Frankfurt 1974.

Frischauer, Willi, *Himmler. The Evil Genius of the Third Reich*, London 1953.

Furtwängler, Wilhelm, *Concerning Music*, London 1953.

Furtwängler, Wilhelm, *Furtwängler on Music*, ed. Ronald Taylor, Aldershot 1991.

Furtwängler, Wilhelm, *Wilhelm Furtwängler. Notebooks 1924–1954*, London 1989.

Gay, Peter, *Freud, Jews and Other Germans: Masters and Victims in a Modernist Culture*, Oxford 1989.

Geissmar, Bertha, *Taktstock und Schaftstiefel. Erinnerungen an Wilhelm Furtwängler*, Cologne 1996; English edn *The Baton and the Jackboot. Recollections of Musical Life*, London 1944.

Germanisches Nationalmuseum (ed.), *Die Meistersinger und Richard Wagner. Die Rezeptionsgeschichte einer Oper von 1868 bis heute*, Nuremberg 1981.

Giesler, Hermann, *Ein anderer Hitler. Bericht seines Architekten*, Leoni am Starnberger See 1977.

Giordano, Ralph, *Wenn Hitler den Krief gewonnen hätte. Die Pläne der Nazis nach dem Endsieg*, Hamburg 1989.

Girard, René, *The Scapegoat*, Baltimore 1995.

Glasenapp, Carl Friedrich, *Das Leben Richard Wagners*, 6 vols, Leipzig 1904–11.

Glasenapp, Carl Friedrich, *Wagner-Enzyklopädie*, vol. 2, Leipzig 1891.

Gobineau, Arthur, *Ein Erinnerungsbild aus Wahnfried (von Cosima Wagner)*, Stuttgart 1907.

Goebbels, Joseph, *The Goebbels Diaries*, ed. Fred Taylor, London 1982.

Goebbels, Joseph, *Reden 1932–1945*, 2 vols, ed. Helmut Heiber, Düsseldorf 1971.

Goebbels, Joseph, *Tagebücher 1924–1925*, 2 vols, ed. Ralf Georg Reuth, Munich 1992.

Goebbels, Joseph, *Tagebücher 1945*, Hamburg 1977.

Goebbels, Joseph, *Die Tagebücher von Joseph Goebbels*, vols 7–10, ed. Eike Fröhlich, Munich 1993–4.

Goebbels, Joseph, *Die Tagebücher von Joseph Goebbels. Sämtliche Fragmente*, 4 vols, ed. Eike Fröhlich, Munich 1987.

Golther, Wolfgang, *Handbuch der germanischen Mythologie*, Rostock 1895.

Goodrick-Clarke, Nicholas, *The Occult Roots of Nazism*, London 1992.

Gossweiler, Kurt, *Kapital, Reichswehr und NSDAP 1919–1924*, Cologne 1982.

Gregor-Dellin, Martin, *Richard Wagner – die Revolution als Oper*, Munich 1973.

Gregor-Dellin, Martin, *Richard Wagner. Sein Leben, sein Werk, sein Jahrhundert*, Munich 1980; English trans.: *Richard Wagner*, London 1983.

Grimm, Jakob, *Deutsche Mythologie*, 3 vols, repr. Frankfurt 1981.

Grosse Deutsche Kunstausstellung 1941 im Haus der Deutschen Kunst zu München (catalogue), Munich 1941.

Grossmann-Vendrey, Susanna (ed.), *Bayreuth in der deutschen Presse*, vol. 2: *Die Uraufführung des Parsifal (1882)*, Regensburg 1977.

Grunberger, Richard, *A Social History of the Third Reich*, London 1971.

Grunfeld, F., *The Hitler File. A Social History of Germany and the Nazis*, London 1974.

Günther, Gitta-Maria, *Weimar. Eine Chronik*, Leipzig 1996.

Gutmann, Robert, *Richard Wagner. The Man, His Mind and His Music*, New York 1968.

Haas, Frithjof, *Zwischen Brahms und Wagner. Der Dirigent Hermann Levi*, Zurich 1995.

Hacker, Rupert (ed.), *Ludwig II von Bayern in Augenzeugenberichten*, Munich 1972.

Haenel, Erich and Eugen Kalckschmidt (eds), *Das alte Dresden. Bilder und Dokumente aus zwei Jahrhunderten*, Bindlach 1995.

Haffner, Sebastian, *Anmerkungen zu Hitler*, Munich 1978; English trans.: *The Meaning of Hitler*, London 1979.

Haffner, Sebastian, *Germany. Jekyll and Hyde*, London 1940.

Hamann, Brigitte, *Hitlers Wien. Lehrjahre eines Diktators*, Munich 1996; English trans.: *Hitler's Vienna: A Dictator's Apprenticeship*, Oxford 1999.

Hammer-Schenk, Harold, *Synagogen in Deutschland*, Hamburg 1981.

Hanfstaengl, Ernst, *Zwischen Weissem und Braunem Haus. Memoiren eines politischen Aussenseiters*, Munich 1970.

Hanslick, Eduard, *Aus meinem Leben*, 2 vols: vol. 1, Berlin 1894; vol. 2: Berlin 1911.

Hartford, Robert (ed.), *Bayreuth: The Early Years. An Account of the Early Decades of the Wagner Festival as Seen by the Celebrated Visitors and Participants*, Cambridge/London/New York/New Rochelle/Melbourne/Sydney 1980.

Heckel, Karl, *Die Bühnenfestspiele in Bayreuth. Authentischer Beitrag zur Geschichte ihrer Entstehung und Entwicklung*, Leipzig 1881.

Heckmann, Hermann, *Matthäus Daniel Pöppelmann und die Barockkunst in Dresden*, Stuttgart 1986.

Heer, Friedrich, *Der Glaube des Adolf Hitler. Anatomie einer politischen Religiosität*, Munich 1968.

Heer, Hannes and Klaus Naumann (eds), *Vernichtungskrieg. Verbrechen der Wehrmacht*, Hamburg 1995.

Heiber, Beatrice and Helmut (eds), *Die Rückseite des Hakenkreuzes. Absonderliches aus den Akten des Dritten Reiches*, Munich 1993.

Heiden, Konrad, *Adolf Hitler*, 2 vols, Zurich 1936; English trans.: *Hitler – A Biography*, London 1936.

Heiden, Konrad, *Geschichte des Nationalsozialismus. Die Karriere einer Idee*, Berlin 1933.

Hermand, Jost, *Der alte Traum vom neuen Reich. Völkische Utopien und Nationalsozialismus*, Frankfurt 1988.

Herz, Rudolf, *Hoffmann und Hitler. Fotographie als Medium des Führer-Mythos*, Munich 1994.

Herzfeld, Friedrich, *Königsfreundschaft. Ludwig II und Richard Wagner*, Leipzig 1939.

Heuss, Theodor, *Hitlers Weg*, ed. Eberhard Jäckel, Tübingen 1968.

Heydick, Lutz, *Leipzig. Historischer Führer zu Stadt und Land*, Leipzig n.d.

Hilberg, Raul, *The Destruction of the European Jews*, London/Chicago 1961.

Hildebrand, Klaus, *Das Dritte Reich*, Munich 1987.

Hillgruber, Andreas, *Die Zerstörung Europas. Beiträge zur Weltkriegsepoche 1914 bis 1945*, Berlin 1988.

Hillgruber, Andreas, *Zweierlei Untergang. Die Zerschlagung des Dritten Reiches und das Ende des europäischen Judentums*, Berlin 1986.

Himmler, Heinrich, *Geheimreden 1933–1945*, ed. Bradley F. Smith and Agnes F. Peterson, Berlin 1974.

Hoffmann, Heinrich, *Hitler Was My Friend*, London 1955.

Höhne, Heinz, *Die Machtergreifung. Deutschlands Weg in die Hitler-Diktatur*, Hamburg 1983.

Höhne, Heinz, *Der Orden unter dem Totenkopf. Die Geschichte der SS*, Gütersloh, 1967.

Hojer, Gerhard (ed.), *König-Ludwig-II-Museum Herrenchiemsee* (catalogue), Munich 1986.

Hollingdale, R.J., *Nietzsche. The Man and His Philosophy*, London 1975.

Hossbach, Friedrich, *Zwischen Wehrmacht und Hitler 1934–1938*, Wolfenbüttel 1949.

Hotter, Hans, *'Der Mai war mir gewogen . . .'. Erinnerungen*, Munich 1996.

Hübinger, Gangolf (ed.), *Versammlungsort moderner Geister. Der Eugen Diederichs-Verlag*, Munich 1996.

Hürlimann, Martin (ed.), *Richard Wagner in Selbstzeugnissen und im Urteil seiner Zeitgenossen*, Zurich 1988.

Hüttl, Ludwig, *Ludwig II, König von Bayern*, Munich 1986.

Ingenschay-Goch, Dagmar, *Richard Wagners erfundener Mythos*, Bonn 1982.

Jäckel, Eberhard, *Das deutsche Jahrhundert. Eine historische Bilanz*, Stuttgart 1996.

Jäckel, Eberhard, *Hitlers Herrschaft. Vollzug einer Weltanschauung*, Stuttgart 1986.

Jäckel, Eberhard, *Hitlers Weltanschauung. Entwurf einer Herrschaft*, Tübingen 1969.

Jäckel, Eberhard and Jürgen Rohwer (eds), *Der Mord an den europäischen Juden im Zweiten Weltkrieg*, Frankfurt 1987.

Jäckel, Günter (ed.), *Dresden zwischen Wiener Kongress und Maiaufstand*, Berlin 1989.

Jäggi, Willy and Hans Oesch (eds), *Der Fall Bayreuth*, Basle 1962.

Jefferson, Alan, *Elisabeth Schwarzkopf*, London 1996.

Jetzinger, Franz, *Hitlers Jugend. Phantasien, Lügen – und die Wahrheit*, Vienna 1956.

Joachimsthaler, Anton, *Korrektur einer Biographie. Adolf Hitler 1908–1920*, Munich 1989.

Johnson, Paul, *A History of the Jews*, London 1987.

Jones, Sidney J., *Hitlers Weg begann in Wien 1907–1913*, Munich 1989.

Kampmann, Wanda, *Deutsche und Juden. Die Geschichte der Juden in Deutschland vom Mittelalter bis zum Beginn des Ersten Weltkriegs*, Frankfurt 1979.

Kapp, Julius, *Wagner. Eine Biographie*, Berlin 1921.

Karbaum, Michael, *Studien zur Geschichte der Bayreuther Festspiele (1876–1976)*, 2 vols, Regensburg 1976.

Katz, Jacob, *The Darker Side of Genius. Richard Wagner's Anti-Semitism*, Hanover/London 1986.

Kerrl, Hanns (ed.), *Reichstagung in Nürnberg 1935. Der Parteitag der Freiheit*, Berlin 1936.

Kershaw, Ian, *Hitler*, London 1991.

Kershaw, Ian, *Hitler 1889–1936*, London 1998.

Kershaw, Ian, *The Hitler Myth. Image and Reality in the Third Reich*, Oxford 1989.

Killian, Herbert, *Gustav Mahler in den Erinnerungen von Natalie Bauer-Lechner*, Hamburg 1984.

Kirchhoff, Jochen, *Nietzsche, Hitler und die Deutschen. Vom unerlösten Schatten des Dritten Reiches*, Berlin 1990.

Kirchmeyer, Helmut, *Das zeitgenössische Wagner-Bild*, vol. 1: *Wagner in Dresden;* vol. 2: *Dokumente 1842–1845;* vol. 3: *Dokumente 1846–1850*, Regensburg 1967–72.

Kirchner, Bertram (ed.), *Das Buch vom Gral. Mythen, Legenden und Dichtungen um das grösste Geheimnis des mittelalterlichen Abendlandes*, Munich 1989.

Klinckerfuss, Margarete, *Aufklänge aus versunkener Zeit*, Urach 1948.

Kloss, Erich, *Wagnertum in Vergangenheit und Gegenwart*, Berlin 1909.

Knopp, Guido, *Hitler. Eine Bilanz*, Berlin 1995.

Koch, H.W., *The Hitler Youth. Origins and Development 1922–1945*, London 1974.

Kogon, Eugen, *Der SS-Staat. Das System der deutschen Konzentrationslager*, Munich 1988.

Köhler, Joachim, *Friedrich Nietzsche und Cosima Wagner. Die Schule der Unterwerfung*, Berlin 1996; English trans.: *Nietzsche and Wagner. A Study in Subjugation*, New Haven/London 1998.

Kohn, Hans, *Karl Kraus, Arthur Schnitzler, Otto Weininger. Aus dem jüdischen Wien der Jahrhundertwende*, Tübingen 1962.

Kohut, Adolph, *Der Meister von Bayreuth. Neues und Intimes aus dem Leben und Schaffen Richard Wagners*, Berlin 1905.

Konzentrationslager. Document No. F 321 for the International Military Tribunal in Nuremberg, ed. French Office of the Information Service on War Crimes 1945, Frankfurt 1988.

Köpnick, Lutz, *Nothungs Modernität. Wagners 'Ring' und die Poesie der Macht im neunzehnten Jahrhundert*, Munich 1994.

Korotin, Ilse (ed.), *Die besten Geister der Nation. Philosophie und Nationalsozialismus*, Vienna 1994.

Krausnick, H., *Anatomy of the SS State*, London 1968.

Kreowski, Ernst and Eduard Fuchs, *Richard Wagner in der Karikatur*, Berlin 1907.

Kretzschmann, Hermann (ed.), *Bausteine zum Dritten Reich. Lehr- und Lesebuch des Reichsarbeitsdienstes*, Leipzig 1933.

Kröplin, Eckart, *Richard Wagner. Theatralisches Leben und lebendiges Theater*, Leipzig 1989.

Kröplin, Karl-Heinz, *Richard Wagner 1813–1883. Eine Chronik*, Leipzig 1983.

Kubizek, August, *Adolf Hitler. Mein Jugendfreund*, Graz 1953.

Kuby, Erich, *Richard Wagner & Co. Zum 150. Geburtstag des Meisters*, Hamburg 1963.

Kunstblätter mit Darstellungen aus Musikdramen und Opern, Munich.

Lange, Walter, *Richard Wagner und seine Vaterstadt Leipzig*, Leipzig 1921.

Langer, Walter C., *The Mind of Adolf Hitler. The Secret Wartime Report*, New York 1972.

Laqueur, Walter and George L. Mosse, *German Intellectuals between the Wars 1919–1939*, London 1962.

Laroche, Bernd, *Der fliegende Holländer. Wirkung und Wandlung eines Motivs*, Frankfurt 1992.

Ley, Michael, *Genozid und Heilserwartung. Zum nationalsozialistischen Mord am europäischen Judentum*, Vienna 1993.

Lilienthal, Georg, *Die 'Lebensborn e. V.'. Ein Instrument nationalsozialistischer Rassenpolitik*, Reinbek 1993.

Lindau, Paul, *Nüchterne Briefe aus Bayreuth*, Breslau 1880.

Lippert, Woldemar, *Richard Wagners Verbannung und Rückkehr 1849–1862*, Dresden 1927.

Lochner, Louis P., *Stets das Unerwartete. Erinnerungen aus Deutschland 1921–1953*, Darmstadt 1955.

Mack, Dietrich, *Der Bayreuther Inszenierungsstil*, Munich 1976.

Mack, Dietrich and Egon Voss (eds), *Richard Wagner. Leben und Werk in Daten und Bildern*, Frankfurt 1978.

Magee, Brian, *Aspects of Wagner*, Oxford 1988.

Mann, Thomas, *Wagner und unsere Zeit. Aufsätze, Betrachtungen, Briefe*, ed. Erika Mann, Frankfurt 1986; English trans.: *Pro and Contra Wagner*, London 1985.

Marcuse, Ludwig, *Das denkwürdige Leben des Richard Wagners*, Munich 1963.

Marek, George R., *Cosima Wagner*, New York 1981.

Marschall, Birgit, *Reisen und Regieren. Die Nordlandfahrten Kaiser Wilhelm II*, Hamburg 1991.

Marsop, Paul, *Studienblätter eines Musikers*, Berlin 1903.

Maser, Werner, *Adolf Hitler. Legende, Mythos, Wirklichkeit*, Munich 1974.

Maser, Werner, *Der Sturm auf die Republik*, Stuttgart 1973.

Mayer, Arno J., *Der Krieg als Kreuzzug. Das Deutsche Reich, Hitlers Wehrmacht und die 'Endlösung'*, Reinbek 1989.

Mayer, Hans, *Richard Wagner*, Reinbek 1959; English trans. 1973.

Mayer, Hans, *Richard Wagner in Bayreuth: 1876–1976*, Frankfurt 1978.

Meier-Gesees, Karl (ed.), *Wahnfried*, Bayreuth 1928.

Mendgen, Eva, *Franz von Stuck 1863–1928*, Cologne 1994.

Metzger, Heinz-Klaus and Rainer Riehn (eds), *Richard Wagner: Wie antisemitisch darf ein Künstler sein? Musikkonzepte 5*, Munich 1981.

Mey, Curt, *Der Meistergesang in Geschichte und Kunst*, Leipzig 1901.

Meyer, Werner, *Götterdämmerung. April 1945 in Bayreuth*, Bayreuth 1975.

Michalka, Wolfgang (ed.), *Deutsche Geschichte 1933–1945. Dokumente zur Innen- und Aussenpolitik*, Frankfurt 1993.

Millenkovich-Morold, Max, *Cosima Wagner. Ein Lebensbild*, Leipzig 1937.

Millenkovich-Morold, Max, *Dreigestirn: Wagner, Liszt, Bülow*, Berlin 1940.

Millington, Barry, *Wagner*, London 1992.

Millington, Barry (ed.), *The Wagner Compendium*, London 1992.

Mitchell, Donald, *Gustav Mahler*, London 1975.

Mitchell, Donald, *Gustav Mahler. The Early Years*, London 1980.

Mitchell, Donald, *Gustav Mahler. Songs and Symphonies of Life and Death*, London 1985.

Mitchell, Donald, *The Wunderhorn Years*, London 1975.

Mommsen, Hans, *Die verspielte Freiheit. Der Weg der Republik von Weimar in den Untergang 1918–1933*, Berlin 1989.

Mork, Andrea, *Richard Wagner als politischer Schriftsteller. Weltanschauung und Wirkungsgeschichte*, Frankfurt 1990.

Mosse, George L., *The Crisis of German Ideology*, New York 1964.

Mosse, George L., *Nazi Culture*, London 1966.

Mosse, George L., *Towards the Final Solution: A History of European Racism*, London 1978.

Mota, Jordi and Maria Infiesta, *Das Werk Richard Wagners im Spiegel der Kunst*, Tübingen 1995.

Müller, Karl Alexander von, *Erinnerungen*, vol. 1: *Aus Gärten der Vergangenheit*, Stuttgart 1951; vol. 2: *Mars und Venus*, Stuttgart 1954; vol. 3: *Im Wandel einer Welt*, ed. Otto Alexander von Müller, Munich 1966.

Müller, Rolf-Dieter, *Hitlers Ostkrieg und die deutsche Siedlungspolitik. Die Zusammenarbeit von Wehrmacht, Wirtschaft und SS*, Frankfurt 1991.

Müller, Ulrich, Franz Hundsnurscher and Cornelius Sommer (eds), *Richard Wagner 1883–1983. Die Rezeption im 19. und 20. Jahrhundert. Gesammelte Beiträge des Salzburger Symposions*, Salzburg 1984.

Müller, Ulrich, Peter Wapnewski and John Deathridge (eds), *Richard-Wagner-Handbuch*, Stuttgart 1986; English trans.: *Wagner Handbook*, Cambridge 1992.

Naegele, Verena, *Parsifals Mission. Der Einfluss Richard Wagners auf Ludwig II und seine Politik*, Cologne 1995.

Neumann, Angelo, *Erinnerungen an Richard Wagner*, Leipzig 1907.

Newman, Ernest, *Fact and Fiction About Wagner*, London 1931.

Newman, Ernest, *The Life of Richard Wagner*, 4 vols, London 1933–47.

Newman, Ernest, *A Study of Wagner*, London 1899.

Newman, Ernest, *Wagner as Man and Artist*, London 1914.

Niedner, Felix and Gustav Neckel (eds), *Thule. Altnordische Dichtung und Prosa*, 24 vols, Jena 1912–30.

Nolte, Ernst, *Der Faschismus in seiner Epoche*, Munich 1963.

Olender, Maurice, *Die Sprachen des Paradieses. Religion, Philologie und Rassentheorie im 19. Jahrhundert*, Frankfurt 1995.

Opitz, Reinhard, *Faschismus und Neofaschismus*, vol. 1: *Der deutsche Faschismus bis 1945*, Cologne 1988.

Orlow, D., *The History of the Nazi Party*, Pittsburgh 1963, 1973.

Otto, Werner (ed.), *Richard Wagner. Ein Lebens- und Charakterbild in Dokumenten und zeitgenössischen Darstellungen*, Berlin 1990.

Pachl, Peter P., *Siegfried Wagner. Genie im Schatten*, Munich 1988.

Papen, Franz von, *Der Wahrheit eine Gasse*, Munich 1952.

Peters, H.F., *Zarathustras Schwester. Fritz und Lieschen Nietzsche – ein deutsches Trauerspiel*, Munich 1983.

Petersen, Julius, *Die Sehnsucht nach dem Dritten Reich in deutscher Sage und Dichtung*, Stuttgart 1934.

Petzet, Detta and Michael, *Die Richard-Wagner-Bühne König Ludwigs II*, Munich 1970.

Petzoldt, Leander (ed.), *Historische Sagen*, vol. 2: *Ritter, Räuber und geistliche Herren*, Munich 1977.

Pfordten, Hermann von der, *Richard Wagners Bühnenwerke*, Berlin 1922.

Philippi, Felix, *Münchner Bilderbogen*, Berlin 1912.

Piekalkiewicz, Janusz, *Die Schlacht um Moskau. Die erfrorene Offensive*, Bergisch Gladbach 1981.

Plewnia, Margarete, *Auf dem Weg zu Hitler. Der 'völkische' Publizist Dietrich Eckart*, Bremen 1970.

Poliakov, Léon, *Der arische Mythos. Zu den Quellen von Rassismus und Nationalismus*, Hamburg 1993.

Poliakov, Léon, *Geschichte des Antisemitismus*, 8 vols, Worms/Frankfurt 1977–88; English trans. of vol. 3: *From Voltaire to Wagner*, London 1975.

Poliakov, Léon and Joseph Wulf, *Das Dritte Reich und seine Denker*, Frankfurt/Berlin 1983.

Pool, James and Suzanne, *Who Financed Hitler. The Secret Funding of Hitler's Rise to Power 1919–1933*, London 1979.

Prawy, Marcel, 'Nun sei bedankt . . .'. Mein Richard-Wagner-Buch, Munich 1983.

Pridham, G., Hitler's Rise to Power, London 1973.

Prieberg, Fred K., Musik im NS-Staat, Frankfurt 1982.

Pulzer, Peter P.J., The Rise of Political Antisemitism in Germany and Austria, New York/London/Sydney 1964.

Rather, L.J., The Dream of Self-Destruction. Wagner's Ring and the Modern World, London 1979.

Rauschning, Hermann, Gespräche mit Hitler, Vienna 1973; English trans.: Hitler Speaks, London 1939.

Rauschning, Hermann, Die Revolution des Nihilismus. Kulisse und Wirklichkeit im Dritten Reich, Zurich 1938.

Reichel, Peter, Der schöne Schein des Dritten Reiches. Faszination und Gewalt des Faschismus, Munich 1991.

Reimann, Heinrich, Hans von Bülow. Sein Leben und sein Wirken, vol. 1: Aus Hans von Bülow's Lehrzeit, Berlin n.d.

Reuth, Ralf Georg, Goebbels, Zurich 1991.

Richter, Karl, Richard Wagner. Visionen, Vilsbiburg 1933.

Roberts, Stephen H., The House that Hitler Built, London 1937.

Roch, Eckhard, Psychodrama. Richard Wagner im Symbol, Stuttgart 1995.

Rose, Paul Lawrence, Revolutionary Antisemitism in Germany from Kant to Wagner, Princeton 1990.

Rose, Paul Lawrence, Wagner. Race and Revolution, London/New Haven 1992.

Rosenberg, Alfred, Der Mythus des 20. Jahrhunderts, Munich 1940.

Rosenberg, Alfred, Das politische Tagebuch Alfred Rosenbergs aus den Jahren 1934–5 und 1939–40, ed. Hans-Günther Seraphim, Göttingen 1956.

Ruprecht, Erich, Der Mythos bei Wagner und Nietzsche. Seine Bedeutung als Lebens- und Gestaltungsproblem, Berlin 1938.

Rützow, Sophie, Richard Wagner und Bayreuth. Ausschnitte und Erinnerungen, Munich 1941.

Sabrow, Martin, Der Rathenaumord. Rekonstruktion einer Verschwörung gegen die Republik in Weimar, Munich 1994.

Schenck, Ernst Günther, Das Notlazarett unter der Reichskanzlei. Ein Arzt erlebt Hitlers Ende in Berlin, Neuried 1995.

Schickling, Dieter, Abschied von Walhall. Richard Wagners erotische Gesellschaft, Munich 1983.

Schirach, Baldur von, Ich glaubte an Hitler, Hamburg 1967.

Schirmag, Heinz, Albert Lortzing. Glanz und Elend eines Künstlerlebens, Berlin 1995.

Schmidt, Paul, Statist auf diplomatischer Bühne 1923–1945, Bonn 1951.

Schneider, Rolf, Die Reise zu Richard Wagner, Vienna 1989.

Schnoor, Hans, Dresden. Vierhundert Jahre deutsche Musikkultur, Dresden 1848.

Schoenberner, Gerhard, Der gelbe Stern. Die Judenverfolgung in Europa 1933–1945, Frankfurt 1991.

Schoeps, Julius H. (ed.), Ein Volk von Mördern? Die Dokumentation zur Goldhagen-kontroverse um die Rolle der Deutschen im Holocaust, Hamburg 1996.

Scholz, Dieter David, Richard Wagners Antisemitismus, Würzburg 1993.

Schönzeler, Hans Hubert, Furtwängler, London 1990.

Schott, Georg (ed.), Houston Stewart Chamberlain. Der Seher des Dritten Reiches, Munich 1934.

Schroeder, Christa, Er war mein Chef: Aus dem Nachlass der Sekretärin von Adolf Hitler, ed. Anton Joachimsthaler, Munich 1985.

Schroeder, Leopold von, *Die Vollendung des arischen Mysteriums in Bayreuth*, Munich 1911.

Schüler, Winfried, *Der Bayreuther Kreis von seiner Entstehung bis zum Ausgang der Wilhelminischen Ära*, Münster 1971.

Schumann, Robert, *Schriften über Musik und Musiker*, Stuttgart 1982.

Schumann, Robert, *Tagebücher, 1836–1854*, 2 vols, ed. Gerd Nauhaus, Leipzig 1987.

Schuster, Peter-Klaus (ed.), *Nationalsozialismus und 'entartete Kunst'*, Munich 1988.

Segnitz, Eugen, *Richard Wagner und Leipzig (1813–1833)*, Liechtenstein 1976.

Seidel, Klaus Jürgen (ed,), *Das Prinzregenten-Theater in München*, Nuremberg 1984.

Seidl, Arthur, *Neue Wagneriana. Gesammelte Aufsätze und Studien*, 3 vols, Regensburg 1914.

Shaw, George Bernard, *The Perfect Wagnerite*, London 1898.

Shirer, W.L., *The Rise and Fall of the Third Reich*, New York 1960.

Siegfried, Walther, *Frau Cosima Wagner. Studie eines Lebens*, Leipzig 1930.

Sigismund, Volker, 'Ein unbehauster Prinz – Constantin von Sachsen-Weimar (1758–1793), der Bruder des Herzogs Carl August' (*Goethe Jahrbuch*, Weimar 1989, p. 250).

Skelton, Geoffrey, *Wagner in Thought and Practice*, London 1991.

Smith, Bradley F., *Heinrich Himmler*, Stanford 1971.

Snyder, L.L., *German Nationalism. The Tragedy of a People*, Harrisburg 1952.

Soden, Michael von (ed.), *Richard Wagner, Lohengrin*, Frankfurt 1980.

Söhnlein, Kurt, *Erinnerungen an Siegfried Wagner und Bayreuth*, ed. Peter P. Pachl, Bayreuth 1980.

Sokoloff, Alice, *Cosima Wagner. Aussergewöhnliche Tochter von Franz Liszt*, Hamburg 1970.

Speer, Albert, *Erinnerungen*, Frankfurt/Berlin/Vienna 1969; English trans.: *Inside the Third Reich*, London 1979.

Speer, Albert, *Spandauer Tagebücher*, Berlin 1975.

Spotts, Frederic, *Bayreuth. A History of the Wagner Festival*, New Haven 1994.

Steiert, Thomas (ed.), *Der Fall Wagner. Ursprünge und Folgen von Nietzsches Wagner-Kritik*, Laaber 1991.

Stein, Heinrich von, *Idee und Welt. Das Werk des Philosophen und Dichters*, ed. Günter Ralfs, Stuttgart 1940.

Stein, Jack M., *Richard Wagner and the Synthesis of the Arts*, Detroit 1960.

Stein, L., *The Racial Thinking of Richard Wagner*, New York 1950.

Steinert, Marlis, *Hitler*, Munich 1994.

Stemplinger, Eduard, *Richard Wagner in München 1864–1870. Legende und Wirklichkeit*, Munich 1933.

Stern, Fritz, *The Politics of Cultural Despair*, Berkeley 1961.

Stern, J.P., *A Study of Nietzsche*, Cambridge 1979.

Stern, J.P., *Hitler. The Führer and His People*, London 1974.

Stock, Richard Wilhelm, *Richard Wagner und seine Meistersinger. Eine Erinnerungsgabe zu den Bayreuther Kriegsfestspielen 1943*, Bayreuth 1943.

Storch, Wolfgang (ed.), *Das Buch des Nibelungen*, Munich 1988.

Strasser, Otto, *Mein Kampf*, Frankfurt 1969.

Strauss, Richard, *Betrachtungen und Erinnerungen*, ed. Willi Schuh, Mainz 1989.

Strobel, Otto (ed.), *Neue Wagner-Forschungen*, Series 1, Karlsruhe 1943.

Syberberg, Hans Jürgen, *Parsifal. Ein Filmessay*, Munich 1982.

Syberberg, Hans Jürgen, 'Winifred Wagner und die Geschichte des Hauses Wahnfried 1914–1975; film interview with Winifred Wagner 1975.

Taylor, Ronald, *Literature and Society in Germany 1918–1945*. Brighton 1980.

Taylor, Ronald, *Richard Wagner. His Life, Art and Thought*, London 1979.

Toland, John, *Adolf Hitler*, London 1997.

Trevor-Roper, Hugh, *The Last Days of Hitler*, London 1966.

Tyrell, Albrecht, *'Führer befiehl . . .': Selbstzeugnisse aus der 'Kampfzeit' der NSDAP*, Düsseldorf 1969.

Tyrell, Albrecht, *Vom 'Trommler' zum 'Führer'. Der Wandel von Hitlers Selbstverständnis zwischen 1919 und 1924*, Munich 1975.

Ueberschär, Gerd R. and Wolfram Wette (eds), *Der deutsche Überfall auf die Sowjetunion. 'Unternehmen Barbarossa' 1941*, Frankfurt 1991.

Umbach, Klaus (ed.), *Richard Wagner. Ein deutsches Ärgernis*, Reinbek 1982.

Uthmann, Jörg von, *Attentat. Mord mit gutem Gewissen*, Berlin 1996.

Vondung, Klaus, *Magie und Manipulation*, Göttingen 1971.

Voss, Egon, *Die Dirigenten der Bayreuther Festspiele*, Regensburg 1976.

Voss, Richard, *Aus einem phantastischen Leben*, Stuttgart 1923.

Wagener, Otto, *Hitler aus nächster Nähe. Aufzeichnungen eines Vertrauten 1929–1932*, ed. Henry A. Turner, Kiel 1987.

Wagner, Cosima, *Die Tagebücher*, 4 vols, ed. Martin Gregor-Dellin and Dietrich Mack, Munich 1982; English trans.: *Cosima Wagner's Diaries*, 2 vols, London 1978–9.

Wagner, Cosima, *Das Zweite Leben. Briefe und Aufzeichnungen 1883–1930*, ed. Dietrich Mack, Munich 1980.

Wagner, Cosima/Daniela von Bülow, *Cosima Wagner. Briefe an ihre Tochter Daniela von Bülow 1866–1885*, ed. Max Freiherr von Waldberg, Stuttgart 1933.

Wagner, Cosima/Houston Stewart Chamberlain, *Briefwechsel 1888–1908*, ed. Paul Pretzsch, Leipzig 1934.

Wagner, Cosima/Fürst Ernst zu Hohenlohe-Langenburg, *Briefwechsel*, ed. Ernst Fürst zu Hohenlohe, Stuttgart 1937.

Wagner, Cosima/Ludwig von Bayern, *Briefe*, ed. Martha Schad, Bergisch Gladbach 1996.

Wagner, Cosima/Ludwig Schemann, *Cosima Wagner. Briefe an Ludwig Schemann*, ed. Bertha Schemann, Regensburg 1937.

Wagner, Friedelind, *Nacht über Bayreuth. Die Geschichte der Enkelin Richard Wagners*, Cologne 1994; English edn: *Heritage of Fire. The Story of Richard Wagner's Granddaughter*, New York 1974.

Wagner, Manfred, *Alfred Roller und seine Zeit*, Salzburg 1996.

Wagner, Nike, *Über Wagner*, Stuttgart 1996.

Wagner, Siegfried, *Erinnerungen*, Stuttgart 1922.

Wagner, Wieland (ed.), *Richard Wagner und das neue Bayreuth*, Munich 1962.

Wagner, Wolf Siegfried, *Die Geschichte unserer Familie in Bildern, Bayreuth 1876–1976*, Munich 1976.

Wagner, Wolfgang, *Bayreuther Leitmotive*, Freiburg 1992.

Wagner, Wolfgang, *Lebens-Akte. Autobiographie*, Munich 1994.

Wagners Werk und Wirkung. Festspielnachrichten Beiträge 1957–1982.

Waite, Robert G.L., *The Psychopathic God. Adolf Hitler*, New York 1977.

Wallrath, Bertram (ed.), *Barbarossa. Sagen, Geschichten und Balladen um Kaiser Friedrich Rotbart und die Staufer*, Munich 1989.

Walter, Michael, *Hitler in der Oper. Deutsches Musikleben 1919–1945*, Stuttgart 1995.

Wapnewski, Peter, *Richard Wagner. Die Szene und ihr Meister*, Munich 1983.

Wapnewski, Peter, *Der traurige Gott. Richard Wagner in seinen Helden*, Munich 1978.

Wapnewski, Peter, *Tristan, der Held Richard Wagners*, Berlin 1981.

Wapnewski, Peter, *Weisst du, wie das wird? Richard Wagner 'Der Ring des Nibelungen'*, Munich 1995.

Wehler, Hans-Ulrich, *Deutsche Gesellschaftsgeschichte*, 2 vols, Munich 1987.

Weigend, Friedrich, Bodo M. Baumunk and Thomas Brune, *Keine Ruhe im Kyffhäuser. Das Nachleben der Staufer*, Stuttgart 1978.

Weiner, Marc A., *Richard Wagner and the Anti-Semitic Imagination*, Lincoln, NB 1995.

Weininger, Otto, *Geschlecht und Charakter. Eine prinzipielle Untersuchung*, Vienna 1905.

Weismüller, Christoph, *Das Drama der Notation. Ein philosophischer Versuch zu Richard Wagners Ring des Nibelungen*, Vienna 1994.

Weissheimer, Wendelin, *Erlebnisse mit Richard Wagner, Franz Liszt und vielen anderen Zeitgenossen nebst ihren Briefen*, Stuttgart 1898.

Weissmann, Karlheinz, *Schwarze Fahnen, Runenzeichen. Die Entwicklung der politischen Symbolik der deutschen Rechten zwischen 1890 und 1945*, Cologne/Düsseldorf 1991.

Wessling, Berndt W. (ed.), *Bayreuth im Dritten Reich: Richard Wagners politisches Erbe. Eine Dokumentation*, Weinheim 1983.

Wessling, Berndt W., *Furtwängler. Eine kritische Biographie*, Stuttgart 1985.

Westernhagen, Curt von, *Die Entstehung des 'Ring'*, Zurich 1972; English trans.: *The Forging of the 'Ring'*, Cambridge 1976.

Westernhagen, Curt von, *Richard Wagner. Sein Werk, sein Wesen, seine Welt*, Zurich 1956.

Westernhagen, Curt von, *Richard Wagners Dresdner Bibliothek 1842–1849*, Wiesbaden 1966.

Westernhagen, Curt von, *Wagner*, Zurich 1979: English trans.: *Wagner*, Cambridge 1979.

Wiesmann, Siegrid (ed.), *Gustav Mahler in Wien*, Stuttgart 1976.

Wilde, Harry, *Die Reichskanzlei 1933–1945*, Bergisch Gladbach 1978.

Wolzogen, Hans von, *Aus Richard Wagners Geisteswelt*, Berlin 1908.

Wolzogen, Hans von, *Bayreuth*, Leipzig n.d.

Wolzogen, Hans von, *Führer durch die Musik zu Richard Wagners Festspiel 'Der Ring des Nibelungen'*, Leipzig n.d.

Wolzogen, Hans von, *Lebensbilder*, Regensburg 1923.

Wolzogen, Hans von, *Wagner und seine Werke*, Regensburg 1924.

Wolzogen, Hans von/Heinrich von Stein, *Heinrich von Steins Briefwechsel mit Hans von Wolzogen. Ein Beitrag zur Geschichte des Bayreuther Gedankens*, ed. Hans von Wolzogen, Berlin 1914.

Wulf, Joseph, *Musik im Dritten Reich. Eine Dokumentation*, Berlin 1989.

Zelinsky, Hartmut, 'Der Dirigent Hermann Levi. Anmerkungen zur verdrängten Geschichte des jüdischen Wagnerianers', in Manfred Treml and Josef Kirmeier (eds), *Geschichte und Kultur der Juden in Bayern*, Munich 1988.

Zelinsky, Hartmut, *Richard Wagner. Ein deutsches Thema. Eine Dokumentation zur Wirkungsgeschichte Richard Wagners 1876–1976*, Frankfurt 1976, new edn Berlin 1983.

Zelinsky, Hartmut, *Sieg oder Untergang: Sieg und Untergang. Kaiser Wilhelm II, die Werk-Idee Richard Wagners und der 'Weltkampf'*, Munich 1990.

Ziegler, Hans Severus, *Adolf Hitler aus dem Erleben dargestellt*, Göttingen 1964.

Zoller, Albert, *Hitler privat. Erlebnisbericht seiner Geheimsekretärin*, Düsseldorf 1949.

INDEX

Act for the Protection of German Blood and German Honour, 248

Ahasverus (the Wandering Jew), 33, 44, 110, 292; annihilation of proposed by Wagner, 88, *see also* 'final solution'; and Flying Dutchman, 284; Kundry as, 227–8

'Alldeutscher Verband', 116–17

Alldeutsches Blatt, 70

Allgemeine Zeitung, 67

Anderson, Warren C., 156, 186

'Anti-Semitic Union', 117

anti-Semitism: and Bayreuth, 111–12, 142, 169, 174, 195, 200; Hitler's, 4, 8, 10–11, 15, 17, 57–8, 68–9, 72–3, 87, 88, 131, 146, 169–70, 201, 202, 203–8, 227, 228, 232–3, 248, 270, 290, 293; in Vienna, 56, 58, 67, 68; Wagner's, 3, 4, 8, 10, 15, 33–4, 43, 44, 56, 58–9, 61, 62–4, 65, 86–8, 93, 94, 100, 110, 119, 143, 146, 173, 200, 203–4, 255–6, 277, 289, 292–4; *see also under* Chamberlain, Houston Stewart; *Ring des Nibelungen*; Wagner, Cosima; Wilhelm II

Arco-Valley, Anton Graf, 149

Arent, Benno von, 55

Auschwitz, 287

Austria, 67–8; Hitler's *Anschluss*, 49, 253

Badenweiler March, 248

Bahr, Hermann, 67–8, 70, 76, 142

Bahr-Mildenburg, Anna, 55, 70

Bakunin, Mikhail, 44, 45

Bartels, Adolf, 156

Baudelaire, Charles, 126

Bayreuth: anti-Semitism, *see* anti-Semitism; 'Awake' slogan, 252; cult, 111, 112–13, 117–18, 119; Festival closed (1914), 165, 178; Festspielhaus, 48, 61, 109, 117, 142, 162, 164, 221, 265; free tickets for, 8, 266–7; and German culture, 8, 61, 143; and German renewal, 142–3, 168; 'German Teachers' Academy', 265–6; and Hitler, 8, 14, 15, 16–17, 20, 25, 110–11, 133–6, 140, 162–5, 168–9, 171–2, 176, 184–5, 195, 196–7, 208, 224, 236, 263, 266–7; Hitler's visits to, 165, 169, 171, 176–7, 193, 224–5, 264; modern productions, 62; and National Socialism, 110, 134, 163, 169, 186, 191–4, 196, 236; and nationalism, 79; Nazi Party branch in, 164, 184; and Nietzsche, 108; and 'Ode to Joy', 39; opening of Festival (1876), 109; political programme, 108, 113, 119, 142–3, 194, 236; programme for 1925 Festival, 236; as religious centre, 112, 119, 221, 226, 237; re-opened (1924), 191, 193; re-opened (1951), 134; secret language of inner circle, 115–16, 192, 290–1; significance to Wagner, 108–10; Wahnfried (Villa), 96, 109, 162; 'Wartime Festivals', 263, 268; and Weimar Republic, 178, 195; *see also individual members of Wagner family*

'Bayreuth Union of German Youth', 111

Bayreuther Blätter, 109, 110, 111, 116, 121, 123, 125, 216, 222

Bechstein Edwin, 159, 160, 160–1

Bechstein, Helene, 159–60, 283; and manuscript of *Mein Kampf*, 160

Beethoven, Ludwig van, 39; Ninth (Choral) Symphony, 40–1, 179, 180, 193

Beidler, Franz Wilhelm, 134–5, 163, 192

Beidler, Isolde (née Wagner), 106, 127, 262

Below, Nicolaus von, 36, 154, 285

Berchtesgaden, 283
Berlin, 1, 109; Brandenburg Gate, 280; Grail Temple planned for, 231, 241; Hitler's disgust at, 227; Holocaust memorial, 4; Ministry of Propaganda bombed, 12; attempted Putsch (1920), 145, 150, 155; re-opening of Staatsoper (1942), 251; Wall, collapse of, 1
Berlin Philharmonic Orchestra, 18
Berlioz, Hector, 32, 126
Beust, Graf Friedrich von, 36, 46, 48
Bie, Oscar, 112
Bismarck, Otto von, 1, 109
Blackshirts, 291
Bloch, Dr Eduard, 69
'Blood Banner', 30, 243, 244
Blood Order, 243, 291
Blum, Robert, 39–40
Bockelmann, Rudolf, 251
Boepple, Ernst, 173
Boisserée, Sulpiz, 230
Bolshevism: and Christianity, 225–6; and Jews, 269, 272, 274, 275, 277; threat to Germany, 275, 276, 285
books, burning of (1934), 31
Borchmeyer, Dieter, 257
Borgia, Cesare: as model for Hitler, 27
Bormann, Martin, 290
Braun, Eva, 8
Breker, Arnold, 95
Breuer, Hans: sings Mime, 70, 203
Brockhaus, Friedrich, 38, 254
Brownshirts, 236
Bruckmann, Elsa, 157–8, 159, 208
Bruckmann, Hugo, 123, 124, 130
Bülow, Hans von, 41, 104, 106, 159, 215; Wagner's correspondence with, 149
Bülow, Paul: The Führer and Bayreuth, 164
Bulwer-Lytton, Edward George Earle Lytton, 31

Carlyle, Thomas: The History of Friedrich II, Called Frederick the Great, 81, 82; Wagner and, 81, 82, 88
Chamberlain, Eva (née Wagner), 14, 120, 122, 123, 126, 132, 164, 171, 175, 222; and Mein Kampf, 208
Chamberlain, Houston Stewart, 8, 77, 120–8, 129, 138, 142, 168, 211; anti-Semitism, 17, 18, 21–2, 33, 126, 142, 170, 173, 174, 270, 276; biography of Wagner, 21–2, 32, 115–16, 123–4, 127; and Carlyle, 81; and Christian Church, 225; and Cosima, 114, 120, 121–3, 124, 131; death, 175; Foundations of the Nineteenth Century, 14, 116, 124–5, 202; and 'German Teachers' Academy', 265–6; and Hitler, 13, 14, 15–16, 123, 124, 125, 131–2, 134, 164, 169, 170, 171–3, 175, 179, 181, 223,

269–70; illness, 14–15, 131–2; awarded Iron Cross, 131; and Kaiser, see under Wilhelm II; and Mein Kampf, 199, 208; and Parsifal, 223; reaction to Wagner's music, 120–1; war essays, 130–1; writing style, 116–17, 121, 123
Charlemagne: imperial insignia, 253
Christian, General Eckhard, 19
Christliche Welt, 125
Class, Heinrich, 117, 157, 160, 166
Confederation of German Industry: and Wagner's manuscripts, 13–14
Conrad, Michael Georg, 163, 164
Constantin von Sachsen-Weimar, Prince, 32, 127

Day of Potsdam, 251
'degenerate art', 246
Deutsches Tageblatt, 222
Devrient, Eduard, 42, 50, 62, 281
Devrient, Paul, 290
Diederichs, Eugen: 'Thule' collection, 149, 263
Diels, Rudolf, 28
Dietrich, Otto, 76, 244–5, 250, 263, 265, 292
Dollfuss, Engelbert: murder, 229–30
Domarus, Max: quoted, 232
Dresden, 1, 40; opera house burnt down, 41, 46–7; Rienzi première, 34–5, 41; revolt (1830), 38; uprising (1849), 44–8, 106
Drexler, Anton, 151
Dürer, Albrecht, 252; The Knight, Death and the Devil, 200, 253

Ebermayer, Erich, 163, 169, 176, 183
Eckart, Dietrich, 164, 186, 283; anti-Semitism, 152, 153, 154, 155; Auf gut deutsch, 154; and Bayreuth, 153–4; 'Call to Arms/Germany Awake!', 153, 168; Heinrich der Hohenstaufe, 263; and Hitler, 151–4, 155, 156, 158, 159, 160, 162; translation of Peer Gynt, 155
Eckhart, Richard du Moulin: biography of Cosima Wagner, 122, 161
Egk, Werner, 155
Eidam, Rosa, 193–4
Eisner, Kurt, 139, 149
Enabling Act (1933), 89, 152, 231
Engel, Gerhard, 286, 290
Erzberger, Matthias, 149
Eulenburg, Prince, 128

Feder, Gottfried, 74
Feingold, Josef, 58
Fest, Joachim C., 92, 285; biography of Hitler, 44, 49, 171, 251
Feustel, Friedrich von, 173
'final solution', 146–7, 209, 235, 249; extermination camps, 286–7; and

'Operation Barbarossa', 286; and
    Wagner's 'grand solution', 110, 147, 176,
    228, 292; see also Holocaust
First World War (Great War), 77, 129, 189;
    and Bayreuth, 129–30; German defeat in,
    1, 78, 80, 131
fliegende Holländer, Der (Wagner), 8, 54, 165;
    ghostly ship like Russia, 284; orchestral
    sketch, 13; in Paris (1940), 266; and
    Wandering Jew, 284
Foerster, Roland, 285
Ford, Henry, 156; funds Hitler, 186–7
Förster, Bernhard, 216–17
Förster-Nietzsche, Elisabeth, 170–1; praises
    Mein Kampf, 198
Franco-Prussian War, 109, 129
François-Poncet, André, 144, 293
Frank, Hans, 151, 182, 235–6
Frankfurter Zeitung, 194
Frederick the Great: Hitler's picture of, 12,
    19, 81
French Revolution, 81; and Germany, 2
Friedrich August, King of Saxony, 35, 38,
    42–3
Friedrich Barbarossa, Emperor, 109, 213;
    legend of reawakening, 85, 223, 281–2,
    283, 284; Wagner plans works on, 282
Friedrich und Freiheit (Wagner), 38
Froebel, Julius, 106
Funk, Walther, 74
Furtwängler, Wilhelm, 55, 162, 247, 268

Gansser, Emil, 156
Geissmar, Bertha, 162
German Fighters against Enslavement to
    Usury, 74
German Workers' Party, 145, 146, 147, 150,
    163
Germanic Order, 148–9, 151; adopts
    swastika, 149; Wagnerian induction
    ceremony, 148
Germany: and Cold War, 1; and collective
    guilt, 4, see also Holocaust; and Great
    Depression, 1; and Lebensraum, 274, 275,
    278; national psyche, 2, 109; nationalism,
    14, 235; political history, 1; and romantic
    tradition, 2, 4; Second Reich, 1; and
    Wagner in interwar period, 78; see also
    Third Reich
Gerstein, Kurt, 287
Gestapo: and Jews, 249
Geyer, Ludwig, 31
Giesler, Hermann, 10, 283–4; model for Linz
    rebuilding, 12–13, 30
Glasenapp, Carl Friedrich: biography of
    Wagner, 259
Gobineau, Arthur, 3, 117, 211; Essai sur
    l'inégalité des races humaines, 116
Gobineau Society, 116, 128

Goebbels, Joseph, 9, 12, 13, 18, 81, 95–6, 142,
    267; and Chamberlain, 175, 277; and
    Meistersinger, 252; quoted, 160, 171, 199,
    222, 251, 263, 277; quotes Wagner, 277;
    and Winifred Wagner, 196, 222
Goering, Hermann, 152; quoted, 248;
    wounded in Munich Putsch, 182, 183–4
gold: linked with Jews, 74–5
Golther, Wolfgang, 222, 229
Götterdämmerung (Wagner), 11, 18, 40, 80;
    death of Siegfried, 10, 18, 22, 40, 59;
    parallels with Hitler's death, 18, 19–20,
    22, 294–5; Roller's production, 91;
    Siegfried's Funeral March, 18, 24, 57, 66,
    67, 80; union of lovers in death, 8, 22;
    Valhalla consumed by fire, 3, 56; see also
    Siegfrieds Tod
Gregor-Dellin, Martin, 45, 109
Grimm, Jakob: German Mythology, 65, 76;
    'Jew in the Thorn Bush', 258, 259
Grossdeutsche Zeitung, 173
Grunsky, Hans Alfred: Bayreuth
    programme (1924), 63, 200; Bayreuth
    programme (1925), 224, 236–7
Gustloff, Wilhelm, 277

Haffner, Sebastian, 293
Hamann, Brigitte, 69
Hammerstein, General Kurt Freiherr von,
    160
Hanfstaengl, Ernst ('Putzi'), 157, 158, 162,
    227, 230; at Bayreuth with Hitler, 165;
    plays Wagner to Hitler, 55, 139, 250;
    quoted, 141, 156, 160
Hanfstaengl, Helene, 69
Hanfstaengl (publishers), 75, 230
Hanisch, Reinhold, 48–9
Hanslick, Eduard, 68, 255, 256, 259;
    criticizes Parsifal, 221
Harden, Maximilian, 149
Harnack, Alfred von, 170
Harrer, Karl, 151
Häusler, Rudolf, 54–5
Hegel, Georg, 93
Heiden, Konrad, 69, 70, 140, 155; praises
    Mein Kampf, 198
Heine, Ferdinand, 165
Heine, Heinrich, 32, 87, 126
Heine, Thomas Theodor: cartoon of Hitler,
    196
Herrig, Hans, 222
Herzl, Theodor, 67
Herzogenberg, Elisabeth von, 221
Hess, Rudolf, 151
Heuss, Theodor, 15, 74, 169, 170
Hey, Julius, 102
Hillgruber, Andreas, 286
Himmler, Heinrich, 13, 18, 151, 234, 290,
    292, 293

Hindenburg, Paul von, 78, 131, 142, 198, 261; quoted, 129
Hitler, Adolf: as architectural patron, 12–13, 30, 49, 79, 81, 95, 230–1, 241, 242; as art lover, 261; as artist, 52, 58; as dog-lover, 18, 265; hatred, 244, 270; as Jesus Christ, 10–11, 167, 181, 227; as Knight of the Grail, 93, 97; as Lohengrin, 238; as Man of Destiny, 276; masks worn by, 144; as Messiah/saviour of Germany, 15, 17, 164, 168, 177, 180, 183, 286; as military commander, 6; as mimic, 52; as orator, 17, 93, 115, 136, 139–41, 145, 147, 176, 181, 290; as Parsifal, 114, 154, 160, 212, 223, 224–5, 237; as politician, 6; secretiveness, 7, 17–18, 232–4, 290; as Siegfried, 9–10, 18, 22, 72, 73, 75, 76, 78–80, 145, 160, 205, 207, 286; as 'Uncle Wolf', 135, 263; as Wagner's heir, 133, 141–2, 196; as Wotan, 9, 75, 76; as writer, 197, 198
Life: at 'Berghof', 283; in bunker, 9–13, 17, 18–20, 22, 81; cartoon of, 196; censorship of press, 256; and Dollfuss murder, 230; as 'education officer', 145–6; in First World War, 55, 77; marries, 8, 22; in Munich, 138–40, 145, 262; orphaned, 51; parallels with Wagnerian heroes, 51, 166, 206–8, 219–20, 242, 293, see also individual operas; parallels with Wagner's life, 3–4, 4–5, 265; physical decay, 12; in Landsberg prison, 3, 55, 123, 159, 160, 183, 193, 196–7, 198, 224; and Munich Putsch (1923), 180–2, 243, 272; and Nazi Party, see National Socialist Party; 'Operation Barbarossa', 284–5; in Paris, 266; 'Polish Operation', 276; as Reich Chancellor, 231; rejected by Viennese Academy of Art, 52; plans religious Order, 239; revolver trademark, 181; rise to power, 1, 16–17, 144–8, 151–2, 155, 156, 158–60, 164, 166; invades Russia, 269, 272, 273, 284; seizes power, 94; SS purges, 229, 235; suicide, 6–7, 8–9, 11, 18–19, 22–3; and Thule Society, see Thule Society; trial, 187–90; and underground lairs, 9; in Vienna, 49, 51, 52–5, 55–6, 57, 201, 202; and Wagner cult, see Bayreuth: and Hitler; at Wagner's grave, 2, 26, 176–7; and Wagner's manuscript scores, 13–14, 19–21, 81; and Wieland libretto, 91–2, 95; and name 'wolf', 19, 283; in 'Wolf's Lair', 56; writes Mein Kampf, 197, 198
Speeches, quoted: 76, 137, 153, 168, 174, 244, 246-7, 251, 273, 274; in Bürgerbräu, Munich (1923), 181; in Hofbräuhaus, Munich (1929), 98; at Kroll Opera House, Berlin (1939), to army officers, 278–80; at Neuschwanstein, 98; at Nuremberg (1937), 277; private (1942), 74–5; radio (1945), 294, 295; to Reichstag (1939), 227; in Sportpalast, Berlin (30 January 1942), 75; in Sportpalast, Berlin (13 February 1942), to officer cadets, 283; see also Hitler, Adolf: as orator
Thought/opinions: animal rights, 265; anti-Semitism, see under anti-Semitism; architecture, 95; and Bayreuth, see under Bayreuth; on Bible, 225–6; 'blood pollution', theory of, 211, 278, see also Parsifal; on Christ, 226; on Christian Church, 73, 110, 225, 226; divine mission, 232, 269–71; drama central to, 242, 295; eastward expansion of Germany, 282, 283; inspired by Frederick the Great, 12; on German culture, 235; on German destiny, 6–7, 11–12, 62, 76; on Greater Germany, 285; on ancient Greek culture, 95–6; on homosexuality, 229; Lebensraum, 274, 275, 278; 'marriage' to Germany, 28; on Marxism, 189, 201; myth, 11–12; paranoia, 10, 27, 28; Peer Gynt, 155; on race, 15, 231–3, 234–5, see also under Parsifal; Russian Revolution, 73–4, 272, 273; self-delusion, 9, 11; on struggle as principle of life, 199–200, 201, see also Mein Kampf; Third Reich symbolism, 95; vegetarianism, 265; equates Wagner with Providence, 271; idolization of Wagner, 7–8, 49, 265; and Wagner's operas, 2–3, 4, 7, 16–17, 25–6, 49, 52–3, 55–8, 61–3, 117, 137, 261, 263, see also under individual operas; inspired by Wagner's writings, 83, 89, 90–1, 92, 93, 115, 218; xenophobia, 96
Works: 'Appeal to the German Nation', 94; Mein Kampf, 3, 10, 17, 25, 26, 78, 94, 116, 147, 196–208, 209, 218, 220, 263; Tischgespräche, 21; 'Why Are We Anti-Semitic?', 246–7
Hitler, Alois, 51
Hitler, Klara, 51
Hitler Youth, 243
Hoffmann, E.T.A., 111
Hoffmann, Heinrich, 163, 283
Hofmann, Julius von, 103
hohe Braut, Die (Wagner), 37
Hohenlohe, Prince, 129, 131
Holocaust, 1, 4, 8, 18, 269, 279–81; army as accomplice in, 279–81; and German people, 287–9, 292, 294; Himmler's responsibility for, 291–2; Hitler and, 4, 17, 189, 289; 'justified' by storyline of Ring des Nibelungen, 205–8; language of murder units, 291; and Parsifal, 241; Wagner's responsibility for, 4, 8, 18, 134, 292–4

idealism, philosophy of, 2

Jäckel, Eberhard, 285
Jahoda, Dr Rudolf, 69
Jews: banned from German cultural life,
    247, 250; blamed for German defeat in
    First World War, 1, 78, 131; blamed for
    sexual depravity, 209–11; boycott (1934),
    231, 287; demonized by Hitler, 11, 16,
    17–18, 57–8, 72–4, 83, 249–50; demonized
    by Wagner, 33, 63–5, 71, 85, 86–7, 110,
    174, 218, 277, see also Ring des Nibelungen;
    emancipation, 142; and German people,
    287–9, 292; linked with gold, 74–5; linked
    with Marxism, 189, 204–5, 271, 272, 274;
    in Poland, 290; as supporters of Wagner,
    87, 107, 143, 222; seen as warmongers,
    273; associated with Weimar Republic,
    94, 172, 178, 180, 236, 272; and yellow
    star, 288; see also anti-Semitism; 'final
    solution'; Holocaust
Joël Karl, 125

Kahr, General Gustav Ritter von, 181
Kainz, Josef, 91
Kalbeck, Max, 219
Kant, Immanuel, 2
Kapp, Wolfgang, 154–5; abortive Putsch
    (Berlin, 1920), 145, 150, 155, 159
Karajan, Herbert von, 266
Karbaum, Michael, 113, 127, 134, 135
Keyserling, Hermann Graf, 125
Kirdorf, Emil, 157–8
Klindworth, Karl, 159, 161
Klintzsch, Hans Ulrich, 156
Kniese, Julius, 70
Knights of the Grail, 93, 97; schoolboys as,
    249; Wagnerians as, 108, 111, 142, 164,
    178, 290–1; see also under Parsifal
Kogon, Eugen, 287
Kristallnacht, 288
Kubizek, August, 25–7, 53, 54, 62, 69, 83, 89,
    91–2, 117, 145
Kuby, Erich, 135

Laube, Heinrich, 39
'League of German Culture', 247
Lechfield: camp, 146
Lehmann, Julius Friedrich, 156–7, 163
Lehrs, Samuel, 87
Leipzig, 1, 37, 40; as revolutionary centre,
    39; Wagner memorial, 137
Leipziger Zeitung, 47–8
Lessing, G.E.: Nathan the Wise, 289
Levi, Hermann, 70, 87, 107, 262
Ley, Robert, 249
Lienhard, Friedrich, 222
Linge, Heinz, 22
Linz, 2; Freinberg, 26, 30; Hitler's plans for,
    12–13, 30, 49, 79, 81
Liszt, Franz, 159; opinion on Parsifal, 217;

Préludes ('Russian Fanfare'), 187, 284
Lohengrin (Wagner), 42, 54, 178, 237;
    Lohengrin, 25, 97, 220–1, 244; miracle, 11;
    at Weimar, 261
Lorenz, Alfred, 225
Lortzing, Alfred: Hans Sachs, 254, 256
Lossow, General Otto von, 177, 181, 187
Louis Philippe, King of France, 37
Lüdecke, Kurt, 143, 186, 187
Ludendorff, General Erich, 78, 142, 166, 182,
    186; at Bayreuth, 192, 193; as Siegfried,
    78
Ludwig II, King of Bavaria, 97, 98, 99, 254;
    and Jews, 34, 87, 103, 107; and Lohengrin,
    25, 97, 99; and Meistersinger, 255; and
    Parsifal, 97, 112, 113, 217, 230; as Siegfried,
    101–2, 103; and Tannhäuser, 97; as
    Wagner's patron, 14, 99, 100–7, 109, 141;
    see also Neuschwanstein castle
Ludwig IV, King of Bavaria, 282
Lueger, Karl, 68, 69, 70
Lüttichau, Wolf von, 35, 41–2, 43–4

Mahler, Gustav, 25, 54, 68, 69, 70–1, 113
Mann, Thomas, 130, 163, 258; quoted, 2; and
    Wagner, 24–5; 'Wagner and Our Time',
    24
Männerlist gegen Frauenlist (Wagner), 33–4
Marienbad: Wagner in, 254
Marx, Karl, 205
Mayr, Captain Karl, 138, 145, 146, 151, 152,
    154
Meier, Mathilde, 101
Meistersinger, Die (Wagner): and anti-
    Semitism, 267–8, see also Beckmesser (this
    entry); at Bayreuth (1943, 1944), 267–8;
    Beckmesser, 153, 250, 256–9, 260; in Berlin
    (1942), 251; Eva, 254, 256, 258; and German
    art/culture, 8, 246–7, 250, 255–6, 257, 261;
    and German reawakening, 180, 251–2;
    and Hitler, 3, 97, 139, 167, 168, 250, 260,
    262, 267; in Munich (1932), 262; at
    Nuremberg (1935), 247; and Nuremberg
    rallies, 267; Prelude, 247, 250; reception of
    revival of Cosima's pre-war production
    (1924), 193–5; Hans Sachs, 167, 193, 250–1,
    252, 253, 254, 255, 256–7, 259, 260;
    Walther von Stolzing, 51, 167, 212, 256,
    258; and Third Reich, 251, 260–1; in
    Vienna, 54; Wagner and, 253
Mendelssohn, Felix, 64, 87
Messmer, Hermann: quoted, 215
Meyerbeer, Giacomo, 34, 35, 36, 64, 87, 259,
    266
Möhl, General Arnold von, 145
Mommsen, Theodor, 257, 277
Morgenstern, Samuel, 58
Muck, Karl, 238
Müller, Karl Alexander von, 141, 167, 168,

181, 208
Munich, 1, 98; 'Brown House', 152, 162;
conservatoire, 105–6; Feldherrnhalle
memorial, 182, 243, 244; 'Haus der
deutschen Kunst', 231, 246, 250; Hitler's
apartment, 262; Hofbräuhaus, 98;
Prinzregententheater, 262–3; proposed
theatre, 48, 106; Putsch (1923), 14, 180–2,
243, 262, 272; St Catherine's, 253;
'Temples of Remembrance', 243; Vier
Jahreszeiten hotel, 150
music: and romantic creativity, 2
Mussolini, Benito, 187

Naegele, Verena, 99
National Socialism, 8; and Christianity, 167,
168, 227; as 'collective will of new race of
men', 234; dogma, 137; Gleichschaltung,
93; goals, 95; ideology, 7, 232, 278;
religious trappings drawn from Parsifal,
221–2, 243, 244; and 'scientific
knowledge' of Jews, 273; and Wagner, 93,
110, 134, 163, 196, 293
National Socialist Party (Nazi Party), 177,
293; anniversary celebrations, 153, 200;
banned, 3, 182, 194; blood symbolism of,
244; commemorates Munich Putsch,
243–4, 262, 273, 288; congress (1933), 247;
congress (1937), 276; Hitler assumes
leadership, 166; Hitler disillusioned with,
238; Horst-Wessel-Song, 266; like
medieval military order, 137, 236, 237;
and Meistersinger, 267; rallies, 3, 29, 167–8,
231, 244, 245, 247–8, 253, 267, 277, 287–8;
re-established (1925), 224; underground
activities, 159; Wagners' fund-raising for,
186
Nazis, see National Socialist Party
Neue Freie Presse, 68
Neue Zeitschrift für Musik, 47
Neue Zürcher Zeitung, 125
Neumann, Angelo, 222
Neumann, Franz, 288
Neuschwanstein castle, 97, 230; Hitler's
visit to, 97–8
New Richard Wagner Society, 56
Newman, Ernest, 41, 44, 48, 111
Nibelungenlied, 60
Nietzsche, Friedrich, 89, 108, 120, 145, 199,
209, 276; anti-Semitism, 111–12; The Birth
of Tragedy from the Spirit of Music, 89, 108;
Thus Spake Zarathustra, 198
November Revolution (1918), 138, 143, 188,
271, 272
Nuremberg: bombed, 249; German cultural
capital, 246, 250, 252, 253, 255; no Jews in,
246, 250; proposed as Ludwig's capital,
107; rallies, 3, 29, 167, 246, 247–9, 267, 277,
287–8; synagogues, 253–4; trials, 249

Nuremberg Race Laws (1935), 211, 247

'Organization Consul', 156

Pan-German Party, 56
Paris: Opéra, 266
Parsifal (Wagner), 16, 17, 54; Amfortas, 14,
132, 214, 215, 217, 223; at Bayreuth, 221,
228–9, 230; blood imagery in, 211, 214,
215, 217–19, 220; 'compassion' in, 214–15,
218, 239; Cosima and, 112, 113, 119; critics
on, 221, 222; as 'devotional festival
drama', 54, 112, 217, 218–22, 228; Eckart's
introduction to, 154; and 'final solution',
227, 241; Hitler's design for Grail Temple,
230–1; Klingsor, 70, 179, 212, 215, 219,
220, 227; Knights of the Grail, 3, 221, 236,
237, 239, 240; Kundry, 33, 44, 67, 214, 215,
220, 222, 227; 'message', 233–4;
Monsalvat, 221, 230; in Munich, 262;
Munich production of 1914, 237; mystical
secret of, as interpreted by Hitler, 238–40;
and National Socialism, 3, 221–2; and
Neuschwanstein castle, 97; planned for
New York, 163; Parsifal, 51, 97, 212,
213–15, 219–20, 222–3, 233; Prelude, 57,
238; première, 219; and racial purity, 211,
215, 217–18, 228, 239–40, 293; religious
tone exploited by Nazis, 168, 222, 236,
238; Roller's 1934 production, 229, 231,
241; storyline, 213–21; Titurel, 243
Pecht, Friedrich, 106
Pfistermeister, Franz Seraph von: as Mime,
103
Pfordten, Adelgunde (née Marx), 104
Pfordten, Ludwig von der, 103–4; as Hagen,
104
Plewnia, Margarete: biography of
Weininger, 156
Pöppelmann, Matthäus Daniel, 46
Possart, Hans von, 262
Preussische Kreuzzeitung, 214–15
Price, Ward, 250

Rathenau, Walther, 78, 149
Rattenhuber, Hans, 8
Raubal, Eli, 262
Rauschning, Hermann, 80, 137, 226, 230,
238–41, 294; comments on Mein Kampf,
198
Reichstag: fire, 3, 27–8; opening, 251
Reinhardt, Max, 98
Rheingold, Das (Wagner), 59, 60, 73, 120;
Alberich as toad, 204; 1851 draft, 71;
manuscript, 13; Prelude, 56–7;
Rhinemaidens, 63
Rhineland: re-occupied, 57, 238
'Richard Wagner Association of German
Women', 111

Rienzi (Bulwer-Lytton), 31
Rienzi (Wagner), 32–3, 34, 47; anti-Semitism, 32, 36; banners, 167; historical Rienzi, 30–1, 35, 282; and Hitler, 2–3, 14, 16–17, 23, 25–30, 36, 51, 180, 237; manuscript, 14; and Nuremberg rallies, 29; Overture, 29, 56; première, 34–5, 165; source, 31
Ring des Nibelungen, Der (Wagner), 13, 17, 51, 54, 84–5, 212; Alberich and Mime, 3, 60, 63, 64–5, 66, 70–3, 74, 75, 79, 174, 179, 200, 203, 204, 207, 258, 272; and anti-Semitism, 3, 56, 63, 64, 70, 71, 72–4, 292, *see also* Alberich and Mime (this entry); Brünnhilde, 65, 66, 101, 102, 178; characters equated with Bavarian ministers, 103; Hagen, 66, 91, 204; and Hitler, 55–8, 68, 69–70, 182–3; as mythological scenario for Germany, 56, 59–60, 61, 70, 71–2, 109, 130, 132, 138, 174, 200; Nibelheim, 8, 57; Nibelungen, *see* Alberich and Mime (this entry); Nibelungen March, 29; Nothung (Siegfried's sword), symbolism of, 79, 93, 128, 132, 145, 168, 191; power of ring, 63, 74; Ride of the Valkyries, 168; Roller's production, 55–6, 57; Siegfried, 52, 59, 60, 65–6, 72, 101–2, 200, 203, 233; Siegmund, 52, 60, 61; as 'statement of faith', 112; storyline, 59–61, 63–6; 'Sword motif', 120–1; Tarnhelm, 74; in Vienna (1879), 68; Wagner as Wotan, 101, 103; Wotan, 52, 64, 65, 121, 200, 206; *see also individual operas*
Roberts, Stephen H., 93; *The House that Hitler Built*, 92
Röchling, Hermann, 275
Röckel, August, 45, 47, 102, 104–5, 106, 199
Röhm, Ernst, 146, 229, 231
Rolland, Romain, 70
Roller, Alfred, 25, 53–4, 55, 68, 91, 229
Roosevelt, President Franklin D., 12
Roselius, Ludwig, 223
Rosenberg, Alfred, 151, 156, 248, 274
Roswaenge, Helge, 229
Rubenstein, Joseph, 87
Russia: Hitler's campaign in, 269, 272, 273, 274–6, 284, 285; Leningrad, 274; 'Operation Barbarossa', 284, 289; Revolution, 73–4, 272, 273; Stalingrad, 30, 270, 274

Sachsenhausen, 19
Salzburg: Wagner productions at, 263
Sarazenin, Die (Wagner), 31
Scharfenberg, Alfred von: 'Jüngerer Titurel', 230
Scheidemann, Philipp, 149
Schelling, Friedrich, 93
Schemann, Ludwig, 116, 117, 119, 222

Schemm, Hans, 266
Scheubner-Richter, Max Erwin von, 183
Schiller, Johann: 'Ode to Joy', 38–9, 40, 89, 106, 179, 294
Schiller Society, 39
Schirach, Baldur von, 244, 254
Schmeitzner, Ernst, 293
Schmidt, Ernest, 139
Schönerer, Georg Ritter von, 68, 69, 70, 91, 117, 128; 'Linz Programme', 68
Schopenhauer, Arthur, 77; anti-Semitism, 257
Schröder-Devrient, Wilhelmine, 47
Schroeder, Christa, 137, 152, 225, 284
Schroeder, Leopold von, 157, 221; *Consummation of the Aryan Mystery*, 118, 157; *Aryan Religion*, 118
Schott (music publishers), 112
Schumann, Clara, 35
Schumann, Robert: review of Meyerbeer, 259–60
Sebottendorf, Rudolf von, 150, 151
Seebach, Albin Leo von, 46–7
Seissen, Hans von, 181
Semper, Gottfried, 48–9, 98, 106, 126
Siegfried (Wagner), 59; at Bayreuth (1914), 128–9, 169; Forging Song, 79–80, 193
Siegfrieds Tod (Wagner), 60, 71, 78, *see also Götterdämmerung*
Simplicissimus, 196, 198
Soviet Union, *see* Russia
Speer, Albert, 3, 9, 26, 31; design for Grail Temple, 231; quoted, 3, 66, 242, 270, 285
Spontini, Gasparo, 35
SS, 229, 243, 291, 292
Stahlhelm, 79
Stalingrad, 30, 270, 274
Stassen, Franz, 143, 169, 191
Stein, Heinrich von, 282
Steinle, Jakob, 230
Stolzing-Czerny, Josef, 163–4, 180, 208; *Friedrich Friesen*, 263
Strasser, Gregor, 27, 141, 235
Strasser, Otto, 27
Strauss, Richard, 193; conducts *Parsifal* (1934), 229
Streicher, Julius, 211, 247, 253
'Strength Through Joy', 262
Stuck, Franz von, 51, 75–6; *Medusa*, 51; *Sin*, 76
Stuckenschmidt, Hans Heinz, 110
swastika, 148, 167
synagogues: destroyed, 254

Tannhäuser (Wagner), 54; Eckart's essay on, 154; and Neuschwanstein castle, 97; in Paris (1861), 266; Pilgrims' Chorus, 56; Tannhäuser, 51, 97
Tausig, Karl, 87

Third Reich: and Jews, 4; and *Meistersinger*, 251, 252; and *Parsifal*, 233–4; symbolism, 95; as Thousand-Year Reich, 281, 294; as Wagnerian opera, 52–3, 66, 242, 245, *see also* Nuremberg: rallies

Thode, Daniela (née Wagner), 117, 127, 164, 184, 267,

Thode, Henry, 125–6

Thule Society, 149–51, 154; and Hitler, 150, 151, 166; martyrs, 150

Tichatschek, Joseph, 31, 47

Tietjen, Heinz, 192–3, 261, 268

Tirpitz, Admiral Alfred von, 131

Todt, Fritz, 284

Treblinka, 287

Tristan und Isolde (Wagner), 25; Hitler's absorption with, 55; Liebestod, 23, 98; 'night of love' staging, 55; in Paris (1940), 266; Roller production, 53, 54, 55, 68; Tristan, 51

'Tunnel über der Spree', 39, 40

Tyrell, Albrecht: *From Drummer Boy to Führer*, 197

Uhlig, Theodor, 90

Vaterlandsverein, 42, 47, 73, 106

Versailles, Treaty of, 1, 28, 94, 143

Vienna: Academy of Art, 52; anti-Semitism, 56, 67, 69; Burgtheater, 49; Heldenplatz, 49; Hofoper, 52, 53, 54, 70; mourns Wagner, 67–8; Ringtheater fire, 289; Secession, 54; sexual immorality, 220; social injustice, 61; Staatsoper, 55; Volksoper, 53

Viereck, Peter: article in *Common Sense*, 93

Völkischer Beobachter, 151, 156, 164, 182; Goebbels in (1937), 252; (1923) quoted, 180, 244; (1933) quoted, 194, 199

Volksblätter: Wagner's article (1849), 43–4

Wagener, Otto, 27, 75, 141, 209–10, 234

Wagner, Cosima (née Liszt, formerly von Bülow), 10, 14, 22, 64, 70, 109, 116, 117, 129, 131, 135, 149, 150, 159; adultery, 104, 106; anti-Semitism, 111–12, 119, 142; and Bayreuth cult, 111, 112–13, 117–19, 121–2; diaries published, 216; and Hitler, 165, 208; and Mussolini, 187; and Nietzsche, 120, 199, 209; and *Parsifal*, 112–13, 119, 213; political views, 113, 119; quoted, 63, 81, 224; religious beliefs, 112

Wagner Daniela, *see* Thode, Daniela

Wagner, Eva, *see* Chamberlain, Eva

Wagner, Friedelind: account of Munich Putsch, 184; relations with Wagner clan, 133–4; source for Bayreuth's relations with Hitler, 161, 162, 163, 165, 176, 177, 179, 230

Wagner, Isolde, *see* Beidler, Isolde

Wagner, Richard:
Life: supposed aristocratic lineage, 32, 127; performs Beethoven's Symphony in Dresden, 40–1; birth and childhood, 31–2; composes *Ring*, 59, 61; death, 18; dream, 223–4; and Dresden uprising (1849), 44–8; exile in Switzerland, 3, 49; 'Flame of Joy' pseudonym, 38; funeral cortège, 67; Kapellmeister in Dresden, 35, 40–2; in London, 64; and Ludwig II's patronage, 99, 100–8; mother, 32; parallels with Hitler's life, 3–4, 4–5; in Paris, 32, 90, 190, 266; as revolutionary, 3, 35, 36, 37–8, 39, 49–50, 180; and historical Rienzi, 31, 119; stepfather, 31; in Vienna, 40

Thought and opinions: anti-Catholicism, 215–16; anti-Semitism, *see under* anti-Semitism; and Carlyle, 81; fire symbolism, 3, 18, 38, 41, 44, 45, 82; and German cultural renewal, 8, *see also under* *Meistersinger;* and Germany's national destiny, 4, 8, 10, 68, 77, 79, 82, 85–6, 99–100, 223–4, 255–6; *Gesamtkunstwerk*, 2, 54, 62, 245, 276; and ancient Greeks, 88–9, 95, 245; and Judaeo-Christian tradition, 110, 216, 225; and Lessing, 289; miscegenation, 100, *see also Parsifal;* political opinions, 42, 50, 62, 81–2; extremist 'religion', 110, 112; and romantic creativity, 2; as Hans Sachs, 253, 254, 255; vegetarianism, 110, 265

Works (literary): *Annals*, 41; 'Art and Revolution', 83, 89, 245; 'Autobiographical Sketch', 206; *Bayreuther Blätter*, 109–10; collected works, 81–2; 'Communication to my Friends', 254; correspondence, burned, 126; 'Heroism and Christianity', 225; 'How Can Republican Impulses be Reconciled with the Monarchy?', 43; influence, 117–18; *Jesus von Nazareth*, 216; 'Know Thyself' (*Bayreuther Blätter*), 110, 126, 203, 225, 228; *Das Liebesmahl der Apostel*, 216; *Mein Leben*, 34, 38, 41, 94, 263; 'Music and the Jews', 3, 34, 64, 86–8, 110, 119, 247, 260, 282, 287; patriotic ode (1871), 129; 'Regeneration Writings', 110; revolutionary poem (1849), 44; 'Shall We Hope?', 138; 'Siegfrieds Tod', 59, 60; style, 93, 115; *Volksblätter* article (1849), 43–4; 'What is German?' (*Bayreuther Blätter*), 109–10; 'Wibelungen', 85, 118, 124, 126, 213, 281; legend of *Wieland der Schmied*, 90, 91, 94–5; 'Work of Art of the Future', 7, 83–4, 86, 92, 99, 123, 135, 202, 235, 242

Works (musical): *Friedrich und Freiheit*, 38; *Die hohe Braut*, 37; *Männerlist gegen Frauenlist*, 33–4; new edition of complete works planned, 20; operas, *see individual operas*; operas viewed by Hitler as prophecy, 271–2; planned works on Barbarossa, 282

Wagner, Rosalie, 39

Wagner Siegfried, 96, 127, 129, 135, 163, 168–9, 178–80, 185–6; in America, 186–7; anti-Semitism, 143, 175, 186, 195, 217; comment on French revolutionaries, 142; *Glück*, 179–80; and Hitler, 79, 134, 164, 170, 178, 179–80, 186, 195; homosexuality, 127, 195; and 1924 *Meistersinger*, 195; and Munich Putsch, 183–4; and Weimar Republic, 192; *see also* Wagner, Winifred

Wagner, Wieland, 20–1, 133–4, 135, 218, 265

Wagner, Winifred (née Williams), 3, 26, 135, 159, 175, 222; in America, 186–7; banished, 133; and Bechsteins, 160–1; and Class, 117; and Hitler, 123, 143, 162–3, 164, 170, 176, 184–5, 197, 229, 263–4, 283; and *Meistersinger* (1943), 267; and Munich Putsch, 183–4; joins Nazi Party, 163; and Wagner's manuscripts, 13, 14, 20, 21

Wagner, Wolfgang, 113, 119, 134, 143, 163, 265; and Hitler, 133, 135–6, 160, 263, 264; quoted, 15

Wahnfried (Bayreuth inner circle), *see* Bayreuth; Chamberlain, Houston Stewart; Wagner, Cosima

Waldersee, Lieutenant-Colonel, 48

Walküre, Die (Wagner), 59; manuscript, 13

Wälsungen Order, 148

Walvater Order, 148

Wandering Jew, *see* Ahasverus

Wapnewski, Peter, 110

Wartenburg, Count Yorck von, 160

Wassermann, Jakob: *My Road as German and Jew*, 120

Weber, Carl Maria von, 34–5

Weber, Friedrich, 157

Weimar Republic, 1, 14, 15, 94, 143, 180, 236, 272; Bayreuth's hostility to, 178, 192; terrorism in, 149, 150

Weingartner, Felix, 56, 57

Weininger, Otto, 155–6; *Race and Character*, 155

Weissheimer, Wendelin, 70

Westernhagen, Kurt von, 251–2, 253

Wilhelm I, Kaiser, 109

Wilhelm II, Kaiser, 14, 114, 129, 131; anti-Semitism, 128; and Chamberlain, 120, 125, 127–8, 130, 131, 141, 172; Charlemagne's imperial insignia, 253; and Eckart, 154

Wisliceny, Dieter, 291

Wittelsbach dynasty, 14

Wittgenstein, Princess Marie, 42

Wolf, Johanna, 152

Wolzogen, Ernst von, 118

Wolzogen, Hans von, 116, 117, 195, 217, 239

Young Germany movement, 35, 36

Zelinsky, Hartmut, 135, 262

Ziegler, Hans Severus, 49, 55, 134, 171, 237, 261–2; and 'Degenerate Music', 261

Zuckmayer, Carl, 136

Zweig, Stefan, 182

Zychlinsky, Leo von, 46, 67